SAP® SD

Handbook

The Jones and Bartlett Publishers SAP® Book Series

SAP® R/3® FI Transactions
V. Narayanan (978-1-934015-01-8) © 2007

Upgrading SAP®
Maurice Sens (978-1-934015-15-5) © 2008

SAP® FI/CO Questions and Answers
V. Narayanan (978-1-934015-22-3) © 2008

SAP® ABAP™ Handbook
Kogent Learning Solutions, Inc. (978-0-7637-8107-1) © 2010

SAP® ABAP™ Questions and Answers
Kogent Learning Solutions, Inc. (978-0-7637-7884-2) © 2010

SAP® MM Questions and Answers
Kogent Learning Solutions, Inc. (978-0-7637-8144-6) © 2010

SAP® SD Questions and Answers
Kogent Learning Solutions, Inc. (978-0-7637-8198-9) © 2010

SAP® ERP® Financials and FICO Handbook
Surya N. Padhi (978-0-7637-8080-7) © 2010

SAP® SD Handbook
Kogent Learning Solutions, Inc. (978-1-934015-34-6) © 2011

For more information on any of the titles above, please visit us online at http://www.jbpub.com/. Qualified instructors, contact your Publisher's Representative at 1-800-832-0034 or info@jbpub.com to request review copies for course consideration.

SAP® SD

Handbook

Kogent Learning Solutions, Inc.

JONES AND BARTLETT PUBLISHERS
Sudbury, Massachusetts
BOSTON   TORONTO   LONDON   SINGAPORE

World Headquarters
Jones and Bartlett Publishers
40 Tall Pine Drive
Sudbury, MA 01776
978-443-5000
info@jbpub.com
www.jbpub.com

Jones and Bartlett Publishers
Canada
6339 Ormindale Way
Mississauga, Ontario L5V 1J2
Canada

Jones and Bartlett Publishers
International
Barb House, Barb Mews
London W6 7PA
United Kingdom

Jones and Bartlett's books and products are available through most bookstores and online booksellers. To contact Jones and Bartlett Publishers directly, call 800-832-0034, fax 978-443-8000, or visit our website www.jbpub.com.

> Substantial discounts on bulk quantities of Jones and Bartlett's publications are available to corporations, professional associations, and other qualified organizations. For details and specific discount information, contact the special sales department at Jones and Bartlett via the above contact information or send an email to specialsales@jbpub.com.

Copyright © 2011 by Jones and Bartlett Publishers, LLC

Reprint & Revision Copyright © 2011 by Jones and Bartlett Publishers, LLC. All rights reserved.
Original Copyright © 2009 by Dreamtech Press.

All rights reserved. No part of the material protected by this copyright may be reproduced or utilized in any form, electronic or mechanical, including photocopying, recording, or by any information storage and retrieval system, without written permission from the copyright owner.

The publisher recognizes and respects all marks used by companies, manufacturers, and developers as a means to distinguish their products. All brand names and product names mentioned in this book are trademarks or service marks of their respective companies. Any omission or misuse (of any kind) of service marks or trademarks, etc. is not an attempt to infringe on the property of others.

Production Credits
Publisher: David Pallai
Editorial Assistant: Molly Whitman
Production Assistant: Ashlee Hazeltine
Production Assistant: Rebekah Linga
Associate Marketing Manager: Lindsay Ruggiero
V.P., Manufacturing and Inventory Control:
    Therese Connell

Composition: diacriTech
Art Rendering: diacriTech
Cover and Title Page Design: Scott Moden
Cover Image: © kentoh/Shutterstock, Inc.
Printing and Binding: Malloy, Inc.
Cover Printing: Malloy, Inc.

Library of Congress Cataloging-in-Publication Data
SAP SD handbook / Kogent Learning Solutions, Inc.
    p. cm.
    Includes index.
    ISBN-13: 978-1-934015-34-6 (hbk.)
    ISBN-10: 1-934015-34-2
    1. SAP ERP. 2. Order picking systems. 3. Business logistics–Computer programs. 4. Management information systems. I. Kogent Learning Solutions, Inc.
    HF5415.7.S27 2011
    658.800285'53–dc22

                                            2009049890

6048
Printed in the United States of America
14 13 12 11 10   10 9 8 7 6 5 4 3 2 1

TRADEMARK ACKNOWLEDGMENT

This publication contains references to the products of SAP AG. SAP, R/3, xApps, xApp, SAP NetWeaver, Duet, PartnerEdge, ByDesign, SAP Business ByDesign, and other SAP products and services mentioned herein are trademarks or registered trademarks of SAP AG in Germany and in several other countries all over the world.

Business Objects and the Business Objects logo, Business Objects, Crystal Reports, Crystal Decisions, Web Intelligence, Xcelsius, and other Business Objects products and services mentioned herein are trademarks or registered trademarks of Business Objects in the United States and/or other countries.

SAP AG is neither the author nor the publisher of this publication and is not responsible for its content, and SAP Group shall not be liable for errors or omissions with respect to the materials.

Contents at a Glance

Introduction		xv
Chapter 1	An Overview of SAP Sales and Distribution	1
Chapter 2	Working with SAP SD Master Data	39
Chapter 3	Working with Sales Documents in SAP SD	79
Chapter 4	Pricing and Taxes in SAP SD	115
Chapter 5	Integration of SAP SD and MM Modules	163
Chapter 6	Shipment, Delivery, and Warehouse Management	259
Chapter 7	Implementing the Billing Process in the SD Module	339
Chapter 8	Credit and Risk Management in SD	405
Chapter 9	Relationship of SD to SM and QM Modules	445
Chapter 10	Working with Reports and Analysis in SD	469
Appendix A	Relevant Transaction Codes for the SD Module	507
Appendix B	Advanced Sales and Distribution Functions	563
	Glossary	603
	Index	611

Table of Contents

Introduction — xv

Chapter 1 An Overview of SAP Sales and Distribution — 1

- Introduction to SAP Applications — 2
    - The Need for SAP Applications — 3
    - History of SAP Software — 5
    - The SAP R/3 Architecture — 7
    - SAP Graphical User Interface (GUI) — 15
    - SAP Customizing Implementation Guide — 18
- Explaining the SAP Modules — 20
    - The Financial/Accounting Module — 21
    - The Controlling Module — 22
    - The Investment Management Module — 23
    - The Project System Module — 24
    - The Human Capital Management Module — 26
    - The Sales and Distribution Module — 26
    - The Materials Management Module — 27
    - The Production Planning Module — 28
    - The Logistics Execution Module — 29
    - The Quality Management Module — 29
    - The Warehouse Management Module — 30
    - The Customer Service Module — 31
- Exploring the SD Module in the SAP Application — 31
    - Classification of Data — 32
    - Role of the SD Module in the SAP System — 33
    - Relationship of SD to Other Relevant Modules — 37
- Summary — 37

Chapter 2	**Working with SAP SD Master Data**	**39**
	Enterprise Structure	40
	Sales Organization	42
	Distribution Channel	44
	Division	45
	SAP Customizing Implementation Guide	47
	Defining Sales Office and Sales Group	48
	Defining Company Code	52
	Organizational Structure in Logistics	54
	Assignment of Organizational Units	58
	Exploring Master Data in SAP SD	68
	Customer Master Data	69
	Material Master Data	73
	Condition Master Data	75
	Customer-Material Info Data	76
	Summary	78
Chapter 3	**Working with Sales Documents in SAP SD**	**79**
	Describing the Sales Order Process	80
	Exploring Sales Documents	80
	Defining the Sales Document Types	81
	Configuring Sales Documents	87
	Controlling the Sales Document with an Item Category	93
	Controlling the Sales Document with a Schedule Line	103
	Working with Different Types of Sales Documents	109
	The Quotation Document	110
	The Cash Sale Document	111
	The Rush Order Document	111
	The Credit Memo Document	111
	The Debit Memo Document	112
	The Standard Order Document	112
	Summary	113

Chapter 4	**Pricing and Taxes in SAP SD**		**115**
	Pricing in SAP SD		116
		Determining the Pricing Procedure	117
		Working with Condition Technique: Basis for Pricing	125
		Creating an Access Sequence	133
		Working with Special Pricing Functions	135
		Working with Special Condition Types	140
		Working with Price Reports	143
	Working with Taxes and Rebates in SAP SD		145
		Determining the Tax	146
		Working with Rebates	158
	Summary		160
Chapter 5	**Integration of SAP SD and MM Modules**		**163**
	Implementing the Availability Check in SD		164
		Working with the Elements of an Availability Check	168
		Configuring an Availability Check	173
	Implementing the Transfer of Requirements in SD		211
		Individual vs. Collective Requirements	212
		Configuring the Transfer of Requirements	212
	Working with Contracts		222
		Quantity Contracts	223
		Value Contracts	225
		Service and Maintenance Contracts	231
		Master Contracts	234
	Working with Scheduling Agreements		243
		Defining Schedule Line Types	243
		Maintaining Planning Delivery Schedule Instructions or Splitting Rules	246
	Working with the Consignment Stock Process		253
		Defining Consignment Fill-up	254
		Displaying Stock Overview	256
	Summary		258

Chapter 6	**Shipment, Delivery, and Warehouse Management**	**259**
	Exploring the Shipment Process	260
	Ways of Shipping	260
	Exploring Different Types of Shipments	263
	Exploring a Shipping Document	269
	Working with the Delivery Process	274
	Configuring a Delivery Document	275
	Determining and Creating the Categories of Delivery Items	278
	Working with Shipping Points	284
	Determining a Picking Location	295
	Working with the Delivery Block Process	302
	Implementing the Delivery Split Process	316
	Exploring Warehouse Management	319
	Exploring the Organizational Structure of a Warehouse	319
	Basic Functions in the Warehouse Management System	320
	Relationship of Warehouse Management to Other Applications	321
	Relationship of Warehouse Management to the Delivery Process	323
	Exploring Decentralized Warehouse Management	327
	Implementing the Packing Process	329
	Packing on the Basis of an Item Category	330
	Packing on the Customer Requirement Basis	332
	Implementing the Returnable Packaging Process	333
	Determining Routes for Transportation	335
	Defining a Route	335
	Determining a Route	337
	Summary	337
Chapter 7	**Implementing the Billing Process in the SD Module**	**339**
	Working with Billing Documents	340
	Defining Billing Types	342
	Categories of Billing Documents	349
	Creating Billing Documents	352
	Modifying Billing Documents	354

	Using the Copying Control Process for Billing	356
	Creating Invoice Lists	362
	Working with Billing Plans	366
	Periodic Billing	368
	Milestone Billing	372
	Working with Rebate Agreements	374
	Defining Rebate Agreement Types	377
	Defining Condition Type Groups	383
	Assigning Condition Types to a Condition Type Group	384
	Assigning Condition Type Groups to a Rebate Agreement Type	386
	Activating Rebate Processing	387
	Working with Rebate Agreements	390
	Exploring Payment Processing in the SD Module	394
	Exploring the Down Payment	395
	Exploring the Installment Payment	396
	Working with Payment Terms	397
	Summary	404
Chapter 8	**Credit and Risk Management in SD**	**405**
	Working with Credit Management	406
	Managing the Credit Control Area	407
	Implementing Automatic Credit Management	413
	Implementing Risk Management in SD	429
	Creating Forms of Payment Guarantee	430
	Implementing the Payment Guarantee Procedure	434
	Summary	444
Chapter 9	**Relationship of SD to SM and QM Modules**	**445**
	Implementing Service Management in SD	446
	Working with Customer Services in SD	448
	Working with Service Orders in SD	455
	Working with Complaints and Returns	459

	Implementing Quality Management in SD	462
	Identifying the Phases of Quality Certification	462
	Managing Quality during Delivery	466
	Summary	467
Chapter 10	**Working with Reports and Analysis in SD**	**469**
	Working with SD Reporting Tools in SAP	470
	Exploring the QuickView Tool	470
	Exploring SAP Query	477
	Exploring Reports and Lists	487
	Working with the Sales Information System	489
	Exploring Standard Analysis	492
	Exploring Flexible Analysis	495
	Creating the Info Structure	496
	Analyzing Data Using SAP Business Information Warehouse	499
	Understanding the Basic SAP BW Concepts	499
	Features of SAP BW	502
	Exploring the BW Architecture	502
	Explaining Business Content	504
	Summary	505
Appendix A	**Relevant Transaction Codes for the SD Module**	**507**
Appendix B	**Advanced Sales and Distribution Functions**	**563**
Glossary		**603**
Index		**611**

Introduction

Congratulations on buying the *SAP® SD Handbook*! This book is designed to provide comprehensive content on the various concepts of the SAP system and the SD module. Introduced by SAP AG, Germany, SAP forms an indispensable part of any business enterprise with respect to enterprise resource planning. The pace of technological enhancements is getting faster day by day, and on similar grounds, SAP is also enhancing day by day. Today, most companies use SAP technology to perform daily business activities.

ABOUT THIS BOOK

In the *SAP® SD Handbook*, you will find as much SAP SD as can fit between the covers. Hundreds of topics are discussed theoretically as well as practically in different chapters of this book. The book also covers SAP R/3®, the relationship and integration of SD with other modules, data access in the SAP system, system architecture, and system administration.

This book is ideal for beginners who intend to familiarize themselves with the SAP SD module, as it covers the very basics that teach you how to perform different tasks in the SAP system. An added advantage is that it also serves professionals, who are already familiar with SAP technologies and want to enhance their skills, as it deals in depth with the advanced concepts of SD. It describes the techniques and procedures that are most frequently employed by users when working with SAP R/3.

The book is divided into easy-to-understand topics, with each topic addressing different programming issues in SAP SD, such as:

- Overview of the SAP SD module
- SD master data
- Sales documents in SD
- Pricing and taxes in SAP SD
- Integration of the SD and MM modules
- Shipment, delivery, and warehouse management processes
- Integration of the SD and FI modules

- Credit and risk management in SD
- Relationship of SD with the SM and QM modules
- Reports and analysis in SD
- Transaction codes related to the SD module
- Advanced sales and distribution functions

This is just an indicative list—there is lot more inside. The book provides special coverage of the SAP SD module implemented in the mySAP™ ERP software, more than any other book dedicated to the subject.

Our sole intent has been to provide a book with in-depth and sufficient information, so that you enjoy reading and learning from it. Happy reading!

HOW TO USE THIS BOOK

In this book, we have employed the mySAP ERP software to run the code. You must, therefore, install the mySAP ERP software on your system to use and implement the applications provided in the book. This book begins with the basics of SAP technology and makes you familiar with its user interface. After that, it discusses the implementation of the concepts in the SAP SD module as well as the relationship of the SAP SD module with other modules. This book consists of 10 chapters and two appendices to provide in-depth knowledge about the SD module.

CONVENTIONS

There are a few conventions followed in this book that need to be taken care of. The *SAP® SD Handbook* provides you with additional information on various concepts in the form of NOTES:

> **Note:** *BEx is a reporting tool in SAP BW that consists of the query designer to create and manipulate queries.*

Introduction xvii

Every figure contains a descriptive caption to enhance clarity:

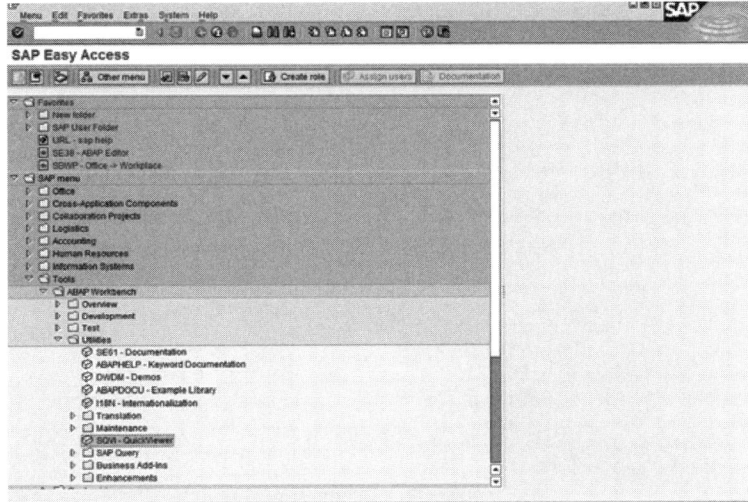

© SAP AG. All rights reserved.

FIGURE 10.1 Displaying the menu path for launching QuickViewer

In this book, table captions are placed immediately after the table, as shown:

Billing Type	Name	Description
F1	Order-related invoice	Generates an invoice on the basis of a sales order
F2	Delivery-related invoice	Generates an invoice on the basis of a delivery
F5	Pro forma invoice for sales orders or delivery	Generates a pro forma invoice on the basis of sales order, for instance in case of Stock Transfer Order or Consignment related transactions

Continued

Billing Type	Name	Description
F8	Pro forma invoice for deliveries	Generates a pro forma invoice related to delivery of goods to the customer
G2	Credit memo	Issues a credit memo to a customer
L2	Debit memo	Issues a debit memo
RE	Credit memo for returns	Generates a return document when a complaint is received from a customer, or when a customer sends the goods back to the company
S1	Cancellation invoice	Cancels an invoice and issues a new one
S2	Cancellation credit memo	Cancels the credit memo of a customer

Table 7.1 Billing Types

OTHER RESOURCES

Other useful HTML links, where you can find texts related to SAP SD with helpful tutorials, are as follows:

- http://help.sap.com/
- http://www.sap.com/solutions/benchmark/sd.epx
- http://www.sap-img.com/sap-sd.htm
- http://sapsdforum.com/

Chapter 1
An Overview of SAP Sales and Distribution

If you need information on:	See page:
Introduction to SAP Applications	2
Explaining the SAP Modules	20
Exploring the SD Module in the SAP Application	31

Systems Applications and Products in Data Processing (SAP) is a business software that can be customized according to the requirements of a user. The SAP application is being used in many organizations today because of its ability to integrate various applications, with each application representing a specific business area, such as planning, manufacturing, and distribution. This integration helps in easy transfer of data among the applications. SAP is a translation of the German term Systeme, Anwendungen, und Produkte in der Datenverarbeitung. SAP provides both functional as well as technical modules. The technical modules, such as Advanced Business Application Programming (ABAP™), help in programming various queries according to what the business requires. However, the functional modules, such as Sales and Distribution (SD), Materials Management (MM), and Production Planning (PP), are used to perform day-to-day business transactions. Depending on the specific activities of each module, the SAP application provides a common platform for different modules within an organization. These modules communicate with each other so that any change made in one module is instantly communicated to the other modules, thereby ensuring effective transfer of information and real-time status information across the organization.

The SAP R/3® software system is a market leader in the SAP® Enterprise Resource Planning (SAP ERP) software. Various activities are performed in an enterprise to complete the business process. Therefore, there is a need for an enterprise-wide information system that can coordinate all the resources, information, and activities needed to complete business processes. ERP best suits this requirement by coordinating the activities needed to complete business processes, such as order fulfillment or billing. It enables an enterprise to coordinate and maintain flow of information between all the processes from purchases to sales, including accounting and human resources. SAP R/3 systems can be broadly classified into various groups: logistics, financial/management accounting and reporting, human resources, and cross-application functions.

This chapter introduces the SAP application and the need for the SAP system in today's businesses. The chapter provides a comprehensive history of the SAP solution, focusing on the circumstances that necessitated its development, and, finally, how its introduction has helped improve system performance and business efficiency. In addition, the chapter focuses on the SAP graphical user interface (GUI), also known as the **SAP** screen, used to perform all tasks, such as creating customer master data and generating bills and invoices. Moreover, the types of data in the SAP application, such as master data and transaction data, are also described. Further, the various functional modules of the SAP R/3 system are introduced. Because this book is mainly focused on the SD module, this chapter introduces the SD module and explains the relationship of the SD module to SAP and its various other modules.

INTRODUCTION TO SAP APPLICATIONS

The SAP application was created and developed by the SAP® AG Company, Weinheim, Germany. The basic idea behind the SAP application was the need to introduce a standard application software that helps in real-time business processing. A standard SAP system is divided into three systems: development, quality assurance, and production. The development system helps customize data in a SAP application; the quality assurance system performs the final testing before using the SAP applications in the production system; and the production system helps perform the day-to-day business activities. The standard SAP software system helps the client to perform daily business activities.

In this section, we discuss the following topics in detail:

- The Need for SAP Applications
- History of the SAP Software
- The SAP R/3 Architecture
- SAP Graphical User Interface
- SAP Customizing Implementation Guide

Now, let's discuss each of them in detail.

The Need for SAP Applications

Before the advent of SAP software, the computer system used to automate and integrate all facets of business operations, including planning, manufacturing, and sales, was known as an ERP system or simply ERP. In the term ERP, E stands for Enterprise, which includes an organization, firm, or company; R stands for Resource, which involves the four M's: man, machine, material, and money; and P stands for Planning, which means efficient use of the available resources.

An ERP system is used to integrate several data sources and processes, such as manufacturing, controlling, and selling and distribution of goods of an organization. This integration is achieved by using various hardware and software components. An ERP system is primarily module based, which implies that it consists of various modular software applications or modules. A software module in an ERP system automates a specific business area or module of an enterprise, such as finance or sales and distribution. A common database is used to store data related to all the modules of an organization, such as sales and distribution (SD), production planning (PP), plant maintenance, and material management (MM). In this way, the data can be accessed, shared, and maintained easily.

Before the advent of the ERP system, each segment of a company had its own customized automation mechanism. As a result, the business modules were not interconnected or integrated, and updating and sharing data across the business modules was a big problem. Let's take an example to better understand this concept. Suppose the finance and SD modules of an enterprise use respective customized automation mechanisms. In such a setup, if a sale is closed, its status would be automatically updated in the SD module. However, the updated status of the sale of an item would not be updated in the finance module automatically. Consequently, the revenue generated from the sale of an item would need to be manually updated in the finance module, resulting in a probability of errors and an asynchronous business process. The problem was fixed with the help of the integration feature built into the ERP system.

Another benefit of an ERP system is that it helps synchronize and update data related to the business modules. Ideally, an ERP system uses only a single, common database to store information related to various modules of an organization, such SD, PP, and MM.

After discussing the benefits of an ERP system, let's now have a look at some of the major drawbacks of a contemporary ERP system, which are as follows:

- Customization of ERP software is restricted because you cannot easily adapt ERP systems to a specific workflow or business process of a company.
- Once an ERP system is established, switching to another ERP system is very costly.
- An ERP system is not clearly associated with the defined roles of employees in an organization. In addition, you do not get the exact status of company resources while an ERP system is processing a transaction. This can cause problems in accountability, lines of responsibility, and employee morale.
- Some large organizations may have multiple departments with separate, independent resources, missions, and chains of command; and their consolidation into a single enterprise may limit the benefits of the ERP system.

SAP software was introduced to overcome the drawbacks of contemporary ERP systems. The introduction of the SAP application not only removed the preceding bottlenecks, but it also led to improved system performance and business efficiency by integrating individual applications. In other words, a SAP system ensures data consistency throughout the system, in addition to removing the drawbacks of contemporary ERP systems.

After discussing the need for SAP, let's analyze the timeline history of SAP—the introduction of SAP® R/1®, R/2®, R/3®, and mySAP™ ERP systems.

History of SAP Software

In this section, we explore the history of SAP based on the various versions of SAP:

- SAP R/1
- SAP R/2
- SAP R/3
- mySAP ERP Application

Introduction of SAP R/1

The development of SAP began in 1972 with five IBM® employees: Dietmar Hopp, Hans-Werner Hector, Hasso Plattner, Klaus Tschira, and Claus Wellenreuther, in Mannheim, Germany. A year later, the first financial and accounting software was developed; it formed the basis for continuous development of other software components that later came to be known as the SAP R/1 system. Here, R stands for real-time data processing and 1 indicates single-tier architecture. This means that the three networking layers, presentation, application, and database, on which the architecture of SAP depends, are implemented in a single system. SAP ensures efficient and synchronous communication among different business modules within an organization. These modules communicate with each other so that any change made in one module is instantly communicated to the other modules, thereby ensuring effective transfer of information and uniform, real-time updates.

Introduction of SAP R/2

The SAP R/2 software system, which is based on two-tiered architecture, was introduced in 1980. SAP R/2 software was implemented on mainframe databases, such as DB/2, IMS, and Adabas. The mainframe computer in SAP R/2 application used the time-sharing feature to integrate the functions or business areas of an enterprise, such as accounting, manufacturing processes, supply chain logistics, and human resources. The two-tiered client–server architecture of the SAP R/2 system enabled a SAP client to connect to a SAP server to access the data stored in the SAP database. Keeping in mind that SAP customers belong to different nations and regions, the SAP R/2 system was designed to handle different languages and currencies. The SAP R/2 system delivered a higher level of stability compared with the earlier version.

> **Note:** Time sharing implies that multiple users can access an application concurrently; however, each is unaware that the operating system is being accessed by other users.

Introduction of SAP R/3

SAP R/3, based on a client–server model, was officially launched on July 6, 1992. This version is compatible with multiple platforms and operating systems, such as UNIX® and Microsoft® Windows®. SAP R/3 introduced a new era of business software, moving from mainframe computing architecture to the three-tiered architecture consisting of the database layer, the application layer (business logic), and the presentation layer. The three-tiered architecture of the client–server model is preferred to the mainframe computing architecture as the standard in business software because a user can make changes or scale a particular layer in the client–server model without making changes in the entire system.

The SAP R/3 system is a customizable software with predefined features that you can turn on or off according to your requirements. The SAP R/3 system contains various standard tables designed to execute various types of processes, such as reading data from database tables or processing the entries stored in a table. You can configure the settings of these tables according to your requirements. The data related to these tables are managed with the help of the dictionary of the SAP R/3 system, which is stored in an SAP database and can be accessed by all the SAP application programs.

The SAP R/3 system integrates all the business modules of a company so that the information, once entered, can be shared across these modules. The SAP R/3 system is a highly generic and comprehensive business application system, especially designed for companies of varied organizational structures and differing lines of business.

The SAP R/3 system runs on various platforms, such as Microsoft® Windows and UNIX. It also supports various relational databases of different database management systems, such as Oracle®, Adabas®, Informix®, and Microsoft® SQL Server®. The SAP R/3 system uses these databases to handle the queries of the users.

With the passage of time, a need for a business suite that would run on a single database and offer a pre-configured system with various scenarios became evident. This led to the introduction of the mySAP™ Business Suite, which provided the mySAP ERP application as a follow-up product to the SAP R/3 software.

Introduction of mySAP ERP Application

The mySAP ERP application is one of the applications within the mySAP Business Suite. Various applications, such as mySAP ERP, mySAP™ Supply Chain Management (SCM), mySAP™ Customer Relationship Management (CRM), mySAP™ Supplier Relationship Management (SRM), and mySAP™ Product Lifecycle Management (PLM), are included in the mySAP Business Suite. The latest release of the mySAP ERP application is SAP® ERP Central Component (SAP ECC 6.0). The mySAP ERP categorizes the applications into the following three core functional areas:

- Logistics
- Financial
- Human Resources

To learn more about the core and other functional areas of mySAP ERP, refer to the *Explaining the SAP Modules* section. This book is focused on the latest release of the mySAP ERP application, ECC 6.0.

Now, let's explore the architecture of the SAP R/3 system.

The SAP R/3 Architecture

As stated earlier, the SAP R/3 system evolved from the SAP R/2 system, which was mainframe based. The SAP R/3 system is based on the three-tiered architecture of the client–server model. Figure 1.1 shows the three-tiered architecture of the SAP R/3 system.

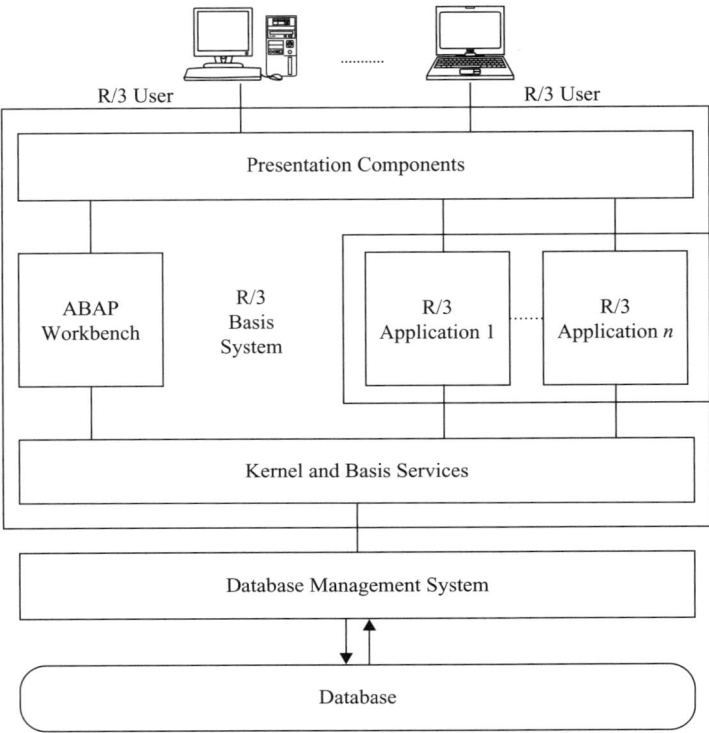

FIGURE 1.1 SAP R/3 architecture

Figure 1.1 shows how the SAP R/3 Basis system forms a central platform within the SAP R/3 system. The architecture of the SAP R/3 system helps distribute the workload to multiple SAP R/3 systems. The links among these systems are established with the help of a network. The SAP R/3 system is implemented in such a way that the presentation, application, and database layers are distributed among individual computers in the SAP R/3 architecture.

The SAP R/3 system consists of the following three types of views:

- Logical view
- Software-oriented view
- User-oriented view

Now, let's describe these views in detail.

The Logical View

The logical view of the SAP system represents the functionality of the SAP system. In this context, the SAP R/3 Basis component controls the functionality and proper functioning of the SAP system. Therefore, in the logical view of the SAP R/3 system, we describe the services provided by the SAP R/3 Basis component that help to execute SAP applications. Following is a description of the various services provided by the SAP R/3 Basis component:

- **Kernel and Basis Services**—Provides a runtime environment for all SAP R/3 applications. The runtime environment may be specific to the hardware, operating system, or database. The runtime environment is mainly written in either C or C++, though some parts are also written in the ABAP programming language. The tasks of the Kernel and Basis services are as follows:
    - Executing all SAP R/3 applications on software processors (virtual machines).
    - Handling multiple users and administrative tasks in the SAP R/3 system, which is a multiuser environment. When users log on to the SAP system and run applications within it, they are not directly connected to the host operating system because the SAP R/3 Basis component is the actual user of the host operating system.
    - Accessing the database in the SAP R/3 system. The SAP R/3 Basis system is connected to a database management system (DBMS) and to the database itself. SAP R/3 applications do not communicate with the database directly; rather, these applications communicate with the database through the administration services provided by the SAP R/3 Basis system.
    - Facilitating communication of SAP R/3 applications with other SAP R/3 systems and with non-SAP systems. You can access SAP R/3 applications from an external system by using the Business Application Programming Interfaces (BAPI®) interface.
    - Monitoring and controlling the SAP R/3 system while the system is running.
- **ABAP Workbench Service**—Provides a programming environment to create ABAP programs using various tools, such as the ABAP Dictionary, ABAP Editor, and Screen Painter.

- **Presentation Components Service**—Facilitates user interaction with SAP R/3 applications using the presentation components (interfaces) of these applications.

The Software-Oriented View

The software-oriented view displays various types of software components that collectively constitute the SAP R/3 system. It consists of SAP GUI components and Application servers as well as a Message server that make up the SAP R/3 system. Since the SAP R/3 system is a multitiered client–server system, the individual software components are arranged in tiers. These components act as either clients or servers based on their position and role in a network. Figure 1.2 shows the software-oriented view of the SAP R/3 architecture.

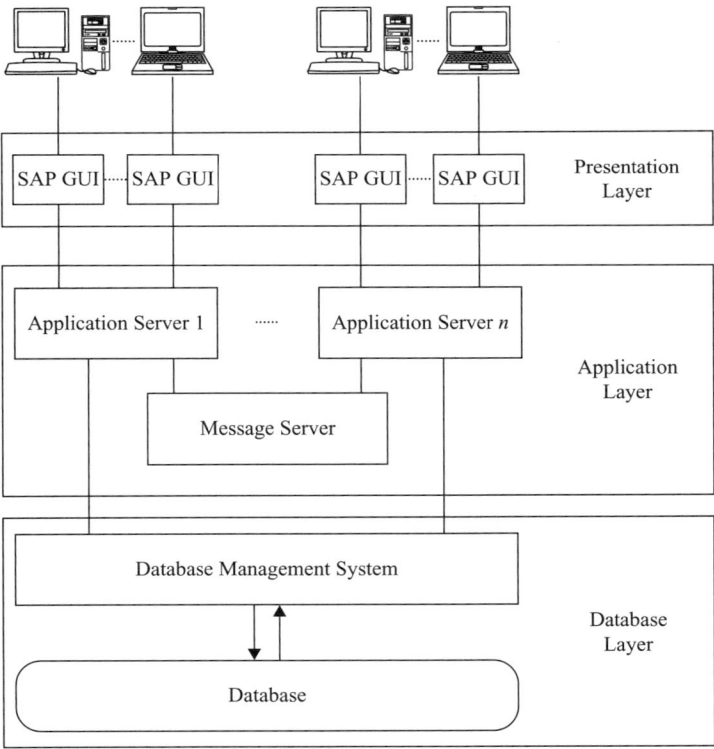

FIGURE 1.2 Software-oriented view

As shown in Figure 1.2, the software-oriented view of the SAP R/3 system consists of the following three layers:

- The Presentation layer
- The Application layer
- The Database layer

Now, let's discuss these layers in detail.

The Presentation Layer

The Presentation layer consists of one or more servers that act as an interface between the SAP R/3 system and its users, who interact with the system with the help of well-defined SAP GUI components. Using these components, users can enter a request, for example, to display the contents of a database table. The Presentation layer then passes the request to the Application server, where it is processed and the result is sent back; the result is then displayed to the user in the Presentation layer. While a SAP GUI component is running, it is also connected to a user's SAP session in the SAP R/3 Basis system.

Note: The servers in the Presentation layer are referred to as Presentation servers in this chapter.

The Application Layer

The Application layer executes the application logic in the SAP R/3 architecture. This layer consists of one or more Application servers and Message servers. Application servers are used to send user requests from the Presentation server to the Database server and to retrieve information from the Database server as a response for these requests. Application servers are connected to Database servers with the help of a local area network (LAN). An Application server provides a set of services, such as processing of the flow logic of screens and updating data in the database of the SAP R/3 system. However, a single Application server cannot handle the entire workload of the business logic on its own. Therefore, the workload is distributed among multiple Application servers. Figure 1.3 shows the location of the Application server between the Database and Presentation servers.

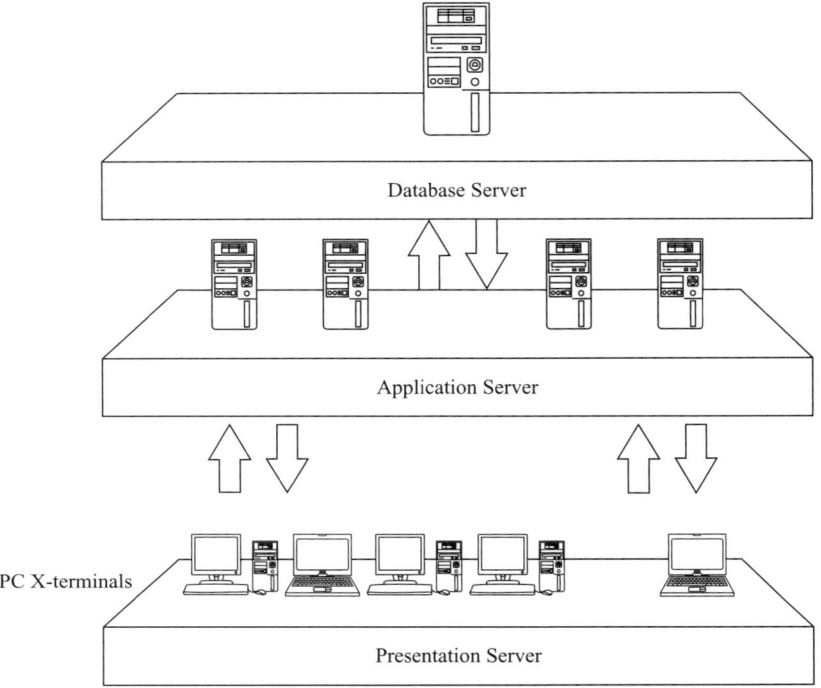

FIGURE 1.3 **Application server**

The Message-server component of the Application layer (Figure 1.3) is responsible for communication among the Application servers. This component also contains information about Application servers and the distribution of load among them. It uses this information to select an appropriate server when a user sends a request for processing.

The separation of the three layers of the SAP R/3 system makes the system highly scalable, with the load being distributed among the layers. This distribution of load enables the SAP R/3 system to handle multiple requests simultaneously. The control of a program moves back and forth among the three layers when a user interacts with the program. When the control of the program is in the Presentation layer, the screen in front of the user is ready to accept input from the user, and during this time, the Application layer becomes inactive for the specific program. This way, any other application can use the Application layer during this time. As soon as the user enters the input on the screen, the control of the program shifts to the Application layer for input processing, and the Presentation layer becomes inactive, which means that the SAP R/3 GUI cannot accept any kind of input. In other words, until the Application layer completes processing the input and calls a new screen, the SAP GUI does not become active. The procedure in which a new screen is presented to the user is known as a dialog step. Dialog steps are processed in the Application layer, as shown in Figure 1.4.

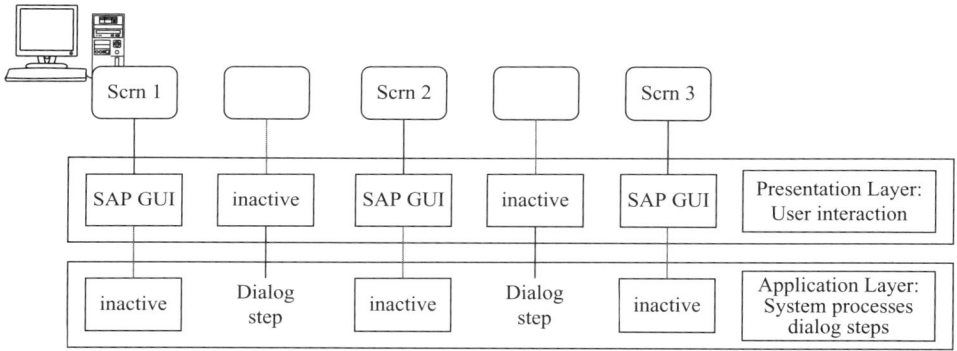

FIGURE 1.4 **A dialog step**

The Database Layer

The Database layer of the SAP R/3 architecture comprises the central database system, which contains two components: DBMS and the database itself. The SAP R/3 system supports various databases, such as Adabas® D™, DB2/400™ (on AS/400), DB2/Common Server™, DB2/MVS™, Informix®, Microsoft® SQL Server®, Oracle®, and Oracle® Parallel™ Server.

The database in the SAP R/3 system stores all of the information of the system except the master and transaction data. Apart from this, the components of ABAP application programs, such as screen definitions, menus, and function modules, are stored in a special section of the database, known as the Repository, and they are also known as Repository Objects. The database also stores control and customized data that govern how the SAP R/3 system functions. Distributed databases are not used in the SAP R/3 system because the system does not support them.

> **Note:** Master data is the core data and is very essential to execute the business logic. Data about customers, products, employees, materials, and suppliers are examples of master data. Transaction data refers to information about an event in a business process, such as generating orders, invoices, and payments.

The User-Oriented View

The user-oriented view displays the GUI of the SAP R/3 system in the form of windows on the screen. These windows are created by the Presentation layer. To view these windows, a user has to start the SAP GUI utility, called the SAP Logon program, or simply SAP Logon. After starting the SAP Logon program, the user selects a SAP R/3 system from the **SAP Logon** screen. The SAP Logon program then connects to the Message server of the SAP R/3 Basis system in the selected SAP R/3 system and retrieves the address of a suitable Application server; that is, the Application server with the lightest load. The SAP Logon program then starts the SAP GUI connected to the Application server.

The SAP GUI starts the **SAP Logon** screen. After the user is successfully logged on, the initial screen of the SAP R/3 system appears. This initial screen starts the first session of the SAP R/3 system. Figure 1.5 shows the user-oriented view of the SAP R/3 system.

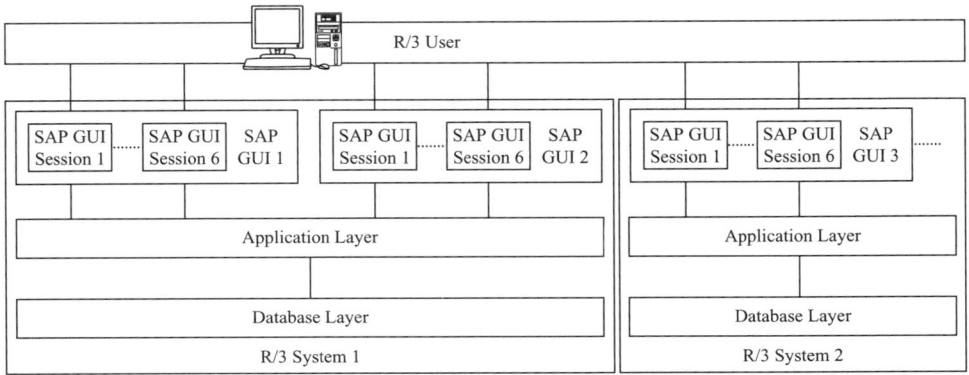

FIGURE 1.5 User-oriented view

A user can open a maximum of six sessions within a single SAP GUI. Each session acts as an independent SAP GUI. Users can simultaneously run different applications on multiple open SAP R/3 sessions. The processing in an opened SAP R/3 session is independent of the other opened SAP R/3 sessions.

We have discussed the SAP architecture; now let's understand SAP GUI used to perform various day-to-day business transactions.

SAP Graphical User Interface (GUI)

The SAP GUI is a standard SAP user interface that displays menus that perform various business activities. The first initial screen of the SAP GUI is known as the **SAP Easy Access** screen. There are numerous SAP GUIs in ECC, such as a standard SAP GUI (also known as the SAP menu) and the Web portal GUI for users who do not access the SAP menu directly from their systems.

Perform the following steps to open the first initial screen (**SAP Easy Access** Screen) of the SAP GUI:

1. Open the **SAP Logon** screen by selecting **Start > All Programs > SAP Front End > SAP Logon**, as shown in Figure 1.6.

FIGURE 1.6 Selecting the SAP Logon option

The **SAP Logon** screen appears as shown in Figure 1.7.

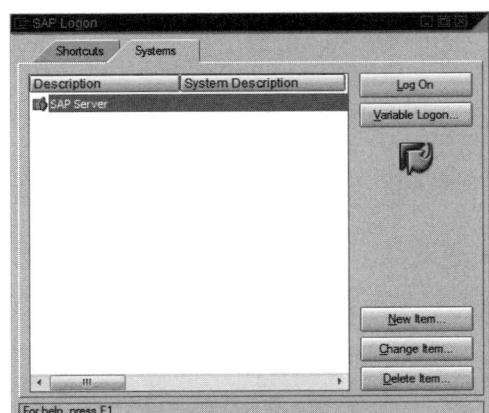

© SAP AG. All rights reserved.

FIGURE 1.7 **The SAP Logon screen**

2. Click the **Log On** button on the **SAP Logon** screen (Figure 1.7).

The **SAP** screen (first screen of the SAP system) to enter the logon details appears as shown in Figure 1.8.

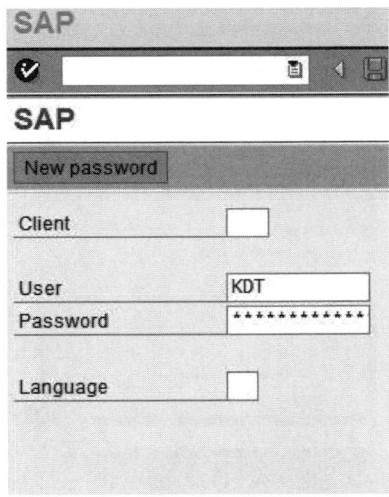

© SAP AG. All rights reserved.

FIGURE 1.8 **The SAP screen for entering the logon details**

Introduction to SAP Applications 17

The **SAP** screen contains the following fields:

- **Client**—The client number is entered here.
- **User**—The user ID is entered here.
- **Password**—The password provided by your system administrator is entered here. You will notice that as you enter the password, asterisks appear in the field rather than the characters you type. As a security measure, the system does not display the values entered in the **Password** field.
- **Language (optional)**—The language you want to be displayed on screens, menus, and fields is entered here.

3. Enter the values in all the fields of the **SAP** screen; for instance, the user name and the password. In our example, we have entered KDT as the user name and sapmac as the password, as shown in Figure 1.8. Now, press the **Enter** key. The **SAP Easy Access** screen or SAP GUI appears as shown in Figure 1.9.

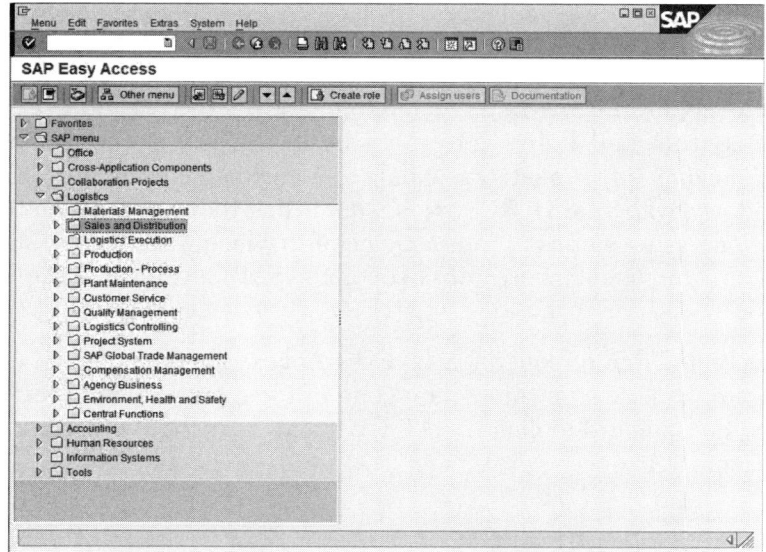

© SAP AG. All rights reserved.

FIGURE 1.9 Displaying the SAP GUI screen

This screen serves as a gateway to working in SAP and contains all the development tools provided by SAP. The standard SAP GUI shown in Figure 1.9 is also known as the **SAP Easy Access** screen. Figure 1.9 shows various SAP menus, such as **Office**, **Cross-Application Components**, **Collaboration Projects**, **Logistics**, and so on.

> **Note:** Since this book focuses on the SD module, we would primarily deal with the **Sales and Distribution** submenu provided under the **Logistics SAP** menu.

Now, after logging on to the **SAP Easy Access** screen, let's discuss the SAP® Customizing Implementation Guide, which provides the subcategories of the three core functional areas discussed previously in the *Introduction of mySAP ERP Application* section.

SAP Customizing Implementation Guide

The SAP Customizing Implementation Guide is the backbone of the mySAP ERP system and helps determine how the system functions. The SAP Customizing Implementation Guide is a customizing screen (T.Code `SPRO`) introduced with the SAP R/3 system. Prior to this, the customization of the system was done using menus or transaction codes, which was time-consuming.

Perform the following steps to open the SAP Customizing Implementation Guide:

1. Open the first screen, the **SAP Easy Access** screen SAP GUI (Figure 1.9).
2. Enter `SPRO` as the transaction code in the command field textbox located on the standard toolbar of SAP GUI, and press the **Enter** key, as shown in Figure 1.10.

Introduction to SAP Applications 19

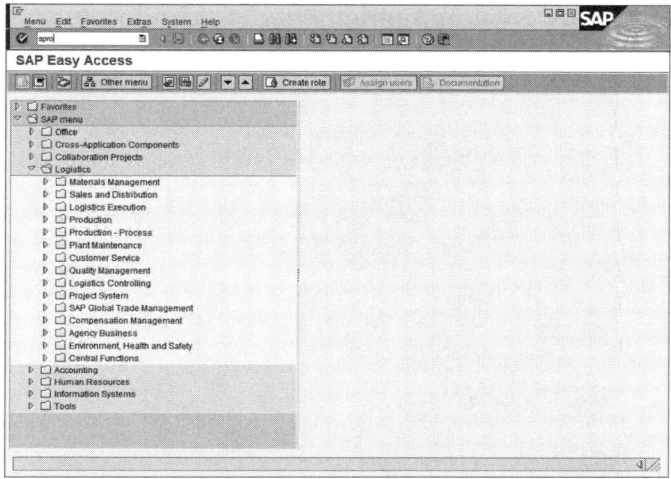

© SAP AG. All rights reserved.

FIGURE 1.10 Entering the transaction code

The **Customizing: Execute Project** screen appears (Figure 1.11).

3. Click the **SAP Reference IMG** button (or press **F5**) as shown in Figure 1.11.

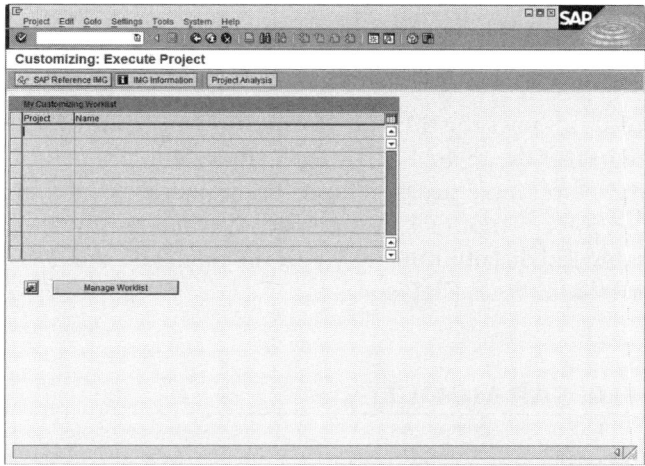

© SAP AG. All rights reserved.

FIGURE 1.11 Displaying the Customizing: Execute Project screen

The **SAP Customizing Implementation Guide** screen appears as shown in Figure 1.12.

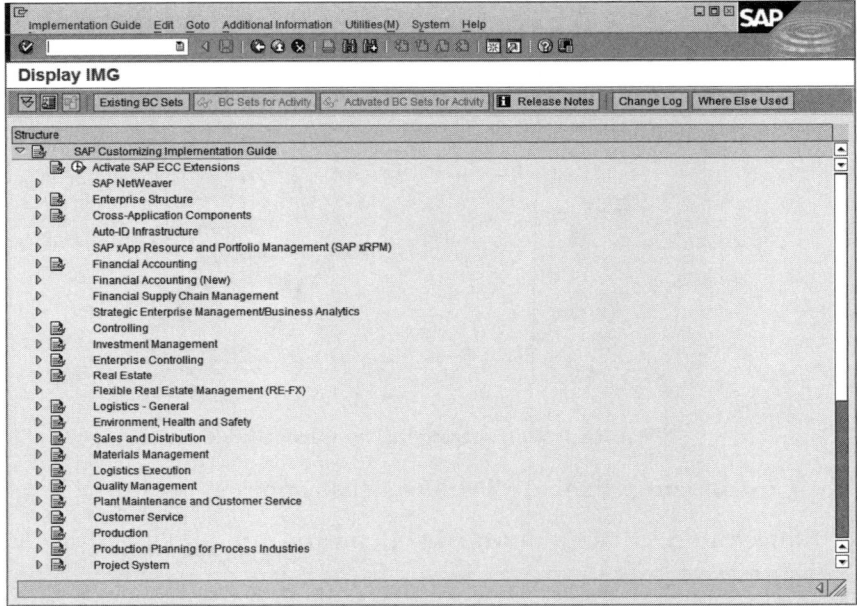

© SAP AG. All rights reserved.

FIGURE 1.12 Displaying the SAP Customizing Implementation Guide screen

Figure 1.12 shows the **SAP Customizing Implementation Guide** screen, which categorizes the mySAP ERP applications into financial, human resources, and logistics functional areas. These functional areas are further subdivided into applications or modules that perform various business operations such as finance, sales and distribution, and material management. Now, let's discuss the modules of the mySAP ERP system.

EXPLAINING THE SAP MODULES

The mySAP ERP application provides various SAP modules, such as MM, SD, and PP, to handle all business activities of an organization, such as recording the payment of invoices, controlling financial accounts, and managing production resources. For example, the SD module is defined to handle sales and distribution tasks, and the MM module is defined to manage the material produced in an organization.

Because the mySAP ERP system works within a single system, the processed data of one module can be used by other modules. The various SAP modules used to perform specific business activities are listed here:

- Financial Accounting
- Controlling
- Investment Management
- Sales and Distribution
- Materials Management
- Logistics Execution
- Quality Management
- Customer Service
- Production Planning for Process Industries
- Project System

Now, let's discuss each of them in detail.

The Financial/Accounting Module

The Financial/Accounting (FI) module is designed to handle financial and accounting-related tasks. This module helps create and maintain financial records, such as general ledger, accounts payable, and accounts receivable. It also helps automatically post journal entries of sales, production, and payments.

The book records designed in this module help the management of a company to access the real financial situation of the company in real time; thereby enabling them to make better decisions and to do better strategic planning. The FI module is also integrated with other SAP modules, such as MM, PP, SD, PM, PS, PM, PY, and PT, depending on the financial activity performed.

Table 1.1 describes the submodules of the FI module.

Now, let's discuss the Controlling (CO) module of the mySAP ERP system.

Submodule	Description
Accounts Payable	Records the account postings for vendor purchase activities and generates automatic postings in the General Ledger module.
Accounts Receivable	Records the account postings for customer sales activities and helps generate customer analysis report. Integrates with the General Ledger, Sales and Distribution, and Cash Management modules to facilitate recording of financial transactions performed in the business.
Asset Accounting	Manages the records related to the fixed assets of a company. Sets a fixed value for depreciation of each fixed asset of the company.
Bank Accounting	Manages all the bank transactions of the company.
Consolidation	Generates a financial overview based on the financial statements defined for various entities of an organization.
Funds Management	Allows the management of a company to set budgets for revenues and expenses.
General Ledger	Records all account postings that display the real-time situation of the financial accounts of a company.
Special Purpose Ledger	Generates ledgers for reporting purposes on the basis of the data collected from both internal and external applications.
Travel Management	Manages the traveling activities, such as booking trips and managing the expenses of a trip.

TABLE 1.1 The submodules of the FI module

The Controlling Module

The CO module is designed for planning, reporting, and monitoring business operations in an organization. This module provides information that helps the management of a company to make important business decisions. It is the most crucial module among all SAP modules because this module helps control transactions made in other modules and also provides the analyses and reports for various business tasks.

Table 1.2 describes the components of the CO module.

Now, let's discuss the Investment Management (IM) module of the mySAP system.

Components	Description
Activity-Based Costing	Provides information in context of costs based on a procedure or activity of a cost center.
Cost Center Accounting	Provides information with regard to costs incurred by the defined cost centers of an organization.
Cost Element Accounting	Provides information in context of costs and revenues of an organization.
Internal Orders	Helps evaluate costs of a specific task in an organization.
Product Cost Controlling	Analyzes the production cost of a product to decide its market price.
Profit Center Accounting	Provides detailed information regarding the profit or loss of an organization.
Profitability Analysis	Allows reviewing information with respect to the profit of a company.

TABLE 1.2 Components of the CO module

The Investment Management Module

The IM module is designed to manage various investment securities, such as shares and bonds, to meet the investment goals for the benefits of the investors of a company. This SAP module enables program management, the process of defining a hierarchy for multiple projects. This ensures effective planning and controlling of the costs that include budget authorization. The IM module also integrates with other modules, such as CO and Asset Management (AM), and helps manage the capital investment and budget of a company. These are the tasks performed in the IM module:

- Appropriation Request (AR) master data
- AR variants and cost or revenue planning
- AR approval and status management
- Implementation of AR through measures
- Periodic processing
- Basic reporting
- Investment Management Program Definition
- Investment Program Structure
- Program Planning
- Program Budgeting

After discussing the IM module, let's describe the roles of the Project System (PS) module in the mySAP ERP system.

The Project System Module

The PS module is designed to handle both small- and large-scale projects. For instance, it can handle large-scale projects, such as building a factory; and small-scale projects, such as organizing a schedule for recruitments. To ensure the completion of a project within time and budget constraints, a project manager in a company needs to define an organizational form for the project, which should be shared by other modules.

The PS module is integrated with other modules of the mySAP ERP system so that users plan and execute all the tasks associated with a project. This integration means that the PS module constantly accesses data of all the departments involved in a project. Moreover, this module includes both technical and commercial aspects of the project. The PS module does not have its own organizational structure; therefore, users must incorporate the project into the existing structure by making assignments to the organizational units in the Accounting and Logistics modules. Figure 1.13 shows the organizational structure of a project defined in the PS module.

Explaining the SAP Modules 25

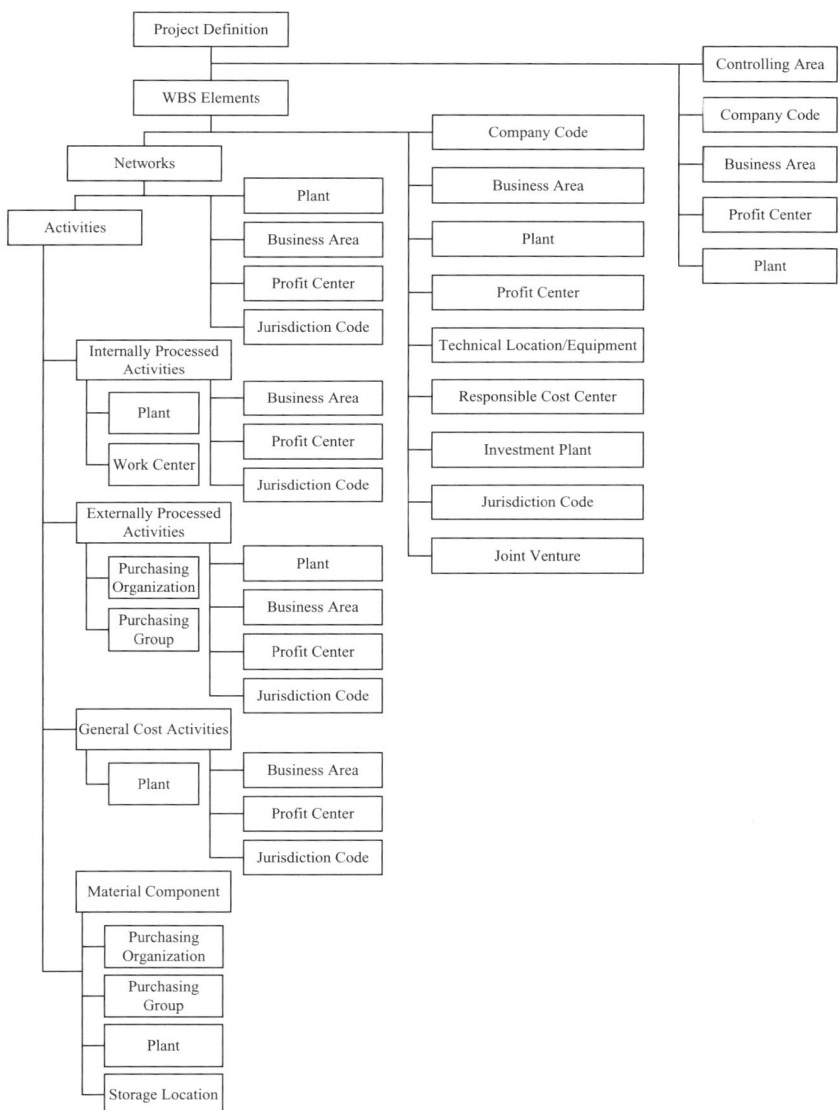

FIGURE 1.13 Displaying organizational structure of a project

Now, after discussing the PS module, let's analyze the role of the Human Capital Management (HCM) module in the mySAP ERP system.

The Human Capital Management Module

The HCM module is designed to plan and control personnel activities. This module is also known as the Human Resources (HR) module, and it is used to perform the HR-related activities of an organization. The employee relations and resource planning tasks are also managed by the HCM module. The objective of this module is to maximize the return on investment from the human capital of an organization and to minimize the risk.

Table 1.3 describes the submodules of the HCM module.

Submodule	Description
Payroll Management (PY)	Maintains all financial records of salaries, wages, bonuses, and deductions of the employees of an organization.
Personnel Administration (PA)	Helps manage and administer the human resources in an organization.
Personnel Development (PD)	Manages the personnel's training for the development of the human resources in an organization.

TABLE 1.3　Submodules of the HCM module

Let's now discuss the Sales and Distribution (SD) module in the mySAP ERP system.

The Sales and Distribution Module

The SD module is one of the logistics modules that helps manage the sales and distribution activities in an organization. A company can input the customer sale price for a product, check for open sales orders, and forecast future requirements using the SD module of the mySAP ERP system. The SD module also helps to regulate all the activities—from receiving the order for a product to product delivery. This module is integrated with other modules, such as MM, FI, and PP modules, and deals with the customer and material master data. The business activities related to sales and distribution, such as setting price quotations for a product and generating sales orders and bills for customers, are managed through the SD module. These are the basic features of the SD module:

- **Pricing and Taxation**—Evaluates the price of a product under various condition types, such as rebate or discount granted to a customer.
- **Availability Check**—Checks the availability of a product in the warehouse.
- **Credit Management**—Defines the credit limit for a customer during the sale of various products by an organization.
- **Billing and Invoice**—Generates bills or invoices after a sales order for a product is placed.
- **Material Determination**—Helps determine the details of materials on the basis of a specific condition type.
- **Account Determination**—Helps determine the details of a customer on the basis of a specific condition type.
- **Text Processing**—Helps copy texts from one document to another.

The other business activities, such as packaging, shipping, and creation of a sales order, are also managed with the help of the SD module.

After discussing the SD module, let's now explore the Materials Management (MM) module of the mySAP ERP system.

The Materials Management Module

The MM module is designed to procure and manage the material resources of a company. This module also handles the inventory functions, such as purchasing, inventory management, and reorder processing, which are performed as daily business operations. This module deals mainly with material data and vendor master data. The MM module is implemented at the following levels of SAP implementation:

- Client
- Company Code
- Plant
- Storage Location
- Purchase Organization

The MM module ensures that the required product is available in an adequate quantity at the right price. Moreover, this module also reduces working capital by monitoring raw and packaged products on a regular basis.

After understanding the MM module, let's discuss the Production Planning (PP) module of the mySAP ERP system.

The Production Planning Module

The PP module is designed to plan the production phase of a product, such as the type of the product and the quantity to be produced on the basis of demand. This module deals with the tasks related to the procurement, warehousing, and transportation of materials in a company. It also plans the transportation of intermediate products from one stage of production to another at the specified time. This module is integrated with other modules, such as MM, FA, HCM, and SD. The basic features provided by the PP module are as follows:

- Capacity planning
- Master production scheduling
- Material requirements planning
- Shop floor

This module also integrates the master data, such as bills of materials, routings, and work centers. Moreover, it also helps plan the business activities at various stages, such as sales, operation planning, and long-term planning.

Table 1.4 describes the submodules of the PP module.

Submodule	Description
PP-Process Industry	Performs business activities of the process industries, such as those associated with oil and gas
Production General	Stores the records of various master data, such as bills of materials, routings, and work centers, in a separate component

TABLE 1.4   Submodules of the PP module

After understanding the role of the PP module in the mySAP ERP system, let's now discuss the Logistics Execution (LE) module.

The Logistics Execution Module

The LE module is designed to implement the shipping and delivery activities of the SD module. This module works closely with the MM and SD modules. In the LE module, the warehouse management concept is implemented from the MM module, while the concepts of delivery, shipping, and transportation are implemented from the SD module. The LE module helps create the delivery document for a vendor who returns goods using the shipping function. It also allows a company to consolidate outbound-delivery activities into the delivery documents. In addition, it helps standardize output of documents and implementation of procedures for the goods returned by a vendor in the Transportation module.

After understanding the LE module, let's now introduce the Quality Management (QM) module of the mySAP ERP system.

The Quality Management Module

The QM module is designed to check and enhance the quality of products produced by a company. Apart from the products, it also monitors the performance of various peripheral processes, such as planning and execution. Quality management is incorporated into each and every step of the supply chain. This module can also be used as a computer-aided quality system and covers the following areas for quality analysis:

- Quality planning
- Quality inspection
- Quality certificates
- Quality notification
- Quality control
- Audit management
- Test equipment management
- Stability study

The QM module is integrated with the MM and SD modules because data is needed from these modules to perform quality inspections. This module allows users to transfer or archive information that is used to plan and trace quality-related activities in an organization. Even the planning, execution, and evaluation of audits are supported by SAP audit management provided by the QM module. Following are the steps for the audit process:

1. Creating an audit plan
2. Creating a question list
3. Executing the audit
4. Capturing corrective and preventive actions
5. Preparing documentation (report)
6. Conducting evaluation

The QM module provides the following interfaces that exchange data with external systems:

- **Inspection Data Interface**—Exchanges data that needs to be inspected between the QM module and external systems.
- **Statistical Data Interface**—Connects the QM module with external evaluation systems.

After understanding the QM module, let's discuss the Warehouse Management (WM) module of the mySAP ERP system.

The Warehouse Management Module

The WM module divides the storage location defined in the Inventory Management submodule into storage types, storage sections, and then into storage bins. This module provides a flexible, automated support that assists users to process movement of all goods and to maintain current stock of the inventory. Following are the functionalities provided by the WM module:

- Defining and managing complex warehousing structures
- Optimizing material flow
- Processing goods receipts, goods issued to customer, and stock transfers
- Characterizing work process in the warehouse
- Performing work efficiently and at a reasonable cost

The WM module integrates with the MM, PP, QM, and SD modules. The stock posted in the WM module is the same as that posted in the IM module. This module also manages hazardous materials, monitors stock movements, and manages stocks at the storage-bin level.

After discussing the WM module, let's now explore the role of the Customer Service (CS) module in the mySAP ERP system.

The Customer Service Module

The CS module provides support for customer services, such as customer support services for computers and equipment. In addition, this module helps a company manage its service department and performs functions such as monitoring service calls. It improves customer service, reduces operating costs, and increases efficiency. This module is linked to the PM module of the mySAP ERP system.

This ends the discussion of the modules in the mySAP ERP system; let's now explore the SD module and understand the types of data in this module as well as its integration with other modules.

EXPLORING THE SD MODULE IN THE SAP APPLICATION

The SD module of SAP processes and tracks all transactions and activities associated with sales and distribution of a product, such as pricing of products, generating bills for customers, and shipping and delivery of products. Since data of one module is used by other modules in SAP, users must store and maintain the data obtained from the processing of all these transactions. Let's discuss the following topics to have a better understanding of the SD module:

- Classification of Data
- Role of the SD Module in SAP
- Relationship of SD to Other Relevant Modules

Now, let's discuss each of them.

Classification of Data

The mySAP ERP system is the latest ERP system used in most organizations. Initially, the data of an organization was maintained on paper; however, the introduction of the SAP system has eased the burden of paper tasks because this system provides real-time information for and about a company. The data in the mySAP ERP system is classified as shown in Figure 1.14.

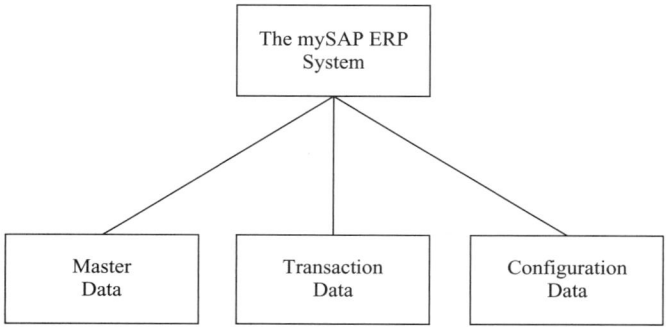

FIGURE 1.14 Classification of data

Figure 1.14 shows the types of data in the mySAP ERP system. Now, let's discuss each in detail.

Master Data

Master data in the mySAP ERP system are data that consist of company codes, cost centers, customer master accounts, and vendor master accounts. Each of these entities in the master data is composed of attributes, hierarchies, and tables. An important characteristic of master data is that it is rarely modified; therefore it is static in nature. For example, if an organization maintains a customer master table containing name, address, and other details of its customers, the chance of modification of these customer details is very small. This type of data serves as the basis for SD processing in a company.

In the mySAP ERP system, every module maintains master data. For example, the SD module maintains the material and customer master data, and the MM module maintains the vendor and material master data. The master data of one module can be used in another module depending upon the customized requirements of the business.

After understanding master data, let's now discuss transaction data.

Transaction Data

Any business activity in an organization generates data that are known as transaction data and are handled by the mySAP ERP system either at the document level or at the summary level. The document-level transaction data represents the detailed data that comprise header line items and schedule lines. The summary-level transaction data are used in the mySAP ERP system mainly for reporting purposes. These types of data normally change on a daily basis.

In mySAP ERP system, transaction data frequently changes (as compared with master data, which remains relatively static). For example, if a company is selling some products to a customer, a sales order for that customer is generated that maintains the sales transaction details. The data from these sales transactions are considered as transaction data, since they may change depending on the need of the customer and the availability of goods. However, customer information may not change frequently, and therefore it is considered to be master data.

After understanding transaction data, let's now discuss configuration data of the mySAP ERP system.

Configuration Data

Configuration data in the mySAP ERP system are linked to the application processing logic and stored in configuration tables. The mySAP ERP system configures the way of processing the data. Users can customize the configuration table according to the requirement of their company.

After understanding all types of data, let's now move ahead to discuss the relationship of the SD module with SAP.

Role of the SD Module in the SAP System

The SD module is one of the oldest SAP modules that serve as an integral part of the SAP ERP system. Let's consider a scenario in which the sale process in a company begins when a customer places an order for goods and services and asks the company to deliver the goods on the due date. The basic information about the customer and the order is used to create a sales order document in the SD module. This SD process is shown in Figure 1.15.

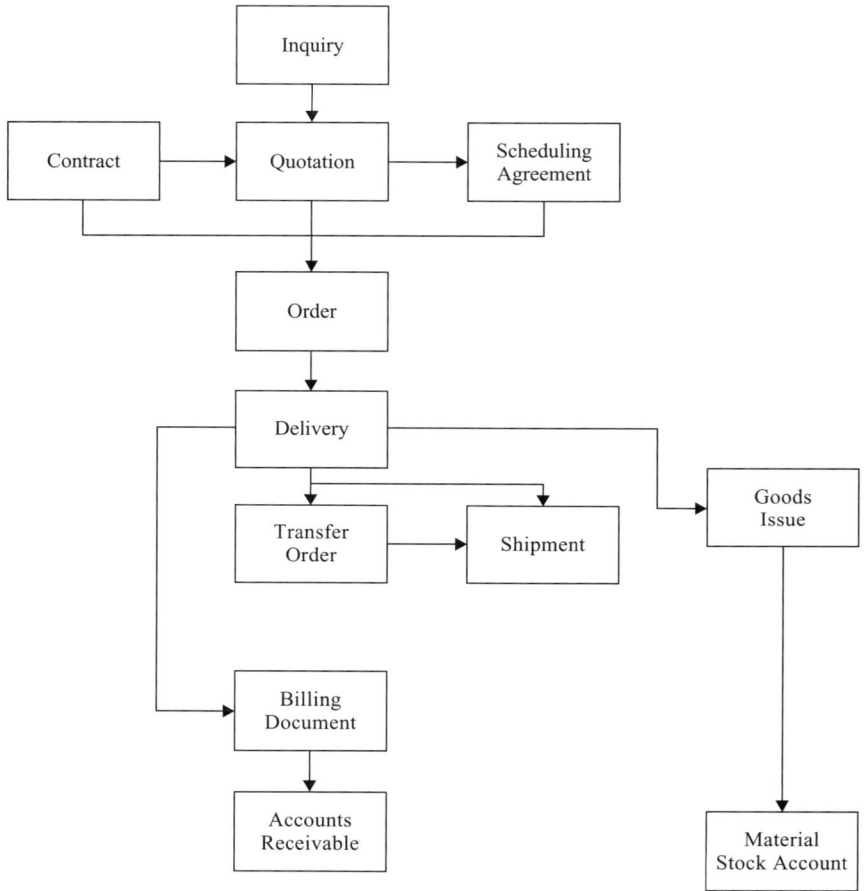

FIGURE 1.15 Displaying the SD process in SAP

Figure 1.15 shows that once the order is placed, you can trigger shipping activities so that the goods are supplied to the customer at the appropriate time. When the products are dispatched from the company, the goods' issue order is posted in the SD module to update the quantity of stock available. Then a billing document for that order is created, and an invoice is sent to the customer.

Finally, the payment is received from the customer, and the amount received is posted in the FI module. In summary, these are the basic functionalities of the SD module in the mySAP ERP system:

- Fulfilling customer requirements
- Shipping or delivering goods to customers (delivery process)
- Receiving payment for goods or services

Now, let's discuss each of them in detail.

Fulfilling Customer Requirements

A sales order in the SD module maintains a customer's request for goods or services to be delivered on a specified date. A standard sales order contains information about the customer and material, price agreement, delivery dates, quantities, shipping processing, and billing. The sales order automatically retrieves data from the master records and controls the table associated with it. Before processing the sales order, the availability of the product ordered by a customer is verified; the sales order is processed if the product is available in stock. However, if the product is not available, the sales order triggers procurement to be fulfilled in one of the following ways:

- Guaranteed Replenishment (purchase order, planned order, or production order)
- Triggers made to production order
- Triggers made for outbound delivery through a third party
- Outbound delivery organized through another warehouse in the form of stock transfer

Note: The creation of master data and control table is discussed in detail in Chapter 2 and Chapter 3.

After the customer requirements are fulfilled, the goods are shipped for delivery on the specified date.

Shipping or Delivering Goods to Customers (Delivery Process)

When goods are available for delivery at the committed time, the shipping process of the SD module begins. In the shipping process, a delivery document is created by copying information, such as material and quantities, from the sales order. The delivery process controls, supports, and monitors numerous subprocesses for shipping, such as picking and confirming the quantity of goods, packing the goods, planning and monitoring the transport facilities, and finally, posting the goods once they are issued out of stock.

These shipping processes are integrated with the LE module of the mySAP ERP system. If a company has implemented warehouse management in the mySAP ERP system, the delivery document is transferred within the warehouse through transfer order. This process of transferring the delivery document helps to control the movement of goods within the warehouse. After the goods are dispatched from the company, the goods issued are posted in ledger accounts to specify that they have been sent for delivery to the customers.

Receiving Payment for Goods or Services

After the customer order is filled, a billing document is created using the information from the sales order and delivery documents. The data in the delivery and order documents serve as a basis for the billing document. These are the important functions of the billing document:

- Serves as the basis to create invoices
- Serves as a data source for financial accounting, which helps monitor and process customer payments

While creating a billing document, the ledger accounts are automatically determined, and the relevant data is posted. Debit posting is done on the receivables accounts; however, credit posting is done on the revenue account. As soon as the customer pays the amount due, the payment is posted against the invoice. The data is automatically posted in the relevant ledger account. Note that debit posting is made on the cash account and credit posting is made on the receivables account.

After understanding the SD process and its role, let's now describe the integration of the SD module with other SAP modules.

Relationship of SD to Other Relevant Modules

The SD module in the mySAP ERP system integrates with other modules, such as the QM, WM, MM, CS, and LE modules. When a customer places an order for goods, the verification of the availability of goods is done from the material master data of the MM module. This depicts the relationship of the SD module with the MM module. Moreover, the shipping and delivery processes of the SD module are configured with the LE module, depicting the relationship of the SD module with the LE module.

The quality management and customer service support for the goods sold to a customer, represented by the sales order document of the SD module, is managed by the QM and CS modules. Similarly, the transfer of delivery documents to warehouse management shows the relationship of the SD and WM modules.

The relationship of these modules with the SD module is discussed in detail in the later chapters of this book.

Let's now summarize the concepts explored in this chapter.

SUMMARY

This chapter discusses the need for, history of, and architecture of the SAP ERP system. The evolution of the SAP ERP system started with the R/1 system, followed by the R/2 and R/3 systems. The mySAP ERP system evolved as a follow-up product of the SAP R/3 system, as described in this chapter. Further, this chapter introduced the SAP GUI, along with the SAP Customizing Implementation Guide that serves as the backbone of the SAP GUI and is used to perform all business operations in the mySAP ERP system.

Moreover, all of the SAP modules, such as FI, CO, MM, and SD, along with their submodules, have been described in this chapter. In addition, this chapter has explored the SD module in detail, describing the types of data in the SD as well as other modules of the mySAP ERP system. Toward the end of the chapter the relationship of the SD module with other modules in the mySAP ERP system is explained.

In the next chapter, we present information about how to define or create the various master data records in the mySAP ERP system.

Chapter 2
Working with SAP SD Master Data

If you need information on:	See page:
Enterprise Structure	40
SAP Customizing Implementation Guide	47
Exploring Master Data in SAP SD	68

Master data refers to a centralized data object that stores information related to the sale of products and services of an organization in the Sales and Distribution (SD) module of the SAP® application. Consequently, master data reduces data redundancy and makes more efficient the transactions related to the customers, business partners, and the goods and services of an organization. Master data form the basis of the entire data processing activities in SD. For example, when a customer places an order to purchase some goods or services, the SD module stores the customer's information in the master data, which are used throughout the process of selling goods and services to that customer. At the same time, the SD module retrieves information about the goods and services sold from master data. It also stores information about the sales agreements made between the organization and the customer. In addition, master data help determine the distribution channel; that is, the division or warehouse from which the goods or services are to be delivered to the customer.

Master data are data about the customers, materials, and the conditions on which sales depend. Therefore, master data are further divided into three subcategories, depending on the source of information: customer master data, material master data, and conditional master data. The maintenance of customer master data and material master data are under the purview of the SD and MM modules, respectively.

In this chapter, enterprise structure (organization structure) and SAP Customized Implementation Guide (IMG) are explained. The chapter also describes the basics of master data and the three types of master data in detail.

Now, let's start our discussion with enterprise structure.

ENTERPRISE STRUCTURE

An organization is divided into small functional units that ensure smooth functioning during sales and distribution and associated activities. These units of the organization, when grouped together, form the structure of an organization. The structure of an organization, along with the data related to this structure, is referred to as enterprise structure. The data stored in master data are retrieved from this structure; it contains the data generated by all the units of the organization.

As learned earlier, an enterprise structure consists of organizational units grouped together for legal or business-specific reasons. These units perform specific functions to fulfill the needs and specifications of an organization. In an SAP system, organizational units in an enterprise structure can be assigned to one or more SAP modules. For example, the sales organization unit is assigned to the SD module, while plants in an organization are assigned to the Production Planning (PP) and Material Management (MM) modules. Figure 2.1 graphically represents the enterprise structure of an organization in an SAP system.

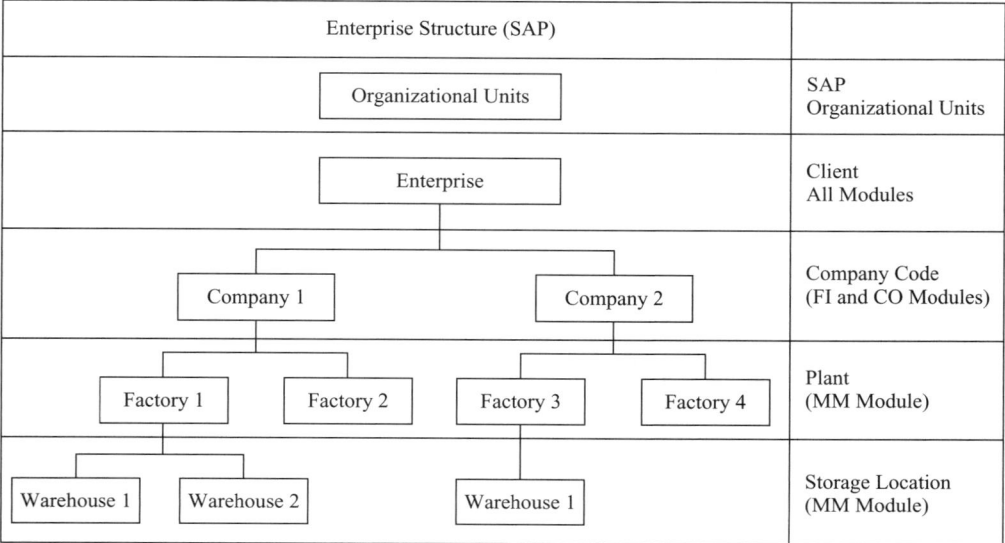

FIGURE 2.1 **SAP enterprise structure**

The units of an enterprise structure, as shown in Figure 2.1, are the following:

- **Client**—Represents the upper-level unit of an enterprise structure. A client is represented by a unique four-character alphanumeric code in the SAP system, and the client has its own master data.
- **Company**—Represents the smallest organizational unit of an enterprise structure for which an independent accounting department can be specified. The company code for a particular client is represented by a unique four-character alphanumeric value; there must be at least one company code for a client.
- **Plant**—Represents the place where production occurs or a group of several locations of material stores. A plant is also represented by a unique four-character alphanumeric value for each client. A plant is assigned a company code; however, many plants can also be assigned to the same company code.
- **Storage Location**—Represents the area where goods are stored and has a warehouse in close proximity. Similar to other organizational units, a storage location is also defined by a unique four-character alphanumeric value for each plant. Storage location is assigned to a plant that can, in turn, have many storage locations.

The enterprise structure links the independent organizational units to each other and provides flexibility while interacting with entities outside the organization. Therefore, an enterprise structure design is the fundamental process while implementing the SAP application in an organization. The enterprise structure design is determined by the business activities performed in an organization. In an enterprise structure design, the most important organizational units are as follows:

- Sales organization
- Distribution channel
- Division

These organizational units are collectively referred to as sales area. Now, let's discuss these organizational units in detail in the following sections.

Sales Organization

In the SAP application, a sales organization unit is used to distribute and sell the goods and services offered by the organization. It can be used to negotiate the sales terms and conditions with customers and process transactions related to the sales and distribution of products and services. Sales organizations are used to process all the business transactions of a company. Therefore, a sales organization must be assigned to at least one company code to process sales and distribution activities in the SAP system.

Perform the following steps to define a sales organization in a SAP system:

1. Navigate the following menu path:

Menu Path

SAP Customizing Implementation Guide > Enterprise Structure > Definition > Sales and Distribution > Define, copy, delete, check sales organization, as shown in Figure 2.2.

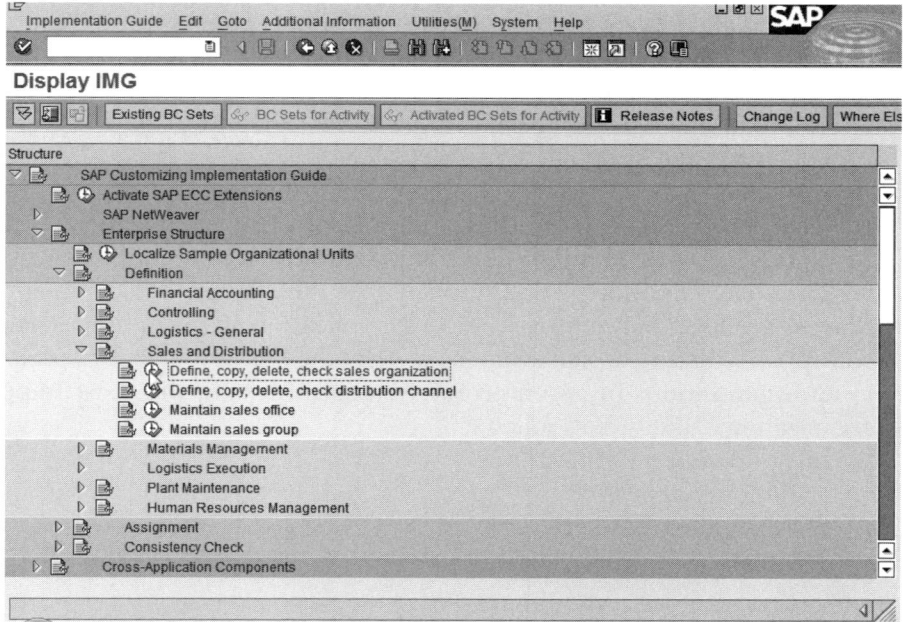

© SAP AG. All rights reserved.

FIGURE 2.2 The Display IMG screen

The **Choose Activity** dialog box appears as shown in Figure 2.3.

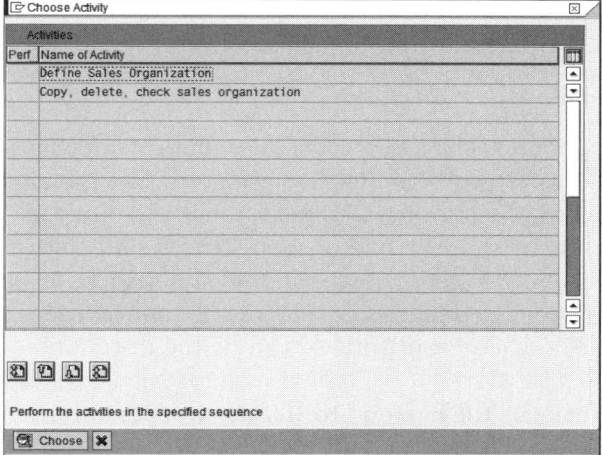

© SAP AG. All rights reserved.

FIGURE 2.3 The Choose Activity dialog box

2. Select the **Define Sales Organization** option and then click the **Choose** button. The **Change View "Sales organizations": Overview** screen appears as shown in Figure 2.4.

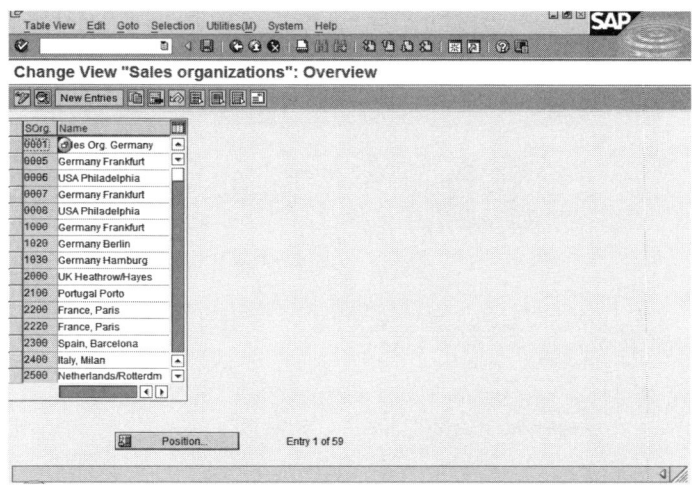

© SAP AG. All rights reserved.

FIGURE 2.4 The Change View "Sales organizations": Overview screen

3. Click the **New Entries** button to define a new sales organization in the **Change View "Sales organizations": Overview** screen.

Now, let's discuss distribution channel.

Distribution Channel

In SAP, a distribution channel specifies a medium by which to supply the products or services of an organization to the customers. Some examples of distribution channels include the Internet, wholesale, retail, and direct sales. While delivering materials to the customers, one or more distribution channels can be used for delivery. In the SAP system, a distribution channel can be assigned to one or more sales organizations to process sales and distribution activities in the SAP system. For example, a dealer or distributor can be the distribution channel in an SAP system.

Let's perform these steps to define a distribution channel in an SAP system:

1. Navigate the following menu path:

Menu Path

SAP Customizing Implementation Guide > Enterprise Structure > Definition > Sales and Distribution > Define, copy, delete, check distribution channel, as shown in Figure 2.5.

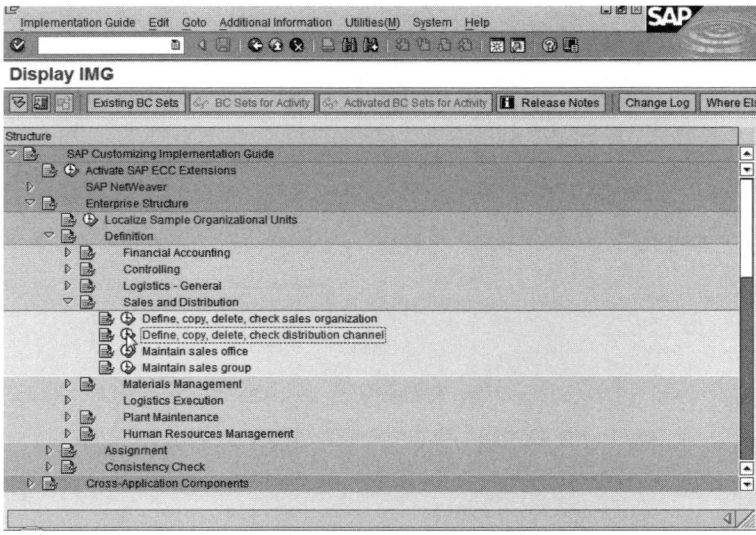

© SAP AG. All rights reserved.

FIGURE 2.5 The Display IMG screen

The **Choose Activity** dialog box appears as shown in Figure 2.3.

2. Select the **Copy, delete, check distribution channel** option and click the **Choose** button. The **Organizational object Distribution channel** screen appears as shown in Figure 2.6.

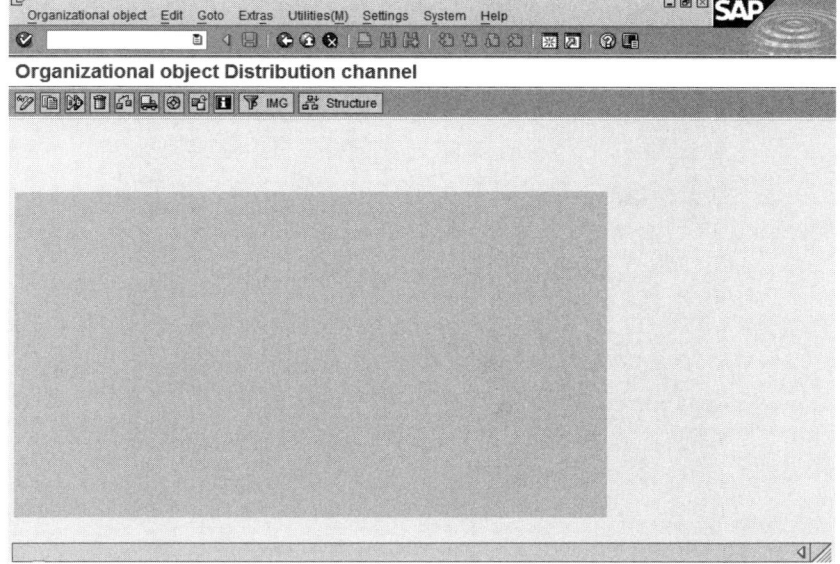

© SAP AG. All rights reserved.

FIGURE 2.6 The Organizational object Distribution channel screen

In the **Organizational object Distribution channel** screen, you can define a new distribution channel.

Now, let's learn about divisions.

Division

A division is an organizational unit in the SD module that is used to logically group products into separate categories. In other words, you can consider a division as a product line that logically groups the products. This process of logically grouping the products can be used to manage materials and services in an organization in separate groups. In the SD module of SAP software, all business transactions are linked to a specific division. In other words, a division can also be considered as a product line.

Let's perform the following steps to create a division:

1. Navigate the following menu path:

Menu Path

SAP Customizing Implementation Guide > Enterprise Structure > Definition > Logistics-General > Define, copy, delete, check division, as shown in Figure 2.7.

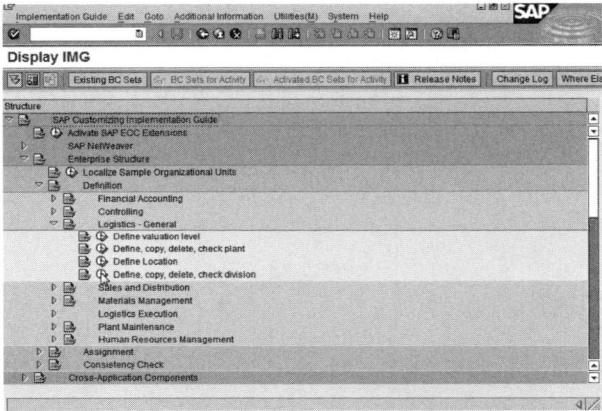

© SAP AG. All rights reserved.

FIGURE 2.7 **The Display IMG screen**

The **Choose Activity** dialog box appears as shown in Figure 2.8.

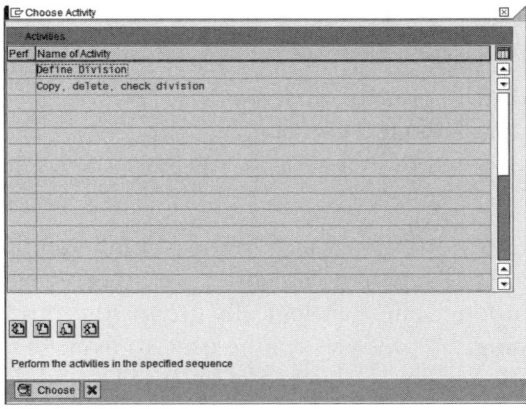

© SAP AG. All rights reserved.

FIGURE 2.8 **The Choose Activity dialog box**

2. Select the **Define Division** option and then click the **Choose** button. The **Change View "Divisions": Overview** screen appears as shown in Figure 2.9.

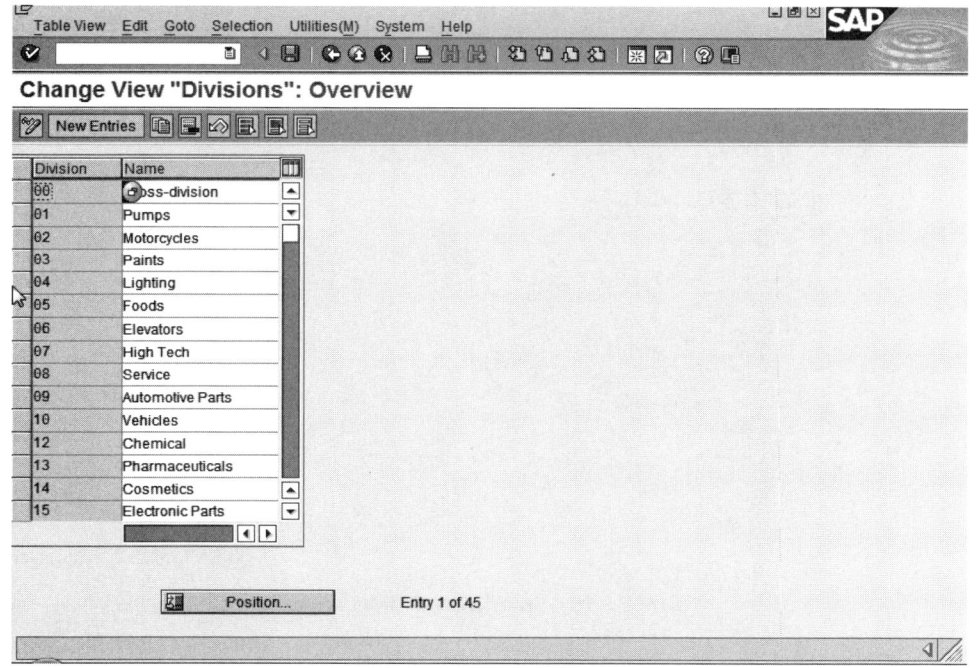

© SAP AG. All rights reserved.

FIGURE 2.9 **The Change View "Divisions": Overview screen**

3. Click the **New Entries** button to define new division-related information.

SAP CUSTOMIZING IMPLEMENTATION GUIDE

SAP Customizing Implementation Guide (IMG) is an interface to customize the functions of an SAP system. It helps implement and define the functionalities in an SAP system in an easy and user-friendly manner. SAP IMG lists all the activities to implement the functionality of each SAP module, such as SD, MM, CO, PS, QM, PP, and FI. It simplifies the way to interact with the SAP system by collectively grouping the areas that must be customized. SAP IMG also forms a structure of documentation, which helps the users to get a brief overview of the concerned functionality. SAP IMG is shown in Figure 2.10.

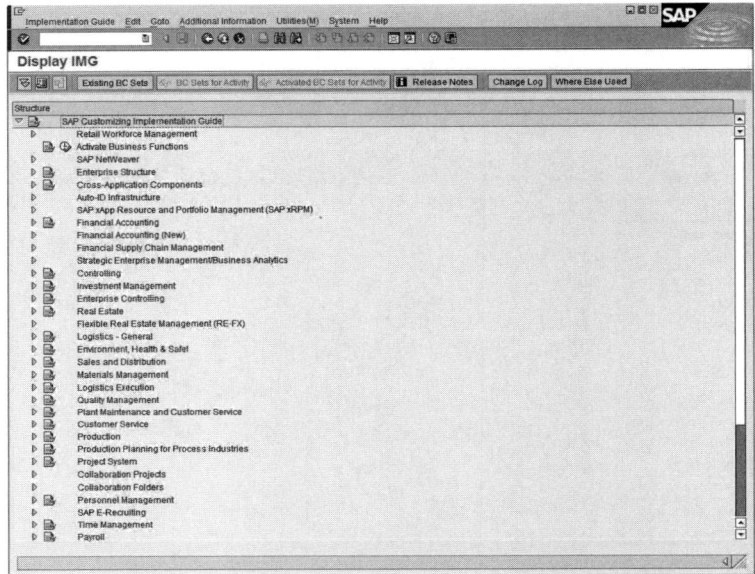

© SAP AG. All rights reserved.

FIGURE 2.10 Standard SAP IMG screen

Using SAP IMG, you can perform the activities related to each module of the SAP system. The following activities can be performed with SAP IMG:

- Defining sales office and sales group
- Defining company code
- Organizational structure in logistics
- Assignment of organizational units

Now, let's discuss how to perform each of these activities.

Defining Sales Office and Sales Group

An organization forms various teams for marketing and selling its products and services. These sales teams, in turn, have their own internal structure that optimizes their functions and reporting based on their activities. This internal organization of the sales teams comprises the following basic organizational units:

- Sales office
- Sales group

Now, let's discuss these units.

Sales Office

Organizations selling their goods and services need to have their sales units or teams in different geographical areas. These geographically separated teams work in separate premises, called sales offices. In the SAP system, these organization units are implemented as sales offices, which are assigned to one or more sales areas. While preparing a sales order, if a sales order is created for a specific sales office, the specific sales office must be assigned to the same sales area to which the sales order is assigned.

Let's perform the following steps to define a sales office:

1. Navigate the following menu path:

Menu Path

SAP Customizing Implementation Guide > Enterprise Structure > Definition > Sales and Distribution > Maintain sales office, as shown in Figure 2.11.

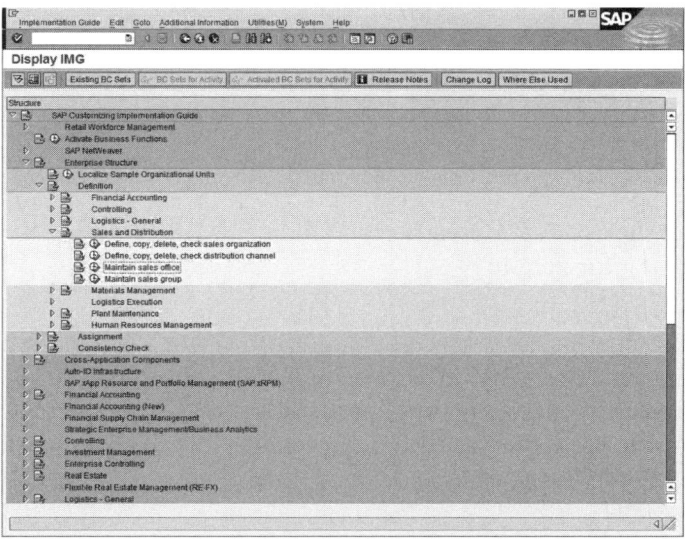

© SAP AG. All rights reserved.

FIGURE 2.11 The Display IMG screen

2. The **Change View "Sales offices": Overview** screen appears as shown in Figure 2.12.

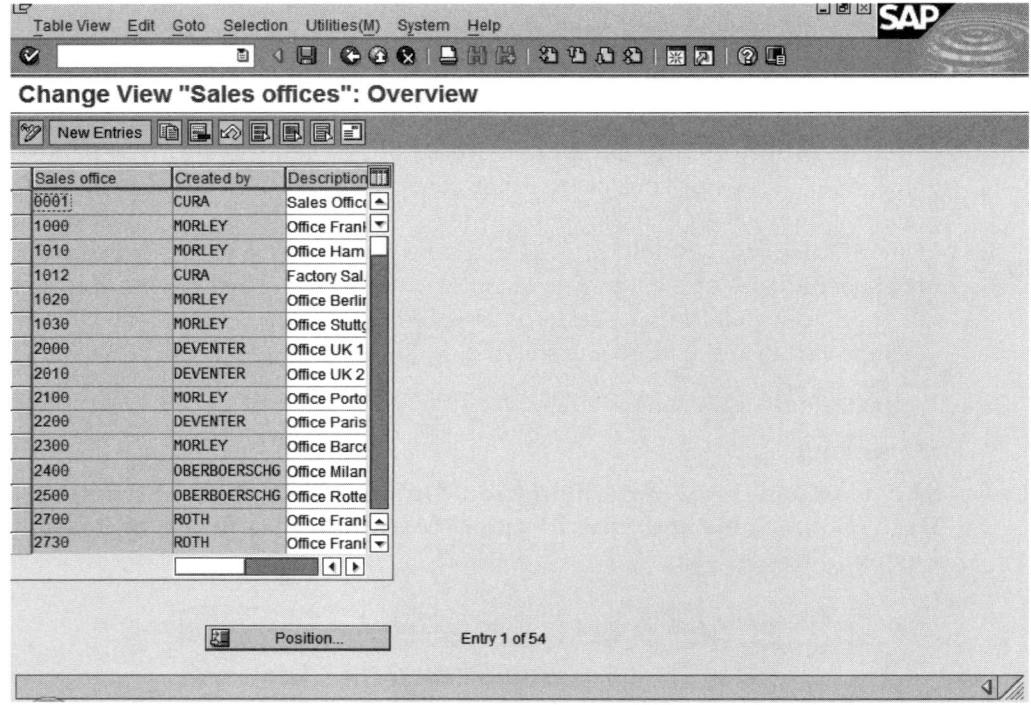

© SAP AG. All rights reserved.

FIGURE 2.12   The Change View "Sales offices": Overview screen

3. Click the **New Entries** button (Figure 2.12) to define new sales office-related information.

Sales Group

A sales group is an organizational unit that represents the group of people involved in the sales activities. A sales office may comprise many sales groups that perform various tasks related to sales activities of an organization. The team members in a sales office are grouped together on the basis of products, divisions, or services. In the SAP system, a sales group is an optional organizational unit that can be defined for a particular market or territory. A sales group is assigned to a sales office.

Let's perform the following steps to define a sales group:

1. Navigate the following menu path:

Menu Path

SAP Customizing Implementation Guide > Enterprise Structure > Definition > Sales and Distribution > Maintain sales group, as shown in Figure 2.13.

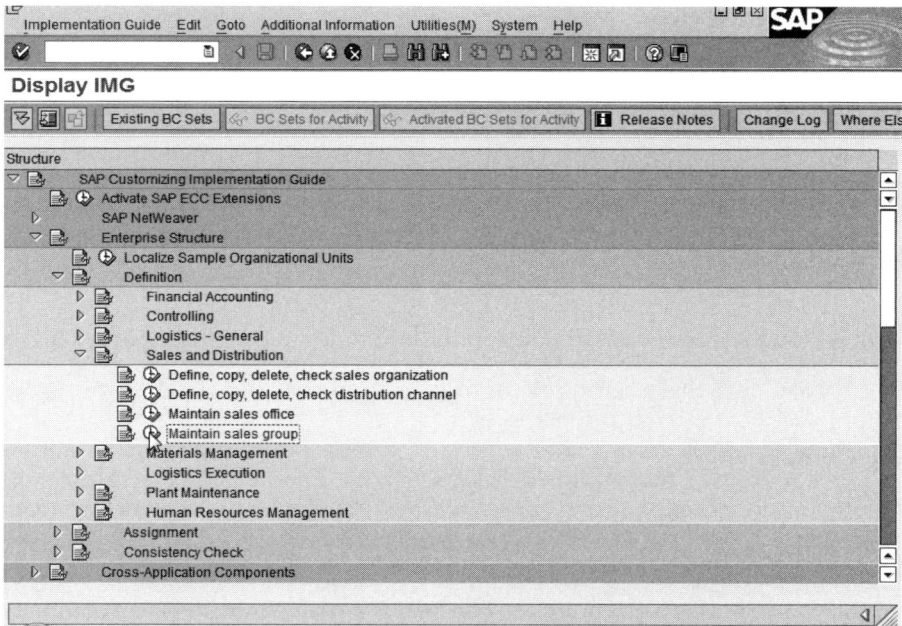

© SAP AG. All rights reserved.

FIGURE 2.13 The Display IMG screen

2. The **Change View "Sales Groups": Overview** screen appears as shown in Figure 2.14.

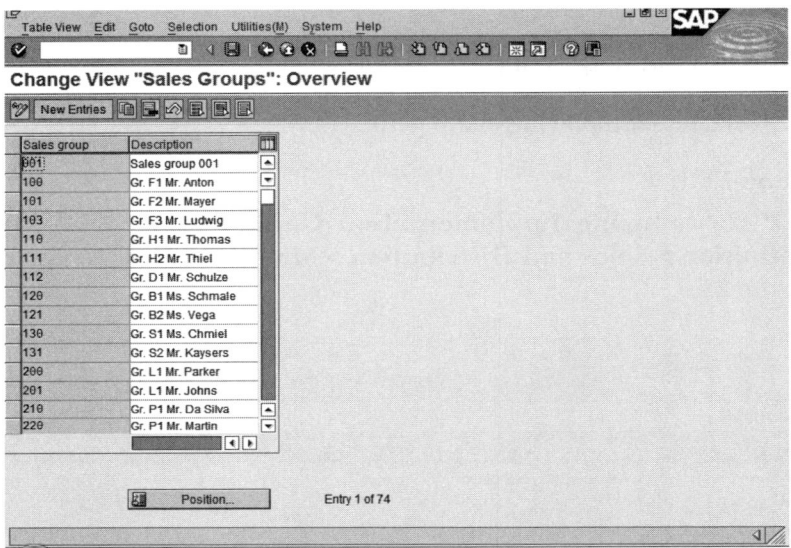

© SAP AG. All rights reserved.

FIGURE 2.14 The Change View "Sales Groups": Overview screen

3. Click the **New Entries** button to define new sales group information.

Now, let's discuss the role of organization structure in accounting.

Defining Company Code

One or more companies, represented by individual company codes, can exist in an SAP system. Each of these company codes can be assigned to one or more sales organizations. All of the company codes are considered to be independent units and entities in accounting. The best approach to configure a company code is to select the existing company code and create a copy for the new company code. You may select a company code according to the country-specific settings of your system.

Let's perform the following steps to define the company code in the SAP system:

1. Navigate the following menu path:

Menu Path

SAP Customizing Implementation Guide > Enterprise Structure > Definition > Financial Accounting > Edit, Copy, Delete, Check Company Code, as shown in Figure 2.15.

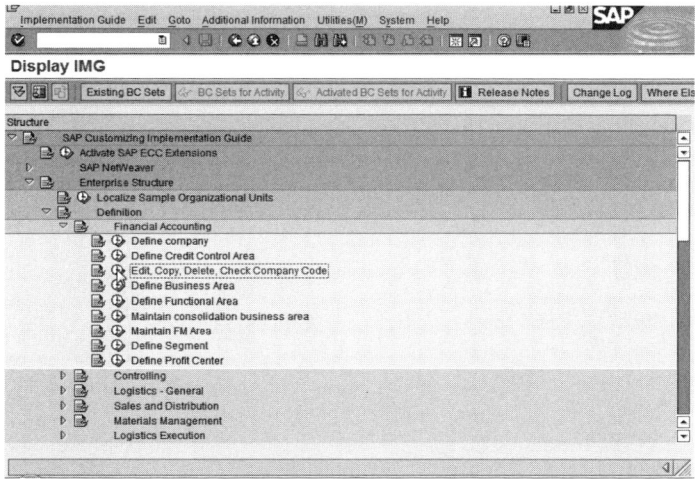

© SAP AG. All rights reserved.

FIGURE 2.15 The Display IMG screen

The **Choose Activity** dialog box appears as shown in Figure 2.16.

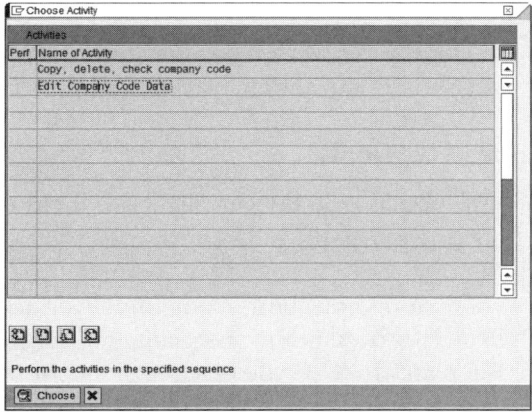

© SAP AG. All rights reserved.

FIGURE 2.16 The Choose Activity dialog box

2. Select the **Edit Company Code Data** option and click the **Choose** button. The **Change View "Company Code": Overview** screen appears as shown in Figure 2.17.

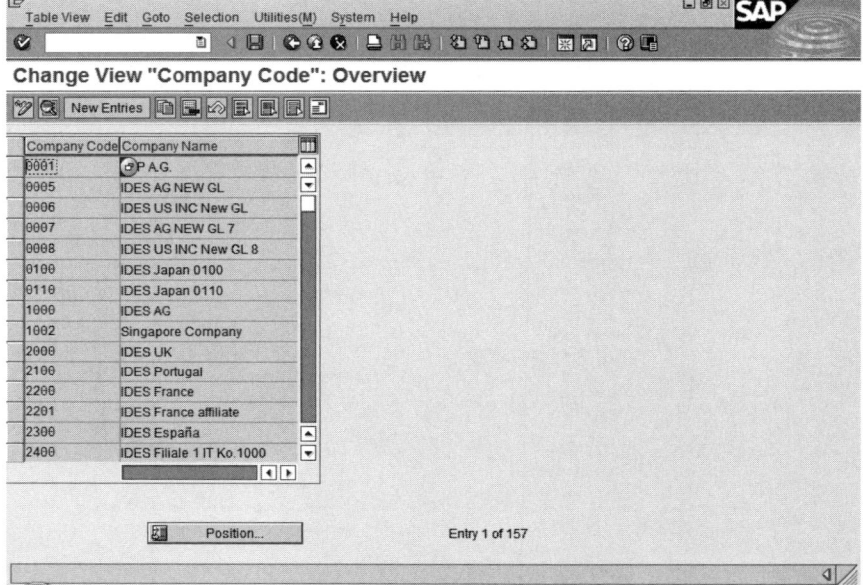

© SAP AG. All rights reserved.

FIGURE 2.17 The Change View "Company Code": Overview screen

3. Click the **New Entries** button to enter the new company code information.

Now, let's discuss an organizational structure in the context of logistics.

Organizational Structure in Logistics

In the SAP organizational structure, a plant is a logistics organizational unit where production, procurement, and material planning activities are executed. In other words, a plant is the place where materials are produced or services are provided. When an organization needs to deliver an order to a customer, an availability check is carried out in the plant, and the goods and services are delivered from the plant. In SAP, you can assign one or more storage locations to a plant and one or more plants to a company code. The following are the points that must be taken care of while assigning plants:

- A plant can be assigned to only one company code.
- A plant can be assigned to more than one sales organization and distribution channel. Stock from the same plant can be distributed in different sales areas.
- A plant may deliver the products and services from more than one shipping point. You can assign a shipping point to more than one plant.

Figure 2.18 graphically represents the assignment of a plant to a company code.

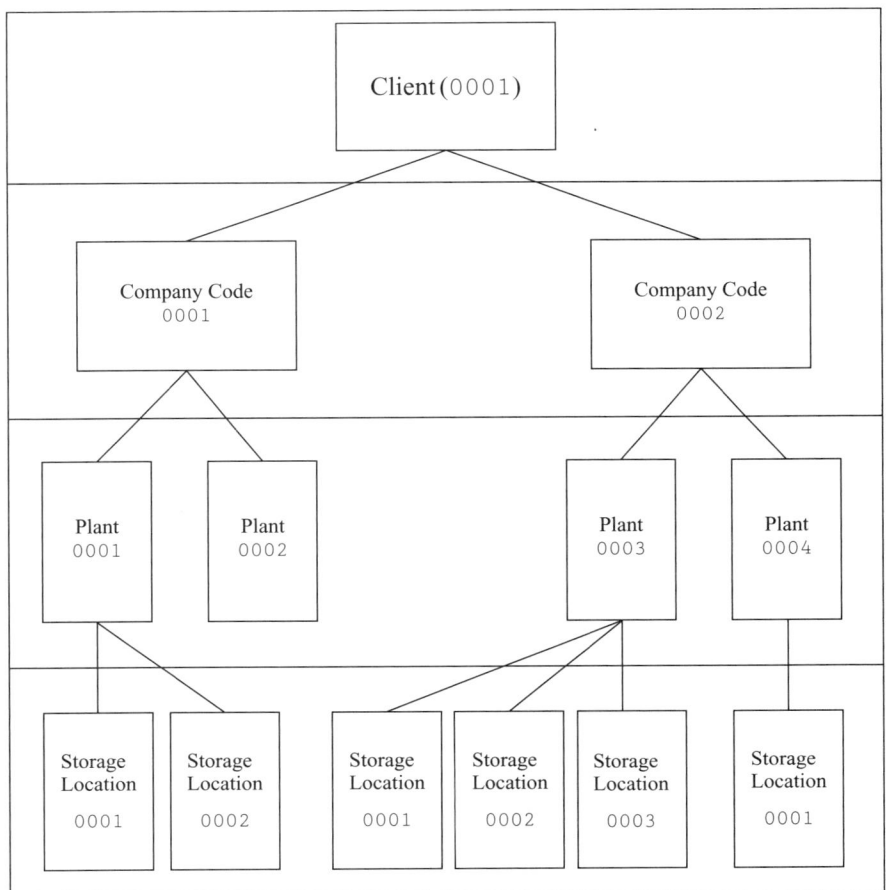

FIGURE 2.18 **Assignment of plants to company code**

In Figure 2.18, the 0001 and 0002 plant numbers are assigned to the 0001 company code, and 0003 and 0004 plant numbers are assigned to the 0002 company code. Similarly, the storage locations, which can be implemented as shipping points for sales transactions, are also assigned to different plants (Figure 2.18).

In the delivery of products and services, shipping points play an important role. A shipping point is a place where the deliveries are processed and from where the goods and services are delivered to the customer. In SAP, one shipping point can be shared by multiple plants. All the deliveries to the customers are initiated from the shipping point, which is why it is placed at the top level in the hierarchy of a shipping organization. A shipping point may have multiple loading points (a subdivision of shipping points where goods are loaded for delivery).

Perform the following steps to define a shipping point:

1. Navigate the following menu path:

Menu Path

SAP Customizing Implementation Guide > Enterprise Structure > Definition > Logistics Execution > Define, copy, delete, check shipping point, as shown in Figure 2.19.

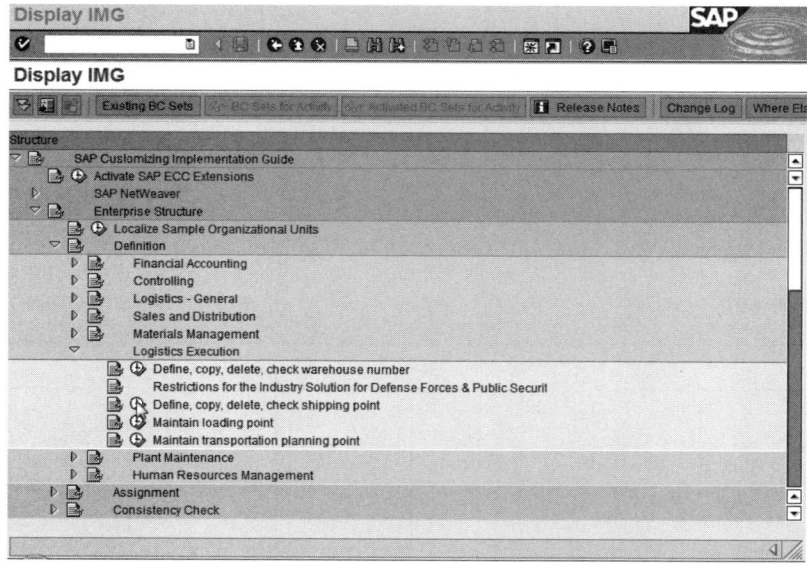

© SAP AG. All rights reserved.

FIGURE 2.19 The Display IMG screen

The **Choose Activity** dialog box appears as shown in Figure 2.20.

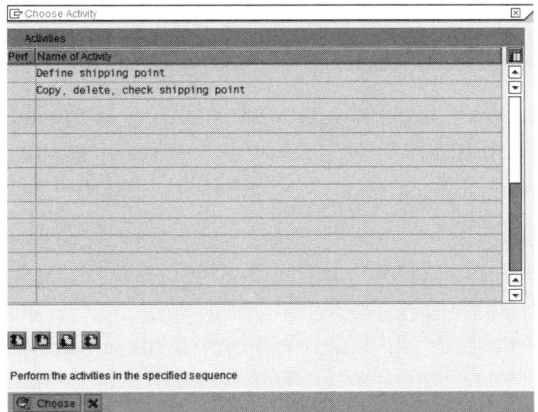

© SAP AG. All rights reserved.

FIGURE 2.20 The Choose Activity dialog box

2. Select the **Define shipping point** option and then click the **Choose** button. The **Change View "Shipping Points": Overview** screen appears as shown in Figure 2.21.

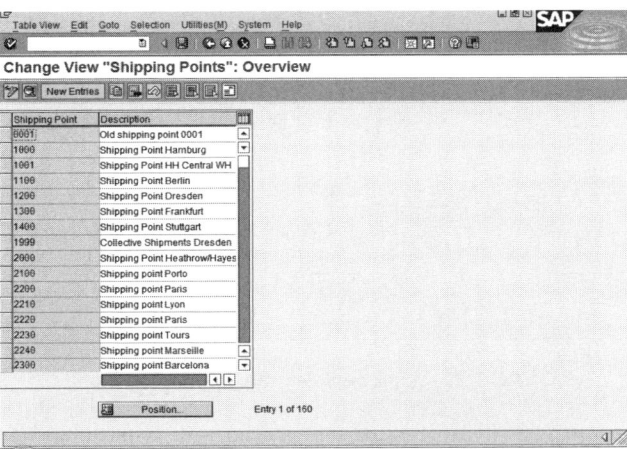

© SAP AG. All rights reserved.

FIGURE 2.21 The Change View "Shipping Points": Overview screen

3. Click the **New Entries** button (Figure 2.18) to enter the new shipping point information.

Now, let's discuss how assignments of different organizational units are achieved.

Assignment of Organizational Units

While assigning the organizational data, different modules of the SAP system are linked on the basis of their interaction with each other. For example, the sales organization and plants are linked together while assigning organizational data. Similarly, a plant can be linked to a company code as well as to several sales organizations at the same time. This means that, although the plant is always controlled by the company code, it can accept orders and deliver goods and services to the customers only within its assigned sales organization. Figure 2.22 graphically represents the link between the organizational units.

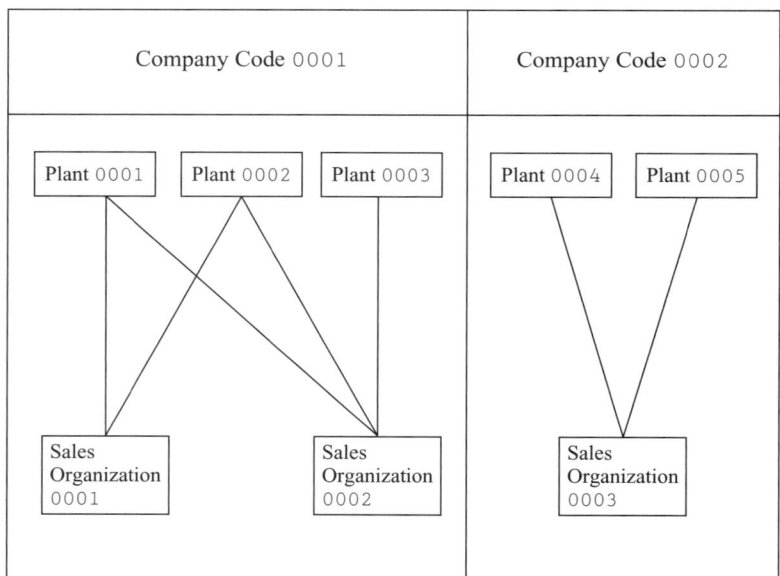

FIGURE 2.22 Link between the organization units

Assignment of different organizational units involves the following:

- Assigning a sales organization to a company code
- Assigning a distribution channel to a sales organization
- Assigning a division to a sales organization

- Setting up a sales area
- Assigning a sales office to a sales area
- Assigning a sales group to a sales office
- Assigning a sales organization, distribution channel, and plant
- Assigning a shipping point to a plant

> **Note:** These assignments are called basic organizational structure in SD, and we always move on as shown in this configuration.

Now, let's discuss each of these in detail.

Assigning a Sales Organization to a Company Code

Navigate the following menu path to assign a sales organization to a company code:

Menu Path

SAP Customizing Implementation Guide > Enterprise Structure > Assignment > Sales and Distribution > Assign sales organization to company code, as shown in Figure 2.23.

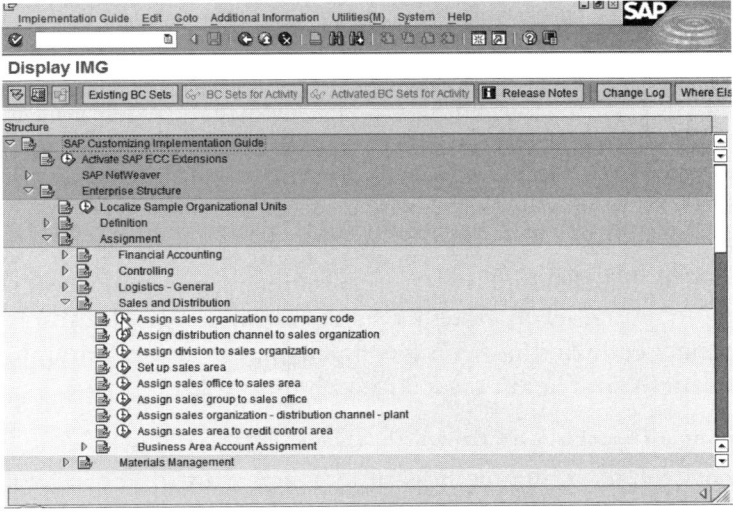

© SAP AG. All rights reserved.

FIGURE 2.23 The Display IMG screen

When the preceding menu path is navigated, the **Change View "Assignment Sales Organization – Company Code": Overview** screen appears as shown in Figure 2.24.

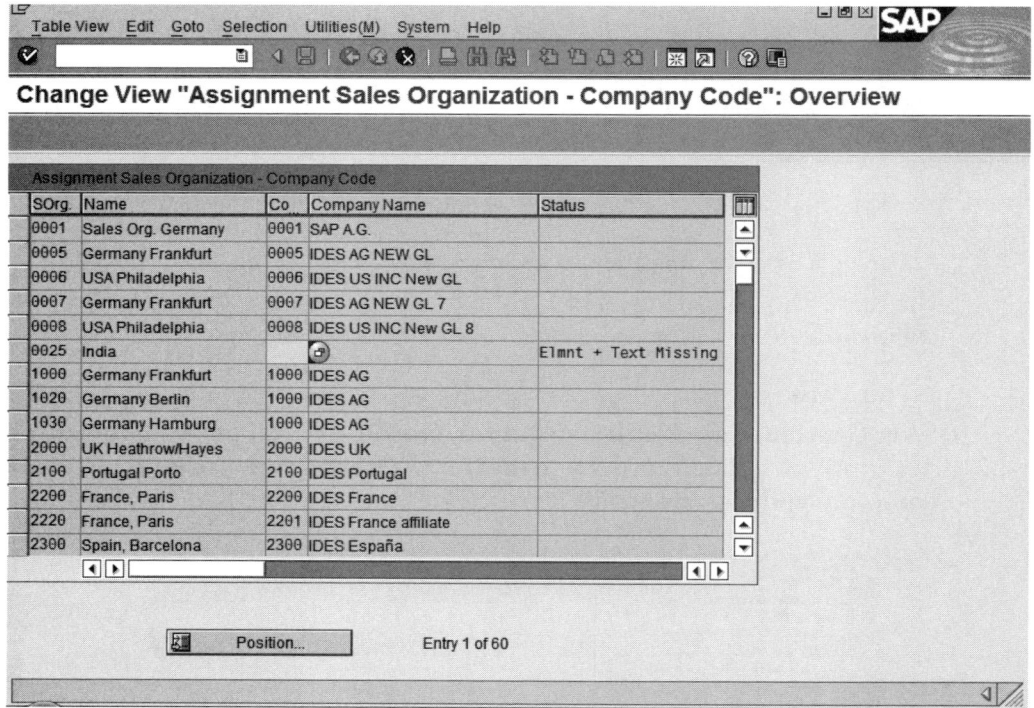

© SAP AG. All rights reserved.

FIGURE 2.24 The Change View "Assignment Sales Organization – Company Code": screen

Notice that the India sales organization, represented in this example by SOrg. No. 0025, has not been assigned a company code. You need to assign a company code and provide a company name in the **Company Code** and **Company Name** fields, respectively (Figure 2.24).

Assigning a Distribution Channel to a Sales Organization

Navigate the following menu path to assign a distribution channel to a sales organization:

Menu Path

SAP Customizing Implementation Guide > Enterprise Structure > Assignment > Sales and Distribution > Assign distribution channel to sales organization, as shown in Figure 2.23.

The **Change View "Assignment Sales Organization – Distribution Channel": Overview** screen appears as shown in Figure 2.25.

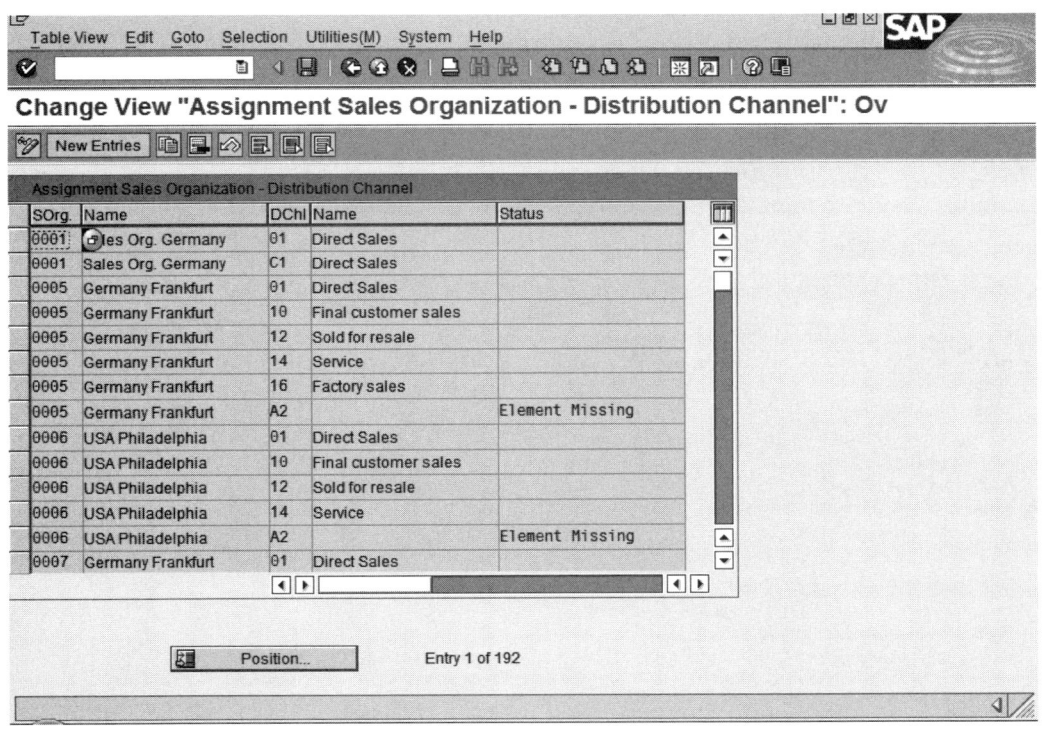

© SAP AG. All rights reserved.

FIGURE 2.25 The Change View "Assignment Sales Organization – Distribution Channel": Overview screen

Click the **New Entries** button (Figure 2.25); the **New Entries: Overview of Added Entries** screen appears. In this screen, you can assign a distribution channel to a sales organization.

Assigning a Division to a Sales Organization

Navigate the following menu path to assign a division to a sales organization:

Menu Path

SAP Customizing Implementation Guide > Enterprise Structure > Assignment > Sales and Distribution > Assign division to sales organization, as shown in Figure 2.23.

The **Change View "Assignment Sales Organization – Division": Overview** screen appears, as shown in Figure 2.26.

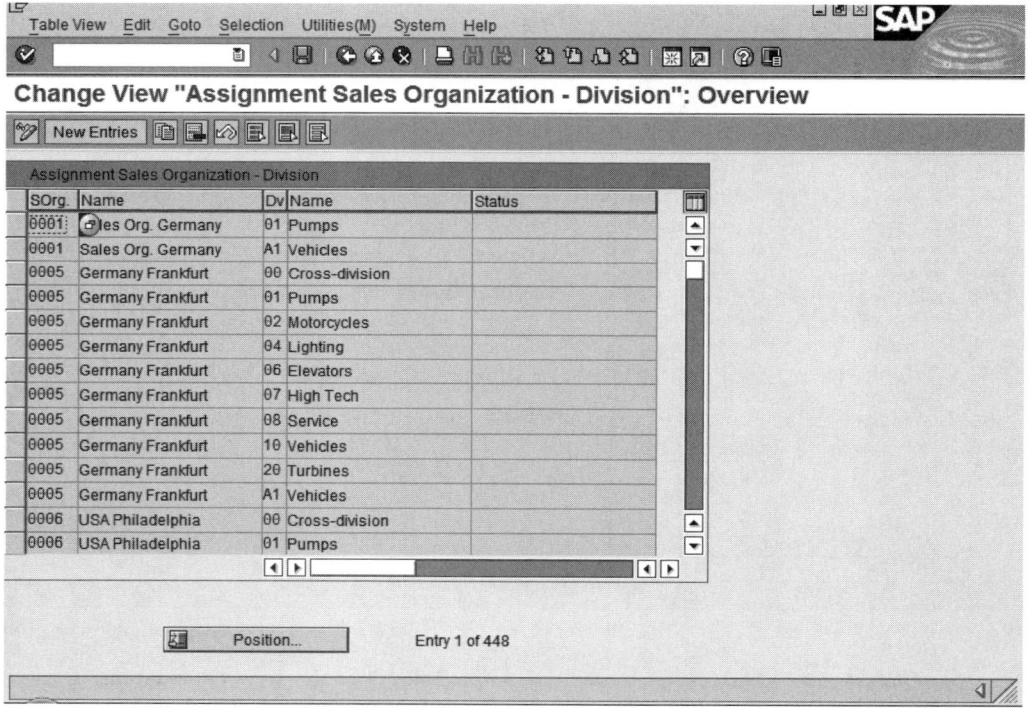

© SAP AG. All rights reserved.

FIGURE 2.26 The Change View "Assignment Sales Organization – Division": Overview screen

Click the **New Entries** button (Figure 2.26): the **New Entries: Overview of Added Entries** screen appears. In this screen, you can assign a division to a sales organization.

Setting Up a Sales Area

As discussed earlier, the combination of sales organization, distribution channel, and division is called a sales area. A sales area must be selected for every sales transaction. Navigate the following menu path to set up a sales area:

Menu Path

SAP Customizing Implementation Guide > Enterprise Structure > Assignment > Sales and Distribution > Set up sales area, as shown in Figure 2.23.

The **Change View "Assignment Sales Org. – Distribution Channel – Division": Overview** screen appears as shown in Figure 2.27.

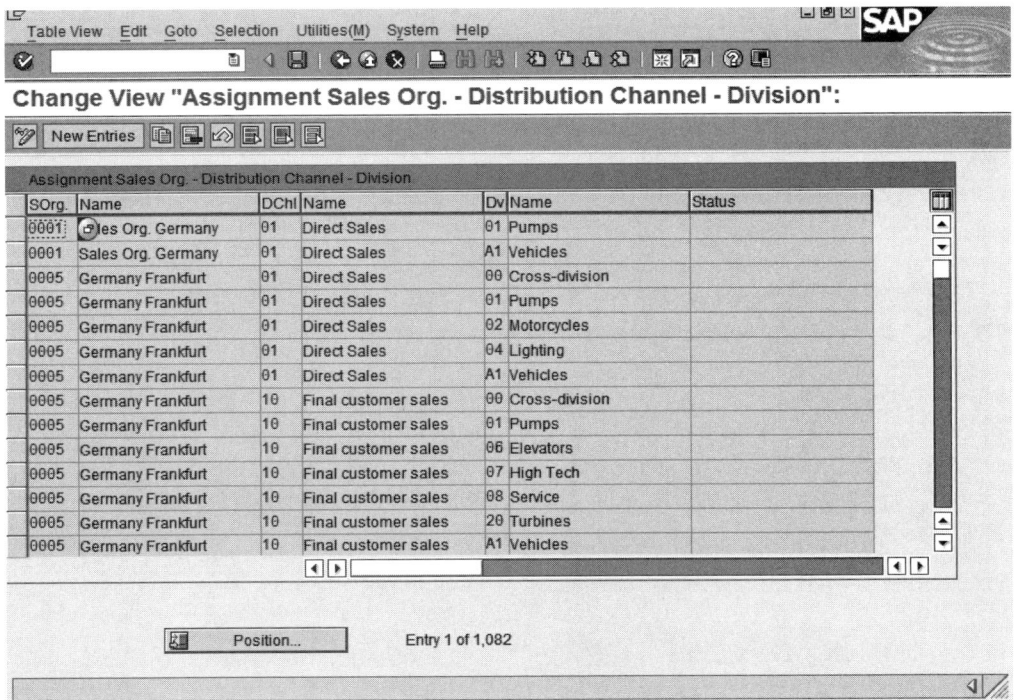

© SAP AG. All rights reserved.

FIGURE 2.27 The Change View "Assignment Sales Org. – Distribution Channel – Division": Overview screen

Click the **New Entries** button (Figure 2.27): the **New Entries: Overview of Added Entries** screen appears. In this screen, you can set up a sales area.

Assigning a Sales Office to a Sales Area

Navigate the following menu path to assign a sales office to a sales area:

Menu Path

SAP Customizing Implementation Guide > Enterprise Structure > Assignment > Sales and Distribution > Assign sales office to sales area, as shown in Figure 2.23.

The **Change View "Assignment Sales Office – Sales Area": Overview** screen appears as shown in Figure 2.28.

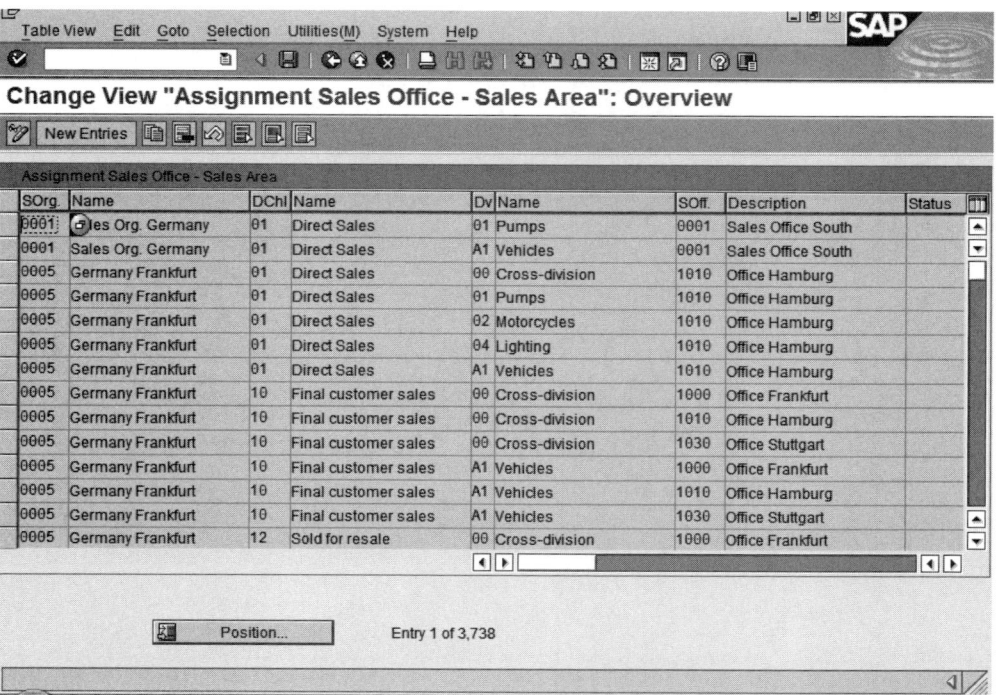

© SAP AG. All rights reserved.

FIGURE 2.28 The Change View "Assignment Sales Office – Sales Area": Overview screen

Click the **New Entries** button (Figure 2.28): the **New Entries: Overview of Added Entries** screen appears. In this screen, you can assign a sales office to a sales area.

Assigning a Sales Group to a Sales Office

Navigate the following menu path to assign a sales group to a sales office:

Menu Path

SAP Customizing Implementation Guide > Enterprise Structure > Assignment > Sales and Distribution > Assign sales group to sales office, as shown in Figure 2.23.

The **Change View "Assignment Sales Office – Sales Groups": Overview** screen appears as shown in Figure 2.29.

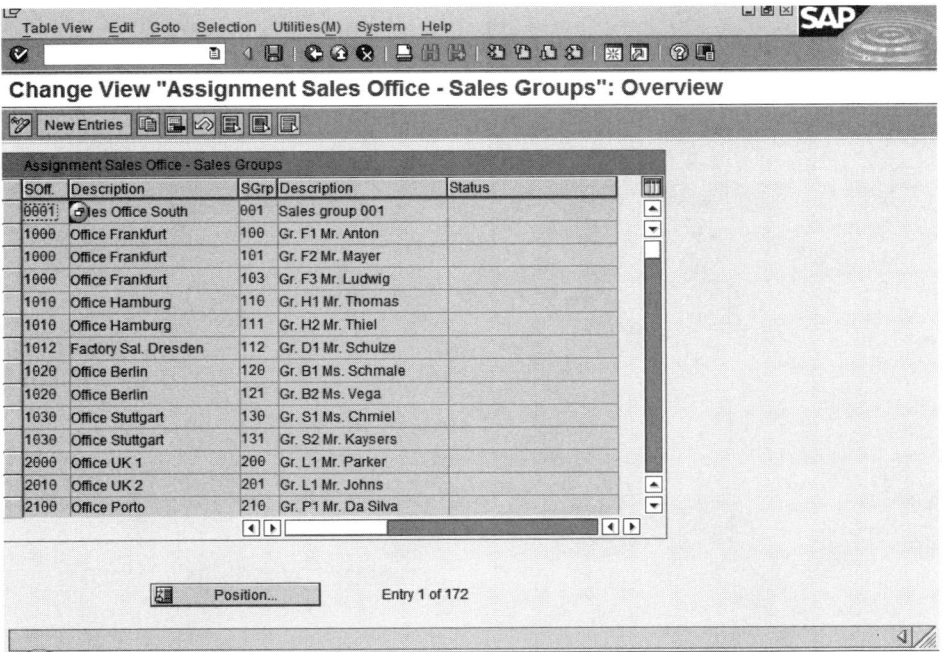

© SAP AG. All rights reserved.

FIGURE 2.29 The Change View "Assignment Sales Office – Sales Groups": Overview screen

Click the **New Entries** button (Figure 2.29): the **New Entries: Overview of Added Entries** screen appears. In this screen, you can assign a sales group to a sales office.

Assigning a Sales Organization, Distribution Channel, and Plant

Navigate the following menu path to assign a sales organization, distribution channel, and plant:

Menu Path

SAP Customizing Implementation Guide > Enterprise Structure > Assignment > Sales and Distribution > Assign sales organization-distribution channel-plant, as shown in Figure 2.23.

The **Change View "Assignment Sales Organization/Distribution Channel – Plan** screen appears as shown in Figure 2.30.

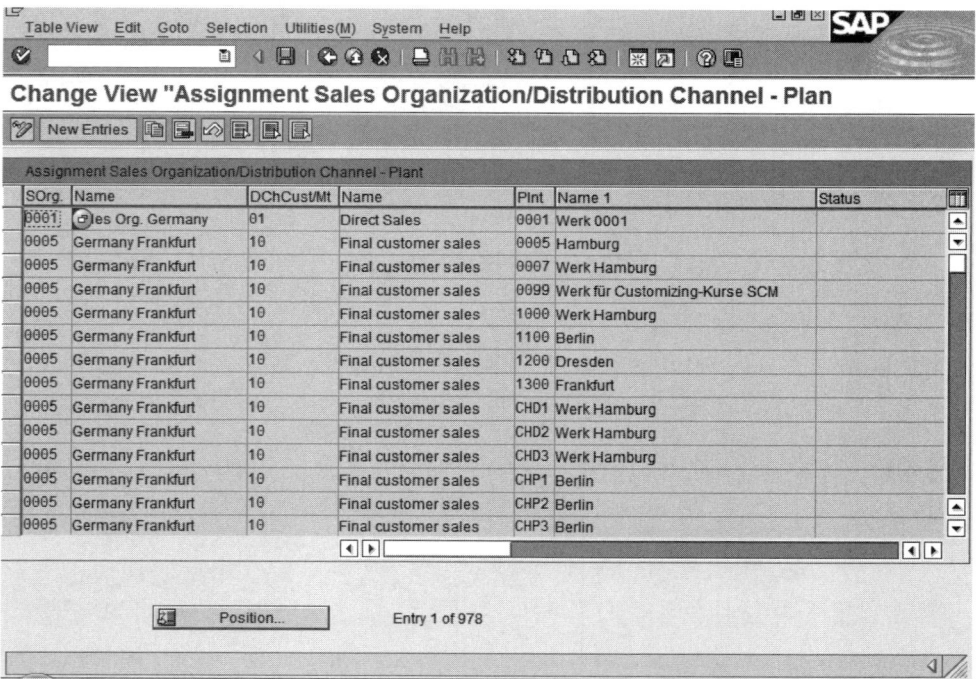

© SAP AG. All rights reserved.

FIGURE 2.30 The Change View "Assignment Sales Organization/Distribution Channel – Plan screen

Click the **New Entries** button (Figure 2.30): the **New Entries: Overview of Added Entries** screen appears, where you can assign a sales organization, distribution channel, and plant.

Assigning a Shipping Point to a Plant

Navigate the following menu path to assign a shipping point to a plant:

Menu Path

SAP Customizing Implementation Guide > Enterprise Structure > Assignment > Logistics Execution > Assign shipping point to plant, as shown in Figure 2.31.

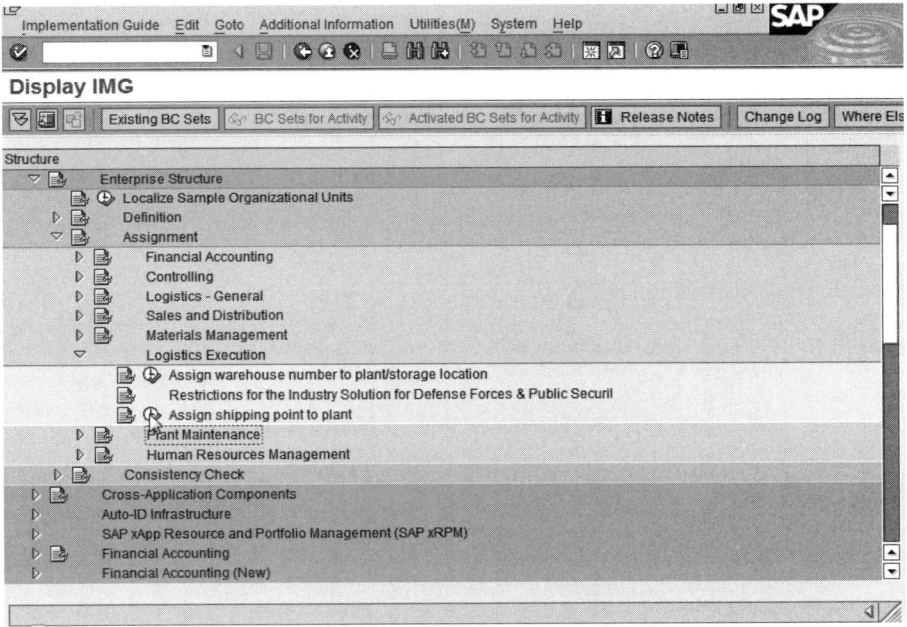

© SAP AG. All rights reserved.

FIGURE 2.31 The Display IMG screen

The **Shipping Points -> Plants: Overview** screen appears as shown in Figure 2.32.

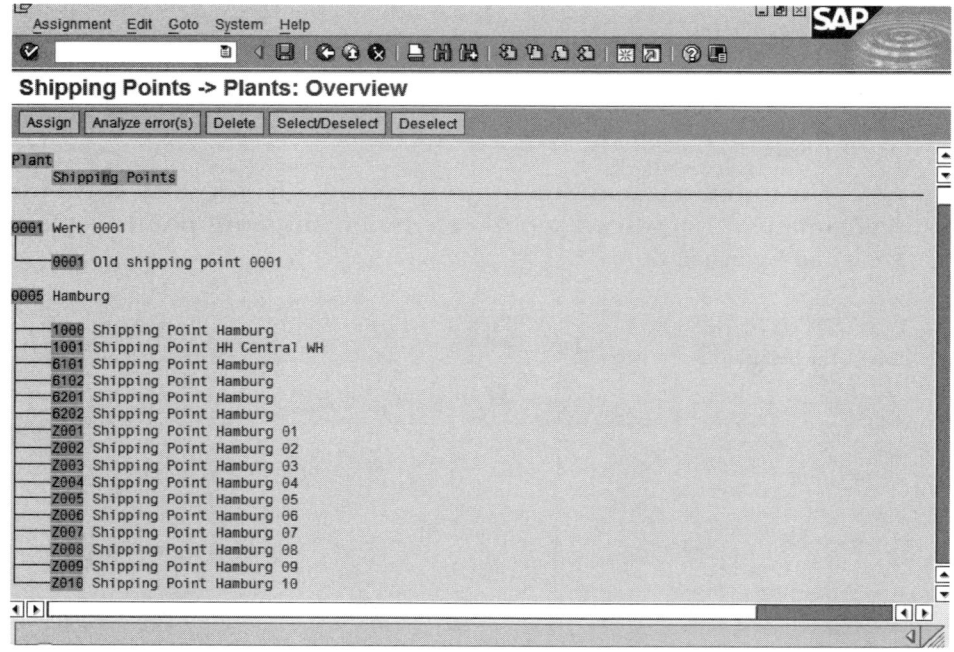

© SAP AG. All rights reserved.

FIGURE 2.32 The Shipping Points -> Plants: Overview screen

Select a shipping point and then click the **Assign** button to assign it to a plant.

Let's now explore master data in SD.

EXPLORING MASTER DATA IN SAP SD

As already discussed, master data are the collection of data related to all the elements of an organization that contribute in the organizational structure. Therefore, this collection of data serves as a central data store from which all the modules of an SAP system can access relevant information. Master data play a vital role for all the transactions performed in the SD module. Figure 2.33 depicts the role of master data in the SD module:

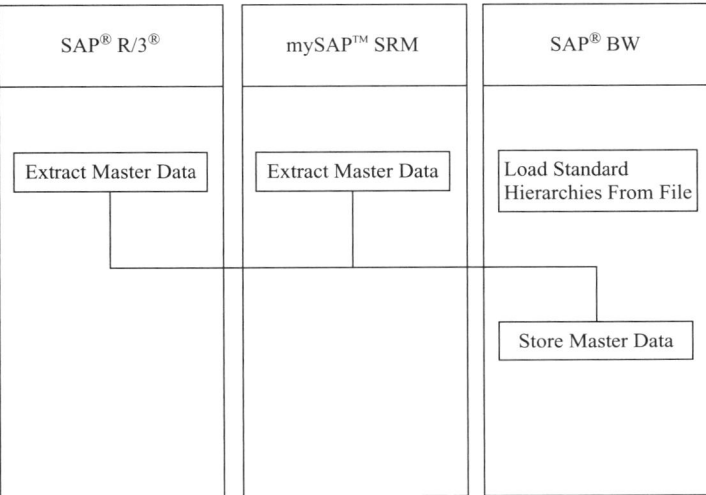

FIGURE 2.33   The role of master data

On the basis of the source of data in the SAP system, master data can be further categorized into the following subcategories:

- Customer master data
- Material master data
- Condition master data
- Customer-material info data

Now, let's discuss these subcategories of master data one by one.

Customer Master Data

Customer master data comprise a collection of records related to a customer, sales area, and other transaction-related units. This type of data helps in carrying out all transactions, delivery, and payment-related functions in the SD module of the SAP system. The data related to all the customers, including intercompany customers and one-time customers, must be stored in customer master data.

Note: Intercompany customers refer to organizational units that behave as a customer while purchasing products from another organizational unit of the same company. One-time customers represent customers who buy products or services infrequently.

Customer master data can be grouped into the following categories:

- **General Data**—A set of data independent of any organizational units of the SAP system. It contains data related to address, control, payment transactions, marketing, uploading points, export, and contact persons. This is the central data set for a customer.
- **Sales Area Data**—A set of data related to the SD module of the SAP system. It consists of data related to orders (sales office, currency, price group), shipping (shipping condition, delivery site, transportation zone), billing document (output tax classification, terms of payment), and partner functions (sold-to party, ship-to party, billing-to party, payer).
- **Company Code Data**—A set of data used by the accounting department of an organization. It consists of data related to account management, payment transactions (payment methods, payment block), correspondence, and insurance.

Figure 2.34 graphically represents these three categories of customer master data.

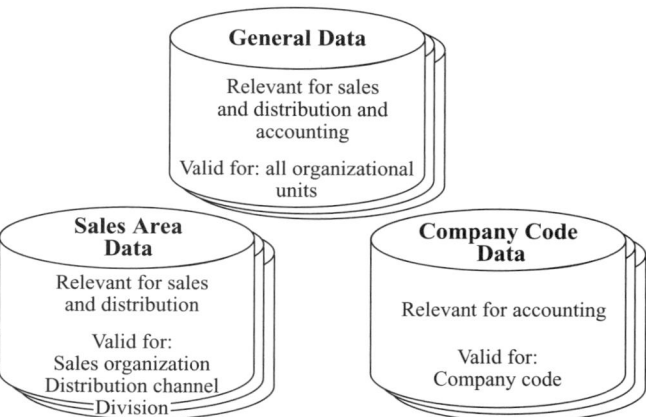

FIGURE 2.34 Categories of customer master data

Now, let's discuss how customer master data is created in the SAP system.

Navigate the following menu path to create customer master data:

Menu Path

SAP Easy Access > SAP menu > Logistics > Sales and Distribution > Master Data > Business Partner > Customer > Create, as shown in Figure 2.35.

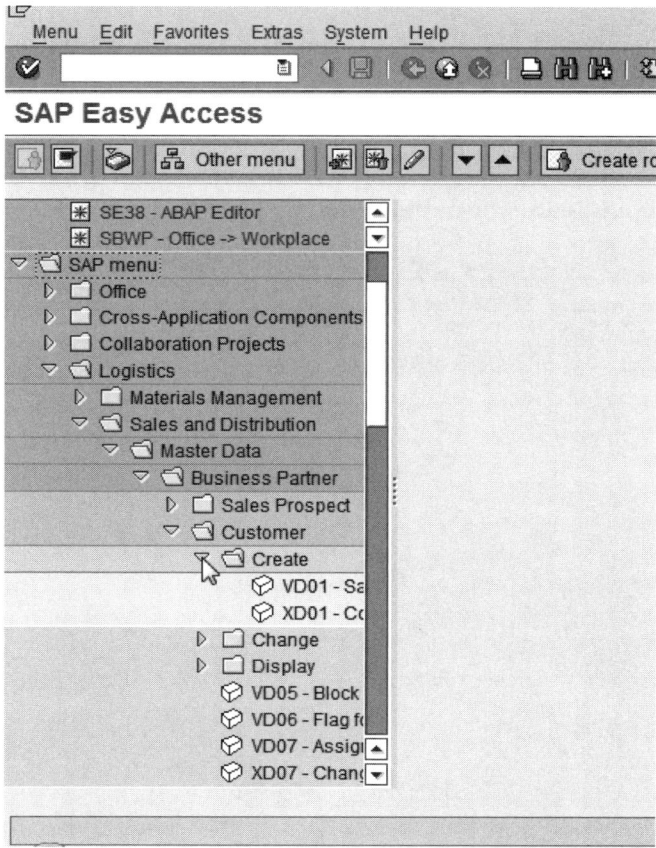

© SAP AG. All rights reserved.

FIGURE 2.35 The SAP Easy Access screen

When the preceding menu path is navigated, two icons to create customer master data are displayed, as shown in Figure 2.36.

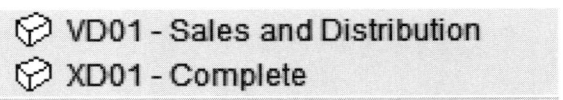

FIGURE 2.36   Options to create customer master data

In Figure 2.36, the **VD01 – Sales and Distribution** icon creates general and SD views of the customer master data, whereas the **XD01 – Complete** icon creates general and central customer master views of the customer master data.

You need to double-click the **VD01 – Sales and Distribution** icon. The **Customer Create: Initial Screen** appears as shown in Figure 2.37.

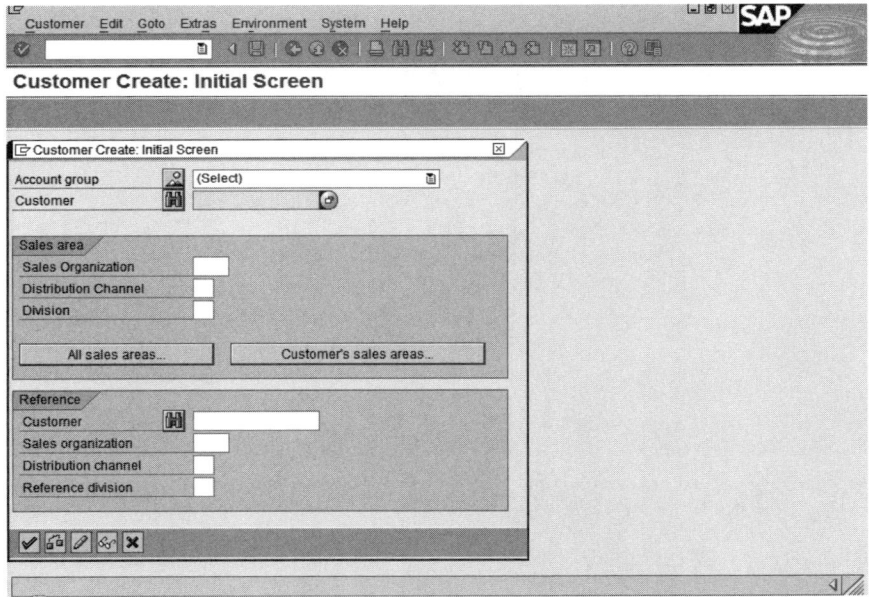

FIGURE 2.37   The Customer Create: Initial Screen

You can now create a new customer master data by specifying the relevant information in the respective fields.

Now, let's discuss the material master data.

Material Master Data

Material master data comprise all the records related to the products/materials and services offered by the organization. Material master data, similar to customer master data, are retrieved and processed from various sources. Material master data can be grouped into the following categories:

- **Basic Data**—A collection of data related to all the organizational units of an SAP system.
- **Sales and Distribution Data**—A collection of data related to the SD module of the SAP system.
- **Purchasing Data**—A collection of data related to the MM module of the SAP system.
- **Accounting Data**—A collection of data related to the FI module of the SAP system.
- **Costing Data**—A collection of data used for cost determination in the SAP system.
- **Warehouse Management**—A collection of data used for warehouse management.

Figure 2.38 graphically represents different categories of material master data.

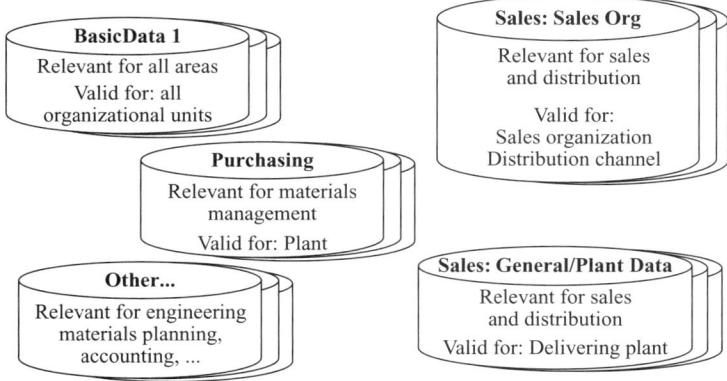

FIGURE 2.38 Categories of material master data

Now, let's discuss how to create material master data.

Navigate the following menu path to create material master data:

Menu Path

SAP Easy Access > SAP Menu > Logistics > Sales and Distribution > Master Data > Products > Material > Other Material > Create, as shown in Figure 2.39.

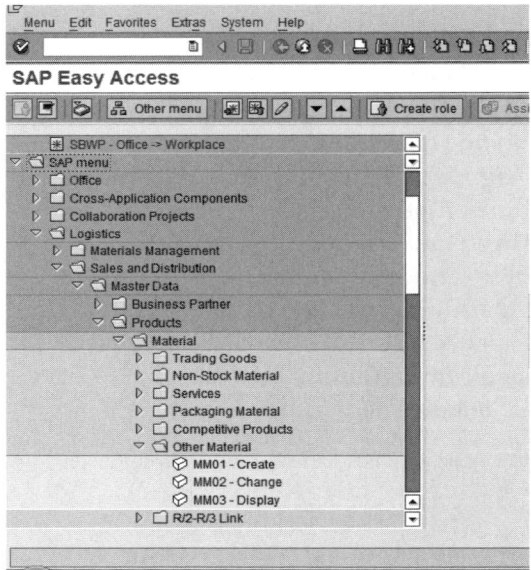

© SAP AG. All rights reserved.

FIGURE 2.39 The SAP Easy Access screen

When the preceding menu path is navigated, the following three icons appear:

- **MM01 – Create**—Creates a new material master data.
- **MM02 – Change**—Modifies the existing material master data.
- **MM03 – Display**—Displays the existing material master data.

Note: A material master is maintained for each combination of plant and distribution channel.

You need to double-click the **MM01** icon to create new material master data. The **Create Material (Initial Screen)** appears, as shown in Figure 2.40.

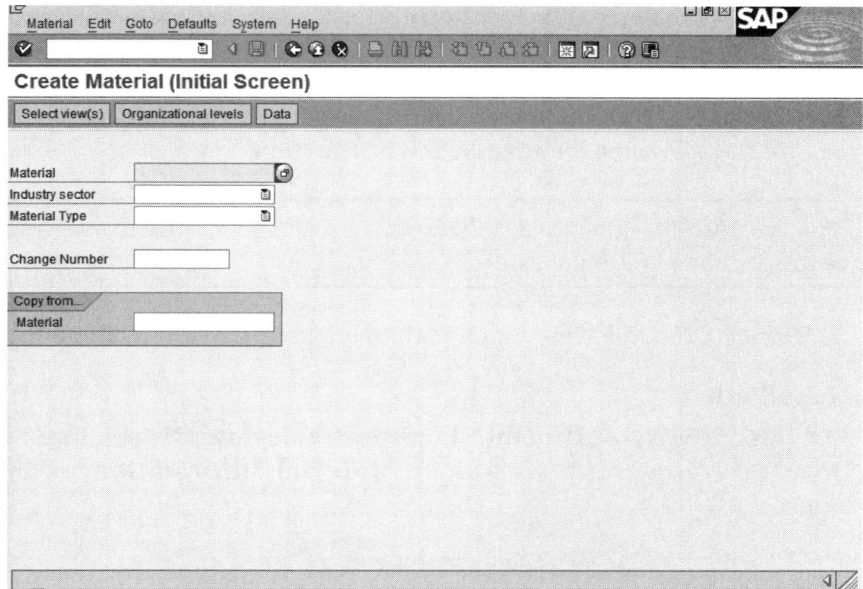

© SAP AG. All rights reserved.

FIGURE 2.40 The Create Material (Initial Screen)

In Figure 2.40, you can create a new material master data by specifying the relevant information in the respective fields.

Now, let's discuss condition master data.

Condition Master Data

Condition master data comprise the business logic or configuration settings. For example, the data related to pricing are determined on the basis of the pricing conditions retrieved through the access sequence. Condition master data are determined using different condition techniques. (For more information, refer to Chapter 4.)

In addition to the three types of master data, customer-material information data are also important for the SD module of the SAP system. Let's now discuss customer-material info data.

Customer-Material Info Data

Customer-material info data are the data related to the material and the customer who buys that material. When customers buy materials, they may have their own specifications for the materials. These specifications can be stored as customer-material info data. When a sales order is created, the default material data are copied from the customer-material info data, if available; otherwise, the material data for the sales area are used by the SAP system.

> **Note:** The master data maintained at various levels are required to fetch the details at the time of creation of sales documents.

Navigate the following menu path to create customer–material info data:

Menu Path

SAP Easy Access > SAP menu > Logistics > Sales and Distribution > Master Data > Agreements > Customer Material Information, as shown in Figure 2.41.

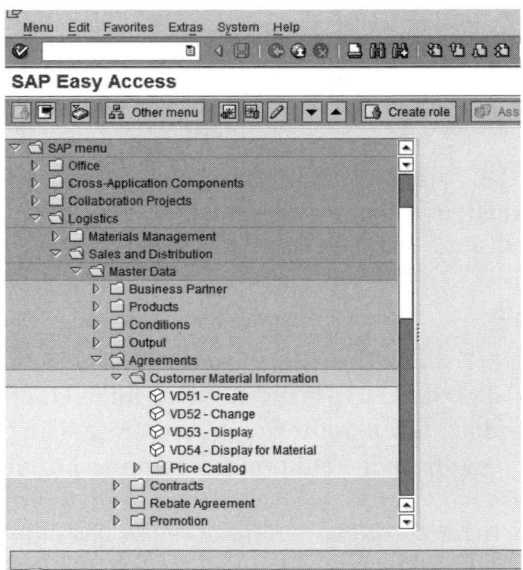

© SAP AG. All rights reserved.

FIGURE 2.41 **The SAP Easy Access screen**

When the preceding menu path is navigated, the following icons appear:

- **VD51 – Create**—Creates customer-material info data.
- **VD52 – Change**—Modifies the existing customer-material info data.
- **VD53 – Display**—Displays the existing customer-material info data.
- **VD54 – Display for Material**—Displays the material-specific customer-material data.

Now double-click the **VD51 – Create** icon. The **Create Customer-Material Info Record** screen appears as shown in Figure 2.42.

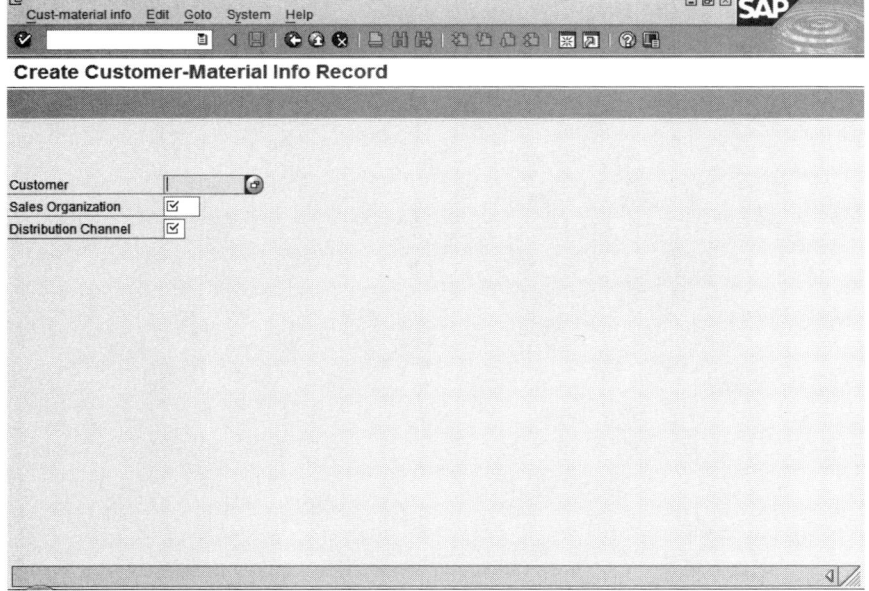

© SAP AG. All rights reserved.

FIGURE 2.42 The Create Customer-Material Info Record screen

Specify the data related to the customer, sales organization, and distribution channel in the **Create Customer-Material Info Record** screen (Figure 2.42) in order to create a new customer-material info data.

Let's now summarize the main concepts of this chapter.

SUMMARY

In this chapter, we have described different types of master data and organizational units of the SAP system. We started our discussion with enterprise structure of different functional units of an organization. In addition, you have learned about the sales organization, distribution channel, and division units in the SD module of SAP. This chapter has also explored SAP IMG and how to define a sales office and sales group in the SAP system. In addition, this chapter has described organizational structure in the context of accounting and logistics and how the assignment of different organizational units is performed. Finally, a detailed description of the customer-material info data has been presented that, in addition to the three types of master data, is also important for the SD module of the SAP system.

In next chapter, the importance of the master data to carry out sales processes is discussed.

Chapter 3
Working with Sales Documents in SAP SD

If you need information on:	See page:
Describing the Sales Order Process	80
Exploring Sales Documents	80
Working with Different Types of Sales Documents	109

When a customer places an order for goods or services in an organization, the organization creates a sales order. This sales order is called a sales document in the Sales and Distribution (SD) module. Let's consider a scenario to help understand the concept of sales document in detail. Suppose you visit a showroom of electronic goods to purchase a refrigerator. After selecting a specific model according to your requirements, you pay for it. When you pay for it, the refrigerator details, such as its model number, color, manufacturer, and price are specified in a document. Such a document containing details of a sold product is called a sales document. This sales document serves as a basis for further processing, if required, for the product.

In the SD module, a sales document is very important because the processing of various other documents, such as invoice, billing, and delivery, depend on the sales document. For example, the delivery document uses data from the sales order document. Therefore, a delivery document cannot be created without a sales order document.

This chapter describes the sales order process in the SD module. The chapter also explores how to create and configure a sales document to use it in any other related documents. Finally, the chapter discusses various types of sales documents in SD, such as quotation, cash sale, and rush order.

DESCRIBING THE SALES ORDER PROCESS

A sales order is a sales document or agreement that is created when a customer places an order in an organization to receive goods or services. While creating a sales order, you need to specify the details of the customer and goods being purchased, along with the quantity and time period required to deliver the goods. Manually specifying all these details to create a sales order is a lengthy and time-consuming process. Therefore, to ease the process of creating a sales order, data from the customer and material master records is automatically transferred to the sales order. The process of extracting the relevant details from customer and material master records and creating a sales order is known as sales order process. The sales order can be customized based on the sales document type, item category, and schedule line category.

Different types of sales documents help identify various business processes. Some of the common sales document types are these:

- Standard Order (SO)
- Returns (RE)
- Free of Charge Delivery (FD)
- Credit Memo
- Debit Memo

Let's now explore sales documents in detail and learn to configure a sales document.

EXPLORING SALES DOCUMENTS

After a sales document is created, the mySAP™ ERP system uses it to create a delivery document, which is then used to create a shipping document. The content of a sales document is divided into the following three levels:

- **Header Level**—Represents the header of a sales document, where the master data, such as the customer material master,

sales area, and organization data of a sales document are stored. Information specified at the header level is stored in the **VBAK** system table. If you make any changes at the header level, all the items in the sales document are affected accordingly.
- **Item Level**—Represents the information about a material or item. All the material or item data, such as the order quantity and the material master data of a sales document, are stored at the item level in the **VBAP** table.
- **Schedule Line**—Represents the date and time when the material has to be delivered to a customer. Information about the material delivery dates and quantity is stated in the schedule line of the **VBEP** table.

The sales document type is defined at the header level of a sales document. A sales document type in SD represents the type of sales document based on a business transaction or process. For example, a quotation sales document type represents the quotation process. A sales document type can be a sales order, a rush order, or a cash sale. We study these sales document types later in this chapter.

Let's now learn how to define and configure the sales document types.

Defining the Sales Document Types

A sales document type specifies the functionality of a sales document. For example, a sales document type, such as free-of-charge delivery and return delivery, specify different functionalities of a sales document. The free-of-charge delivery document type specifies the items that a company provides free-of-charge, whereas the return delivery document type specifies the items that a customer returns to a company.

While choosing a sales document type, you need to specify a number of entries, such as the sales document type key, its description, and category. You should be careful when specifying entries in a sales document type because a sales document may be related to other subsequent documents, such as billing, delivery, and shipping.

You can define a sales document type in the following two ways:

- Creating a new sales document type
- Copying and modifying an existing sales document type

Let's describe these ways in detail next.

Creating a New Sales Document Type

When a new sales document type is created, the sales document type key, its description, and the screen sequence group must be specified. The sales document type key is a unique, four-character, alphanumeric key used to identify a sales document. The screen sequence group shows the sequence in which the data in a sales document is displayed and processed. Let's perform the following steps to create a new sales document:

1. Select **Sales and Distribution > Sales > Sales Documents > Sales Document Header > Define Sales Document Types** in the **Display IMG** screen, as shown in Figure 3.1.
2. Click the **IMG Activity** icon (⊕) beside the **Define Sales Document Types** option, as shown in Figure 3.1.

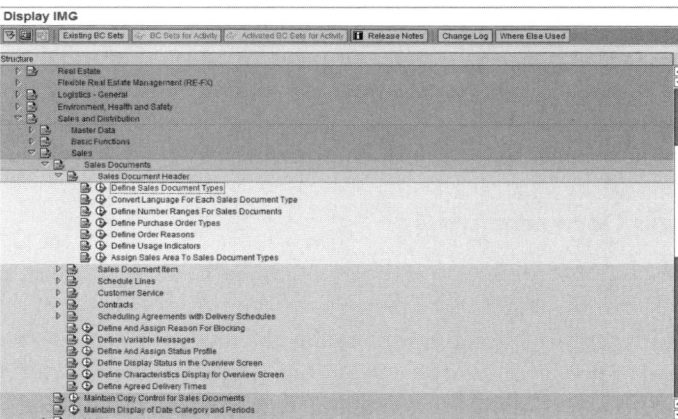

© SAP AG. All rights reserved.

FIGURE 3.1 Selecting Define Sales Document Types option

The **Change View "Maintain Sales Order Types": Overview** screen appears. This screen displays the existing sales document types as shown in Figure 3.2.

3. Click the **New Entries** button to create a new sales document type, as shown in Figure 3.2.

Exploring Sales Documents 83

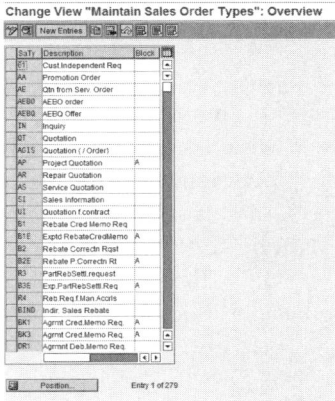

© SAP AG. All rights reserved.

FIGURE 3.2 Displaying existing sales document types

The **New Entries: Details of Added Entries** screen appears as shown in Figure 3.3.

4. Specify all the required fields in the **New Entries: Details of Added Entries** screen, and click the **Save** icon (🖫) on the standard toolbar to save the new sales document type, as shown in Figure 3.3.

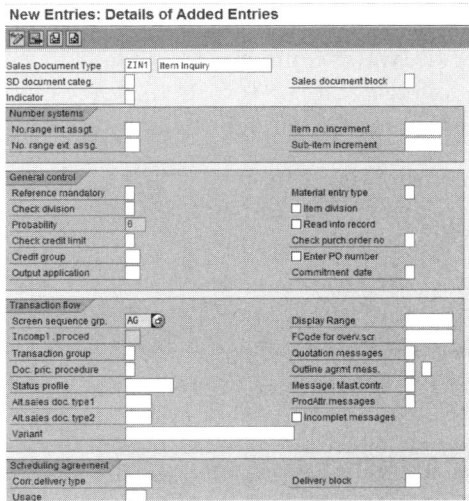

© SAP AG. All rights reserved.

FIGURE 3.3 Specifying entries for a new sales document type

In our case, we have specified the following entries:

- **Sales Document Type**—Represents the sales document type key and its description. The sales document type is ZIN1 (sales document type key), which represents **Item Inquiry**. When specifying the sales document type key, ensure that the key must either start with 9, Y, or Z. You can use these keys to define your own sales document types.
- **Screen Sequence Grp**—Represents the sequence group according to which a sales document screen appears. The screen sequence group we have entered is AG, which represents the inquiry and quotation.

Now, let's discuss how to create a new sales document type by copying and modifying an existing sales document type.

Copying and Modifying an Existing Sales Document Type

You can also create a new document type by modifying a few details of an existing sales document type according to your requirements. In such a case, the existing sales document type serves as a template to create a new sales document type. For example, if certain fields in an existing sales document type are similar to the fields that you want to enter in a new sales document type, you can simply create a copy of an existing sales document type. After creating a copy of the existing sales document type, you can modify it to create a new sales document type.

Perform the following steps to create a sales document type by copying and modifying an existing sales document type:

1. Select **Sales and Distribution > Sales > Sales Documents > Sales Document Header > Define Sales Document Types** in the **Display IMG** screen (Figure 3.1).
2. Click the **IMG Activity** icon (⊕) beside the **Define Sales Document Types** option (Figure 3.1). The **Change View "Maintain Sales Order Types": Overview** screen appears. This screen displays the existing sales document types (Figure 3.2).
3. Select the sales document type whose copy you want to create (Figure 3.2). In our example, we have selected the QT (Quotation) sales document type.

4. Click the **Copy** icon (■) (Figure 3.2). A copy of the selected sales document type is created (Figure 3.4).
5. Make the required changes in this copy. We have changed the sale document type key from QT to ZQT, as shown in Figure 3.4:

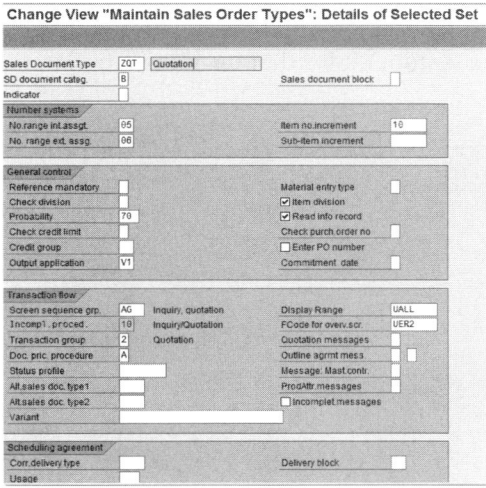

© SAP AG. All rights reserved.

FIGURE 3.4 Displaying the copy of the QT sales document

6. Click the **Copy** icon on the standard toolbar. The **Dependent entries for copying control** dialog box appears (Figure 3.5) and prompts you to save the relevant changes for copying the control rules.
7. Click the **Yes** button to make sure that the changes made are relevant for copying control rules, as shown in Figure 3.5:

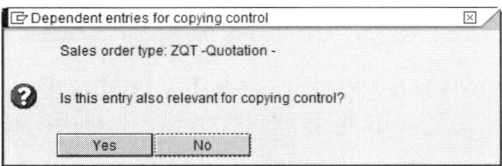

© SAP AG. All rights reserved.

FIGURE 3.5 Confirming copying control rules

The **Change View "Maintain Sales Order Types": Overview** screen appears (Figure 3.2), showing the new created sales order type.

8. Click the **Save** icon (🖫) on the standard toolbar to save the sales document type.

The **Maintain Table Views: Initial Screen** appears as shown in Figure 3.6, which shows the system tables that have been updated due to the changes that have been made.

9. Click the **Continue** icon (✓) to complete the process of creating a new sales document, as shown in Figure 3.6:

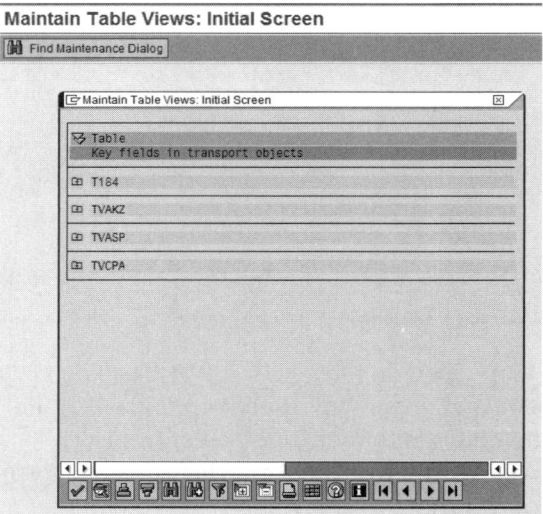

© SAP AG. All rights reserved.

FIGURE 3.6 **Displaying the updated tables**

The **Change View "Maintain Sales Order Types": Overview** screen appears (Figure 3.2), which shows the newly created sales document type.

After creating a sales document type, you can configure it to specify entries such as sales area and order reasons.

Configuring Sales Documents

A sales document is configured to make its data available in subsequent documents, such as delivery and billing documents. If a sales document is not properly configured, then its data cannot be used in any subsequent document. Configuring a sales document includes the following tasks:

- Assigning sales area to a sales document
- Creating order reasons
- Defining purchase order types

Let's explore these tasks next.

Assigning Sales Area to a Sales Document

A sales area must be assigned to a sales document in order to specify various parameters:

- **Sales Organization**—Represents an organizational unit responsible for the selling and distribution of goods.
- **Distribution Channel**—Represents a channel used to deliver goods to customers. A distribution channel can be assigned to multiple sales organizations. For example, a distributor, dealer, and institution can be distribution channels in the SAP system.
- **Division**—Represents the logical grouping of products into various categories such as refrigerator, color TV, and washing machine.

Perform the following steps to assign a sales area to a sales document:

1. Select **Sales and Distribution > Sales > Sales Documents > Sales Document Header > Assign Sales Area To Sales Document Types** in the **Display IMG** screen (Figure 3.1).

2. Click the **IMG Activity** icon (⊕) beside the **Assign Sales Area To Sales Document Types** option. The **Choose Activity** dialog box appears as shown in Figure 3.7.

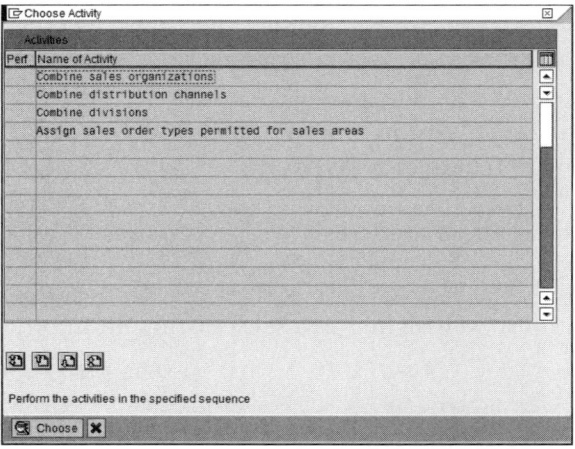

© SAP AG. All rights reserved.

FIGURE 3.7 Displaying the Choose Activity dialog box

In the **Choose Activity** dialog box, you can select an activity, such as **Combine sales organizations** and **Combine divisions**, that you want to perform. After selection, you need to click the **Choose** button to assign a sales area to a sales document.

Creating Order Reasons

An order reason is a parameter that specifies the reasons that make a customer place an order in an organization. Some common examples of order reasons are newspaper advertisement, attractive item price, and television advertisements. An order reason helps you generate sales statistics. For example, while creating a sales statistic, you can generate a separate sales statistic for the orders that were placed due to any specific advertisement.

You specify the order reasons at the header level of a sales document so that they can be automatically applied to all of the items of the sales document.

Let's now perform the following steps to create an order reason:

1. Select **Sales and Distribution > Sales > Sales Documents > Sales Document Header > Define Order Reasons** in the **Display IMG** screen (Figure 3.1).
2. Click the **IMG Activity** icon (⊕) beside the **Define Order Reasons** option (Figure 3.1).

The **Change View "Sales Documents: Order Reasons": Overview** screen appears (Figure 3.8). This screen displays the existing order reasons and their descriptions.

3. Click the **New Entries** button to create a new order reason, as shown in Figure 3.8.

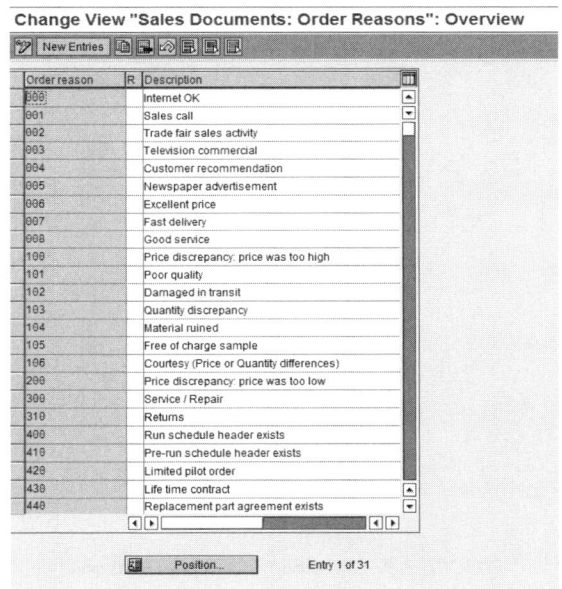

© SAP AG. All rights reserved.

FIGURE 3.8 Displaying the order reasons and descriptions

When you click the **New Entries** button, the **New Entries: Overview of Added Entries** screen appears (Figure 3.9).

4. Type an order reason number in the **Order reason** column (Figure 3.9). The order reason number should be unique for each order reason. In our example, the order reason number is 500.
5. Specify the order description in the **Description** column (Figure 3.9). In our example, the order description is Technical Support, as shown in Figure 3.9.

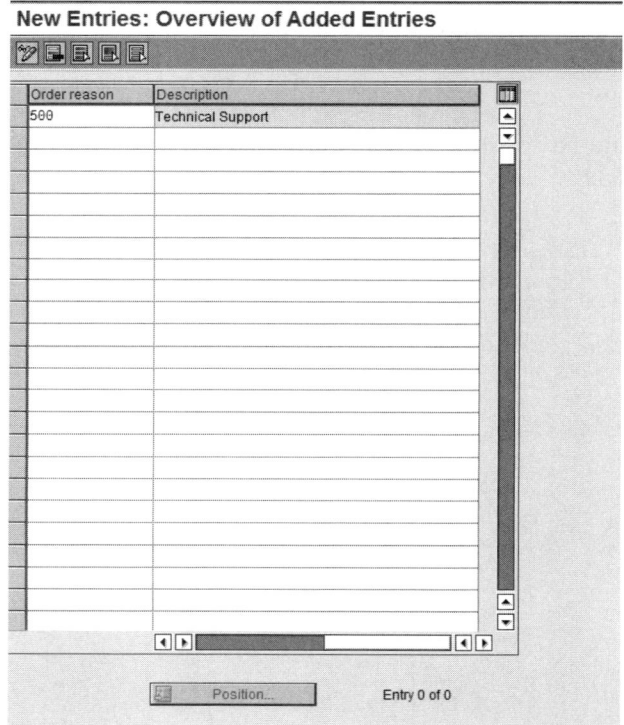

© SAP AG. All rights reserved.

FIGURE 3.9 Specifying the order reasons

6. Click the **Save** icon (🖫) on the standard toolbar to save the order reason. You can see the newly created order reason in the **Change View "Sales Documents: Order Reasons": Overview** screen.

Defining Purchase Order Types

A purchase order type is a parameter that a customer uses to place an order in an organization. The purchase order type parameter can refer to telephone call, fax, or email. You specify the purchase order type at the header level of a sales document. A purchase order type helps you generate sales statistics. For example, while creating a sales statistics, you can generate a separate set of sales statistics for the orders that were placed through phone calls.

Let's now perform the following steps to define a purchase order type:

1. Select **Sales and Distribution > Sales > Sales Documents > Sales Document Header > Define Purchase Order Types** in the **Display IMG** screen (Figure 3.1).
2. Click the **IMG Activity** icon (⊕) beside the **Define Purchase Order Types** option (Figure 3.1). The **Change View "Sales Documents: Customer Order Types": Overview** screen appears (Figure 3.10). This screen displays the existing purchase order types and their descriptions.
3. Click the **New Entries** button to create a new purchase order type, as shown in Figure 3.10.

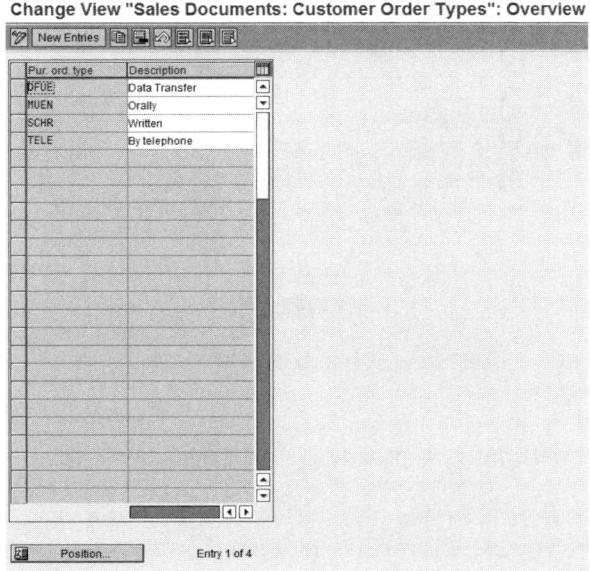

© SAP AG. All rights reserved.

FIGURE 3.10 Displaying the purchase order types and their description

When you click the **New Entries** button, the **New Entries: Overview of Added Entries** screen appears (Figure 3.11).

4. Specify a unique four-character alphanumeric key for the purchase order type in the **Pur. ord. type** column (Figure 3.11). In our example, the purchase order type key is INET.
5. Specify the purchase order type description in the **Description** column (Figure 3.11). In our case, the order description is Email.

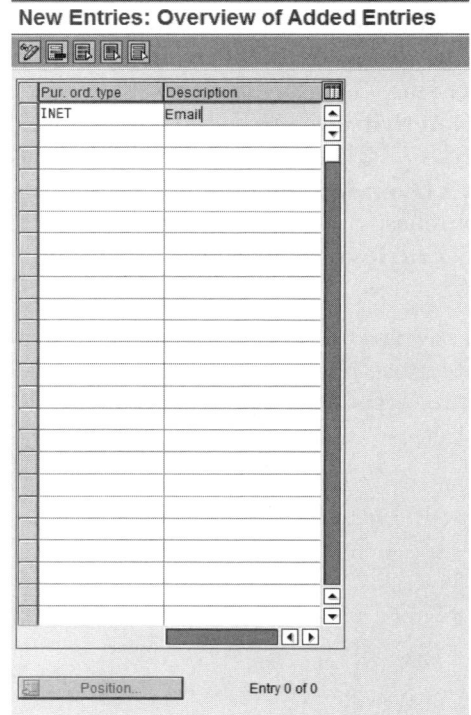

© SAP AG. All rights reserved.

FIGURE 3.11 Specifying the purchase order types

6. Click the **Save** icon (🖫) on the standard toolbar to save the purchase order type. Now you can see the newly created purchase order type in the **Change View "Sales Documents: Customer Order Types": Overview** screen.

Controlling the Sales Document with an Item Category

An organization divides its goods and services into various categories, such as free-of-charge items or items affected by some specific discounts. The categories under which the items are placed are known as item categories. The mySAP™ ERP system provides various item categories, such as inquiry item and free-of-charge items, which can be added in a sales document. The item category, along with the sales document type, controls the flow of a sales document. You can use a single item category for multiple sales documents depending on the sales document types. The item categories provided by the mySAP ERP system can be used to define customized item categories.

Let's study the item categories under the following sections:

- Defining an item category
- Assigning an item category
- Creating an item category group

Defining an Item Category

You can define an item category by customizing the item categories provided by the mySAP ERP system or by creating your own item category depending on your requirements. When you define a new item category, you must specify the item category key, which is a four-character alphanumeric key. Whether you define a new item category or modify an existing category, the item category key must start with 9, Y, or Z; otherwise, the item category will not be defined. The first two characters in the item category key represent the sales documents. These two characters refer to the item category while the remaining two characters represent the functionality of the item category.

You can define an item category using either of two methods:

- Defining a new item category
- Copying and modifying an existing item category

Let's discuss these processes in the next section.

Defining a New Item Category

You define a new item category when your business requirements do not match the already existing item categories. Perform the following steps to define a new item category:

1. Select **Sales and Distribution > Sales > Sales Documents > Sales Document Item > Define Item Categories** in the **Display IMG** screen (Figure 3.12).
2. Click the **IMG Activity** icon (⊕) beside the **Define Item Categories** option, as shown in Figure 3.12.

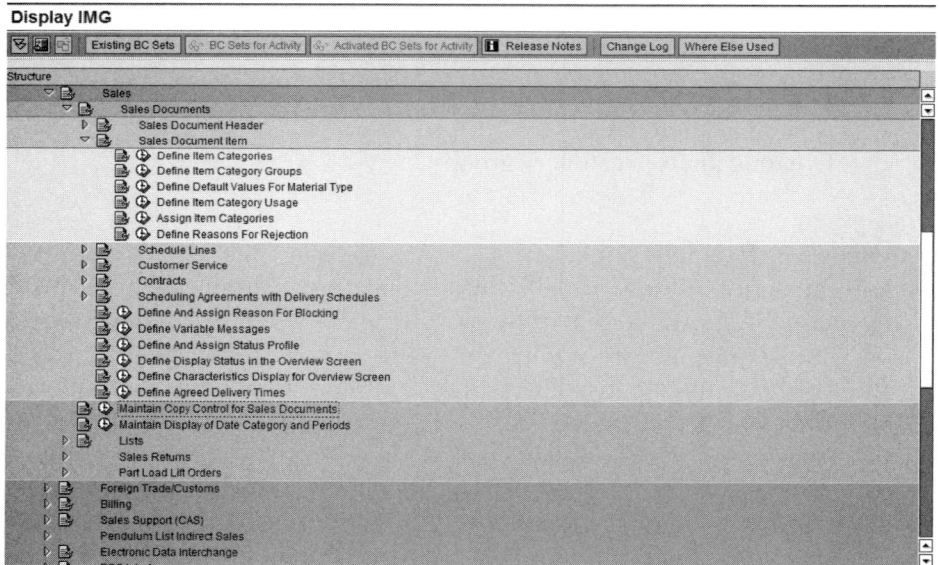

© SAP AG. All rights reserved.

FIGURE 3.12 Selecting the Define Item Categories option

The **Change View "Maintain Item Categories": Overview** screen appears (Figure 3.13), which displays the existing item categories.

3. Click the **New Entries** button, as shown in Figure 3.13.

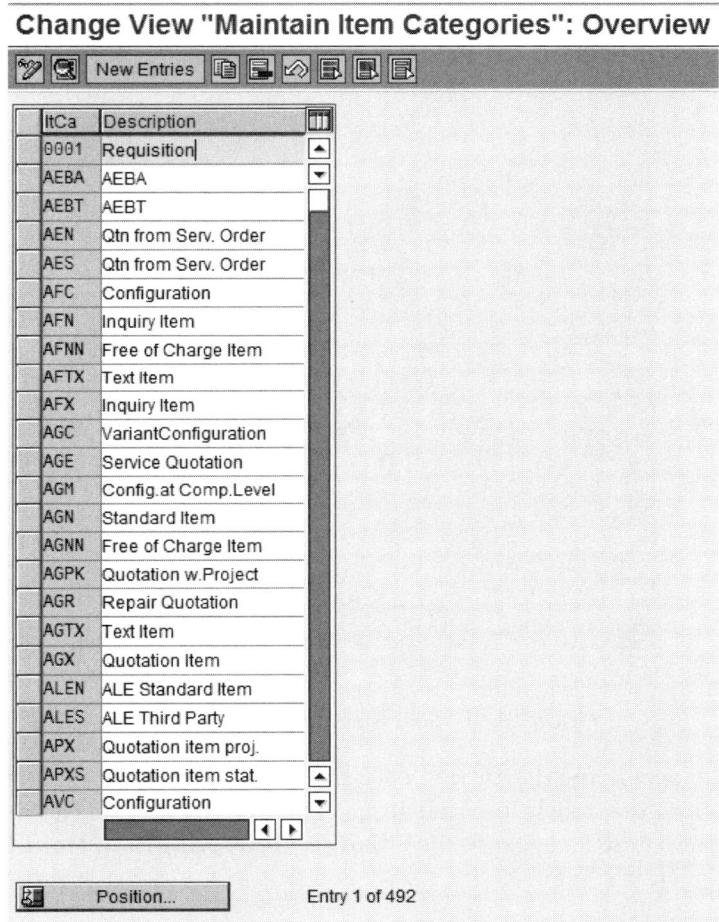

FIGURE 3.13 Displaying the existing item categories

The **New Entries: Details of Added Entries** screen appears (Figure 3.14).

4. Specify the required entries. We have specified the item category key as `ZFC1`, its description as `Free Items`, and pricing as `B`, which represents a 100% discount (Figure 3.14).

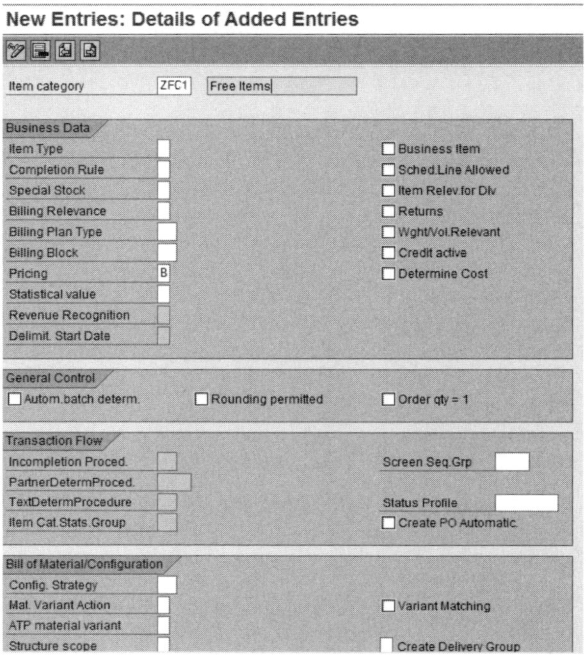

FIGURE 3.14 Specifying the required entries

5. After specifying the entries, click the **Save** icon (🖫) on the standard toolbar to save the newly created item category. Now, you can see the newly created item category in the **Change View "Maintain Item Categories": Overview** screen.

Copying and Modifying an Existing Item Category

You copy and modify an existing category to create a new item category when your business requirements closely match the details specified in an existing document. The best approach to defining item categories is by copying and modifying an existing item category. In this case, an existing item category works as a template to create a new item category. While modifying an existing item category, ensure that the item category key starts with 9, Y, or Z; otherwise the item category cannot be saved.

Let's now perform the following steps to define a new item category by copying and modifying an existing item category:

1. Select **Sales and Distribution > Sales > Sales Documents > Sales Document Item > Define Item Categories** in the **Display IMG** screen (Figure 3.12).
2. Click the **IMG Activity** icon (⊕) beside the **Define Item Categories** option (Figure 3.12). The **Change View "Maintain Item Categories": Overview** screen appears (Figure 3.13), which displays the existing item categories.
3. Select the item category according to your requirement (Figure 3.13), and click the **Copy** icon (📋) to create a copy of the selected item category (Figure 3.13). We have selected the ZEQU (Container Item) item category. The **Change View "Maintain Item Categories": Details of Selected Set** screen appears (Figure 3.15).
4. Modify the entries in this screen according to your business requirements. We have changed the item category key from ZEQU to ZEQ1, as shown in Figure 3.15.

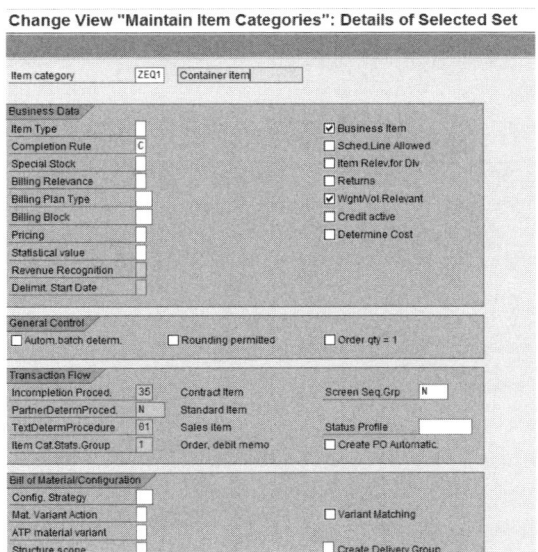

© SAP AG. All rights reserved.

FIGURE 3.15 Displaying an existing item category

5. After modifications, click the **Copy** icon (■) on the standard toolbar. The **Dependent entries for copying control** dialog box appears (Figure 3.5), which prompts you to specify whether the changes you have made are relevant for the copying control rules.
6. Click the **Yes** button to specify that the changes are relevant (Figure 3.5). The **Change View "Maintain Item Categories": Overview** screen opens again. You can now see the newly defined item category among the existing item categories on this screen.
7. Click the **Save** icon (■) on the standard toolbar to save the changes. The **Display IMG** screen appears, which shows the tables that are updated due to the modifications (Figure 3.16).
8. Click the **Continue** icon (✓) to complete the process of creating an item category through copying and modifying an existing item category, as shown in Figure 3.16.

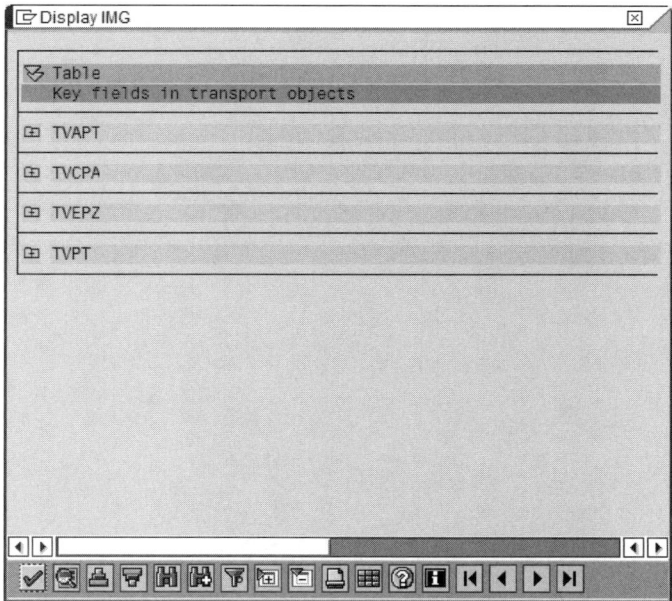

© SAP AG. All rights reserved.

FIGURE 3.16 Displaying the updated tables

The **Change View "Maintain Item Categories": Overview** screen appears, which contains the newly defined item category.

Assigning an Item Category

After defining an item category, it must be assigned to a sales document type. An item category is assigned to a sales document type to let the mySAP ERP system automatically suggest item categories when a document is created, such as billing and delivery. Perform the following steps to assign an item category to a sales document type:

1. Select **Sales and Distribution > Sales > Sales Documents > Sales Document Item > Assign Item Categories** in the **Display IMG** screen (Figure 3.12).
2. Click the **IMG Activity** icon (⊕) beside the **Assign Item Categories** option (Figure 3.12). The **Change View "Item Category Assignment": Overview** screen appears (Figure 3.17), which displays the available entries such as sales document types and item categories in their respective columns.
3. Click the **New Entries** button to assign an item category to a sales document type, as shown in Figure 3.17.

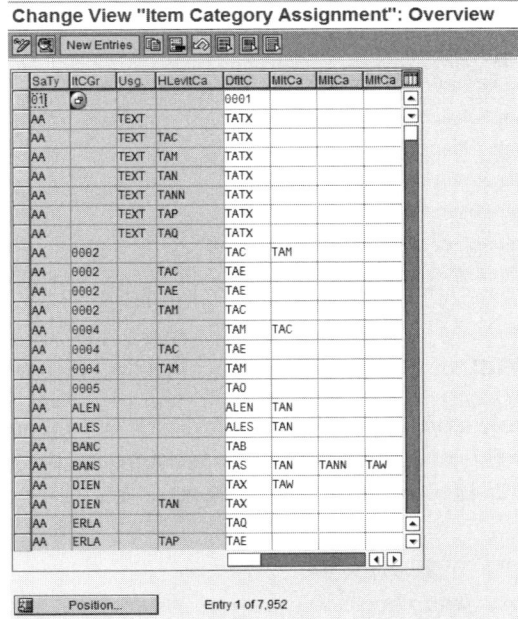

© SAP AG. All rights reserved.

FIGURE 3.17 Displaying the Item Category Assignment screen

The **New Entries: Details of Added Entries** screen appears (Figure 3.18).

4. Specify the required entries, such as sales document type and item category to complete the process of assigning an item category to a sales document. We have specified IN (Inquiry) as the sales document type and AGNN (Free-of-Charge Item) as the item category, as shown in Figure 3.18.

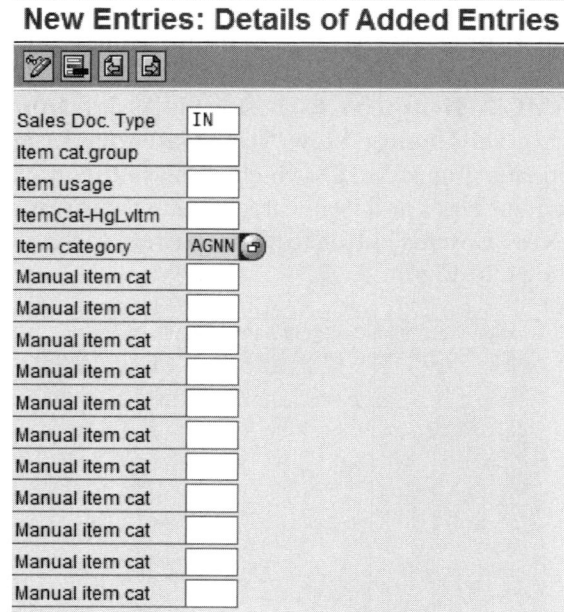

© SAP AG. All rights reserved.

FIGURE 3.18 Specifying the assignment entries

5. Click the **Save** icon (🖫) on the standard toolbar to save the assignment. Now, you can see the newly assigned item category in the **Change View "Item Category Assignment": Overview** screen.

Creating an Item Category Group

An item category group helps to group various related item categories in a sales document. The material master record maintains the item category group. During the process of creating a sales document, the mySAP ERP system automatically finds item categories in the material master record and assigns them to the sales document being created. When you create an item category group, you must specify the item category group key, which is an alphanumeric key. The key cannot have more than four alphanumeric characters and must start with 9, Y, or Z; otherwise, the item category group will not be saved.

Perform the following steps to create an item category group:

1. Select **Sales and Distribution > Sales > Sales Documents > Sales Document Item > Define Item Category Groups** in the **Display IMG** screen (Figure 3.12).
2. Click the **IMG Activity** icon ( ) beside the **Define Item Category Groups** option (Figure 3.12). The **Change View "Materials: Item Category Groups in Material Master": Overview** screen appears (Figure 3.19), which displays the available item category groups and their descriptions.
3. Click the **New Entries** button to create a new item category group, as shown in Figure 3.19.

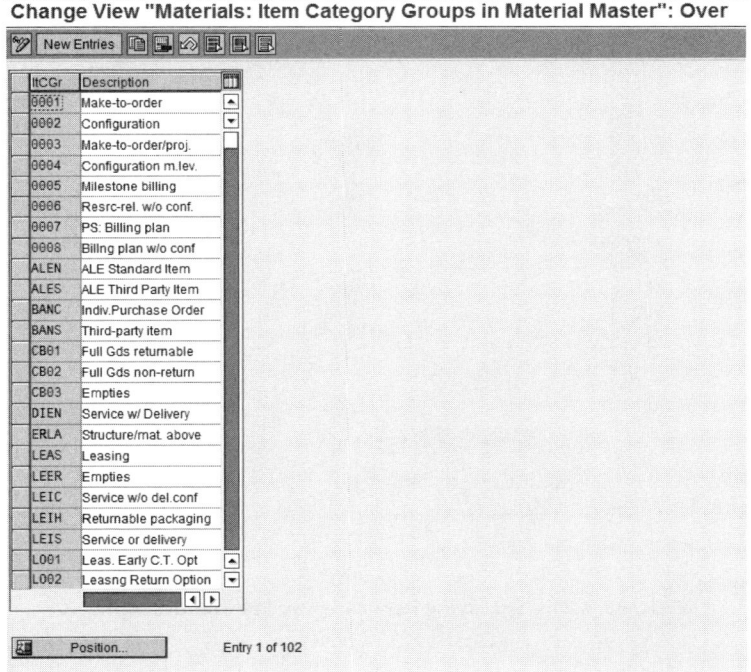

© SAP AG. All rights reserved.

FIGURE 3.19 Displaying the existing item category groups

The **New Entries: Overview of Added Entries** screen appears (Figure 3.20).

4. Specify the item category group key and its description in their respective columns. We have specified ZSAM as item category group key and Samples as its description, as shown in Figure 3.20.

© SAP AG. All rights reserved.

FIGURE 3.20 Specifying item category key and description

5. Click the **Save** icon (▣) on the standard toolbar to save the newly created item category group.

Now, you can see the newly created item category in the **Change View "Materials: Item Category Groups in Material Master": Over** screen.
Let's now explore how to control sales documents with schedule line.

Controlling the Sales Document with a Schedule Line

A schedule line in a sales document specifies the date and quantity of items to be delivered on the specified date. For example, suppose you need to deliver 500 pieces of a specific product and 50 of these pieces need to be delivered on a specified date. You can specify the number of pieces that you need to deliver on a specific date and time using schedule lines. Items are delivered based on the date, time, and quantity assigned in a schedule line in a sales document. After an item category is defined, you should assign the schedule line to it, because if you do not assign the schedule line to an item category, the mySAP ERP system cannot automatically transfer the data from a sales document to the delivery document. This is because the schedule line is determined in the sales order itself for a line item of a material; then it is copied to the delivery document. The schedule line that is needed to define an item category is determined on the basis of the item category and the Material Requirements Planning (MRP) of material master record.

Let's next explore how to define and assign a schedule line.

Defining Schedule Line Category

The schedule line category, along with the sales document type and item category, controls the way in which the available data need to be transferred to the next document. When the schedule line category is defined a schedule line category key, which is two characters, along with its description must also be specified. According to the standard naming conventions of the mySAP ERP system, the first character of the key indicates the sales process, while the second character represents the logistics process. Table 3.1 lists the characters that can be used to specify the first character of the schedule line category key.

Character	Indicates To
A	Inquiry
B	Quotation
C	Order
D	Returns

TABLE 3.1　First character of the schedule line category key

Table 3.2 lists the characters that can be used to specify the second character of the schedule line category key.

Character	Indicates To
T	No inventory management
X	No inventory management with goods issue
N	No material planning
P	Material requirements planning
V	Consumption-based planning

TABLE 3.2　Second character of the schedule line category key

The characters listed in Table 3.1 are reserved for the default mySAP ERP system keys; therefore, while creating your own schedule line category, you cannot use these characters. When you define your own schedule line category, the first character of the schedule line category must start with either Y or Z. Let's now perform the following steps to define a schedule line category.

1. Select **Sales and Distribution > Sales > Sales Documents > Schedule Lines > Define Schedule Line Categories** in the **Display IMG** screen (Figure 3.21).
2. Click the **IMG Activity** icon (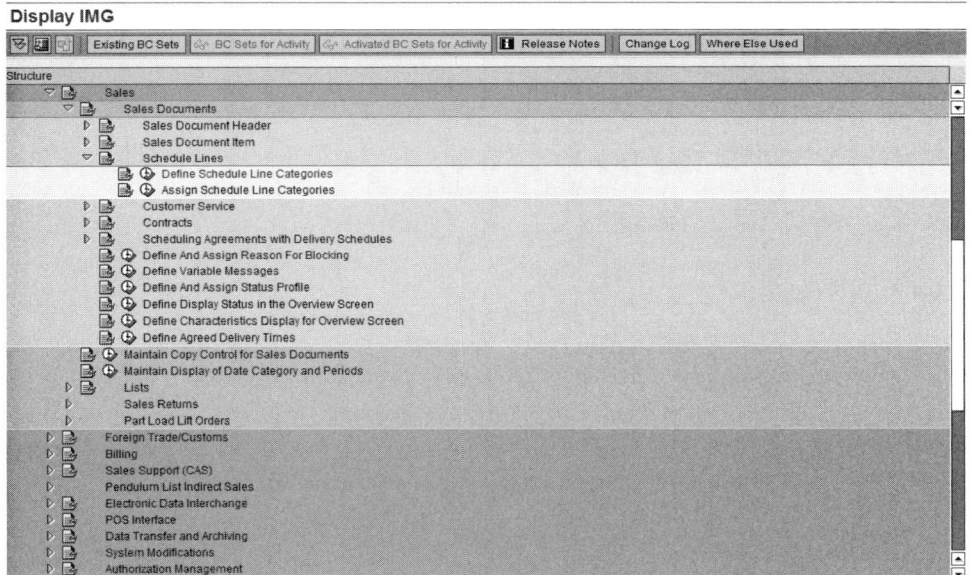) beside the **Define Schedule Line Categories** option, as shown in Figure 3.21.

© SAP AG. All rights reserved.

FIGURE 3.21 Selecting the Define Schedule Line Categories option

The **Change View "Maintain Schedule Line Categories": Overview** screen appears (Figure 3.22), which displays the available schedule line categories and their descriptions.

3. Click the **New Entries** button to create a new schedule line category, as shown in Figure 3.22.

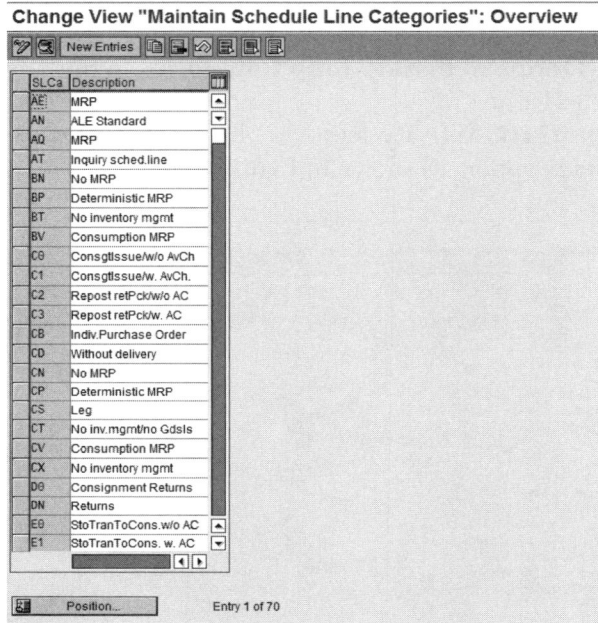

© SAP AG. All rights reserved.

FIGURE 3.22 Displaying existing schedule line categories

The **New Entries: Details of Added Entries** screen appears (Figure 3.23), where you can specify the required entries, such as schedule line categories group, its description, and the item category.

4. Specify the entries according to your business requirements. We have specified ZN as the schedule line category key and No Material Planning as its description. We have also selected the **Availability** checkbox, which indicates the goods availability for other transactions (Figure 3.23).

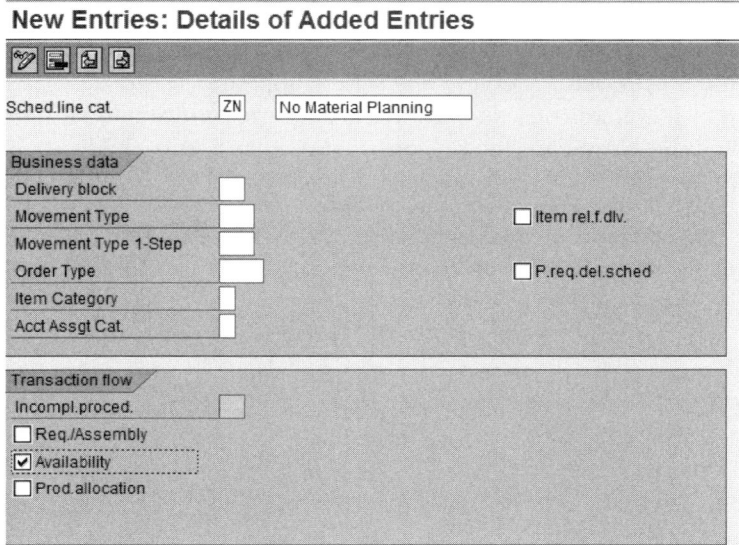

FIGURE 3.23 Specifying schedule line category entries

5. Click the **Save** icon (🖫) on the standard toolbar to save the newly created schedule line category.

Now, you can see the newly created schedule line category in the **Change View "Maintain Schedule Line Categories": Overview** screen.

Assigning Schedule Line Category

Schedule line categories are assigned to item categories so that the mySAP ERP system can automatically suggest a schedule for items delivery during document entry. You allocate a schedule line category to item categories on the basis of the MRP specified in the material master record for a material. Let's perform the following steps to assign a schedule line category to the item categories:

1. Select **Sales and Distribution > Sales > Sales Documents > Schedule Lines > Assign Schedule Line Categories** in the **Display IMG** screen (Figure 3.21).

2. Click the **IMG Activity** icon (◉) beside the **Assign Schedule Line Categories** option (Figure 3.21). The **Change View "Assign Schedule Line Categories": Overview** screen appears (Figure 3.24), which displays the available entries, such as item categories and schedule line categories.
3. Click the **New Entries** button, as shown in Figure 3.24.

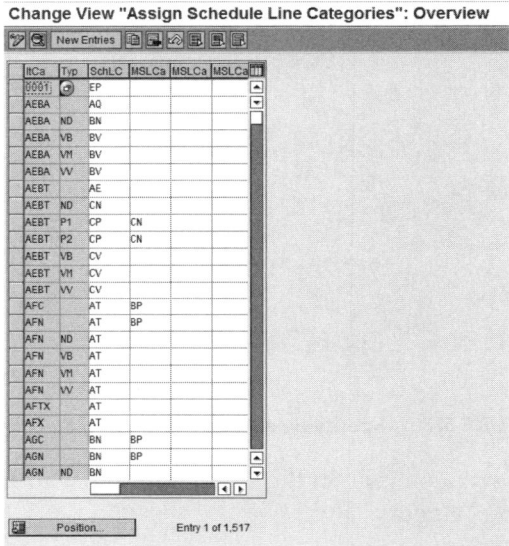

© SAP AG. All rights reserved.

FIGURE 3.24 **Displaying the existing schedule line categories**

The **New Entries: Details of Added Entries** screen appears (Figure 3.25).

4. Specify the required fields (Figure 3.25). We have specified the following fields:

    - **Item Category**—Represents the item category with which you need to assign a schedule line. In our example, the item category is AGX, which represents the quotation item.

    - **MRP Type**—Represents material requirement planning. In our case, MRP type is ND, which means no material requirement planning is required.

- **PropSchdLneCat**—Represents the proposed schedule line. In our case, it is BN, which stands for no MRP.

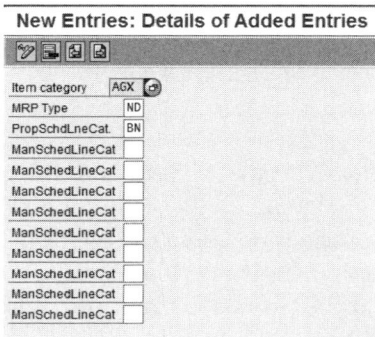

© SAP AG. All rights reserved.

FIGURE 3.25 Specifying the schedule line entries

5. Click the **Save** icon (📄) on the standard toolbar to save the entries. Now you can see the newly assigned schedule line to the specified item category in the **Change View "Assign Schedule Line Categories": Overview** screen.

Now, let's discuss various types of sales documents in detail.

WORKING WITH DIFFERENT TYPES OF SALES DOCUMENTS

Sales documents in the mySAP ERP system are of various types. For example, the quotation sales document helps process the quotation for goods or services. The mySAP ERP system provides various standard sales documents that can be modified according to your requirements; however, if your requirements do not match the available sales documents, you can create your own sales documents. This section discusses a few variations used to create a specific sales document as opposed to the general procedure to create a sales document. The following are the types of sales documents of the standard mySAP ERP system:

- Quotation
- Cash Sale
- Rush Order

- Credit Memo
- Debit Memo
- Standard Order

Let's next discuss these types of sales documents.

The Quotation Document

A quotation in the mySAP ERP system is defined as a sales document. The quotation document is created after a customer makes an inquiry. The quotation document contains information about the goods or services, quantity and price of goods, and the proposed delivery time. It also contains information about the material availability at the proposed price and delivery date.

When creating a quotation document for some specific goods or services, you must ensure that you have assigned an SD document category, screen sequence group, transaction group, and item category according to the mySAP ERP system's standards. Table 3.3 lists the notations for the entries that you should specify while creating a quotation document.

Entry	Notation
SD Document Category	B
Screen Sequence Group	AG
Transaction Group	2
Item Category	AGN

TABLE 3.3 Notations for the quotation document

When creating a quotation, you should also provide information about the credit limit, which can be customer specific. On the basis of the quotation document, you can check the order probability; that is, how likely it is that the customer will place an order on this quotation.

The mySAP ERP system calculates the probability percentage of the order on the basis of the customer master record and combines it with the probability percentage of the sales document type. On the basis of both the percentages, the mySAP ERP system calculates the order probability. The quotation document can also retrieve data from the inquiry document.

> **Note:** The process to create a document type is similar to the process of creating a sales document, which has been already discussed in the section *Defining the Sales Document Types* of this chapter.

The Cash Sale Document

A cash sale document is created when a customer places an order for goods or services, collects the ordered item, and pays the proposed amount at the same time. Let's take an example. When you visit a grocery store, a cash sale document is created that specifies the amount to be paid in cash. While creating a cash sale document, the mySAP ERP system automatically specifies the current date as the delivery and billing date.

The mySAP ERP system's standard sales document type for this document is `BV`.

The Rush Order Document

A rush order document is created when the goods need to be delivered or shipped immediately after the order is received. A rush order document is similar to a cash sale document; the only difference being that in a cash sale document, the invoice is generated along with the delivery, while in the rush order document the invoice is generated later.

The sales document type for the rush order document is `SO`. While creating the rush order sales document, the mySAP ERP system automatically creates a delivery document when the sales order is saved.

The Credit Memo Document

A credit memo document is created when a good is sold to a customer on credit. In the mySAP ERP system, the credit memo document is created when one of the following two conditions is met:

- When the customer returns the previously purchased goods.

- When the customer has not returned the goods, but the order is credited as in the following two cases:

  - The defective goods are delivered to the customer, but the cost to repair the goods is more than the manufacturing cost of the goods. In this case, the company asks the customer to destroy the defective goods, and the customer is credited for the destroyed goods.
  - The customer is overcharged for the goods. When a customer is overcharged for the goods, the customer is credited according to the corrected amount.

When creating a credit memo document, a record of the goods specification should be maintained, such as goods price, delivery date, and reason for order. You can use this record in the future whenever required. The sales document type for the credit memo document is G2, and the item category is G2N.

The Debit Memo Document

The debit memo sales document is created when you need to debit a customer for the goods or services that have not been fully billed. You create the debit memo sales document according to the standard billing and invoice procedure. While creating the debit memo sales document, you increase the customer's accounts receivable by the amount that needs to be debited to the customer.

The sales document type for a debit memo document is L2, and the standard item category is L2N. While creating a debit memo document, you may set a condition that the debit memo request can be created only with the reference of the defective invoice document. A customer may have paid the full amount for the goods and services; however, due to the wrong price of goods and services entered in the material master record, full payment might not be reflected in the mySAP ERP system. Therefore, in such a case, we must not debit the customer, but rather correct the price of the goods and services in the material master record.

The Standard Order Document

The standard order is an ordinary sales order with no specific requirement. In routine process a standard order is created, and the standard order type in a standard system is OR.

SUMMARY

In this chapter you have learned about sales order processing, and we have examined how to define and configure a new sales document. In addition, the chapter has described item category and schedule line, which are used to manage a sales document. Toward the end, various sales document types, such as cash sale, rush order, debit memo, have been discussed.

The next chapter describes the pricing procedure in the SD module.

Chapter 4
Pricing and Taxes in SAP SD

If you need information on:	See page:
Pricing in SAP SD	116
Working with Taxes and Rebates in SAP SD	145

In the real world, the pricing of goods and services is determined on the basis of certain conditions, such as the cost of raw material, manufacturing, and shipping. In the SAP SD module, the pricing function determines the prices of goods and services. The prices of goods and services are specified while preparing the sales document. The pricing function is a method of determining the prices of goods and services using condition techniques that are related to the cost of the goods and services. In the mySAP™ ERP system, the pricing function is also termed as pricing procedure. It is associated with the sales document and provides the input data required to determine the final agreement with the customers regarding the price of goods and services.

The costs and the data related to pricing, such as surcharge and discount on goods and services, are stored in the condition table in the form of condition records. These condition records consist of condition types that represent the price, discount, and surcharge on goods and services as a separate condition type. These condition types are finally used by the condition technique to determine the price of goods and services in the mySAP ERP system.

The SD module of SAP also accounts for the taxes levied on the sale and purchase of goods and services. The amount or percentage of tax depends on the region or country where the goods and services are sold or bought. Therefore, while determining the price of goods and services, the tax imposed on sales or purchases is also determined on the basis of these conditions.

In addition to taxes, the SAP SD module accounts for the rebates provided to the customer, based on conditions such as the region, amount of goods, and services procured, type of goods and services sold, and frequency of buying a specific good or service.

In this chapter, the pricing function in the mySAP ERP system is explored in detail. The price determination processes, along with their practical implementations are explained. Next, the chapter describes various types of taxes and the procedure used for tax determination in the mySAP ERP system. Finally, implementing rebates and discounts on goods and services in the SAP SD module are demonstrated.

Now, let's start the chapter with a discussion on the pricing function in SAP SD.

PRICING IN SAP SD

In the mySAP ERP system, a vendor uses the pricing function to create the purchase document. The mySAP ERP system automatically determines the gross price of the goods or services by calculating the surcharges and discounts applied on a particular vendor on the basis of a specific condition type. The net price of the goods and services are calculated after adjusting the surcharges and discounts.

> **Note:** Condition types are discussed in detail later in this chapter.

During the price determination process, the information about the product for which the price is to be determined is entered in the mySAP ERP system, which checks for the appropriate pricing procedures. The other factors that influence the price determination process include the following:

- Determining the pricing procedure
- Condition technique: Basis for pricing

- Access sequence
- Special pricing functions
- Special condition types
- Price reports

Let's next explore each of these in detail.

Determining the Pricing Procedure

Pricing procedure is a technique used to determine the price of goods and services in the mySAP ERP system. It is a collection of condition types specified for a customer or the sales document used to determine the price. For example, suppose the sales department of your organization categorizes the customers on the basis of city and defines a separate pricing procedure for each. Each of these pricing procedures will contain its own set of condition types to determine the price of goods and services for the respective customer category. Pricing procedure determination is the process that the mySAP ERP system uses to determine which pricing procedure is to be used for a customer or sales document. The mySAP ERP system automatically determines the pricing procedure on the basis of the following:

- Customer master data
- Sales area
- The sales document

The data are retrieved from the headers of the sales document. Once the mySAP ERP system ascertains the adequate pricing procedure, it performs the following functions:

1. Retrieves condition types from the pricing procedure.
2. Determines the access sequence based on the condition type selected.
3. Locates the valid condition records according to the access sequence selected.
4. Retrieves the condition record and copies into the sales document.

This determination process is repeated until the mySAP ERP system finishes the entire pricing procedure. The pricing process is graphically represented in Figure 4.1.

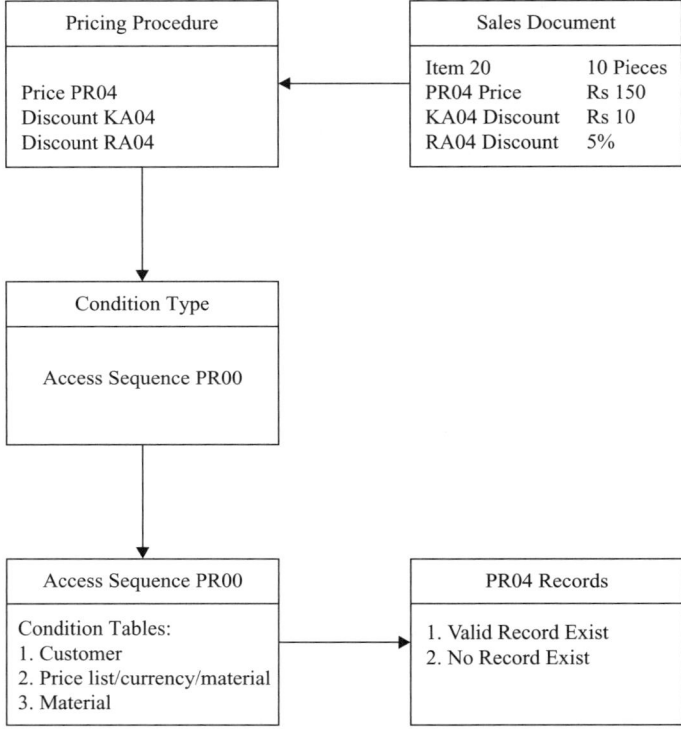

FIGURE 4.1 Pricing process

The broad-level steps to create the pricing procedure are the following:

1. Creating the customer pricing procedure indicator.
2. Creating the document pricing procedure indicator.
3. Defining the pricing procedure determination.

Let's now explore the broad-levels steps to create the pricing procedure in detail.

Creating the Customer Pricing Procedure

The customer pricing procedure represents the collection of condition types specified for a customer buying the goods or services. The mySAP ERP system processes these condition types to determine the price of goods and services for that customer. Perform the following steps to create the customer pricing procedure indicator:

1. Navigate the menu path to create the customer pricing procedure indicator:

Menu Path

SAP Customizing Implementation Guide > Sales and Distribution > Basic Functions > Pricing > Pricing Control > Define and Assign Pricing Procedures. Figure 4.2 shows the preceding menu path.

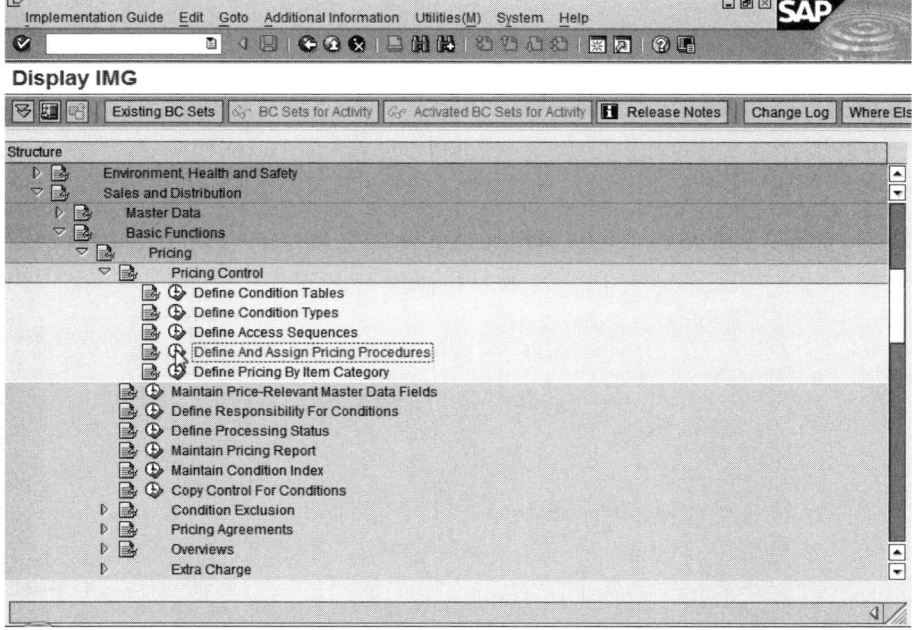

© SAP AG. All rights reserved.

FIGURE 4.2 The Display IMG screen

2. Click the **Activity** icon (⊕) beside the **Define and Assign Pricing Procedures** activity. The **Choose Activity** dialog box appears, as shown in Figure 4.3.

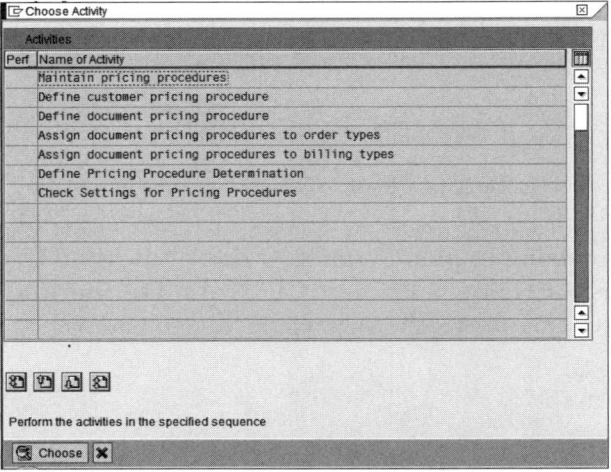

© SAP AG. All rights reserved.

FIGURE 4.3 The Choose Activity dialog box

3. Select the **Define customer pricing procedure** option and click the **Choose** button. The **Change View "Customer Pricing Procedures": Overview** screen appears as shown in Figure 4.4.

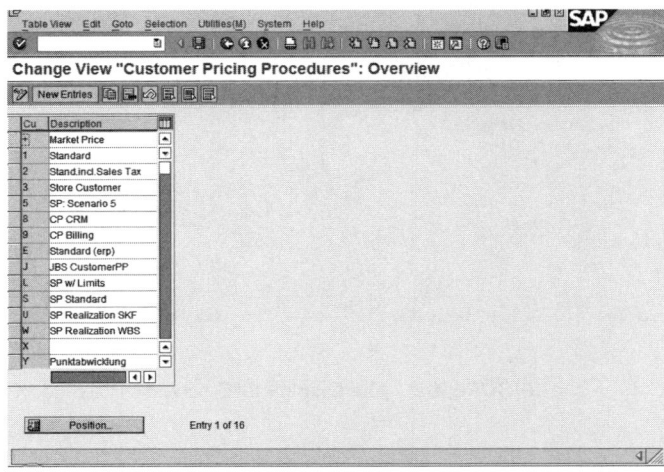

© SAP AG. All rights reserved.

FIGURE 4.4 The Change View "Customer Pricing Procedures": Overview screen

4. Click the **New Entries** button (Figure 4.4) to create a new customer pricing procedure. The **New Entries: Overview of Added Entries** screen appears as shown in Figure 4.5.

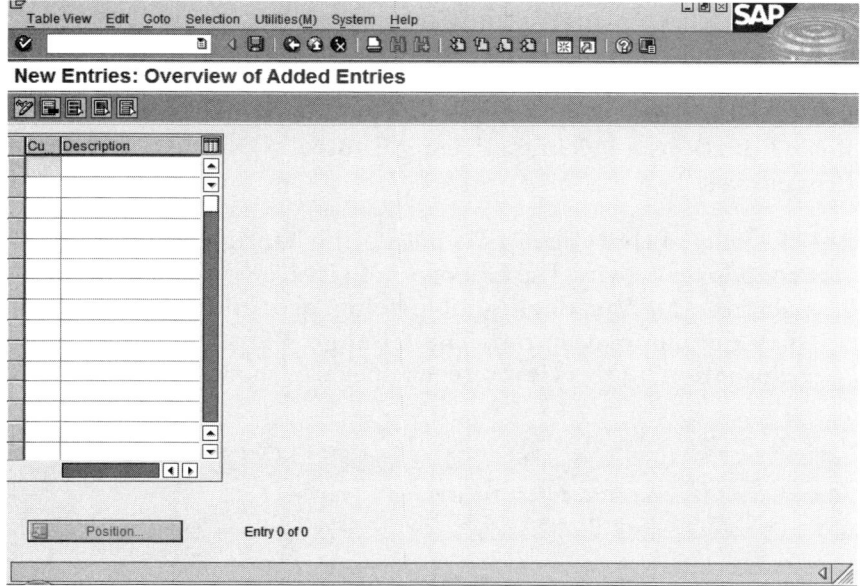

© SAP AG. All rights reserved.

FIGURE 4.5 The New Entries: Overview of Added Entries screen

5. Enter the customer-related information in the **New Entries: Overview of Added Entries** screen (Figure 4.5) to create the new customer pricing procedure indicator.

The new customer pricing procedure indicator is created. Let's now learn how to create the document pricing procedure.

Creating the Document Pricing Procedure

The document pricing procedure represents the collection of condition types specified in a sales document. The mySAP ERP system uses these condition types to determine the price of goods and services for each sales document. Different document pricing procedures are defined for each sales document type. Perform the following steps to create the document pricing procedure indicator:

1. Navigate the following menu path to create the document pricing procedure indicator:

Menu Path

SAP Customizing Implementation Guide > Sales and Distribution > Basic Functions > Pricing > Pricing Control > Define and Assign Pricing Procedures (Figure 4.2).

2. Click the **Activity** icon (⊕) beside the **Define and Assign Pricing Procedures** activity. The **Choose Activity** dialog box appears (Figure 4.3).
3. Select the **Define document pricing procedure** option (Figure 4.3). Click the **Choose** button. The **Change View "Pricing Procedures: Transaction": Overview** screen appears as shown in Figure 4.6.

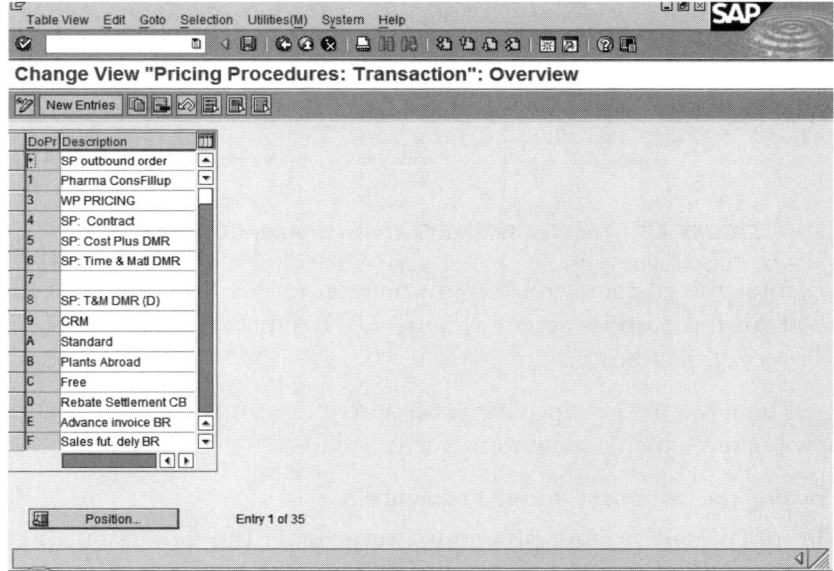

© SAP AG. All rights reserved.

FIGURE 4.6   The Change View "Pricing Procedures: Transaction": Overview screen

4. Click the **New Entries** button to create a new document pricing procedure (Figure 4.6). The **New Entries: Overview of Added Entries** screen appears as shown in Figure 4.7.

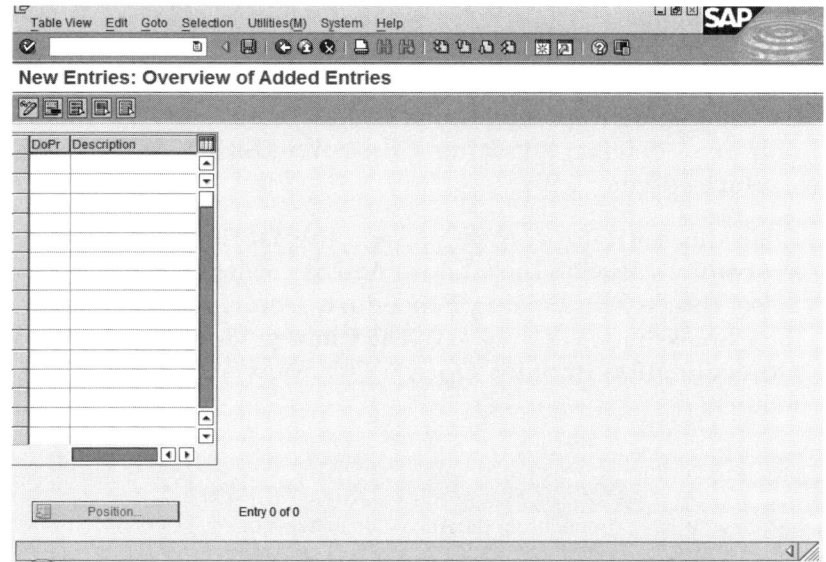

© SAP AG. All rights reserved.

FIGURE 4.7 The New Entries: Overview of Added Entries screen

5. Specify the **Document Procedure (DoPr)** and the **Description** in the **New Entries: Overview of Added Entries** screen to create a new document pricing procedure.

Defining the Pricing Procedure Determination

After creating the customer pricing procedure and document pricing procedure indicators, the customer pricing procedure must be assigned to the customer master and the document pricing procedure must be assigned to the sales document type while defining the sales document type, respectively. Let's define the pricing procedure determination to determine the prices of goods and services. Perform the following steps to define the pricing procedure determination:

1. Navigate the following menu path to define the pricing procedure determination:

Menu Path

SAP Customizing Implementation Guide > Sales and Distribution > Basic Functions > Pricing > Pricing Control > Define and Assign Pricing Procedures (Figure 4.2).

2. Click the **Activity** icon (⊕) beside the **Define and Assign Pricing Procedures** activity. The **Choose Activity** dialog box appears (Figure 4.3).
3. Select the **Define Pricing Procedure Determination** option and click the **Choose** button (Figure 4.3). The **Change View "Pricing Procedures: Determination in Sales Docs.": Overview** screen appears as shown in Figure 4.8.

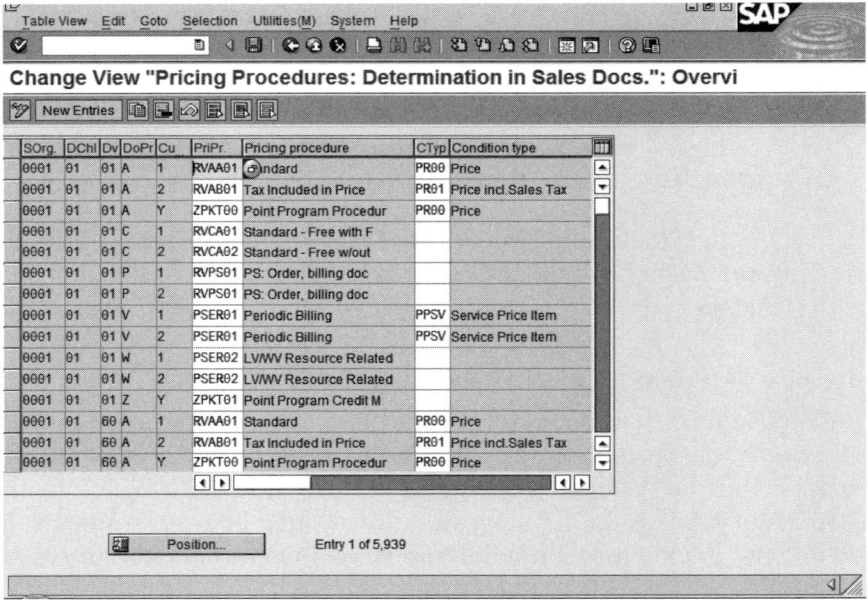

© SAP AG. All rights reserved.

FIGURE 4.8 The Change View "Pricing Procedures: Determination in Sales Docs.": Overview screen

4. Click the **New Entries** button (Figure 4.8). The **New Entries: Overview of Added Entries** screen appears as shown in Figure 4.9.

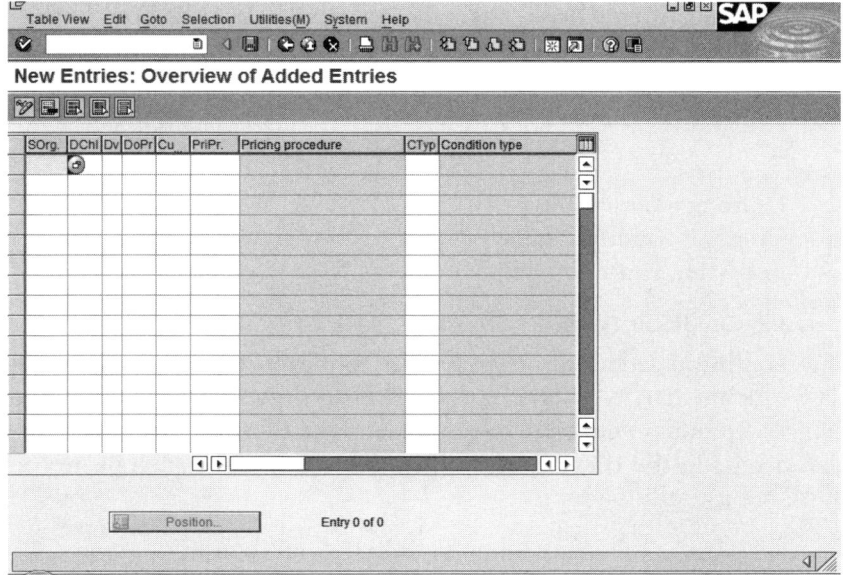

FIGURE 4.9 The New Entries: Overview of Added Entries screen

5. Enter relevant information in the respective fields (Figure 4.9) to define the new pricing procedures.

You have learned to determine the pricing procedure. Next, we discuss the next factor responsible for price determination—condition technique.

Working with Condition Technique: Basis for Pricing

The condition technique refers to a method that the mySAP ERP system uses to determine the price of goods and services for a customer. The mySAP ERP system determines a price structure for goods and services by selecting a set of condition types among various condition types. These options, such as base price, surcharges, discounts, freight, and taxes, are variables that may change for each customer at the time of sale. Therefore, the price of goods and services determined by the mySAP ERP system also varies for each customer.

To understand the condition technique, let's consider a scenario. Imagine that a customer is buying a book that has the standard selling price of $ 50.00 per book for all customers. However, if the customer is a large corporation and is buying many books at an instance, a cheaper price structure is used, such as $ 40.00 per book. On the other hand, if the customer is a general customer and is buying a single book, he or she will have to buy the book at the standard selling price. This is because the former customer is a large corporation and buying many books in single slot, which is a condition type used for price determination in this case.

Now let's discuss how to manage conditions in the following ways:

- Defining condition types
- Creating condition tables
- Accessing condition tables

Defining Condition Types

The condition technique is based on condition types, which represent the daily pricing activity of goods and services in the mySAP ERP system. There can be separate condition types for each type of price, surcharge, or discount that occurs in the transaction performed. The following steps are performed to define a condition type:

1. Navigate the following menu path to define a condition type:

Menu Path

SAP Customizing Implementation Guide > Sales and Distribution > Basic Functions > Pricing > Pricing Control > Define Condition Types. Figure 4.10 shows the preceding menu path.

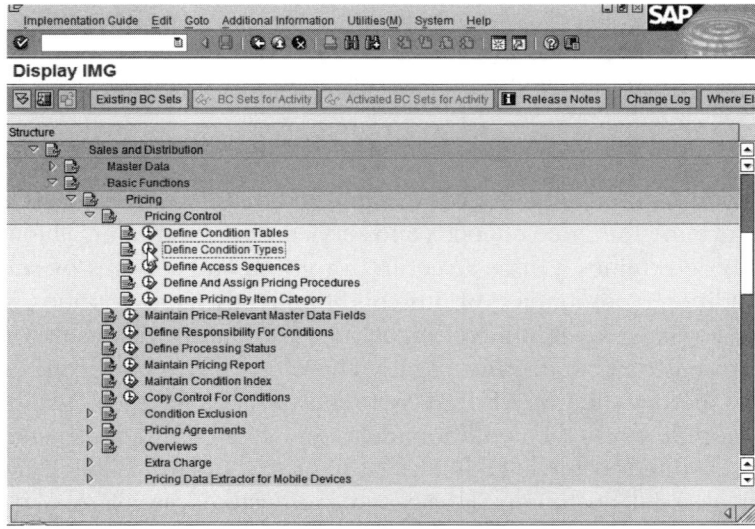

© SAP AG. All rights reserved.

FIGURE 4.10 The Display IMG screen

2. Click the **Activity** icon (⊕) beside the **Define Condition Types** activity. The **Choose Activity** dialog box appears as shown in Figure 4.11.

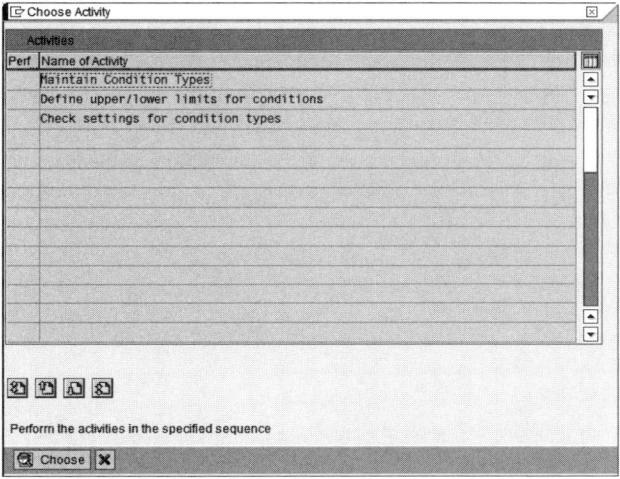

© SAP AG. All rights reserved.

FIGURE 4.11 The Choose Activity dialog box

3. Select the **Maintain Condition Types** option and click the **Choose** button. The **Change View "Conditions: Condition Types": Overview** screen appears as shown in Figure 4.12.

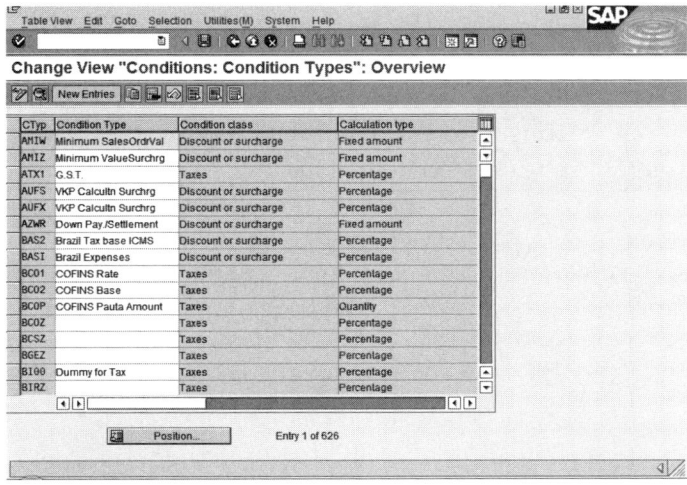

© SAP AG. All rights reserved.

FIGURE 4.12 The Change View "Conditions: Condition Types": Overview screen

4. Click the **New Entries** button (Figure 4.12). The **New Entries: Details of Added Entries** screen appears as shown in Figure 4.13.

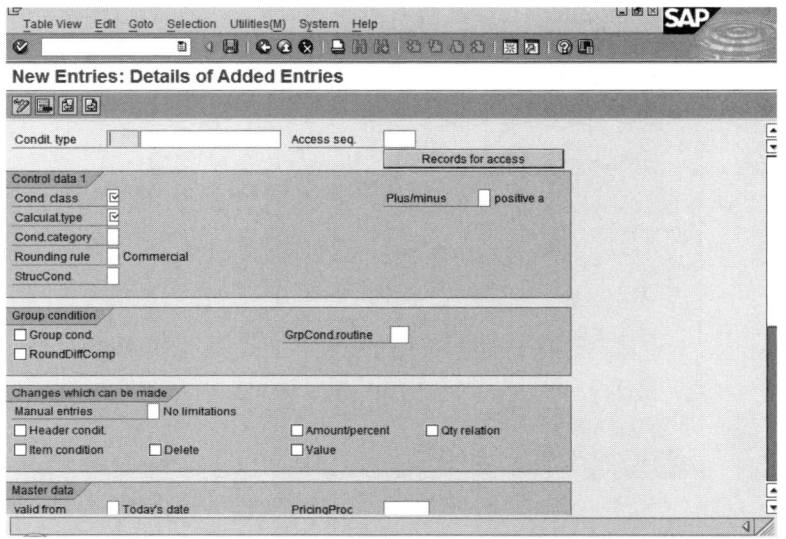

© SAP AG. All rights reserved.

FIGURE 4.13 The New Entries: Details of Added Entries screen

5. In the **New Entries: Details of Added Entries** screen, enter the relevant information in the respective fields to define a new condition type (Figure 4.13).

> **Note:** In normal practice you can create a new condition type by taking the reference from an existing standard condition type and thereby make the changes according to your requirement.

The condition types are defined.
Now, let's learn to create a condition table in the following section.

Creating Condition Tables

In day-to-day business activities, different types of prices, discounts, and surcharges are levied on goods provided to the customers. Each kind of price, discount, and surcharge in a transaction is represented as a condition type, and these condition types collectively form a condition record. A condition table represents a collection of condition records in the mySAP ERP system.

Perform the following steps to create a condition table:

1. Navigate the following menu path to create a condition table:

Menu Path

SAP Customizing Implementation Guide > Sales and Distribution > Basic Functions > Pricing > Pricing Control > Define Condition Tables. Figure 4.14 shows the preceding menu path.

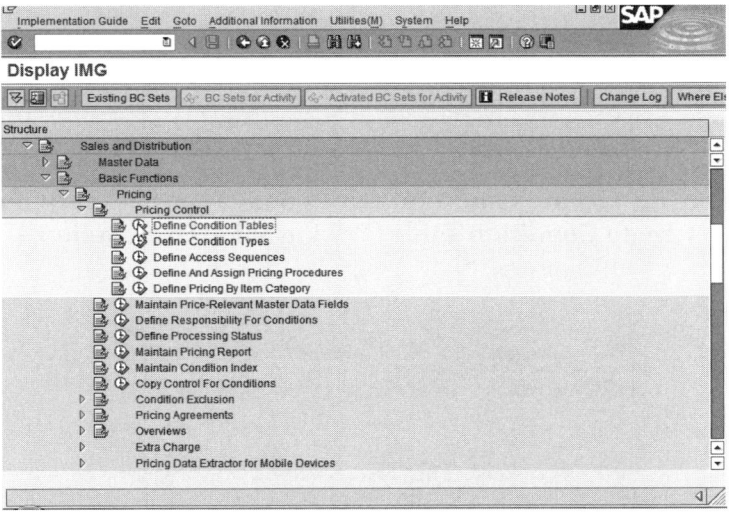

© SAP AG. All rights reserved.

FIGURE 4.14 The Display IMG screen

2. Click the **Activity** icon (⊕) beside the **Define Condition Tables** activity. The **Choose Activity** dialog box appears as shown in Figure 4.15.

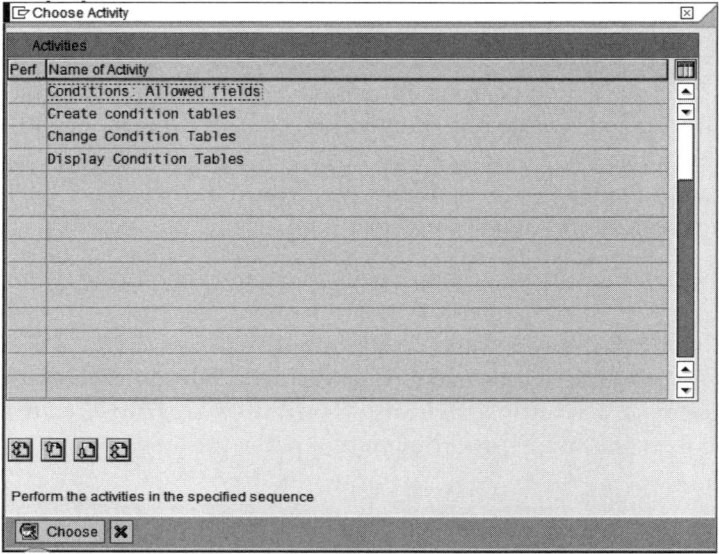

FIGURE 4.15   The Choose Activity dialog box

3. Select the **Create condition tables** option and click the **Choose** button. The **Create Condition Table (Pricing Sales/Distribution)** screen appears as shown in Figure 4.16.

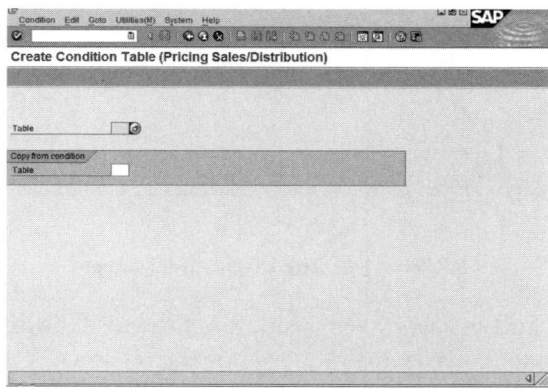

FIGURE 4.16   The Create Condition Table (Pricing Sales/Distribution) screen

4. Enter the relevant information in the respective fields of the **Create Condition Table (Pricing Sales/Distribution)** screen (Figure 4.16) to create the condition table.

After creating a condition table, we need to access the condition types from the condition table. Let's discuss how to access the condition tables in the following section.

Accessing Condition Tables

After creating the condition table, you can access the existing condition table for determining the price of goods and services. Perform the following steps to access an existing condition table:

1. Navigate the following menu path to access an existing condition table:

Menu Path

SAP Customizing Implementation Guide > Sales and Distribution > Basic Functions > Pricing > Pricing Control > Define Condition Tables. Figure 4.17 shows the preceding menu path.

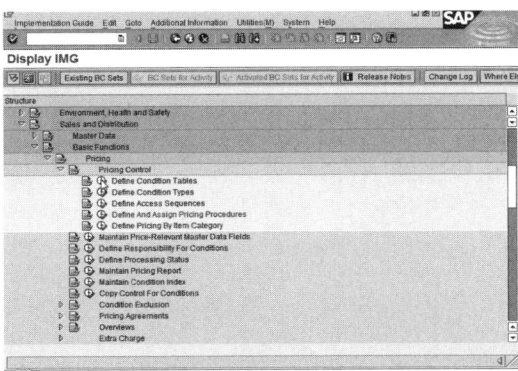

© SAP AG. All rights reserved.

FIGURE 4.17 The Display IMG screen

2. Click the **Activity** icon (⊕) beside the **Define Condition Tables** activity. The **Choose Activity** dialog box appears (Figure 4.15).
3. Select the **Display Condition Tables** option and click the **Choose** button. The **Display Condition Table (Pricing Sales/Distribution)** screen appears as shown in Figure 4.18.

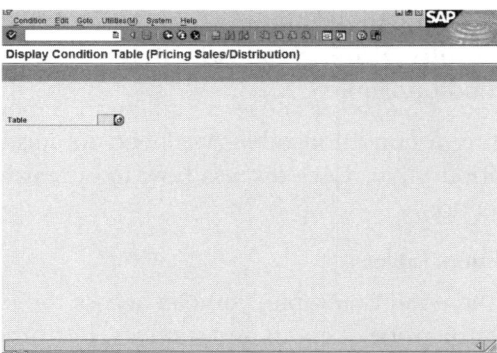

© SAP AG. All rights reserved.

FIGURE 4.18 The Display Condition Table (Pricing Sales/Distribution) screen

4. Enter the table number of an existing table in the **Table** field.

> **Note:** In case you are unable to recall the table number, click the icon to get a list of tables from which you can select a table to be displayed.

Press the **Enter** key after specifying a table number for selecting a table. The selected condition table is displayed as shown in Figure 4.19.

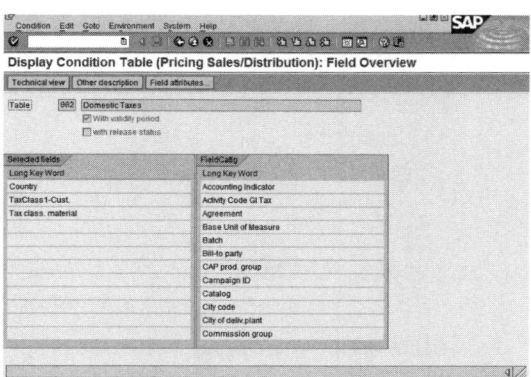

© SAP AG. All rights reserved.

FIGURE 4.19 The Display Condition Table (Pricing Sales/Distribution): Field Overview screen

In this section, we have learned to define condition types and condition tables and to access existing condition tables. These condition tables are maintained with the help of the access sequence.

Let's next learn to create an access sequence.

Creating an Access Sequence

An access sequence refers to the creation and arrangement of condition records in a logical sequence. Access sequence plays an important role in the price determination procedure. An access sequence defines the sequence in which the mySAP ERP system searches for condition records. This implies that an access sequence must be created to use condition records.

In the pricing procedure, the access sequence is first assigned to the condition type. Assigning an access sequence to condition types allows the values to be retrieved from the condition table in a logical sequence. Next, this condition type is selected for the price determination procedure. Perform the following steps to create an access sequence:

1. Navigate the following menu path to create an access sequence:

Menu Path

SAP Customizing Implementation Guide > Sales and Distribution > Basic Functions > Pricing > Pricing Control > Define Access Sequences, as shown in Figure 4.17.

2. Click the **Activity** icon (⊕) beside the **Define Access Sequences** activity. The **Choose Activity** dialog box appears as shown in Figure 4.20.

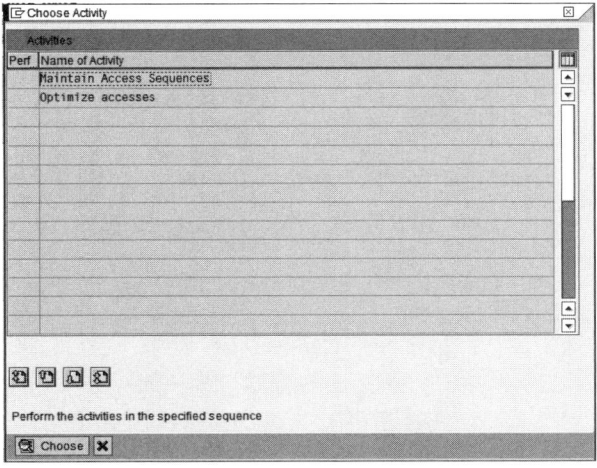

© SAP AG. All rights reserved.

FIGURE 4.20 The Choose Activity dialog box

3. Select the **Maintain Access Sequences** option and click the **Choose** button (Figure 4.20). The **Information** dialog box appears as shown in Figure 4.21.

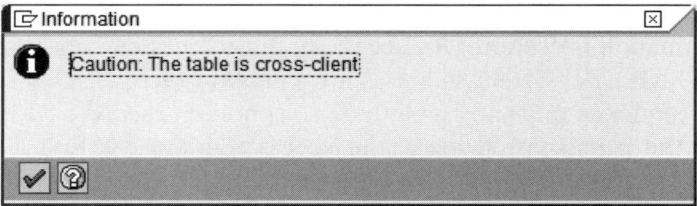

© SAP AG. All rights reserved.

FIGURE 4.21 The Information dialog box

The **Information** dialog box displays a caution message that the table is cross-client (Figure 4.21).

4. Click the **Continue** icon (☑) to proceed (Figure 4.21). The **Change View "Access sequences": Overview** screen appears as shown in Figure 4.22.

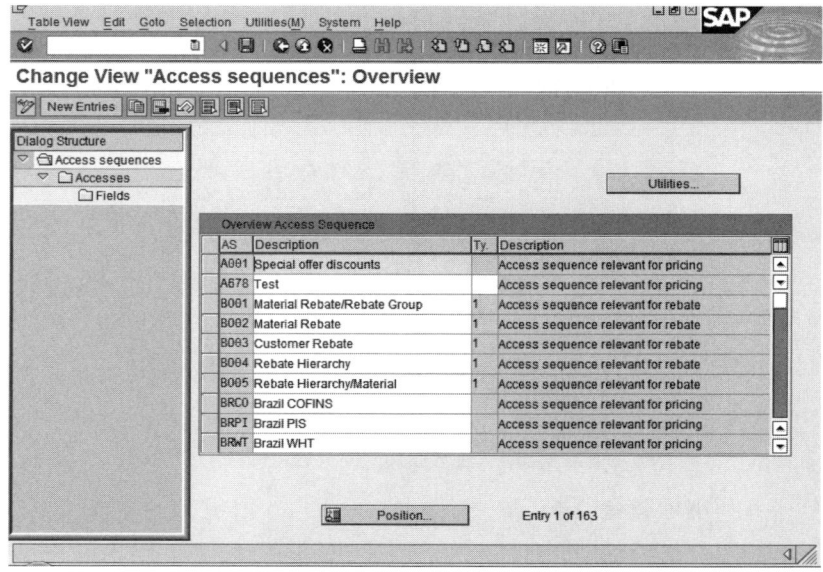

© SAP AG. All rights reserved.

FIGURE 4.22 The Change View "Access sequences": Overview screen

5. Click the **New Entries** button to create an access sequence. The **New Entries: Overview of Added Entries** screen appears as shown in Figure 4.23.

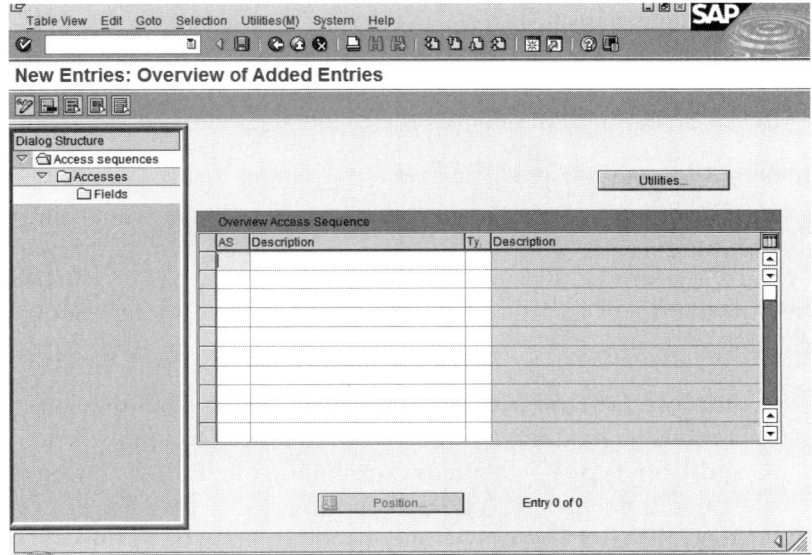

© SAP AG. All rights reserved.

FIGURE 4.23 The New Entries: Overview of Added Entries screen

6. Now, enter relevant information in the respective fields of the **New Entries: Overview of Added Entries** screen (Figure 4.23) to create an access sequence.

After learning how to create an access sequence, let's now discuss special pricing functions, such as group conditions, in the following section.

Working with Special Pricing Functions

As presented earlier, the price of goods and services are determined using the condition technique. In certain cases, the price of goods and services is determined on the basis of specific pricing procedures, such as the comparison between condition types and condition updates for price determination. These pricing procedures are known as special pricing functions.

The noteworthy special pricing functions are these:

- Group conditions
- Condition exclusion
- Comparison of condition types

Let's discuss these in detail in the following section.

Exploring Group Conditions

A group condition is a collection of condition types. While customizing the pricing function for goods and services, various condition types are grouped together to create a group condition, which forms the basis for price determination. The different types of group keys used to create the group condition are the following:

- **Complete Document**—Contains information of all the quantities of goods and services with the same condition type.
- **Condition Types**—Contains information of all the quantities of the condition types with group condition.
- **Material Price Group**—Contains information of all the quantities with the same condition type and same material pricing group.

The Condition Exclusion

You can use more than one condition during price determination. For example, while determining the price of a good or service for a customer, more than one type of discount may be used. The condition exclusion function ensures that only one type of condition or condition record is used for price determination. In our example, the best discount type is used for price determination with the help of the condition exclusion procedure. Condition exclusion function can be used for both, groups of conditions as well as condition types and records. Perform the following steps to set the condition exclusion for groups of conditions:

1. Navigate the following menu path to set the condition exclusion for groups of conditions:

Menu Path

SAP Customizing Implementation Guide > Sales and Distribution > Basic Functions > Pricing > Condition Exclusion > Condition Exclusion For Groups Of Conditions. Figure 4.24 shows the preceding menu path.

PRICING IN SAP SD   137

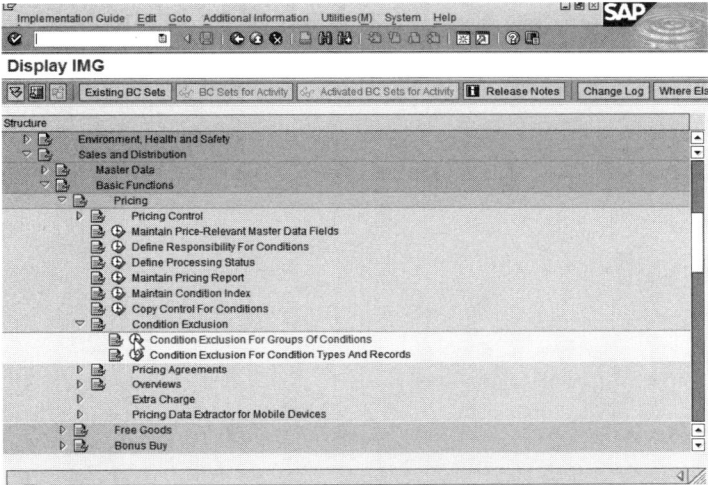

© SAP AG. All rights reserved.

FIGURE 4.24 The Display IMG screen

2. Click the **Activity** icon (⊕) beside the **Condition Exclusion For Groups Of Condition** activity. The **Choose Activity** dialog box appears as shown in Figure 4.25.

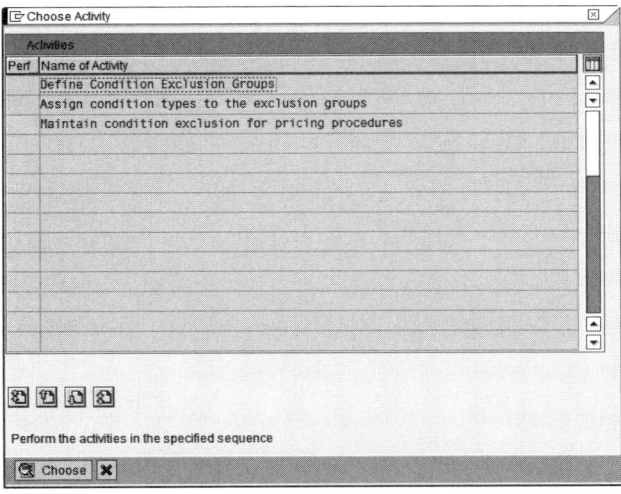

© SAP AG. All rights reserved.

FIGURE 4.25 The Choose Activity dialog box

3. Select the **Define Condition Exclusion Groups** option and click the **Choose** button. The **Change View "Condition Exclusion Groups": Overview** screen appears as shown in Figure 4.26.

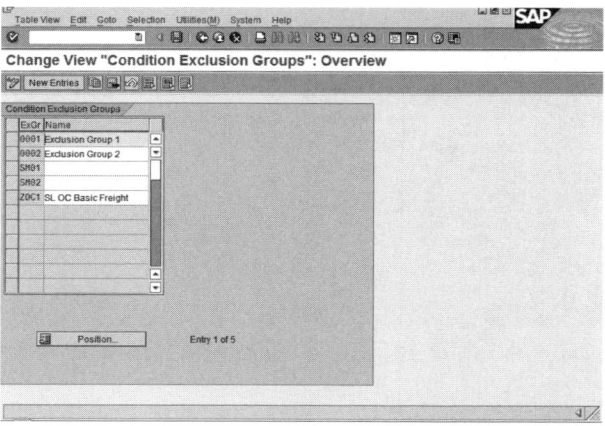

© SAP AG. All rights reserved.

FIGURE 4.26 The Change View "Condition Exclusion Groups": Overview screen

4. Click the **New Entries** button to define the new condition exclusion (Figure 4.26). The **New Entries: Overview of Added Entries** screen appears as shown in Figure 4.27.

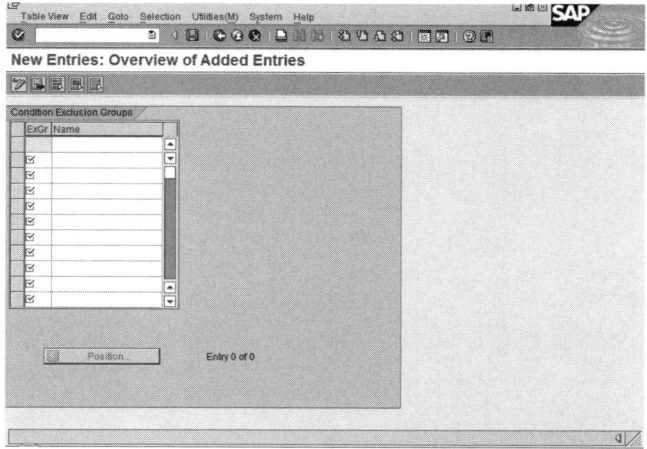

© SAP AG. All rights reserved.

FIGURE 4.27 The New Entries: Overview of Added Entries screen

5. Enter the relevant information in the respective fields of the **New Entries: Overview of Added Entries** screen. The new condition exclusion group is defined.

In this section, we have created a condition exclusion for groups of conditions. Similarly, you can also create condition exclusions for condition types and records. Apart from creating condition exclusion groups, you can also assign condition types to exclusion groups and maintain condition exclusion functions for pricing procedures by selecting the appropriate option from the **Choose Activity** dialog box (Figure 4.25).

Next, we discuss the third special pricing function—Comparison of Condition Types.

Comparison of Condition Types

You can compare the condition types during the price determination process. Condition types that need to be compared are placed in an exclusion group. The approaches for comparing condition types are these:

- **A**—The conditions within the first exclusion group are compared and the condition with the best price is selected; the rest of the conditions are considered as declarative.
- **B**—The condition records in a condition table are compared and the best price is selected; the rest of the condition records are considered declarative.
- **C**—The condition records of the total of the first and second exclusion groups are compared, and the group that provides the best price is selected. The conditions from the other group are considered to be declarative.
- **D**—Two exclusion groups are compared; if a condition record is determined for the condition type of the first exclusion group, then all the condition records for the second exclusion group are considered to be declarative.
- **E**—This approach is similar to comparing approach D; however, in this case, either the highest cost or the lowest discount is selected.
- **F**—This approach is similar to approach C; however, in this case, either the higher cost or lowest discount condition group is selected.

In this section, we discussed various special pricing functions that are used to determine the price of goods and services.

Let's now explore the special condition types.

Working with Special Condition Types

The standard condition types present in the mySAP ERP system are known as special condition types. The standard condition types, such as HM00 and AMIW, are automatically used for price determination without any editing. However, there are a few standard condition types that help you create your own custom condition types that, in turn, help you meet your business requirements. The special condition types are helpful in the following areas of the SD module of the mySAP ERP system:

- Manual pricing
- Minimum price value pricing
- Hierarchy pricing
- Discount and surcharges
- Rounding difference
- Statistical condition types

Let's discuss these in detail in the following sections.

Manual Pricing

During price determination, using the HM00 header condition type, the order value in the mySAP ERP system is manually entered. This process of manually entering the order value is known as manual pricing. After the order value is entered, the new order value is distributed proportionately among the items of the order by the mySAP ERP system. Moreover, the PN00 standard condition type helps to manually specify the net price for an item. Remember that the header conditions are manual conditions.

Minimum Price Value Pricing

The AMIW standard condition type is a group condition type used to get the minimum order value in the mySAP ERP system. During pricing, if the value in the order header is less than the minimal order value retrieved through the AMIW condition type, the minimum order value is used as the net order value by the mySAP ERP system. This process of pricing is called the minimum price value pricing.

The `AMIW` condition type consists of the `AMIZ` condition type. The `AMIZ` condition type works with the calculation formula 13 and is used in minimum price value pricing to calculate the minimum value surcharge. It calculates the minimum value surcharge by subtracting the net item value from the minimum order value, retrieved by the `AMIW` condition type. This formula calculates the minimum value surcharge, which is retrieved by subtracting the net item value from the minimum order value.

The `PMIN` condition type is used for the material minimum price. The `PMIN` condition type is also used by the mySAP ERP system to get the difference if the minimum price is not met during the pricing function.

Hierarchy Pricing

Flexible hierarchies are created in the mySAP ERP system to represent the customer organization with the help of customer hierarchies available in Sales Order Management. The different customer groups within a company can be represented in the mySAP ERP system by using these hierarchies and can be used to determine prices and runtime statistics during the sales order and billing processes. This mode of pricing is known as hierarchy pricing, and it helps improve sales order management.

Using the customer hierarchy of an organization, the price and rebate agreement can be assigned to a higher-level node. The customer hierarchy consists of the following elements:

- Master record for each node
- Assignment of nodes
- Assignment of customer master record to node

The price and rebate agreement assigned to a higher-level node is valid for all the subordinate nodes below the higher-level node. However, pricing condition records, which are relevant for pricing, can also be created for each node (as previously discussed in this chapter).

Discount and Surcharges

Special condition types in the mySAP ERP system, such as `KP00` and `KP01`, help you to work with discount and surcharges during price determination. The `KP00` condition type takes the number of the complete pallet as input to determine the pallet-level discount. The `KP00` condition type is controlled by formula 22 in the pricing procedure.

The `KP01` condition type is used to charge the customers with surcharges for incomplete pallets. This special condition type is also controlled by formula 22 in the pricing procedure.

The `KP02` special condition type is used to determine the mixed pallet discount. It retrieves the quantity of individual items and calculates the discount for the complete pallet. This condition type is controlled by formula 23.

The Rounding Difference

Rounding difference is a technique used to round off a fraction number to the nearest integer. In the mySAP ERP system, the following three rounding rules are available:

- **Commercial Rounding**—Rounds down the values that are less than 5 to the nearest integer, while the values that are greater than 5 are rounded up to the nearest integer. For example, the commercial rounding of 5.014 will be rounded down to 5.01; and the value 5.016 will be rounded up to 5.02.
- **Always Round Up**—Rounds up the value up to the next integer. For example, 5.014 and 5.016 will both be rounded up to 5.02.
- **Always Round Down**—Rounds the value down to the next integer. For example, 5.014 and 5.016 will both be rounded down to 5.01.

> **Note:** The rounding difference condition updates the G/L maintenance for the rounding difference.

Statistical Condition Types

During price determination in the mySAP ERP system, you may need to determine prices of goods and services for statistical purposes. The condition types used for determining prices for statistical purposes are known as statistical condition types. A few examples of the statistical condition types are listed here:

- **VPRS Condition Type**—Retrieves the standard cost of the material. The retrieved cost of the material is used as a statistical condition. To get the standard or moving average cost, the **VPRS** condition type uses the condition category **G**. The use of condition category **G** allows it to access the valuation segment of

material master, which helps to calculate the standard or moving average cost. The **VPRS** condition type uses the condition category **T**, when it has to access only moving average cost.
- **SKTO Condition Type**—Retrieves the cash discount rate. This condition type is used as a statistical value in pricing procedure.
- **EDI1 and EDI2 Condition Types**—Compares the net price with the price expected by the customer. This comparison is achieved with the help of the **EDI1** condition type. The **EDI2** condition type is used to compare the overall item value, where the overall item value is the product of net price and the quantity. The **EDI1** condition type uses the calculation formula 9 with a maximum deviation of 0.05 currency, whereas the **EDI2** condition type uses the calculation formula 8 with a maximum deviation of 1.0 currency.

> **Note:** Statistical condition types do not play any role in determining the price of a commodity by a pricing procedure, but they are used for internal analysis and for report development.

After completing the price determination procedure, we create price reports. Therefore, after discussing the important special condition types used in price determination procedure, let's now discuss the price reports in the following section.

Working with Price Reports

Pricing reports are ABAP/4 programs used in the SD module of SAP to analyze condition records based on different criteria. The reports, which are developed by using an ABAP program, are called Z-Reports. This is because we start their T.Codes with the letter Z, which is reserved in the SAP system for the customized development of reports. Perform the following steps to create a pricing report:

1. Navigate the following menu path to create a pricing report:

Menu Path

SAP Customizing Implementation Guide > Sales and Distribution > Basic Functions > Pricing > Maintain Pricing Report. Figure 4.28 shows the preceding menu path.

144 Chapter 4 Pricing and Taxes in SAP SD

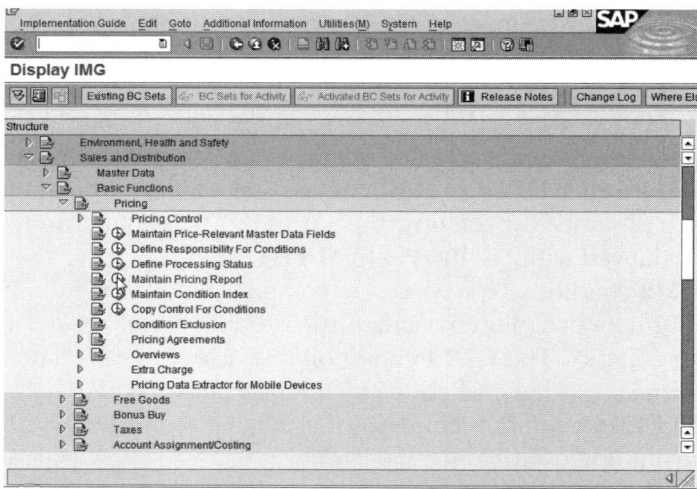

FIGURE 4.28 The Display IMG screen

2. Click the **Activity** icon (⊕) beside the **Maintain Pricing Report** activity. The **Choose Activity** dialog box appears as shown in Figure 4.29.

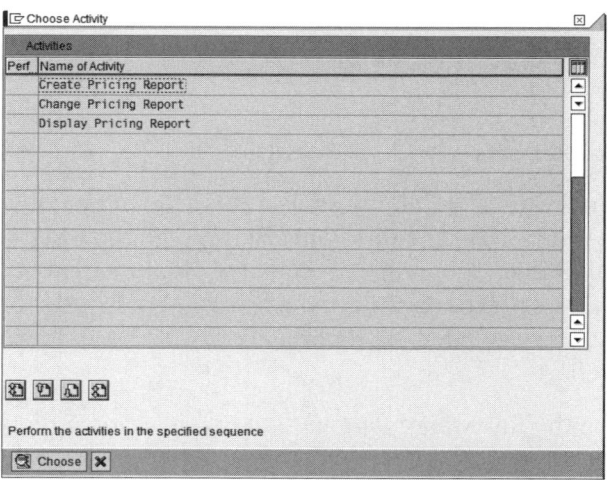

FIGURE 4.29 The Choose Activity dialog box

3. Select the **Create Pricing Report** option and click the **Choose** button (Figure 4.29). The **Create Pricing Report** screen appears as shown in Figure 4.30.

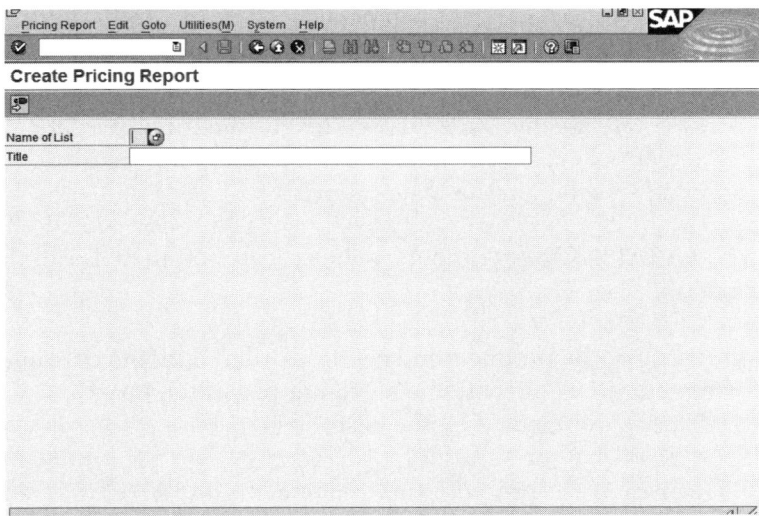

© SAP AG. All rights reserved.

FIGURE 4.30 The Create Pricing Report screen

4. Specify the **Name of List** and **Title** in the **Create Pricing Report** screen. A new price report is created.

Next, let's explore taxes and rebates in the following section.

WORKING WITH TAXES AND REBATES IN SAP SD

Tax and rebate are an integral part of SAP SD. Taxes are the amount paid by the customer as well as the seller of the goods and services. The tax amount paid varies with the nature of the product being sold and bought as well as the region in which it is being sold or bought.

Rebates are the amount deducted from the price of goods and services on the basis of certain criteria.

After the price determination functions are completed, the tax and rebates for goods and services are decided. The mySAP ERP system determines tax on the following bases:

- The departure country specified in the sales document.
- The destination country specified as the ship-to party in the sales document.
- The tax classification specified in the customer master data.
- The material tax classification accessed using the departure country, specified in the material master.

The mySAP ERP system determines rebates on the basis of the following information:

- Quantity of the products and services ordered by the customer.
- Frequency; i.e., how often a customer places the order.
- Delivery date selected by the customer.

On the basis of the preceding information, the mySAP ERP system calculates taxes and rebates. The two basic functions performed by the mySAP ERP system while calculating taxes are these:

- Tax determination
- Rebates

Let's discuss these functions in detail in the following sections.

Determining the Tax

Tax determination is a function performed by the mySAP ERP system to determine the taxes paid for the goods and services sold and bought. For tax determination, the mySAP ERP system uses some rules and criteria. These rules vary from country to country. In some countries, a single-level tax, such as Value Added Tax (VAT), is charged per sale. In other countries, multilevel taxes such as state, city, and several other taxes are levied. In several countries, country-level tax is also applied for sales. During tax determination, the data relevant to taxes must be maintained in coordination with the Financial Accounting (FI) module. The mySAP ERP system determines the tax rate and the billing document on the following bases:

- **Business Transaction**—Domestic or export–import
- **Tax Liability**—Of the ship-to party
- **Tax Liability**—Of the material

Let's now discuss the tax determination rules in the following section.

Defining the Rules for Tax Determination

The tax determination rules must be defined for appropriate and correct tax determination. The mySAP ERP system calculates the taxes according to the following parameters:

- Country of the plant from where the delivery of goods takes place.
- Country of the buyer of the goods.
- Tax indicator of the customer master record in coordination with the tax indicator of the material master record in the mySAP ERP system.

The preceding factors help define the tax determination rules. Perform the following steps to define the tax determination rule:

1. Navigate the following menu path to define the tax determination rule:

Menu Path

SAP Customizing Implementation Guide > Sales and Distribution > Basic Functions > Taxes > Define Tax Determination Rules. Figure 4.31 shows the preceding menu path.

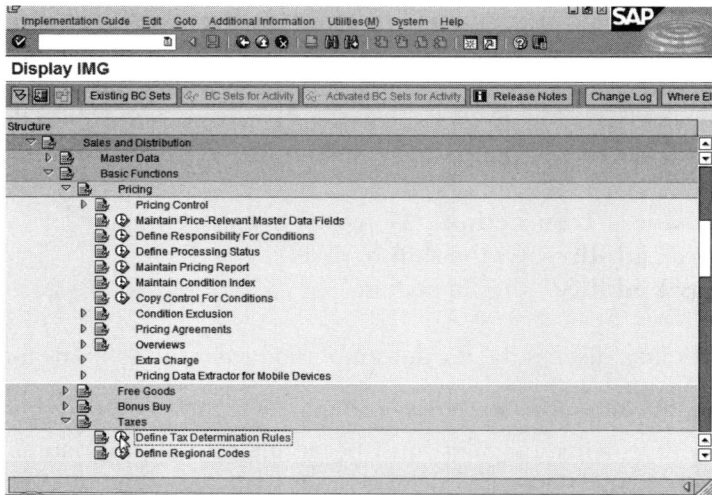

FIGURE 4.31   The Display IMG screen

2. Click the **Activity** icon (⊕) beside the **Define Tax Determination Rules** activity. The **Change View "Taxes: Tax Categories by Country": Overview** screen appears as shown in Figure 4.32.

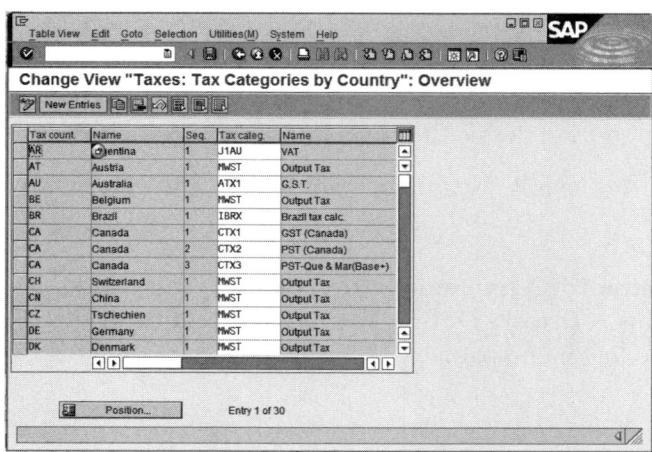

FIGURE 4.32   The Change View "Taxes: Tax Categories by Country": Overview screen

3. Click the **New Entries** button (Figure 4.32). The **New Entries: Overview of Added Entries** screen appears as shown in Figure 4.33.

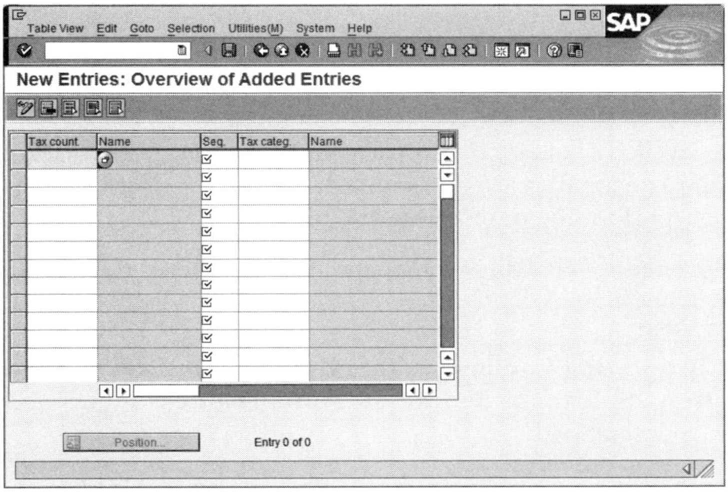

© SAP AG. All rights reserved.

FIGURE 4.33 The New Entries: Overview of Added Entries screen

4. Specify the relevant information in the respective fields of the **New Entries: Overview of Added Entries** screen to define the new tax determination rule.

An organization may be dealing with countries where taxes are applied at the regional level. In such a case, regional codes are used by the mySAP ERP system for tax determination. Let's discuss how to define regional codes in the following section.

Defining Regional Codes

During tax determination in the mySAP ERP system, the tax can be applied at the regional level. More than one country can be defined in a region. Simultaneously, you can also directly define cities in a region. Consequently, the regional codes can be defined in two ways:

- Defining a country code
- Defining a city code

> **Note:** The region and country codes are defined to use in the tax structure development apart from the other usage in the system.

Let's next discuss these functions in detail.

Defining a Country Code

Country code is a four-character alphanumeric value that defines a country in the mySAP ERP system. Because a country can have regions, it is also necessary to define a regional code to determine taxes. We now learn to define the country codes by performing the following steps:

1. Navigate the following menu path to define the country code:

Menu Path

SAP Customizing Implementation Guide > Sales and Distribution > Basic Functions > Taxes > Define Regional Codes. Figure 4.34 shows the preceding menu path.

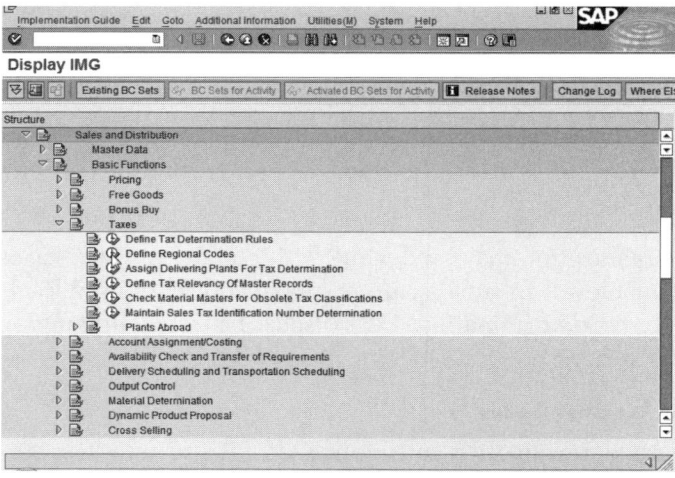

© SAP AG. All rights reserved.

FIGURE 4.34 **The Display IMG screen**

2. Click the **Activity** icon (⊕) beside the **Define Regional Codes** activity. The **Choose Activity** dialog box appears as shown in Figure 4.35.

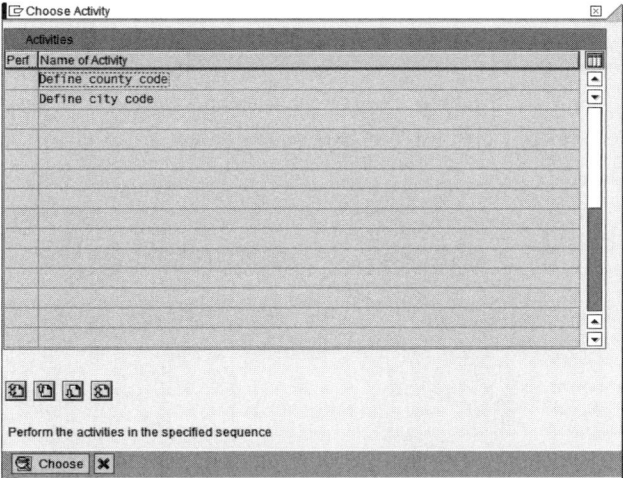

© SAP AG. All rights reserved.

FIGURE 4.35 The Choose Activity dialog box

3. Select the **Define county code** option, and click the **Choose** button. The **Change View "County": Overview** screen appears as shown in Figure 4.36.

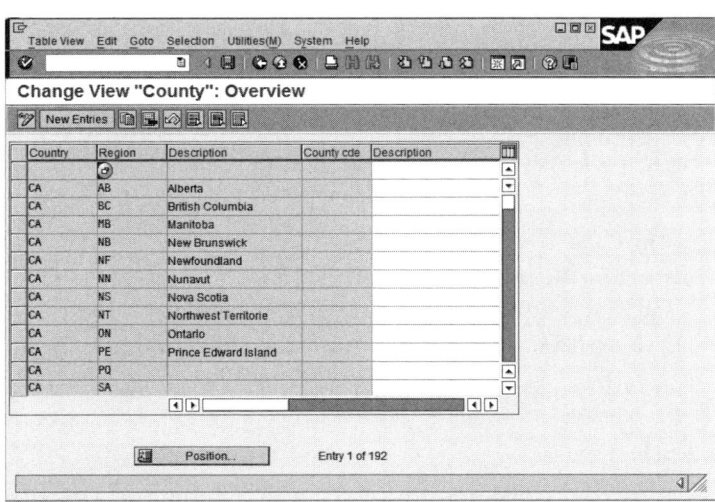

© SAP AG. All rights reserved.

FIGURE 4.36 The Change View "County": Overview screen

The **Change View "County": Overview** screen displays predefined country codes.

4. Click the **New Entries** button to define a new country code. The **New Entries: Overview of Added Entries** screen appears as shown in Figure 4.37.

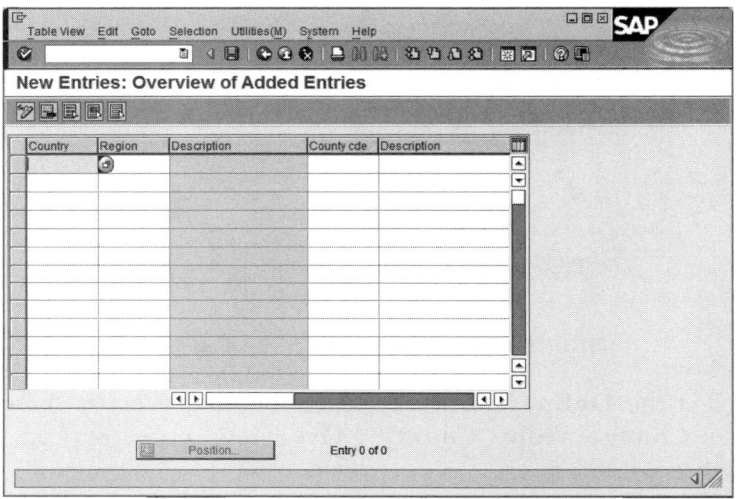

© SAP AG. All rights reserved.

FIGURE 4.37 The New Entries: Overview of Added Entries screen

5. Specify the relevant details in the respective fields of the **New Entries: Overview of Added Entries** screen (Figure 4.37). The country code is defined.

Defining a City Code

Within a region in the mySAP ERP system, one or more city codes can be defined. City codes play a vital role in the tax determination process of the mySAP ERP system. Perform the following steps to define a city code:

1. Navigate the following menu path to define a city code:

Menu Path

SAP Customizing Implementation Guide > Sales and Distribution > Basic Functions > Taxes > Define Regional Codes, as shown in Figure 4.34.

2. Click the **Activity** icon (⊕) beside the **Define Regional Codes** activity. The **Choose Activity** dialog box appears (Figure 4.35).
3. Select the **Define city code** option, and click the **Choose** button (Figure 4.35). The **Change View "City": Overview** screen appears as shown in Figure 4.38.

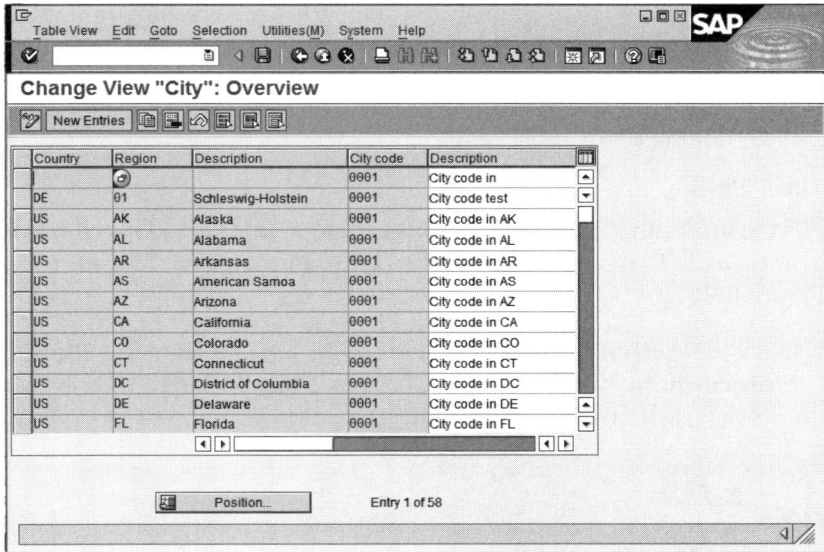

© SAP AG. All rights reserved.

FIGURE 4.38 The Change View "City": Overview screen

The **Change View "City": Overview** screen displays the existing city codes.

4. Click the **New Entries** button to define a new city code (Figure 4.38). The **New Entries: Overview of Added Entries** screen appears (Figure 4.37). Specify the relevant details in the respective fields to define a new city code.

The goods and services are delivered from the delivery plant to the customers. Therefore, the details of delivery plant to the city or the country code must be specified in the mySAP ERP system. In other words, apart from the country code and city code, the delivering plant is also an important organizational unit for tax determination.

Now, let's discuss how to assign delivering plants for tax determination in the following section.

Assigning a Delivering Plant for Tax Determination

The plant from where the goods and services are delivered also plays an important and crucial role in determining the taxes to be paid. Therefore, it is essential to assign the delivering plant for tax determination. Perform the following steps to assign the delivering plant for tax determination:

1. Navigate the menu path provided to assign the delivering plant for tax determination:

Menu Path

SAP Customizing Implementation Guide > Sales and Distribution > Basic Functions > Taxes > Assign Delivering Plants For Tax Determination (Figure 4.34).

2. Click the **Activity** icon ( ) beside the **Assign Delivering Plants For Tax Determination** activity. The **Change View "Plants": Overview** screen appears as shown in Figure 4.39.

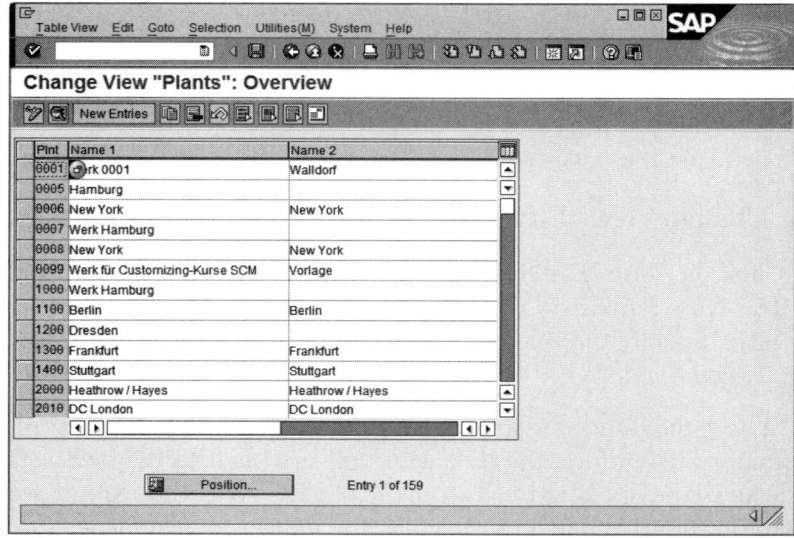

© SAP AG. All rights reserved.

FIGURE 4.39 The Change View "Plants": Overview screen

The **Change View "Plants": Overview** screen displays the existing plants detail (Figure 4.39).

3. Click the **New Entries** button (Figure 4.39) to enter a new plant in the existing list of plants. The **New Entries: Details of Added Entries** screen opens, as shown in Figure 4.40.

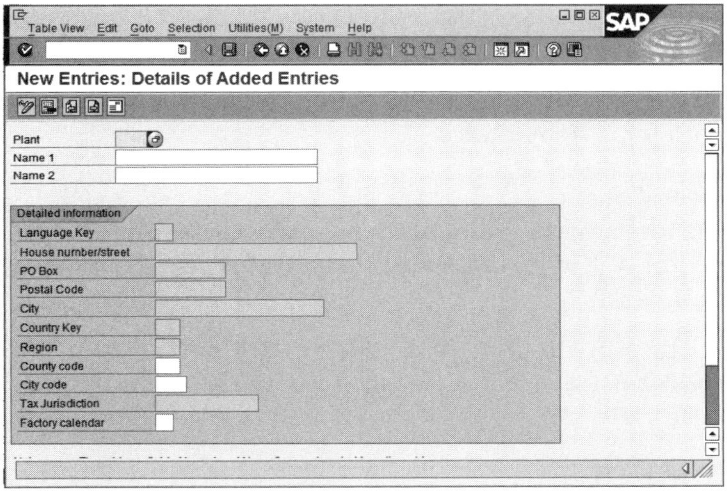

© SAP AG. All rights reserved.

FIGURE 4.40 The New Entries: Details of Added Entries screen

4. Specify the relevant information required in the respective fields of the **New Entries: Details of Added Entries** screen (Figure 4.40) to assign the plant for tax determination.

When a customer buys goods and services, a certain amount of tax is levied on the basis of the type of customer. Therefore, tax relevancy of the Master Records–Customer Taxes is also considered during tax determination. Let's discuss defining tax relevancy of Master Records–Customer Taxes in the following section.

Defining the Tax Relevancy of Master Records–Customer Taxes

During the tax determination process, it is essential to determine whether a particular customer is liable to pay tax. While determining the price of goods and services for a customer, the mySAP ERP system accesses the records of the customer from master data and determines whether the customer is liable for

156 CHAPTER 4 PRICING AND TAXES IN SAP SD

tax. Therefore, to determine the tax liability of a customer, the tax relevancy of master record for customer taxes must be defined in the mySAP ERP system.

> **Note:** The region of a customer is defined in the Customer Master Record, which serves as the basis for the tax rates that appear in a sales order.

Perform the following steps to define the tax relevancy of master record for customer taxes:

1. Navigate the following menu path to define the tax relevancy of master record for customer taxes:

Menu Path

SAP Customizing Implementation Guide > Sales and Distribution > Basic Functions > Taxes > Define Tax Relevancy Of Master Records (Figure 4.34).

2. Click the **Activity** icon ( ) beside the **Define Tax Relevancy Of Master Records** activity. The **Choose Activity** dialog box appears as shown in Figure 4.41.

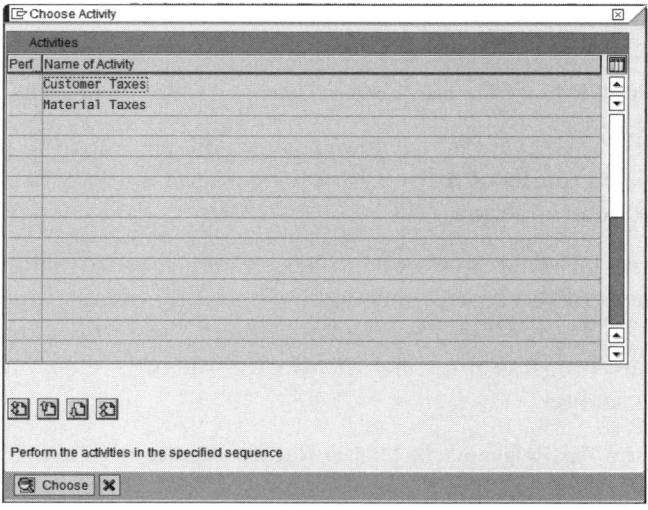

© SAP AG. All rights reserved.

FIGURE 4.41 **The Choose Activity dialog box**

3. Select the **Customer Taxes** option and click the **Choose** button. The **Change View "Customer Taxes": Overview** screen appears as shown in Figure 4.42.

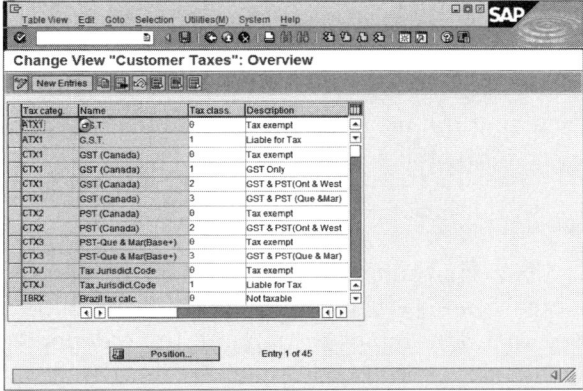

© SAP AG. All rights reserved.

FIGURE 4.42 The Change View "Customer Taxes": Overview screen

The **Change View "Customer Taxes": Overview** screen (Figure 4.42) shows all the predefined entries.

4. Click the **New Entries** button (Figure 4.42) to define the new tax relevancy of master record for customer taxes. The **New Entries: Overview of Added Entries** screen appears as shown in Figure 4.43.

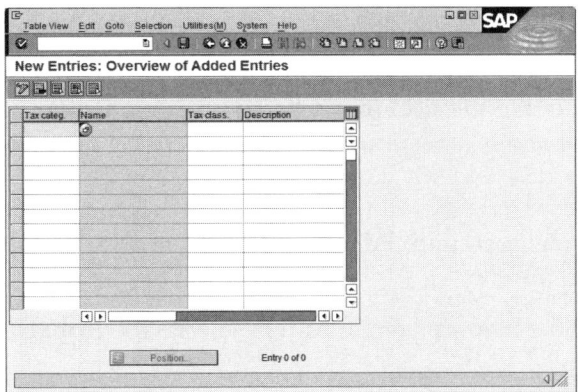

© SAP AG. All rights reserved.

FIGURE 4.43 The New Entries: Overview of Added Entries screen

5. Specify the relevant information in the respective fields of the **New Entries: Overview of Added Entries** screen to define the new tax relevancy of the master record for customer taxes.

> **Note:** Similar to defining tax relevancy of master record for customer taxes, you can also define the tax relevancy for material taxes.

After discussing the tax determination process in detail, let's discuss the rebates in detail in the following section.

Working with Rebates

In real life, a rebate is an amount deducted from the price of goods and services from specific customers. In the mySAP ERP system, a rebate is a pricing condition type that determines the amount to be deducted from the price of the goods and services purchased by a customer. Rebates are provided on the basis of rebate agreements established between the organization (seller of the goods and services) and the customer. The rebate agreement must be created according to a specific rebate agreement type. The following are the standard agreement types that the mySAP ERP system provides.

- Material
- Customer
- Customer hierarchy
- Material group rebate
- Independent of sales volume

Rebates differ from discounts because the discounts are calculated irrespective of the sales volume, whereas the amount of rebate depends on the sales volume and is passed to the customer after a predefined volume of sales or time period is reached. The rebate conditions appear in the sales order.

To work with rebates in the mySAP ERP system, the **Rebate Processing** option must be activated. Perform the following steps to activate the **Rebate Processing** option:

1. Navigate the following menu path to activate the **Rebate Processing** option:

Menu Path

SAP Customizing Implementation Guide > Sales and Distribution > Billing > Rebate Processing > Activate Rebate Processing. Figure 4.44 shows the preceding menu path.

Working with Taxes and Rebates in SAP SD

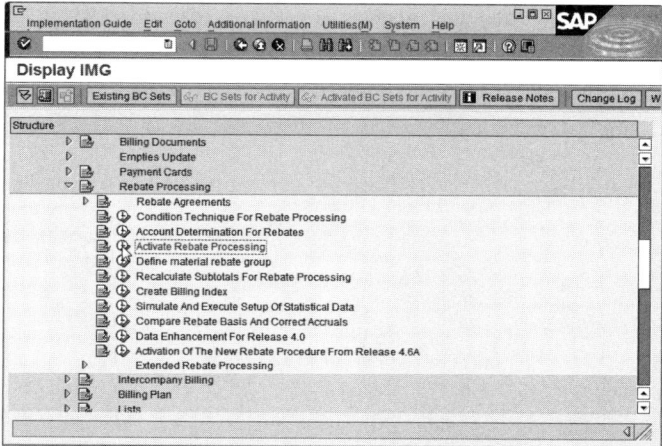

FIGURE 4.44 The Display IMG screen

2. Click the **Activity** icon (🔄) beside the **Activate Rebate Processing** activity. The **Choose Activity** dialog box appears as shown in Figure 4.45.

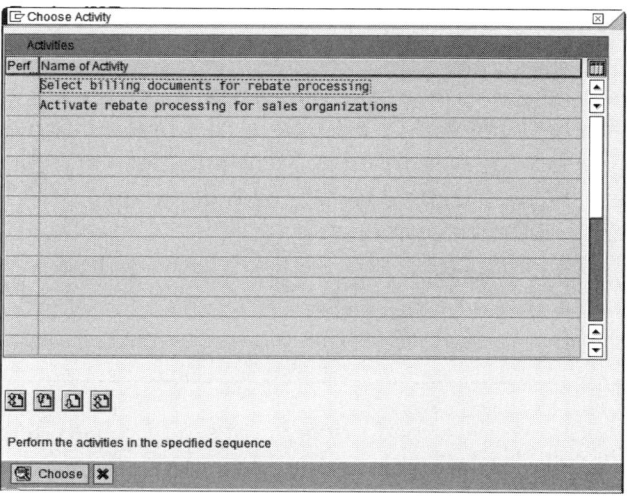

FIGURE 4.45 The Choose Activity dialog box

3. Select the **Activate rebate processing for sales organizations** option and click the **Choose** button. The **Change View "Sales Organization – Rebate": Overview** screen appears as shown in Figure 4.46.

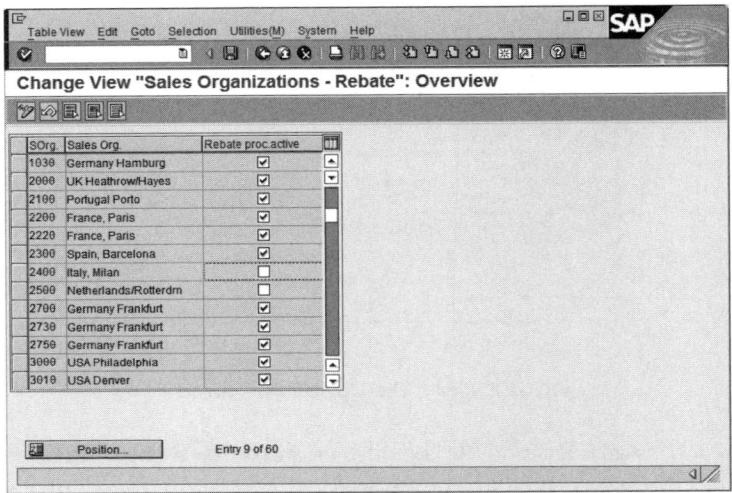

© SAP AG. All rights reserved.

FIGURE 4.46 The Change View "Sales Organization – Rebate": Overview screen

You can activate or deactivate the rebate processing by either selecting or clearing the check box for the respective sales organization.

In this section, we discussed tax determination and rebates in the mySAP ERP system. We also learned to define tax determination rules and to activate and deactivate the rebate process.

Finally, let's summarize what we have discussed in this chapter.

SUMMARY

In this chapter, we described pricing, taxes, and rebate functions in the SAP SD module. The chapter has explored the price determination function in the mySAP ERP system, in addition to the aspects that help in the price determination procedure. Next, the chapter described the taxes applicable to sales and specified that the tax is determined on the basis of the delivering country, country of the customer, and other criteria. The chapter also explored some standard conditional codes provided by the mySAP ERP system that are essential for the tax determination functions. Finally, the chapter explored the concepts of rebate and how the rebate processing option is activated in the mySAP ERP system.

The next chapter discusses the relationship of the SD module with the MM module of SAP.

Chapter 5
Integration of SAP SD and MM Modules

If you need information on:	See page:
Implementing the Availability Check in SD	164
Implementing the Transfer of Requirements in SD	211
Working with Contracts	222
Working with Scheduling Agreements	243
Working with the Consignment Stock Process	253

The Sales and Data (SD) module of SAP® software is cohesively related to the Material Management (MM) module. Various activities performed during the life cycle of a sales order are implemented in the SD and MM modules. To understand the concept better, let's briefly explore the sales order life cycle. The sales order life cycle starts with a sales order being placed in the SD module of the SAP application. The sales order is further processed by verifying the availability of stock, which is implemented in the MM module. If the stock availability check specifies that the required goods are available, the sales order is processed, and the goods are delivered to the customer. At times, the stock availability check might specify that the required goods are not available. In such a situation, the required material is delivered by following a specific process called cross-company sales (a concept presented later in this chapter). Consequently, cross-company sales are implemented in the MM module of SAP.

Sometimes a sales order means delivering the required goods after procuring them from a third-party vendor. This requires that the delivery of material request be transferred to an external vendor, which in turn delivers the material to the customer. Since the material is being delivered by a third-party vendor, the vendor might put an additional charge for delivering the material to the customer. To avoid this additional charge, the organization can provide the material required to manufacture the final product to the external vendor. This process of providing the raw material to the vendor, known as subcontracting the procurement process, is also implemented in the MM module. In addition to this, the MM module also plays a role in scheduling various agreements and contracts between customers and third-party vendors.

This chapter explores the concept of the availability check and describes various processes, such as cross-company sales and cross-company stock transfer orders. In addition, the chapter also explores the process of defining various types of contracts and scheduling agreements, and it explores the consignment stock process.

IMPLEMENTING THE AVAILABILITY CHECK IN SD

An availability check is an integral part of sales order processing. It helps determine whether the requested deliverable quantity would be available for shipping on the delivery due date. This process of availability check is performed at the plant level in an organization and returns the material availability date; that is, the due date on which the material would be available. The picking and packing time as well as the transportation scheduling time are added to the material availability date determined by the mySAP™ ERP system. After adding packaging and transportation time, the planned goods issue date is determined. The shipping time is further added to the planned goods issue date, resulting in the final delivery date to the customer.

Before starting the discussion on the basic elements of availability check, let's discuss the terminologies that will be used throughout the chapter:

- **Backorder Processing**—Represents the processing of a sales order that has either not been fully confirmed or has not been confirmed at a specific date.
- **Rescheduling**—Represents a proposal for reassigning a sales order. It replaces one sales order with another sales order due to higher priority. For example, the sales order given by the ABC customer can be replaced with the sales order of the XYZ customer because the sales order of the XYZ customer has a higher priority.
- **Availability to Promise (ATP)**—Serves as the basis for an availability check in which the mySAP ERP system automatically evaluates the available quantity to promise or commit to a sales document on the basis of the inward and outward movement of goods.

- **Replenishment Lead Time**—Represents the time required to produce or procure the required stock. It includes the time consumed by a company, either to produce the material or to externally procure the material from the third party.

After understanding the basic terminologies that have been used to describe availability check, let's now discuss how to examine the stock on hand in an organization. Use the following menu path to evaluate the stock on hand:

Menu Path

SAP menu > Logistics > Sales and Distribution > Sales > Environment > Availability Overview. Figure 5.1 shows the preceding menu path accessed to examine the stock on hand.

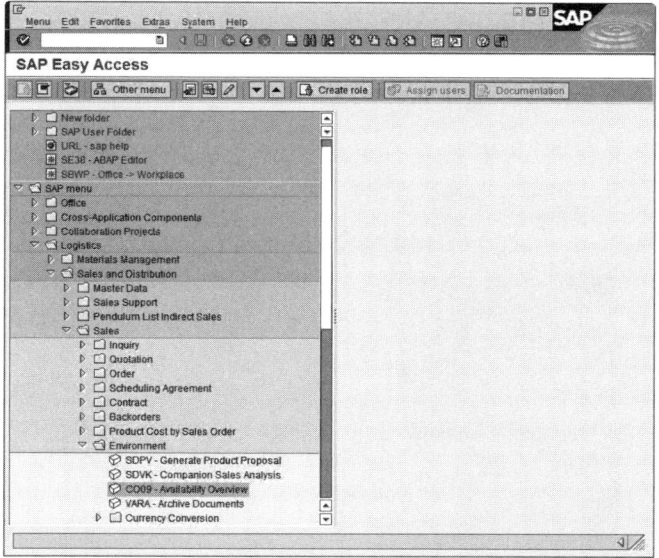

© SAP AG. All rights reserved.

FIGURE 5.1 Displaying menu path for availability overview

Note: You can also use the `CO09` transaction code to examine the stock in hand in the system.

Chapter 5 Integration of SAP SD and MM Modules

After selecting the menu path shown in Figure 5.1, the **Availability Overview** screen is displayed, as shown in Figure 5.2.

Now, enter the details in the following text fields, as shown in the **Availability Overview** screen:

- **Material**—Accepts the material number of the material that you want to check. In our example, we entered CPD20008 in the **Material** text field (Figure 5.2).
- **Plant**—Accepts the plant code in which the associated material (entered in the **Material** text field) is available. In our example, we entered CPF3 in the **Plant** text field (Figure 5.2).
- **MRP Area**—Accepts the MRP area associated with the material number and plant entered by you. In our example, we entered CPF3 in the **MRP Area** text field (Figure 5.2).
- **Checking Rule**—Accepts the checking code associated with the checking condition. In our example, we entered 01 in the **Checking Rule** text field (Figure 5.2).

Figure 5.2 shows the fields entered by us in the **Availability Overview** screen:

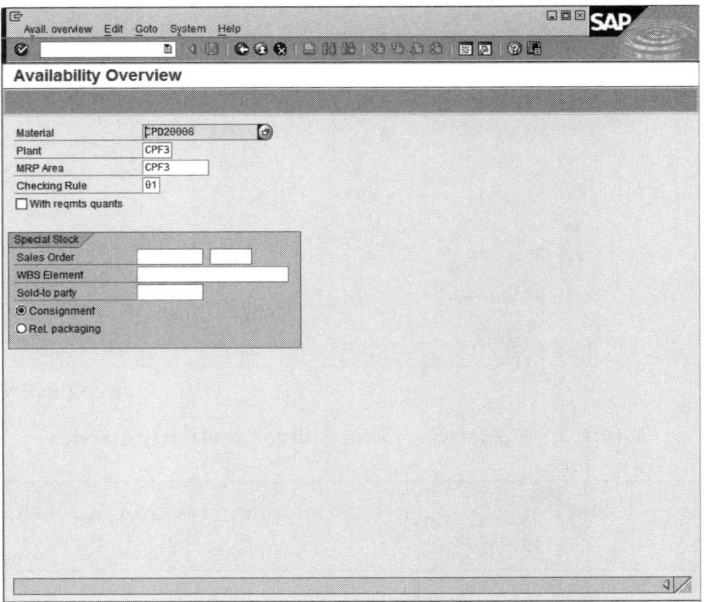

© SAP AG. All rights reserved.

FIGURE 5.2 Displaying the Availability Overview screen

After you have entered the details, either press the **Enter** key or click the **Execute** icon ( ), shown on the standard toolbar of the SAP GUI. The **Availability Overview** screen changes and displays the details of the material entered (Figure 5.2), as shown in Figure 5.3.

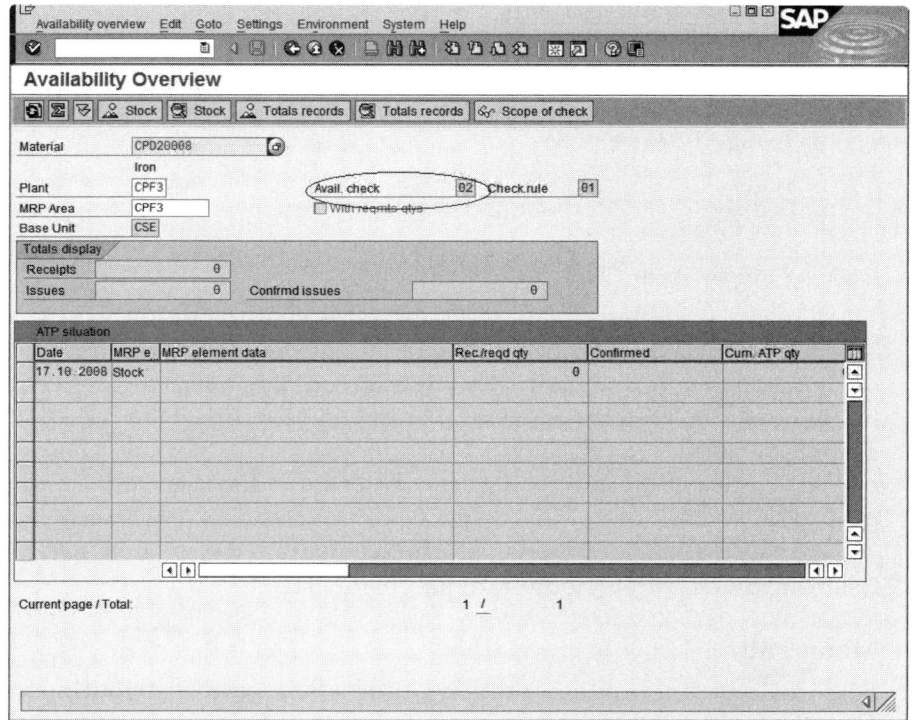

© SAP AG. All rights reserved.

FIGURE 5.3 Displaying the details of a specific material

Figure 5.3 shows the details of the CPD20008 material, where the **Aval. check** field displays the available stock on hand.

After learning how to examine stock on hand, let's discuss the basic elements of configuring availability check.

Working with the Elements of an Availability Check

Before configuring an availability check, its various elements must be understood. Following are the elements of an availability check:

- Requirement class
- Requirement types
- Checking group
- Checking rules
- Schedule line category

Let's discuss each of them in detail.

Defining Requirement Class

The process of defining a requirement class controls the processes of the availability check and the transfer of requirements (TOR) for all of the sales document types. Whenever a sales order is received, the list of goods required is entered in the requirement class that is defined in the mySAP ERP system. The entries at the requirement class level are used as default values by the mySAP ERP system, and the data is transferred to the sales order. Generally, instead of creating a new requirement class for business processing, you copy and rename the most appropriate existing requirement class. Let's navigate the following menu path to define a requirement class:

Menu Path

SAP Customizing Implementation Guide > Sales and Distribution > Basic Functions > Availability Check and Transfer of Requirements > Transfer of Requirements > Define Requirements Classes

Figure 5.4 shows the preceding menu path to define the requirement class.

Implementing the Availability Check in SD

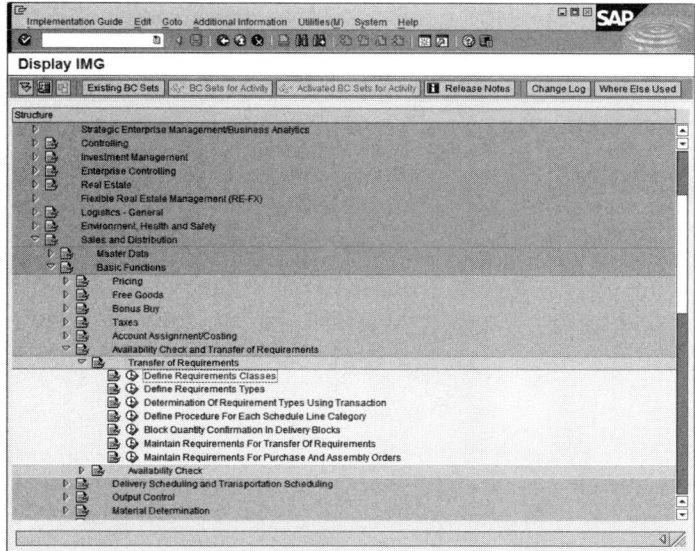

FIGURE 5.4   Displaying the menu path to define requirement class

Now click the **Activity** icon (☑) to display the **Change View "Requirements Classes": Overview** screen, as shown in Figure 5.5.

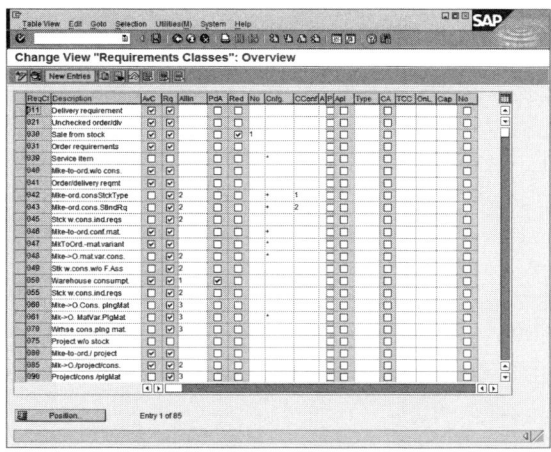

FIGURE 5.5   Displaying the Change View "Requirements Classes": Overview screen

Figure 5.5 shows the details of the existing requirement classes defined in the mySAP ERP system. To define a new requirement class, click the **New Entries** button (Figure 5.5) and enter the details of the new requirement class, as shown in Figure 5.6.

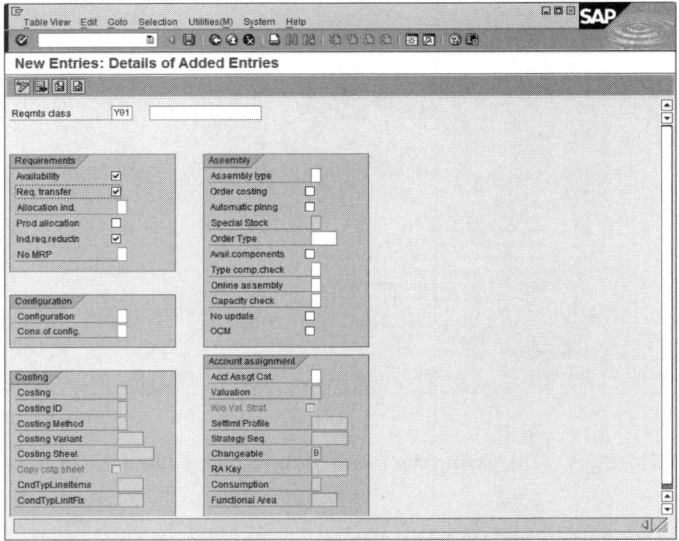

© SAP AG. All rights reserved.

FIGURE 5.6 Displaying details entered for a new requirement class

After entering the details as shown in Figure 5.6, click the **Save** icon (🖫) to save the details of the newly defined requirement class.

> **Note:** Remember that the name of the new requirement class should have Y or Z as the initial letter, followed by numbers, because it is a user-defined requirement class. However, the name of a system-defined requirement class starts either with a number or with any letter between A and X.

After understanding how to define a requirement class, let's now discuss requirement types.

Defining Requirement Type

Requirement types are defined in relation to the requirement class and its features. While transferring requirements from one location to another in a company, a requirement class is assigned to one or more requirement types. Requirement types can be allocated only to a single requirement class, whereas a requirement class can be allocated to multiple requirement types. Moreover, a requirement type is displayed in the sales order and is based on the item category as well as the MRP type of a material.

In this section, we discuss how to define a requirement type and assign a requirement class to it. Let's navigate the following menu path to define a requirement type (Figure 5.4):

Menu Path

SAP Customizing Implementation Guide > Sales and Distribution > Basic Functions > Availability Check and Transfer of Requirements > Transfer of Requirements > Define Requirements Types

After navigating through the preceding menu path, click the **Activity** icon (🕭) to display the **Change View "Requirements Types": Overview** screen, as shown in Figure 5.7.

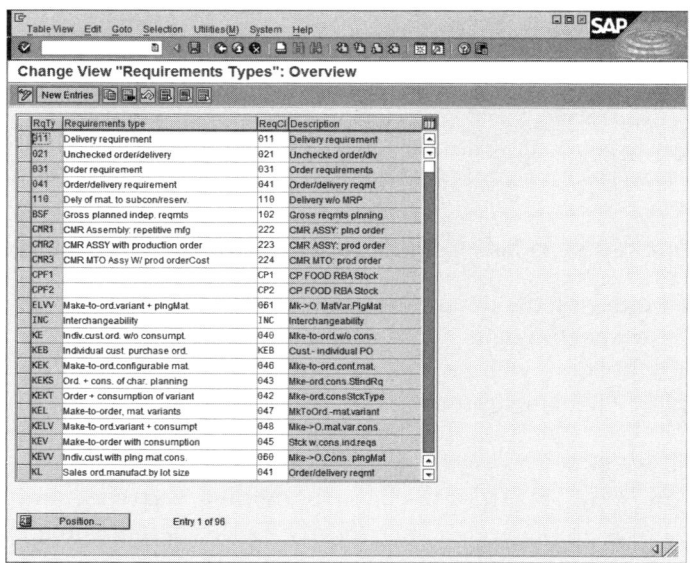

© SAP AG. All rights reserved.

FIGURE 5.7 Displaying the Change View "Requirements Types": Overview screen

Figure 5.7 shows the details of all the requirement types along with their associated requirement classes. Click the **New Entries** button (Figure 5.7) to add a new requirement type. Enter the details of the new requirement type, as shown in Figure 5.8.

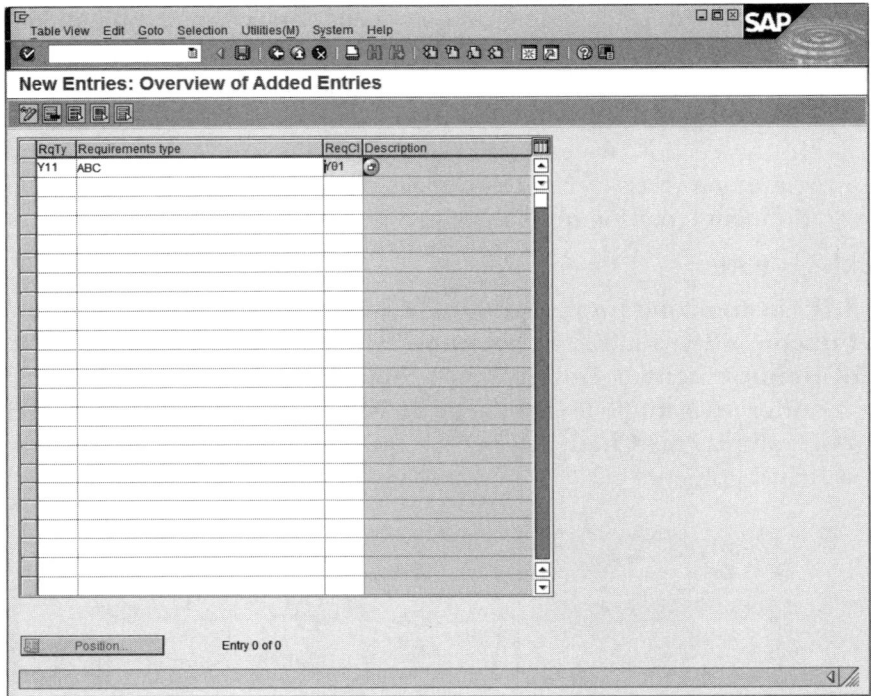

© SAP AG. All rights reserved.

FIGURE 5.8 Displaying details entered for a new requirement type

After entering the details to define a new requirement type, click the **Save** icon (🖫) to save the data.

In this section, you have learned how to define a requirement type. Now let's explore checking groups in detail.

Checking Group

A checking group provides the basis for defining the type of requirement to be passed. For example, a checking group checks whether you need to record the requirements in the stock requirement list as daily requirements or as weekly summed up requirements. You can also record individual requirements for each sales order and line items in the stock requirement list. However, there are pros and cons of both individual and summarized requirements. You can implement backorder processing for individual requirements instead of the summarized requirements. However, since an individual requirement is based on each sales order and lined items, it may lead to greater impact on the system performance as compared to the summarized requirement. The SAP standard uses `01` to represent daily requirements and `02` to represent individual requirements.

After discussing the checking group, let's discuss checking rules as the basic elements of an availability check.

Checking Rules

A checking rule is a rule that determines the scope of an availability check for each transaction in SD processing. For example, if the checking rule `01` is assigned to the `Z001` transaction, the availability check of the material associated with the `Z001` transaction is controlled on the basis of the `01` checking rule. You can also control the availability check on the material master record based on the checking group.

After discussing the checking rule, let's now discuss the schedule line category, another basic element of the availability check.

Schedule Line Category

The schedule line level fine-tunes the availability check and deactivates the schedule lines that are not relevant for a particular availability check by ensuring that the availability check indicator is not checked. For example, the transactions that have already been processed are discarded from the schedule line category; there is no need to process them again or to reschedule them.

This concludes the discussion on the basic elements of availability check. Now, let's learn how to configure an availability check.

Configuring an Availability Check

An availability check is performed to determine whether the required material can be supplied to a customer on the customer's requested delivery date. With the release of 3.0E, orders can be confirmed not only by order entries but also through the product allocation. Therefore, in this section we discuss how to configure an availability check based on the following three types:

- Availability check with ATP or against planning
- Availability check against product allocation
- Rule-based availability check

Let's discuss each of them in detail.

Availability Check with ATP or against Planning

An availability check with ATP or against planning is a type of availability check that helps configure the mySAP ERP system to perform an availability check on the basis of either planning made against availability check or ATP logic. ATP refers to Available to Promise, which also considers inward and outward movement of material. This may be configured with or without Replenishment Lead Time (RLT). To configure the availability check with ATP or against planning, use the following menu path from the SAP® Customizing Implementation Guide:

Menu Path

SAP Customizing Implementation Guide > Sales and Distribution > Basic Functions > Availability Check and Transfer of Requirements > Availability Check > Availability Check with ATP Logic or Against Planning

Figure 5.9 shows the preceding menu path in the mySAP ERP system:

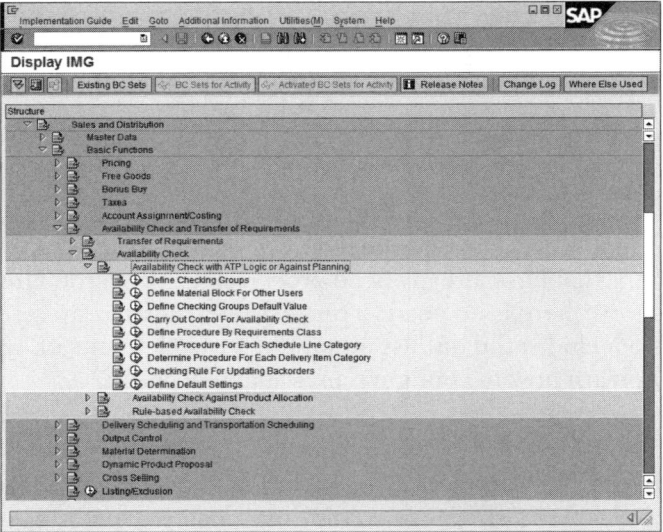

© SAP AG. All rights reserved.

FIGURE 5.9 Displaying IMG path for availability check with ATP logic or planning

Figure 5.9 also shows the list of activities needed to configure the availability check with ATP logic or planning. The list of activities includes the following:

- Define Checking Groups
- Define Material Blocks For Other Users
- Define Checking Groups Default Value
- Carry Out Control For an Availability Check
- Define Procedure By Requirements Class
- Define Procedure For Each Schedule Line Category
- Determine Procedure For Each Delivery Item Category

- Checking Rule For Updating Backorders
- Define Default Settings

Let's discuss each of these activities in detail.

Define Checking Groups

In the mySAP ERP system, you can define the checking groups by specifying the type of requirements that the mySAP ERP system creates while processing sales orders or deliveries. The requirement types for sales order processing are known as sales order requirements, and the requirement types for delivery processing are known as delivery requirements. Now, let's navigate the following menu path to define the checking groups (Figure 5.9):

Menu Path

SAP Customizing Implementation Guide > Sales and Distribution > Basic Functions > Availability Check and Transfer of Requirements > Availability Check > Availability Check with ATP Logic or Against Planning > Define Checking Groups

After navigating through the preceding menu path, click the **IMG Activity** icon () beside the **Define Checking Groups** activity. The **Change View "Availability Check Control": Overview** screen appears as shown in Figure 5.10.

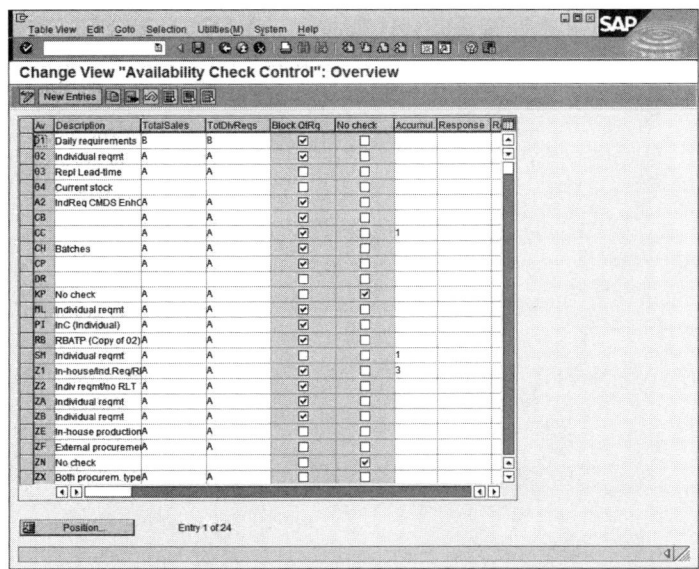

© SAP AG. All rights reserved.

FIGURE 5.10 Displaying the Change View "Availability Check Control": Overview screen

Figure 5.10 displays the list of existing checking groups. However, you can also define a new checking group by clicking the **New Entries** button.

After learning how to define checking groups, let's now learn how to define material blocks for other users.

Define Material Block for Other Users

Sometimes, a material may be reserved for a specific customer. In such a case, the material is not available for other users who place their sales orders. The **Defining Material Block for Other Users** activity allows you to decide whether to block the material master record for other orders during the availability check. If the material is not blocked during the availability check, the other orders are confirmed because the quantity is sufficient for all orders. Use the following menu path to define the material block for other users (Figure 5.9):

Menu Path

SAP Customizing Implementation Guide > Sales and Distribution > Basic Functions > Availability Check and Transfer of Requirements > Availability Check > Availability Check with ATP Logic or Against Planning > Define Material Block For Other Users

After navigating through the preceding menu path, click the **IMG Activity** icon (🔧) beside the **Define Material Block for Other Users** activity. The **Change View "Availability Check: Checking Criteria": Overview** screen appears as shown in Figure 5.11.

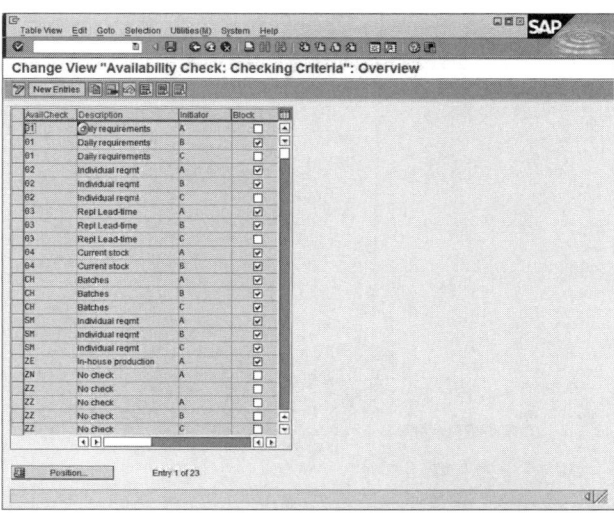

© SAP AG. All rights reserved.

FIGURE 5.11 Displaying the Change View "Availability Check: Checking Criteria": Overview screen

Figure 5.11 shows the list of existing blocked materials for other users during the availability check. You can also block some other material by clicking the **New Entries** button and then entering details in the **New Entries: Overview of Added Entries** screen, as shown in Figure 5.12.

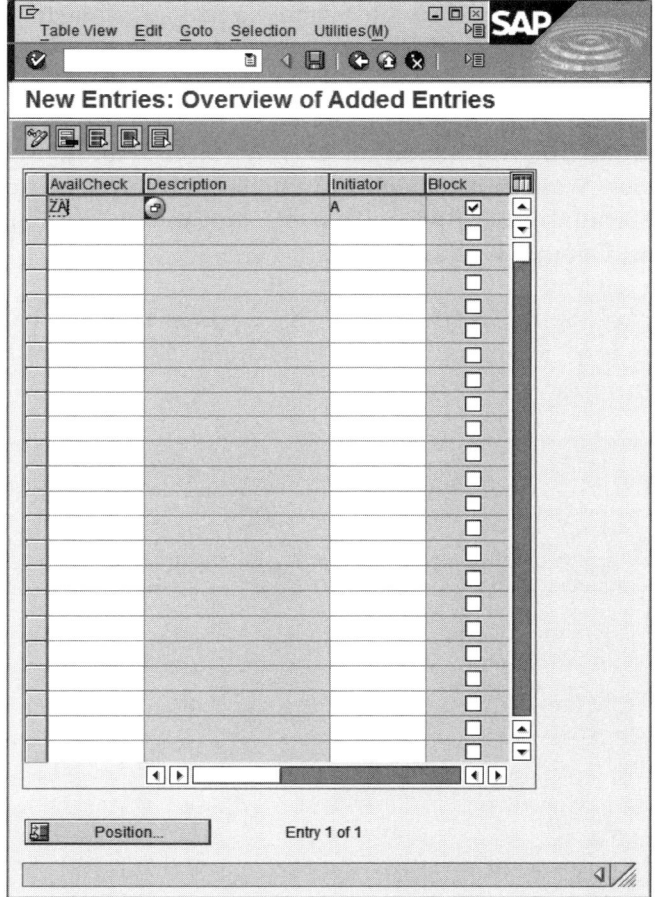

FIGURE 5.12 Entering details for blocking materials for others

Figure 5.12 shows that the ZA material is blocked for other users during the availability check. Now click the **Save** icon (🖫) to save the entered data.

After discussing how to block the material for other users, let's describe how to define a default value for a checking group.

Define Checking Groups Default Value

If you do not provide a value for a checking group, the mySAP ERP system accepts the default value. You can define a default value for a checking group, depending upon the material type and plant. When you create a new material master record, you define the checking group that the mySAP ERP system specifies. Let's navigate the following menu path to define the default value for a checking group (Figure 5.9):

Menu Path
SAP Customizing Implementation Guide > Sales and Distribution > Basic Functions > Availability Check and Transfer of Requirements > Availability Check > Availability Check with ATP Logic or Against Planning > Define Checking Groups Default Value

After navigating through the preceding menu path, click the **IMG Activity** icon (⊕) beside the **Define Checking Groups Default Value** activity. The **Change View "Scope of Availability Check (Default Values)": Overview** screen appears as shown in Figure 5.13.

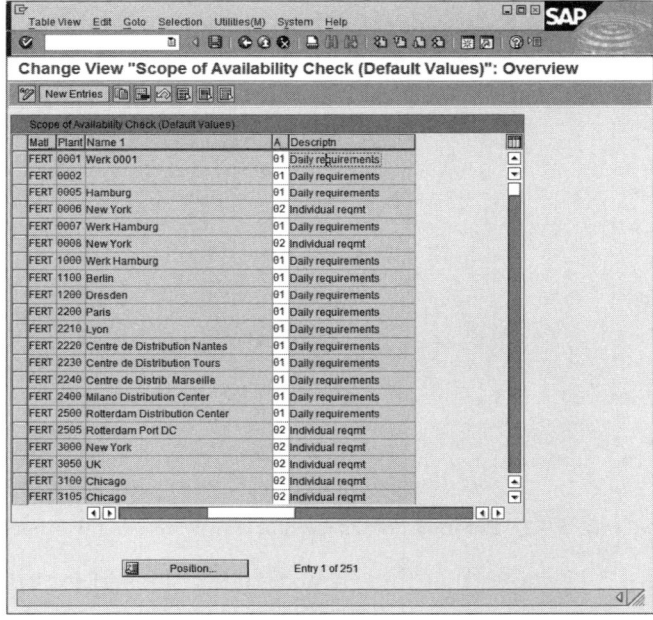

© SAP AG. All rights reserved.

FIGURE 5.13 Displaying the Change View "Scope of Availability Check (Default Values)": Overview screen

Figure 5.13 shows the list of default values for checking groups. To define a new default value for a checking group, click the **New Entries** button and enter details in the **New Entries: Overview of Added Entries** screen as shown in Figure 5.14.

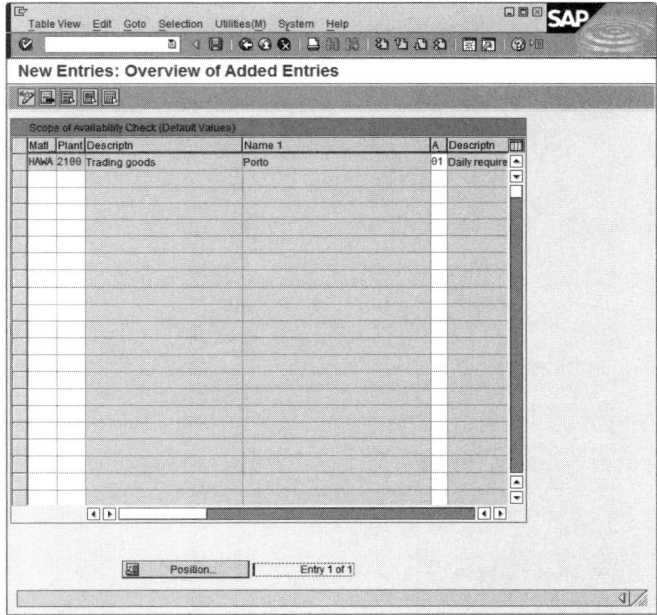

© SAP AG. All rights reserved.

FIGURE 5.14 Displaying the New Entries: Overview of Added Entries screen

After entering the details, click the **Save** icon (🖫) to save the data.

Now, let's move ahead to explore the next activity, **Carry Out Control for an Availability Check**.

Carry Out Control for an Availability Check

The **Carry Out Control for Availability Check** activity allows you to allocate a checking rule to a checking group. For this, you need to define a checking rule to specify the scope of the availability check for each transaction. Let's navigate the following menu path to perform this activity (Figure 5.9):

Menu Path

SAP Customizing Implementation Guide > Sales and Distribution > Basic Functions > Availability Check and Transfer of Requirements > Availability Check > Availability Check with ATP Logic or Against Planning > Carry Out Control For Availability Check

After navigating through the preceding menu path, click the **IMG Activity** icon ( ) beside the **Carry Out Control for Availability Check** activity. The **Change View "Availability Check Control": Overview** screen appears as shown in Figure 5.15.

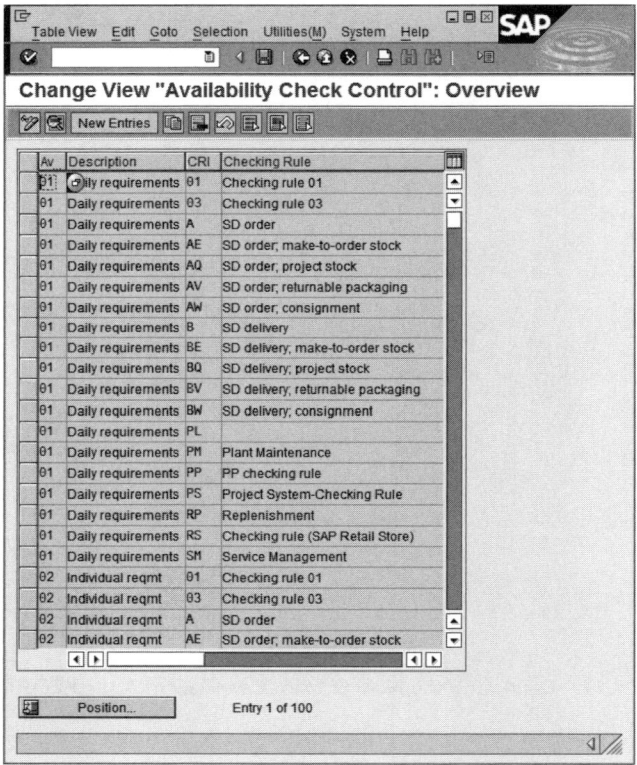

© SAP AG. All rights reserved.

FIGURE 5.15 Displaying the Change View "Availability Check Control": Overview screen

Figure 5.15 shows the list of existing checking rules defined for checking groups. To define a new checking rule for an availability check, click the **New Entries** button and enter details in the **New Entries: Details of Added Entries** screen as shown in Figure 5.16.

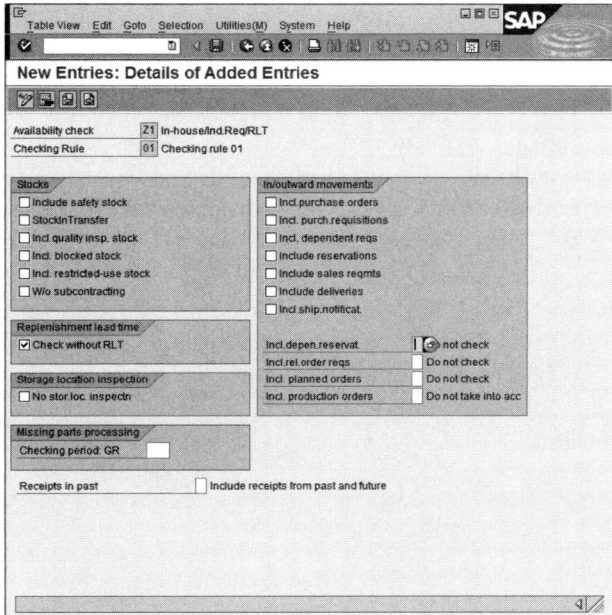

FIGURE 5.16 **Displaying the New Entries: Details of Added Entries screen**

Figure 5.16 shows the details entered to define a new checking rule for an availability check. Click the **Save** icon (🖫) to save the details entered for the Z1 availability check.

After understanding how to control the availability check on the basis of a checking rule, let's now learn how to define a procedure by the requirements class.

Define Procedure by Requirements Class

The **Define Procedure by Requirements Class** activity allows you to specify whether availability check needs to be performed for a requirement class. The settings that you define in the **Define Procedure by Requirements Class** activity correspond to the requirement class settings globally. These settings are automatically copied to the requirement class for which the settings have been made. To define the availability check for a requirement class, navigate the following menu path (Figure 5.9):

Menu Path

SAP Customizing Implementation Guide > Sales and Distribution > Basic Functions > Availability Check and Transfer of Requirements > Availability Check > Availability Check with ATP Logic or Against Planning > Defining Procedure By Requirements Class

After navigating through the preceding menu path, click the **IMG Activity** icon ( ) beside the **Defining Procedure by Requirements Class** activity. The **Change View "Availability and Transfer of Requirements by Req. Type": Overview** screen appears as shown in Figure 5.17.

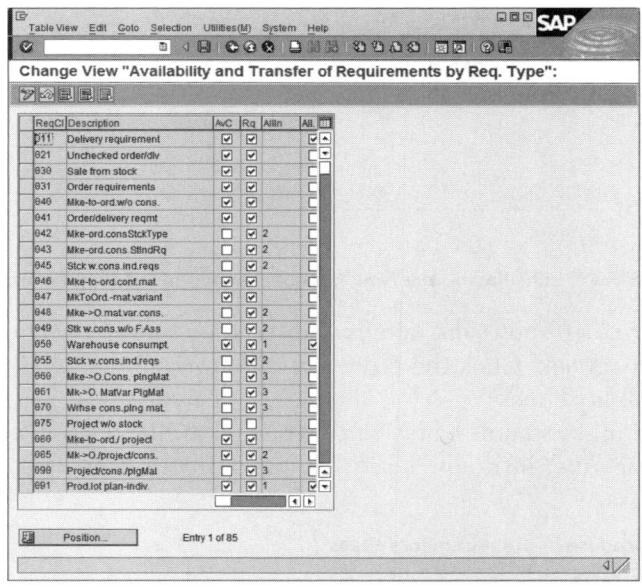

© SAP AG. All rights reserved.

FIGURE 5.17 Displaying the Change View "Availability and Transfer of Requirements by Req. Type": Overview screen

Figure 5.17 shows the existing list of procedures defined for various requirement classes. However, you can change the details for any requirement class by editing the data displayed in various columns, as shown in Figure 5.17.

After understanding how to define a procedure by a requirement class, let's now explore how to define the procedure for each schedule line category.

Define Procedure for Each Schedule Line Category

The **Define Procedure for Each Schedule Line Category** activity allows you to define the availability check with respect to a schedule line category of SD documents. Before defining an availability check procedure for a schedule line category, you must ensure that the schedule line categories are already defined. Now, to define the availability check for a schedule line category, navigate the following menu path (Figure 5.9):

Menu Path

SAP Customizing Implementation Guide > Sales and Distribution > Basic Functions > Availability Check and Transfer of Requirements > Availability Check > Availability Check with ATP Logic or Against Planning > Define Procedure For Each Schedule Line Category

After navigating through the preceding menu path, click the **IMG Activity** icon (🔵) beside the **Define Procedure For Each Schedule Line Category** activity. The **Change View "Rel. Requirements and Availability for Sched. Line Categories": Overview** screen appears as shown in Figure 5.18.

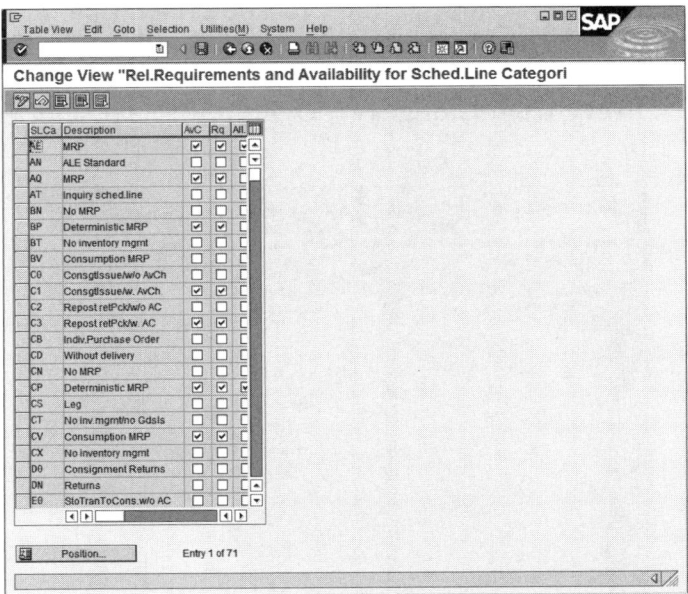

© SAP AG. All rights reserved.

FIGURE 5.18 Displaying the Change View "Rel. Requirements and Availability for Sched. Line Categories": Overview screen

Figure 5.18 shows the list of existing availability check procedures defined for various schedule line categories. The details for any schedule line category can be changed by editing the data provided in the various columns shown in Figure 5.18.

After understanding how to define a schedule line category, let's discuss how to determine the procedure for each delivery item.

Determine Procedure for Each Delivery Item Category

While performing the **Determine Procedure for Each Delivery Item Category** activity, you can disable the availability check for a specific deliverable item category. For example, the availability check should be disabled for the transaction in which the delivered goods are returned. To determine the availability check procedure for a specific item category, navigate the following menu path (Figure 5.9):

Menu Path

SAP Customizing Implementation Guide > Sales and Distribution > Basic Functions > Availability Check and Transfer of Requirements > Availability Check > Availability Check with ATP Logic or Against Planning > Define Procedure For Each Delivery Item Category

After navigating through the preceding menu path, click the **IMG Activity** icon (⊕) beside the **Determine Procedure for Each Delivery Item Category** activity. The **Change View "Availability Check for Each Delivery Item Category": Overview** screen appears as shown in Figure 5.19.

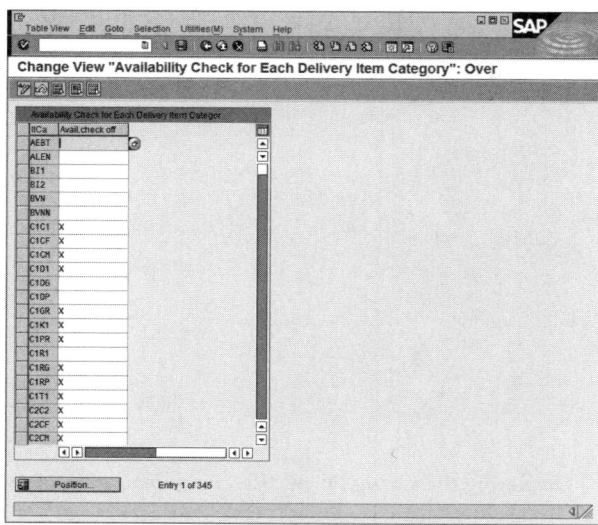

© SAP AG. All rights reserved.

FIGURE 5.19 Displaying the Change View "Availability Check for Each Delivery Item Category": Overview screen

Figure 5.19 displays the list of existing deliverable item categories for which the availability check is disabled. You can edit the **Avail. Check off** column with respect to the **Item Category** column.

After understanding how to determine the availability check for various item categories, let's now learn about the **Checking Rule for Updating Backorders** activity.

Checking Rule for Updating Backorders

In the mySAP ERP system, checking rules can also be used to update the backorders. In this activity, you specify the checking rule for a plant, which serves as the basis of the availability check. Now, navigate the following menu path to define the checking rule for updating backorders (Figure 5.9):

Menu Path

SAP Customizing Implementation Guide > Sales and Distribution > Basic Functions > Availability Check and Transfer of Requirements > Availability Check > Availability Check with ATP Logic or Against Planning > Checking Rule For Updating Backorders

After navigating through the preceding menu path, click the **IMG Activity** icon (🔍) beside the **Checking Rule for Updating Backorders** activity. The **Change View "Checking Rule for Updating Backorders": Overview** screen appears as shown in Figure 5.20.

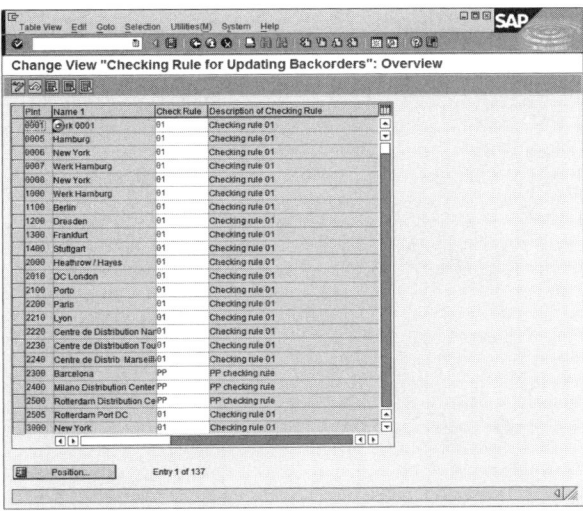

© SAP AG. All rights reserved.

FIGURE 5.20 Displaying the Change View "Checking Rule for Updating Backorders": Overview screen

Figure 5.20 lists the existing checking rules defined for various plants. After understanding the **Checking Rule for Updating Backorders** activity, let's now discuss how to define default settings for the results of the availability check.

Define Default Settings

You can customize the settings for the results of an availability check; however, if you do not specify the settings, the mySAP ERP system accepts the default settings. The **Define Default Settings** activity allows you to specify the default settings for the results of an availability check. For every sales area, an indicator can be set to fix the date, the quantity, and the rule to transfer the results of the availability check to the sales order documents. To define the default settings for the results of the availability check, let's navigate the following menu path (Figure 5.9):

Menu Path

SAP Customizing Implementation Guide > Sales and Distribution > Basic Functions > Availability Check and Transfer of Requirements > Availability Check > Availability Check with ATP Logic or Against Planning > Define Default Settings

After navigating through the preceding menu path, click the **IMG Activity** icon (⊕) beside the **Define Default Settings** activity. The **Change View "Sales Area: Default Values for Availability Check": Overview** screen appears as shown in Figure 5.21.

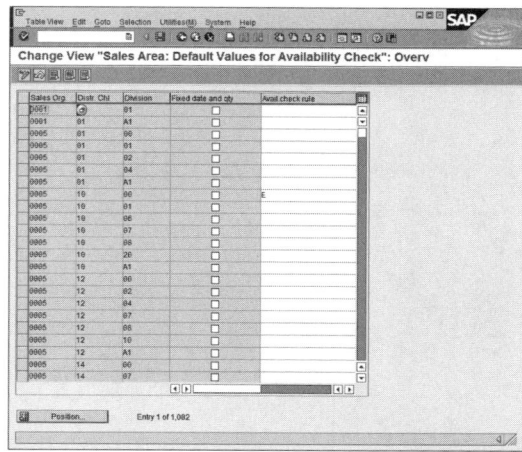

© SAP AG. All rights reserved.

FIGURE 5.21 Displaying the Change View "Sales Area: Default Values for Availability Check": Overview screen

Figure 5.21 shows the list of existing default values for the results of the availability check.

We now conclude the discussion on the configuration of an availability check with ATP logic or planning. Apart from this, you can also configure availability check against production allocation, which is discussed in the next section.

Availability Check against Product Allocation

SAP release 3.0E provides the facility to perform an availability check against product allocation. The availability check against product allocation implies that the availability of material can be checked while processing sales orders. This kind of availability check is configured for a scenario where the material is in short supply and you need priority for some set of customers. To perform this type of availability check, you must ensure that the following conditions are met:

- The user must have entered a product allocation determination procedure in the material master record.
- The user must have made the settings for statistics update in the info structure.

To perform the availability check against product allocation, let's navigate the following menu path:

Menu Path

SAP Customizing Implementation Guide > Sales and Distribution > Basic Functions > Availability Check and Transfer of Requirements > Availability Check > Availability Check Against Product Allocation

Figure 5.22 shows the preceding menu path in the mySAP ERP system:

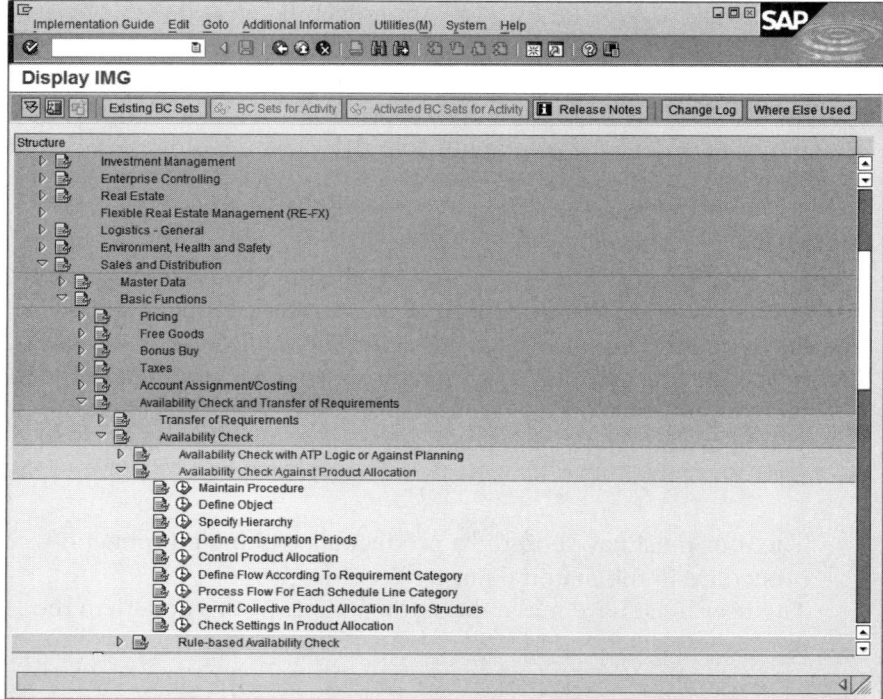

FIGURE 5.22 Displaying menu path for availability check against product allocation

Figure 5.22 shows the following SAP IMG activities or steps that you can perform to configure availability check against product allocation:

- Maintain Procedure
- Define Object
- Specify Hierarchy
- Define Consumption Periods
- Control Product Allocation
- Define Flow According to Requirement Category
- Process Flow for Each Schedule Line Category
- Permit Collective Product Allocation in Info Structures
- Check Settings in Product Allocation

Now, let's perform each of these activities one by one.

Maintain Procedure

The **Maintain Procedure** activity allows you to define a product allocation procedure for the availability check against product allocations. The product allocation procedure that you define must be entered in the material master record. Moreover, an information structure must also be assigned to the product allocation procedure. To maintain or define this procedure, let's navigate the following menu path (Figure 5.22):

Menu Path

SAP Customizing Implementation Guide > Sales and Distribution > Basic Functions > Availability Check and Transfer of Requirements > Availability Check > Availability Check Against Product Allocation > Maintain Procedure

After navigating through the preceding menu path, click the **IMG Activity** icon (🔘) beside the **Maintain Procedure** activity. The **Change View "Procedure Allocation: Definition of Procedure": Overview** screen appears as shown in Figure 5.23.

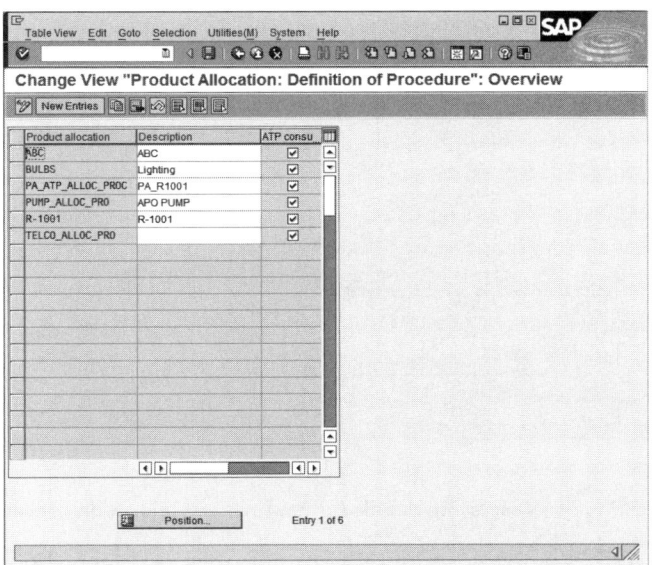

© SAP AG. All rights reserved.

FIGURE 5.23 Displaying the list of existing procedures against product allocation

Figure 5.23 shows the existing product allocation procedure defined for a specific product allocation. You can define a new product allocation by clicking the **New Entries** button. The **New Entries: Overview of Added Entries** screen appears as shown in Figure 5.24.

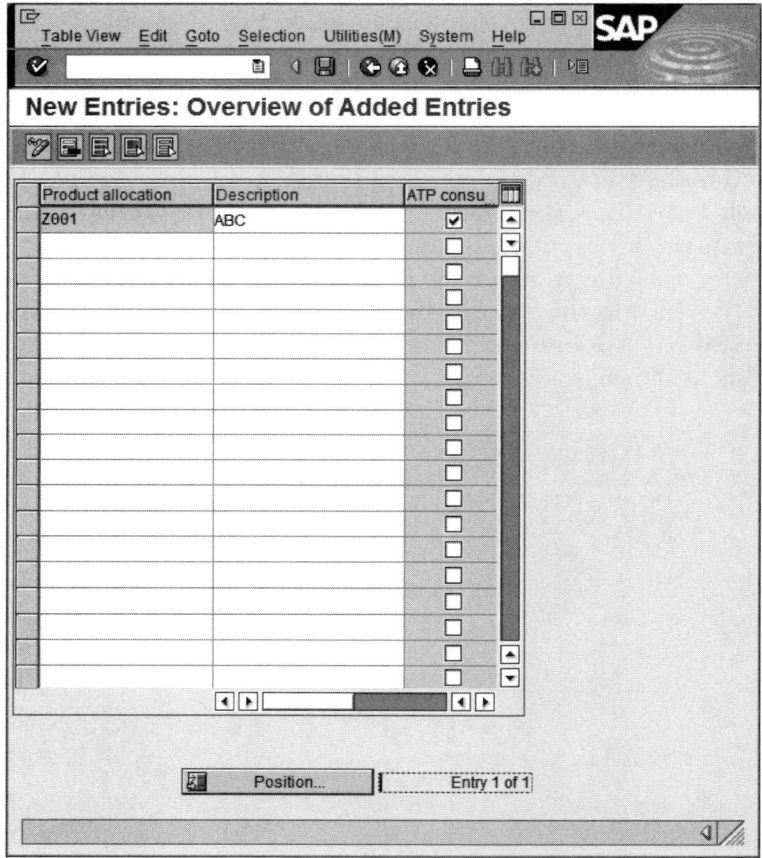

© SAP AG. All rights reserved.

FIGURE 5.24 **Displaying details for new product allocation procedure**

Figure 5.24 shows the details for the new product allocation procedure for availability check against product allocation. The **New Entries: Overview** of Added Entries screen shown in the preceding figure has the following fields:

- **Product Allocation**—Specifies the code representing the name of the product allocation procedure. In our example we entered Z001 in the **Product allocation** field (Figure 5.24).
- **Description**—Contains the details to describe the product allocation procedure that you have defined. In our example, we entered ABC in the **Description** field (Figure 5.24).
- **ATP Consumption**—Enables ATP consumption for the defined product allocation by checking the **ATP consumption** checkbox (Figure 5.24).

After understanding how to maintain a product allocation procedure for availability check against product allocation, let's learn how to define objects for the same.

Define Object

The **Define Object** activity allows you to define the product allocation object while determining the product allocation procedure. You need to perform this activity because product allocations are stored in the form of objects in the planning hierarchy. To define an object in the product allocation determination procedure, let's navigate the following menu path (Figure 5.22):

Menu Path

SAP Customizing Implementation Guide > Sales and Distribution > Basic Functions > Availability Check and Transfer of Requirements > Availability Check > Availability Check Against Product Allocation > Define Object

After navigating through the preceding menu path, click the **IMG Activity** icon (⊕) beside the **Define Object** activity. The **Change View "SD Product Allocation Objects": Overview** screen appears as shown in Figure 5.25.

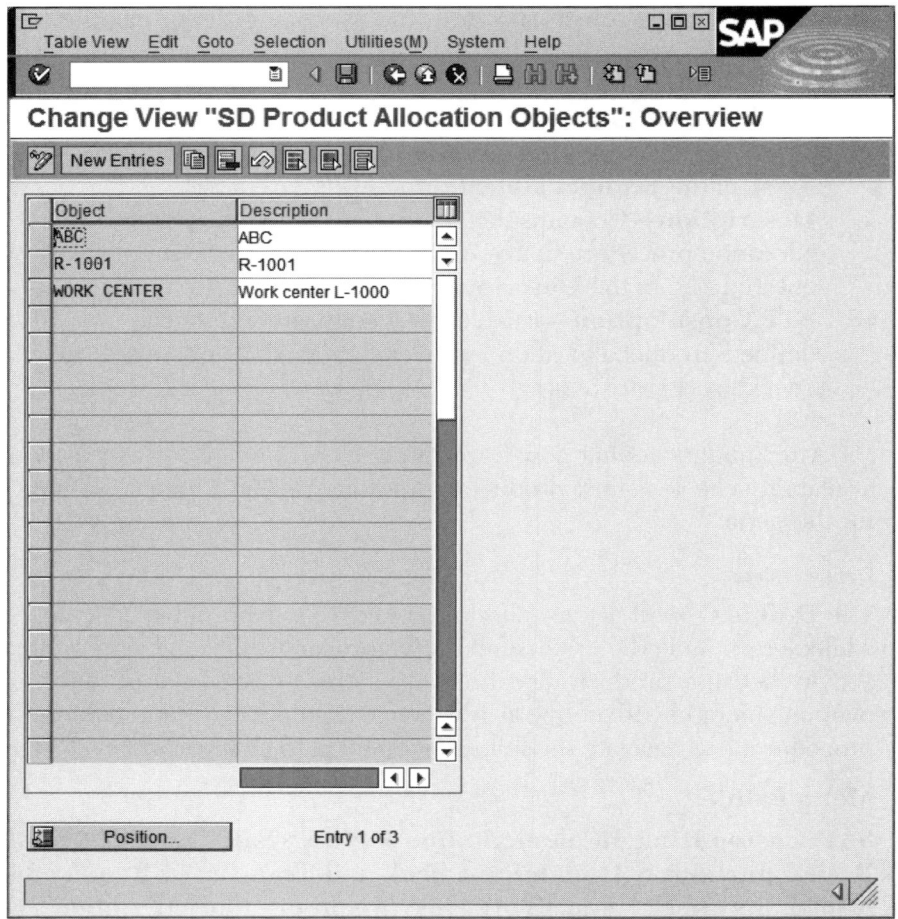

FIGURE 5.25   Displaying the list of existing product allocation objects

Figure 5.25 displays the existing product allocation objects in the mySAP ERP system. To define a new product allocation object, click the **New Entries** button and enter the details in the **New Entries: Overview of Added Entries** screen as shown in Figure 5.26.

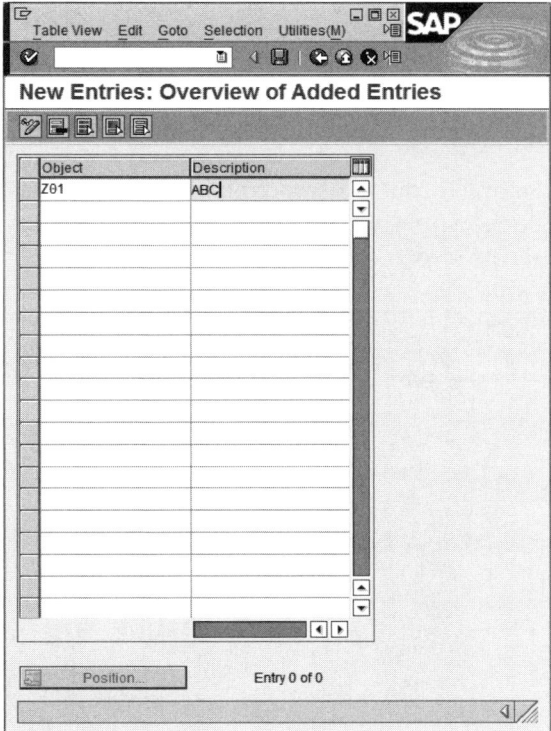

FIGURE 5.26 Displaying details for new product allocation object

Figure 5.26 shows the details entered for a new product allocation object (Z01). Click the **Save** icon ( ) to save the entered data.

After understanding how to define objects for product allocation, let's move ahead to discuss the next activity, which involves specifying the hierarchy of each product allocation determination procedure.

Specify Hierarchy

The **Specify Hierarchy** activity allows you to define an information structure against each product allocation determination procedure. Apart from the info structure, the mySAP ERP system also allows you to specify the formatting character for each info structure. To specify an info structure against each product allocation determination procedure, let's navigate the following menu path (Figure 5.22):

Menu Path

SAP Customizing Implementation Guide > Sales and Distribution > Basic Functions > Availability Check and Transfer of Requirements > Availability Check > Availability Check Against Product Allocation > Specify Hierarchy

After navigating through the preceding menu path, click the **IMG Activity** icon (🕭) beside the **Specify Hierarchy** activity. The **New Entries: Overview of Added Entries** screen appears as shown in Figure 5.27.

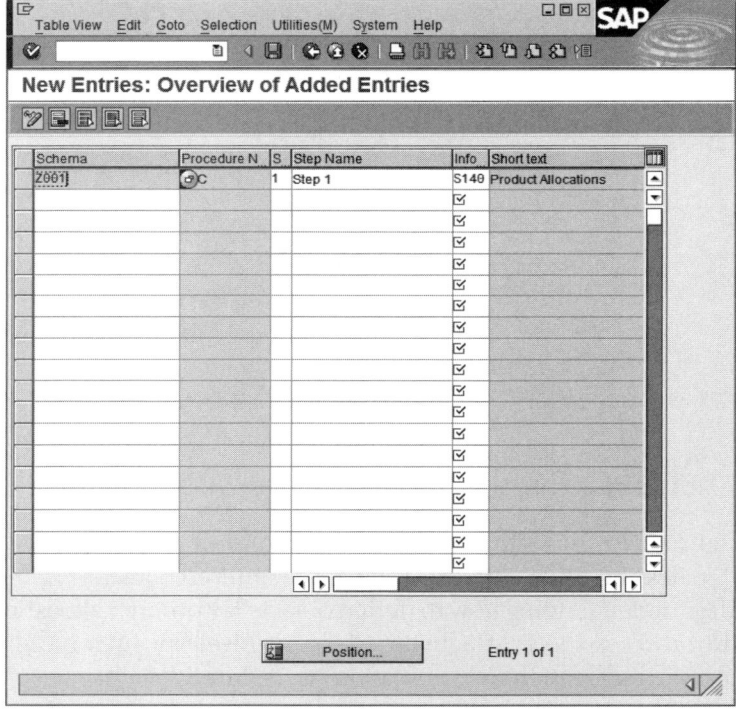

© SAP AG. All rights reserved.

FIGURE 5.27 Displaying the New Entries: Overview of Added Entries screen

Figure 5.27 shows the details of the new info structure defined for the product allocation determination procedure. After understanding how to define an info structure against the product allocation determination procedure, let's explore how to define consumption periods.

Define Consumption Periods

The mySAP ERP system allows you to define the time duration before and after the availability check. This time duration is known as the consumption period. You can also define the past and future consumption periods for product allocation quantities. In the mySAP ERP system, the past consumption period is also known as the backward consumption period, and the future consumption period refers to the forward consumption period. To define the consumption period for each product allocation determination procedure, let's navigate the following menu path (Figure 5.22):

Menu Path

SAP Customizing Implementation Guide > Sales and Distribution > Basic Functions > Availability Check and Transfer of Requirements > Availability Check > Availability Check Against Product Allocation > Define Consumption Periods

After following the preceding menu path, click the **IMG Activity** icon (⊕) beside the **Define Consumption Periods** activity. The **Change View "SD Allocation: Consumption Period in Number of Periods": Overview** screen appears as shown in Figure 5.28.

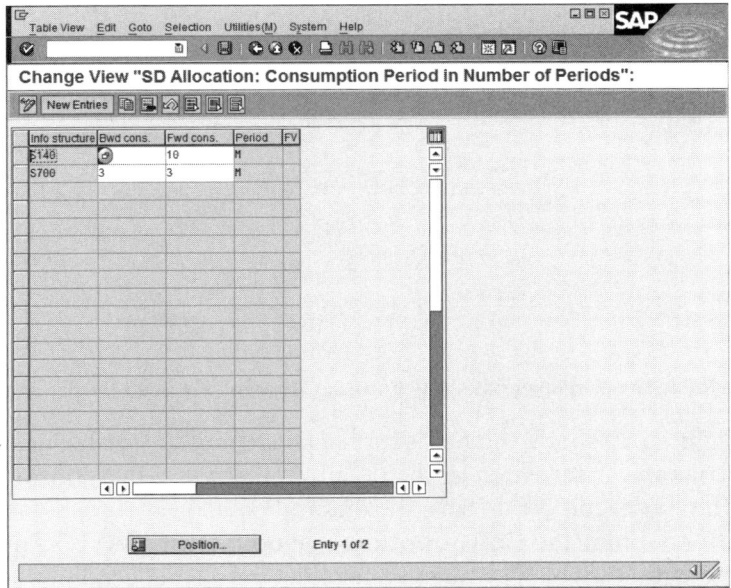

© SAP AG. All rights reserved.

FIGURE 5.28 Displaying existing consumption periods for various info structures

Figure 5.28 shows the list of existing consumption periods. To define the past and future consumption periods, click the **New Entries** button. The **New Entries: Overview of Added Entries** screen appears as shown in Figure 5.29.

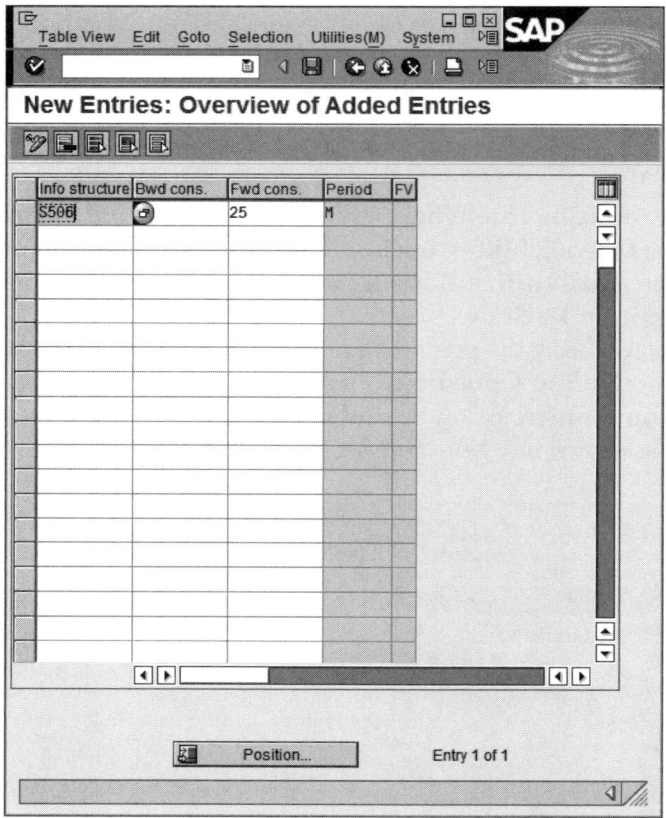

© SAP AG. All rights reserved.

FIGURE 5.29 **Displaying the New Entries: Overview of Added Entries screen**

Figure 5.29 shows the fields for backward and forward consumption of an info structure. After entering the details in the respective consumption fields, click the **Save** icon (🖫) to save the entered data.

After defining the **Consumption Periods** activity, let's now move ahead to the next activity, which involves controlling product allocation.

Control Product Allocation

The **Control Product Allocation** activity allows you to assign one or more objects with varying validity periods to the product allocation determination procedures. The validity period of one procedure cannot overlap with that of another. A product allocation check is not performed for the validity periods that are not active or that have expired. To control product allocation, use the following menu path (Figure 5.22):

Menu Path

SAP Customizing Implementation Guide > Sales and Distribution > Basic Functions > Availability Check and Transfer of Requirements > Availability Check > Availability Check Against Product Allocation > Control Product Allocation

After navigating through the preceding menu path, click the **IMG Activity** icon (🔹) beside the **Control Product Allocation** activity. The **Determine Work Area: Entry** dialog box appears as shown in Figure 5.30.

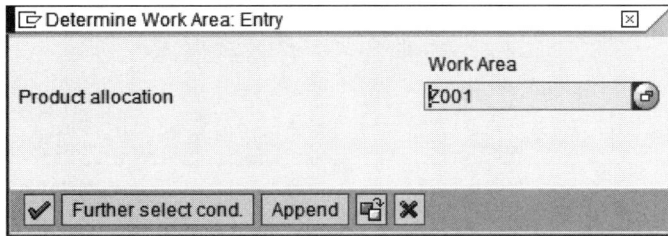

© SAP AG. All rights reserved.

FIGURE 5.30 Displaying the Determine Work Area: Entry dialog box

Figure 5.30 shows the Z001 product allocation entered to control its product allocation. After specifying the product allocation, click the **Continue** icon (✓). The **Change View "Customizing for Product Allocation": Overview** screen appears as shown in Figure 5.31.

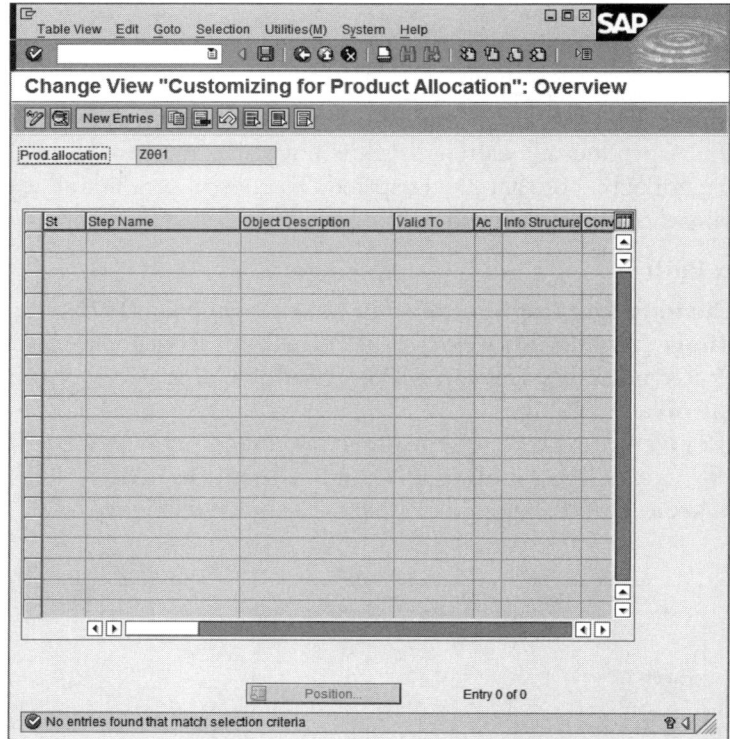

FIGURE 5.31 Displaying the customized view for specified product allocation procedure

Figure 5.31 shows the details of a specific product allocation determination procedure, such as Z001 in our example. However, since there are no details specified for Z001, no details are displayed in Figure 5.31. You can define the objects with varying periods by clicking the **New Entries** button. The **New Entries: Details of Added Entries** screen appears as shown in Figure 5.32.

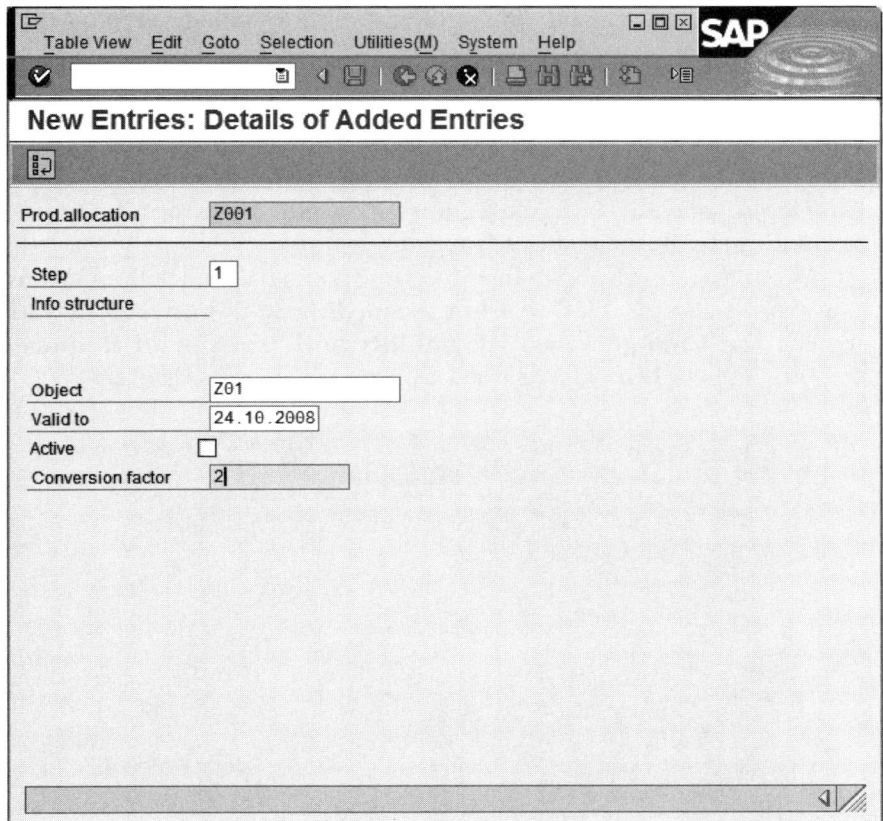

© SAP AG. All rights reserved.

FIGURE 5.32 Displaying the New Entries: Details of Added Entries screen

Figure 5.32 shows the details for the objects of the Z001 procedure. Click the **Save** icon ( ) to save the details.

Let's now explore the **Define Flow According to Requirement Category** activity.

Define Flow According to Requirement Category

The **Define Flow According To Requirement Category** activity allows you to determine whether the mySAP system should run an availability check for product allocation. You can determine this in each requirement class. Navigate the following menu path to define the flow of product allocation according to requirement category (Figure 5.22):

Menu Path

SAP Customizing Implementation Guide > Sales and Distribution > Basic Functions > Availability Check and Transfer of Requirements > Availability Check > Availability Check Against Product Allocation > Define Flow According To Requirement Category

After navigating through the preceding menu path, click the **IMG Activity** icon (🕮) beside the **Define Flow According to Requirement Category** activity. The **Change View "Availability and Transfer of Requirements by Req. Type": Overview** screen appears as shown in Figure 5.33.

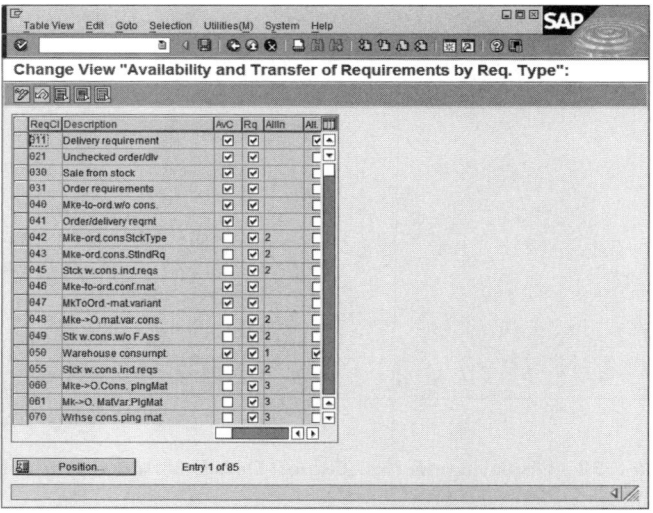

© SAP AG. All rights reserved.

FIGURE 5.33 Displaying the Change View "Availability and Transfer of Requirements by Req. Type": Overview screen

Figure 5.33 shows the existing list of flow defined on the basis of requirement classes.

After understanding the **Define Flow According to Requirement Category** activity, let's now explore the **Process Flow for Each Schedule Line Category** activity.

Process Flow for Each Schedule Line Category

Similar to the activity discussed in the preceding section, the **Process Flow for Each Schedule Line category** activity allows you to determine whether the system would perform the availability check for each schedule line category. You can also deactivate the availability check. To determine the process flow for each schedule line, let's navigate the following menu path (Figure 5.22):

Menu Path

SAP Customizing Implementation Guide > Sales and Distribution > Basic Functions > Availability Check and Transfer of Requirements > Availability Check > Availability Check Against Product Allocation > Process Flow For Each Schedule Line Category

After navigating through the preceding menu path, click the **IMG Activity** icon (🌀) beside the **Process Flow for Each Schedule Line Category** activity. The **Change View "Rel. Requirements and Availability for Sched. Line Categories": Overview** screen appears as shown in Figure 5.34.

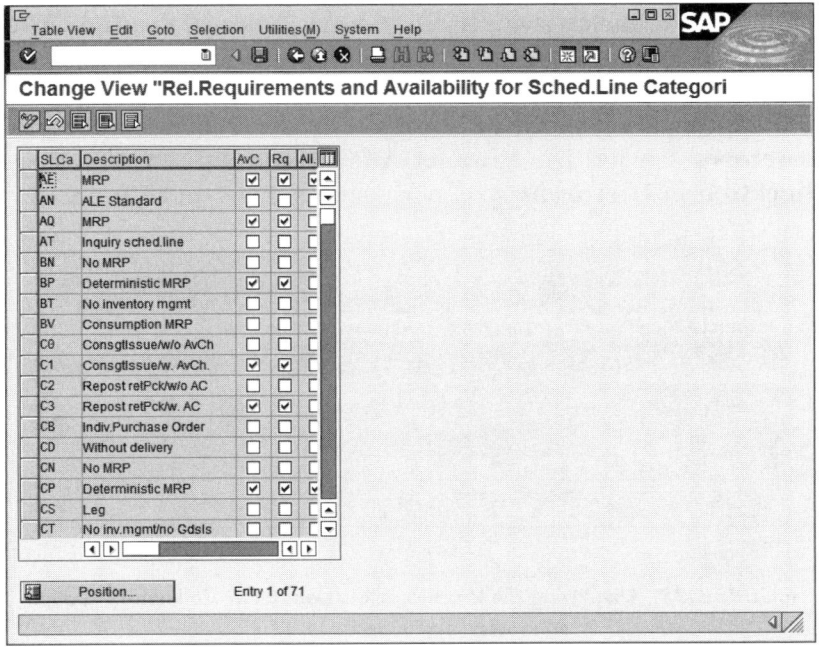

© SAP AG. All rights reserved.

FIGURE 5.34 Displaying the availability check for each schedule line category

Figure 5.34 shows whether the availability check is to be performed for a specific schedule line category. If the **AvC** (Availability Check) column beside a schedule line category is checked, an availability check is performed for that schedule line category.

After understanding how to determine the process flow for each schedule line category, let's learn about the **Permit Collective Product Allocation in the Info Structures** activity.

Permit Collective Product Allocation in Info Structures

The **Permit Collective Product Allocation in Info Structures** activity allows you to enter the info structure of the planning hierarchy to collectively allocate multiple products. This activity also creates general entries in the planning hierarchy. To permit collective production allocation in an info structure, let's navigate the following menu path (Figure 5.22):

Menu Path

SAP Customizing Implementation Guide > Sales and Distribution > Basic Functions > Availability Check and Transfer of Requirements > Availability Check > Availability Check Against Product Allocation > Permit Collective Product Allocation in Info Structures

After navigating through the preceding menu path, click the **IMG Activity** icon (⊕) beside the **Permit Collective Product Allocation in Info Structures** activity. The **Product Allocation: Enter Collective Product Allocation in Hierarchy** screen appears as shown in Figure 5.35.

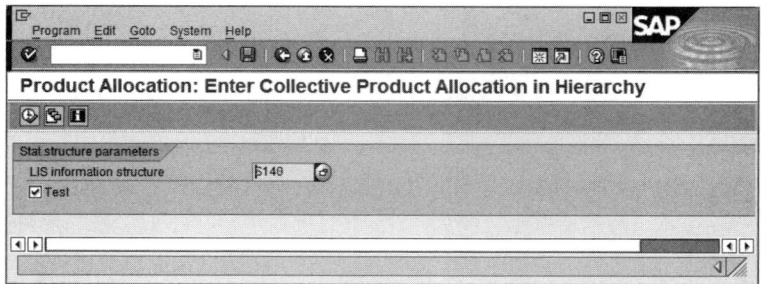

© SAP AG. All rights reserved.

FIGURE 5.35 Displaying the Product Allocation: Enter Collective Product Allocation in Hierarchy screen

Figure 5.35 shows the screen in which to enter the info structure. In Figure 5.35, we have entered S140 as the info structure. Now, after entering the info structure, click the **IMG Activity** icon (). The view of the screen changes and displays the details of the key for the entered collective product allocations, as shown in Figure 5.36.

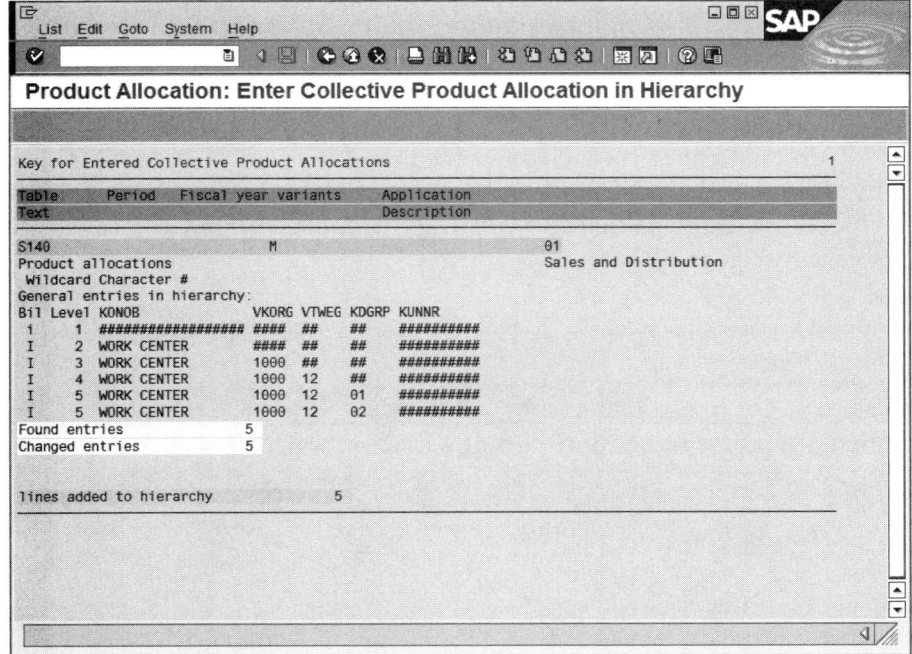

© SAP AG. All rights reserved.

FIGURE 5.36 Displaying the key for entered collective product allocations

Figure 5.36 shows collective product allocations for the S140 info structure. This concludes the discussion on the **Permit Collective Product Allocation in Info Structures** activity.

Now, let's analyze the **Check Settings in Product Allocation** activity.

Check Settings in Product Allocation

In the **Check Settings in Product Allocation** activity you enter the details of product allocation determination procedure and the product allocation object for which you want to check the settings. It also allows you to check whether the settings for the following are consistent:

- Product allocation determination procedure
- Product allocation objects

To check the settings in product allocation, navigate the following menu path (Figure 5.22):

Menu Path

SAP Customizing Implementation Guide > Sales and Distribution > Basic Functions > Availability Check and Transfer of Requirements > Availability Check > Availability Check Against Product Allocation > Check Settings in Product Allocation

After navigating through the preceding menu path, click the **IMG Activity** icon (⊕) beside the **Check Settings in Product Allocation** activity. The **Check Product Allocation Settings in Customizing** screen appears as shown in Figure 5.37.

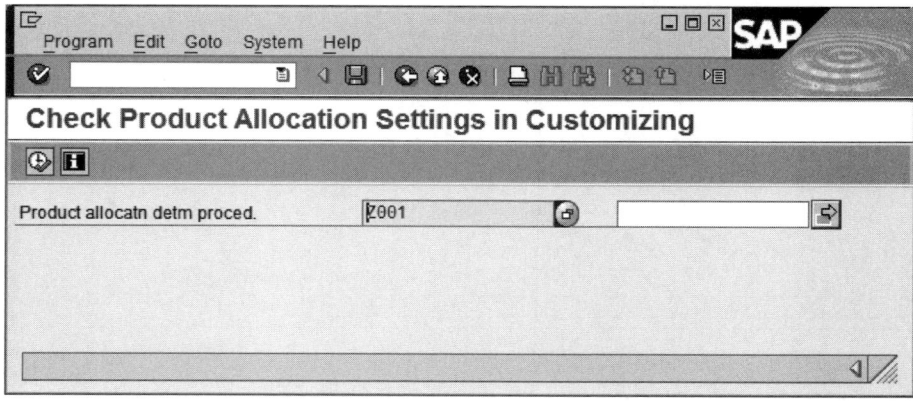

© SAP AG. All rights reserved.

FIGURE 5.37 Displaying the Check Product Allocation Settings in Customizing screen

Enter the product allocation determination procedure in the text field shown in Figure 5.37. In our example, we have entered Z001 as the product allocation determination procedure. Click the **IMG Activity** icon (⊕). The **Check**

Product Allocation Settings in Customizing screen appears as shown in Figure 5.38.

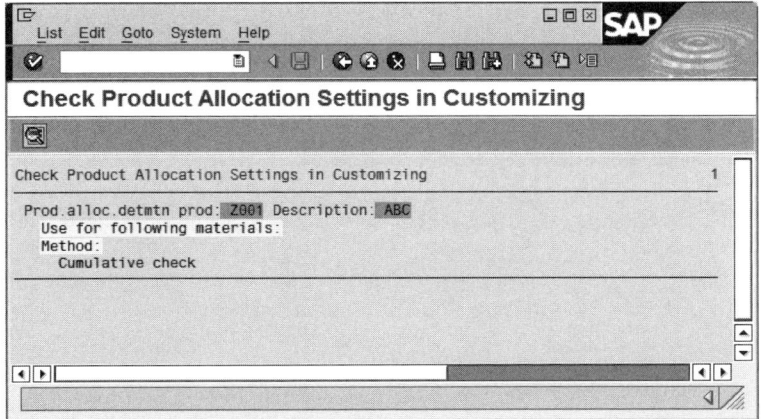

FIGURE 5.38 Displaying the production allocation settings of Z001

Figure 5.38 shows the production allocation settings for the Z001 product allocation determination procedure. With this, we complete the discussion on the configuration of the availability check against product allocation.

After exploring the two approaches to configuring an availability check (an availability check with ATP logic or planning and an availability check against product allocation), let's move ahead to discuss the third approach; that is, a rule-based availability check.

Rule-Based Availability Check

A rule-based availability check allows the mySAP ERP system to perform the availability check for materials on the basis of the rules defined. For example, you can define a rule to perform an availability check in various plants and on multiple materials. The rule-based availability check is performed in the stand-alone Advanced Planner and Optimizer (APO) of SAP. Under this availability check, the source system triggers the check in the SAP APO system and then provides the result to the source system. The result of the SAP APO availability check comprises a list of materials, plants, and quantities. To perform a rule-based availability check, you can navigate the following menu path:

Menu Path

SAP Customizing Implementation Guide > Sales and Distribution > Basic Functions > Availability Check and Transfer of Requirements > Availability Check > Rule-based Availability Check

Figure 5.39 shows the preceding navigation path in the mySAP ERP system.

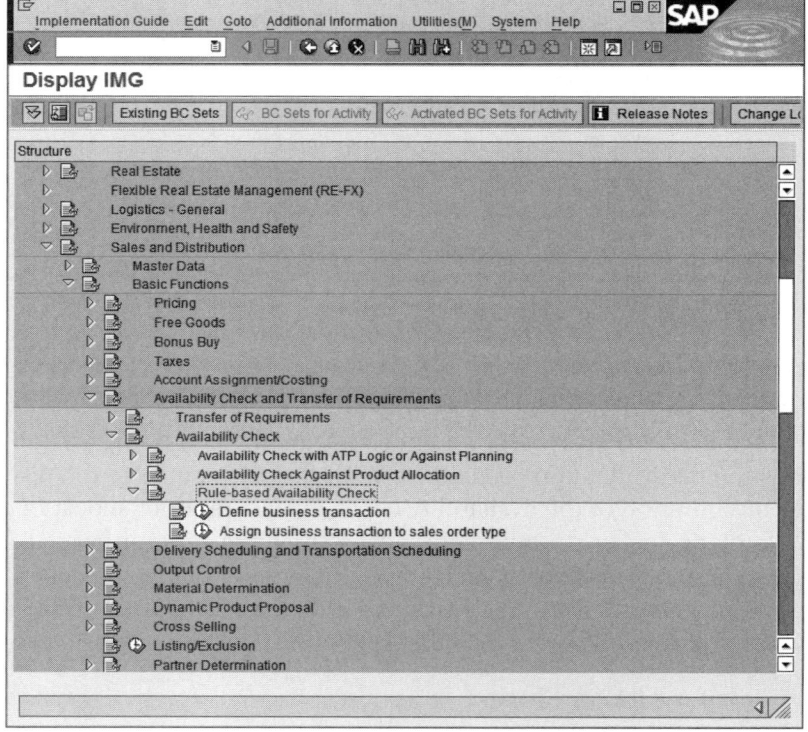

© SAP AG. All rights reserved.

FIGURE 5.39 Displaying the menu path for the rule-based availability check

After navigating the menu path shown in Figure 5.39, you must perform the following activities or steps for the rule-based availability check:

- Define a business transaction.
- Assign the business transaction to a sales order type.

Now, let's discuss each of these activities.

Defining a Business Transaction

The **Define Business Transaction** activity allows you to define a business transaction that must be available in the SAP APO planning system. In the **Define Business Transaction** activity, an availability check control is performed for the defined transactions. Let's navigate the following menu path to define a business transaction (Figure 5.39):

Menu Path

SAP Customizing Implementation Guide > Sales and Distribution > Basic Functions > Availability Check and Transfer of Requirements > Availability Check > Rule-based Availability Check > Define business transaction

After navigating the preceding menu path, click the **IMG Activity** icon (⊕) beside the **Define Business Transaction** activity. The **Change View: "ATP Business Transaction": Overview** screen appears as shown in Figure 5.40.

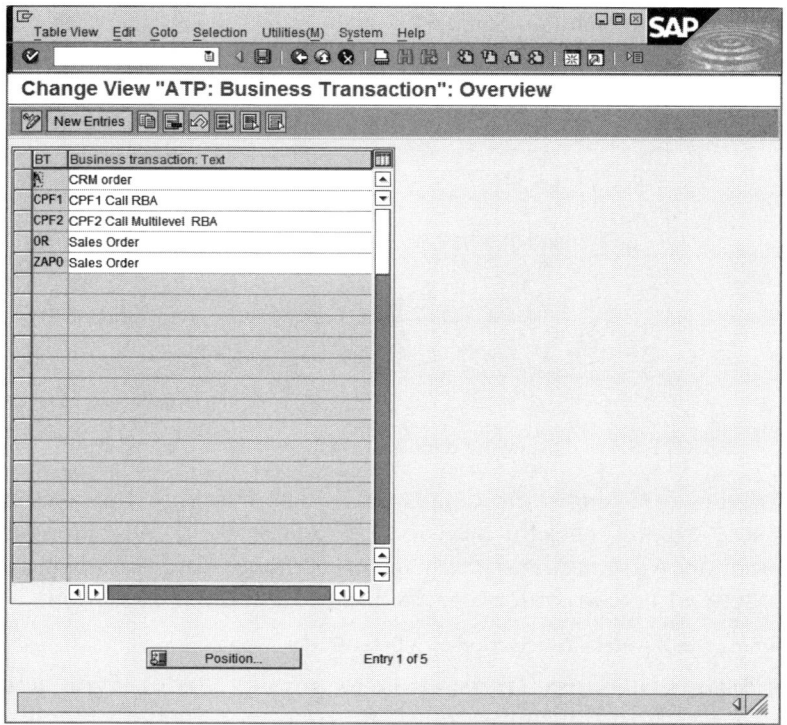

© SAP AG. All rights reserved.

FIGURE 5.40 Displaying the Change View: "ATP Business Transaction": Overview screen

Figure 5.40 shows the existing business transactions defined in the mySAP ERP system. To define a new business transaction, click the **New Entries** button. The **New Entries: Overview of Added Entries** screen appears as shown in Figure 5.41.

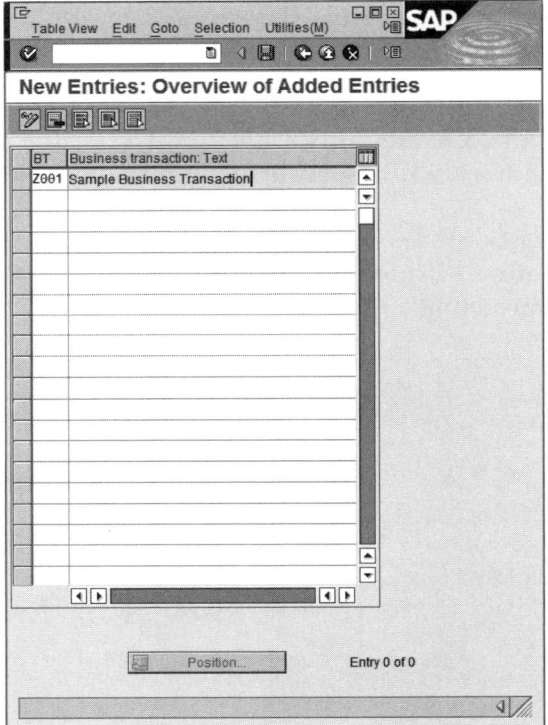

© SAP AG. All rights reserved.

FIGURE 5.41 Displaying details of the new business transaction

Figure 5.41 shows the details entered for the new business transaction; that is, Z001. Now click the **Save** icon (🖫) to save the details of the new business transaction. After defining a new business transaction, you need to assign this transaction to a sales order type, as discussed in the next section.

Assigning the Business Transaction to a Sales Order Type

The **Assign Business Transaction to a Sales Order Type** activity allows you to assign the business transaction, defined in the preceding section, to a sales order type. Assigning the business transaction to sales order type activates the availability check process for the sales order type that was maintained in the SAP APO planning system. Now let's navigate the following menu path to assign the business transaction to the sales order type (Figure 5.39):

Menu Path

SAP Customizing Implementation Guide > Sales and Distribution > Basic Functions > Availability Check and Transfer of Requirements > Availability Check > Rule-based Availability Check > Assign business transaction to sales order type

After navigating through the preceding menu path, click the **IMG Activity** icon (🔵) beside the **Assign Business Transaction to the Sales Order Type** activity. The **Change View: "Maintain Sales Order Types": Overview** screen appears as shown in Figure 5.42.

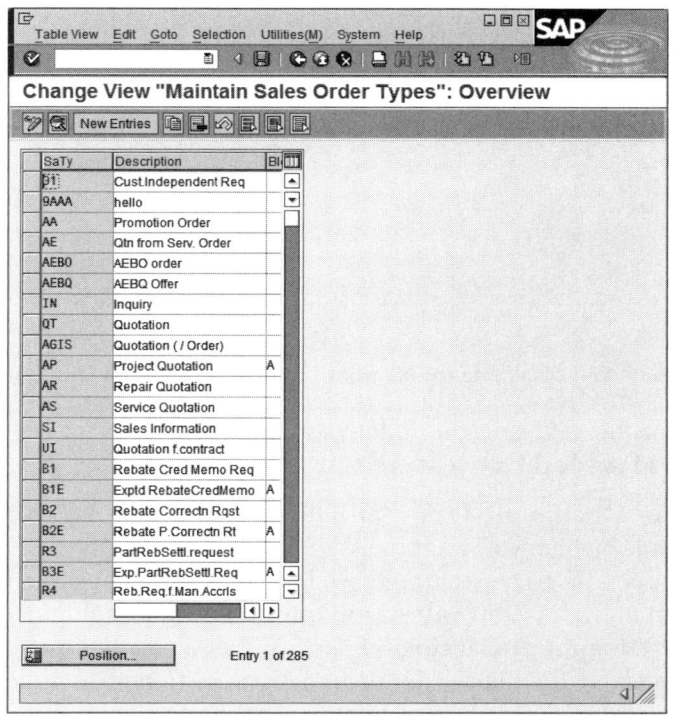

© SAP AG. All rights reserved.

FIGURE 5.42 Displaying the Change View: "Maintain Sales Order Types": Overview screen

Figure 5.42 shows the list of existing business transactions assigned to the sales order type. To assign a new business transaction, click the **New Entries** button. The **New Entries: Details of Added Entries** screen appears as shown in Figure 5.43.

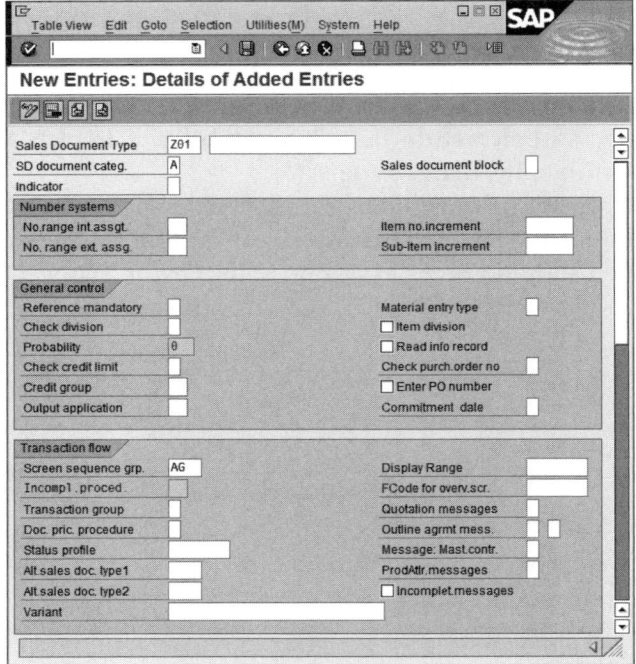

© SAP AG. All rights reserved.

FIGURE 5.43 Displaying the New Entries: Details of Added Entries screen

Enter the values in the following mandatory fields of the **New Entries: Details of Added Entries** screen:

- **Sales Document Type**—Specifies the sales order document type for which you want to assign the defined business transaction. In our example, we have entered Z01 in the text field in front of the **Sales Document Type** label (Figure 5.43).
- **SD Document Catalog**—Specifies the sales order document catalog for the sales order document type. In our example, we have entered A, implying **Inquiry** as the **SD document categ.** (Figure 5.43).

- **Screen Sequence Grp**—Specifies the screen you wish to see during a specific transaction. In our example, we have entered AG, specifying inquiry quotation screen (Figure 5.43).
- **Business Transaction**—Specifies the business transaction you wish to allocate for a specific sales order document type. In our example, we have entered Z001 as the business transaction that we have defined in the *Define Business Transaction* section (Figure 5.43).

Now, after entering the preceding mandatory details, click the **Save** icon (🖫) to save the entered data.

With this, we conclude our discussion on the three ways of configuring an availability check by performing various activities under each approach. Now, let's discuss the concept of transfer of requirements in detail.

IMPLEMENTING THE TRANSFER OF REQUIREMENTS IN SD

In sales and distribution processing, the Material Requirement Planning (MRP) department needs to be informed about the deadlines and quantities to be delivered for a sales order. This process of intimation about the deadlines and quantity-related information is done with the help of the transfer of requirements mechanism. The transfer of requirements mechanism is crucial. The availability check of the material is done on the basis of the delivery dates requested by a customer. It ensures that the material is transferred to the customer on the delivery due date. Transfer of requirements is based on the following factors:

- Requirement types
- Requirement class
- Check group
- Schedule line category

> **Note:** The *Working with the Elements of an Availability Check* section has discussed these factors in detail.

As you transfer requirements, you create MRP records in the Material Management (MM) module. Then these MRP records are passed to the

Production Planning (PP) module, so that the material can be properly planned and made available on time. Therefore, the transfer of requirement mechanism is integrated with the MM and PP modules. In this section, we discuss the following topics to understand the transfer of requirements in detail:

- Individual vs Collective Requirements
- Configuring the Transfer of Requirements

Now, let's discuss each of them in detail.

Individual vs. Collective Requirements

Transfer of requirements can be divided into two categories: transfer of requirement with an individual requirement or collective requirements.

In the individual transfer of requirements, a single transfer of demand occurs in the MRP department for each schedule line. In the case of individual transfer, the requirement overview shows the order quantity, sales document number, item number, and requirement class for each schedule line for which the demand has been created.

Collective requirements are a group of requirements, created over a certain period of time, such as on a daily, weekly, or monthly basis, and are transferred to the MRP department. In this case, the requirement overview screen does not show the requirement details related to a single transaction; rather, it shows the details of a group of requirements. Collective requirement is beneficial for the organizations that deal with large volumes of sales orders on a daily basis.

After discussing the individual and collective requirements, let's now configure the transfer of requirements in the mySAP ERP system.

Configuring the Transfer of Requirements

In the SAP system, the transfer of requirements is mainly controlled by the requirement class, which is derived from the requirement type for all the sales document types. To implement transfer of requirements, navigate the following menu path:

Menu Path

SAP Customizing Implementation Guide > Sales and Distribution > Basic Functions > Availability Check and Transfer of Requirements > Transfer of Requirements

Figure 5.44 shows the preceding navigated menu path in the mySAP ERP system.

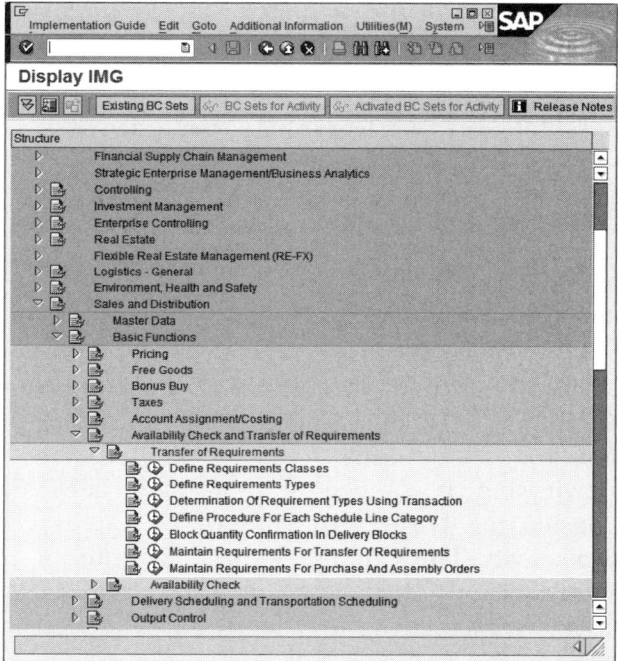

© SAP AG. All rights reserved.

FIGURE 5.44 **Displaying the menu path for transfer of requirements**

Figure 5.44 shows the following activities related to the transfer of requirements:

- Define Requirements Classes
- Define Requirements Types
- Determination of Requirement Types Using Transaction
- Define Procedure for Each Schedule Line Category
- Block Quantity Confirmation in Delivery Blocks
- Maintain Requirements for the Transfer of Requirements
- Maintain Requirements for Purchase and Assembly Orders

214 CHAPTER 5 INTEGRATION OF SAP SD AND MM MODULES

> **Note:** To learn more about defining the requirements classes, refer to the *Defining Requirement Class* section of this chapter. To learn more about defining requirement types, refer to the *Defining Requirement Type* section of this chapter.

Let's now discuss these activities, (except the first two) one by one.

Determination of Requirement Types Using Transaction

A requirement type can be determined on the basis of a specific search strategy or transaction. For example, in the mySAP ERP system, the 021 requirement type is based on the 0001 requirement type. To determine the requirement type using transaction, use the following menu path (Figure 5.44):

Menu Path

SAP Customizing Implementation Guide > Sales and Distribution > Basic Functions > Availability Check and Transfer of Requirements > Transfer of Requirements > Determination Of Requirement Types Using Transaction

After navigating the preceding menu path, click the **IMG Activity** icon ( ) beside the **Determination of Requirement Types Using Transaction** activity. **The Change View: "Assignment of Requirements Types to Transaction": Overview** screen appears as shown in Figure 5.45.

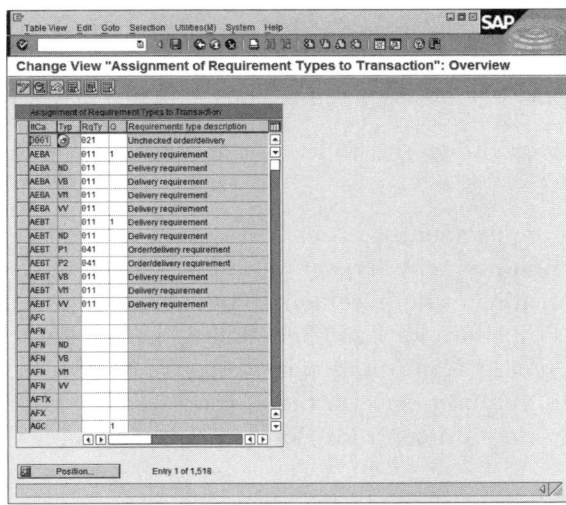

© SAP AG. All rights reserved.

FIGURE 5.45 Displaying the existing assigned requirement types to transactions

Figure 5.45 shows the list of existing requirement types assigned to different transactions. You can view the details of each requirement type by first selecting the appropriate row for which you want to view the details, and then by clicking the **Details** icon (). The **Change View "Assignment of Requirement Types to Transaction": Details** screen appears as shown in Figure 5.46.

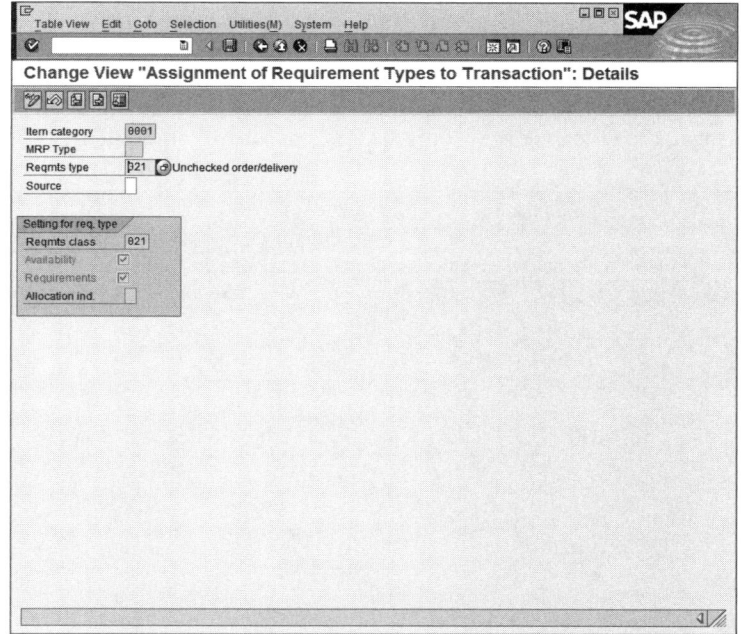

© SAP AG. All rights reserved.

FIGURE 5.46 Displaying the transaction details of the requirement type

Figure 5.46 shows the transaction details of the 021 requirement type.

After determining the requirement types used in transactions, let's now discuss how to define a procedure for each schedule line category.

Defining Procedure for Each Schedule Line Category

The **Define Procedure for Each Schedule Line Category** activity allows you to define a procedure by verifying whether the transfer of requirements should be processed for each schedule line category. The procedure defined for each schedule line category is relevant only for the sales documents. If you do not want to perform the transfer of requirement for a specific schedule line category, you need to deactivate the transfer of requirements for that schedule line category. To define the procedure for each schedule line category, navigate the following menu path (Figure 5.44):

Menu Path

SAP Customizing Implementation Guide > Sales and Distribution > Basic Functions > Availability Check and Transfer of Requirements > Transfer of Requirements > Defining Procedure For Each Schedule Line Category

After navigating the preceding menu path, click the **IMG Activity** icon ( ) beside the **Define Procedure for Each Schedule Line Category** activity. The **Change View: "Rel. Requirements and Availability for Sched. Line Categories": Overview** screen appears as shown in Figure 5.47.

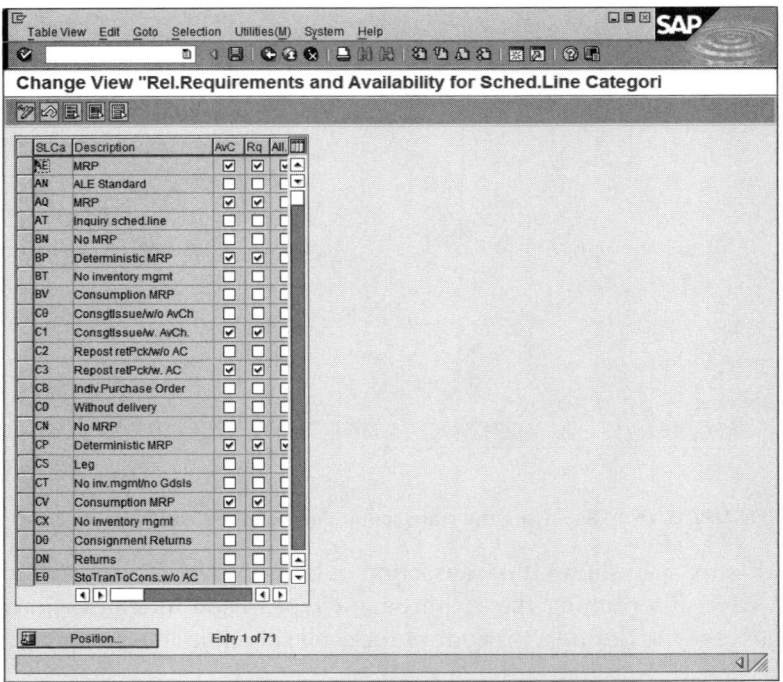

© SAP AG. All rights reserved.

FIGURE 5.47 Displaying the activation or deactivation for transfer of requirements

In Figure 5.47, if the **Rq** column corresponding to the **SLCa** column is checked, it implies that the transfer of requirement is active for that schedule line category.

After defining the procedure for each schedule line category, let's now explore the next activity for the transfer of requirements, **Block Quantity Confirmation in Delivery Blocks**.

Blocking Quantity Confirmation in Delivery Blocks

After transferring the requirements to the MRP department, the confirmed quantity is reserved for a confirmed sales document. If a transaction is blocked for delivery, the required stock is also blocked. In spite of such blockage, if the transaction permits, you can perform availability checks at any time. In such a case, the mySAP ERP system creates temporary schedule lines with confirmed quantities, which are removed when the sales document is saved. To block the confirmation of quantities in delivery blocks, navigate the following menu path (Figure 5.44):

Menu Path

SAP Customizing Implementation Guide > Sales and Distribution > Basic Functions > Availability Check and Transfer of Requirements > Transfer of Requirements > Block Quantity Confirmation in Delivery Blocks

After navigating the preceding menu path, click the **IMG Activity** icon ( ) beside the **Block Quantity Confirmation in Delivery Blocks** activity. The **Choose Activity** dialog box appears as shown in Figure 5.48.

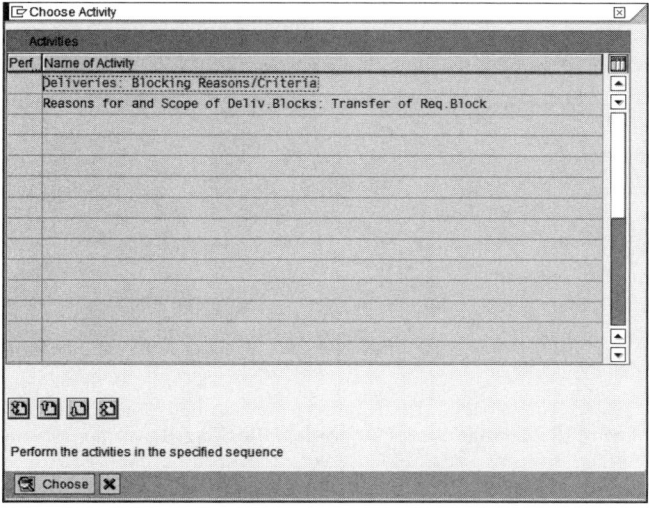

© SAP AG. All rights reserved.

FIGURE 5.48 Displaying the Choose Activity dialog box

Figure 5.48 shows the following activities:

- **Deliveries**—Blocking Reasons/Criteria.
- **Reasons for and Scope of Deliv. Blocks**—Transfer of Req. Block.

In our case, we have selected the **Deliveries: Blocking Reasons/Criteria** activity. The **Change View "Deliveries: Blocking Reasons/Criteria": Overview** screen appears as shown in Figure 5.49.

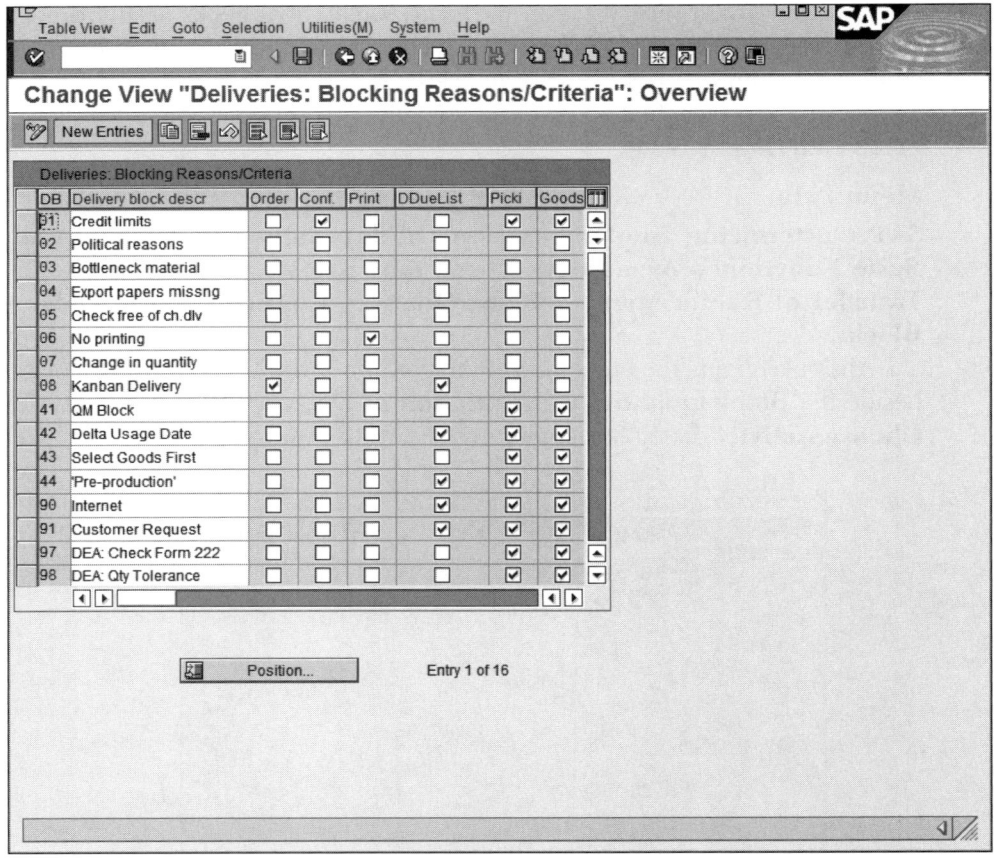

© SAP AG. All rights reserved.

FIGURE 5.49 Displaying the Change View "Deliveries: Blocking Reasons/Criteria": Overview screen

Figure 5.49 shows the existing delivery blocks along with their descriptions. To define a new delivery block, click the **New Entries** button. The **New Entries: Overview of Added Entries** screen appears as shown in Figure 5.50.

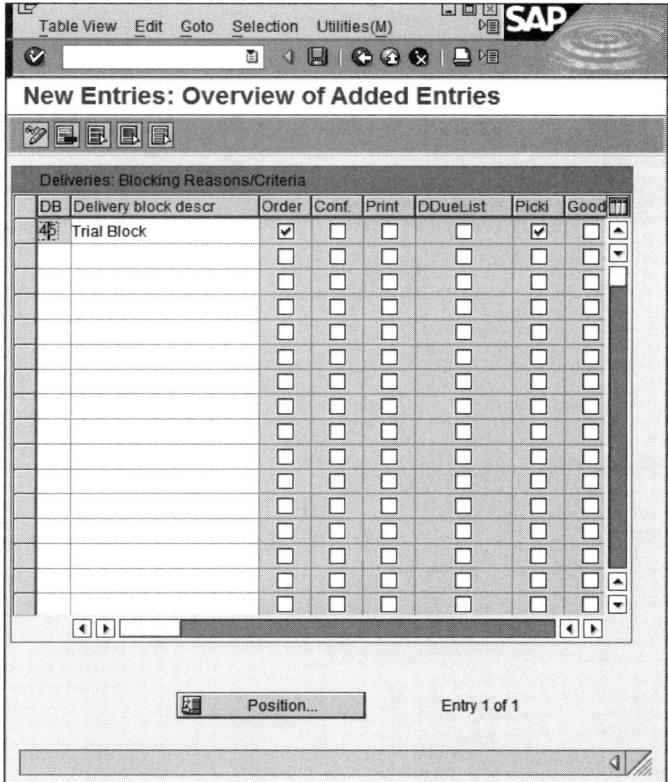

FIGURE 5.50 Displaying details of block quantity for delivery

Figure 5.50 shows the details of the new block quantity for delivery. Click the **Save** icon (🖫) to save the details entered in Figure 5.50.

After discussing the **Block Quantity Confirmation in Delivery Blocks** activity, let's move ahead to discuss the next activity for transfer of requirements, **Maintain Requirements for Transfer of Requirements**.

Maintaining Requirements for the Transfer of Requirements

In the **Maintain Requirements for Transfer of Requirements** activity, you list and maintain your own requirements for the transfer of requirements. By specifying the requirements, you can avoid reservations of large quantities, thereby saving your expenditure. To maintain your requirements, navigate the following menu path (Figure 5.44):

Menu Path

SAP Customizing Implementation Guide > Sales and Distribution > Basic Functions > Availability Check and Transfer of Requirements > Transfer of Requirements > Maintain Requirements For Transfer Of Requirements

After navigating the preceding menu path, click the **IMG Activity** icon ( ) beside the **Maintain Requirements for Transfer of Requirements** activity. The **Change View Criteria for Creating Requirements (Availability) for Orders: Overview** screen appears as shown in Figure 5.51.

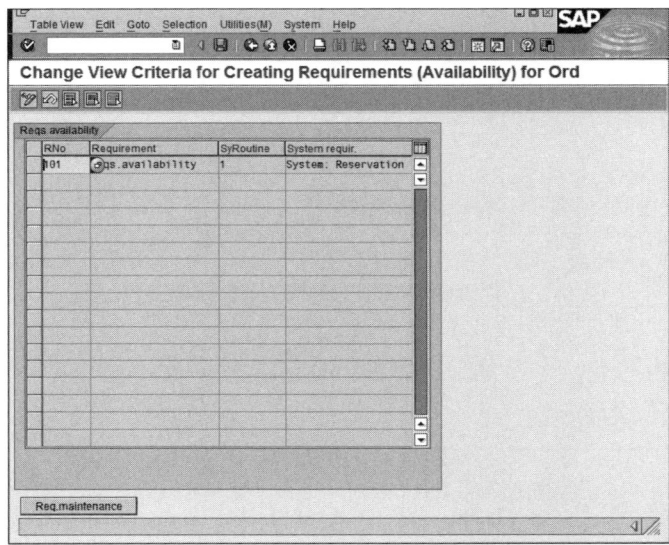

© SAP AG. All rights reserved.

FIGURE 5.51 Displaying the Change View Criteria for Creating Requirements (Availability) for Orders: Overview screen

Figure 5.51 shows the existing requirements for transfer of requirements.

After understanding the **Maintain Requirements for Transfer of Requirements** activity, let's explore the **Maintain Requirements for Purchase and Assembly Orders** activity.

Maintaining Requirements for Purchase and Assembly Orders

The **Maintain Requirements for Purchase and Assembly Orders** activity allows you to maintain your own requirements so that you can purchase the required quantities of goods in a flexible and economic manner. To maintain requirements and assemble orders for the products to be purchased, navigate the following menu path (Figure 5.44):

Menu Path

SAP Customizing Implementation Guide > Sales and Distribution > Basic Functions > Availability Check and Transfer of Requirements > Transfer of Requirements > Maintain Requirements For Purchase and Assembly Orders

After navigating through the preceding menu path, click the **IMG Activity** icon (🔘) beside the **Maintain Requirements for Purchase and Assembly Orders** activity. The **Change View "Req. for Creating Purch. Requisition/Assembly for Order": Overview** screen appears as shown in Figure 5.52.

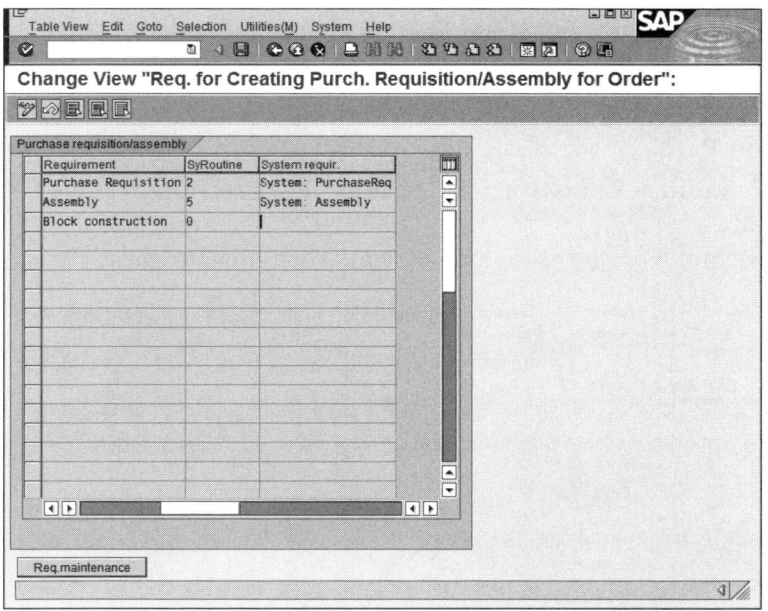

© SAP AG. All rights reserved.

FIGURE 5.52 Displaying the Change View "Req. for Creating Purch. Requisition/Assembly for Order": Overview screen

Figure 5.52 shows the existing requirements for purchase requisition.

This concludes the section on configuring the transfer of requirements. Let's now discuss the concept of contracts in detail.

WORKING WITH CONTRACTS

In an organization, under special conditions, such as lack of supply of goods corresponding to the demand and allowing special discounts to a few customers, a contract is created between a vendor and a customer. This contract is a sales agreement valid for a specified period. It depicts the conditions that may affect the price, target value, or target quantity related to the goods. Creating and working with contracts in the mySAP ERP system refer to aspects of contract processing. Contracts facilitate planning and guarantee a fixed agreement with a customer. A contract does not contain details regarding schedule line, delivery quantities, or delivery dates; instead, it is an agreement that represents specific price agreements. The data from a contract are copied to the special agreements related to prices or delivery deadlines. Release orders are also created with reference to a contract, and in turn, they generate a document flow record that allows updating the released quantities and values in a contract. To create a contract, navigate the following menu path:

Menu Path

SAP menu > Logistics > Sales and Distribution > Sales > Contract > Create

Figure 5.53 shows the preceding navigated menu path.

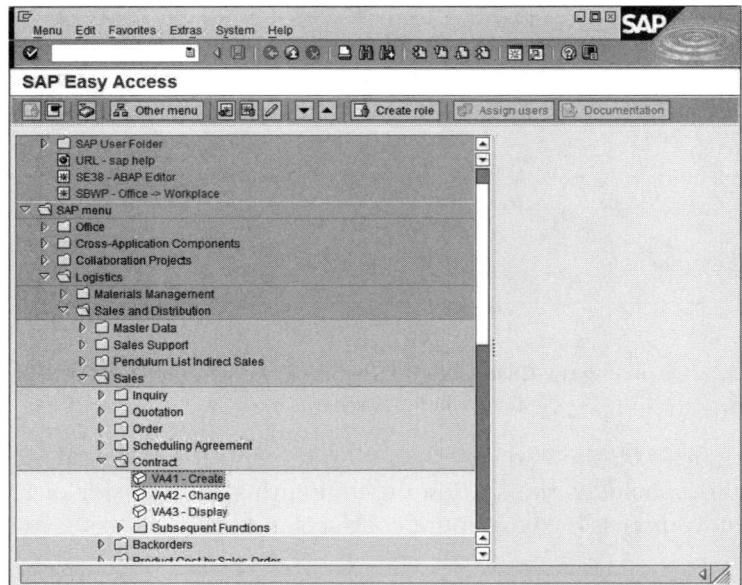

© SAP AG. All rights reserved.

FIGURE 5.53 Displaying the menu path for creating a contract

Next, click the **Create** activity. The **Create Contract: Initial Screen** appears as shown in Figure 5.54.

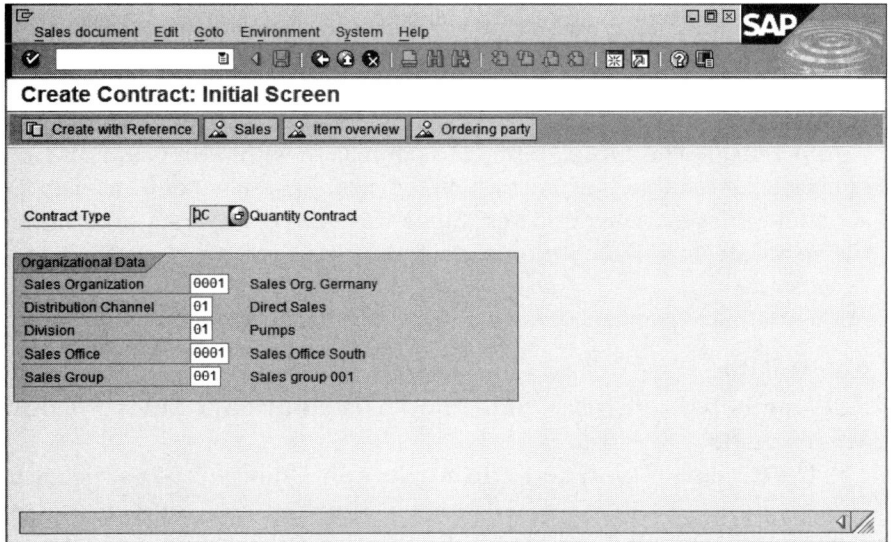

© SAP AG. All rights reserved.

FIGURE 5.54 Displaying the details for creating a contract

Figure 5.54 shows the **Contract Type** field, which accepts the type of contract you want to create. In the mySAP ERP standard system, these are the types of contracts:

- Quantity Contracts (QC)
- Value Contracts (WK)
- Service and Maintenance Contracts (SC)
- Master Contracts (QP)

Let's discuss each of them in detail.

Quantity Contracts

During a recession period or under any other critical situation, it is possible that the supply of a particular product is less than its demand. In such a situation, an organization can restrict the quantity of goods and services that a customer can buy in order to evenly distribute products among customers. The restriction on the quantity of goods and services is implemented by using quantity contracts. These contracts are defined after the quotation of a product is specified but before an order is placed. The SAP system defines the **KM** or **CQ SAP** standard sales documents for quantity contracts.

In a quantity contract, transfer requirements cannot be transferred. This implies that the quantity contract does not create a requirement for stock within a plant. Therefore, no stock is confirmed within the plant for a quantity contract. The contracts against which the products are not delivered do not have schedule lines or delivery dates. Since this type of contract does not contain delivery dates, a release order is created from the contract, and the delivery is processed.

To define a quantity contract, navigate the following menu path (Figure 5.53):

Menu Path

SAP menu > Logistics > Sales and Distribution > Sales > Contract > VA41-Create

The **Create Contract: Initial Screen** (Figure 5.54) appears to help you create the contract. After creating the contract, you can navigate the following menu path to create a release order with a reference to the contract (Figure 5.53):

Menu Path

SAP menu > Logistics > Sales and Distribution > Sales > Order > Create

After creating the release order, the available quantity of material delivered to a customer decreases. This decrement of the quantity of material can be analyzed while creating a new order. (The contract and the release order must have been created already.) Next, you can set up the quantity contract by navigating through the following menu path:

Menu Path

SAP Customizing Implementation Guide > Sales and Distribution > Sales > Sales Documents > Sales Document Header > Define Sales Document Types

Now you can view the details of the quantity contract using the following menu path (Figure 5.53):

Menu Path

SAP menu > Logistics > Sales and Distribution > Sales > Contract > Display

The example in Figure 5.55 shows the details of the `40000089` quantity contract.

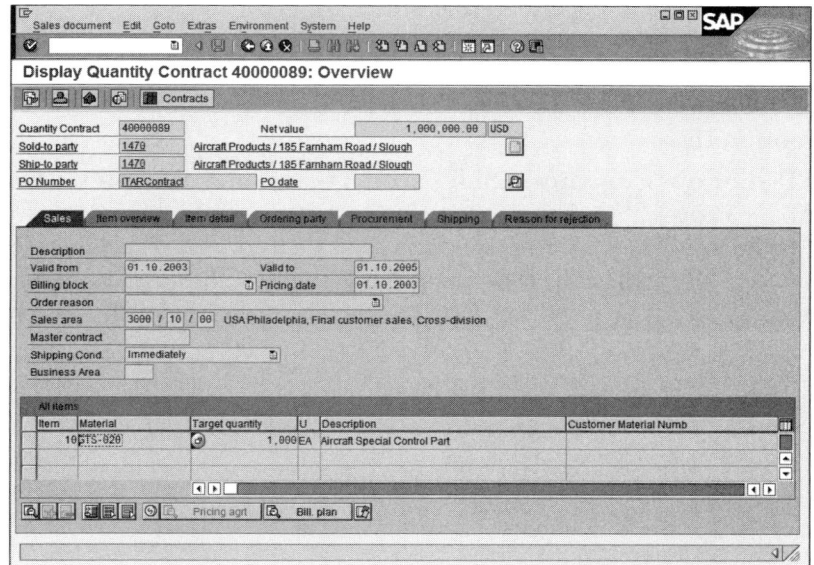

FIGURE 5.55   Displaying the details of a quantity contract

Figure 5.55 shows the **Sales, Item overview**, and **Item detail** tabs in reference to the `40000089` quantity contract. In a quantity contract, the quantity available in a contract is known as the target quantity and the quantity that has been utilized by the sales orders refers to the order quantity. The **All items** section in Figure 5.55 displays the target quantity associated with the `GTS-020` material.

After understanding the quantity contract, let's move ahead to discuss the value contract.

Value Contracts

A value contract limits the amount or quantity of material or services to a customer, depending upon the total value of the material or services mentioned in the contract. In SAP, there are two types of value contracts:

- **Standard Value Contract**—A contract based on the total value of an assortment of materials.
- **Material-Related Value Contract**—Restricts the use of a contract to a single material.

Similar to other contracts, you can also define the value contract by navigating through the following menu path (Figure 5.53):

Menu Path

SAP menu > Logistics > Sales and Distribution > Sales > Contract > VA41-Create

Similarly, you can enter WK1 or WK2 beside the **Contract type** textbox in the **Create Contract: Initial Screen** to create the value contract. After entering the contract type, press the **Enter** key. The **Create Value contract-gen.: Overview** screen appears as shown in Figure 5.56.

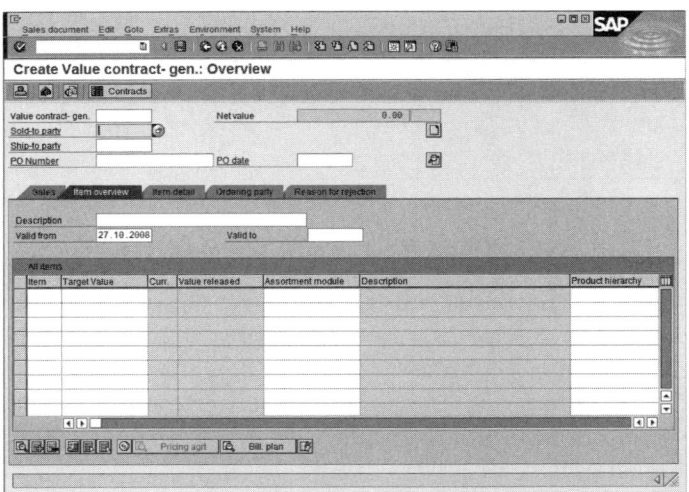

© SAP AG. All rights reserved.

FIGURE 5.56 Displaying the Create Value contract-gen.: Overview screen

Enter the required details beside the **Value contract.gen.**, **Sold-to party**, **Ship-to party**, and **PO Number** fields in the screen shown in Figure 5.56. An order entry in the assortment module must be created to display the list of materials and services that can be released from a value contract. This module has a validity date and displays only those materials and services that belong to the same sales organization and distribution channel. To define an assortment module, navigate the following menu path:

Menu Path

SAP menu > Logistics > Sales and Distribution > Master Data > Products > Assortments > Assortment > Module > Create

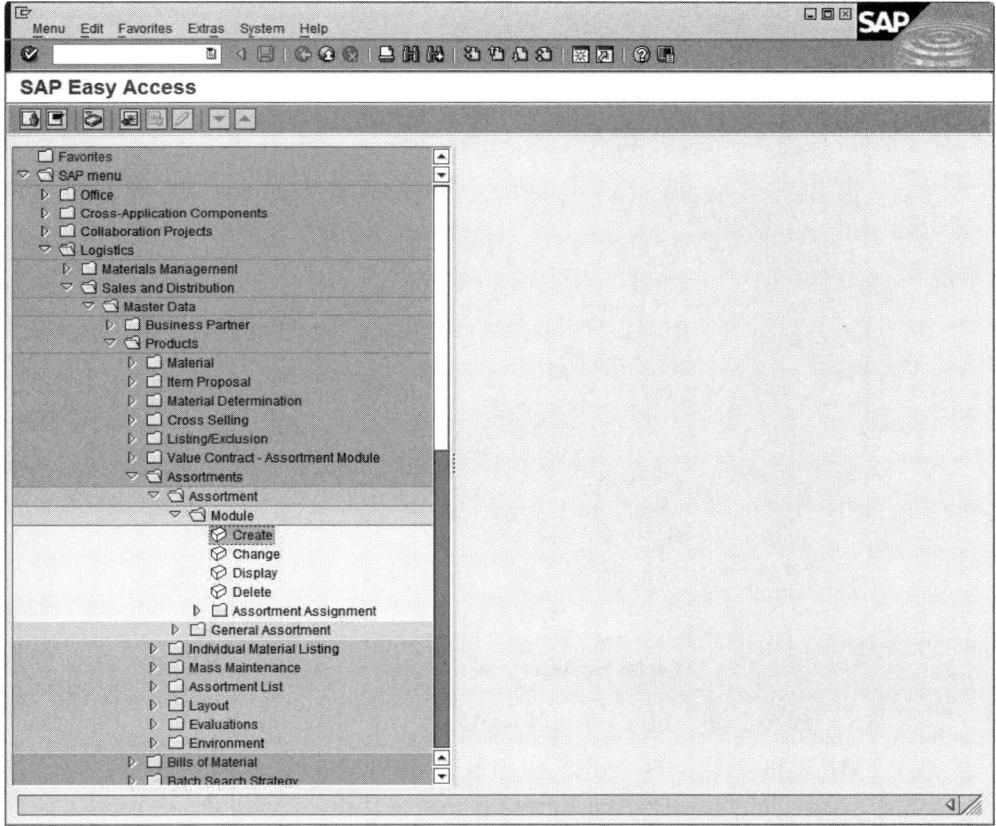

© SAP AG. All rights reserved.

FIGURE 5.57 Displaying the menu path for defining assortment module

After navigating the preceding menu path, the **Assortment Module Create: Initial Screen** appears as shown in Figure 5.58.

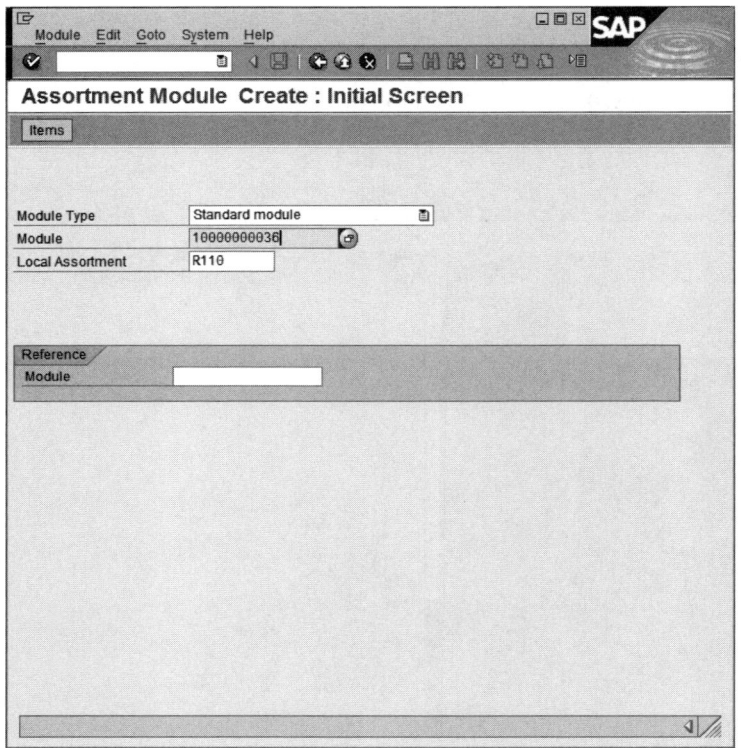

© SAP AG. All rights reserved.

FIGURE 5.58   Displaying Assortment Module Create: Initial Screen

In Figure 5.58, enter the following details in the corresponding fields:

- **Module Type**—Specify which type of module you want to create, such as **Exclusion** module or **Standard** module. In our example, we entered Standard module.

- **Module**—Specify the module number, which serves as an object used to list the materials that are either in store or distribution center assortments. In our example, we entered `10000000036` as the module number.
- **Local Assortment**—Specify the local assortment, which serves as an object to which materials are assigned. In our example, we entered `R110` as the local assortment.

By entering the details, you define the assortment module that is used while defining a value contract.

After creating the value contract, you may call it off using a release order. To call it off, navigate the following menu path:

Menu Path

SAP menu > Logistics > Sales and Distribution > Sales > Contract > Subsequent Functions > V-01-Order

Figure 5.59 shows the preceding navigated menu path.

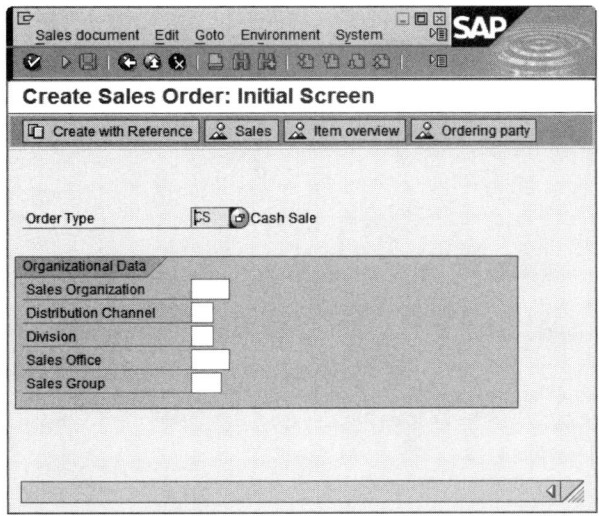

© SAP AG. All rights reserved.

FIGURE 5.59 Displaying the menu path for defining order

After navigating the preceding menu path, the **Create Sales Order: Initial Screen** appears as shown in Figure 5.60.

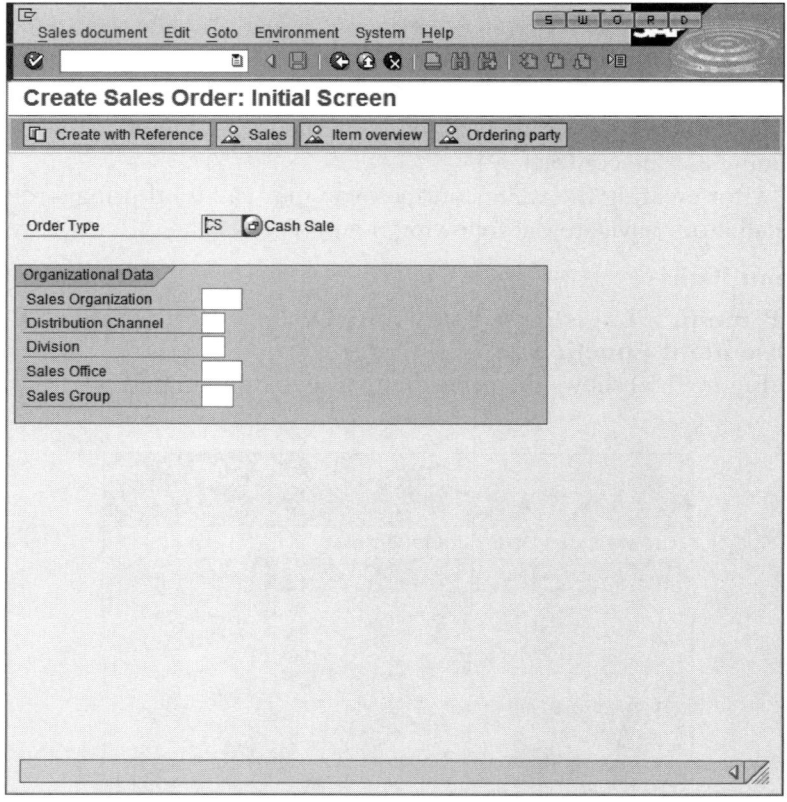

© SAP AG. All rights reserved.

FIGURE 5.60 Displaying Create Sales Order: Initial Screen

In Figure 5.60, CS has been entered as the order type. Now click the **Create with Reference** button. The **Create with Reference** dialog box appears as shown in Figure 5.61.

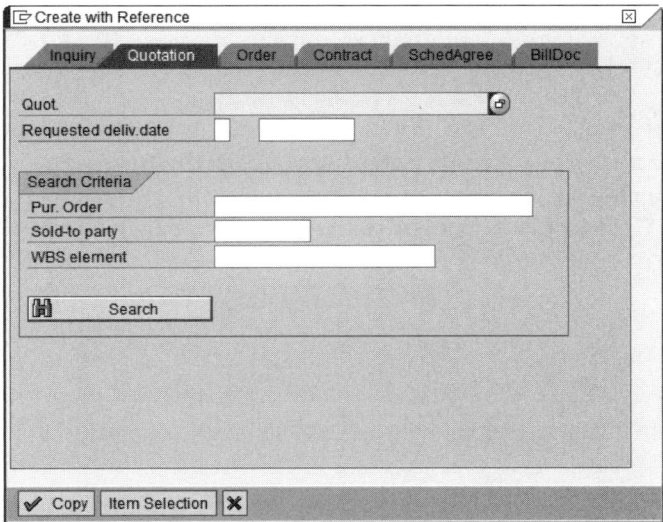

FIGURE 5.61 Displaying the Create with Reference dialog box

In this dialog box, select the **Contract** tab, enter the contract number to be called off, and also enter the call-off party in the textbox beside the **Releasing partner** label. After entering the details, click the **Copy** button.

This concludes the discussion on the value contract; now let's discuss the service contract.

Service and Maintenance Contracts

A legal agreement between the service receiver and the service provider is known as a service and maintenance contract. For a supplier the basic need of a service order is to initiate automatic billing of regular services at fixed intervals. Moreover, with the help of this contract, an organization can also determine whether a cancellation request of the contract is valid.

Apart from the supplier, the receiver also requires this contract to claim for services and the set prices on specific services. For this type of contracts, the mySAP ERP system uses the WV standard SAP sales document. Moreover, there is no need to have call-offs or release orders or references to other sales documents. This type of contract has either periodic or milestone billing. To define a service and maintenance contract, navigate the following menu path (Figure 5.53):

Menu Path

SAP menu > Logistics > Sales and Distribution > Sales > Contract > VA41-Create

The **Create Contract: Initial Screen** appears, in which you need to enter the type of contract, as shown in Figure 5.62.

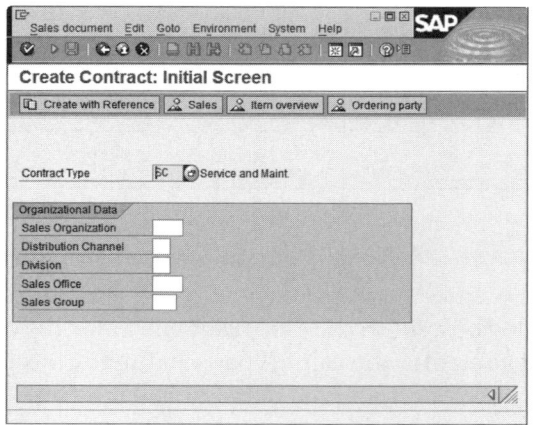

© SAP AG. All rights reserved.

FIGURE 5.62 Displaying the Create Contract: Initial Screen

Enter SC as the contract type and press the **Enter** key; the **Create Service and Maintenance: Overview** screen appears. Now, enter the details for the service and maintenance contract in order to define the service and maintenance contract. Apart from defining this contract, you can view the details of this contract by navigating the following menu path (Figure 5.53):

Menu Path

SAP Menu > Logistics > Sales and Distribution > Sales > Contract > VA43-Display

The **Display Contract: Initial Screen** appears; now enter the service and maintenance contract number for which you want to display the details, as shown in Figure 5.63.

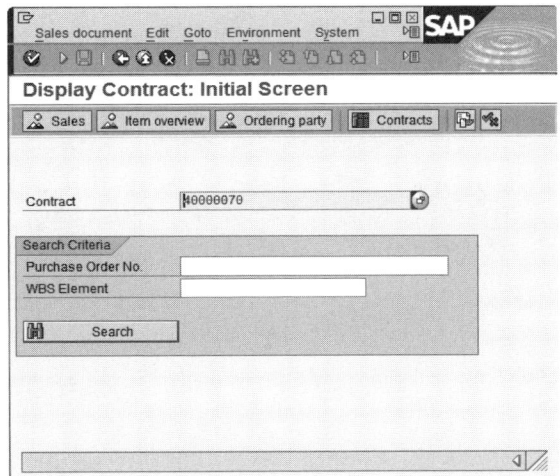

© SAP AG. All rights reserved.

FIGURE 5.63 Displaying the Display Contract: Initial Screen

After entering the service and maintenance contract number, (in our example, we have entered 40000070 as the contract number) press the **Enter** key. The **Display Service and Maint. 40000070: Overview** screen appears as shown in Figure 5.64.

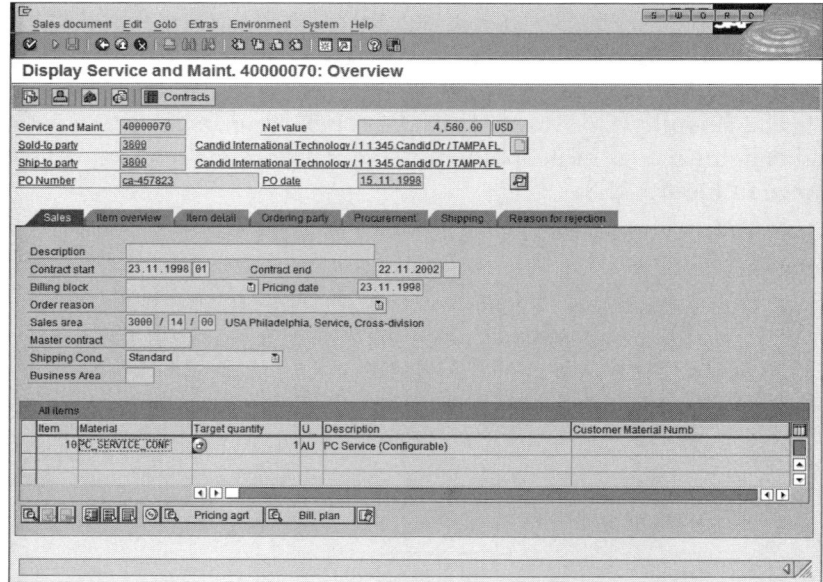

FIGURE 5.64 Displaying details of a specific value contract

Figure 5.64 shows the details of the 40000070 contract, such as the sales, items, shipping, and ordering-party details.

After defining the service and maintenance contract, let's move ahead to discuss master contracts.

Master Contracts

In SAP, you can group the quantity, service, or value contracts under one main contract, known as the master contract. During the process of grouping, the contracts that are grouped are known as lower-level contracts. The rules defined in the master contract are inherited by all the lower-level contracts as well.

This process of grouping various lower-level contracts under a single master contract to facilitate data consistency is known as contract grouping. While linking a lower-level contract to a master contract, the header data of the master contract is transferred into the lower-level contracts. In this process, you must ensure that the lower-level contracts and the master contract are allocated to the same sales area.

Now, after understanding the concept of contract grouping, let's explain the following activities required to define a master contract:

- Define Reference Sales Document Types
- Define Referencing Procedures
- Define a Master Contract
- Define Workflow for Master Contracts

Now let's discuss each of them in detail.

Defining Reference Sales Document Types

You can refer various sales documents to a master contract on the basis of certain defined rules. The rules used to refer to the sales documents are known as referencing requirements. The **Defining Reference Sales Document Types** activity helps to define referencing requirements. Referencing requirements are useful while defining a master contract.

Now, let's navigate the following menu path to define the referencing requirements for sales documents:

Menu Path

SAP Customizing Implementation Guide > Sales and Distribution > Sales > Sales Documents > Contracts > Master Contract > Define Referencing Requirements > Define Reference Sales Document Types

Figure 5.65 shows the preceding menu path.

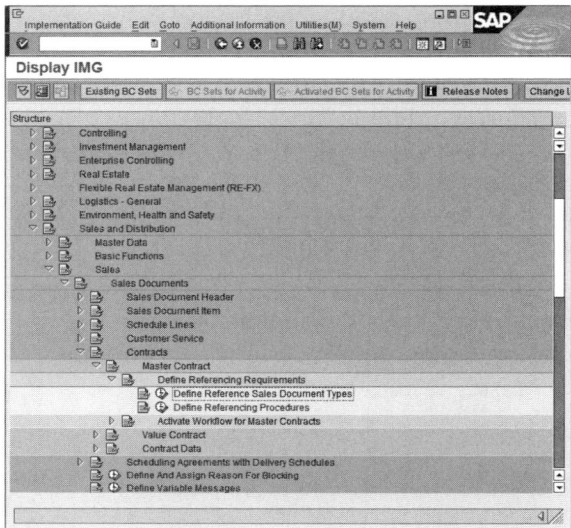

© SAP AG. All rights reserved.

FIGURE 5.65 Displaying the menu path for defining referencing requirements

After navigating the menu path shown in Figure 5.65, click the **IMG Activity** icon ( ) beside the **Define Reference Sales Document Types** activity. The **Change View "Group Referencing Requirement: Sales Document Type": Overview** screen appears as shown in Figure 5.66.

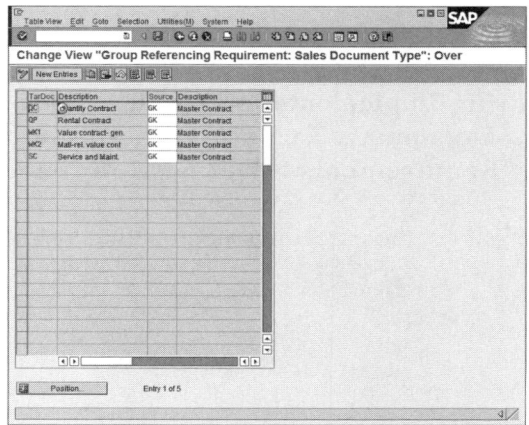

© SAP AG. All rights reserved.

FIGURE 5.66 Displaying the group referencing requirement

Figure 5.66 shows the existing sales documents defined for referencing requirement. Now click the **New Entries** button to define the sales document for group referencing. The **New Entries: Overview of Added Entries** screen appears. Figure 5.67 shows the details of the new group referencing requirements.

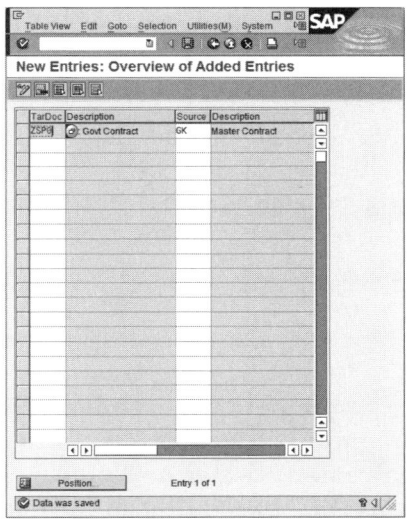

© SAP AG. All rights reserved.

FIGURE 5.67 **Displaying the details for a group referencing requirements**

Enter the following details in their respective columns:

- **TarDoc**—Specify the sales document type that can reference the master contract type.
- **Source**—Specify the master contract type to which a sales document type can refer.

Click the **Save** icon (■) to save the configuration.

Now, after defining the reference sales document types, let's now discuss how to define referencing procedures.

Defining Referencing Procedures

The **Define Referencing Procedures** activity allows you to define the fields relevant for contract grouping. It defines the rules on the basis of which the mySAP ERP system copies data from a master contract to lower-level contracts. Following are the classifications of the fields relevant for contract grouping:

- **Identical Fields**—Specifies that a contract can refer a master contract if the value of the identical field in the master contract identically matches with the fields of the contract that you define.
- **Copy Fields**—Specifies that the values of the copy fields are copied from the master contract to the lower-level contracts. However, the copied values are not overwritten in the lower-level contracts.
- **Proposal Fields**—Specify that the values of the proposal fields are copied from the master contract to the lower-level contracts. However, the copied values can be overwritten in the lower-level contracts.

To define the referencing procedure, navigate the following menu path (Figure 5.65):

Menu Path

SAP Customizing Implementation Guide > Sales and Distribution > Sales > Sales Documents > Contracts > Master Contract > Define Referencing Requirements > Define Referencing Procedures

After navigating the preceding menu path, the **Change View "Procedures": Overview** screen appears as shown in Figure 5.68.

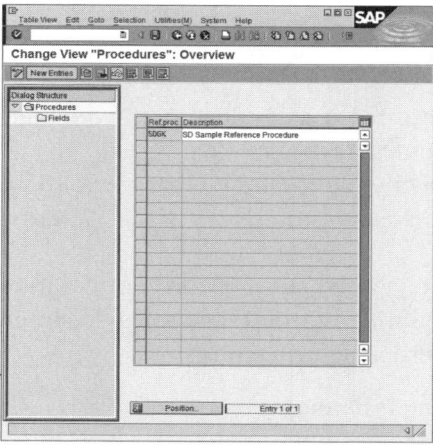

© SAP AG. All rights reserved.

FIGURE 5.68 Displaying the existing referencing procedures

Figure 5.68 shows the existing referencing procedures. To define a new referencing procedure, click the **New Entries** button. The **New Entries: Overview of Added Entries** screen appears as shown in Figure 5.69.

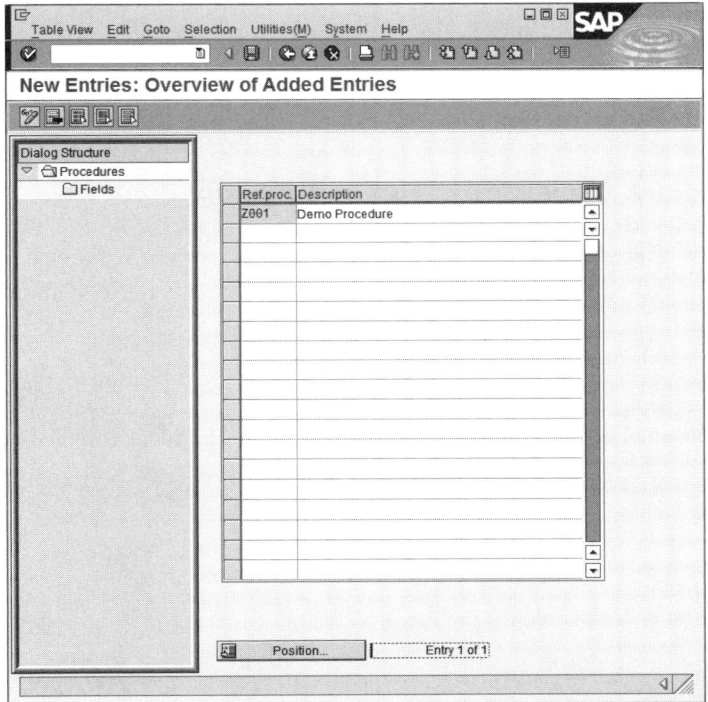

© SAP AG. All rights reserved.

FIGURE 5.69 Displaying the details of a new referencing procedure

After entering the details for a new referencing procedure, click the **Save** icon (🖫) to save the data.

Let's now discuss how to define a master contract in the following section.

Defining a Master Contract

You can define a master contract in the same way that a sales document is defined. Out of various sales document types, you can choose the GK sales document type to define a master contract that is a standard sales document type for a master contract. However, to copy or change the standard sales document, you must ensure the following:

- For the master contract, the sales document category must be 0.
- The screen sequence group must either be GK or a copy of GK.
- To represent a contract, the transaction group must be 4.

You must remember that first you need to define a master contract and then define other individual lower-level contracts because you can assign the higher-level contract to lower-level contracts. To define the master contract, navigate the following menu path (Figure 5.53):

Menu Path

SAP Menu > Logistics > Sales and Distribution > Sales > Contract > VA41-Create

The **Create Contract: Initial Screen** appears. Now enter GK as the contract type, and enter other details related to the sales organization, as shown in Figure 5.70.

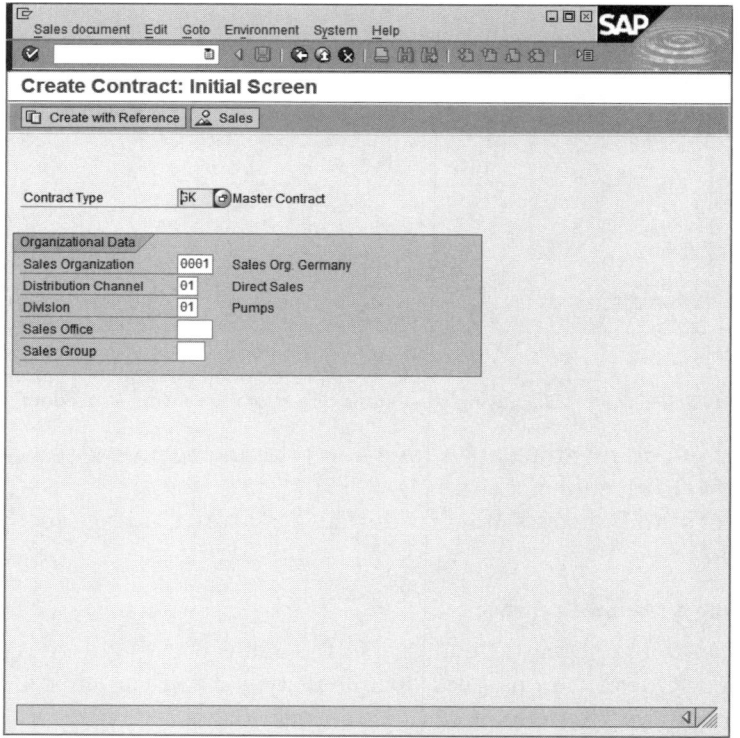

© SAP AG. All rights reserved.

FIGURE 5.70 Displaying the Create Contract: Initial Screen

Figure 5.70 displays the sales organization data and contract type for creating the master contract. After entering the details, press the **Enter** key. The **Create Master Contract: Overview** screen appears as shown in Figure 5.71.

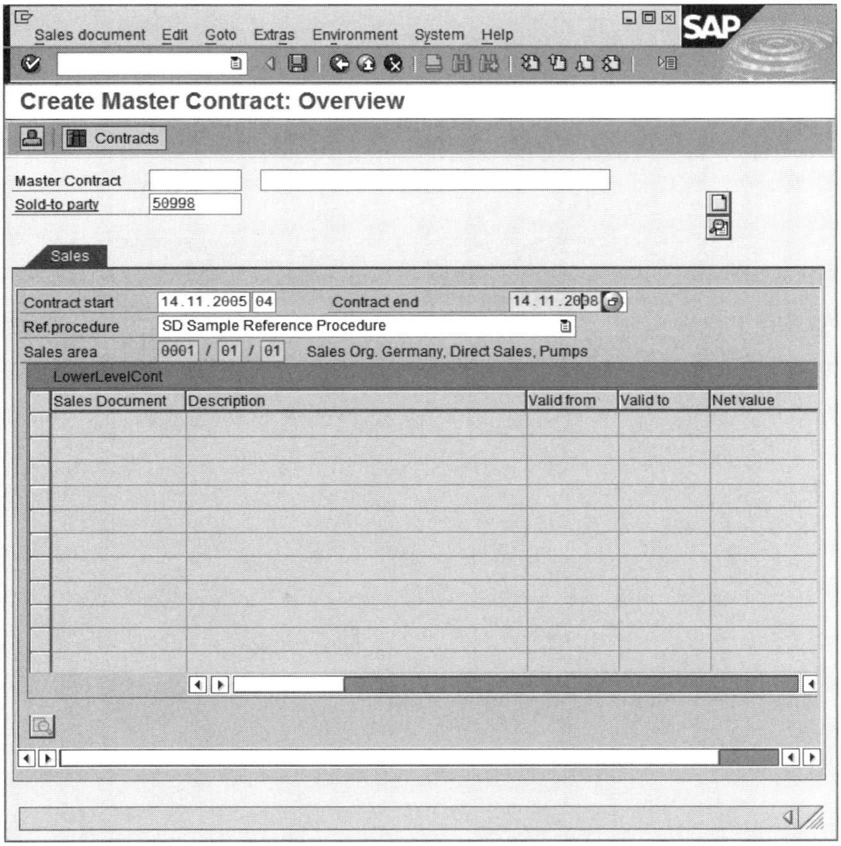

© SAP AG. All rights reserved.

FIGURE 5.71 Displaying the Create Master Contract: Overview screen

After entering the details, such as **Sold-to party**, **Contract start** date, and **Contract end** date, click the **Save** icon () to save the details.

After defining a master contract, let's now discuss the workflow of master contracts.

Defining Workflow for Master Contracts

The term workflow implies sequential steps that are performed to accomplish a task. The workflow in an enterprise is either carried out manually by the user or processed automatically by the SAP system. Navigate the following menu path to define the workflow for master contracts (Figure 5.65):

Menu Path

SAP Customizing Implementation Guide > Sales and Distribution > Sales > Sales Documents > Contracts > Master Contract > Activate Workflow for Master Contracts

Figure 5.72 shows the preceding navigated menu path.

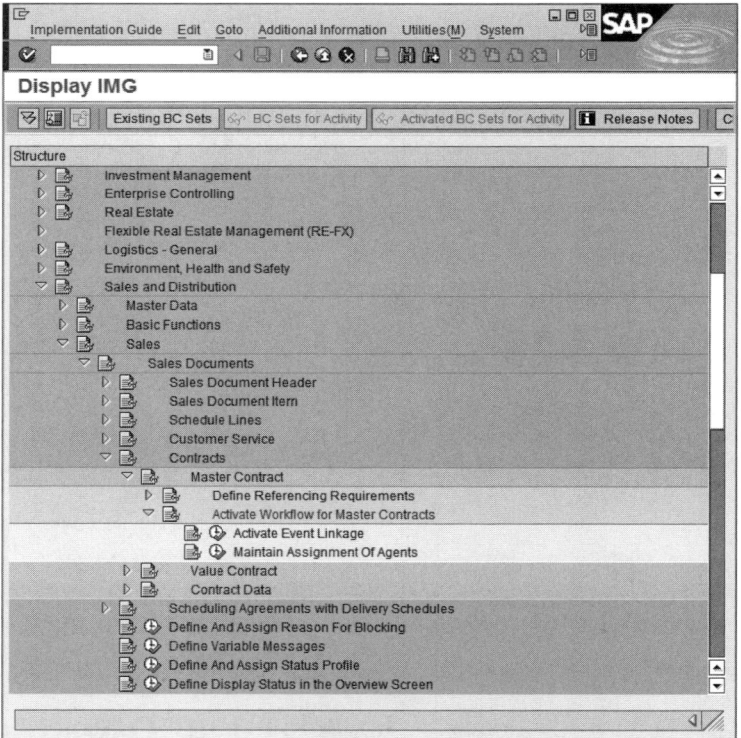

© SAP AG. All rights reserved.

FIGURE 5.72 Displaying the menu path for workflow of master contracts

You must perform the following tasks to create the settings for the workflow scenario in the mySAP ERP system:

- Activate the event that triggers the workflow scenarios.
- Define the receiver when the scenario begins.

This section concludes the discussion on contracts. Now, let's explore scheduling agreements.

WORKING WITH SCHEDULING AGREEMENTS

Scheduling agreements are detailed agreements between an organization and a customer. These agreements contain the delivery dates along with the specified quantity of a material to be delivered. The dates specified in the scheduling agreements are entered as schedule lines, and therefore, the agreement is processed by delivering the schedule lines on the due date. For scheduling agreements, you need to perform the following activities:

- Define Schedule Line Types
- Maintain Planning Delivery Schedule Instructions or Splitting Rules
- Define Scheduling Agreements

Now, let's discuss each of them in detail.

Defining Schedule Line Types

In a scheduling agreement, the schedule line type is defined for information purposes. Following are the schedule line types, already defined in the mySAP ERP system:

- Normal Schedule Line
- Backlog
- Immediate Requirement

- Forecast Delivery Schedule
- Just In Time (JIT) Delivery Schedule

To define a new schedule line type, navigate the following menu path:

Menu Path

SAP Customizing Implementation Guide > Sales and Distribution > Sales > Sales Documents > Scheduling Agreements with Delivery Schedules > Define Schedule Line Types

Figure 5.73 shows the preceding navigated menu path.

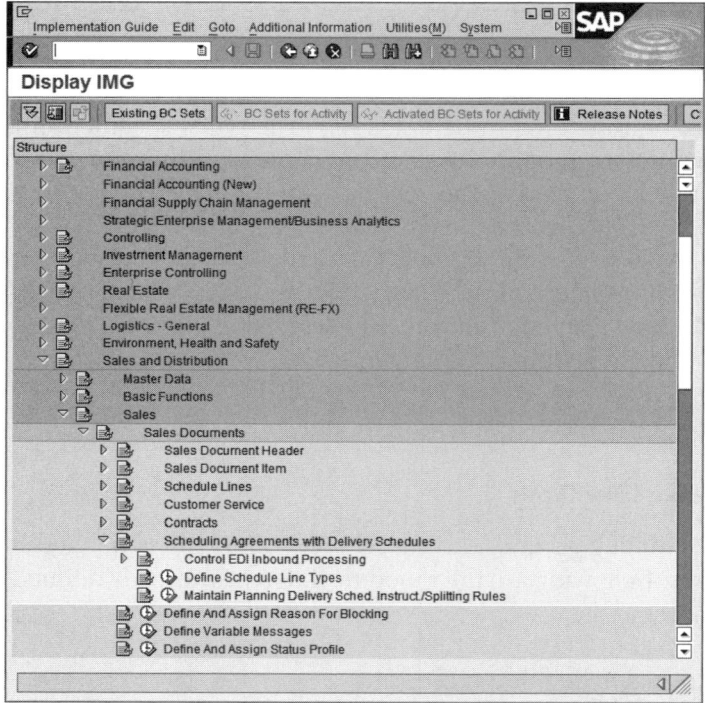

© SAP AG. All rights reserved.

FIGURE 5.73 Displaying menu path to define schedule line types

After navigating through the preceding menu path, click the **IMG Activity** icon (🌀) beside the **Define Schedule Line Types** activity. The **Change View "Schedule Line Types for Scheduling Agreements": Overview** screen appears as shown in Figure 5.74.

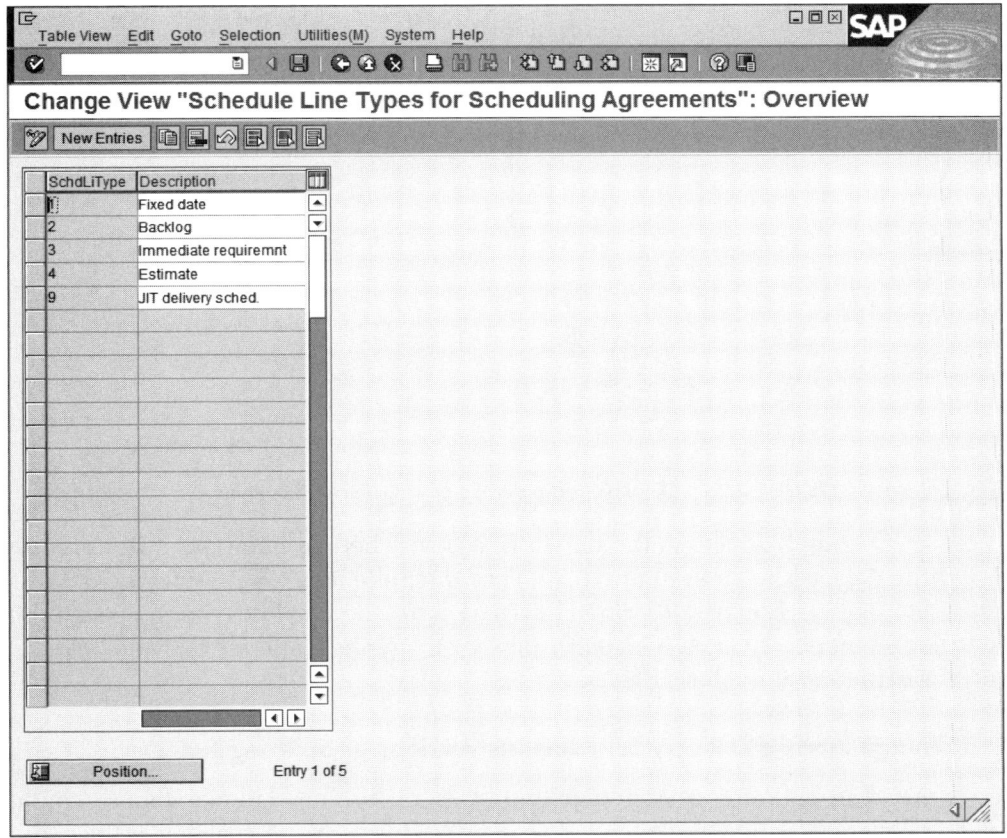

© SAP AG. All rights reserved.

FIGURE 5.74 Displaying the existing schedule line types

Figure 5.74 shows the existing schedule line types defined in the mySAP ERP system, such as **Fixed date** and **Backlog**. To define a new schedule line type, click the **New Entries** button. The **New Entries: Overview of Added Entries** screen appears as shown in Figure 5.75.

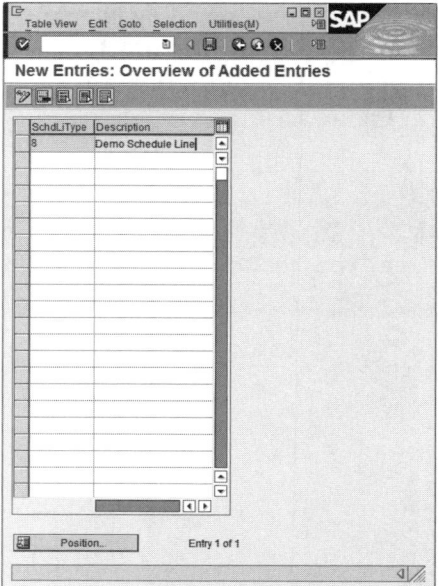

© SAP AG. All rights reserved.

FIGURE 5.75 **Displaying the details of a new schedule line type**

Figure 5.75 shows the details of a new schedule line type. After entering the data as shown in Figure 5.75, click the **Save** icon ( ) to save the details.

This section has described how to define schedule line types for scheduling agreements. Let's now explore how to maintain planning delivery schedule instructions or splitting rules.

Maintaining Planning Delivery Schedule Instructions or Splitting Rules

Apart from defining a schedule line type, you also need to maintain a planning delivery schedule. A planning delivery schedule is an internal delivery schedule necessary to plan the requirements of an organization more efficiently. This activity is divided into the following subactivities:

- Defining planning delivery schedule instructions
- Defining delivery schedule splitting rules
- Assigning delivery schedule splitting rules

Let's now explore each of the following subactivities in detail.

Defining Planning Delivery Schedule Instructions

The planning delivery schedule instructions are helpful in determining the details of planning delivery schedules. To maintain planning delivery schedule instructions, navigate the following menu path (Figure 5.73):

Menu Path

SAP Customizing Implementation Guide > Sales and Distribution > Sales > Sales Documents > Scheduling Agreements with Delivery Schedules > Maintain Planning Delivery Sched. Instruct./Splitting Rules

The **Change View "Maintain Planning Delivery Schedule Instructions": Overview** screen appears as shown in Figure 5.76.

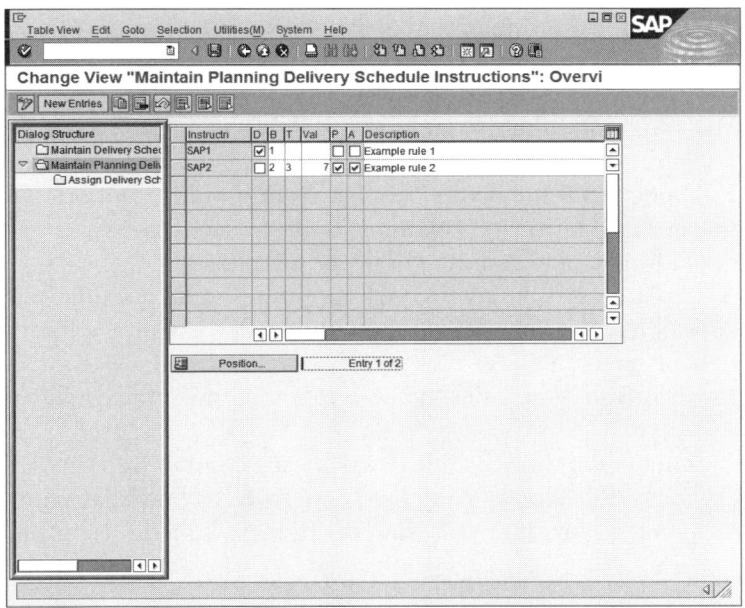

© SAP AG. All rights reserved.

FIGURE 5.76   Displaying planning delivery schedule splitting rules

Figure 5.76 displays the existing splitting rules, **SAP1** and **SAP2**, defined for the planning delivery schedule. The column **D** for **SAP1** instruction is checked, which indicates that the schedule lines in the planning delivery schedule are relevant for delivery and should replace the schedule lines in the forecast delivery schedule. However, for **SAP2**, the column **D** is cleared indicating that the schedule lines in the planning delivery schedule are not relevant for delivery.

Following are the detailed descriptions of the columns shown in Figure 5.76:

- **Instructn**—Specifies the name of the instruction defined.
- **D**—Depicts whether the schedule lines in the planning delivery schedule are relevant for delivery.
- **B**—Specifies the date accepted by the mySAP ERP system as the initial date for planning delivery schedule.
- **T**—Specifies whether the delivery schedule split validity period is measured in weeks or months.
- **Val**—Specifies the time period (weeks or months) for which the delivery schedule split is valid.
- **P**—Specifies if the mySAP ERP system should adopt schedule lines from the previous planning delivery schedule while generating a new planning delivery schedule.
- **A**—Examines if the mySAP ERP system should automatically generate a planning delivery schedule while creating a forecast delivery schedule.
- **Description**—Specifies the description of the defined splitting rule.

After understanding the relevance of each column, you can define planning delivery instructions by clicking the **New Entries** button (Figure 5.76).

Let's now discuss how to define the delivery schedule splitting rules.

Defining Delivery Schedule Splitting Rules

The delivery schedule splitting instructions help define the split of schedule line quantities between various days in the forecast delivery schedules and planning delivery schedules. To maintain the delivery schedule splitting rules, double-click the **Maintain Delivery Schedule Splitting Rules** folder from the **Dialog Structure** section (Figure 5.76). After selecting the **Maintain**

Delivery Schedule Splitting Rules folder, the **Change View "Maintain Delivery Schedule Splitting Rules": Overview** screen appears as shown in Figure 5.77.

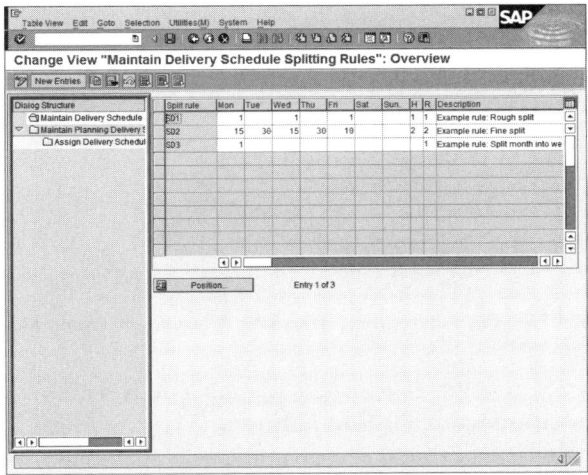

© SAP AG. All rights reserved.

FIGURE 5.77 Displaying the delivery schedule splitting rules

Figure 5.77 shows the following columns:

- **Split rule**—Specifies how the mySAP ERP system must split schedule lines from the current forecast delivery schedule and assign them to the new planning delivery schedule.
- **Mon–Sun**—Maintains how the mySAP ERP system must split weekly (Monday to Sunday) schedule lines in a forecast delivery schedule into daily schedule lines in the planning delivery schedule.
- **H**—Specifies the holiday rule for delivery schedule split.
- **R**—Specifies the split quantity rounding.
- **Description**—Specifies the description of a defined split rule.

You can also define the delivery schedule splitting rules by clicking the **New Entries** button (Figure 5.77). and entering the relevant details in the previously discussed columns.

Let's now discuss how to assign delivery schedule splitting rules.

Assigning Delivery Schedule Splitting Rules

Since there are various splitting rules for each instruction, you can assign a date, type, and range for each splitting rule. To assign the delivery schedule splitting rules to a scheduling agreement, click the **Assign Delivery Schedule Splitting Rules** folder (Figure 5.76). The **Determine Work Area: Entry** dialog box appears. Now, enter the planning delivery schedule instruction, as shown in Figure 5.78:

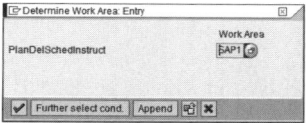

© SAP AG. All rights reserved.

FIGURE 5.78 Displaying the Determine Work Area: Entry dialog box

In Figure 5.78, enter SAP1 as the planning delivery schedule instruction then click the **Continue** icon (✔). **The Change View "Assign Delivery Schedule Splitting Rules": Overview** screen appears as shown in Figure 5.79.

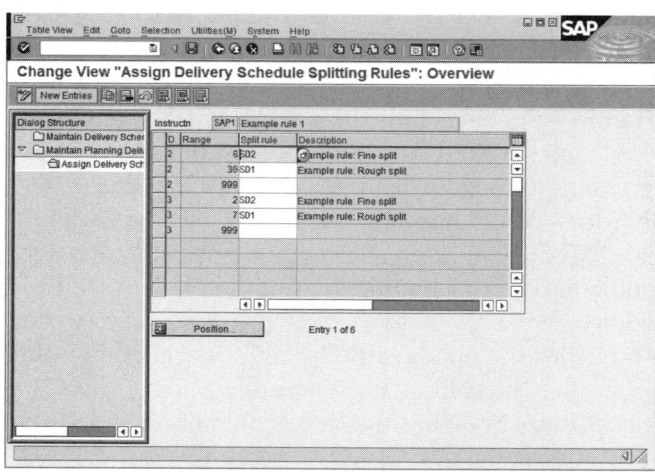

© SAP AG. All rights reserved.

FIGURE 5.79 Displaying the Change View "Assign Delivery Schedule Splitting Rules": Overview screen

Figure 5.79 displays the split rules assigned to the **SAP1** delivery schedule.

This concludes the discussion on maintaining a planning delivery schedule; let's now define the scheduling agreements.

Defining Scheduling Agreements

To define a scheduling agreement, navigate through the following menu path:

Menu Path

SAP menu > Logistics > Sales and Distribution > Sales > Scheduling Agreement > VA31-Create

Figure 5.80 shows the preceding navigated menu path.

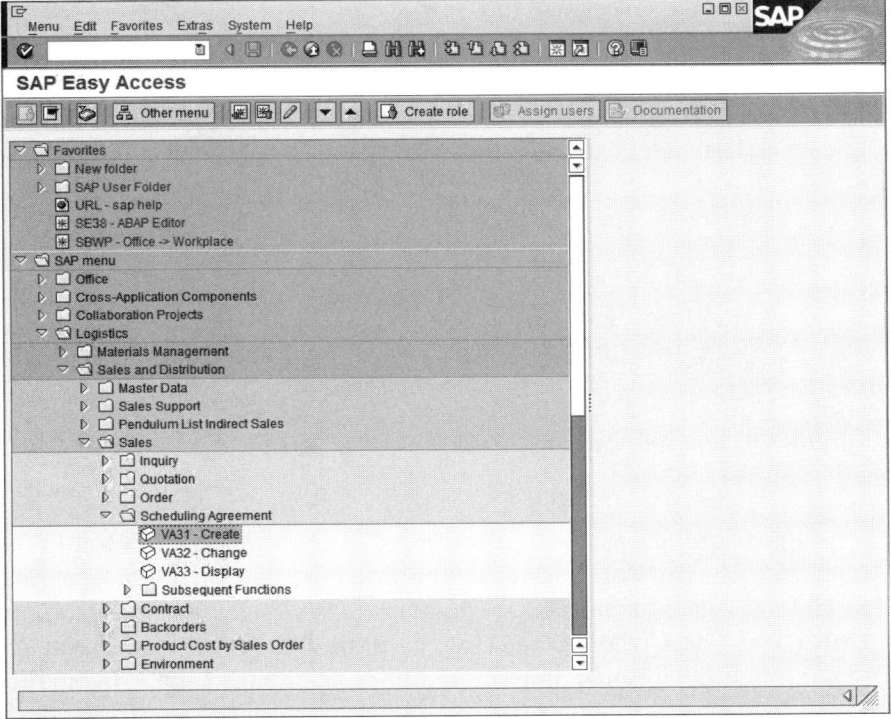

© SAP AG. All rights reserved.

FIGURE 5.80 Displaying the menu path for defining scheduling agreements

After navigating the preceding menu path, click the **VA31-Create** activity. The **Create Scheduling Agreement: Initial Screen** appears as shown in Figure 5.81.

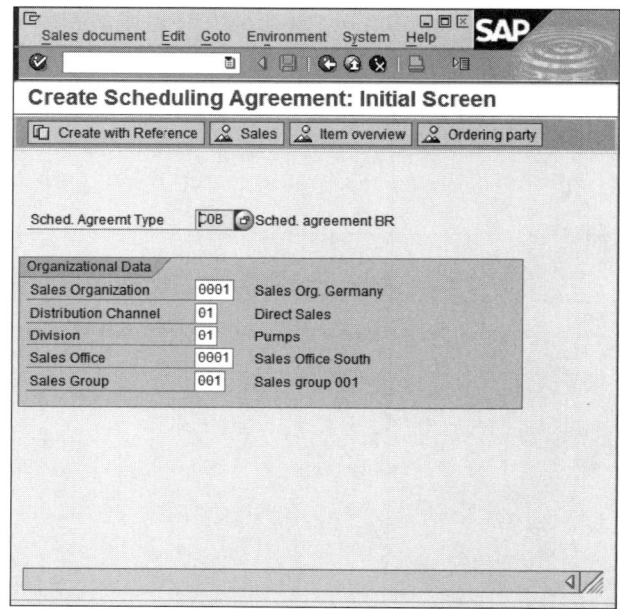

© SAP AG. All rights reserved.

FIGURE 5.81 Displaying the Create Scheduling Agreement: Initial Screen

Figure 5.81 shows the organizational data for which you want to define a scheduling agreement. In our example, we have specified organizational data for the 0001 sales organization. After entering the organizational data, press the **Enter** key. The **Create Sched. agreement BR: Overview** screen appears. Now enter the relevant details for new scheduling agreements. In our example, we have created the `35000090` scheduling agreement. Figure 5.82 shows the header data of this scheduling agreement.

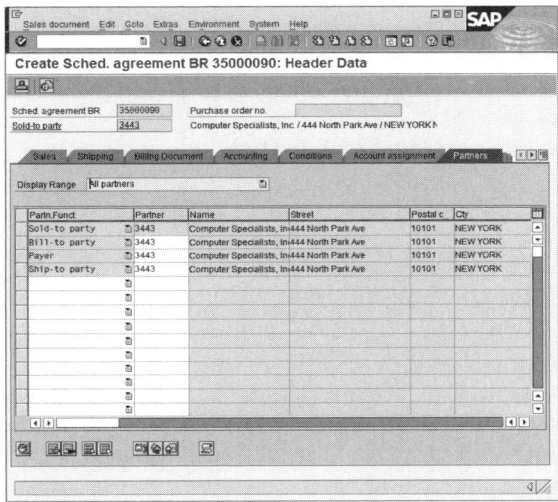

© SAP AG. All rights reserved.

FIGURE 5.82 **Displaying the scheduling agreement header data**

Let's now discuss the consignment stock process.

WORKING WITH THE CONSIGNMENT STOCK PROCESS

Consignment stock process is a special process that is used to place the stock or material reserved for a customer at the customer's or organization's end. This process is performed on the basis of an agreement with the customer, stating that the customer can sell the specified quantity of material. After the customer either consumes or sells the material, the customer informs the organization, the stock is transferred to the customer's ownership, and an invoice is issued. However, if the customer is not able to consume or sell the material, then the organization is also informed, and the stock is taken back.

The requirements transferred from consignment sales orders to materials planning are transferred to sales order documents as individual requirements, irrespective of the group settings of the availability checking. In this process, the consignment stock is controlled in the mySAP ERP system by the customer, and the material is monitored separately from the available stock for standard sales orders. In this section, we discuss the following activities with respect to the consignment stock process:

- Define Consignment Fill-up
- Display Stock Overview

Now, let's discuss each of them in detail.

Defining Consignment Fill-up

When the stock ordered by a customer is delivered to the customer on the basis of the order placed, this is known as consignment fill-up. This process uses the KB standard sales order document type. The KB sales document type and other consignment-related sales document types should have C as the sales document category setting. The KBN is used as the standard item category for consignment fill-up. To define the consignment fill-up order, navigate the following menu path:

Menu Path

SAP menu > Logistics > Sales and Distribution > Sales > Order > VA01-Create

The **Create Sales Order: Initial Screen** appears as shown in Figure 5.83.

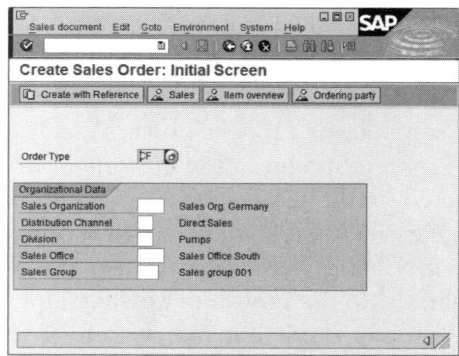

© SAP AG. All rights reserved.

FIGURE 5.83 **Displaying the Create Sales Order: Initial Screen**

Figure 5.83 shows `CF`, representing consignment fill-up, as the order type. Now, press the **Enter** key. The **Create Consignment Fill-up: Overview** screen appears, and you can enter the relevant details here. In our example, we have entered `35000094` as the consignment fill-up number and `40005` as the **Sold-to party** as well as the **Ship-to party**, as shown in Figure 5.84.

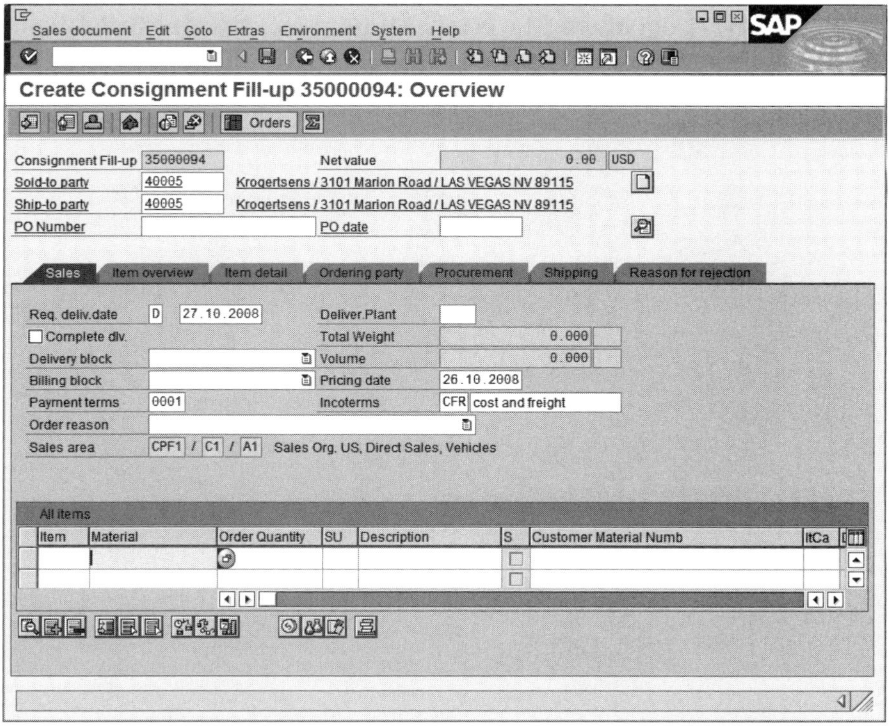

© SAP AG. All rights reserved.

FIGURE 5.84 Displaying details of new consignment fill-up

Figure 5.84 shows the consignment fill-up screen for the `35000094` consignment. After entering the details, click the **Save** icon (🖫) to save the details of the new consignment fill-up.

After discussing the consignment fill-up process, let's now move ahead to discuss how to display stock overview.

Displaying Stock Overview

This section explains how to view the stock provided to a customer on a consignment basis. Let's navigate the following menu path to display the stock overview:

Menu Path

SAP menu > Logistics > Materials Management > Physical Inventory > Environment > MMBE-Stock Overview

Figure 5.85 shows the preceding navigated menu path.

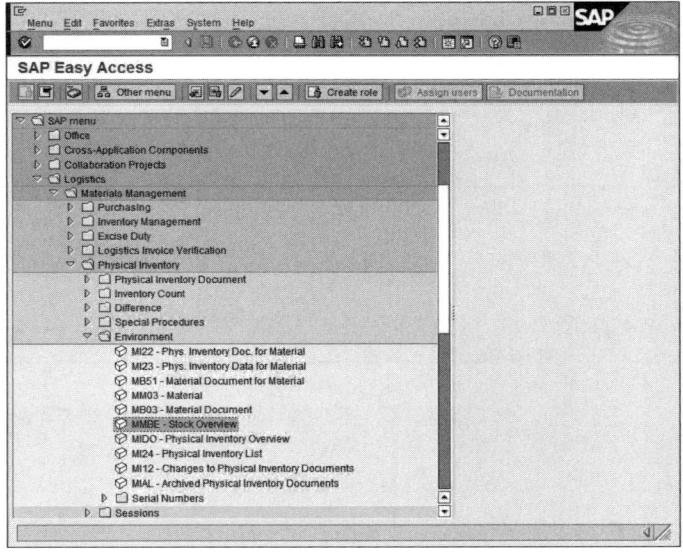

© SAP AG. All rights reserved.

FIGURE 5.85 Displaying the menu path of stock overview

After navigating the preceding menu path, click the **MMBE-Stock Overview** activity. The **Stock Overview: Company Code/Plant/Storage Location/Batch** screen appears as shown in Figure 5.86.

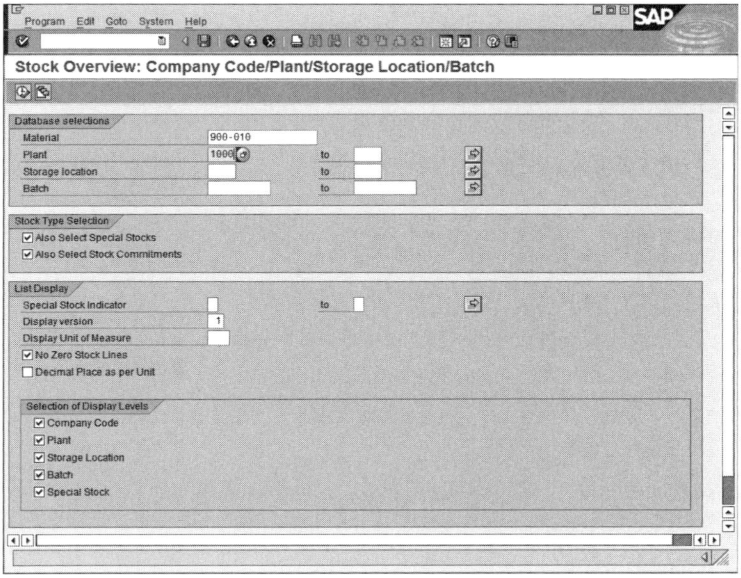

FIGURE 5.86   Displaying stock overview

You must enter the material and plant details in the **Stock Overview: Company Code/Plant/Storage Location/Batch** screen. In our example, we have entered DPC2 as material and 1000 as plant. Now, after entering the details, click the **Execute** icon ( ). The **Stock Overview: Basic List** screen appears as shown in Figure 5.87.

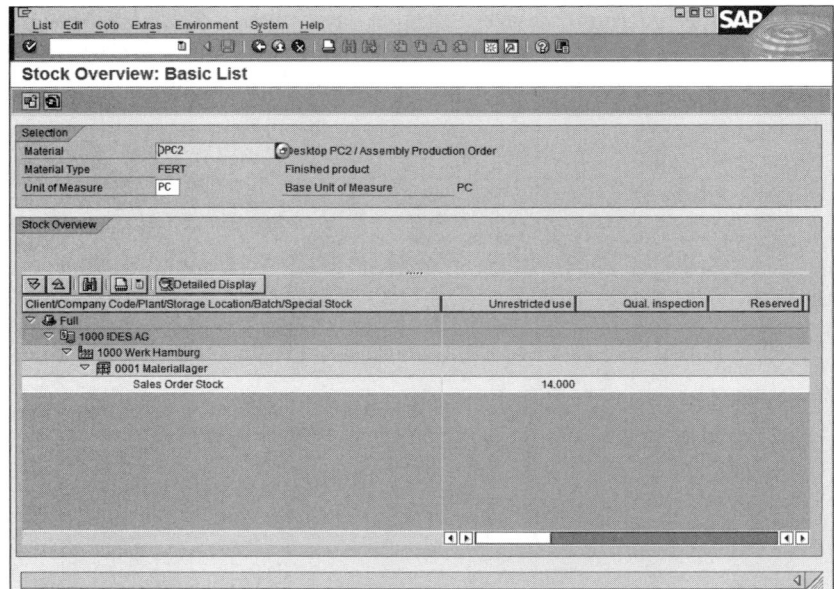

FIGURE 5.87   Displaying the Stock Overview: Basic List screen

Figure 5.87 shows the stock overview of the DPC2 material.
Now, let's summarize this chapter.

SUMMARY

This chapter described how the availability check of products can be performed on the basis of the ATP logic, product allocation, and rules. Apart from these three approaches to availability check, the concept of transfer requirements has also been discussed in the chapter, focusing the discussion on individual and collective requirements. Moreover, the chapter also explored the various types of contracts, such as quantity, value, service and maintenance, and master contract, which serve as the basis for all other contracts. Toward the end of the chapter, the process of scheduling agreements and consignment stock was discussed.

The next chapter discusses the shipment, delivery, and warehouse management process in the SD module.

Chapter 6
Shipment, Delivery, and Warehouse Management

If you need information on:	See page:
Exploring the Shipment Process	260
Working with the Delivery Process	274
Exploring Warehouse Management	319
Implementing the Packing Process	329
Implementing the Returnable Packaging Process	333
Determining Routes for Transportation	335

Shipping and delivery of goods is one of the many functions managed by the Sales and Distribution (SD) module of SAP®. As you know, a sales order is generated when a customer places an order for the required goods. The ordered goods are then assembled and packed in a warehouse before being sent to the customer. The location from where the packed items are dispatched is known as the shipping point, and the process of dispatching the packed items is known as shipping. Depending upon various factors, such as distance between the departure and destination points and change in the mode of transport, there can be one or more shipping points. After the goods reach the final shipping point, they are dispatched for their respective destinations. This process of transferring goods from the final shipping point to the customer's destination is known as the delivery process.

The SD module facilitates the shipping, delivery, and warehouse management processes in the mySAP™ ERP system. In the SD module, the sales order information, such as the quantity of goods ordered by the customer, is retrieved to create a delivery document. After creating the delivery document, the shipping process begins with the dispatch of goods to one or more shipping points. The delivery document helps manage the delivery and warehouse processes, including picking and confirming the quantity of goods, packing the materials, and planning and monitoring the transport.

In this chapter, you learn about the shipment process, which describes the inbound and outbound shipment of goods. In addition, you learn about different types of shipment, such as individual and collective shipments. Apart from the shipment process, this chapter also explores the delivery and warehouse management processes. Toward the end of the chapter, you learn how to implement the returnable packaging process in the SAP SD module and determine the modes of transportation for shipping goods. Now, let's explore the shipment process.

EXPLORING THE SHIPMENT PROCESS

Shipment refers to the process of transporting goods from one place to another. The company that issues the goods can be either a manufacturer of raw materials or a finished product exporter. If the issuing goods are raw materials, they are delivered from the warehouse of the manufacturing company to the premises of the receiving company. On the other hand, when the goods being issued are finished products, the goods are delivered from a manufacturing company to the customer.

Let's now explore the different ways of shipping goods.

Ways of Shipping

The goods can be shipped in different ways and can be categorized as follows:

- **Inbound**—Transports the goods from a vendor to a plant or from a customer to the plant in case the product delivered to the customer is rejected because of any specific valid reason.
- **Outbound**—Transports the goods from a plant to a customer.
- **For Stock Transfer**—Transports the goods from one plant to another.

Figure 6.1 shows the three ways in which goods can be shipped.

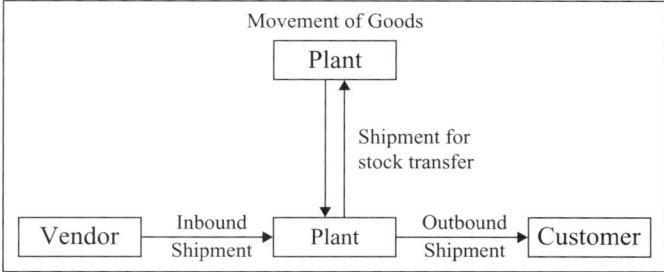

FIGURE 6.1 Displaying different ways of shipment

After discussing various ways of shipment, let's now explore the inbound and outbound shipment processes to understand the shipment process in detail.

Inbound Shipment Process

The inbound shipment process is an important part of the procurement process, which is related to the Material Management (MM) module. First of all, a purchase order is generated that includes all the details and the specifications of the product that needs to be purchased. Next, an inbound delivery document is created in the mySAP ERP system using the reference number of the purchase order. The inbound delivery document is required to implement the inbound shipment process. During this process, an inbound delivery notice document is created, which is used to confirm the inbound delivery by a vendor. Figure 6.2 shows the flow of inbound shipment process.

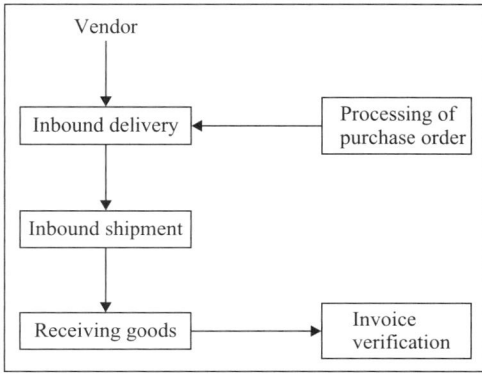

FIGURE 6.2 Inbound shipment process

Outbound Shipment Process

The outbound shipment process is the reverse of the inbound shipment process, where finished goods are transported from a company to the customer's destination. The process of outbound shipment starts with the processing of the associated sales order, which leads to the creation of the outbound delivery document. In addition, the documents containing the shipping details, such as shipping point, modes of transport, and shipping types are also created. The outbound delivery document serves as the basis for the implementation of the outbound shipment process. Finally, the issuing goods are posted in the book of accounts, and their bills are generated.

Figure 6.3 shows the flow of the outbound shipment process.

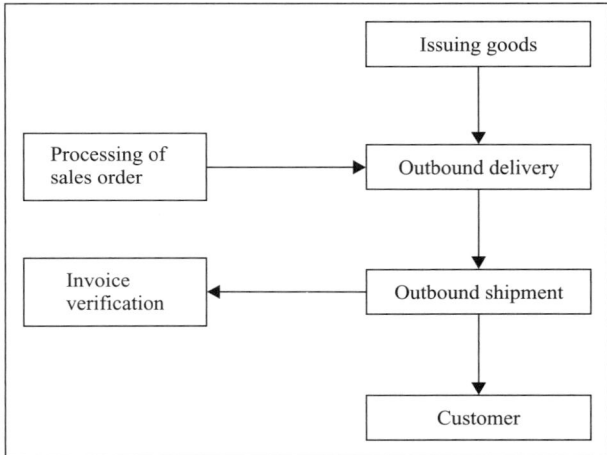

FIGURE 6.3 Outbound shipment process

The receiving party needs to provide the following details to the sending party so that the goods are delivered on the due date, on time, and at the appropriate location:

- **Address**—Refers to the address where goods need to be delivered.
- **Receiving Time**—Refers to the ideal time for sending or receiving the goods.

- **Contact Person**—Specifies the authorized personnel to receive the goods.
- **Notification**—Refers to the information that is sent to the receiving party about the dispatch or delivery of the product.
- **Postage**—Specifies the cost of the postage of goods.
- **Customs**—Specifies the details of the custom duties, in case the goods are being shipped outside the country.
- **Delivery**—Specifies the guidelines regarding the delivery of the goods.
- **Unloading**—Specifies the rules for unloading the goods.

Let's now explore the different types of shipments.

Exploring Different Types of Shipments

The shipments can be divided into various categories based on various factors, such as quantity of goods, production types, modes of transportation, number of shipping or destination points, and shipping types.

These are the shipment categories:

- Individual shipment
- Collective shipment
- Transportation chain

Let's explore each of these shipment categories in detail.

Individual Shipment

A shipment that has a single departure point and a destination point is referred to as an individual shipment. Usually, only one consignment of items is sent in this type of shipment.

The individual shipment category is characterized in the following ways:

- A collection of one or more inbound or outbound deliveries
- Single point of departure
- Single point of destination
- One mode of transport
- A single shipment document

Figure 6.4 depicts the concept of individual shipment.

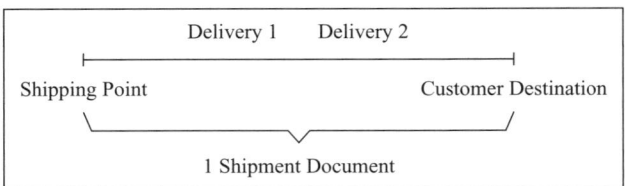

FIGURE 6.4 Displaying individual shipment

According to the customer preference, individual shipment is carried out in order to do the following:

- Process the delivery in a short span of time
- Transport sensitive items, such as glassware, chemicals, crackers, and petroleum products
- Minimize the risk of damage that can occur in case of an accident
- Maintain a tight vigilance on the delivery process

After understanding the concept of individual shipment, let's explore how to implement it in the mySAP ERP system.

Navigate the following menu path to configure individual shipment in the mySAP ERP system:

Menu Path

SAP menu > Logistics > Logistics Execution > Transportation > Transportation Planning > Create > VT01N-Single Documents

Figure 6.5 shows the navigated menu path in the **SAP Easy Access** screen.

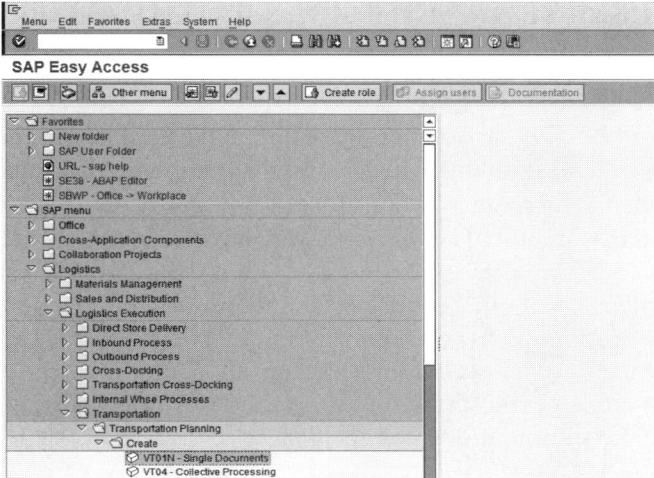

FIGURE 6.5 Displaying the menu path for individual shipment configuration

The **Create Shipment: Initial Screen** appears as shown in Figure 6.6.

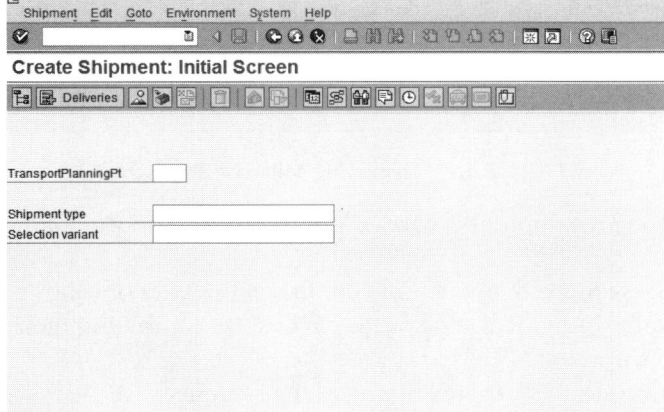

FIGURE 6.6 Displaying the Create Shipment: Initial Screen

The **Create Shipment: Initial Screen** is used to enter the initial shipment details for an individual shipment.

Collective Shipment

A shipment having one or more departure and destination points is referred to as the collective shipment. However, only one mode of transportation is used in this type of shipment.

Collective shipment is characterized in the following ways:

- A collection of one or more inbound or outbound deliveries
- One or more points of departure
- One or more points of destination
- One mode of transport
- A single shipment document

Figure 6.7 shows the concept of collective shipment.

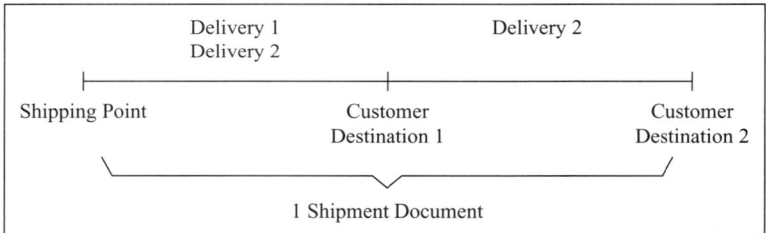

FIGURE 6.7 **Displaying collective shipment**

Collective shipment is carried out in order to do the following:

- Process more than one delivery in a short span of time
- Reduce individual transportation cost by combining more than one shipment
- Reduce the risk of unshipped delivery items
- Increase the revenue with the processing of multiple orders at a time

After exploring the collective shipment, let's now discuss how to implement it in the mySAP ERP system.

Navigate the following menu path to configure collective shipment in the mySAP ERP system:

Menu Path

SAP menu > Logistics > Logistics Execution > Transportation > Transportation Planning > Create > VT014-Collective Processing

Figure 6.8 shows the navigated menu path in the **SAP Easy Access** screen.

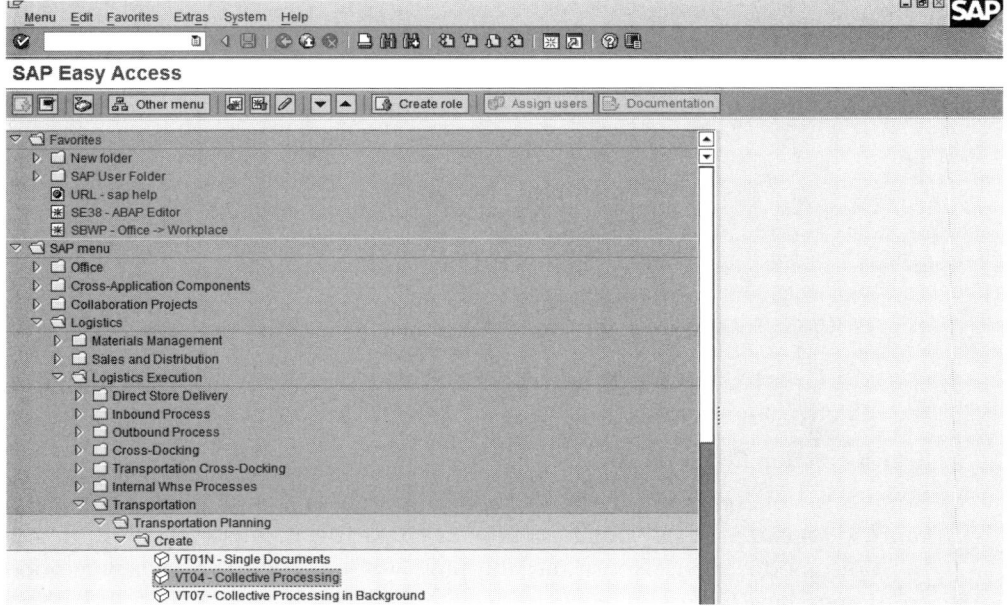

© SAP AG. All rights reserved.

FIGURE 6.8 Displaying the menu path to configure collective shipment

The **Create shipments in collective proc.** screen appears as shown in Figure 6.9.

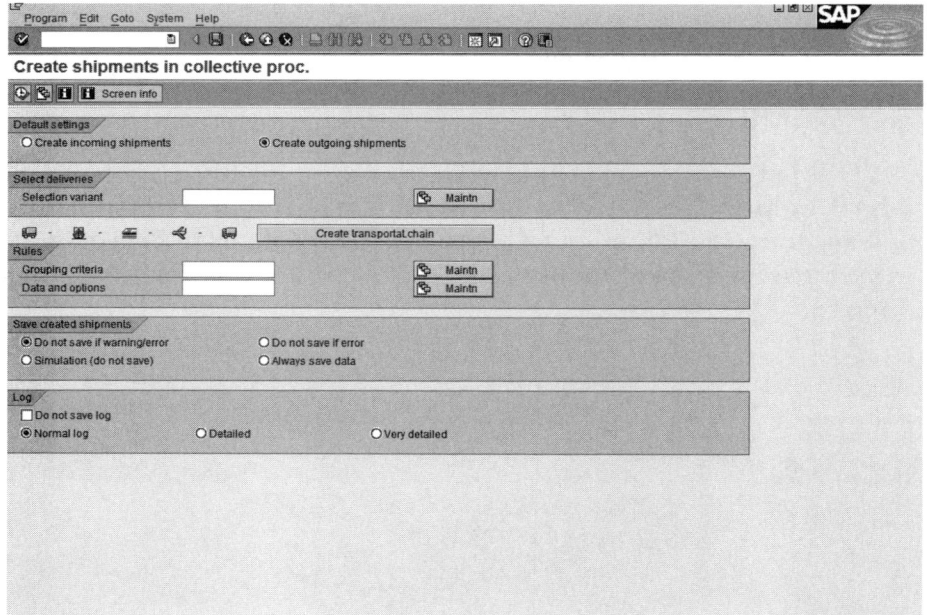

FIGURE 6.9 Displaying the Create shipments in collective proc. screen

The **Create shipments in collective proc.** screen stores the details related to collective shipment.

Transportation Chain

Similar to collective shipment, transportation chain shipment also has one or more departure and destination points. However, in this type of shipment, multiple modes of transport and shipping types are used to transport goods from one place to another.

Transportation chain shipment is characterized in the following ways:

- A collection of one or more inbound or outbound deliveries
- One or more points of departure
- One or more points of destination

- Two or more modes of transport
- Multiple shipment documents

Figure 6.10 shows the concept of transportation chain in shipment.

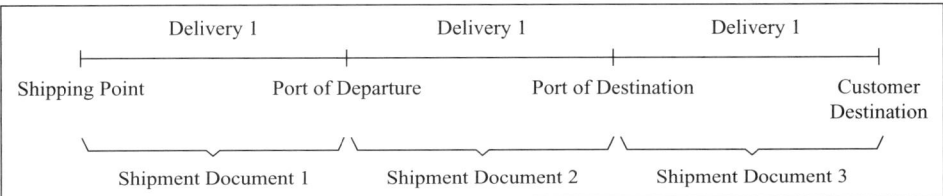

FIGURE 6.10 **Displaying transportation chain in shipment**

Now, let's discuss how to display the details of a shipping document.

Exploring a Shipping Document

A shipping document contains all the necessary information and details required to transport the goods from one place to another. The shipping document includes the following details:

- **Means of Transport**—Specifies the transportation details, such as weight and quantity of the goods allowed in a particular means of transport, details of the driver, and time of travel.
- **Service Agents**—Specifies the information about the service agents, such as forwarding agents or customs agents, who are involved in the transportation process.
- **Deadlines**—Specifies the planned as well as the actual date and time by which all activities related to the transportation of the goods must be completed.
- **Status**—Specifies the current status of the shipping activities in the shipping document. For example, when the planning activities for a shipping document are completed, the status in

the shipment document is set as **Planned**. Consequently, when the status is set as **Planned**, no planning activities can be further performed for this shipment document. The color of the light icon in the SAP Graphical User Interface (GUI) indicates the overall status of the shipment document.

Table 6.1 lists the various colors of the light icon and their respective interpretation.

Color of the Light Icon	Description
Red	Indicates that the transportation planning is complete.
Yellow	Indicates that the loading at the plant has either started or is complete.
Green	Indicates that the shipment has been processed.
No color	Indicates that no planning activities have been performed.

TABLE 6.1 Colors of the light icon for shipment document

- **Tendering Status**—Provides the updated status of a shipment through the Internet.
- **Route**—Specifies country-specific restrictions regarding the total weight of the shipment allowed on a particular route. If the total weight of goods to be shipped exceeds the allowed weight on a particular route, the mySAP ERP system issues a warning message. The weight of the goods to be shipped is then reduced accordingly to map the allowed weight.
- **Texts**—Specifies any essential information for smooth performance of the transportation process.
- **Output**—Specifies the types of output that have been set for transportation in the **SAP Customizing** screen. You can set the output types only if the condition records for these output types are already created.

- **Dangerous Goods**—Defines the legal requirements to transport dangerous goods. For example, you can indicate whether the transportation of certain materials, such as wine and armaments, are allowed in certain modes of transport.

A shipment document is used for the following purposes:

- Combining one or more deliveries into inbound or outbound shipment
- Specifying the shipment stages that include legs, border crossing points, and load transfer points
- Assigning goods to the units that handle the shipping activities in the mySAP ERP system
- Assigning service agents in the mySAP ERP system
- Specifying the deadlines while planning the transportation process
- Recording the time actually taken in the transportation process
- Specifying the type of output required for transportation, such as shipping papers
- Defining the text related to the transportation of goods in the mySAP ERP system

Note: You will read more about shipment stages in the *Exploring the Stages of Shipment* section of this chapter.

Let's perform the following steps to display the details related to a shipment document:

1. Double-click **SAP Menu > Logistics > Logistics Execution >Transportation > Transportation Planning > Change > VT03N-Display**, as shown in Figure 6.11.

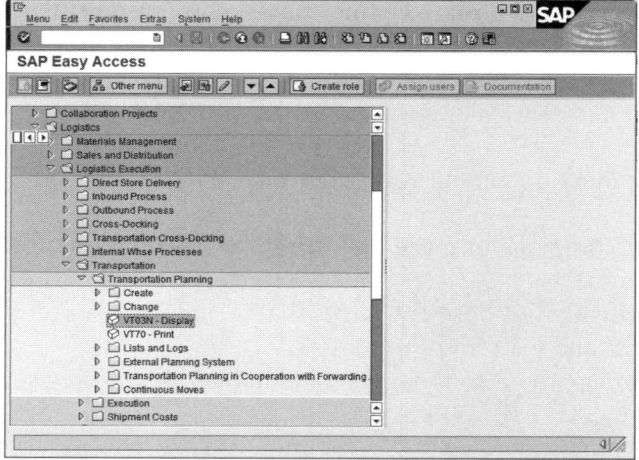

© SAP AG. All rights reserved.

FIGURE 6.11   Displaying menu path to display a shipping document

The **Display Shipment: Initial Screen** appears (Figure 6.12).

2. Enter a shipment number in the **Shipment Number** field of the **Display Shipment: Initial Screen** to display the details of the shipment document. In our case, we have entered 1245 as the shipment number, as shown in Figure 6.12.

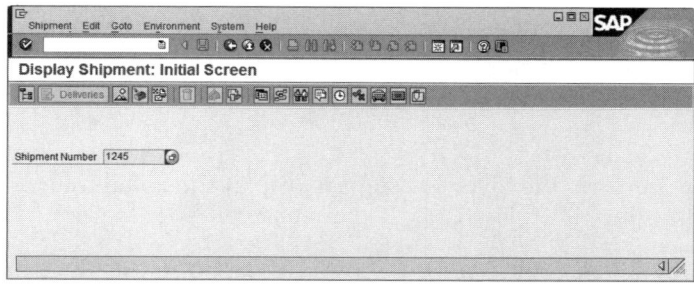

© SAP AG. All rights reserved.

FIGURE 6.12   Displaying the Display Shipment: Initial Screen

3. Press the **Enter** key to continue the process.

The **Indiv.Shipmt-Road 1245 Display: Overview** screen appears as shown in Figure 6.13.

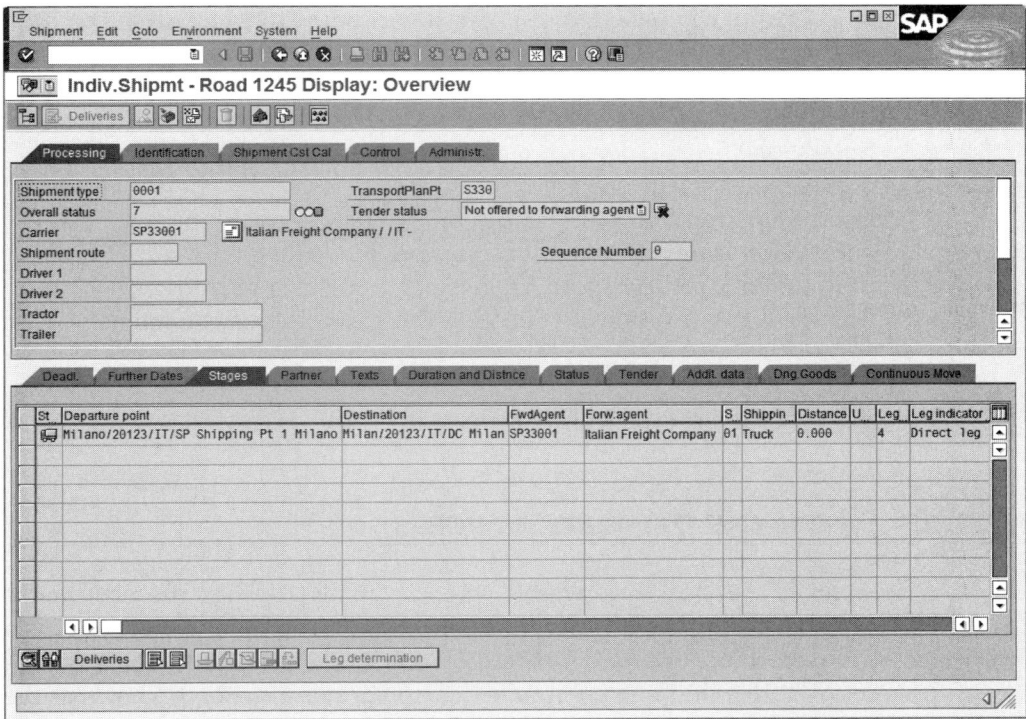

FIGURE 6.13 Displaying the Indiv.Shipmt-Road 1245 Display: Overview screen

Figure 6.13 shows the shipping document for the individual shipment, displaying all the details, such as mode of transport, departure point, destination point, and the forwarding agent of the shipment. However, if you need to edit the details of a shipment, you can do it in the Change mode.

Let's now discuss the stages involved in the shipment of goods.

Exploring the Stages of Shipment

A shipment sometimes needs to pass through various stages before being delivered to its final destination. The current stage of a shipment can be identified based on the various departure and destination points, such as shipping or loading point, transportation connection point, and customer location. A proper knowledge of these stages helps in calculating the total cost of the shipment. The following are the different types of shipment stages:

- **Leg**—Specifies the departure and destination points of a shipment along with the entire route.
- **Load Transfer Point**—Specifies the points where a shipment is unloaded from one means of transport and loaded onto another means of transport, for instance from a ship to a truck.
- **Border Crossing Point**—Specifies the point where a shipment crosses the border.

Let's now explore the delivery process in detail.

WORKING WITH THE DELIVERY PROCESS

A product is said to be delivered when it finally reaches the customer's destination. The shipment process usually ends at a shipping point, such as a harbor, a post office, or a local distribution office. The process of delivering the product from this shipping point to the customer's destination is known as the delivery process.

Based on the movement of goods, the delivery process is categorized as inbound and outbound. In the inbound delivery process, the goods are received by the company either from a vendor or a customer and are posted as goods received in the books of accounts. In the outbound delivery process, the goods are sent to the customer and are posted as goods issued.

In the mySAP ERP system, a delivery document is created using a reference to either a sales document or to an inbound return sales document. The creation of a delivery document signifies the beginning of the delivery process.

Let's explore the following topics to better understand the delivery process:

- Delivery document
- Categories of delivery items

- Shipping points for transportation
- Picking process
- Delivery block process
- Delivery split process

Now, first of all, let's discuss how to configure a delivery document.

Configuring a Delivery Document

The delivery document, similar to a sales order, has a header as well as an item structure. A delivery document deals with delivery functions; for example, the delivery document uses the outbound delivery split function to divide an outbound delivery into various shipments.

Note: A delivery can be split into two or more shipments if the number of goods to be delivered is large. This depends on various factors, such as mode of transportation and number of goods to be delivered or as per customer preferences.

The delivery document is created with reference to one of the following documents:

- Sales document order
- Sales document scheduling agreement
- Sales return

Some standard delivery documents are available in the mySAP ERP system:

- Standard delivery (LF)
- Delivery without reference (LO)
- Returns delivery (LR)
- Returned delivery from a purchase order (RL)
- Delivery for stock replenishment (NL)

Perform the following steps to configure a delivery document in the mySAP ERP system:

1. Select **SAP Customizing Implementation Guide > Logistics Execution > Shipping > Deliveries > Define Delivery Types**, as shown in Figure 6.14.

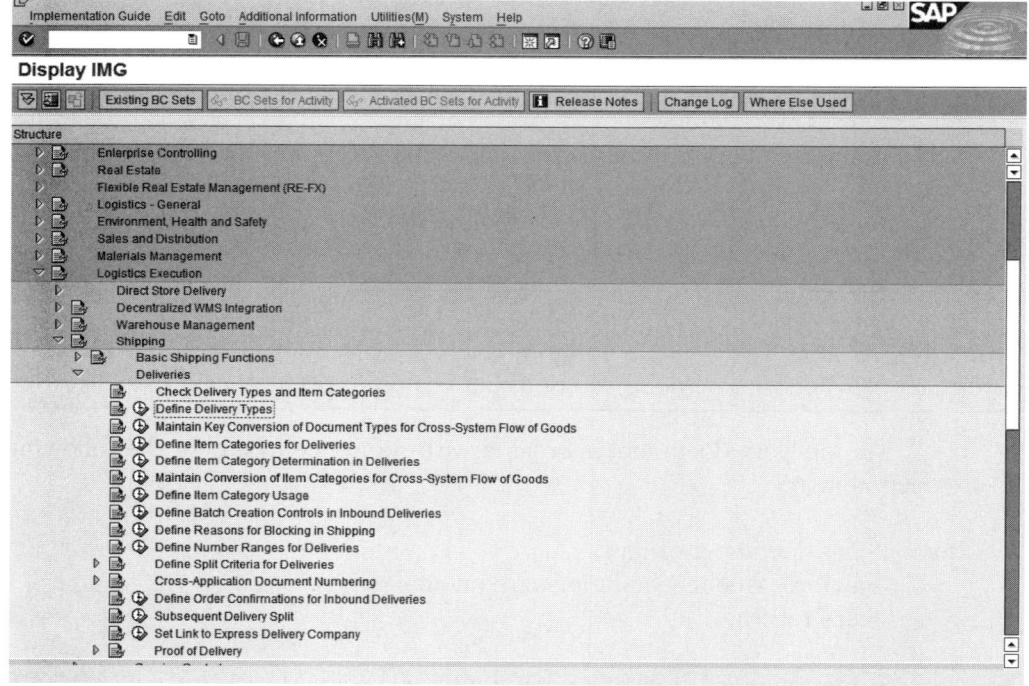

© SAP AG. All rights reserved.

FIGURE 6.14 Displaying the menu path to configure a delivery document

2. Click the **IMG Activity** icon (⊕) beside the **Define Delivery Types** activity in the **Display IMG** screen. The **Change View "Delivery types": Overview** screen appears as shown in Figure 6.15.

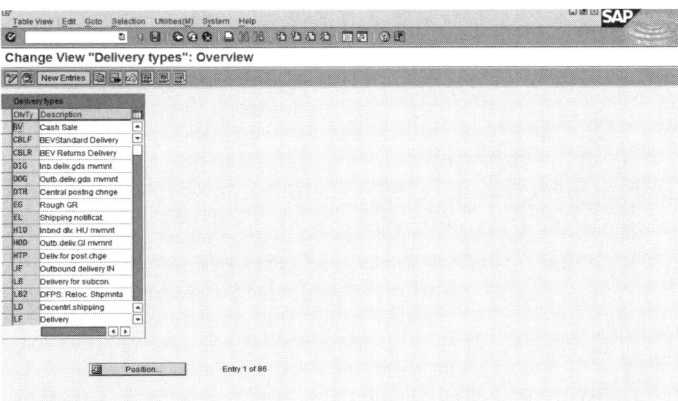

© SAP AG. All rights reserved.

FIGURE 6.15 Displaying the Change View "Delivery types": Overview screen

You can view different delivery types and their descriptions in the **Change View "Delivery types": Overview** screen.

3. Click the **New Entries** button to create a new delivery type. The **New Entries: Details of Added Entries** screen appears as shown in Figure 6.16.

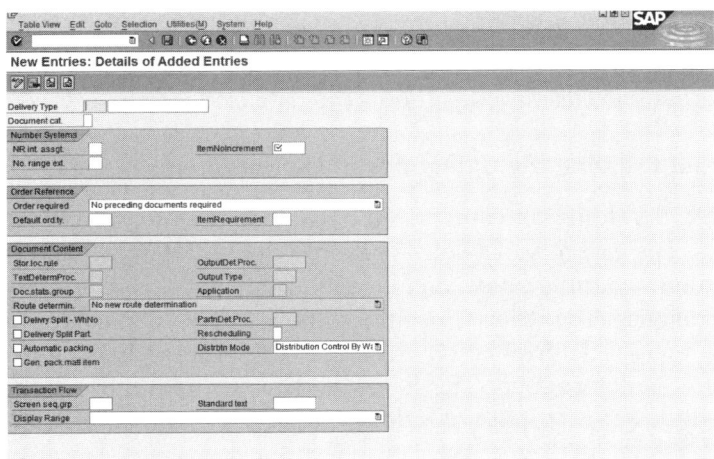

© SAP AG. All rights reserved.

FIGURE 6.16 Displaying New Entries: Details of Added Entries screen

To create a new delivery document, you need to provide the following details in the **New Entries: Details of Added Entries** screen:

- **Delivery Type**—Specifies the document types associated with the delivery of a product.
- **Number Systems**—Specifies the number of items to be delivered. You can define the number range for the delivery document type by providing a **Number Range Object** while creating a new delivery type, by navigating through the following menu path:

Menu Path

SAP Customizing Implementation Guide > Logistics Execution > Shipping > Deliveries > Define Number Ranges for Deliveries

- **Order Reference**—Creates a delivery document without the reference of a sales document type by specifying an arbitrary sales document type in the **Default ord ty.** field.
- **Document Contents**—Specifies that the delivery process is carried out without referring to a sales order. The **Document Contents** section provides the information related to the warehouse and additional details, such as product specifications and delivery dates.
- **Transaction Flow**—Determines the sequence in which the screens are displayed and how the data is placed in a screen.

Determining and Creating the Categories of Delivery Items

The delivery items are categorized to provide better control over the delivery process. The category of a delivery item contains the information regarding the item, such as number, type, and location from where the item has to be picked up for delivery. To retrieve this information, you need to configure the delivery item categories determination process. In this process, first a source (document or entity) is determined. The following sources help retrieve the information of the different categories of delivery items:

- Order item
- Schedule line

Note: The categories of the delivered items can be created, modified, and changed in the mySAP ERP system.

If an order item or schedule line is used to determine the delivery item, the item category used in the sales order is copied in the delivery document. If the delivery item is independent of the sales order, the delivery item is determined by the delivery item category determination table, which is a standard table in the mySAP ERP system.

Let's first discuss how to configure the delivery item categories determination process and then create a new delivery item category.

Perform the following steps to configure the delivery item categories determination process:

1. Navigate the following menu path to determine the item category:

Menu Path

SAP Customizing Implementation Guide > Logistics Execution > Shipping > Deliveries > Define Item Category Determination in Deliveries

Figure 6.17 shows the **Display IMG** screen that appears after navigating the preceding menu path.

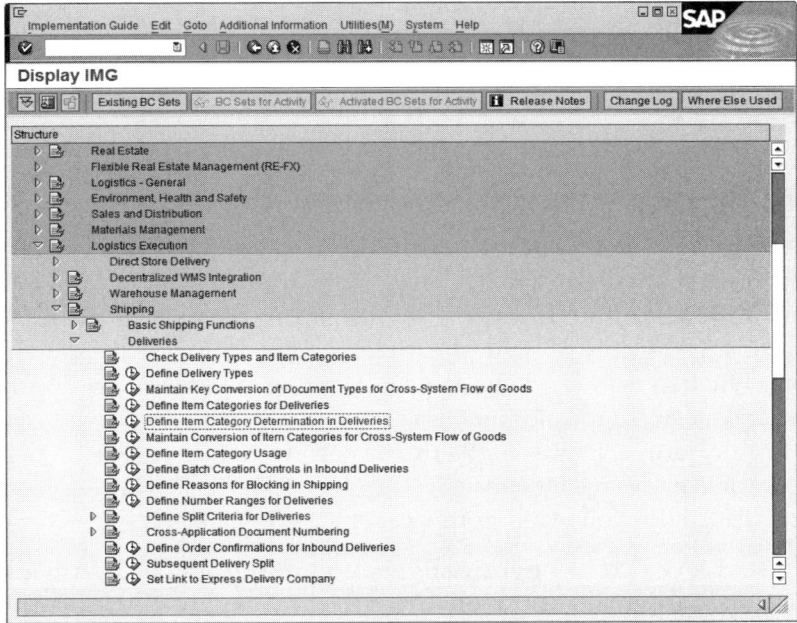

© SAP AG. All rights reserved.

FIGURE 6.17 Displaying the menu path for determination of delivery item categories

2. Click the **IMG Activity** icon (⊕) beside the **Define Item Category Determination in Deliveries** activity in the **Display IMG** screen. The **Change View "Delivery item category determination": Overview** screen appears as shown in Figure 6.18.

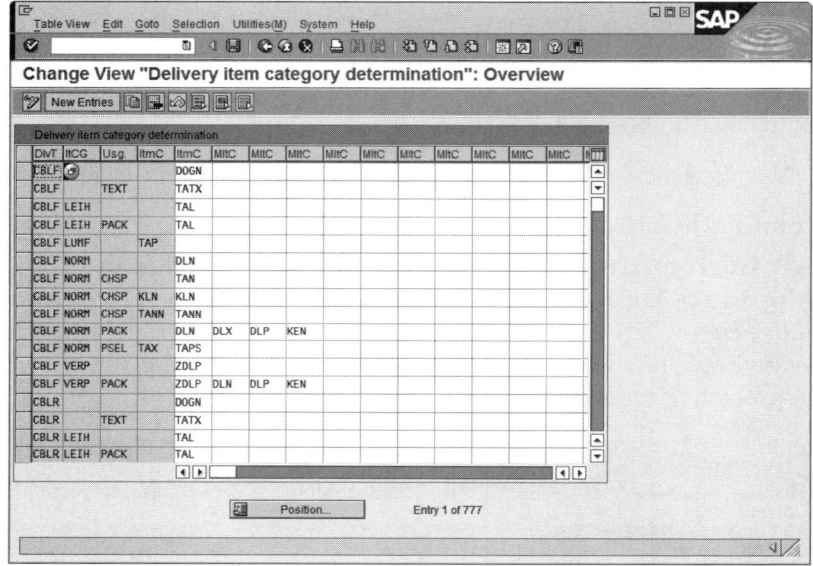

© SAP AG. All rights reserved.

FIGURE 6.18 Displaying the Change View "Delivery item category determination": Overview screen

Figure 6.18 shows the existing delivery item categories in the mySAP ERP system. You can create a new delivery item category by clicking the **New Entries** button (Figure 6.18) and entering the relevant details in the **New Entries: Overview of Added Entries** screen. In Figure 6.18, notice that the determination rule for delivery item category is followed by document type, item category group, and item usage.

After learning how to configure the delivery item categories, let's now create a new delivery item category.

Perform the following steps to create a new category of delivery items:

1. Select **SAP IMG > Logistics Execution > Shipping > Deliveries > Define Item Categories for Deliveries** in the **Display IMG** screen, as shown in Figure 6.19.

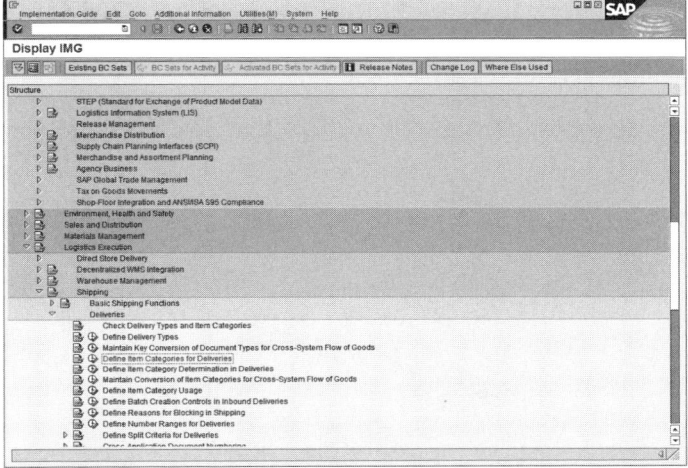

FIGURE 6.19 Displaying the menu path for defining delivery item categories

2. Click the **IMG Activity** icon (&) beside the **Define Item Categories for Deliveries** activity in the **Display IMG** screen. The **Change View "Delivery item categories": Overview** screen appears as shown in Figure 6.20.

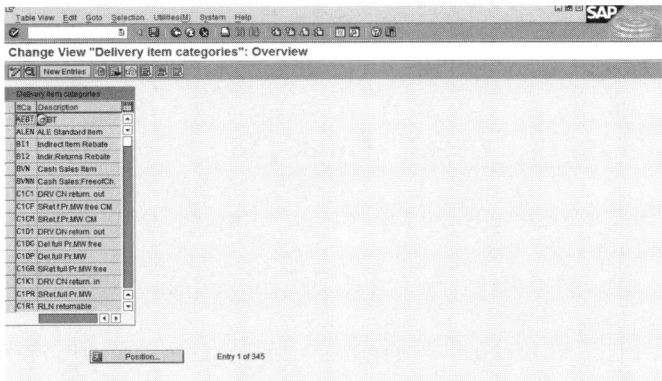

FIGURE 6.20 Displaying the Change View "Delivery item categories": Overview screen

Figure 6.20 shows the existing categories of delivery items.

3. Click the **New Entries** button to create new delivery categories for a particular item in the **Change View "Delivery item categories": Overview** screen (Figure 6.20).

The **New Entries: Details of Added Entries** screen appears as shown in Figure 6.21.

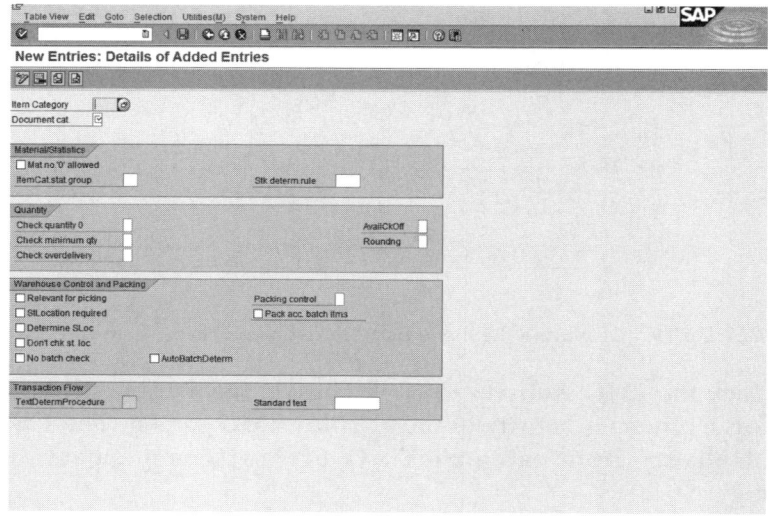

© SAP AG. All rights reserved.

FIGURE 6.21 Displaying the details for a new item category

A new item category is created by providing the details in the following sections of the **New Entries: Details of Added Entries** screen:

- **Item Category**—Specifies different items, such as a return or outbound delivery item.
- **Document Category**—Specifies the different types of delivery items.
- **Material Statistics**—Specifies additional information about the material statistics, such as material number and stock determination date.
- **Quantity**—Specifies the quantity of the material delivered to a particular customer.
- **Warehouse Control and Packing**—Specifies information related to the picking and storage locations. You can select the

Relevant for picking check box for an item in order to display it in the picking list. The checked item indicates that the item can now be transferred to the warehouse.
- **Transaction Flow**—Specifies a name for a group of text types, such as standard header and standard pricing.

4. Enter the required details in the **New Entries: Details of Added Entries** screen and click the **Save** icon (🖫) on the standard toolbar to save the entered details.

Figure 6.22 shows the details of the new item category, C1D1, in the mySAP ERP system.

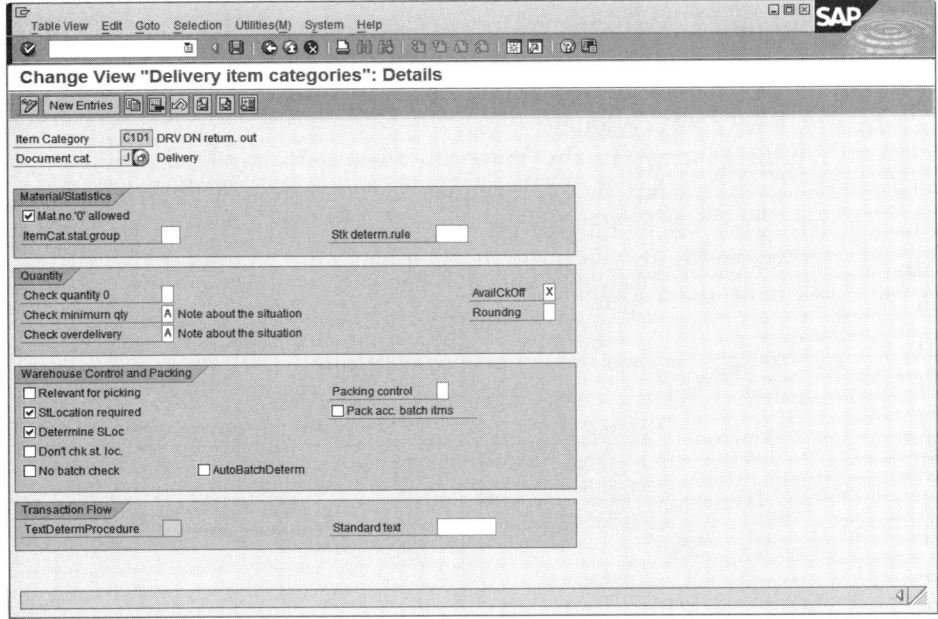

© SAP AG. All rights reserved.

FIGURE 6.22 Displaying the delivery item category details for the C1D1 item code

> **Note:** You can display or change the details of an item category by selecting it in the **Change View "Delivery item categories": Overview** screen and clicking the **Display/Change** icon (🖉) (Figure 6.20).

After configuring the delivery items determination process and creating the delivery item, let's now discuss how to determine the shipping point for the goods.

Working with Shipping Points

A shipping point is either a departure or a destination point for the goods. In other words, it is the location from where goods are sent or received in a company's plant. A plant can receive goods from more than one shipping point; however, at one instance, it can deliver goods only from a single shipping point.

A shipping point can be determined based on the following factors:

- **Shipping Conditions from the Customer Master Table**—Provides the delivery details from the customer master table. The agreement for urgent delivery of products is finalized based on these delivery details.
- **Loading Group in the Material Master Record**—Specifies the loading group that determines the medium to load the goods, such as crane or truck.
- **Delivery Plant**—Determines the plant from where the delivery of the product originates.

Figure 6.23 displays the process to determine a shipping point based on a combination of factors:

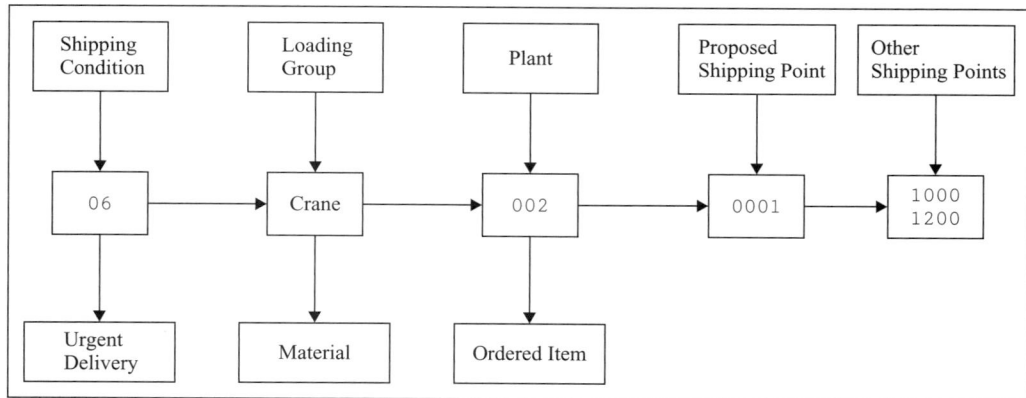

FIGURE 6.23 **Displaying determination of shipping point**

Figure 6.23 displays the determination of the 0001 shipping point based on a combination of factors; that is shipping condition, loading group, and plant.

Perform the following steps to define a new shipping point:

1. Select **SAP Customizing Implementation Guide > Enterprise Structure > Definition > Logistics Execution > Define copy, delete, check shipping point**, as shown in Figure 6.24.

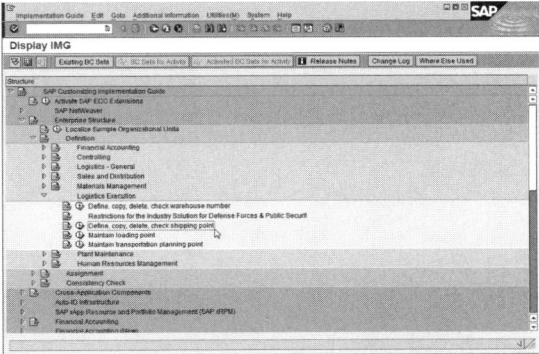

© SAP AG. All rights reserved.

FIGURE 6.24 Displaying the menu path for defining shipping points

2. Click the **IMG Activity** icon (⊕) beside the **Define, copy, delete, check shipping point** activity in the **Display IMG** screen. The **Choose Activity** dialog box appears as shown in Figure 6.25.

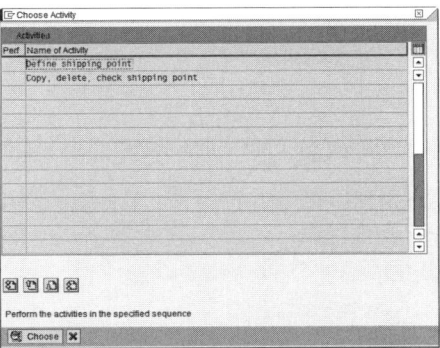

© SAP AG. All rights reserved.

FIGURE 6.25 Displaying the Choose Activity dialog box

3. Select the **Define shipping point** activity and click the **Choose** button to define a shipping point.

   The **Change View "Shipping Points": Overview** screen appears as shown in Figure 6.26.

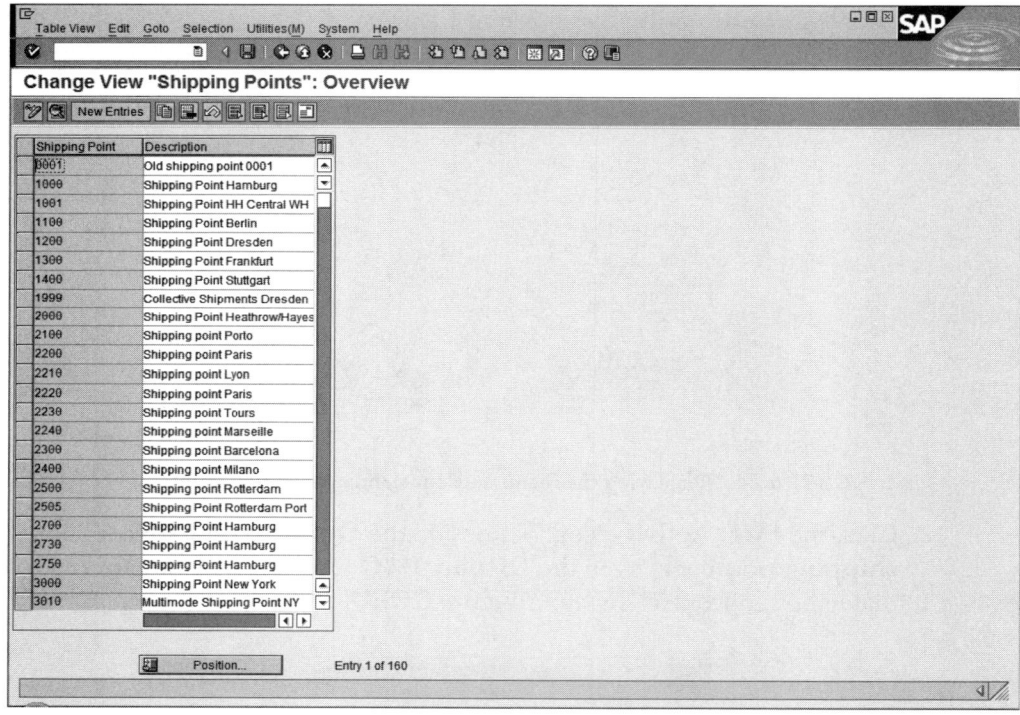

© SAP AG. All rights reserved.

FIGURE 6.26 Displaying the Change View "Shipping Points": Overview screen

4. Click the **New Entries** button in the **Change View "Shipping Points": Overview** screen (Figure 6.26). The **New Entries: Details of Added Entries** screen appears as shown in Figure 6.27.

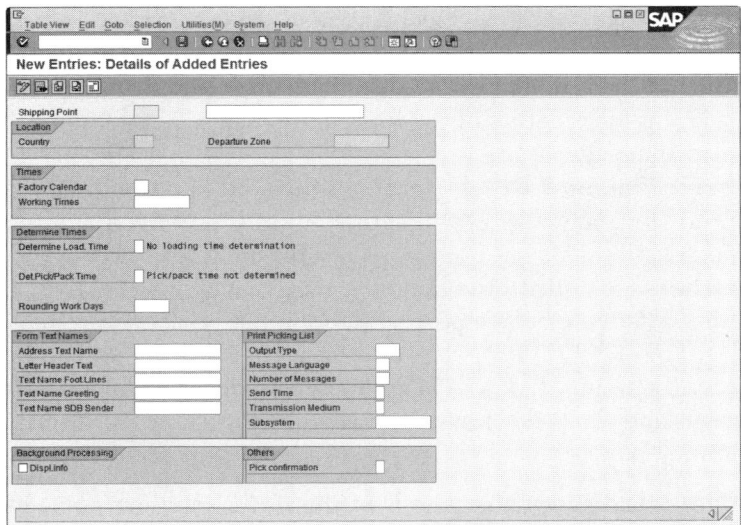

FIGURE 6.27 Displaying the New Entries: Details of Added Entries screen

Figure 6.27 shows the **New Entries: Details of Added Entries** screen, in which you need to enter the relevant details to create a new shipping point. A new shipping point is created by entering the details in the following sections of the **New Entries: Details of Added Entries** screen:

- **Shipping Point/Receiving Point**—Specifies a physical location; for instance, a warehouse where items are shipped or received.
- **Location**—Specifies the country and the departmental zone from where the delivery process begins. Different countries have different country keys, which are specified in the **Country** field.
- **Times**—Stores the timetable of working days according to the specified country key.
- **Determine Times**—Helps in determining whether the loading or picking time is defined.

- **Form Text Names**—Specifies the name for address, letter header, footer lines, greetings, and other relevant details.
- **Background Processing**—Contains the options to display relevant information in the form of messages, in addition to the error message.
- **Print Picking List**—Determines the kind of output to be produced, language in which the output is produced, number of copies produced, and other related information.
- **Others**—Confirms the quantity of items that need to be picked up for delivery before posting them in the book of accounts.

5. Enter the required details in the **New Entries: Details of Added Entries** screen and click the **Save** icon (🖫) on the standard toolbar to create a shipping point.

Figure 6.28 shows the details of the 0001 shipping point in the mySAP ERP system.

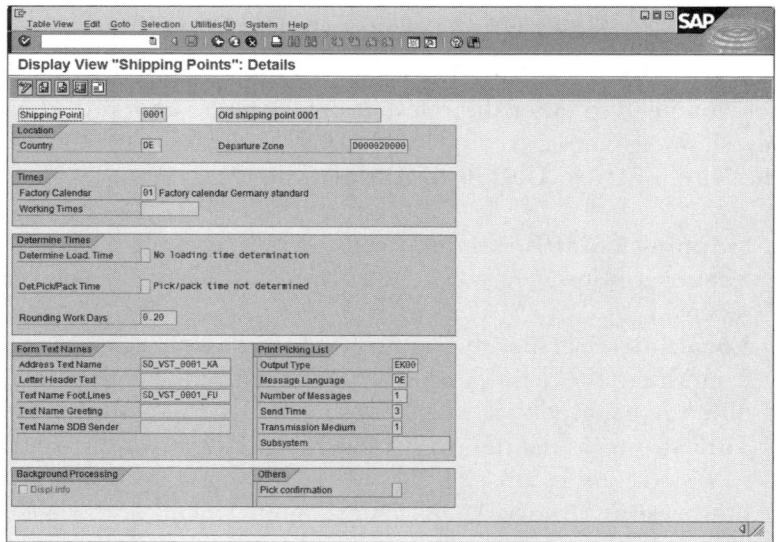

© SAP AG. All rights reserved.

FIGURE 6.28 Displaying the Display View "Shipping Points": Details screen

> **Note:** You can display or change the details of a shipping point by selecting a shipping code in the **Change View "Shipping Points": Overview** screen and clicking the **Display/Change** icon ( ) (Figure 6.26).

After creating a new shipping point, let's perform the following steps to determine and assign a shipping point to a specific delivery (through its assignment to a delivery plant):

1. Select **SAP Customizing Implementation Guide > Logistics Execution > Shipping > Basic Shipping Functions > Shipping Point and Goods Receiving Point Determination > Assign Shipping Points**, as shown in Figure 6.29.

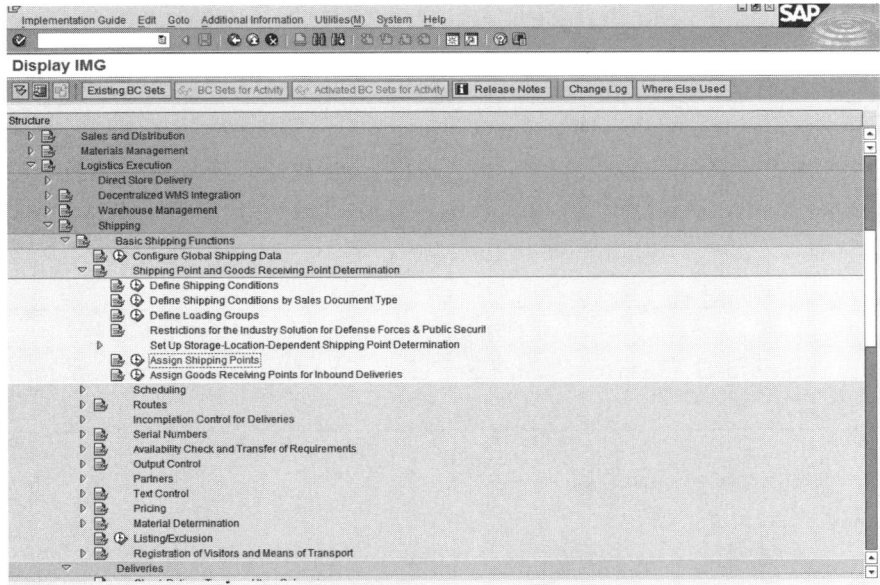

© SAP AG. All rights reserved.

FIGURE 6.29 Displaying the menu path for determination of shipping points

2. Click the **IMG Activity** icon ( ) beside the **Assign Shipping Points** activity in the **Display IMG** screen. The **Change View "Shipping Point Determination": Overview** screen appears as shown in Figure 6.30.

Chapter 6 Shipment, Delivery, and Warehouse Management

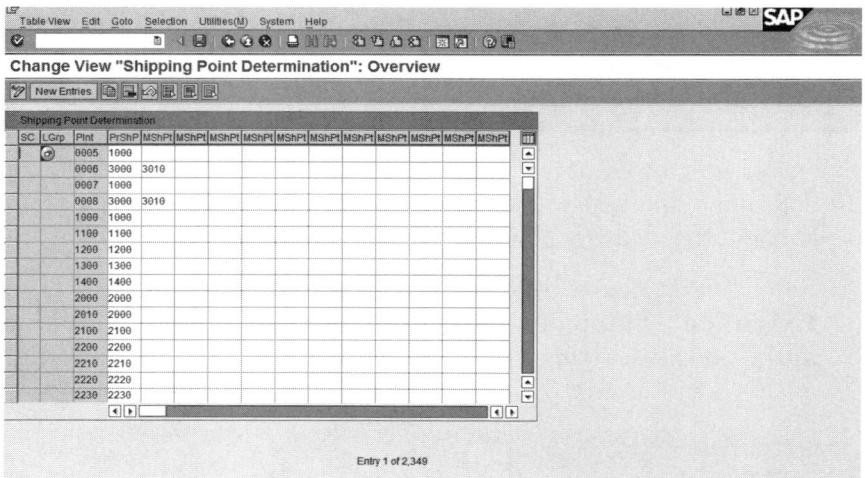

FIGURE 6.30   Displaying the Change View "Shipping Point Determination": Overview screen

Figure 6.30 shows that a shipping point is allocated on the basis of the combination of shipping conditions and loading group factors.

Let's now configure a shipping point based on the following factors:

> **Note:** You can copy, modify, or delete an existing shipping point by selecting the **Copy, delete, check shipping point activity** in the **Choose Activity** dialog box (Figure 6.25).

- Shipping conditions
- Loading groups
- Assignment of shipping points to delivery plants or a delivery plant

Defining Shipping Conditions

Shipping conditions are entered in the customer master table in the mySAP ERP system. Navigate the following menu path to define the shipping conditions:

Menu Path

SAP Customizing Implementation Guide > Logistics Execution > Shipping > Basic Shipping Functions > Shipping Point and Goods Receiving Point Determination > Define Shipping Conditions, as shown in Figure 6.31.

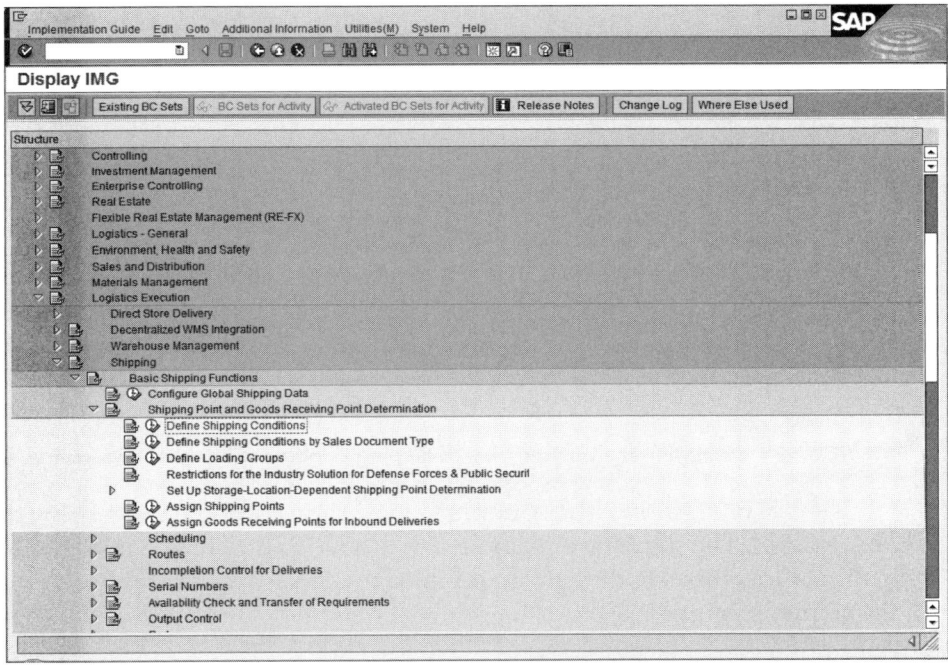

© SAP AG. All rights reserved.

FIGURE 6.31 Displaying the menu path to define a shipping condition

Click the **IMG Activity** icon (⊕) beside the **Define Shipping Conditions** activity in the **Display IMG** screen. The **Change View "Shipping Conditions": Overview** screen appears as shown in Figure 6.32.

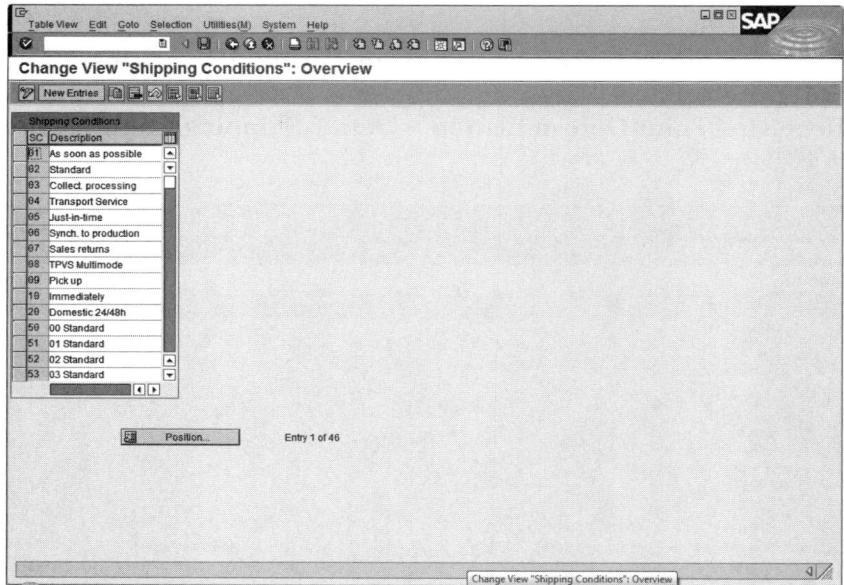

FIGURE 6.32 Displaying the Change View "Shipping Conditions": Overview screen

Figure 6.32 shows the shipping condition codes, followed by their descriptions. The shipping conditions are entered in the customer master table in the shipping screen; they are then copied to the sales document to determine the shipping point.

Defining a Loading Group

A loading group factor for the items to be delivered varies depending on the characteristics of the items, such as fragile, explosive, and heavy. Depending upon the loading factor, the items are grouped together and a single medium can be used to load those items. For instance, breakable items, such as glassware and chinaware, are grouped together because they need to be manually loaded. In other words, this is a process of grouping materials on the basis of their loading execution mode. Navigate the following menu path to define a loading group for a delivery item (Figure 6.32):

Menu Path

SAP Customizing Implementation Guide > Logistics Execution > Shipping > Basic Shipping Functions > Shipping Point and Goods Receiving Point Determination > Define Loading Groups

The navigated menu path is shown in the **Display IMG** screen (Figure 6.31).

Click the **IMG Activity** icon (⊕) to define a loading group. The **Change View "Routes: Loading Groups": Overview** screen appears as shown in Figure 6.33.

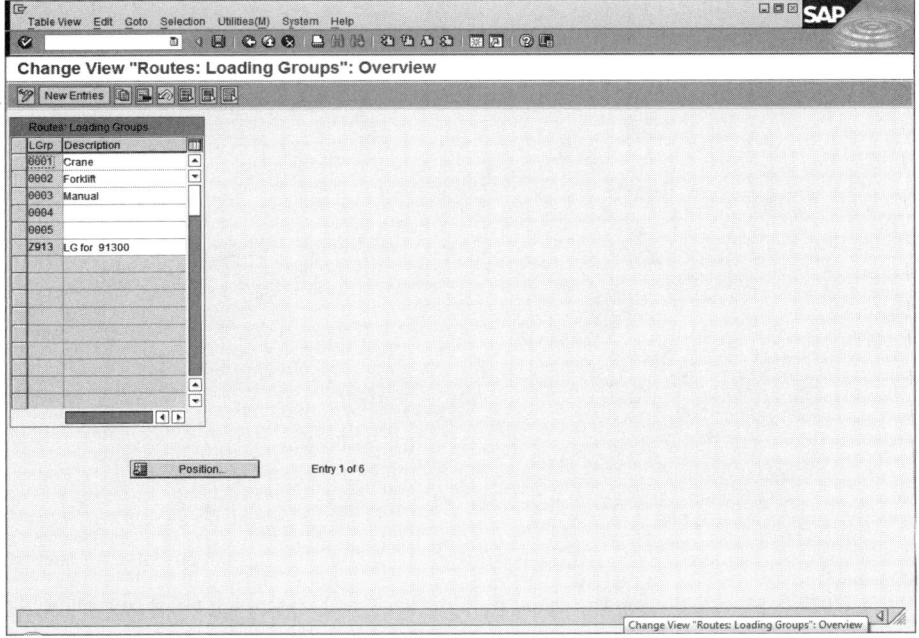

© SAP AG. All rights reserved.

FIGURE 6.33 Displaying the Change View "Routes: Loading Groups": Overview screen

Figure 6.33 shows the different loading groups, such as crane, forklift, and manual.

Assigning a Shipping Point to a Delivery Plant

Another important factor in determining the shipping point is to select the plant from where the goods are to be delivered. Navigate the following menu path to assign a shipping point to a plant:

Menu Path

SAP Customizing Implementation Guide > Enterprise Structure > Assignment > Logistics Execution > Assign shipping point to plant

Figure 6.34 shows the navigated menu path in the **Display IMG** screen.

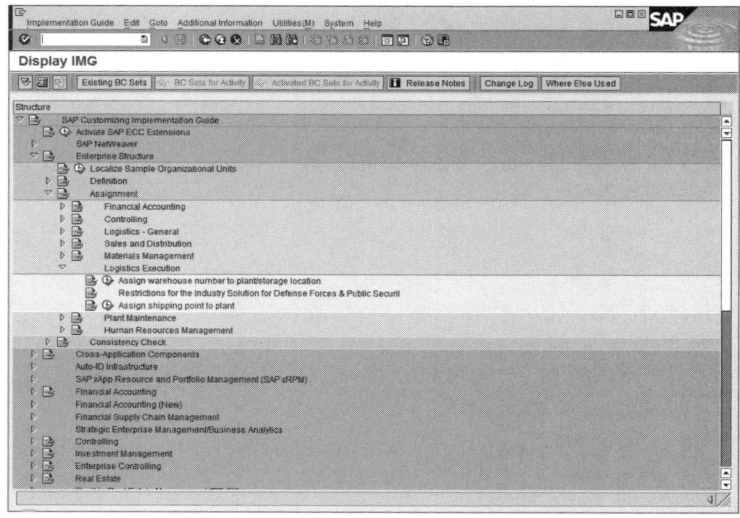

© SAP AG. All rights reserved.

FIGURE 6.34 Displaying the menu path for assigning a shipping point to a plant

Click the **IMG Activity** icon (☺) beside the **Assign shipping point to plant** activity in the **Display IMG** screen (Figure 6.34). The **Shipping Points-> Plants: Overview** screen appears as shown in Figure 6.35.

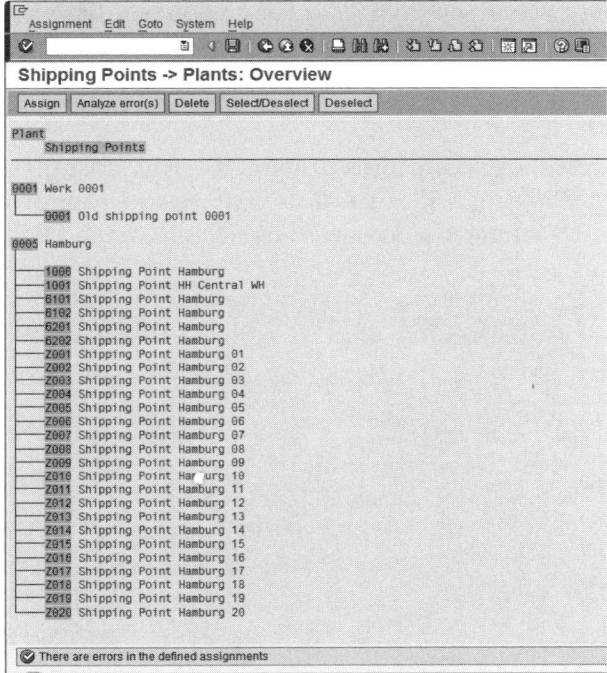

FIGURE 6.35 Displaying the Shipping Points->Plants: Overview screen

Figure 6.35 shows the shipping points followed by the names of the plants.

After determining the shipping point, you can assign the determined shipping point to a delivery. To assign a shipping point, select the shipping point and click the **Assign** button (Figure 6.35).

Let's now discuss the picking location determination activity.

Determining a Picking Location

A picking location refers to a place from where the goods ordered by a customer are picked to be transported to another place. For example, if the goods are loaded from a warehouse to deliver to a customer's destination, the warehouse is considered as the picking location.

Navigate the following menu path to configure a picking location:

Menu Path

SAP Customizing Implementation Guide > Logistics Execution > Shipping > Picking > Define Relevant Item Categories

Figure 6.36 shows the navigated menu path in the **Display IMG** screen.

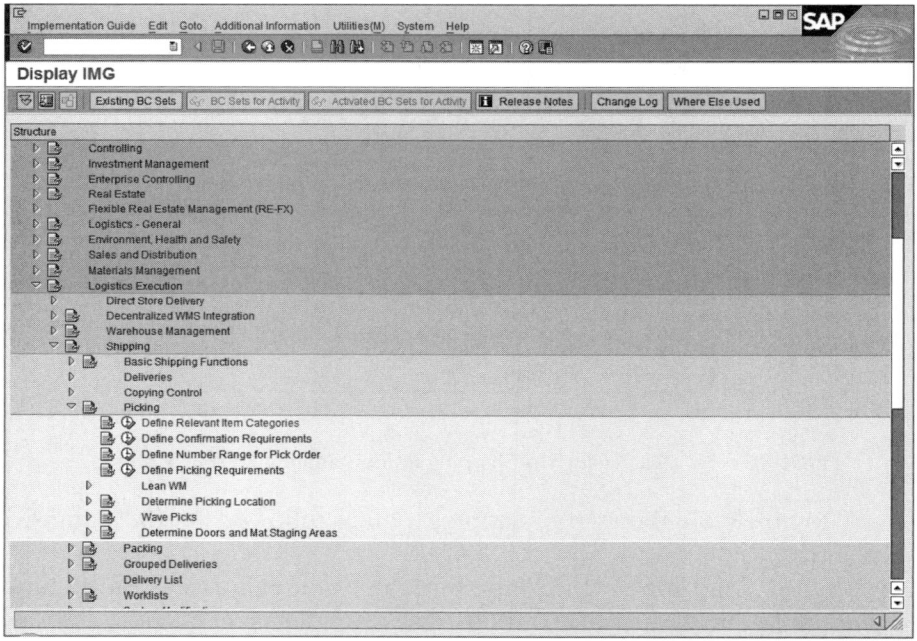

© SAP AG. All rights reserved.

FIGURE 6.36 Displaying the menu path for defining relevant item categories for picking

Click the **IMG Activity** icon (◉) beside the **Define Relevant Item Categories** activity in the **Display IMG** screen (Figure 6.36). The **Change View "Deliveries: Item categories - picking": Overview** screen appears as shown in Figure 6.37.

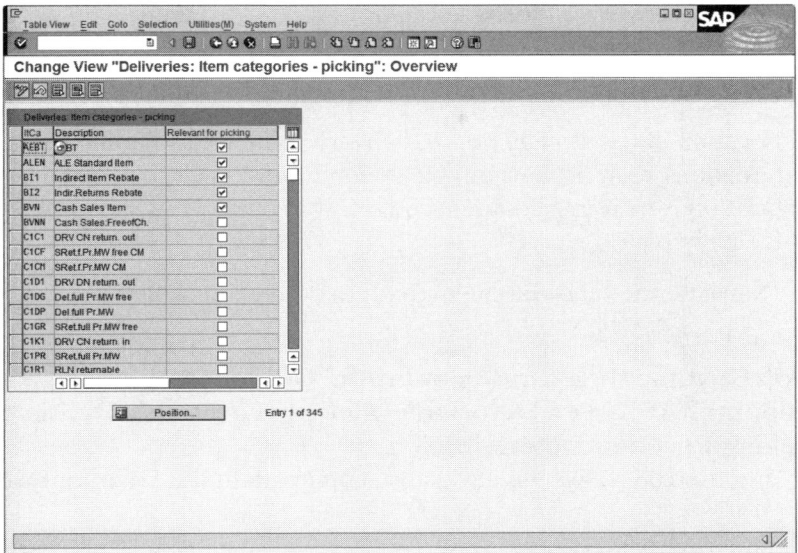

© SAP AG. All rights reserved.

FIGURE 6.37 Displaying the Change View "Deliveries: Item categories - picking": Overview screen

Figure 6.37 shows that the items within the selected item categories need to be picked.

The picking location can be determined depending on the following factors:

- **Shipping Point**—Helps determine a picking location that is closer to the shipping point from where the goods have been shipped.
- **Plant**—Helps identify a picking location near the plant.
- **Storage Location**—Specifies that the storage location should be compatible with the picking location in terms of distance and efficiency in picking of goods.

You need to perform the following tasks to determine a picking location (also called picking location determination):

- Define the rule for a picking location
- Define a storage condition
- Assign a picking location

Defining the Rule for a Picking Location

To determine a picking location, you first need to define a picking rule. This picking rule is defined depending on the following parameters:

1. Location of the storage house, delivery plant, and shipping point
2. Situations relating to the picking conditions, such as whether the picking location is near to a company's plant
3. Delivery type

Navigate the following menu path to define a picking rule:

Menu Path

SAP Customizing Implementation Guide > Logistics Execution > Shipping > Picking > Determine Picking Location > Define Rules for Picking Location Determination

Figure 6.38 shows the navigated menu path in the **Display IMG** screen.

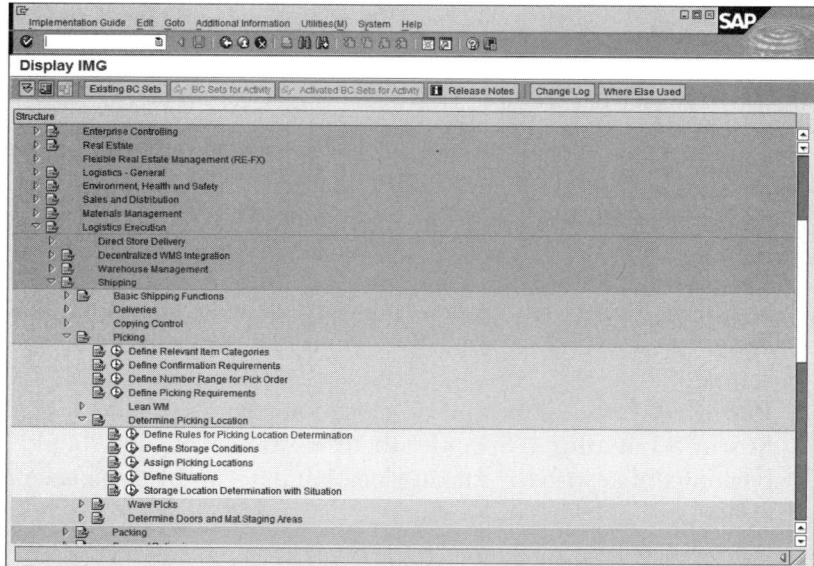

© SAP AG. All rights reserved.

FIGURE 6.38 Displaying the menu path for determining rules for a picking location

Click the **IMG Activity** icon (⊕) beside the **Define Rules for Picking Location Determination** activity in the **Display IMG** screen. The **Change**

View **"Deliveries: Dlv.types - Purchase Order Storage Location R** screen appears as shown in Figure 6.39.

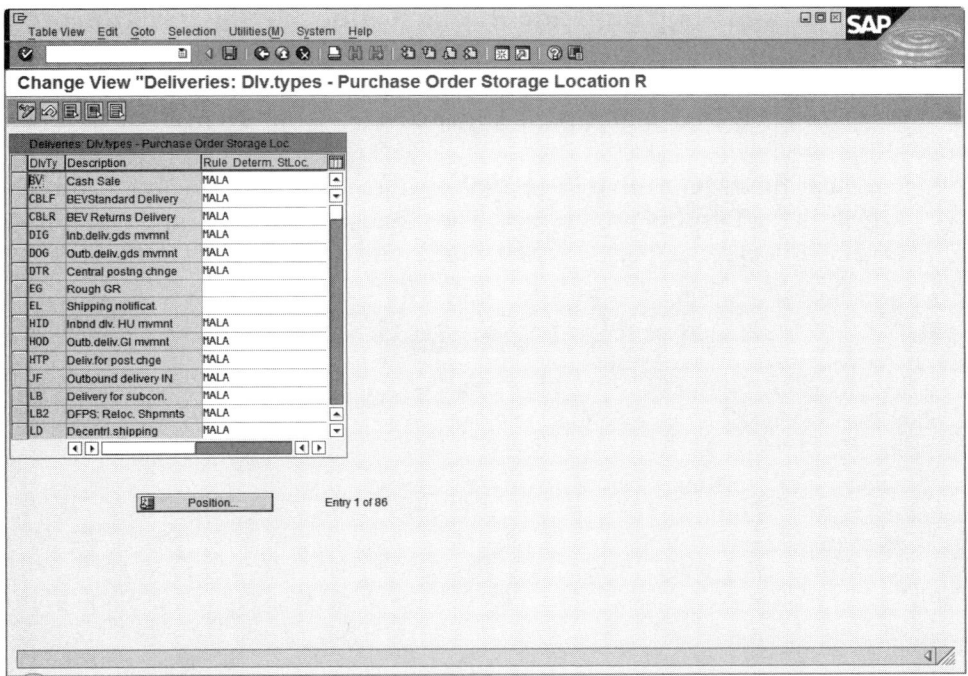

FIGURE 6.39 Displaying the Change View "Deliveries: Dlv.types - Purchase Order Storage Location R screen

Figure 6.39 displays the delivery types, their descriptions, and the picking rules. You can click the **Change/Display** icon ( ) to edit the rules on the basis of delivery types.

Defining a Storage Condition

Depending upon the physical and chemical composition of goods, their storage or picking conditions are defined. For example, a chemically reactive substance such as phosphorous needs to be stored in a dark and cool place. Storage condition is based on the nature of a material and the conditions required to store that material. These storage conditions are defined in the Material Master table, and are retrieved to determine a storage location.

Navigate the following menu path to define a storage condition:

Menu Path

SAP Customizing Implementation Guide > Logistics Execution > Shipping > Picking > Determine Picking Location > Define Storage Conditions

The navigated menu path is displayed in the **Display IMG** screen (Figure 6.38).

Click the **IMG Activity** icon (🔘) beside the **Define Storage Conditions** activity in the **Display IMG** screen. The **Change View "Storage Conditions": Overview** screen appears as shown in Figure 6.40.

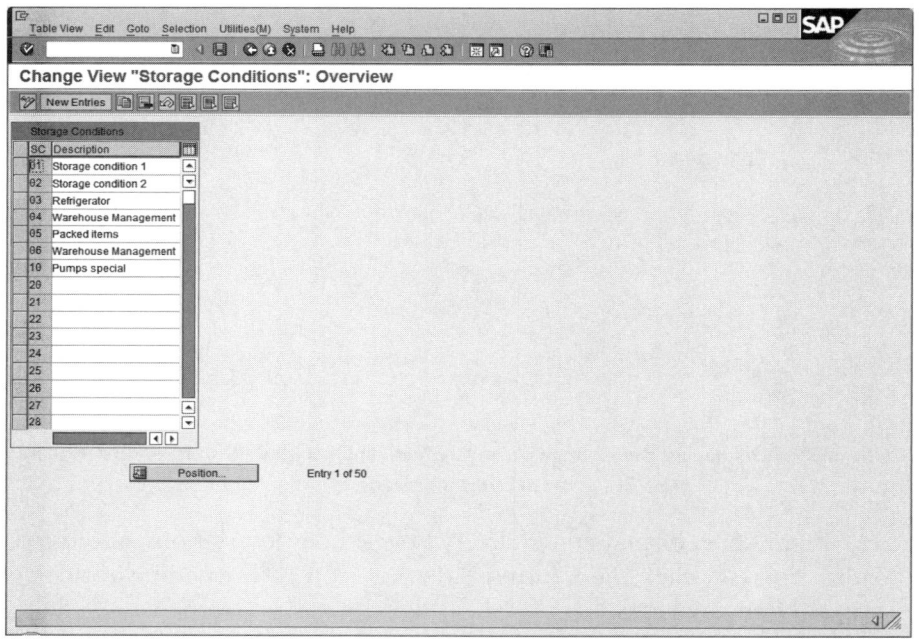

© SAP AG. All rights reserved.

FIGURE 6.40 Displaying the Change View "Storage Conditions": Overview screen

Figure 6.40 shows storage conditions for the storage of various products. You can define a new storage condition by clicking the **New Entries** button. Next, enter the details required to define the storage condition and click the **Execute** icon (✓) to save the entered details.

Assigning a Picking Location

The my SAP ERP system determines the storage or picking location for an item on the basis of its storage conditions defined in the **Define Storage Conditions** activity. You can then assign the determined location. In other words, the mySAP ERP system automatically determines the storage or picking locations when you assign the picking locations for the items. This process is called picking location determination rule. Navigate the following menu path to assign the picking location:

Menu Path

SAP Customizing Implementation Guide > Logistics Execution > Shipping > Picking > Determine Picking Location > Assign Picking Locations

The **Change View "Picking Location Determination": Overview** screen appears as shown in Figure 6.41.

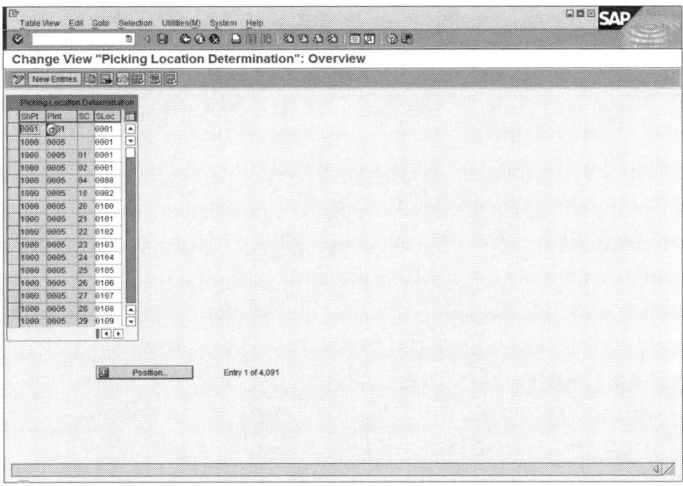

© SAP AG. All rights reserved.

FIGURE 6.41 Displaying the Change View "Picking Location Determination": Overview screen

In Figure 6.41, note that the picking location has been assigned on the basis of the shipping point and the storage location. Also note that you need to define a plant, storage conditions, and a shipping location before allocating the picking location.

The goods, once picked, need to be delivered to the specified destination. However, sometimes the management blocks the delivery of goods for unavoidable reasons. Let's now discuss the reasons for and types of blocking the delivery process.

Working with the Delivery Block Process

A delivery block refers to a situation in which the delivery of the ordered goods is blocked. In normal circumstances, the delivery processes function smoothly. However, in some undesirable or inevitable situations, the management might decide to block the delivery. In this section, we discuss the following in the context of delivery blocks:

- Reasons for blocking the delivery process
- Define the delivery blocks

Let's discuss each of them in detail.

Exploring Reasons for Delivery Blocks

The following are some of the reasons that lead to delivery blocks:

- **Credit Limits**—Blocks the delivery if the cost of the items exceeds the credit limit allowed to the customer.
- **Political Reasons**—Blocks the delivery due to government orders or any other political factor.
- **Bottleneck Material**—Blocks the delivery if defective material is produced or if the material is destroyed due to improper handling.
- **Export Papers Missing**—Blocks the delivery if the relevant documents for exporting the goods are not available.
- **Change in Quantity**—Blocks the delivery due to an unexpected change in the material quantity.
- **Printing Issues**—Blocks the delivery if the required documents are not printed.
- **Customer Request**—Blocks the delivery if the customer requests the blockage.
- **Free of Cost Sales**—Blocks delivery to avoid further processing until the delivery is released by the competent authority.

Now, let's perform the following steps to define the reasons for blocking a delivery:

1. Navigate the following menu path to define the reasons for delivery block:

Menu Path
SAP Customizing Implementation Guide > Logistics Execution > Shipping > Deliveries > Define Reasons for Blocking in Shipping

Figure 6.42 shows the navigated menu path in the **Display IMG** screen.

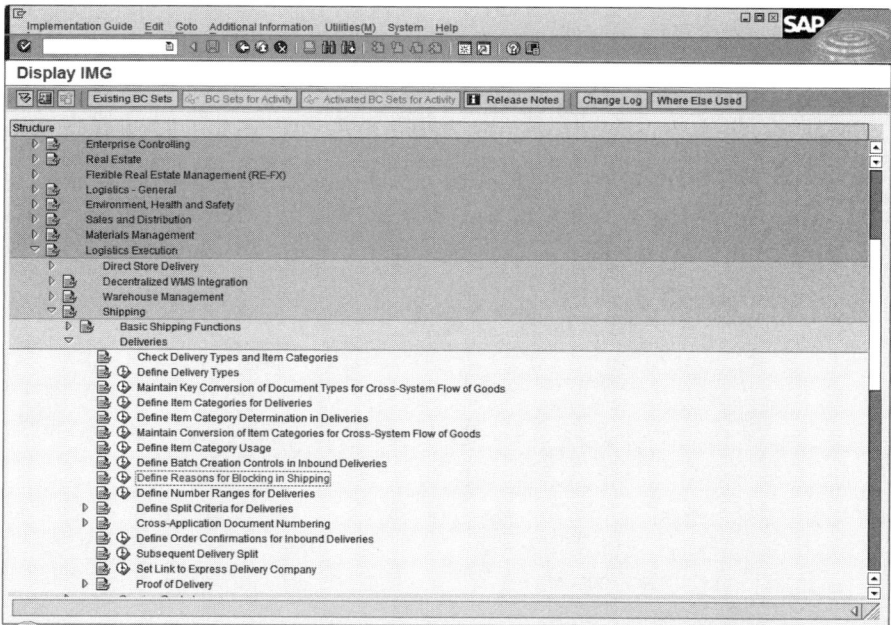

© SAP AG. All rights reserved.

FIGURE 6.42 Displaying the menu path to define reasons for blocking a delivery

2. Click the **IMG Activity** icon ( ) beside the **Define Reasons for Blocking in Shipping** activity. The **Choose Activity** dialog box appears as shown in Figure 6.43.

304   Chapter 6   Shipment, Delivery, and Warehouse Management

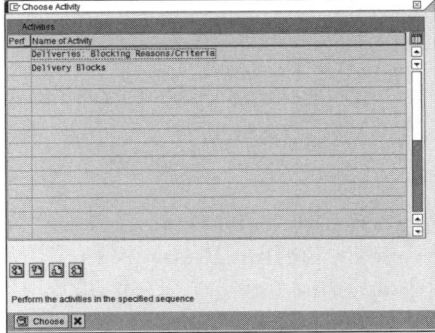

© SAP AG. All rights reserved.

FIGURE 6.43   Displaying the Choose Activity dialog box

Figure 6.43 shows the two activities associated with the blocking of a delivery process—**Deliveries: Blocking Reasons/Criteria** and **Delivery Blocks**.

3. Select the **Deliveries: Blocking Reasons/Criteria** activity and click the **Choose** button. The **Change View "Deliveries: Blocking Reasons/Criteria": Overview** screen appears as shown in Figure 6.44.

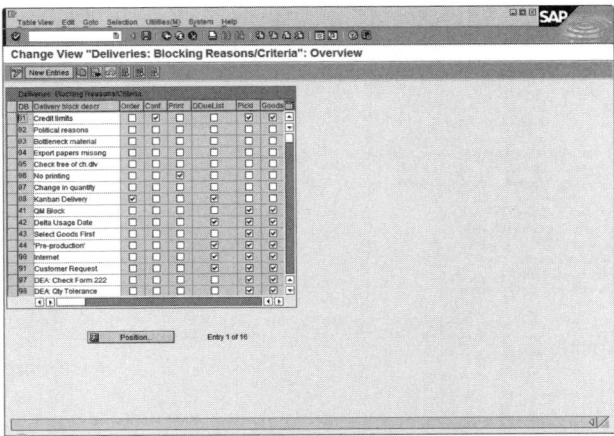

© SAP AG. All rights reserved.

FIGURE 6.44   Displaying the Change View "Deliveries: Blocking Reasons/Criteria": Overview screen

Figure 6.44 shows the list of delivery block codes along with their descriptions. The check boxes beside the relevant delivery block codes are checked to specify the reason for blocking the delivery.

The various check boxes that need to be checked are the following:

- **Order**—Blocks the sales order for delivery processing.
- **Conf.**—Blocks the delivery after confirmation of the sales order.
- **Print**—Blocks the printing of the document.
- **DDueList**—Blocks the delivery by automatic processing in the delivery due list.
- **Picking**—Blocks the picking of goods.
- **Goods Issue**—Blocks the issuing of goods.

> **Note:** Select the **Delivery Blocks** activity in the **Choose Activity** dialog box (Figure 6.44) and click the **Choose** button. The **Change View "Delivery Blocks": Overview** screen appears, displaying the list of the existing blocked deliveries, as shown in Figure 6.45.

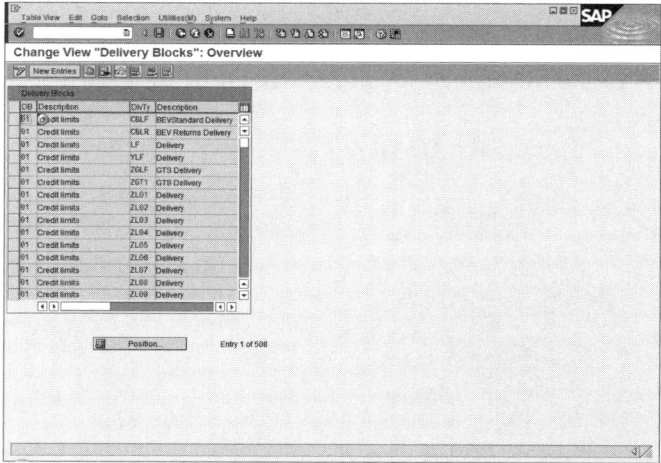

© SAP AG. All rights reserved.

FIGURE 6.45 Displaying delivery blocking criteria

Figure 6.45 shows the list of blocked deliveries and the criteria due to which they are blocked.

After discussing the reasons for delivery blocks, let's discuss the types of delivery blocks.

Defining Delivery Blocks

After defining the reasons for blockage of the delivery process, the administrative personnel implements the delivery blocking process in the mySAP ERP system. The delivery block can be defined at any of the following levels:

- Header level
- Schedule line level
- Customer/header level

Defining a Delivery Block at the Header Level

You can define a delivery block at the header level by entering the block into the sales order header. Perform the following steps to define a delivery block at the header level:

1. Navigate the following menu path in order to open a sales order header:

Menu Path

SAP Customizing Implementation Guide > Sales and Distribution > Sales > Sales Documents > Sales Document Header > Define Sales Document Types

Figure 6.46 shows the **Display IMG** screen after navigating the menu path.

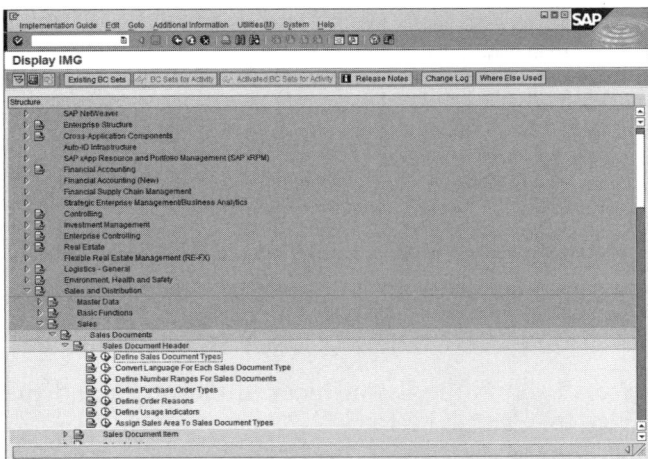

© SAP AG. All rights reserved.

FIGURE 6.46 Displaying the menu path to define delivery blocks at the header level

2. Click the **IMG Activity** icon (🔘) beside the **Define Sales Document Types** activity in the **Display IMG** screen. The **Change View "Maintain Sales Order Types": Overview** screen appears as shown in Figure 6.47.

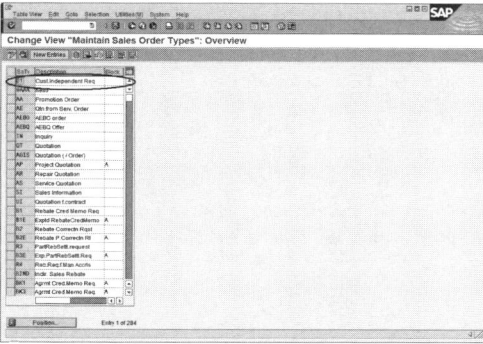

© SAP AG. All rights reserved.

FIGURE 6.47 Displaying the Change View "Maintain Sales Order Types": Overview screen

Figure 6.47 shows the existing sales document types, along with the **Block** header, displaying the blocked sales documents. In Figure 6.48, the **Block** header of the **Cust Independent Req** sales order type is blank, which denotes that no delivery with respect to the **Cust Independent Req** sales order type (sales order type 01) is blocked.

3. Double-click the **Cust Independent Req** sales order type to block it. The **Change View "Maintain Sales Order Types": Details** screen appears as shown in Figure 6.48.

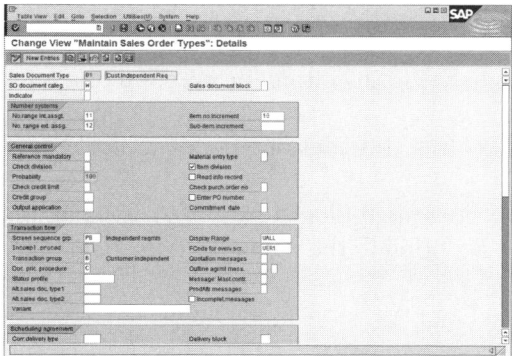

© SAP AG. All rights reserved.

FIGURE 6.48 Displaying the Change View "Maintain Sales Order Types": Details screen

Figure 6.48 shows the details of the `01` sales document type. The **Sales document block** field denotes the blocking status of the document.

4. Select the **Sales document block** check box. The **Sales document block (1)** dialog box appears as shown in Figure 6.49.

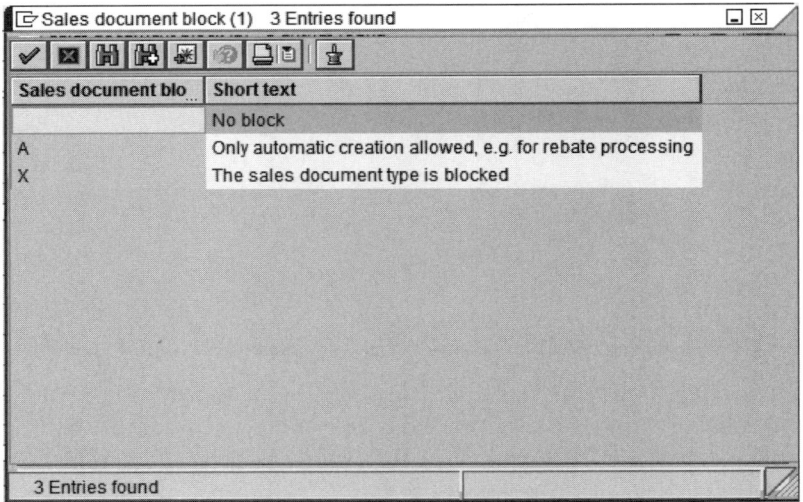

© SAP AG. All rights reserved.

FIGURE 6.49 Displaying the Sales document block (1) dialog box

In Figure 6.49, you can see that the sales document blocks are denoted by the following:

- **None**—Specifies that no delivery is blocked.
- **A**—Specifies that only automatic creation of a sales document is allowed.
- **X**—Specifies that the sales document is blocked.

5. Select a sales document block to apply a particular blocking. In our case, we selected the **X** option in the dialog box, as shown in Figure 6.50.

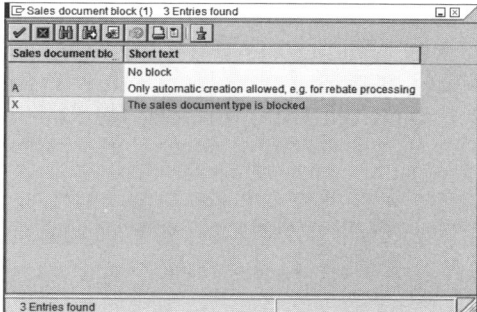

FIGURE 6.50 Selecting X option from the Sales document block dialog box

6. Double-click a blocking type to apply the selected blocking. The **Change View "Maintain Sales Order Types": Details** screen appears as shown in Figure 6.51.

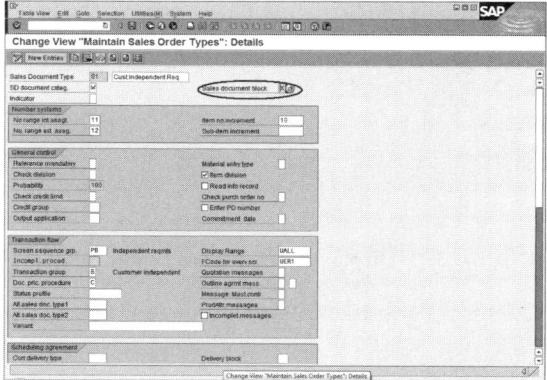

FIGURE 6.51 Displaying the blocked state of a sales order type

Note that in Figure 6.51, the **X** option is displayed in the **Sales document block** field. In the preceding figure, the **Sales document block** field specifies that the blocking is done on the **Cust Independent Req** sales order type.

You can navigate to the **Change View "Maintain Sales Order Types": Overview** screen by clicking the **Back** icon ( ) on the standard toolbar. The **Change View "Maintain Sales Order Types": Overview** screen appears, displaying the **Cust Independent Req** sales order type, as shown in Figure 6.52.

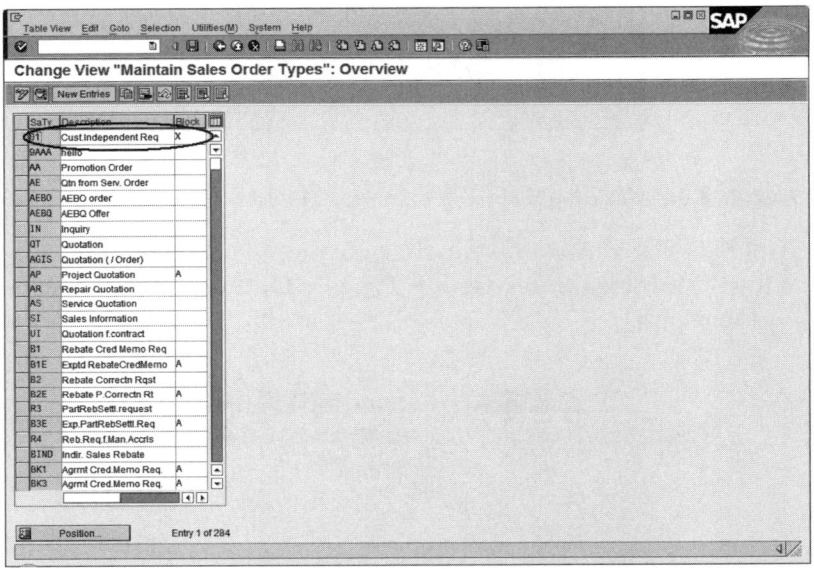

© SAP AG. All rights reserved.

FIGURE 6.52 **Displaying the blocked sales order type**

Figure 6.52 shows the blocked sales order type denoted by **X** against the sales document type 01.

Defining Delivery Block at the Schedule Line Level

A delivery block implemented in a sales document at the schedule line level is known as schedule line level delivery blocking. This type of blocking does not depend on whether the delivery block is assigned to the respective delivery document. In a schedule line level block, the blocking of delivery is not copied in the sales documents; instead, the sales order item and the delivery blocks can be created manually.

> **Note:** The delivery or schedule line blocks are introduced in configuration strictly according to the need of the business process.

Perform the following steps to define delivery block at the schedule line level:

1. Navigate the following menu path to open the schedule line categories:

Menu Path

SAP Customizing Implementation Guide > Sales and Distribution > Sales > Sales Documents > Schedule Lines > Define Schedule Line Categories

Figure 6.53 shows the navigated menu path in the **Display IMG** screen.

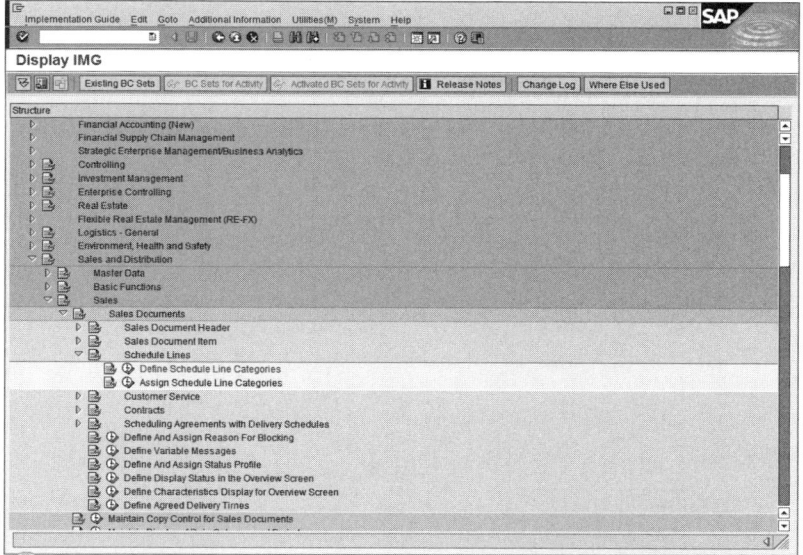

© SAP AG. All rights reserved.

FIGURE 6.53 Displaying the menu path to define a delivery block at the schedule line level

2. Click the **IMG Activity** icon (⊕) beside the **Define Schedule Line categories** activity in the **Display IMG** screen. The **Change View**

"Maintain Schedule Line Categories": Overview screen appears as shown in Figure 6.54.

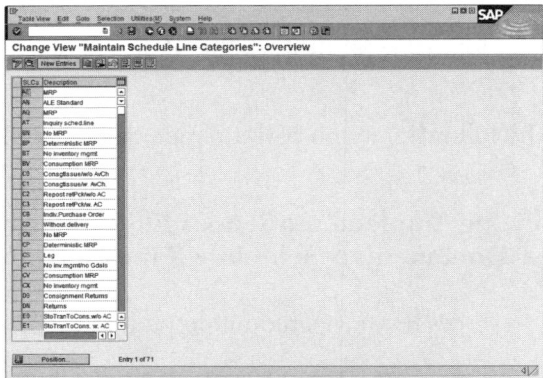

© SAP AG. All rights reserved.

FIGURE 6.54 Displaying the Change View "Maintain Schedule Line Categories": Overview screen

Figure 6.54 shows the schedule line categories along with their descriptions.

3. Double-click an item to view the details of the particular schedule line. In our case, we double-clicked the **MRP** schedule line category. The details of the **MRP** schedule line category are displayed in Figure 6.55.

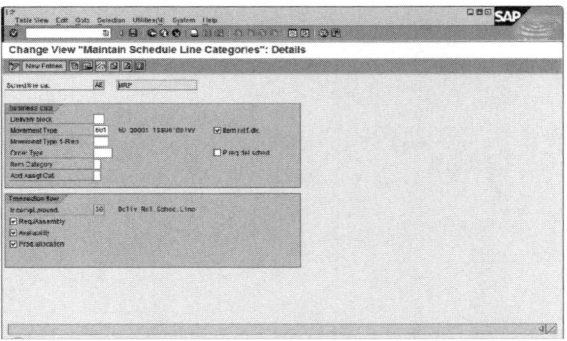

© SAP AG. All rights reserved.

FIGURE 6.55 Displaying the Change View "Maintain Schedule Line Categories": Details screen

In Figure 6.55, you can see that the **Delivery block** field under the **Business data** section is blank. This means that the delivery with respect to the **MRP** schedule line category is not yet blocked.

4. Click the **Delivery block** field. The **Default delivery block (1)** dialog box appears as shown in Figure 6.56.

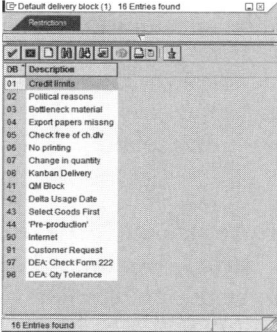

© SAP AG. All rights reserved.

FIGURE 6.56 **Schedule line restrictions**

In Figure 6.56, the different schedule line restrictions are displayed. You need to select a schedule line restriction to apply the delivery block at the schedule line level.

In our case, we selected the **Credit limits** restriction option represented by delivery block 01 (Figure 6.56). The modified view of the **Change View "Maintain Schedule Line Categories": Details** screen appears as shown in Figure 6.57.

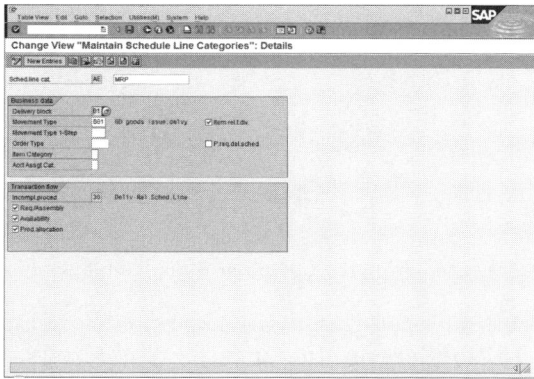

© SAP AG. All rights reserved.

FIGURE 6.57 **Displaying the selected delivery block**

Figure 6.57 shows the blocked delivery of the **MRP** schedule line.

Defining Delivery Block at the Customer/Header Level

The delivery blocking process used to block the records for a particular sales area in the Customer Master table is known as customer/header level delivery blocking. Perform the following steps to define delivery block at the customer/header level:

1. Navigate the following menu path to open the **Customer Block/Unblock: Initial Screen**, representing schedule line categories:

Menu Path

SAP Customizing Implementation Guide > Logistics > Sales and Distribution > Master Data > Business Partner > Customer > Block

(Or you can directly use the Transaction Code VD05.)

The **Customer Block/Unblock: Initial Screen** appears as shown in Figure 6.58.

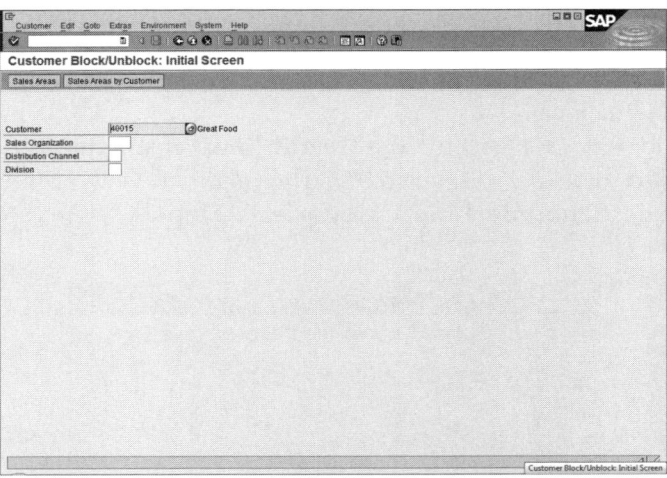

© SAP AG. All rights reserved.

FIGURE 6.58 Displaying the Customer Block/Unblock: Initial Screen

2. Enter the customer code in the Customer text box of the **Customer Block/Unblock: Initial Screen**. In our case, we entered 40015 as the customer code.
3. Press the **Enter** key. The **Customer Block/Unlock: Details Sales Area** screen is displayed, as shown in Figure 6.59.

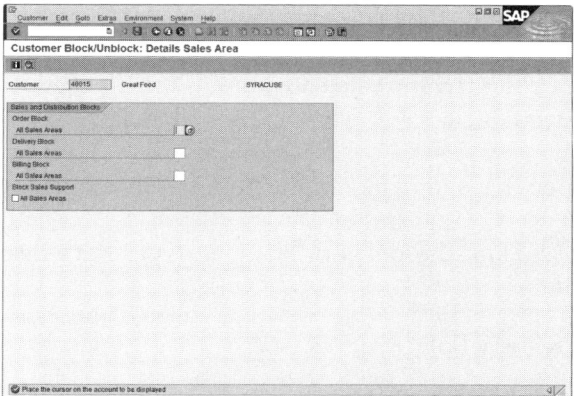

FIGURE 6.59   Displaying the Customer Block/Unblock Details Sales Area screen

Figure 6.59 shows various blocking options under the **Sales and Distribution Blocks**, which may be a block for the entered sales area or for all the sales areas for which this customer code has been created.

4. Enter the blocking code for each of the options and press the **Enter** key. The various blocks for the 40015 customer code, such as **Order Block**, **Delivery Block**, and **Billing Block**, are displayed in Figure 6.60.

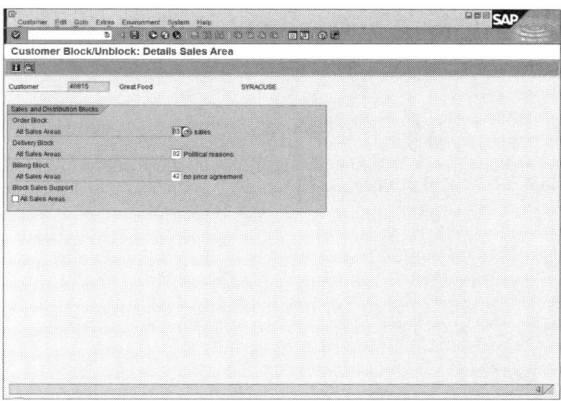

FIGURE 6.60   Displaying the details of a specific customer

Figure 6.60 shows the following blocking codes for the `40015` customer code:

- **03**—Specifies that no sales documents are blocked.
- **02**—Specifies that a delivery has been blocked due to political reasons.
- **42**—Specifies billing blocks due to no price agreement.

After discussing the delivery blocking types, let's discuss the concept of delivery split.

Implementing the Delivery Split Process

The process of splitting one consignment of delivery into multiple shipments is known as delivery split. A delivery might need to be split due to various reasons, such as excess weight of goods, carrying cost, and loading problems. Before performing the delivery split process, you must ensure that you have selected the items to be split from the delivery item list in the mySAP ERP system. Perform the following steps to learn how to split a delivery:

1. Open the **Change View "Split profile": Overview** screen by navigating the following menu path:

Menu Path

SAP Customizing Implementation Guide > Logistics Execution > Shipping > Deliveries > Subsequent Delivery Split

Figure 6.61 shows the **Change View "Split profile": Overview** screen.

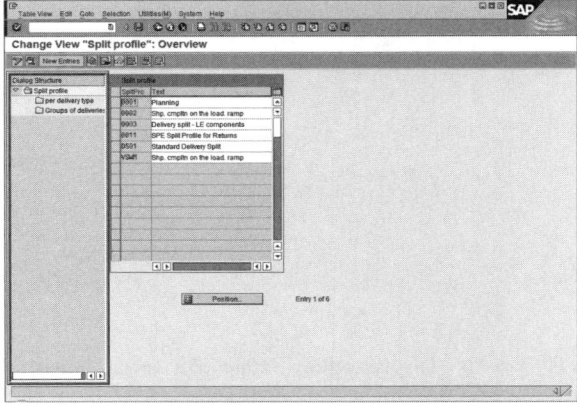

© SAP AG. All rights reserved.

FIGURE 6.61 Displaying the Change View "Split profile": Overview screen

In Figure 6.61, the left pane of the **Change View "Split profile": Overview** screen displays the **Dialog Structure** pane of the split profiles. The right pane displays various split profiles, along with their descriptions. For example, 0001 represents a split profile based on planning. The **Dialog Structure** pane allows you to view single as well as grouped delivery types of a split profile.

2. Double-click the 0001 split profile. The **Change View "Split profile": Details** screen appears as shown in Figure 6.62.

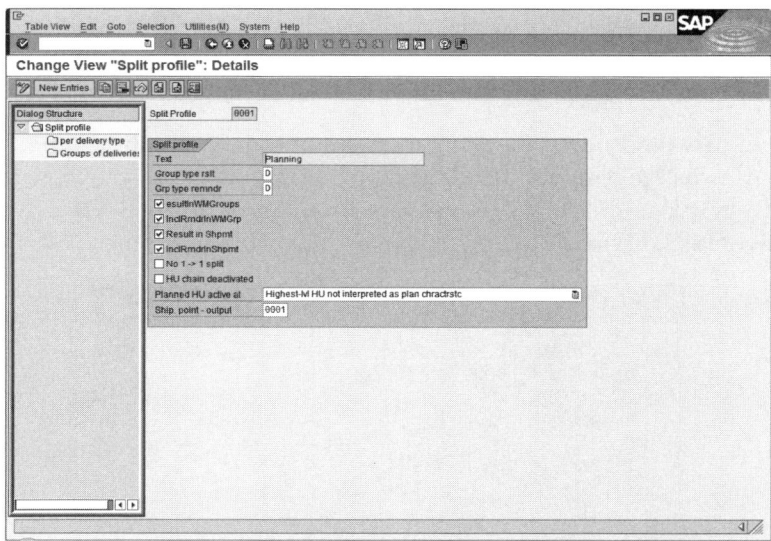

© SAP AG. All rights reserved.

FIGURE 6.62 Displaying the Change View "Split profile": Details screen

Figure 6.62 displays the details of the 0001 split profile.

3. Double-click the **per delivery type** folder in the **Dialog Structure** pane to display the delivery types of the 0001 split profile. The **Change View "per delivery type": Overview** screen appears as shown in Figure 6.63.

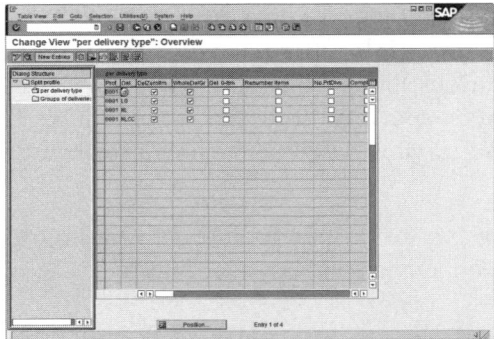

FIGURE 6.63   Displaying the Change View "per delivery type": Overview screen

Figure 6.63 shows the delivery types of the 0001 split profile.

Alternatively, select the **Groups of deliveries** folder to view the grouped delivery types of the 0001 split profile. The **Change View "Groups of deliveries": Overview** screen appears as shown in Figure 6.64.

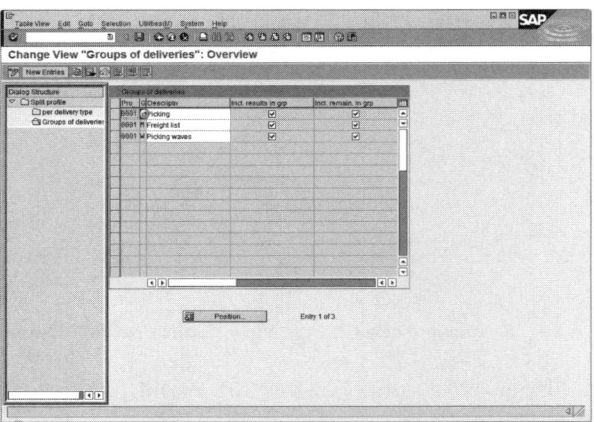

FIGURE 6.64   Displaying the Change View "Groups of deliveries": Overview screen

Now, after discussing the delivery process in detail, let's discuss the warehouse management process in the following section.

EXPLORING WAREHOUSE MANAGEMENT

Warehouse management works closely with the shipping and delivery processes. Warehouse management refers to the process of managing, storing, and facilitating the movement of goods in and out of the warehouse of an organization. Let's explore the following concepts related to the warehouse management process:

- The organizational structure of a warehouse
- Basic functions performed by warehouse management system
- Relationship of warehouse management to other applications
- Relationship of warehouse management to the delivery process
- The concept of decentralized warehouse management

Exploring the Organizational Structure of a Warehouse

A warehouse is organized into a hierarchical structure, including one or more multilevel organizational units. Figure 6.65 shows the organizational structure of a warehouse.

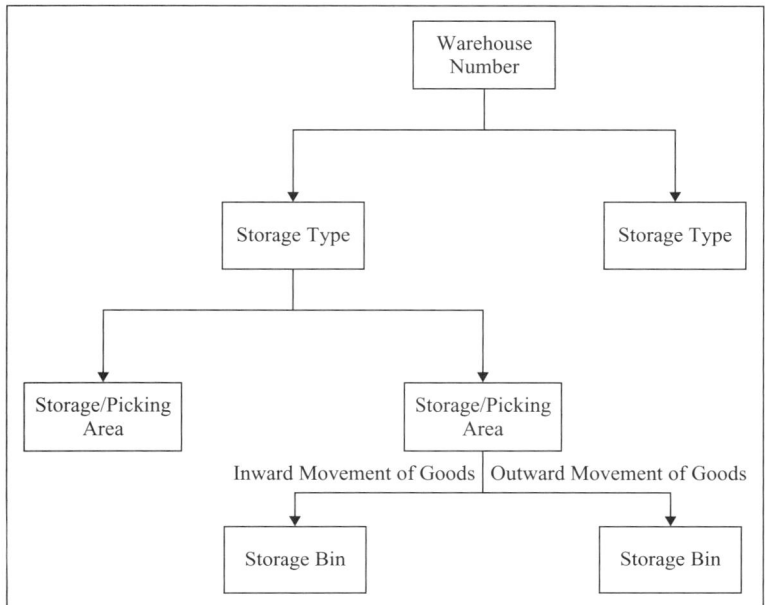

FIGURE 6.65 **Organizational structure of a warehouse**

As you can see in Figure 6.65, the topmost node in the hierarchy of the organizational structure is the warehouse number. This number represents a warehouse, which has various storage types to store different items. There can be multiple warehouses identified by their numbers in an organization. Similarly, depending upon the nature of items, each warehouse can have one or more storage types to store these items.

The next level in the warehouse organizational structure is occupied by storage/picking area, where the physical inventories are stored. In the mySAP ERP system, each storage/picking area is identified by a code and also contains the information related to the respective storage type. Depending upon the inward or outward movement of goods, the storage area is divided into two parts—goods received and goods issued. This storage area is further organized into lower-level units known as storage bins.

The storage bin is at the last level and is the smallest storage area in the organizational structure of a warehouse.

In the absence of warehouse management the storage bin is not important. The attributes that characterize a storage bin are these:

- **Maximum Weight**—Specifies the maximum weight of items that can be stored in a storage bin.
- **Total Capacity**—Specifies the total number of items that can be stored in a storage bin.
- **Fire Containment Section**—Specifies a place to hold fire safety equipment.
- **Storage Type**—Specifies the type of storage items that can be stored in a storage bin.

Basic Functions in the Warehouse Management System

Warehouse management refers to the process of managing the resources of a warehouse. It provides the following functions to facilitate the movement of goods in and out of a warehouse:

- **Consistency in Inventory Management and Storage of Goods**—Ensures that the available stock shown in the mySAP ERP system matches the goods available in the storage bins of the warehouses.

- **Mapping the Movement of Goods**—Maintains the transfer order document to verify the movement of goods. The transfer order document consists of goods-related details, such as the source, destination, date, and quantity of goods being transferred from one location to another. Mapping the movement of goods is performed on the basis of the details of the goods entered in the mySAP ERP system.
- **Monitoring the Goods Movement Process**—Monitors the quantity of goods and ensures that the quantity of goods available in a warehouse matches the amount of goods shown in the books of accounts (inventory management). Inventory management provides the estimated quantity of materials in stock; whereas warehouse management provides the exact location of the goods and their current status.
- **Mobile Data Entry Collection Centers**—Allows the WMS to automatically collect the details of the goods stored in a warehouse. Automatic data collection terminals are installed in a warehouse to collect the data in the form of radio frequency. Today, highly customized software, such as mySAP ERP system and Smart Turn®, is available for warehouse management.
- **Connections to the External System**—Connects a warehouse with an external software system, using an appropriate interface, such as Business Application Programming Interface (BAPI). Such connections provide the following benefits:
    - Smoother data sharing between warehouses
    - Elimination of waste
    - Efficient decision-making process

Let's now proceed to discuss how various applications help the proper functioning of the warehouse management process.

Relationship of Warehouse Management to Other Applications

In the mySAP ERP system, the warehouse management process works in close coordination with many applications, such as production planning and finance, to facilitate the smooth function of the business processes related to WMS.

The mySAP ERP system maintains the uniformity and consistency of data by communicating and exchanging data among these applications.

The following applications are linked with the warehouse management process:

- **Inventory Management**—Maintains the stock of goods (in the books of accounts) that are stored in a warehouse. In other words, any modification or addition to the materials in the inventory management has a direct impact on the warehouse management process.
- **Delivery Processing**—Allows the outbound movement of goods from the warehouse to the customer's destination. As a result, the quantity of goods in the warehouse is reduced, making it necessary to reorder the items in advance so that the warehouse activities do not remain idle. In other words, the inbound and outbound movement of goods should be streamlined and maintained to reduce waste and to improve the efficiency of the business as well as the delivery processes.
- **Production Planning**—Plans the production of the goods so that the produced goods can be effectively handled in a warehouse. If the number of produced items is higher than the items that a warehouse can manage, the items cannot be stored and managed properly. In contrast, if the number of items produced is less than the estimated quantity, the personnel associated with the warehouse management remains idle, increasing the overall production cost. This, in turn, also delays the delivery process, resulting in customer dissatisfaction.
- **Quality Management**—Ensures the quality of the items stored in a warehouse. In the absence of a strong quality control process, the goods might be tampered with or stolen from the warehouse, resulting in loss of precious items, loss of revenue, and possible delay in the delivery process.

Let's now discuss how the warehouse management process is related to the delivery process.

Relationship of Warehouse Management to the Delivery Process

As you know, there are two types of delivery processes—inbound and outbound. In case of inbound delivery, the information regarding the storage types, storage section, and storage bins for the items are stored in the transfer order. The inbound delivery process is completed with the posting of the goods received in the inventory management system. This information, received by the inventory management system, is used by the WMS to manage the goods stored in the warehouse and also for further delivery processing.

Perform the following steps to create an inbound delivery reference to a sales order:

1. Navigate the following menu path:

Menu Path

SAP menu > Logistics > Logistics Execution > Inbound Process > Goods Receipt for Inbound Delivery > Inbound Delivery > Create > VL31N- Single Documents

Figure 6.66 shows the navigated menu path in the **SAP Easy Access** screen.

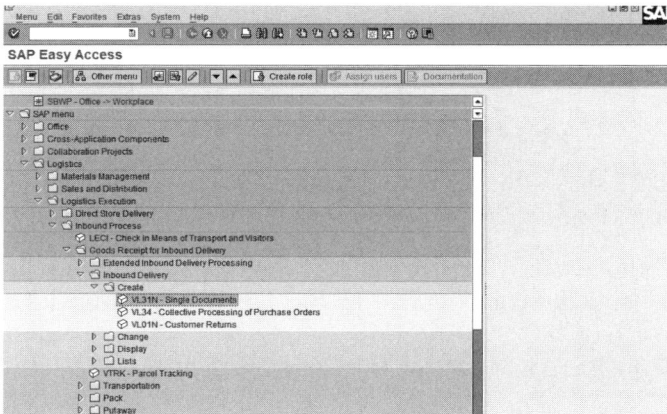

© SAP AG. All rights reserved.

FIGURE 6.66 Displaying the menu path for creating inbound delivery

2. Double-click the **VL31N-Single Documents** activity on the **SAP Easy Access** screen. The **Create Inbound Delivery** screen appears as shown in Figure 6.67.

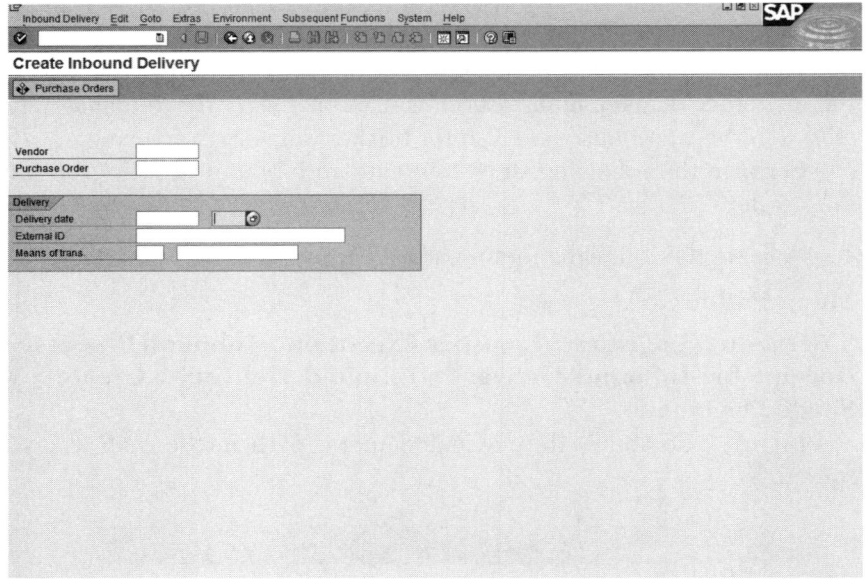

© SAP AG. All rights reserved.

FIGURE 6.67 Displaying the Creating Inbound Delivery screen

Figure 6.67 shows the **Create Inbound Delivery** screen, which is used to create an inbound delivery with reference to the sales order.

3. Enter the details related to inbound delivery, such as purchase order, vendor name, and delivery details, in the **Create Inbound Delivery** screen (Figure 6.67).
4. Click the **Save** icon (🖫) on the standard toolbar to save the entered data.

In case of outbound delivery, the transfer order is created with reference to the sales order, which is used to remove the stock from the storage location. After completion of the picking process, the information about outbound delivery is posted in the inventory management. Perform the following steps to create an outbound delivery reference:

1. Navigate the following menu path:

Menu Path

SAP menu > Logistics > Logistics Execution > Outbound Process > Goods Issue for Outbound Delivery > Outbound Delivery > Create > Single Document > VL01N-With Reference to Sales Order

Figure 6.68 shows the navigated menu path in the **SAP Easy Access** screen.

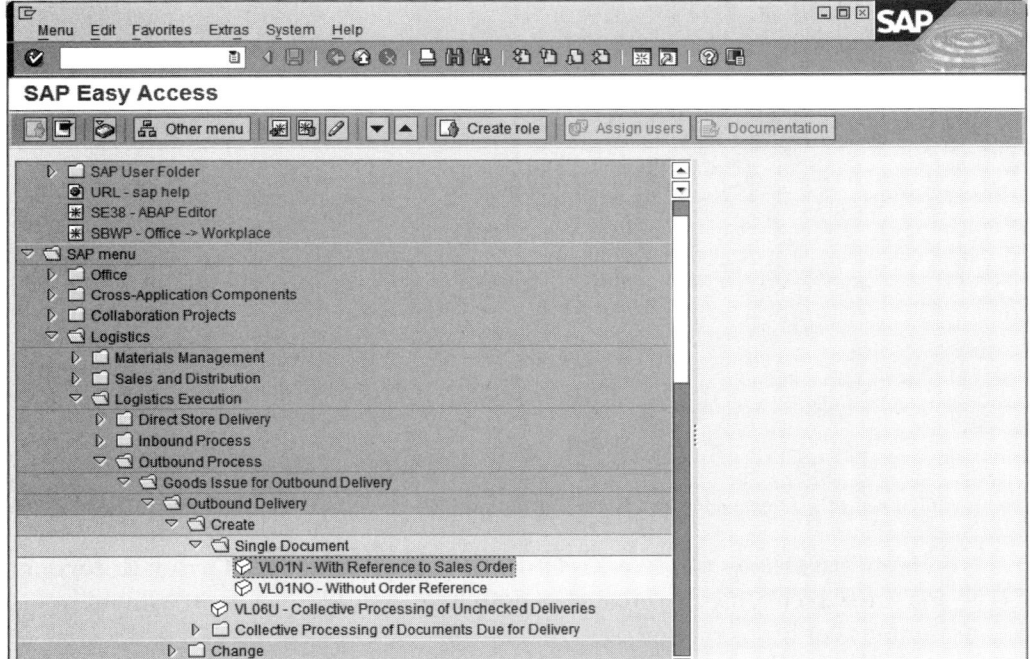

© SAP AG. All rights reserved.

FIGURE 6.68 Displaying the menu path to create an outbound delivery

An outbound delivery can be created with or without the reference to the sales order. In our example, we selected the creation of outbound delivery with reference to the sales order.

2. Double-click the **VL01N-With Reference to Sales Order** activity (Figure 6.68). The **Create Outbound Delivery with Order Reference** screen appears as shown in Figure 6.69.

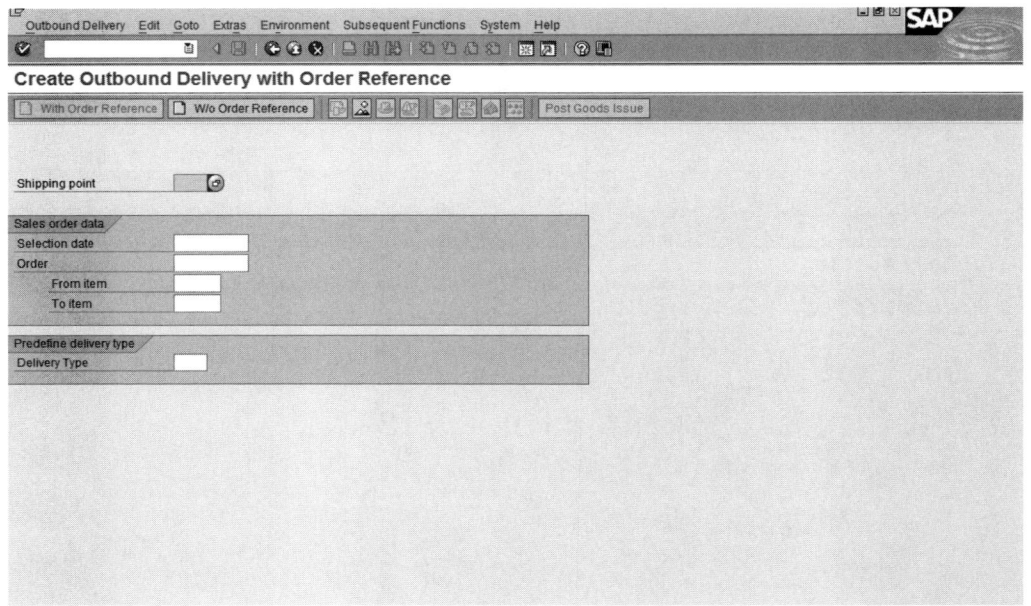

© SAP AG. All rights reserved.

FIGURE 6.69 Displaying the Create Outbound Delivery with Order Reference screen

Figure 6.69 shows the **Create Outbound Delivery with Order Reference** screen, which is used to create the outbound delivery document with reference to the sales order.

3. Enter the relevant details, such as shipping point, selection date, order number (from item to item), and delivery type (optional, as this is determined automatically based on the configuration done for copy controls), in the **Create Outbound Delivery with Order Reference** screen.
4. Click the **Save** icon ( ) on the standard toolbar to save the entered data.

Let's now discuss the concept of decentralized warehouse management.

Exploring Decentralized Warehouse Management

Decentralized warehouse management is the process of implementing the warehouse management system on another system instead of the mySAP ERP system. This type of warehouse management provides the flexibility to execute warehouse processes that are independent of the mySAP ERP system. The communication between the mySAP ERP system and WMS is done with the help of BAPI. The decentralized WMS structure is shown in Figure 6.70.

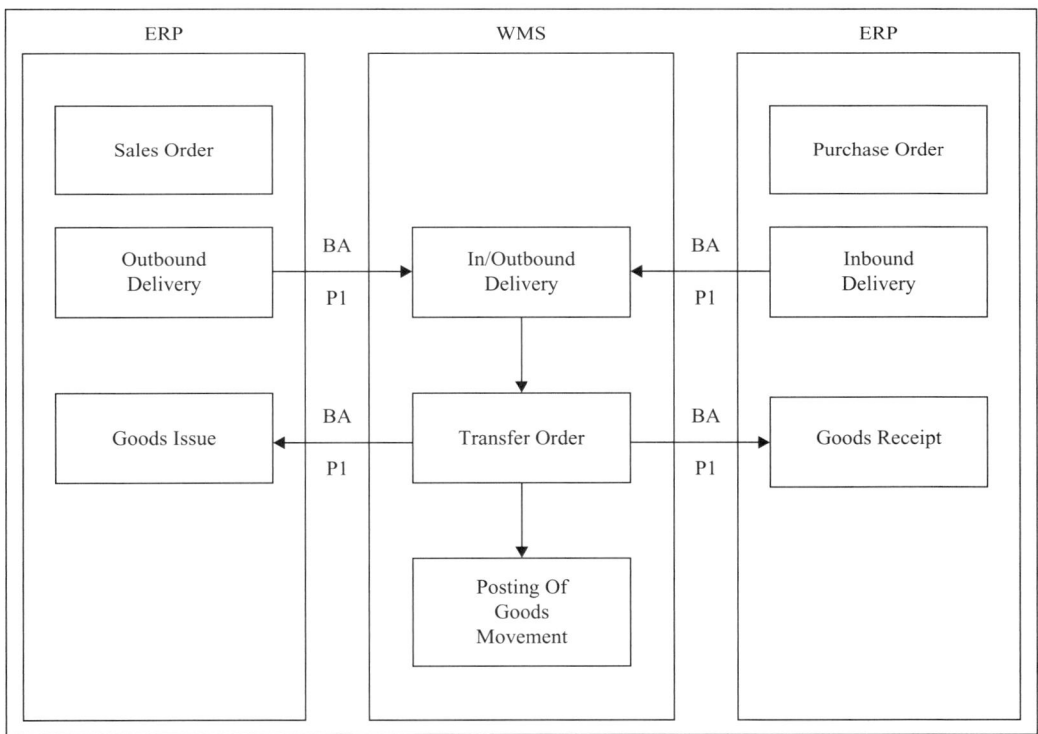

FIGURE 6.70 Displaying the decentralized WMS

In Figure 6.70, the decentralized WMS acts as an interface between the inbound and outbound delivery processes. BAPI is used for communication between the WMS and ERP systems.

In the case of an outbound delivery process, first an outbound delivery document is created by the supplier or the vendor on the basis of the sales order, and the details of the outbound delivery document are then transferred to the WMS. Next, the transfer order is created, and goods are eliminated from the stock. Finally, the information about the movement of goods is posted in the inventory management system.

Similarly, in the case of an inbound delivery process, the inbound delivery document is created on the basis of the purchase order, and its details are transferred to the WMS. The transfer order is then created based on the inbound delivery. The inbound delivery process is completed with the posting of the goods received in the inventory management system. The inbound delivery document is used by the customer to receive the goods from the supplier or the vendor.

In decentralized WMS, the posting of goods is automatically done in the case of both inbound and outbound movement of goods. After the posting is done in the book of accounts, it is not possible to change it because it is an automated process in WMS.

Let's now see how a decentralized WMS is different from the conventional centralized WMS, as described in Table 6.2.

Centralized WMSs	Decentralized WMSs
Simplified order processing.	Complex order processing, due to large volume of data from more than one warehouse.
Less capital required to set up a centralized warehouse environment.	More capital required, because various separate environments need to be set up for the decentralized warehouse system.
Lower cost of inventory holding.	Higher cost of inventory carrying, handling, and management.
Lower outbound transportation costs.	Higher outbound cost, due to transfer of goods from factory to multiple warehouses.

Continued

Centralized WMSs	Decentralized WMSs
Better use of overall business potential.	Difficulty in allocating the material and staff to multiple warehouses, leading to a situation where the business potential is overused, affecting the workers' productivity.
Difficulty in analyzing the needs of the customers, resulting in limited scope of providing the goods of their choice. As a result, sales and profit do not meet expectations.	Better opportunity to understand the needs of customers. This leads to an increase in profit margin.
Requires high investment at one place.	No compulsion of high investment in decentralized warehouse setup.
Fear of being affected by market fluctuations.	No fear of market fluctuations.
Requires large establishments to store inventories related to customers from various countries.	Requires no large establishments because products can be sent directly to the warehouse in a certain country.

TABLE 6.2 Comparing the centralized and decentralized WMSs

After discussing the centralized and decentralized warehouse management systems, let's discuss the process of packing goods.

IMPLEMENTING THE PACKING PROCESS

The packing process is done just before an item is shipped. According to the requirements, an item can be packed into one or more packing units. The criteria to implement the packing process in the mySAP ERP system are these:

- Item category
- Customer requirements

Let's discuss each of these criteria in detail.

Packing on the Basis of an Item Category

You learned earlier that items are placed under various item categories depending upon their basic configuration. The category of an item determines whether the item needs to be packed before being delivered. Navigate the following menu path to learn how to control the process of packing items:

Menu Path
SAP Customizing Implementation Guide > Logistics Execution > Shipping > Packing > Packing Control By Item Category

Figure 6.71 shows the navigated menu path in the **Display IMG** screen.

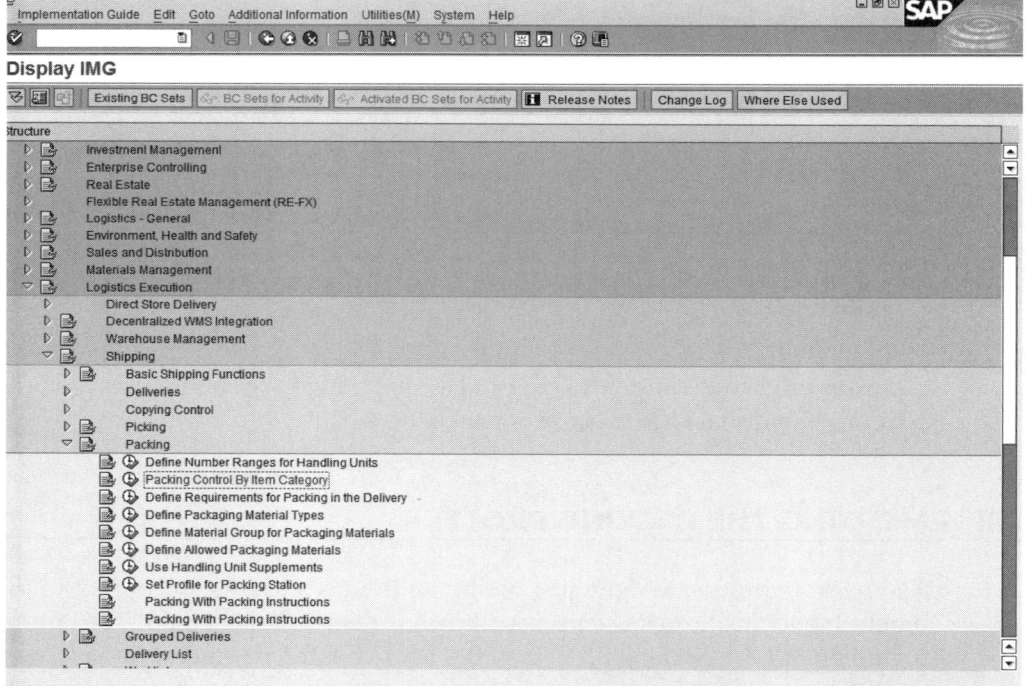

© SAP AG. All rights reserved.

FIGURE 6.71 Displaying the Packing Control By Item Category activity

Click the **IMG Activity** icon (⊕) beside the **Packing Control By Item Category** activity in the **Display IMG** screen. The **Change View "Packing Requirement for Item Categories": Overview** screen appears as shown in Figure 6.72.

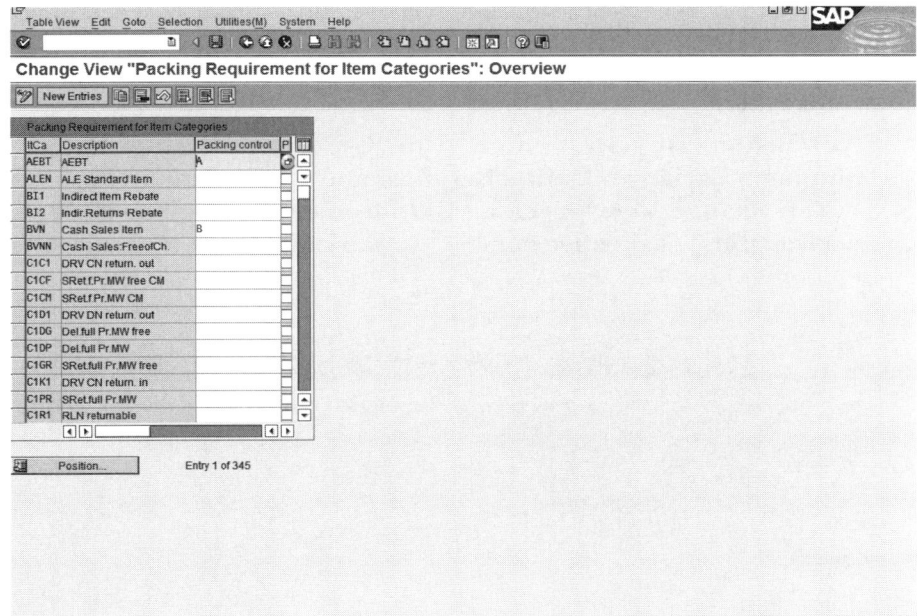

© SAP AG. All rights reserved.

FIGURE 6.72 Displaying the Change View "Packing Requirement for Item Categories": Overview screen

Figure 6.72 shows the different item categories, along with their descriptions. Various packing control keys are allotted to the item categories under the **Packing control** header. For example, the A packing code is allotted to the items that are referenced by the **AEBT** item category; and the B code is allocated to the items referenced by the **BVN** item category.

Let's now discuss the process of packing items depending on the customer's requirements.

Packing on the Customer Requirement Basis

Apart from the item categories, you can also pack the items based on the customer's requirements. The customer's packing requirements are defined in the form of routines in the mySAP ERP system. Navigate the following menu path to control the packing process of an item based on customer requirements:

Menu Path

SAP Customizing Implementation Guide > Logistics Execution > Shipping > Packing > Define Requirement for Packing in the Delivery

The **Change View" Packing Requirements in Delivery": Overview** screen appears. The routine number 112 indicates the packing code, as shown in Figure 6.73.

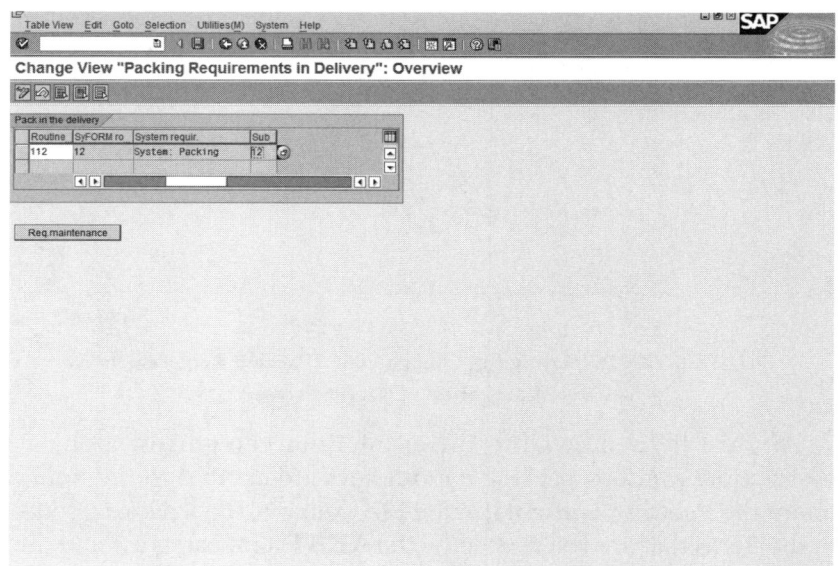

© SAP AG. All rights reserved.

FIGURE 6.73 The Change View "Packing Requirement in Delivery": Overview screen

You can view the details of the packing requirements by selecting a routine and clicking the **Req. maintenance** button. You can also edit the details by clicking the **Change/Display** icon ( ).

In the next section, let's discuss the returnable packaging process.

IMPLEMENTING THE RETURNABLE PACKAGING PROCESS

A special type of packaging process, in which the packing material used for packaging is returned by the customer after the delivery of goods, is known as the returnable packaging process. The returned packaging material is reused for delivering the next lot of items. For example, in the case of soft drinks, crates are returnable material. They are returned by the customer after the delivery of the soft drinks. Even though returnable packaging is the property of the vendor, it is stored by the customer. In the case of unreturned or destroyed packaging material, the customer has to pay a penalty. This packaging is different from nonreturnable packaging. Now, perform the following steps to implement the returnable packaging process in the mySAP ERP system:

1. Navigate the following menu path:

Menu Path

SAP menu > Logistics > Material Management > Inventory Management > Environment > Consignment at Customer

Figure 6.74 shows the navigated menu path in the **SAP Easy Access** screen.

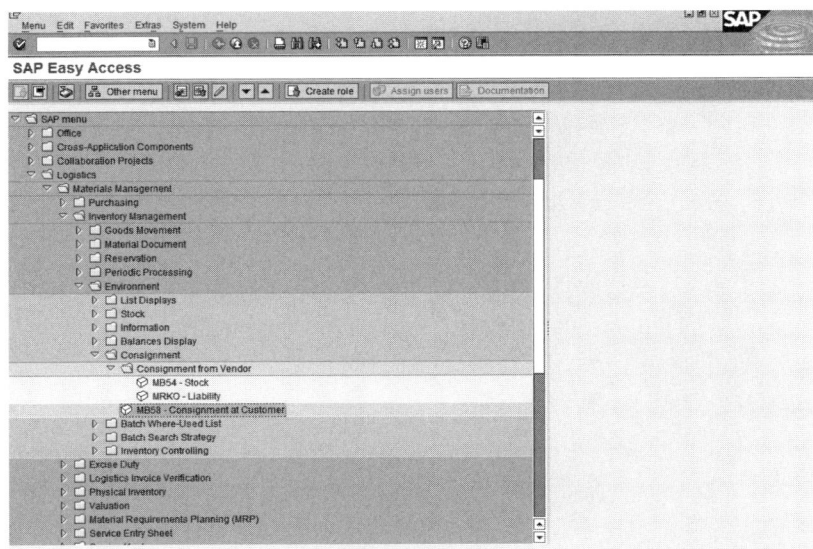

© SAP AG. All rights reserved.

FIGURE 6.74 Displaying the returnable packaging menu path

2. Double-click the **Consignment at Customer** activity in the **SAP Easy Access** screen. The **Display Consignment and Returnable Packaging Stocks at Customer** screen appears as shown in Figure 6.75.

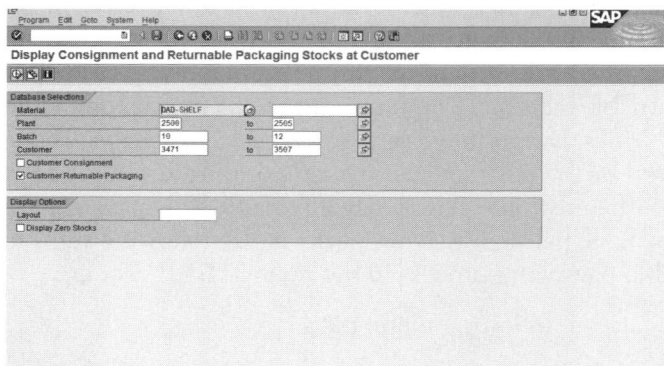

© SAP AG. All rights reserved.

FIGURE 6.75 Displaying the Display Consignment and Returnable Packaging Stocks at Customer screen

3. Click the **Execute** icon ( ) on the **Display Consignment and Returnable Packaging Stocks at Customer** screen. The details of returnable packaging are displayed as shown in Figure 6.76.

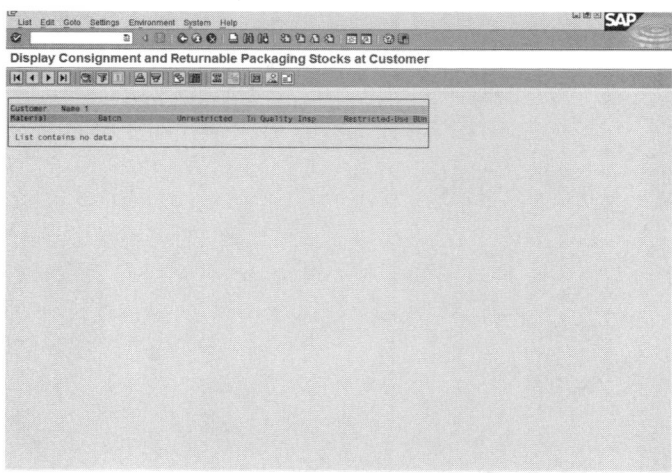

© SAP AG. All rights reserved.

FIGURE 6.76 Displaying consignment and returnable packaging stock at customer details

Figure 6.76 displays the packaging stock that needs to be returned by the customer. In our case, none of the packages are returnable. However, if any packaging material needs to be returned by a customer, it is displayed on the **Display Consignment and Returnable Packaging Stocks at Customer** screen.

Let's now proceed to discuss routing, which is one of the major elements of the shipping and delivery process.

DETERMINING ROUTES FOR TRANSPORTATION

Route refers to the itinerary followed by a transportation medium, such as a public carrier, to transport goods from the shipping point to the customer's destination. This route is specified in the sales document of an item. The correct determination of routes not only reduces the delivery time, but also ensures the safety of the goods. However, prior to determining a route, you need to define a route. Let's discuss how to define a route.

Defining a Route

A route is defined by providing details for one or more of the following parameters (called the determination rule):

- Transportation modes
- Shipping types
- Transportation connection points
- Routes
- Stages

Perform the following steps to define a route to ship an item to its destination:

1. Navigate the following menu path to define a route:

Menu Path

SAP Customizing Implementation Guide > Sales and Distribution > Basic Functions > Routes > Define Routes

Figure 6.77 shows the navigated menu path in the **Display IMG** screen.

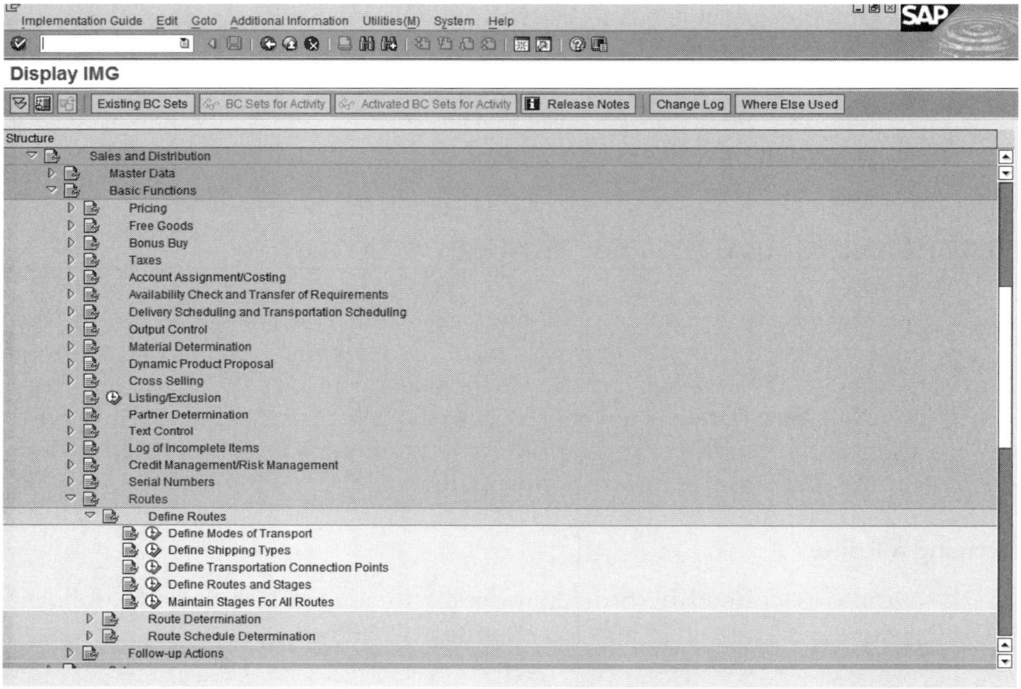

FIGURE 6.77 Displaying the menu path to define routes

© SAP AG. All rights reserved.

Figure 6.77 shows the following activities used to define a route:

- **Define Modes of Transport**—Specifies the modes of transport, such as road, air, and post, which are used to ship goods to the customer's destination. A mode of transport is defined by entering two alphanumeric characters and a description.
- **Define Shipping Types**—Defines the shipping types based on the mode of transport. For example, if the mode of transport is road, the shipping type can be truck, truck with trailer, or crane. A shipping type is defined by entering two alphanumeric

characters and a description. A shipping type can also be associated with one or more modes of transport.

- **Define Transportation Connection Points**—Defines the points that connect two or more shipping types. For example, an item can be transported first by plane and then delivered to the customer by truck. In this case, the airport is considered as the transportation connection point. A connection point is created by entering 10 alphanumeric characters and a text description.
- **Define Routes and Stages**—Defines routes and route stages. A route is defined by entering six alphanumeric characters, a text description, and a shipping type (optional). The route stages are defined by entering a starting point and a destination point (optional).
- **Maintain Stages For All Routes**—Maintains the detailed information of various stages of shipment for all routes.

Let's now learn the process to determine a defined route.

Determining a Route

After defining the routes, you can determine the routes defined in the mySAP ERP system on the basis of various details, such as the transportation groups for each country, for each department zone, and according to the weight of the items being shipped. Perform the following steps to determine a route:

1. Define the route determination process in the mySAP ERP system.
2. Assign the departure routes to the shipping points.
3. Define the transportation groups for the materials.
4. Select the routes according to the criteria defined in the sales processing.

Now, let's summarize all that we have learned in this chapter.

SUMMARY

In this chapter, you learned about the shipment, delivery, and warehouse management processes in detail. First, the shipment process has been described, and you explored different types of shipments, such as individual, collective, and transportation chain. Next, you learned how to create a shipping document by providing relevant transportation details. In addition, the various shipment stages have been discussed. You also learned how to configure a delivery document and how to determine the categories of delivery items, a shipping point, and a picking location. The chapter also discussed various activities performed by WMS, such as managing, storing, and facilitating the movement of goods inside and outside a warehouse. Toward the end of the chapter, you learned about the packing process and the returnable packaging process, and finally, you learned how to define and determine the routes for transportation.

The next chapter describes the integration of the SD module with the FI module.

Chapter 7
Implementing the Billing Process in the SD Module

If you need information on:	See page:
Working with Billing Documents	340
Using the Copying Control Process for Billing	356
Creating Invoice Lists	362
Working with Billing Plans	366
Working with Rebate Agreements	374
Exploring Payment Processing in the SD Module	394

Billing refers to the process of creating a legal document that contains the details of quantity, price, discounts, and taxes for the materials sold or services rendered to a customer. This legal document, known as a billing document, is sent to the customer as an invoice against which the customer has to pay the amount due for the goods purchased or services received. A billing document can be created as an individual billing document or as a collective billing document. If individual or collective billing documents are combined into one billing document, it is known as an invoice list. The Sales and Distribution (SD) module of the mySAP™ ERP system helps you to create and manage billing documents. In addition to billing documents, the SD module also allows you to create and manage billing plans. A billing plan includes the billing dates on which partial payments of goods or services are to be made.

The SD module also enables you to create a rebate agreement, which is an agreement between a sales organization (or a company) and a party (or a customer) who has purchased the goods over a specific period of time. This agreement includes various conditions of sale, such as amount of rebate and quantity of items. After a rebate agreement is finalized, a customer needs to pay the bill of the purchased goods. A customer can pay the bill using any mode, such as credit card, cash, check, or demand draft. Note that paying a bill is also known as payment processing. In the SD module, there are two types of payment processing: down payment and installment payment.

In this chapter, you learn how bills are processed in the mySAP ERP system. In addition, you learn about the billing process; that is, how bills are created, displayed, modified, and processed in the mySAP ERP system. You also learn how to generate billing documents on the basis of sales documents or delivery documents by using the copying control process. Next, you learn to create invoice lists, billing plans, and rebate agreements. The chapter provides a detailed discussion on rebate agreements covering their various aspects, such as rebate types, condition types, and condition-type groups. Finally, you learn about payment processing in the SD module.

Let's begin by discussing the billing documents.

WORKING WITH BILLING DOCUMENTS

Billing is the final processing stage of a business transaction in the SD module of SAP®. In this process, you can perform the following functions:

- Create invoices on the basis of delivered goods or services
- Create and issue credit and debit memos
- Create pro forma invoices
- Cancel billing transactions
- Work with pricing functions
- Issue rebates
- Transfer the billing data to the Financial Accounting (FI) module

Note: In the billing process, the transfer of the billing data to the FI module is achieved by creating an accounting document released to FI. This accounting document is created by the mySAP ERP system after you have saved a billing document. This accounting document is released to FI immediately after the invoice is created; it could be released later as well, depending upon the business requirement.

In the SAP® SD module, a billing document is created on the basis of a sales order, delivery, or external transaction. When you create a billing document, you can refer to an entire document, to individual items of the document, or to some specific quantity of the items.

In the billing process, you can create the billing documents by any of the following methods:

- **Individual Billing Documents**—Creates an individual billing document as per a sales document.
- **Collective Billing Documents**—Creates a collective billing document for several sales documents.
- **Invoice Split**—Creates multiple billing documents for one or more sales documents.

The structure of all the billing documents is the same; it includes a header and an items area as shown in Figure 7.1.

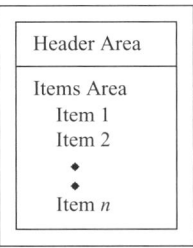

FIGURE 7.1 Displaying the structure of a billing document

The header area of a billing document contains general data related to the entire document, such as the identification number of the customer, billing date, document currency, terms of payment, and pricing elements. The items area, on the other hand, includes the data related to a particular item, such as the material description and code value of the individual items, and the total quantity of the items.

In the mySAP ERP system, a billing document is created on the basis of certain types of billing. Let's now discuss these billing types in detail.

Defining Billing Types

To work with different types of business transactions, an organization needs to create different types of billing documents, such as invoices, credit memos, debit memos, and cancellation documents. These billing documents are created on the basis of certain predefined billing types provided by the mySAP ERP system.

Table 7.1 lists the billing types provided by the mySAP ERP system.

Billing Type	Name	Description
F1	Order-related invoice	Generates an invoice on the basis of a sales order.
F2	Delivery-related invoice	Generates an invoice on the basis of a delivery.
F5	Pro forma invoice for sales orders or delivery	Generates a pro forma invoice on the basis of a sales order; for instance, a Stock Transfer Order or a Consignment-related transaction.
F8	Pro forma invoice for deliveries	Generates a pro forma invoice related to delivery of goods to the customer.
G2	Credit memo	Issues a credit memo to a customer.
L2	Debit memo	Issues a debit memo to a customer.
RE	Credit memo for returns	Generates a return document when a complaint is received from a customer or when a customer sends the goods back to the company.
S1	Cancellation invoice	Cancels an invoice and issues a new one.
S2	Cancellation credit memo	Cancels the credit memo of a customer.

TABLE 7.1   Billing types

Now let's perform the following steps to define a billing type:

1. Select **SAP Customizing Implementation Guide > Sales and Distribution > Billing > Billing Documents > Define Billing Types**, as shown in Figure 7.2.

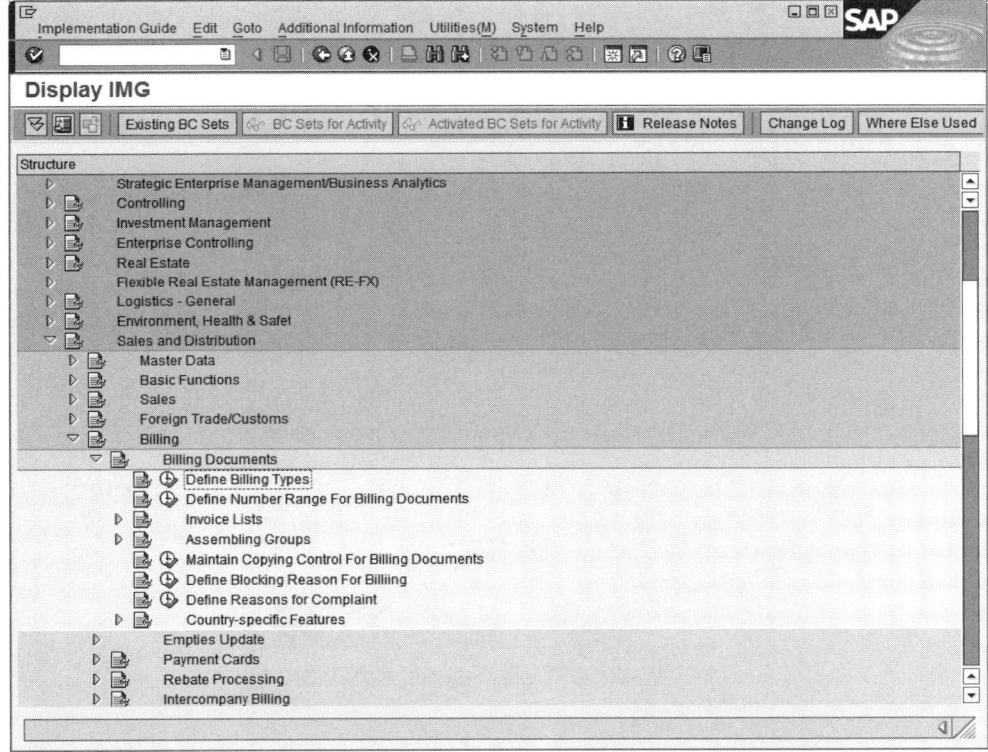

© SAP AG. All rights reserved.

FIGURE 7.2 Displaying the Define Billing Types activity

Note: You can access the SAP Customizing Implementation Guide by using the SPRO transaction code.

2. Click the **IMG Activity** icon (⊕) beside the **Define Billing Types** activity (Figure 7.2). The **Choose Activity** dialog box appears as shown in Figure 7.3.

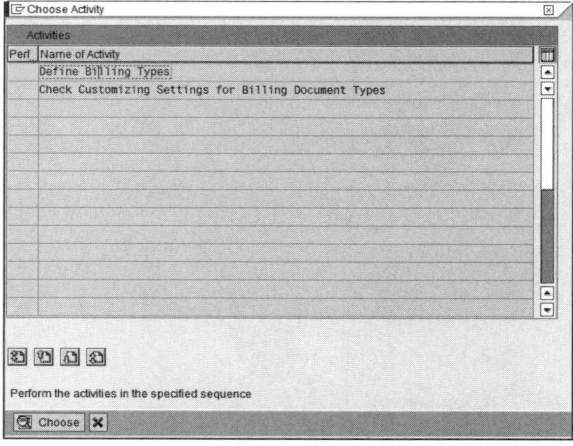

© SAP AG. All rights reserved.

FIGURE 7.3 Displaying the Choose Activity dialog box

3. Select the **Define Billing Types** activity and click the **Choose** button (Figure 7.3). The **Change View "Billing: Document Types": Overview** screen appears as shown in Figure 7.4.

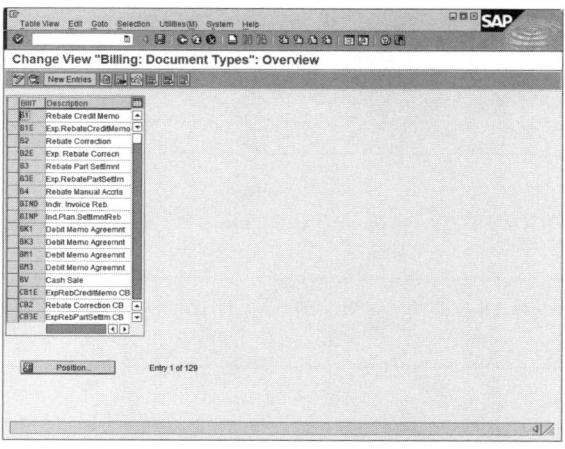

© SAP AG. All rights reserved.

FIGURE 7.4 Displaying the Change View "Billing: Document Types": Overview screen

4. Click the **New Entries** button in the **Change View "Billing: Document Types": Overview** screen (Figure 7.4). The **New Entries: Details of Added Entries** screen appears as shown in Figure 7.5.

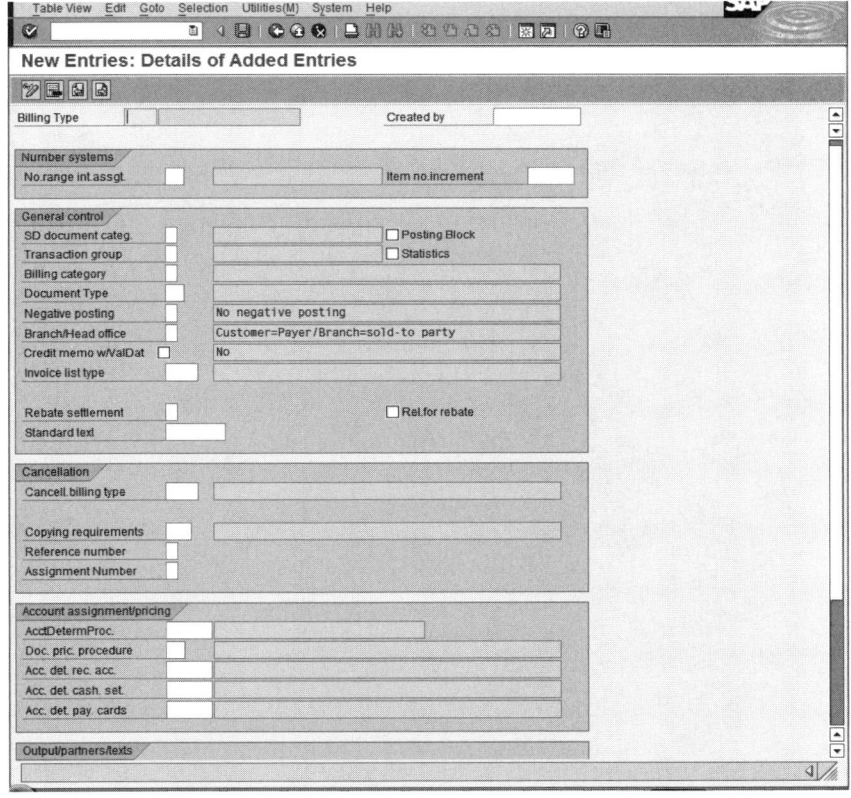

© SAP AG. All rights reserved.

FIGURE 7.5 Displaying the New Entries: Details of Added Entries screen

Note: You can create a new billing type by entering its name, which must be prefixed with a Y or Z letter.

The **New Entries: Details of Added Entries** screen contains the following group boxes:

- **Number systems**—Assigns a number range to the document type.
- **General control**—Specifies the general data related to a billing type.

- **Cancellation**—Specifies the details of the cancellation data.
- **Account assignment/pricing**—Determines the condition types for various types of accounts or pricing procedures.
- **Output/partners/texts**—Defines the header and item levels of a billing type.

Figure 7.6 shows a billing type, **F5**, in the display mode.

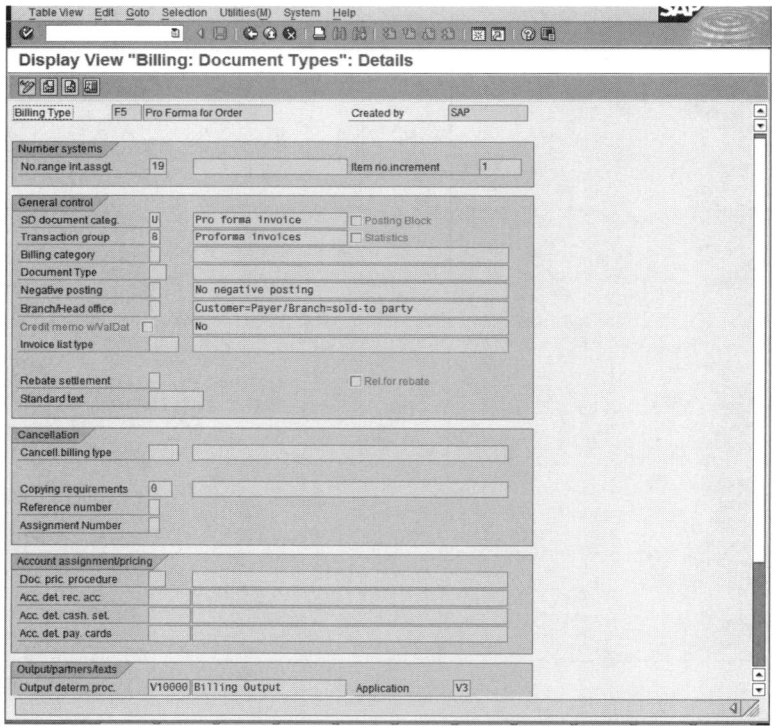

© SAP AG. All rights reserved.

FIGURE 7.6 Displaying the details of the F5 billing document type

> **Note:** To open a billing type in the display mode, as shown in Figure 7.6, click the **Display/Change** icon ( ) in the **Change View "Billing: Document Types": Overview** screen (Figure 7.4), and then click the **Details** icon ( ).

Table 7.2 lists the controls used to create a billing type.

Control	Description
Billing Type	Specifies the type of billing document.
Created by	Specifies the name of the person who created the billing type.
No. range int.assgt.	Specifies a number that determines a number range for the billing documents.
Item no. increment	Specifies the increment number used by the mySAP ERP system while generating an item number for a sales, delivery, or billing document.
SD document categ.	Determines how the mySAP ERP system stores and maintains the document data on the basis of different types of documents.
Posting Block	Allows blocking of automatic transfer of the billing document to accounting.
Transaction group	Allows control of the features of transaction flow by sales, shipping, and billing documents.
Statistics	Allows the mySAP ERP system to store the information from billing documents for statistical analysis.
Billing category	Differentiates the billing documents to be used for various tasks, such as invoice printing, billing document creation, or forwarding to FI.
Document Type	Specifies the code of an accounting document.
Negative posting	Specifies that the transaction figures have to be reset for a document item.
Branch/Head office	Controls the partner functions of the billing document, which can be forwarded to FI.
Credit memo w/ValDat	Signifies that the VALDT (fixed value date) field in the credit memo request is filled with the payment deadline baseline date of the base billing document if the reference billing document is not set, and the payment deadline date for the base billing document appears after the billing date for the credit memo.

Continued

Control	Description
Invoice list type	Specifies the type of invoice list.
Rebate settlement	Specifies whether the billing type is used when a rebate is processed.
Rel. for rebate	Specifies whether the billing document type is relevant when a rebate is processed.
Standard text	Specifies a number for the standard text.
Cancell.billing type	Specifies the default cancellation data for the billing type.
Copying requirements	Specifies a copying routine to check whether some specific requirements are met when a document is copied from another document.
Reference number	Specifies a number that is sent from SD to FI as additional information.
Assignment number	Specifies an allocation number that is sent from SD to FI as additional information.
Account assignment/pricing	Specifies the condition types for a specific type of document, which determines the general ledger (G/L) accounts to which amounts should be posted.
Doc. pric. procedure	Specifies a key that is used to define the pricing procedure for a sales document.
Acc. det. rec. acc.	Specifies the condition types that are used by the mySAP ERP system to determine the reconciliation account, which is used for a specific type of document; for instance, an invoice.
Acc. det. cash. set	Specifies the condition types that are used by the mySAP ERP system to determine the G/L account for cash settlement, which is used for a specific type of document such as an invoice.
Acc. det. pay. cards	Specifies the condition types that are used by the mySAP ERP system to determine the G/L account for document types used in payment card transactions.

Continued

Control	Description
Output determ.proc.	Defines the output categories, such as order confirmation and electronic mail message for a document, and the sequence of the output categories in which they appear in the document.
Application	Specifies the applications from which output is sent, such as sales order processing or invoice processing.
Item output proc.	Refers to a combination of output categories that are used to process the output at the items level in a document; for instance, the output for a sales order item.
Output Type	Defines the required kind of output.
Header partners	Refers to a group of partner functions that the mySAP ERP system proposes for the header level of a type of billing document.
Item partners	Refers to a group of partner functions that the mySAP ERP system proposes for the item level of a type of billing document.
TextDetermProcedure	Refers to a group of text types that is used in the header of a document. This field also determines the sequence of text types in which they appear in the document.
Text determ.proc.itm	Refers to a procedure that determines the texts, which are assigned to an item in a billing document.
Delivery text	Refers to the text that is copied from a delivery note.

TABLE 7.2   Controls to create a billing type

Now, let's explore the categories of the billing documents.

Categories of Billing Documents

The billing types can be divided into various categories, depending upon the task they are designed to perform. Some of the most commonly used categories of billing documents are as follows:

- Standard invoice
- Credit and debit memos

- Pro forma invoices
- Cancellation invoices

Let's discuss these categories in detail.

Standard Invoices

A standard invoice is a sales document that contains the sales records of a customer. In other words, it is a bill given to a customer against the delivery of goods or services. It is created by referring either to a sales order or to a delivery. You create an invoice on the basis of a delivery if you want to ensure that goods are sent before the invoice is created. However, you create an invoice on the basis of a sales order if you want to receive the cost of the goods before sending the goods to the customer, or in the case of a service item, where a delivery document is not relevant. Consequently, you need to refer to a sales order, instead of a delivery order, to create an invoice in case you have to bill a customer for a service.

Credit and Debit Memos

A credit memo is a sales document that is created on the basis of a customer's complaint, such as defective goods or overcharging of the goods or services by the vendor. A debit memo, on the other hand, is a sales document that is created because the customer was not charged enough by the vendor. A credit or debit memo is created by referring to an invoice or to a credit memo request. It can include all items, selected items, or a certain quantity of items.

Pro Forma Invoices

A pro forma invoice is an invoice that needs to be created when you need to export your goods. It contains the details regarding the quantity and cost of the goods. It is created on a paper and is provided to the customs/governing authorities of the receiving country, so that they can verify the forthcoming shipments. A pro forma invoice is created on the basis of a sales order or a delivery. If a pro forma invoice is created from a sales order, the billing type is **F5**. On the other hand, if it is created from a delivery, the billing type is **F8**.

Figure 7.7 shows the billing types of pro forma invoices.

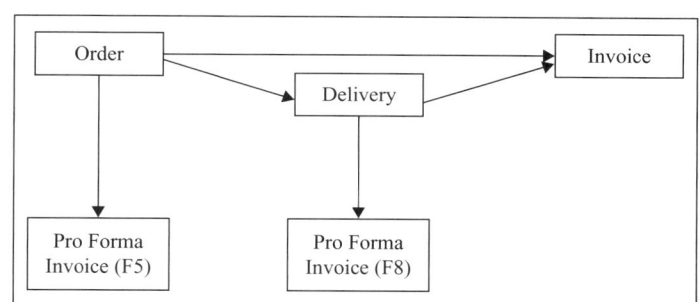

FIGURE 7.7 The billing types of pro forma invoices

Some features of a pro forma invoice, which differentiate it from a normal invoice, are listed in Table 7.3.

Parameter	Pro Forma Invoice	Normal Invoice
Payment	Payment is not necessary	Payment is necessary
Statistical data	Not required	May be required
Issuing goods	Not required	May be required
Multiple documents creation	May be more than one	Generally, one document is created
Data transfer to the FI module	Not required	Required
Accounting document	Not generated	Generated

TABLE 7.3 Differences between pro forma and normal invoices

Note: A pro forma invoice is not used to record accounts receivable for the seller and accounts payable for the buyer. Therefore, it is not considered as a true invoice.

Cancellation Invoices

A cancellation invoice is an invoice that is created when a billing document is found to have errors and needs to be cancelled or recreated. For example, a cancellation invoice is generated if the purchased goods are not mentioned in an invoice. In such a case, the original billing document is cancelled, and a new document is sent to the customer. A cancellation invoice is displayed by entering MR8M in the transaction code field of the standard toolbar of the mySAP ERP system.

Let's now learn how to create billing documents.

Creating Billing Documents

We learned earlier that a billing document contains the details of the goods purchased or services rendered by a company to a customer. You can create different types of billing documents depending on the type of business transaction, such as the sale or delivery of goods. To create a billing document, you first need to open the **Create Billing Document** screen. For this, navigate the following menu path:

Menu Path
SAP menu > Logistics > Sales and Distribution > Billing > Billing Document

Now, double-click the **VF01 – Create** option, as shown in Figure 7.8.

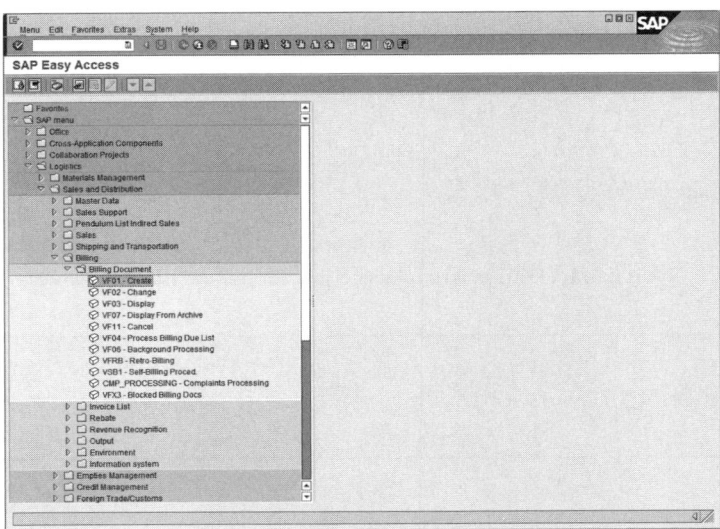

© SAP AG. All rights reserved.

FIGURE 7.8 Displaying the VF01 – Create option

The **Create Billing Document** screen appears as shown in Figure 7.9.

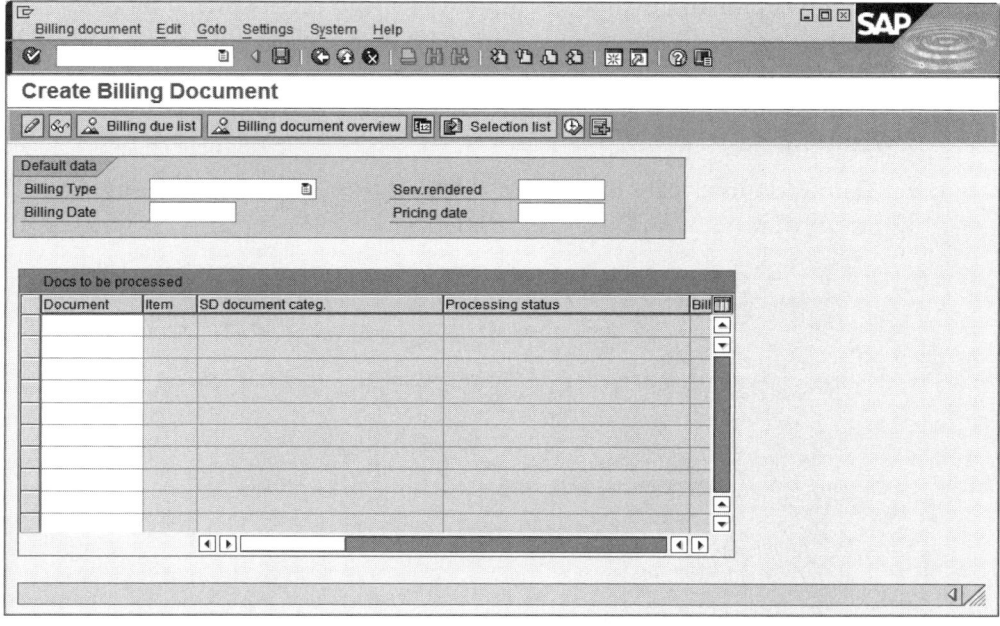

FIGURE 7.9 Displaying the Create Billing Document screen

Figure 7.9 displays the following fields, which need to be filled in order to create a billing document:

- **Billing Type**—Specifies the type of billing document required for the billing process.
- **Serv.rendered (services rendered)**—Specifies the date when the goods have been supplied or the date the services have been rendered to the customer.
- **Billing Date**—Specifies the date on which the billing document was generated.
- **Pricing date**—Represents the date on which the price of goods was entered in the mySAP ERP system.
- **Document**—Specifies the number of the sales or distribution document. This number must be unique because it helps to identify the type of document, such as sales, delivery, or billing.

Let's now learn how to modify the billing documents.

Modifying Billing Documents

To modify an existing billing document, navigate the following menu path:

Menu Path

SAP menu > Logistics > Sales and Distribution > Billing > Billing Document

Then, double-click the **VF02 – Change** option. The **Change Billing Document** screen appears as shown in Figure 7.10.

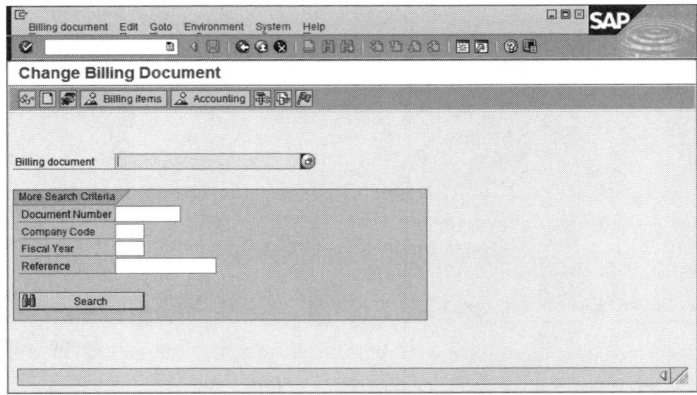

© SAP AG. All rights reserved.

FIGURE 7.10 Displaying the Change Billing Document screen

The following fields are displayed in the **Change Billing Document** screen:

- **Billing document**—Specifies the type of billing document you want to change.
- **Document Number**—Specifies the number of the billing document you want to change.
- **Company Code**—Specifies the company code to which the billing document belongs.

- **Fiscal Year**—Specifies the year in which the billing document was created.
- **Reference**—Specifies a reference number of the billing document.

Table 7.4 shows the important transaction codes and menu paths that are used to perform operations related to a billing document.

Transaction Code	Menu Path	Description
VF01	SAP menu > Logistics > Sales and Distribution > Billing > Billing Document > Create	Creates a billing document.
VF02	SAP menu > Logistics > Sales and Distribution > Billing > Billing Document > Change	Modifies a billing document.
VF03	SAP menu > Logistics > Sales and Distribution > Billing > Billing Document > Display	Displays a billing document.
VF04	SAP menu > Logistics > Sales and Distribution > Billing > Billing Document > Process Billing Due List	Processes a pending billing document from the billing due list. A billing due list is a collection of transactions and deliveries for which bills can be generated. In addition, during the process of billing, billing documents are created on the basis of items listed in the billing due list.
VF06	SAP menu > Logistics > Sales and Distribution > Billing > Billing Document > Background Processing	Performs background processing for a billing document.
VF07	SAP menu > Logistics > Sales and Distribution > Billing > Billing Document > Display From Archive	Displays the billing documents that have been archived.

Continued

Transaction Code	Menu Path	Description
VF11	SAP menu > Logistics > Sales and Distribution > Billing > Billing Document > Cancel	Cancels a billing document.
VFRB	SAP menu > Logistics > Sales and Distribution > Billing > Billing Document > Retro-Billing	Creates and executes the credit and debit memos after retroactive price adjustments.
VSB1	SAP menu > Logistics > Sales and Distribution > Billing > Billing Document > Self-Billing Proced.	Monitors the self-billing procedures. In this procedure, the customer provides the billing document to the company.
VFX3	SAP menu > Logistics > Sales and Distribution > Billing > Billing Document > Blocked Billing Docs	Displays the billing documents that cannot be transferred to an account.

TABLE 7.4 Transaction codes and menu paths to work with billing documents

Let's now discuss the concept of copying control in the SD module.

USING THE COPYING CONTROL PROCESS FOR BILLING

Copying control is a process in which some important transaction parameters are copied from an original document to a target document. It controls the flow of data from one document to another. For example, you can use the copying control process to create a new billing document from an existing billing or sales document. You can use the copying control process to create sales documents and deliveries as well. When creating billing documents, copying control is divided into three copy control rules that define the copy rules for the header and item levels between the documents. The three copy control rules are as follows:

- **Sales Document to Billing Document**—Creates a billing document by copying data from a sales document.
- **Billing Document to Billing Document**—Creates a billing document by copying data from another billing document.

- **Delivery Document to Billing Document**—Creates a billing document by copying data from a delivery document.

The following features are considered when the copying control process is used to create billing documents from other documents:

- **Reference Documents**—Signifies the documents that may be used as reference documents to create billing documents. Some examples of these documents are invoices, credit and debit memos, pro forma invoices, and cancellation documents. For example, invoices are based on deliveries or services; credit and debit memos are based on their requests, pro forma invoices are based on sales documents or deliveries; and cancellation documents are based on billing documents or credit memos.
- **Flow of Data**—Signifies the data that has to be copied from reference documents to billing documents. You can refer to the entire reference document, or to its individual items, or to some specific quantities of items from the reference document. An example is a delivery-related billing document, where quantities are copied from the delivery and prices are copied from the sales order.
- **Billing Quantity**—Signifies either the order quantity or the delivery quantity that has to be invoiced.
- **Requirements for Copying**—Signifies the requirements according to which a sales document is billed.
- **Pricing**—Signifies whether the pricing should be carried out again or should be copied from a sales order.

In the SD module, you can access the copying control by navigating the following menu path:

Menu Path

SAP Customizing Implementation Guide > Sales and Distribution > Billing > Billing Documents > Maintain Copying Control For Billing Documents

Figure 7.11 shows the preceding menu path.

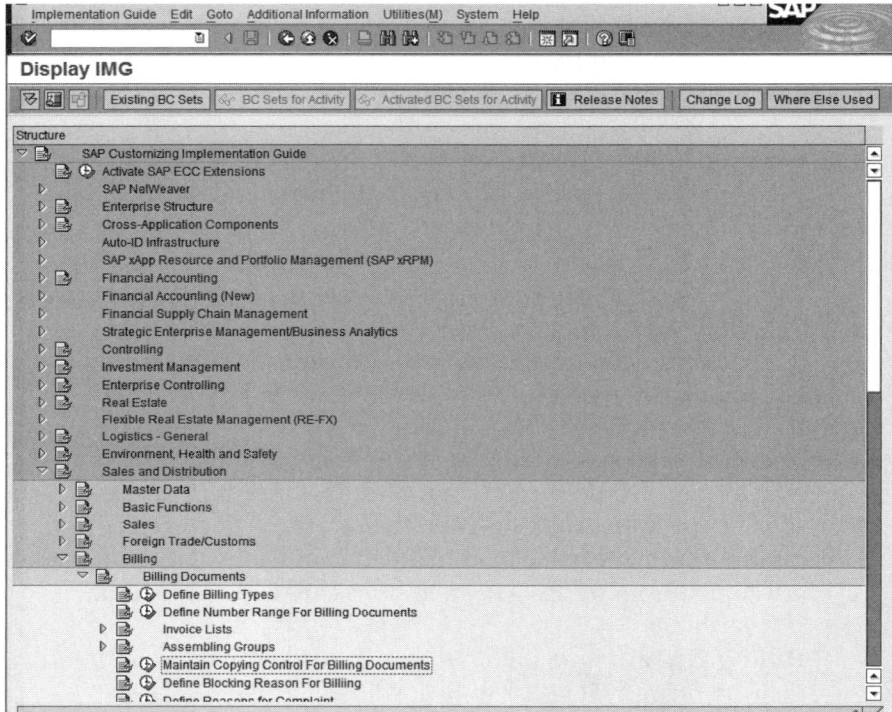

FIGURE 7.11   Displaying the Maintain Copying Control For Billing Documents activity

Click the **IMG Activity** icon (⊕) beside the **Maintain Copying Control For Billing Documents** activity (Figure 7.11). The **Choose Activity** dialog box is displayed as shown in Figure 7.12.

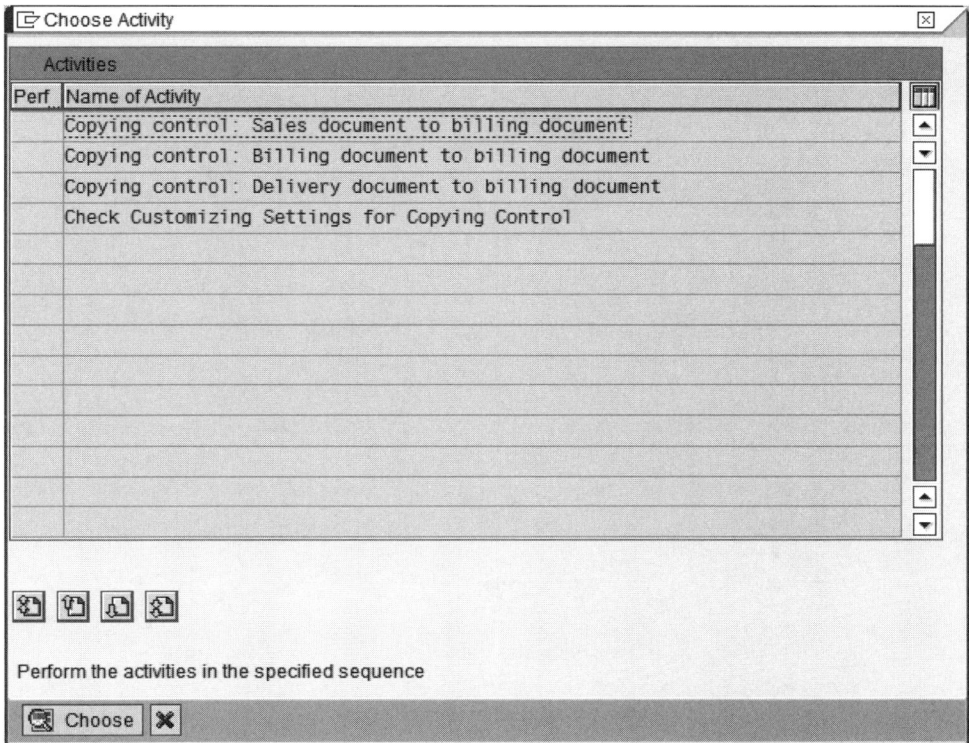

FIGURE 7.12 Displaying the Choose Activity dialog box

Figure 7.12 displays the following options used by the copying control process to copy different types of billing documents:

- **Copying control**: Sales document to billing document
- **Copying control**: Billing document to billing document
- **Copying control**: Delivery document to billing document

You can select any of the three options to use the copying control process, depending upon the requirement. Let's select the **Copying control: Sales document to billing document** option and then click the **Choose** button

(Figure 7.12). The **Display View "Header": Overview** screen is displayed as shown in Figure 7.13.

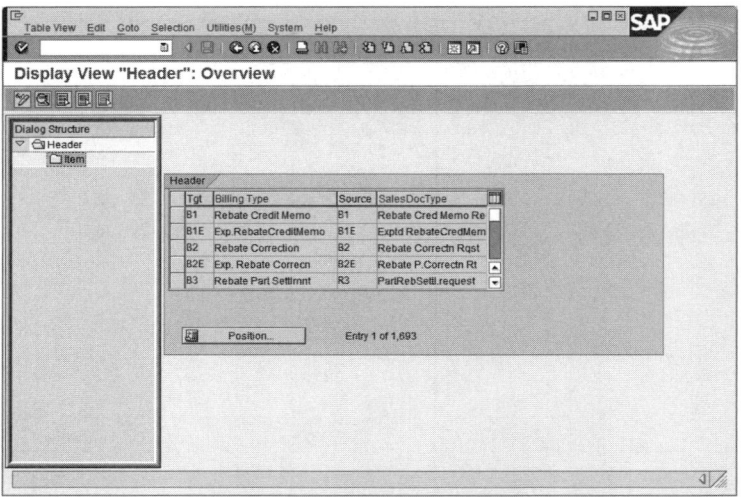

FIGURE 7.13   Displaying the View "Header": Overview screen

The following fields are displayed in Figure 7.13:

- **Tgt (Target)**—Specifies the type of billing that is being copied.
- **Source**—Specifies the type of billing document from which a target billing document type is copied.
- **Billing Type**—Describes the billing type document that is copied.
- **SalesDocType**—Describes the type of a sales document that you want to copy.

When you select the **Copying control: Billing document to billing document** option and click the **Choose** button in the **Choose Activity** dialog box (Figure 7.12), the corresponding screen appears, as shown in Figure 7.14.

Using the Copying Control Process for Billing 361

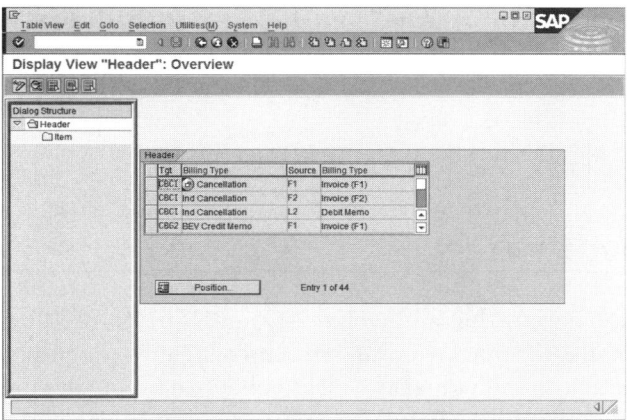

FIGURE 7.14 Displaying the View "Header": Overview screen for the second option

Note: The fields displayed in Figure 7.14 are the same as those in Figure 7.13 and have already been described earlier.

Similarly, when you select the **Copying control: Delivery document to billing document** option and click the **Choose** button in the **Choose Activity** dialog box (Figure 7.12), the corresponding screen appears, as shown in Figure 7.15.

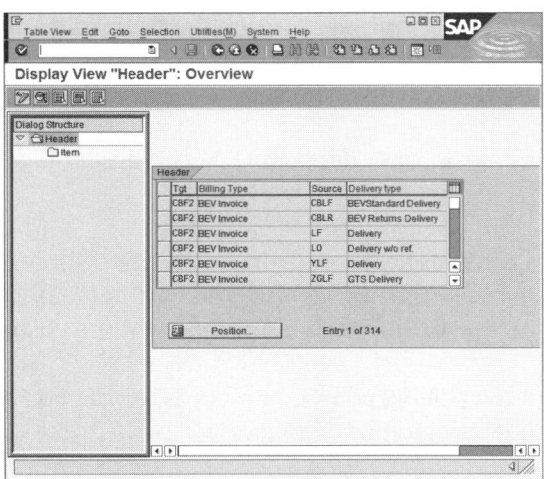

FIGURE 7.15 Displaying the Display View "Header": Overview screen for the third option

In Figure 7.15, you see four fields: **Tgt**, **Billing Type**, **Source**, and **Delivery type**. The first three fields are the same as those in Figure 7.15 and have already been described. The **Delivery type** field specifies the mode of delivery of goods.

Next, let's learn how to create invoice list types.

CREATING INVOICE LISTS

We learned earlier that an invoice list signifies a list of individual or collective billing documents that are combined into one billing document. One invoice list can contain both individual as well as collective billing documents. The mySAP ERP system provides the following two types of invoice lists:

- Invoice list for the invoices and debit memos (LR)
- Invoice list for credit memos (LG)

You need to perform the following steps before using invoice lists:

- Assign an invoice list to a billing document type that you want to use. You should use the LR invoice list type for invoices and debit memos and the LG invoice list type for credit memos.
- Maintain the **RL00** (factoring discount) condition type, and the **MW15** (factoring discount tax) condition type, if required.
- Define copying requirements, such as the payer and terms of payment, which must be similar in the billing documents that are included in the invoice list.

The following master data must be maintained for the functioning of invoice lists:

- Define a customer calendar, which specifies the time interval or dates to process the invoice list. The customer calendar must be entered in the **Billing Sales Area** view of the customer master record.
- Maintain the pricing condition records for the **RL00** and **MW15** condition types (if required).

- Create the output condition records for the **LR00** and **RD01** condition types.

The structure of an invoice list contains header data and item data. The header data contains information, such as the net value of the billing documents and the discount provided, as well as the tax levied on the list of goods in the invoice list. The item data, on the other hand, is the data pertaining to an item, such as purchased goods, their quantity, and their net price.

An invoice list contains various billing documents, such as credit and debit memos, which are used for the payment of the purchased goods. You can create an invoice list for a customer at either specific intervals or specific dates. Navigate the following menu path to create an invoice list:

Menu Path

SAP menu > Logistics > Sales and Distribution > Billing > Invoice List > VF21 – Create

Figure 7.16 shows the preceding menu path.

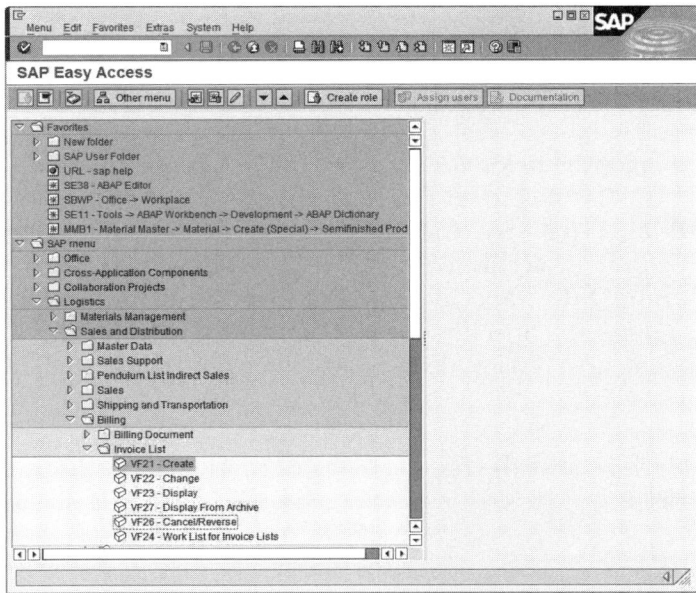

© SAP AG. All rights reserved.

FIGURE 7.16 Displaying the VF21 – Create activity to create an invoice list

Double-click the **VF21 – Create** option shown in Figure 7.16. The **Create Invoice List** screen is displayed as shown in Figure 7.17.

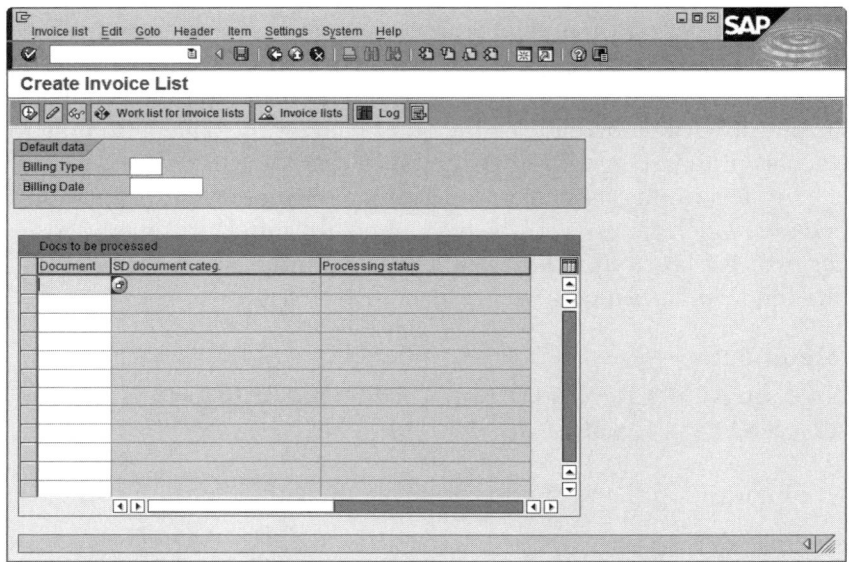

FIGURE 7.17 Displaying the Create Invoice List screen

The following fields are displayed in the **Create Invoice List** screen:

- **Billing Type**—Specifies the types of billing documents to create an invoice list.
- **Billing Date**—Specifies the date to create an invoice list.
- **Document**—Specifies a unique number to identify the document as a sales, delivery, or billing document, to create an invoice list.

Table 7.5 shows the transaction codes and menu paths used to work with invoice lists.

Transaction Code	Menu Path	Description
VF21	SAP menu > Logistics > Sales and Distribution > Billing > Invoice List > Create	Creates an invoice list
VF22	SAP menu > Logistics > Sales and Distribution > Billing > Invoice List > Change	Modifies an invoice list
VF23	SAP menu > Logistics > Sales and Distribution > Billing > Invoice List > Display	Displays an invoice list
VF24	SAP menu > Logistics > Sales and Distribution > Billing > Invoice List > Work List for Invoice Lists	Displays a work list for an invoice list
VF26	SAP menu > Logistics > Sales and Distribution > Billing > Invoice List > Cancel/Reverse	Cancels or reverses an invoice list
VF27	SAP menu > Logistics > Sales and Distribution > Billing > Invoice List > Display From Archive	Displays an archived invoice list

TABLE 7.5 Transaction codes and menu paths used to work with invoice lists

Use the **Assign Invoice List Type to Each Billing Type** activity for assigning an invoice list type to a billing document type. You can access the **Assign Invoice List Type to Each Billing Type** activity by navigating the following menu path:

Menu Path

SAP Customizing Implementation Guide > Sales and Distribution > Billing > Billing Documents > Invoice Lists

Figure 7.18 shows the assigned invoice list type to various billing document types.

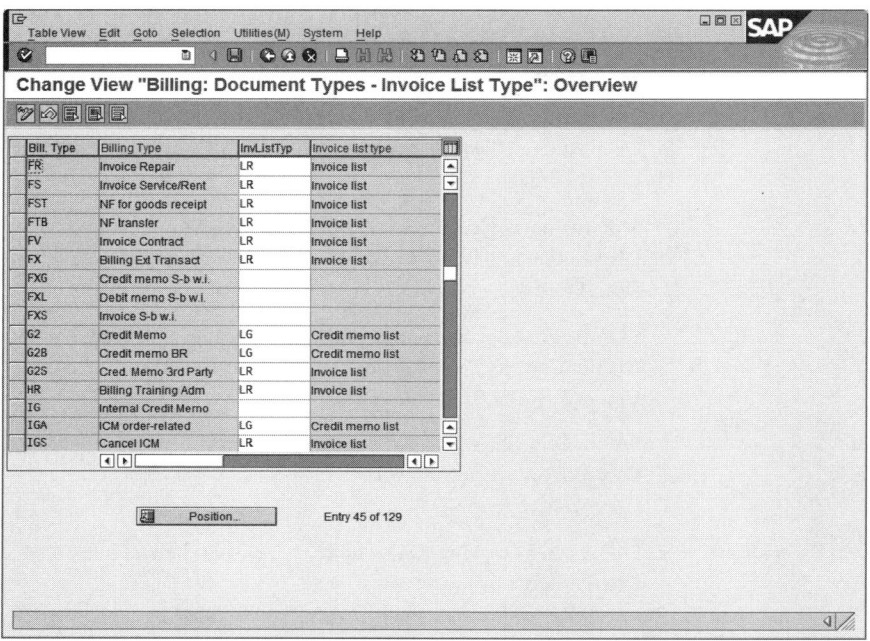

© SAP AG. All rights reserved.

FIGURE 7.18 **Displaying the assigned invoice list type to various billing document types**

Now, let's discuss the billing plans used in the mySAP ERP system.

WORKING WITH BILLING PLANS

A billing plan is a plan that contains a list of dates according to which the mySAP ERP system generates billing request items. After generating billing request items, the mySAP ERP system also creates a billing document based on each billing request item. Note that if a billing plan is defined at the header level of a sales document, the billing plan is valid for all the items that are assigned to it. Moreover, each billing plan has a unique billing plan number that is used to generate a billing document. This unique billing plan number is assigned to a billing plan internally by the mySAP ERP system.

> **Note:** A billing request item is an item for billing, which is generated on the basis of specific criteria of a billing plan.

The menu path to define a billing plan type in the mySAP ERP system is **SAP Customizing Implementation Guide > Sales and Distribution > Billing > Billing Plan > Define Billing Plan Types**

Figure 7.19 shows the preceding menu path.

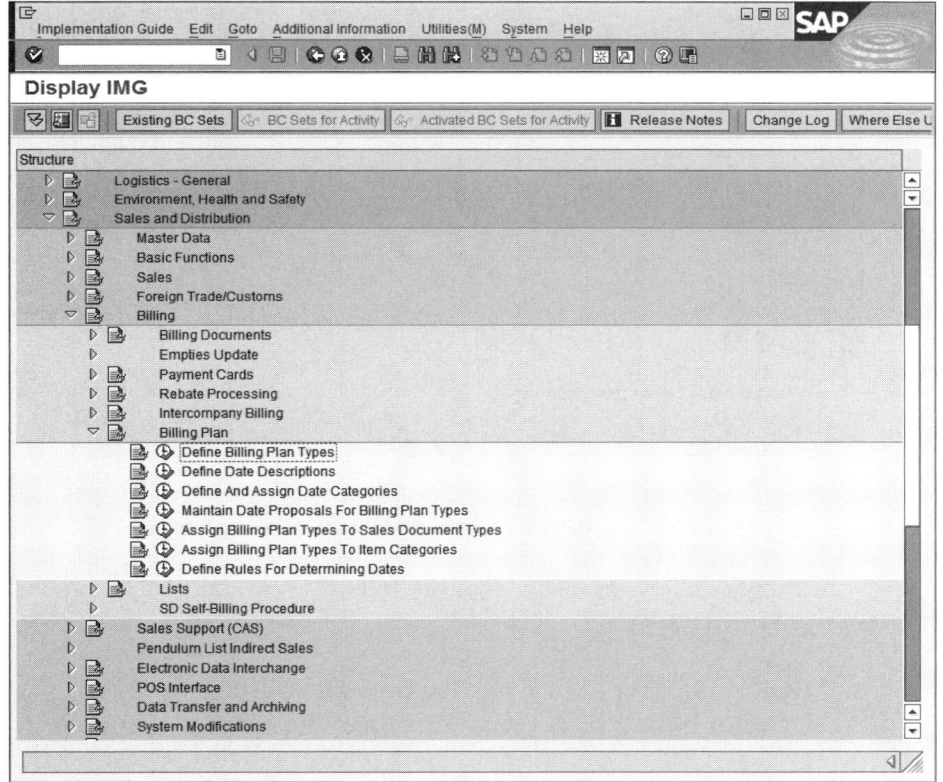

© SAP AG. All rights reserved.

FIGURE 7.19 Displaying the Define Billing Plan Types activity for a billing plan

When you click the **IMG Activity** icon (⊕) beside the **Defining Billing Plan Types** activity in Figure 7.19, the **Choose Activity** dialog box is displayed, as shown in Figure 7.20.

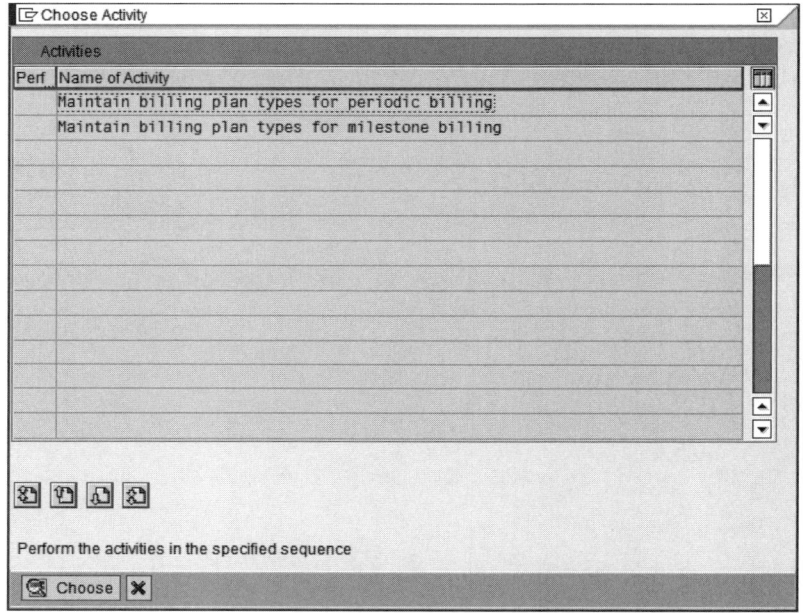

© SAP AG. All rights reserved.

FIGURE 7.20 Displaying the Choose Activity dialog box

In Figure 7.20, you can see that the following two options are available in the mySAP ERP system:

- **Maintain billing plan types for periodic billing**
- **Maintain billing plan types for milestone billing**

Let's next create these billing plans in the SD module.

Periodic Billing

Billing for a good or service might be distributed over a period of time, where the customer has to pay a specific predefined amount at predefined periods or intervals. This type of billing arrangement is called periodic billing.

Note that the installment amounts and dates of payment may not be equal, but they are always predefined in the periodic billing. For example, a customer may enter into a periodic billing arrangement to pay a total amount due of $1,000 in three installments within 12 months. The customer could pay $500 in the sixth month, $200 in the eighth month, and $300 in the twelfth month. In periodic billing a billing document is generated after the end of every predefined period.

To create a billing plan for periodic billing, select the **Maintain billing plan types for periodic billing** option (Figure 7.20) and click the **Choose** button. The **Change View "Maintain Billing Plan Types for Periodic Billing": Overview** screen is displayed as shown in Figure 7.21.

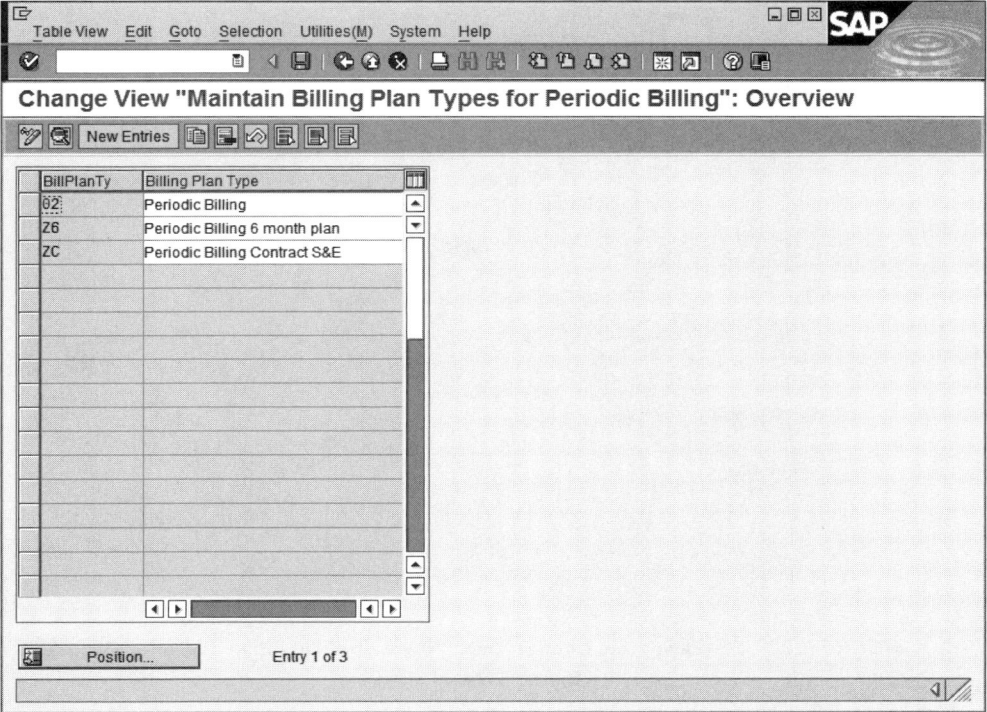

© SAP AG. All rights reserved.

FIGURE 7.21 Displaying the Change View "Maintain Billing Plan Types for Periodic Billing": Overview screen

The following fields are displayed in the **Change View "Maintain Billing Plan Types for Periodic Billing": Overview** screen:

- **BillPlanTy**—Specifies the code to create the periodic billing plan.
- **Billing Plan Type**—Describes the type of periodic billing plan.

Now, if you select any entry in the **Change View "Maintain Billing Plan Types for Periodic Billing": Overview** screen and click the **Details** icon ( ) (Figure 7.21), the **Change View "Maintain Billing Plan Types for Periodic Billing": Detail** screen appears. In our case, we select the entry having the **BillPlanTy** as **Z6** (Figure 7.21). The **Change View "Maintain Billing Plan Types for Periodic Billing": Detail** screen appears, as shown in Figure 7.22.

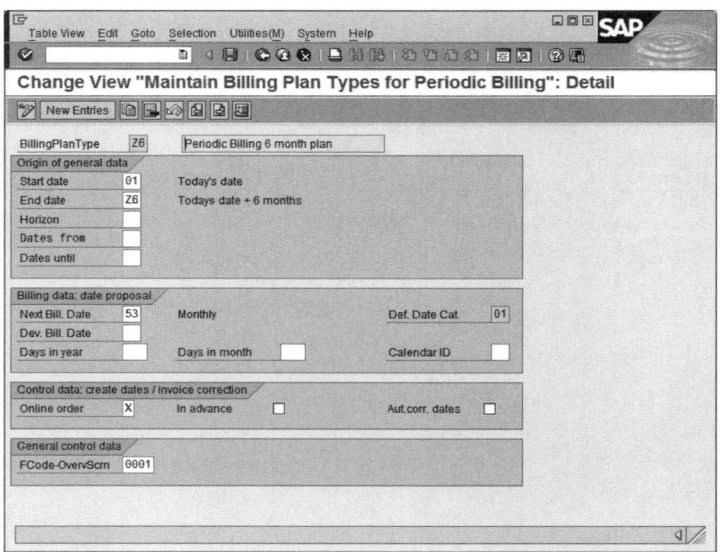

© SAP AG. All rights reserved.

FIGURE 7.22 Displaying the Change View "Maintain Billing Plan Types for Periodic Billing": Detail screen

In the **Change View "Maintain Billing Plan Types for Periodic Billing": Detail** screen, you see the following fields:

- **Start date**—Specifies the date on which the periodic billing plan is created.
- **End date**—Specifies the date on which the periodic billing plan is scheduled to end.
- **Horizon**—Specifies the end date of the previous periodic billing plan stored in the mySAP ERP system. This field is used by the mySAP ERP system to determine the last date of the present periodic billing plan.
- **Dates from**—Specifies a unique number for setting the start date of the periodic billing plan.
- **Dates until**—Specifies a unique number for setting the end date of the periodic billing plan.
- **Next Bill. Date**—Specifies the date of the next periodic billing plan.
- **Def. Date Cat.**—Specifies a unique number used to set a billing rule for a periodic billing plan.
- **Dev. Bill. Date**—Specifies a date on which a customer wants his or her bill for the purchased goods. For example, a customer might want his or her bill 2 days before the end of the month.
- **Days in year**—Specifies the number of days in a year, in the context of the periodic billing plan.
- **Days in month**—Specifies the number of days in a month, in the context of the periodic billing plan.
- **Calendar ID**—Specifies the factory calendar for defining the days, which are relevant for billing or invoicing. A factory calendar is a collection of days on which billing should be carried out.
- **FCode-OvervScrn**—Specifies a unique number of a screen that a user wants to navigate after entering the data on the initial screen of the periodic billing plan.

The **Change View "Maintain Billing Plan Types for Periodic Billing": Detail** screen also displays the following check boxes:

- **Online order**—Specifies the values (X, Y, or blank) to determine whether the mySAP ERP system generates an online bill for the periodic billing plan.
- **In advance**—Specifies whether a bill for the periodic billing plan is created in advance.

- **Aut.corr. dates**—Activates automatic creation of credit memo dates in the periodic billing plan.

Let's now explore milestone billing.

Milestone Billing

Milestone billing is a billing arragement in which a customer is billed in installments spread over a specific period of time on the achievement of a predefined milestone for a work.

The difference between milestone and periodic billing is that in milestone billing, the customer has to pay the total amount in parts or installments that are not fixed because it depends on the achievement of a milestone. For example, rental billing is an example of periodic billing, and billing done on the achievment of predefined milestones during the construction of a bridge is an example of milestone billing. In milestone billing, a billing document is generated on the achievement of predefined milestones.

To create a milestone billing plan in the mySAP ERP system, select the **Maintain billing plan types for milestone billing** option (Figure 7.20) and click the **Choose** button. The **Change View "Maintain Billing Plan Types for Milestone Billing": Overview** screen is displayed as shown in Figure 7.23.

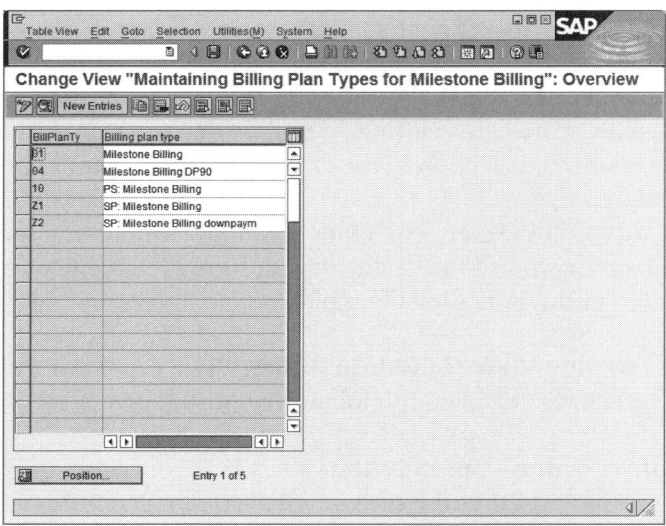

© SAP AG. All rights reserved.

FIGURE 7.23 Displaying the Change View "Maintain Billing Plan Types for Milestone Billing": Overview screen

The following fields are displayed in Figure 7.23:

- **BillPlanTy**—Specifies the types of billing plans, such as 01, 04, 10, Z1, and Z2, to create the milestone billing plan.
- **Billing plan type**—Describes the types of billing plans corresponding to the **BillPlanTy** field (Figure 7.23), such as **Milestone Billing, Milestone Billing DP90**, and **PS: Milestone Billing**.

Select the **Milestone Billing** option and click the **Details** icon ( ) (Figure 7.23). The **Change View "Maintain Billing Plan Types for Milestone Billing": De** screen is displayed as shown in Figure 7.24.

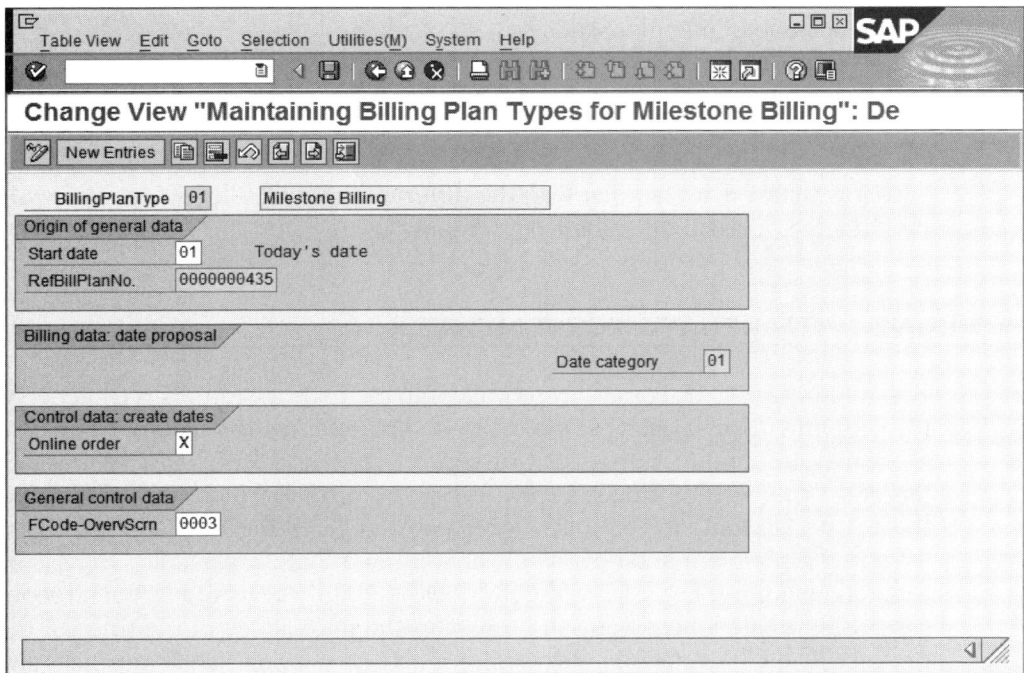

© SAP AG. All rights reserved.

FIGURE 7.24 Displaying the Change View "Maintain Billing Plan Types for Milestone Billing": De screen

The following fields are displayed in Figure 7.24:

- **BillingPlanType**—Specifies the type of billing plan to create the milestone billing plan.
- **Start date**—Specifies the start date of the milestone billing plan.
- **RefBillPlanNo.**—Specifies the billing plan number.
- **FCode-OvervScrn**—Specifies a unique number of a screen that a user wants to navigate, after entering the data on the initial screen of the milestone billing plan.

The following check boxes are also displayed in Figure 7.24:

- **Date category**—Specifies the billing plan type number of the milestone billing plan, such as 01, 02, 03, and 04.
- **Online order**—Specifies the values (X, Y, or blank) to determine whether the mySAP ERP system generates an online bill for the milestone billing plan.

Now that you are familiar with the different types of billing plans of the SD module, let's learn about rebate agreements.

WORKING WITH REBATE AGREEMENTS

Rebate is a special discount given by a company to its customers retroactively; the agreement of rebate between the company and the customer is called a rebate agreement. The special discount is based on the sales volume (or target) of the customer over a specific period of time, which is configured in the rebate agreement. A rebate agreement includes the details of a rebate, such as the recipient and criteria of rebate. In a rebate agreement, you create separate condition records for the product bought by a customer. Each record shows the rebate amount and the rebate as the percentage of the price of the product. The billing documents used for rebate processing, such as invoices and credit and debit memos, are managed by the mySAP ERP system. In addition, a rebate agreement is finally settled and reflected in a credit memo issued to a customer for the total accumulated rebate. A rebate in a rebate agreement can be based on some levels that include a material, a customer, a customer hierarchy, or a group of materials.

The following prerequisites must be configured for the processing of rebate agreements:

- A sales organization, in which you process the sales orders
- A payer
- A billing type, which includes invoices, credit memos, or debit memos

A rebate agreement is created based on the rebate agreement type, which specifies the data proposed by the mySAP ERP system for processing rebate agreements. The data proposed by the mySAP ERP system can have the following parameters:

- Condition types that can be used in a rebate agreement
- Validity period of the rebate agreement
- The required status that must be met by the rebate agreement
- Rebate agreement types that are defined in the SD module of the mySAP ERP system

Table 7.6 describes various rebate agreement types provided by the mySAP ERP system:

Rebate Agreement Type	Description
0001	Represents a group of rebates
0002	Represents a material rebate
0003	Represents a customer rebate
0004	Represents a customer hierarchy rebate
0005	Represents a rebate that is independent of sales volume

TABLE 7.6 Describing rebate agreement types

In a rebate agreement, a rebate can be offered at the following levels:

- **Material**—Implies that a rebate is based on the purchased/sold material. If the rebate is based on the percentage rate, the rebate agreement type is `0001`; whereas, if the rebate is based on the quantity of material, the rebate agreement type is `0002`.
- **Customer**—Implies that a rebate is based on the customer. The rebate agreement type for this level is `0003`. You have to specify a material for settlement when creating a condition record for a rebate at this level.
- **Customer Hierarchy**—Implies that a rebate is based on customer hierarchy. The rebate agreement type for this level is `0004`. You have to specify a material for settlement when creating a condition record for a rebate at this level.
- **A Group of Materials**—Implies that a rebate is based on a group of materials. In this level, you assign more than one material to a single rebate group. You have to specify a material for settlement when creating a condition record for a rebate at this level.

> **Note:** You must specify a material for settlement in case you create rebates that are not based on materials. The mySAP ERP system uses this material for settlement to implement the rebate. In addition, you need to create a special material master record for this material for settlement.

A rebate agreement consists of multiple individual agreements in the form of condition records. It is identified by a unique rebate agreement number. A rebate agreement contains the following data, which applies to all its condition records as well:

- The validity period of an agreement
- The status of the agreement, for instance, whether the agreement is released for settlement
- Recipient, who receives the credit memo
- Currency, which is retrieved from the sales organization
- A method of payment, such as check or draft

Each condition record can have the following data:

- The base of a rebate; for example, a customer, a material, or a customer hierarchy

- The validity period, which must be same as the validity period of the rebate agreement
- A condition rate for the condition record
- Material for settlement
- Accural rate
- Other control data; for instance, pricing scale type

Let's now learn about defining rebate agreement types.

Defining Rebate Agreement Types

As described earlier, a rebate agreement is created based on a rebate agreement type. The menu path to define a rebate agreement type in the mySAP ERP system is the following:

Menu Path

SAP Customizing Implementation Guide > Sales and Distribution > Billing > Rebate Processing > Rebate Agreements > Define Agreement Types

Figure 7.25 shows the preceding menu path.

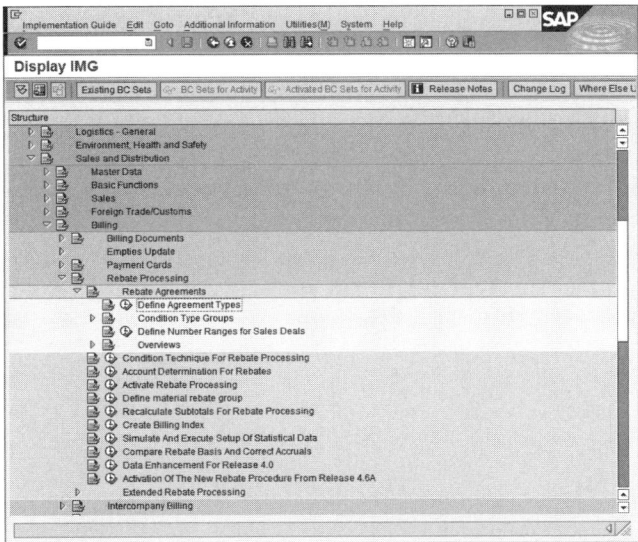

© SAP AG. All rights reserved.

FIGURE 7.25 Displaying the Define Agreement Types activity for a rebate agreement

Now, click the **IMG Activity** icon (⊕) beside the **Defining Agreement Types** activity. The **Choose Activity** dialog box appears as shown in Figure 7.26.

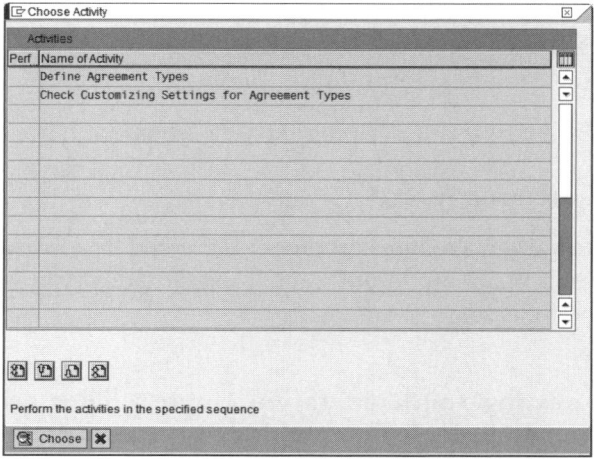

© SAP AG. All rights reserved.

FIGURE 7.26 Displaying the Choose Activity dialog box

In the **Choose Activity** dialog box (Figure 7.26), you see the following options:

- **Define Agreement Types**—Defines the type of rebate agreement.
- **Check Customizing Settings for Agreement Types**—Customizes the rebate agreement.

Next, select the **Define Agreement Types** option and click the **Choose** button (Figure 7.26). The **Change View "Rebate Agreement Types": Overview** screen appears as shown in Figure 7.27.

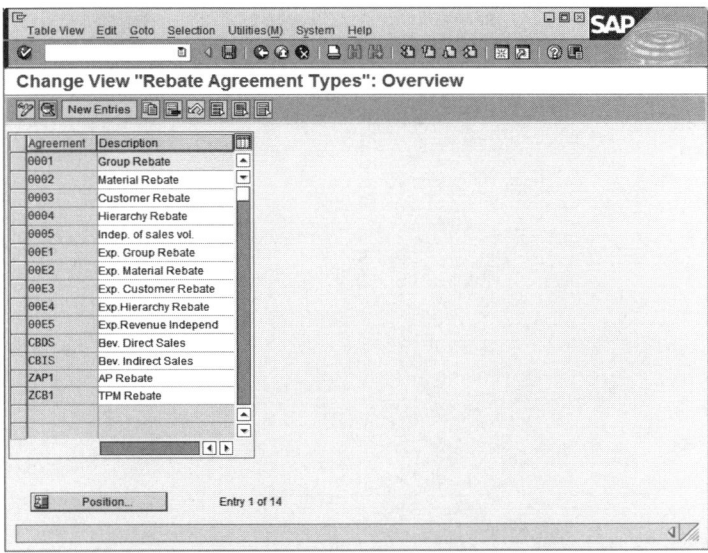

FIGURE 7.27 Displaying the Change View "Rebate Agreement Types": Overview screen

The **Change View "Rebate Agreement Types": Overview** screen displays a list of the rebate agreement types that you can use to define the rebate agreement. If you need to create a new rebate agreement type, click the **New Entries** button to open the **New Entries: Details of Added Entries** screen. Figure 7.28 shows the **New Entries: Details of Added Entries** screen.

In Figure 7.28, you see the following controls for creating a new rebate agreement type:

- **Proposed valid-from**—Specifies the starting date of the rebate validity period.
- **Proposed valid-to**—Specifies the end date of the rebate validity period.

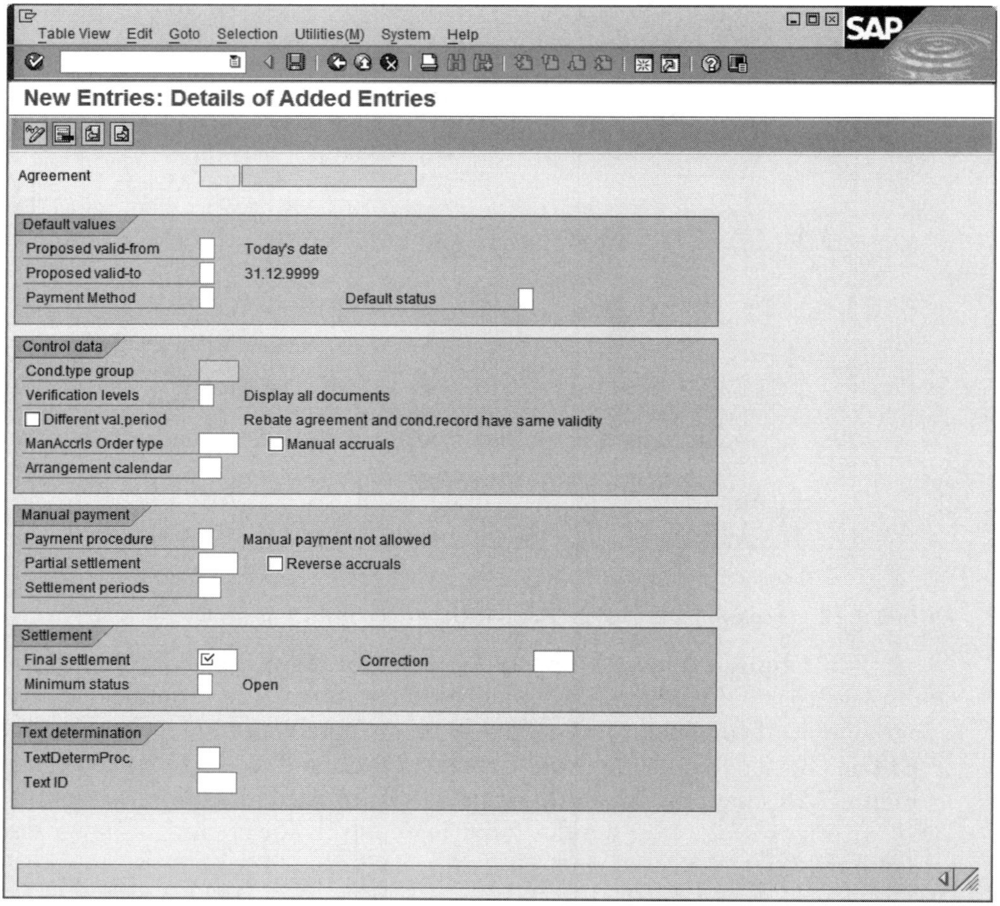

FIGURE 7.28 Displaying the New Entries: Details of Added Entries screen

- **Payment Method**—Determines how payments are to be made; that is, by check or draft.
- **Default status**—Specifies a character that denotes the default status of the rebate agreement. For example, if you don't want an agreement to be released individually for settlement, set its default status to B.
- **Cond.type group**—Specifies a group of condition types and condition tables that are used to process a rebate.
- **Verfication levels**—Determines the type of information to display or print for a particular rebate agreement. This field provides the **totals by sold-to party/material/validity period (A)** and **totals by sold-to party/material (B)** options.
- **Different val.period**—Specifies whether the validity period of a rebate is different from the condition specified in the rebate agreement.
- **ManAccris Order type**—Specifies the sales document, which is assigned to a rebate agreement and is used to perform manual accruals (the amount that is not paid by the end of the financial year) in the rebate agreement.
- **Manual accruals**—Specifies whether the manual accruals are activated in a rebate agreement.
- **Arrangement calendar**—Specifies the date until which a rebate agreement is valid.
- **Payment procedure**—Specifies the procedure of payment for a rebate agreement.
- **Partial settlement**—Specifies the sales document used for partial settlement of a rebate agreement.
- **Reverse accruals**—Specifies whether a manual payment is made for a rebate agreement.
- **Settlement periods**—Defines the period, such as arrangement yearly (**AJ**) and agreement monthly (**AM**), for settling the rebate agreement.
- **Final settlement**—Specifies the sales document used to request the final settlement of a rebate agreement.
- **Minimum status**—Defines the status the rebate agreement must reach before the final settlement may be carried out.

- **Correction**—Specifies the sales document used to correct the base values, such as sales volume, on which a payment is made for a rebate agreement.
- **TextDetermProc.**—Specifies a unique number used in the text determination procedure to create a rebate agreement.
- **Text ID**—Specifies a unique number used to denote different types of text objects, such as **TDSTYLE** (default style), **TDFORM** (default form), and **TDTEXTTYPE** (text format).

> **Note:** In the **Change View "Rebate Agreement Types": Overview** screen (Figure 7.27), you can click the **Display/Change** icon ( ) to open the list of rebate agreement types in the **Display** mode. In addition, you can click the **Details** icon ( ) to view or modify the details of any payment terms.

Figure 7.29 shows the details of the 0003 rebate agreement type in the **Display** mode:

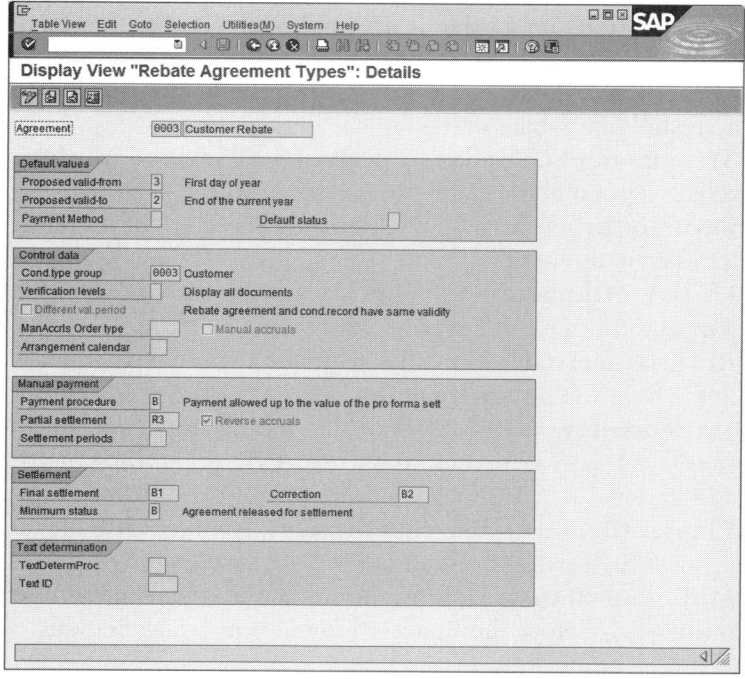

© SAP AG. All rights reserved.

FIGURE 7.29 Displaying the details of the 0003 rebate agreement type

Next, let's discuss about condition type groups, and how to define them in the SD module.

Defining Condition Type Groups

A condition type group is a group of condition records. You can define a condition type group by using the following menu path:

Menu Path

SAP Customizing Implementation Guide > Sales and Distribution > Billing > Rebate Processing > Rebate Agreements > Condition Type Groups

The **Change View "Condition Type Groups": Overview** screen appears as shown in Figure 7.30.

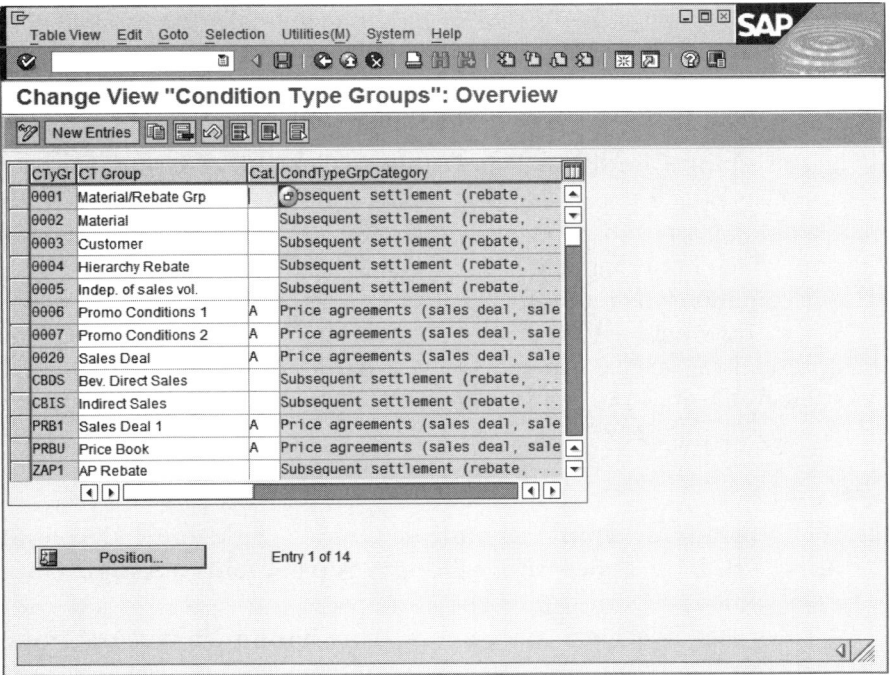

© SAP AG. All rights reserved.

FIGURE 7.30 Displaying the Change View "Condition Type Groups": Overview screen

Figure 7.30 displays the following fields:

- **CTyGr**—Specifies a group of condition types and condition tables that are used to process rebates.
- **CT Group**—Describes a condition type.
- **Cat**—Specifies the category of a condition type group.
- **CondTypeGrpCategory**—Describes a category group categorized on the basis of a conditon type.

You can copy a condition type group and then change its name by using the prefix, Z. However, note that when a condition type group is created by copying another condition type group, the mySAP ERP system does not copy the associated assignments of condition types.

Next, let's discuss how to assign various condition types to a condition type group.

Assigning Condition Types to a Condition Type Group

The **Assigning Condition Type/Table to Condition Type Groups** activity is used for rebate processing of purchased goods. In this activity, you assign the condition types that appear on the pricing procedure to the condition type group, which in turn appears on the rebate agreement type.

A condition type represents the factors, such as freight costs, custom duties, taxes, or discounts, which are used to determine the pricing procedure and output control mechanism required for particular goods in the mySAP ERP system. You can assign condition types to a condition type group by using the following menu path:

Menu Path

SAP Customizing Implementation Guide > Sales and Distribution > Billing > Rebate Processing > Rebate Agreements > Assign Condition Types/Tables to Condition Type Groups

The preceding menu path opens the **Change View "Assignment of Condition Type/Table for agreement": Overview** screen, as shown in Figure 7.31.

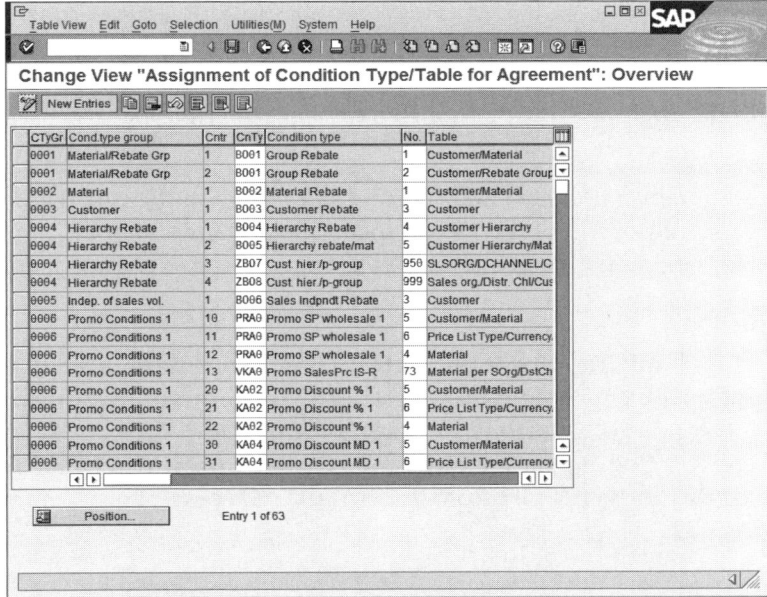

FIGURE 7.31 Displaying the "Assignment of Condition Type/Table for Agreement": Overview screen

The following fields are displayed in Figure 7.31:

- **CTyGr**—Specifies a group of condition types and condition tables used to process rebates.
- **Cond.type group**—Describes a condition type.
- **Cntr**—Specifies a unique number used to create a condition type.
- **CnTy**—Specifies a key to uniquely identify a condition type.
- **Condition type**—Specifies the type of condition in which the factors affecting the pricing of goods, such as freight cost, custom duties, or taxes, are provided.
- **No.**—Specifies a unique number of a condition record.
- **Table**—Describes a condition table, such as **Customer/Material**, and **Customer Hierarchy**.

Next, let's discuss how to assign various condition type groups to a rebate agreement type.

Assigning Condition Type Groups to a Rebate Agreement Type

As presented earlier, a condition type group consists of condition types and condition tables that are used to process a rebate in the mySAP ERP system. You can assign condition type groups to rebate agreement types by using the following menu path:

Menu Path

SAP Customizing Implementation Guide > Sales and Distribution > Billing > Rebate Processing > Rebate Agreements > Assign Condition Type Groups to Rebate Agreement Types

The preceding menu path opens the **Change View "Allocation of Condition Type Group/Agreement": Overview** screen, as shown in Figure 7.32.

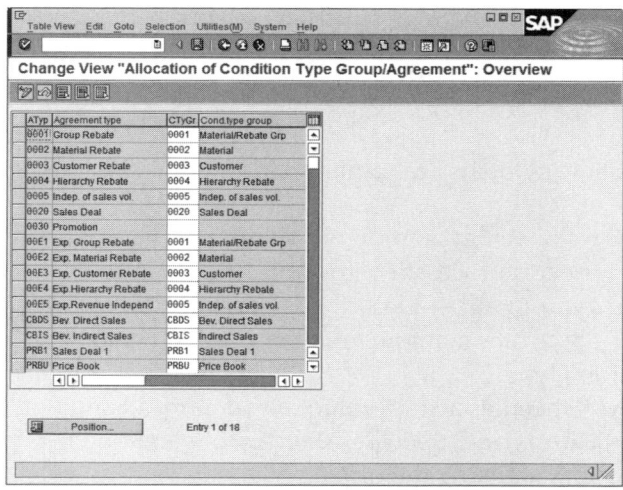

© SAP AG. All rights reserved.

FIGURE 7.32 Displaying the Change View "Allocation of Condition Type Group/Agreement": Overview screen

Figure 7.32 displays the following fields:

- **ATyp**—Specifies the type of rebate agreement, such as 0001, 0002, and 0004.

- **Agreement type**—Describes the type of rebate assigned to a rebate agreement, such as group rebate, material rebate, or customer rebate.
- **CTyGr**—Specifies a group of condition types and condition tables used to process rebates.
- **Cond.type group**—Describes a condition type group assigned to a rebate agreement, such as material/rebate group, customer, and price book.

Next, let's discuss how to activate rebate processing.

Activating Rebate Processing

You can activate rebate processing for billing types or sales organizations by navigating the following menu path:

Menu Path

SAP Customizing Implementation Guide > Sales and Distribution > Billing > Rebate Processing > Activate Rebate Processing

The **Choose Activity** dialog box appears as shown in Figure 7.33.

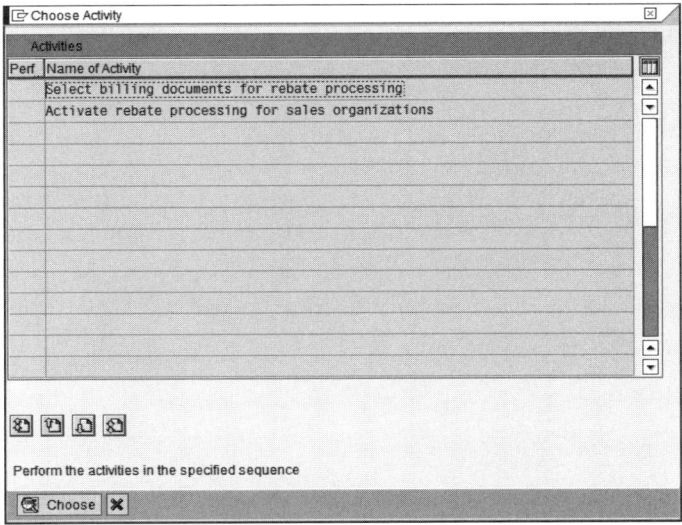

© SAP AG. All rights reserved.

FIGURE 7.33 Displaying the Choose Activity dialog box

The **Choose Activity** dialog box shows the following activities:

- **Select billing documents for rebate processing**
- **Activate rebate processing for sales organizations**

Let's learn about the preceding options one by one in the following sections.

Selecting the Billing Documents for Rebate Processing

The **Select billing documents for rebate processing** activity helps you to select the billing document types, such as credit demo and delivery-related invoice, for activating rebate processing. However, not all billing documents are relevant for rebate processing; pro forma invoices, for example.

Select the **Select billing documents for rebate processing** option (Figure 7.33) and click the **Choose** button. The **Change View "Billing: Document Types": Overview** screen appears as shown in Figure 7.34.

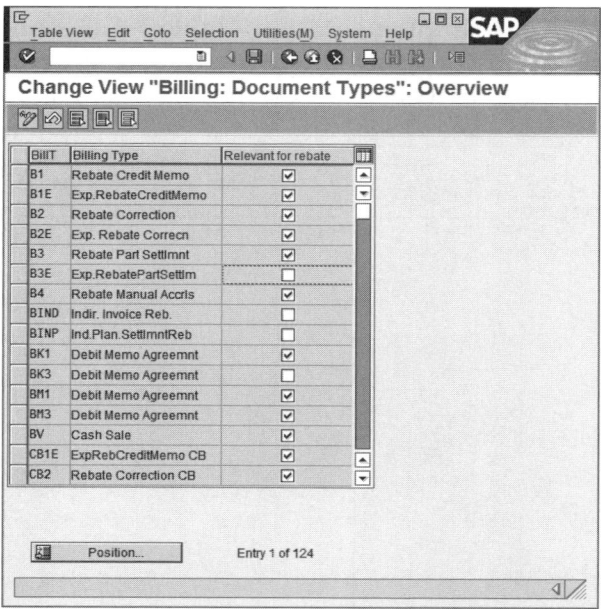

© SAP AG. All rights reserved.

FIGURE 7.34 Displaying the Change View "Billing: Document Types": Overview screen

The following fields are displayed in Figure 7.34.

- **BillT**—Specifies the types of billing documents required for rebate processing.
- **Billing Type**—Describes the billing document for rebate processing.
- **Relevant for rebate**—Indicates whether the billing documents are required for rebate processing.

Activating Rebate Processing for Sales Organizations

You can also activate rebate processing for sales organizations. Select the **Activate rebate processing for sales organizations** activity (Figure 7.33) and click the **Choose** button. The **Change View "Sales Organizations - Rebate": Overview** screen appears as shown in Figure 7.35.

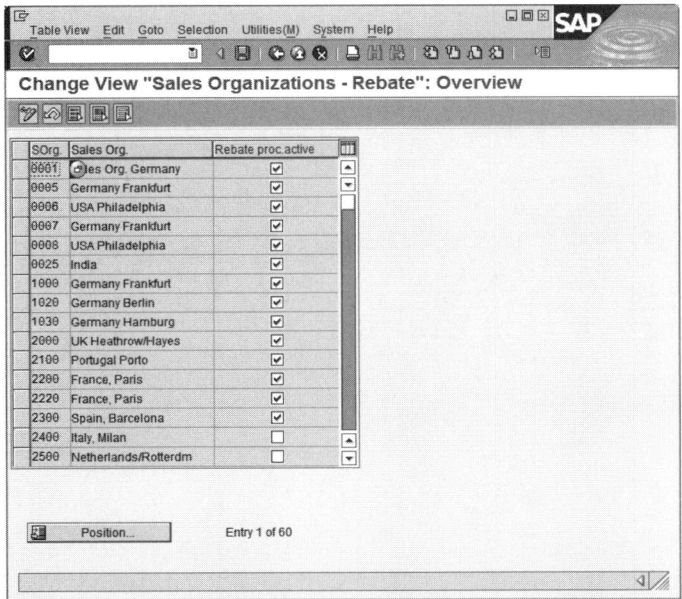

© SAP AG. All rights reserved.

FIGURE 7.35 Displaying the Change View "Sales Organizations - Rebate": Overview screen

The following fields are displayed in Figure 7.35:

- **SOrg.**—Specifies the unique number of the organizational unit offering a rebate.

- **Sales Org.**—Specifies the name of the organizational unit offering the rebate.
- **Rebate proc.active**—Indicates whether the sales organization offers rebates.

Next, let's learn to create, renew, and delete rebate agreements.

Working with Rebate Agreements

As we learned earlier, a rebate agreement is a contract or an agreement between two business partners that contains the terms and conditions of a discount that is paid after the purchase of a product. These terms and conditions include the rebate recipient, rebate value, and the criteria of the rebate.

Let's perform the following steps to create a new rebate agreement:

1. Navigate to **SAP menu > Logistics > Sales and Distribution > Master Data > Agreements > Rebate Agreement**, as shown in Figure 7.36.
2. Double-click the **VBO1 – Create** option, as shown in Figure 7.36.

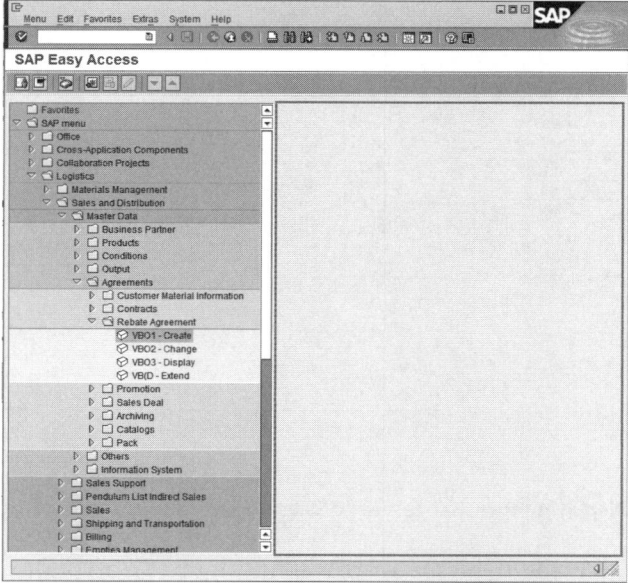

© SAP AG. All rights reserved.

FIGURE 7.36   Displaying the VBO1 – Create option

The **Create Rebate Agreement** screen appears as shown in Figure 7.37.

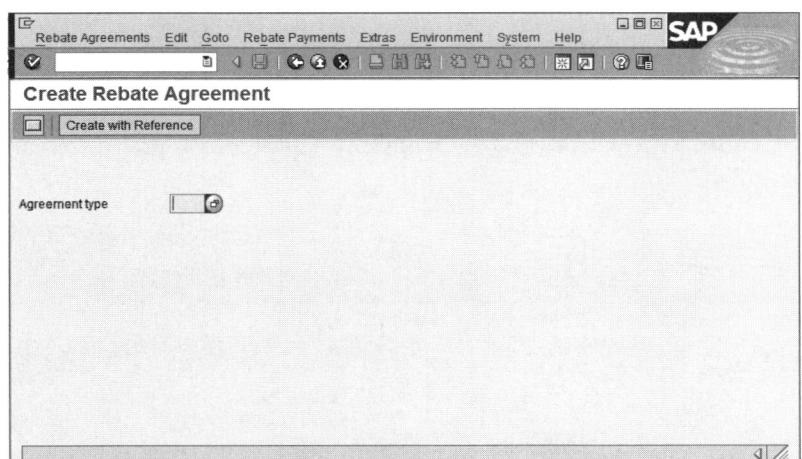

© SAP AG. All rights reserved.

FIGURE 7.37 Displaying the Create Rebate Agreement screen

3. Select an agreement type from the list of agreement types. In our case, we have selected the `0002` agreement type.
4. Click the **Organization data** icon (🗔). The **Organizational Data** dialog box appears as shown in Figure 7.38.

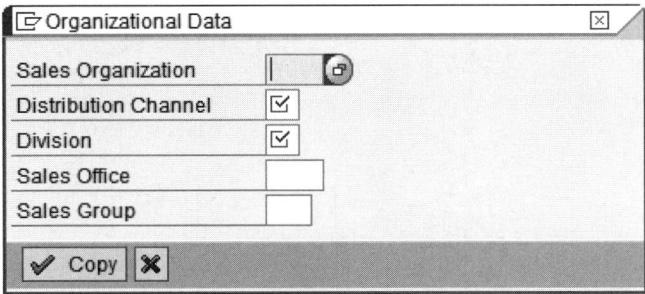

© SAP AG. All rights reserved.

FIGURE 7.38 Displaying the Organizational Data dialog box

5. Enter the data in the required fields of the **Organizational Data** dialog box, such as **Sales Organization** and **Division**.

Note that the data for the required field is automatically proposed by the mySAP ERP system. After entering the data, click the **Copy** button. The **Overview** screen related to the selected agreement type appears. In our case, the **Create Material Rebate: Overview Agreement** screen appears as shown in Figure 7.39.

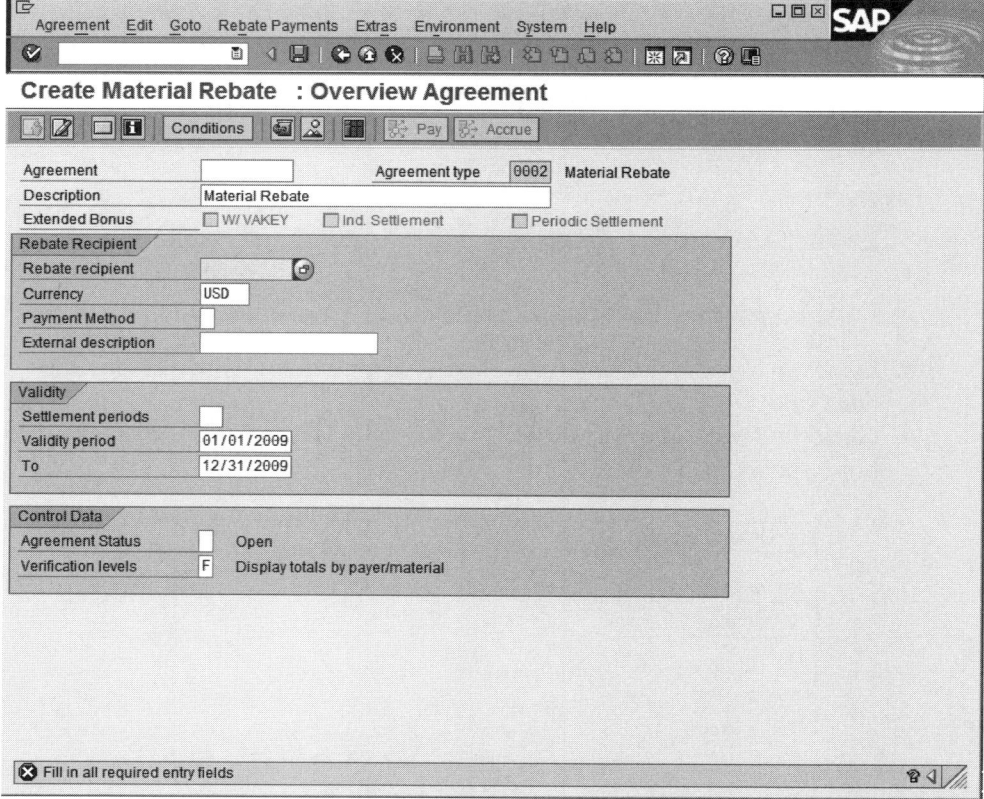

© SAP AG. All rights reserved.

FIGURE 7.39 Displaying the Create Material Rebate: Overview Agreement screen

Figure 7.39 displays the following fields:

- **Agreement**—Signifies a number that uniquely identifies the rebate agreement.
- **Agreement type**—Signifies the type of rebate agreement; for instance, whether a rebate is based on a customer or a material.
- **Description**—Signifies the description of the agreement, such as sales deal and promotion.
- **Extended Bonus**—Indicates the extended bonus information of an agreement. For instance, this control can specify whether an indirect agreement type or an enhanced rebate procedure is used to create the rebate agreement.
- **Rebate recipient**—Signifies a customer who receives the rebate specified by a rebate agreement.
- **Currency**—Represents a code denoting the currency being used.
- **Payment Method**—Determines the mode of payments, such as check, bank transfer, or bill of exchange.
- **External description**—Represents the customer's description of a rebate agreement.
- **Settlement periods**—Defines a periodic partial settlement that has to be carried out for a rebate agreement, at the relevant settlement dates.
- **Validity period**—Signifies the start date of the validity period for the agreement.
- **To**—Signifies the end date of the validity period for the agreement.
- **Agreement Status**—Signifies the current status of a rebate agreement or arrangement.
- **Verification levels**—Signifies the type of information regarding the verification for a specific rebate agreement that you can view or print.

Note: You can create condition records for a rebate agreement by clicking the **Conditions** button (Figure 7.39).

Table 7.7 shows the transaction codes and menu paths used in rebate agreements in the SD module.

Transaction Code	Menu Path	Description
VBO1	SAP menu > Logistics > Sales and Distribution > Master Data > Agreements > Rebate Agreement > Create	Creates a rebate agreement
VBO2	SAP menu > Logistics > Sales and Distribution > Master Data > Agreements > Rebate Agreement > Change	Changes an existing rebate agreement
VBO3	SAP menu > Logistics > Sales and Distribution > Master Data > Agreements > Rebate Agreement > Display	Displays a rebate agreement
VB(D)	SAP menu > Logistics > Sales and Distribution > Master Data > Agreements > Rebate Agreement > Extend	Extends an existing rebate agreement

TABLE 7.7 Transaction codes and menu paths for working with rebate agreements

Now that you have a good idea about rebate agreements, let's learn about payment processing in the SD module.

EXPLORING PAYMENT PROCESSING IN THE SD MODULE

A payment that is received from a customer must be processed in the mySAP ERP system. However, the payment that is not processed or entered in the mySAP ERP system appears in the accounts receivable as the payment to be processed or posted.

The following are the two types of payments that can be processed in the mySAP ERP system:

- **Down Payment**—Refers to partial payment, which is paid by customers at the time of purchasing the goods.

- **Installment Payment**—Specifies the payments that are paid by a customer in installments. Only one billing document is created for all the installment payments.

Let's explore these types of payments in the following sections.

Exploring the Down Payment

Down payment is the partial payment of goods paid by a customer at the time of purchasing of goods. For example, a customer may purchase plant engineering and construction or capital goods on installment. The customer is required to pay a one-time initial amount at the time of purchasing the goods, which is known as a down payment.

Down payments are saved in a sales order, and they act as a component of the agreement with the customer. A down payment agreement is created as a deadline in the billing plan, which enables a customer to agree to multiple down payments payable at different dates. The date for the down payment request is specified in the deadline of the billing plan, and the value of the agreed down payment can be created either as an amount or as a percentage value of the good.

A down payment request is sent to the customer at the specified deadline. This down payment request can be automatically generated by the mySAP ERP system from the billing due list, or it can be entered manually. While processing a down payment, a down payment request is sent to a customer at the time of the corresponding due date. This down payment request is automatically posted in the FI module. When you need to post an incoming payment for a down payment, the mySAP ERP system automatically proposes and assigns the available down payment requests.

For the partial invoice and the final invoice, the down payments that are copied to the billing document are considered as down payments for clearing. The value of these down payments for clearing is displayed in the customer invoices. However, you can modify the down payment amounts for clearing in the partial or final invoice. Moreover, you can cancel a down payment request for an invoice, along with down payment clearing.

Exploring the Installment Payment

When a customer makes a payment in installments, it is known as an installment payment. Only one billing document is created for all of the installments. Then a printed invoice is created on the basis of the billing document, which includes a list of all the individual payment dates, the total amount to be paid by the customer, and the terms and conditions of the installment.

Navigate the following menu path to define the terms of an installment payment in the SD module:

Menu Path

SAP Customizing Implementation Guide > Financial Accounting > Accounts Receivable and Accounts Payable > Business Transactions > Incoming Invoices/Credit Memos > Define Terms of Payment for Installment Payments

The **Change View "Terms of Payment for Holdback/Retainage": Overview** screen appears as shown in Figure 7.40.

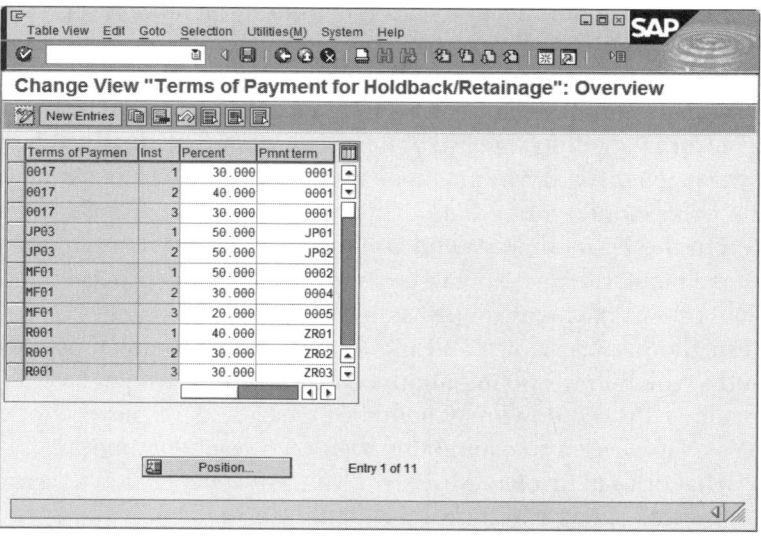

© SAP AG. All rights reserved.

FIGURE 7.40 Displaying the Change View "Terms of Payment for Holdback/Retainage": Overview screen

Figure 7.40 displays the following fields:

- **Terms of Payment**—Specifies payment terms, such as cash discounts in percentages, and payment periods.
- **Inst**—Specifies the number of installments to be paid by the customer.
- **Percent**—Specifies the percentage rate of the amount that is payable by the customer.
- **Pmnt term**—Specifies the terms of payment for a holdback or retainage. Retainage payment refers to a payment that is witheld and is paid at a later stage.

> **Note:** When an invoice has to be paid in installments, you must create several invoice items with the appropriate partial amounts and related due dates when entering payment details in a billing document. You can perform this task either by entering several items manually or by entering only one item for the entire invoice amount and using a terms of payment key for holdback or retainage payment.

Now, let's learn about payment processing.

Working with Payment Terms

The terms of payment that specify the conditions agreed between a company and a customer for the payment of invoices are known as payment terms. In SAP, payment terms determine the due date of payment for customer or vendor invoices. These payment terms can also determine when a discount is availed by a customer or granted by a vendor, and the percentage of the given discount. In other words, the mySAP ERP system can calculate the cash discount and due date for paying the invoice. In the mySAP ERP system, payment terms are maintained in the customer master record.

You can specify the terms of payment for the payment of invoices by using the **New Entries: Details of Added Entries** screen. To access the **New Entries: Details of Added Entries** screen, navigate the following menu path:

Menu Path

SAP Customizing Implementation Guide > Financial Accounting (New) > Accounts Receivable and Accounts Payable > Business Transactions > Outgoing Invoices/Credit Memos > Maintain Terms of Payment

Figure 7.41 shows the preceding menu path.

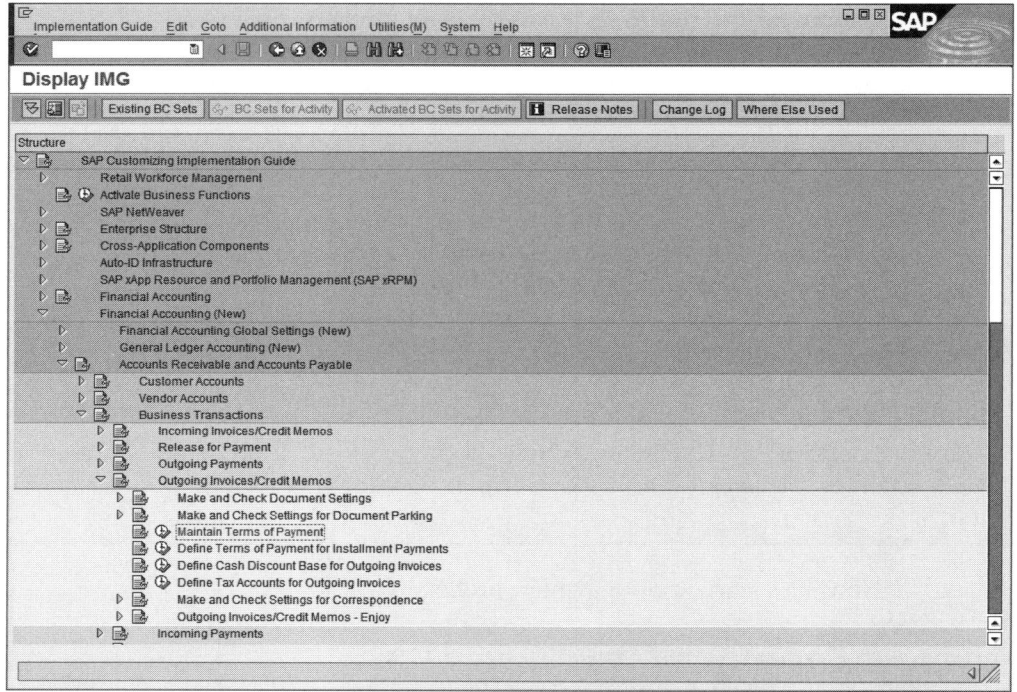

© SAP AG. All rights reserved.

FIGURE 7.41   Displaying the Maintain Terms of Payment activity for payment terms

Click the **IMG Activity** icon ( ) beside the **Maintain Terms of Payment** activity. The **Change View "Terms of Payment": Overview** screen appears as shown in Figure 7.42.

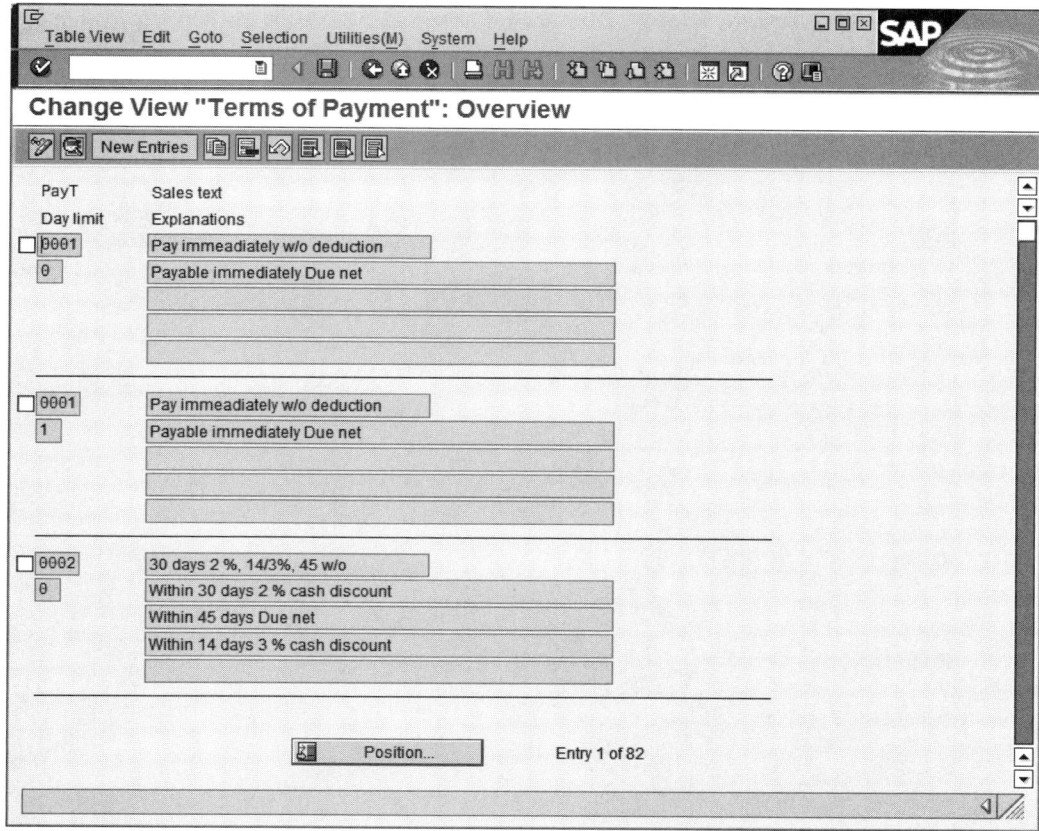

FIGURE 7.42 Displaying the Change View "Terms of Payment": Overview screen

Note: You can also open the **Change View "Terms of Payment": Overview** screen by executing the OBB8 transaction code.

In the **Change View "Terms of Payment": Overview** screen, you see a list of payment terms already created in the mySAP ERP system. Click the **New Entries** button to create a new payment term. The **New Entries: Details of Added Entries** screen appears as shown in Figure 7.43.

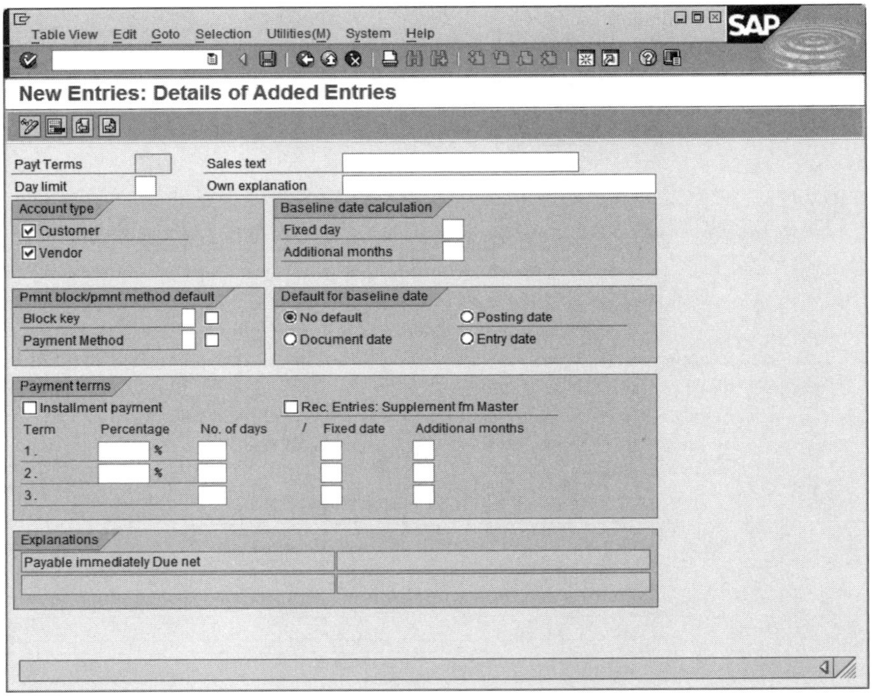

© SAP AG. All rights reserved.

FIGURE 7.43 Displaying the New Entries: Details of Added Entries screen

In Figure 7.43, you see various controls, such as text fields, check boxes, and radio buttons, in the **New Entries: Details of Added Entries** screen. Table 7.8 describes the controls that appear in the **New Entries: Details of Added Entries** screen.

Control Name	Control Type	Description
Payt terms	Text field	Specifies a unique number for specific payment terms.
Sales text	Text field	Describes the details of payment terms.
Day limit	Text field	Specifies the number of day(s) in which the payment has to be made.
Own explanation	Text field	Includes information related to a term of payment.
Customer	Check box	Specifies whether the customer account type is displayed in a payment term.
Vendor	Check box	Specifies whether the vendor account type is displayed in a payment term.
Fixed day	Text field	Specifies the due date for the payment.
Additional months (Baseline date calculation)	Text field	Specifies the number of months for which the mySAP ERP system adds the baseline date (date from which the terms of payment apply) to make a payment.
Block key	Check box	Specifies whether a payment is transferred to an invoice list.
Block key	Text field	Specifies the default value used for a term of payment.
Payment method	Check box	Specifies whether the payment method is transferred between a customer and a vendor, and if the terms of payment are changed in an invoice item.

Continued

Control Name	Control Type	Description
Payment method	Text field	Specifies how the payment is made, such as check or bank transfer.
No default	Radio button	Specifies whether a default value is required for a baseline date for a payment.
Posting date	Radio button	Specifies that the posting date is proposed in the baseline date for payment, which means the date from which the terms of payment apply.
Document date	Radio button	Specifies that the document date is proposed in the baseline date for payment.
Entry date	Radio button	Specifies that the entry date is proposed in the baseline date for payment.
Installment payment	Check box	Specifies whether the installment can be made for an invoice amount.
Rec. entries: supplement fm master	Check box	Specifies whether a term of payment is received from the customer or the vendor master record.
Percentage	Text field	Specifies the cash discount (in percentage) that is granted if the payment is made during a specified period.
No. of days	Text field	Specifies the number of days within which the payment must be made.

Continued

Control Name	Control Type	Description
Fixed date	Text field	Specifies the due date for the payment.
Additional months (Payment terms)	Text field	Specifies the total number of months within which the payment must be made.
Explanations	Text field	Describes a term of payment.
Customer	Check box	Specifies whether the customer account type is displayed in a payment term.
Vendor	Check box	Specifies whether the vendor account type is displayed in a payment term.
Block key	Check box	Specifies whether a payment is transferred to an invoice list.
Payment method	Check box	Specifies whether the payment method is transferred between a customer and a vendor, and if the terms of payment are changed in an invoice item.
Installment payment	Check box	Specifies whether the installment can be made for an invoice amount.
Rec. entries: supplement fm master	Check box	Specifies whether a term of payment is received from the customer or the vendor master record.
No default	Radio button	Specifies whether a default value is required for a baseline date for a payment.

Continued

Control Name	Control Type	Description
Posting date	Radio button	Specifies that the posting date is proposed in the baseline date for payment, which means the date from which the terms of payment apply.
Document date	Radio button	Specifies that the document date is proposed in the baseline date for payment.
Entry date	Radio button	Specifies that the entry date is proposed in the baseline date for payment.

TABLE 7.8 Controls required creating terms of payment

> **Note:** In the **Change View "Terms of Payment": Overview** screen (Figure 7.42), you can click the **Display/Change** icon (▣) to open the listed terms of payment in the **Display** mode. In addition, you can click the **Details** icon (▣) to view or modify the details of any payment terms.

With this, we come to the end of this chapter. Let's now summarize the main points of this chapter.

SUMMARY

In this chapter, you learned about billing processing. The chapter started by describing the billing documents, the structure of a billing document, different types of billing document types, different types of billing documents, and how to create, display, or modify the billing documents. You also learned how to use the copying control process for billing. Next, we described how to create an invoice list. You learned about different billing plans: periodic and milestone. Then, you learned about rebate processing, different types of rebate agreements, condition types and condition type groups for rebate agreements, and the procedures to activate rebate processing and create rebate agreements. Finally, we described payment processing in the SD module.

The next chapter describes credit and risk management in the SD module.

Chapter 8
Credit and Risk Management in SD

If you need information on:	See page:
Working with Credit Management	406
Implementing Risk Management in SD	429

We know that goods or services from an organization are purchased at a predetermined price. Sometimes, instead of making an immediate payment, the customer pays the amount at a predetermined time after purchasing the goods or services. This process of procuring goods or services from an organization before paying for the same is called credit. The purchase of a good or service from an organization on credit is restricted to a maximum amount, which is called the credit limit of the customer. The predefined time period in which the customer can pay the credit amount is called the credit period. Consider a situation where a customer wants to purchase goods worth $12,000 from an organization. However, if the credit limit assigned by an organization for the customer is worth $10,000, the customer can purchase goods on credit up to the assigned credit limit only. In this situation, if the organization has set the credit period of, say, 6 months for the customer, the customer is liable to pay the credit amount within the credit period.

In the mySAP™ ERP system, credit limit is managed through the credit management system of the mySAP ERP system. The credit management system helps you to apply checks on customers' credit limits, so that when a credit limit expires, the mySAP ERP system prompts you to take the necessary actions with regard to the set credit limit.

In this chapter, we learn how credit management and risk management are handled in the Sales and Distribution (SD) module of the mySAP ERP system.

WORKING WITH CREDIT MANAGEMENT

The credit management system in the SD module of the mySAP ERP system allows you to manage each customer's credit limit and credit period specified in the Customer Master Record.

You can use the mySAP ERP system's credit management to perform the following tasks:

- Set different credit limits for different customers
- Customize the mySAP ERP system to display information on the expiry of a customer's credit limit
- Check whether the customer has paid the entire credit amount within the specified credit period
- Block a customer from further purchasing goods or services if the credit amount is not paid within the credit period

However, before managing a customer's credit details, you need to specify a credit control area for each customer in the SAP® SD module. The credit control area helps in grouping the customers into various risk categories, such as high risk or low risk. This grouping is done on the basis of the previous payment records of the customers or on the basis of the requirement of the business process. For example, if the payment record of a customer is good, the customer can be placed in the low-risk category; whereas a customer having a bad payment record can be placed in the high-risk category. On the basis of these risk categories, you can assign different credit limits to different customers. For instance, the credit limit for a low-risk customer would be more than that of a high-risk customer. Moreover, the low-risk category offers lower restrictions for the sales process of these customers. However, the high-risk category imposes various restrictions for the sales process of high-risk customers.

You can manage credit details only after assigning a credit limit to a customer. Navigate through the following menu path to assign a credit limit:

Menu Path

SAP menu > Accounting > Financial Accounting > Accounts Receivable > Credit Management > Master Data > FD32-Change

After assigning the credit limit, you can manage the credit details of a customer on the basis of the credit control area assigned for the customer in customer master. Now, let's proceed to discuss the following processes of the credit management system:

- Managing the credit control area
- Implementing automatic credit management

Managing the Credit Control Area

In the SD module, each customer is assigned an area, known as the credit control area, which helps to manage the credit details of the customer. This credit control area helps the mySAP ERP system to automatically determine the credit limits to be assigned to a customer. You must assign company codes to the credit control area to centralize the credit management. Centralizing the credit management means assigning a single credit limit for multiple companies. You can also assign separate credit limits for various companies. However, one client or customer cannot use the credit amount assigned to another client or customer. For example, suppose you have three companies as your customers, x, y, and z, and the credit limit for each company is \$5 million per month. In this case, if the credit limit of the x company is exhausted but the credit limits of the y and z companies are not, you cannot use the credit amount allotted to the y and z companies for the x company.

You can manage the credit control area either by modifying an existing credit control area or by defining a new credit control area.

Creating a New Credit Control Area

Perform the following steps to create a new credit control area:

1. Select **SAP Customizing Implementation Guide > Enterprise Structure > Definition > Financial Accounting > Define Credit Control Area** (Figure 8.1).
2. Click the **IMG Activity** icon ( ) beside the **Define Credit Control Area** option as shown in Figure 8.1.

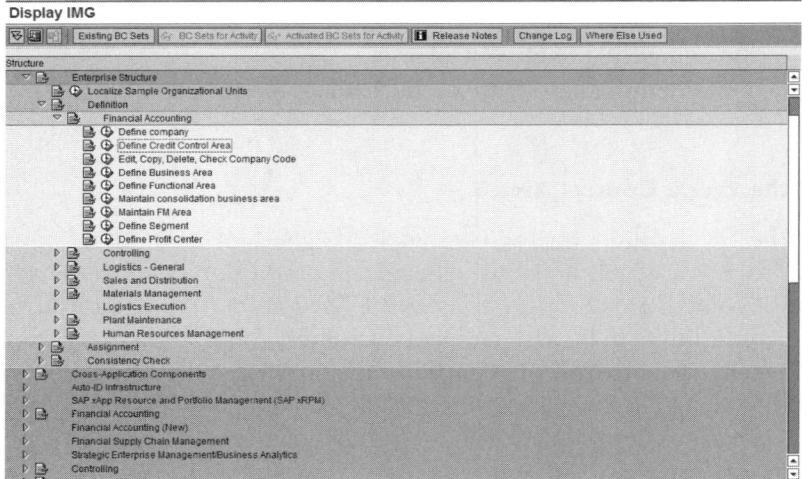

© SAP AG. All rights reserved.

FIGURE 8.1 Selecting the Define Credit Control Area option

The **Change View ""Credit Control Areas"": Overview** screen appears as shown in Figure 8.2.

3. Click the **New Entries** button on the **Change View ""Credit Control Areas"": Overview** screen (Figure 8.2).

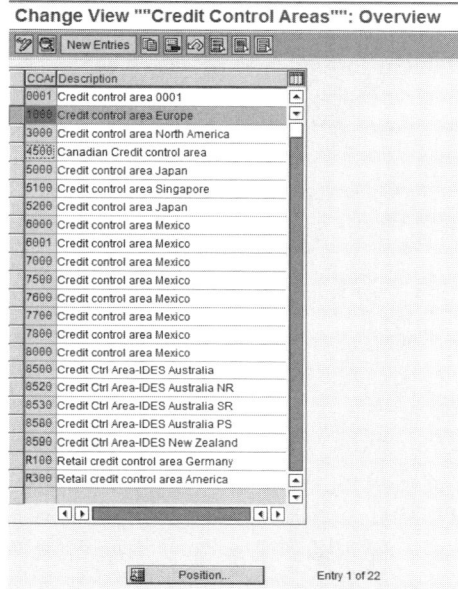

© SAP AG. All rights reserved.

FIGURE 8.2 Clicking the New Entries button

The **New Entries: Details of Added Entries** screen appears as shown in Figure 8.3.

4. Specify the required entries. In this case, we have specified 1100 as the credit control area key and CAD (**Canadian dollar**) as currency type (Figure 8.3).
5. Click the **Save** icon ( ) on the standard toolbar to save the changes, as shown in Figure 8.3.

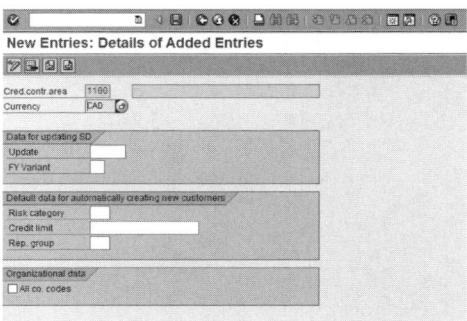

© SAP AG. All rights reserved.

FIGURE 8.3   Specifying and saving new credit control area entries

After creating a credit control area, you can assign company codes to it. The company code is an alphanumeric key that helps the mySAP ERP system to identify the company.

Perform the following steps to assign a company code to a credit control area:

1. Select **SAP Customizing Implementation Guide > Enterprise Structure > Assignment > Financial Accounting > Assign company code to credit control area** (Figure 8.4).
2. Click the **IMG Activity** icon (🔘) beside the **Assign company code to credit control area** option, as shown in Figure 8.4.

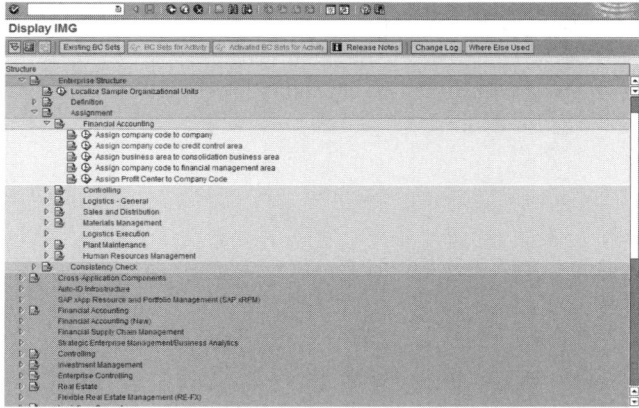

© SAP AG. All rights reserved.

FIGURE 8.4   Selecting the Assign company code to credit control area option

The **Change View "Assign company code -> credit control area": Overview** screen appears (Figure 8.5).

3. Specify the credit control area to which you want to assign a company code. In this case, we have specified 5100 as the credit control area (Figure 8.5).
4. Click the **Save** icon (🖫) on the standard toolbar to save the changes, as shown in Figure 8.5.

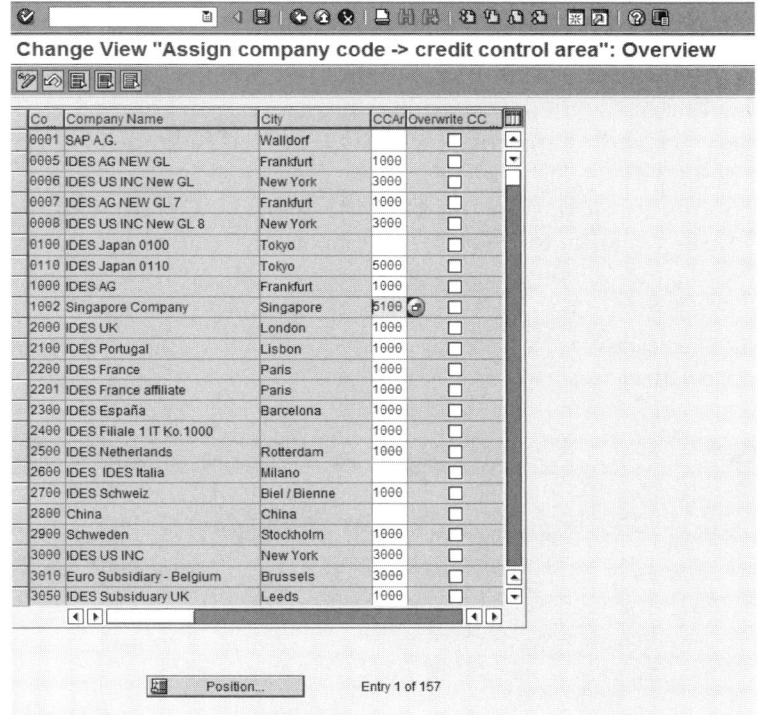

© SAP AG. All rights reserved.

FIGURE 8.5 Assigning company code to credit control area

Let's now learn how to modify an existing credit control area.

Modifying an Existing Credit Control Area

In order to modify a credit control area, you need to create a copy of the existing credit control area. You can make the required changes according to your business requirements in that copy.

Perform the following steps to modify an existing credit control area:

1. Select **SAP Customizing Implementation Guide > Enterprise Structure > Definition > Financial Accounting > Define Credit Control Area** (Figure 8.1).
2. Click the **IMG Activity** icon (⊕) beside the **Define Credit Control Area** option (Figure 8.1).

The **Change View ""Credit Control Areas""**: **Overview** screen appears (Figure 8.2).

3. Select the credit control area that matches to your requirement and click the **Copy As** icon (▣). In this case, we have selected the credit control area that has 1000 as the credit control area key (Figure 8.2). The **Change View ""Credit Control Areas""**: **Details of Selected Set** screen appears (Figure 8.6).
4. Modify the entries on the **Change View ""Credit Control Areas""**: **Details of Selected Set** screen according to your requirements. In this case, we have changed the value of the credit control area key to 1050 from 1000 (Figure 8.6).
5. Click the **Copy** icon (⊕) on the standard toolbar to create a modified credit control area, as shown in Figure 8.6.

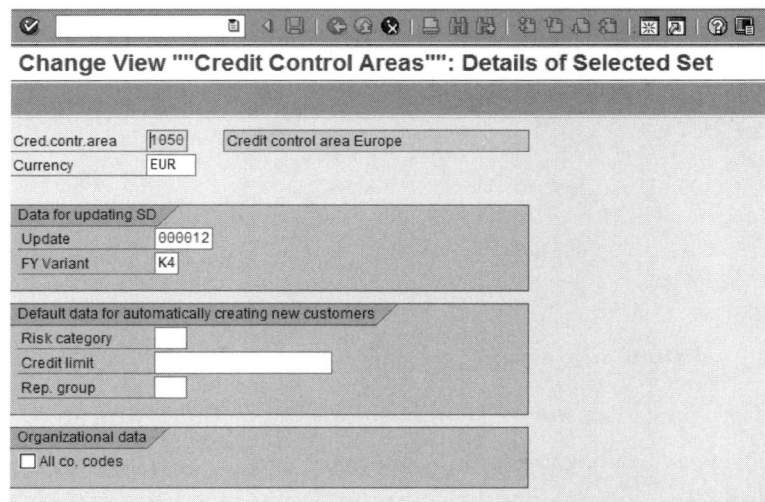

© SAP AG. All rights reserved.

FIGURE 8.6 Modifying the Credit Control Area key

This takes you back to the **Change View ""Credit Control Areas""**: **Overview** screen (Figure 8.2).

6. Click the **Save** icon (🖫) on the standard toolbar to save the credit control area.

After learning the process to create and modify a credit control area, let's discuss automatic credit management.

Implementing Automatic Credit Management

Automatic credit management is a process that helps the mySAP ERP system to automatically determine the action to be taken for a customer who has reached the credit limit. The action can be to allow or block the customer from further purchasing goods and services on credit. The mySAP ERP system suggests the necessary actions, such as allowing or blocking the credit of a customer, on the basis of the risk category assigned to the customer.

Let's perform the following tasks to implement automatic credit management in the mySAP ERP system:

- Creating customer risk category
- Creating credit groups
- Assigning sales and delivery documents
- Creating automatic credit control
- Creating master data for customer credit management

Creating Customer Risk Category

You can segregate customers into various risk categories, such as new, low risk, medium risk, and high risk, in order to let the mySAP ERP system decide the action that should be taken when a customer reaches the credit limit. For example, a high-risk customer should be blocked for further purchasing until the receivable amounts are paid. The mySAP ERP system's Financial Accounting (FI) module is used to create the customer's risk category. Let's now perform the following steps to create the customer's risk category:

1. Select **SAP Customizing Implementation Guide > Financial Accounting > Accounts Receivable and Accounts Payable > Credit Management > Credit Control Account > Define Risk Categories** (Figure 8.7).

2. Click the **IMG Activity** icon (⊕) beside the **Define Risk Categories** option, as shown in Figure 8.7.

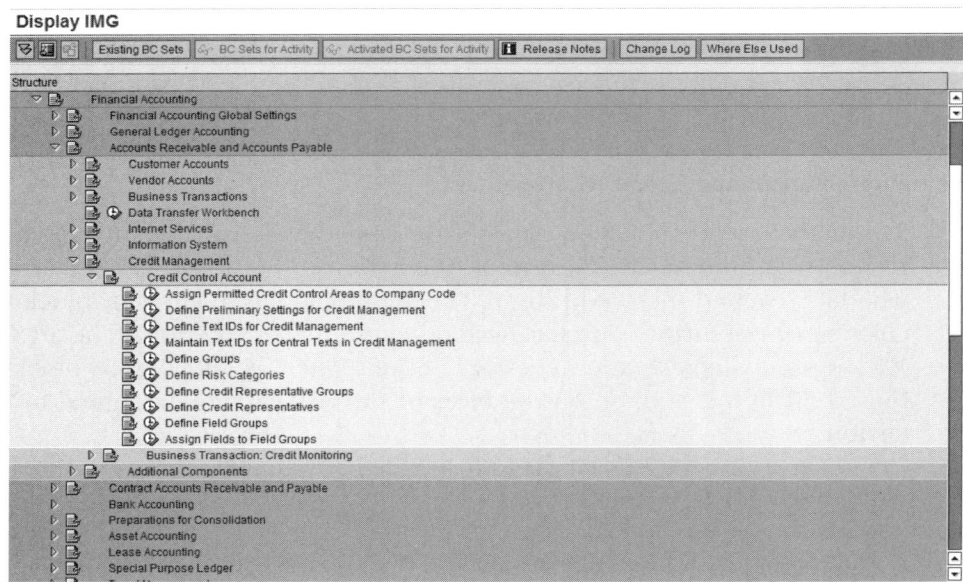

FIGURE 8.7 Selecting the Define Risk Categories option

The **Change View "Credit Management Risk Categories": Overview** screen appears (Figure 8.8). This screen shows the already created risk categories. However, you can also create a new risk category by specifying the following:

- **Risk Category**—Refers to an alphanumeric key that can be a maximum of three characters.
- **CCAr**—Refers to an alphanumeric key that represents the customer's credit control area.
- **Name**—Refers to the name of the risk category in which the customer is placed, such as low risk or high risk.

3. Click the **New Entries** button, as shown in Figure 8.8.

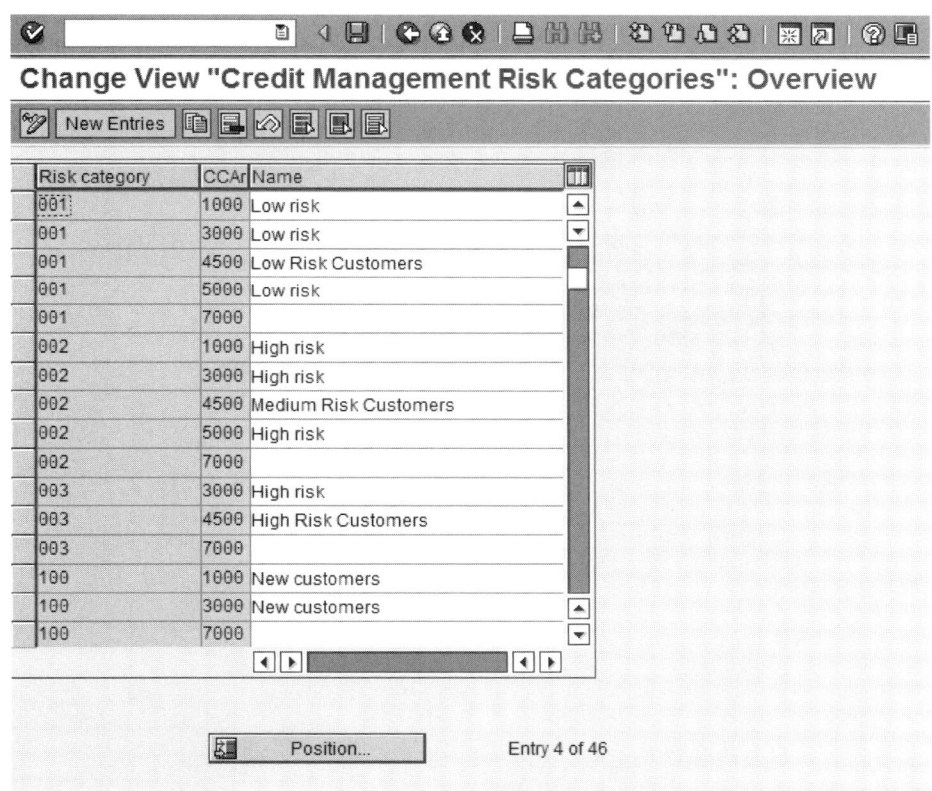

FIGURE 8.8 Creating a new risk category

The **New Entries: Overview of Added Entries** screen appears (Figure 8.9).

4. Specify the risk category, the credit control area, and the name of the risk category in the **New Entries: Overview of Added Entries** screen (Figure 8.9). In this case, we have specified 004 as the risk category, 6001 as the customer credit control area, and High-risk as the risk category name (Figure 8.9).
5. Click the **Save** icon (🖫) on the standard toolbar to save the newly created risk category, as shown in Figure 8.9.

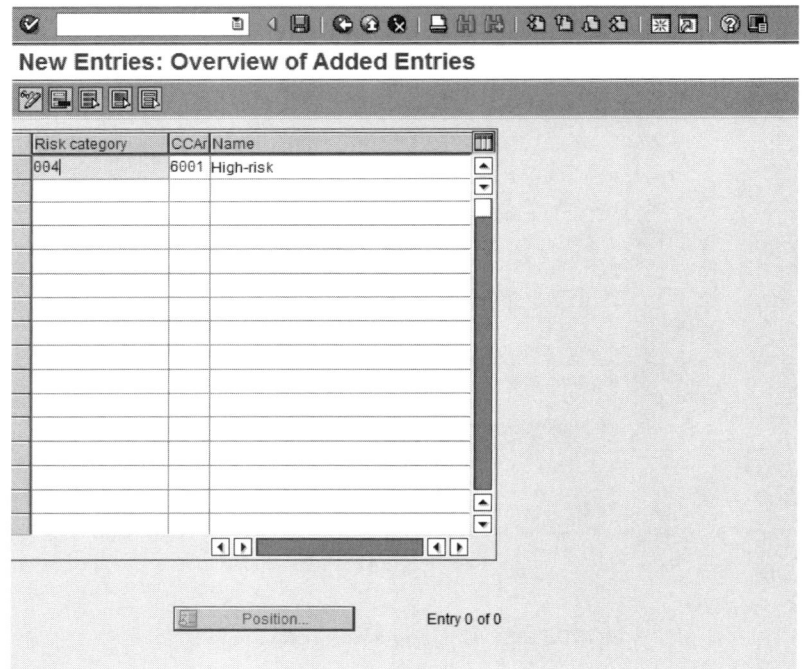

© SAP AG. All rights reserved.

FIGURE 8.9 Saving the newly created risk category

The newly created risk category can now be viewed in the **Change View "Credit Management Risk Categories": Overview** screen.

Creating Credit Groups

A credit group is created in the SD module of the mySAP ERP system to group various business documents, such as quotation and sales order. The credit limit check is performed on the basis of the information provided in these documents. The information, such as total amount of goods or services purchased and type of product purchased helps determine the amount of credit limit that can be assigned. Grouping these documents is essential to ensure that the relevant information can be retrieved from a single source.

While creating a credit group, you need to specify a credit check group key, which is a two-character alphanumeric key. Let's perform the following steps to create a credit group:

1. Select **SAP Customizing Implementation Guide > Sales and Distribution > Basic Functions > Credit Management/Risk Management > Credit Management > Define Credit Groups** (Figure 8.10).
2. Click the **IMG Activity** icon (⊕) beside the **Define Credit Groups** option, as shown in Figure 8.10.

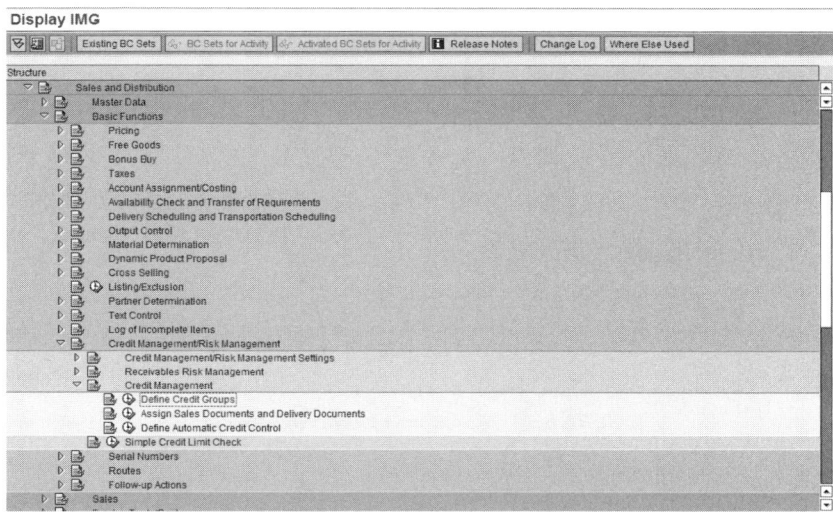

© SAP AG. All rights reserved.

FIGURE 8.10 Selecting the Define Credit Groups option

The **Change View "Credit Groups Transaction Types": Overview** screen appears (Figure 8.11) showing the already created transaction groups.

3. Click the **New Entries** button to create a new credit group, as shown in Figure 8.11.

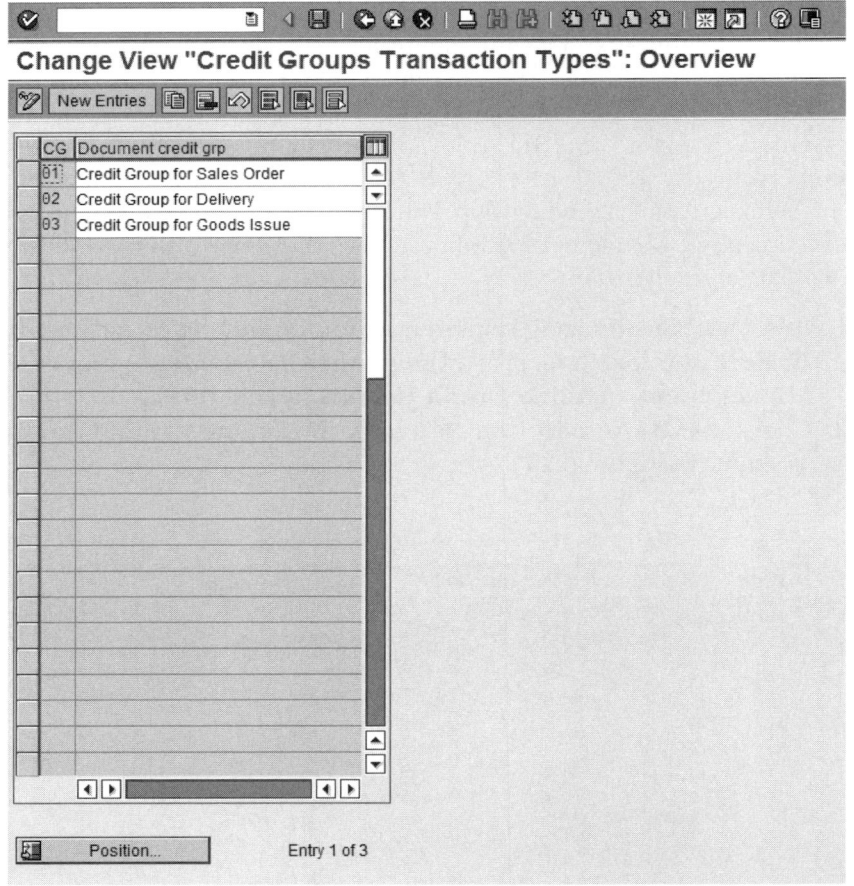

FIGURE 8.11 Creating a new credit group

The **New Entries: Overview of Added Entries** screen appears (Figure 8.12).

4. Specify the required entries. In this case, we have specified 04 as the credit group key and Credit grp for Standard Order as the credit group's description (Figure 8.12).
5. Click the **Save** icon (🖫) on the standard toolbar to save the newly created credit group, as shown in Figure 8.12.

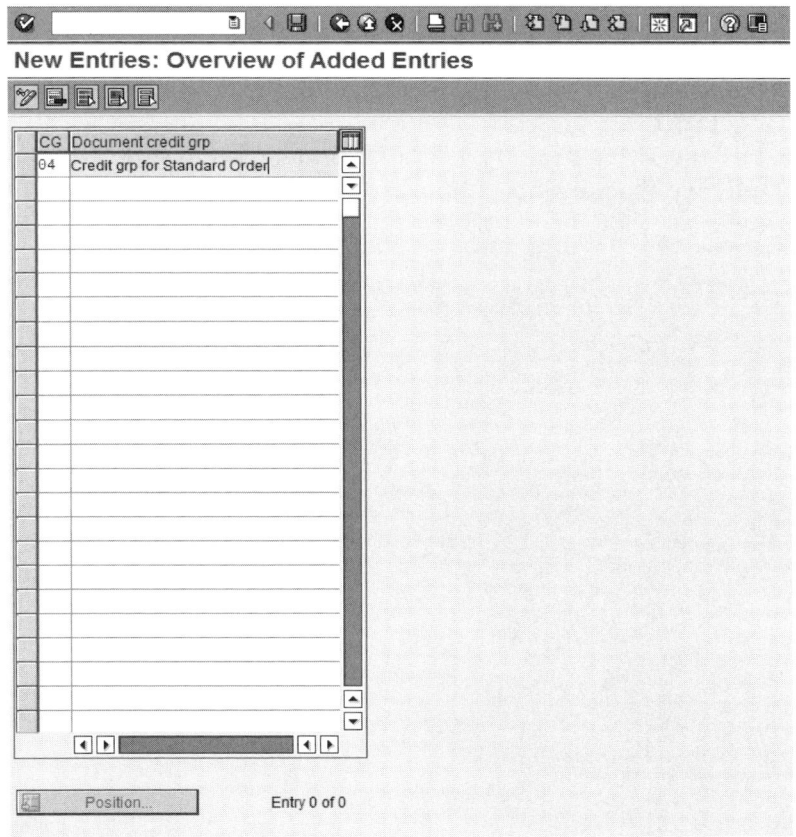

© SAP AG. All rights reserved.

FIGURE 8.12 Saving the newly created credit group

The newly created credit group can now be viewed in the **Change View "Credit Groups Transaction Types": Overview** screen.

Assigning Sales and Delivery Documents

After a credit group is created, you can assign the sales and delivery document types to it. On the basis of the document type, the mySAP ERP system determines the credit group during the sales order processing.

Let's now perform the following steps to assign the sales and delivery documents to a credit group:

1. Select **SAP Customizing Implementation Guide > Sales and Distribution > Basic Functions > Credit Management/Risk Management > Credit Management > Assign Sales Documents and Delivery Documents** (Figure 8.13).
2. Click the **IMG Activity** icon ( ) beside the **Assign Documents and Delivery Documents** option, as shown in Figure 8.13.

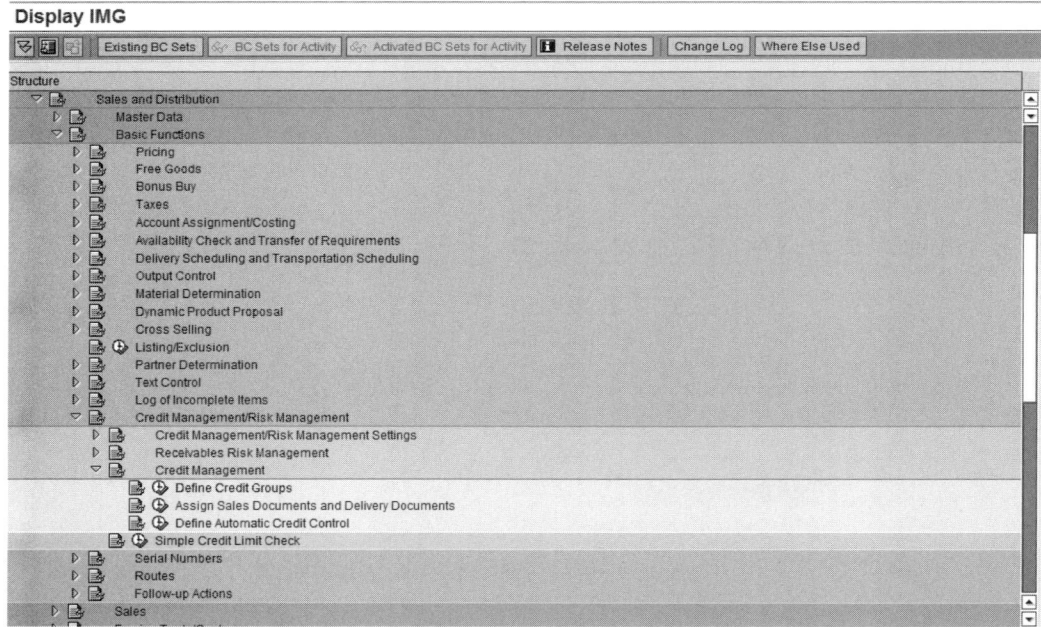

© SAP AG. All rights reserved.

FIGURE 8.13 Selecting the Assign Sales Documents and Delivery Documents option

The **Choose Activity** dialog box appears (Figure 8.14). This dialog box allows you to perform the following activities:

- **Credit Limit Check for Order Types**—Assigns a credit group to the sales document type that is a sales order type.
- **Credit Limit Check for Delivery Types**—Assigns a credit group to the delivery document type that is a delivery document type.

3. Select the entity according to your business requirements in the **Choose Activity** dialog box (Figure 8.14). In this example, we chose the **Credit limit check for order types** activity.
4. Click the **Choose** button, as shown in Figure 8.14.

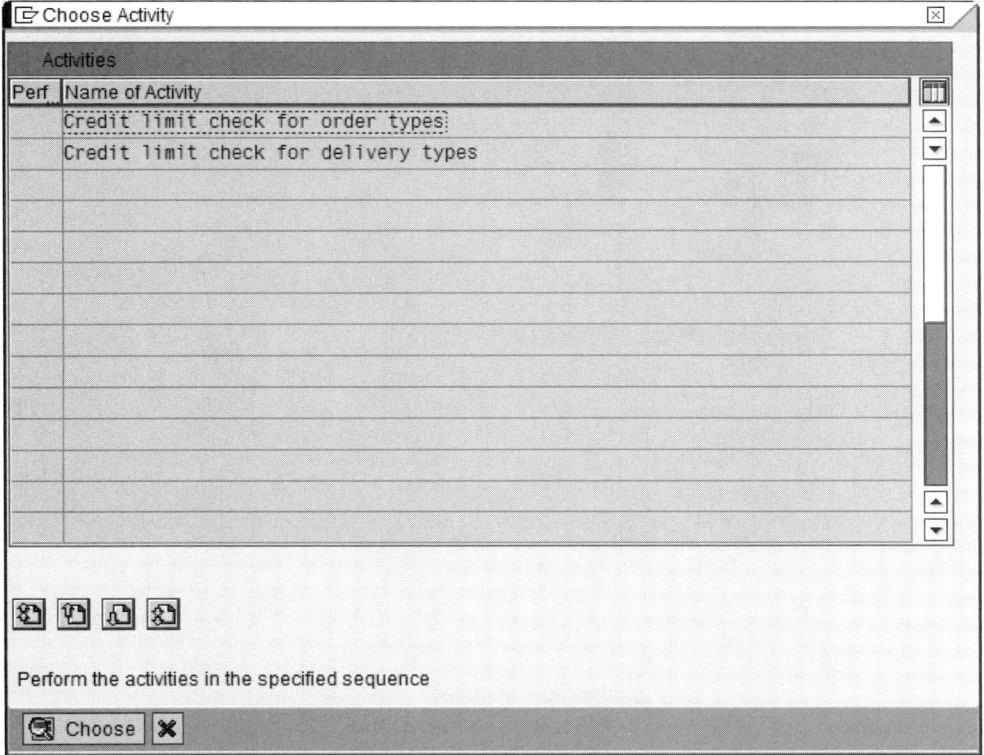

© SAP AG. All rights reserved.

FIGURE 8.14 Selecting an activity

The **Change View "Sales Document Types - Credit Limit Check": Overview** screen appears (Figure 8.15).

5. Select the sales document type. In this example, we selected the **IN (Inquiry)** document (Figure 8.15).
6. Specify the credit group in the **Credit group** column for the selected document type. In this example, we have specified 01 as the credit group (Figure 8.15).

> **Note:** If you want the mySAP ERP system to automatically check the customer's credit limit, then specify D in the **Check credit** column for the selected sales document types.

7. Click the **Save** icon (🖫) on the standard toolbar to save the changes, as shown in Figure 8.15.

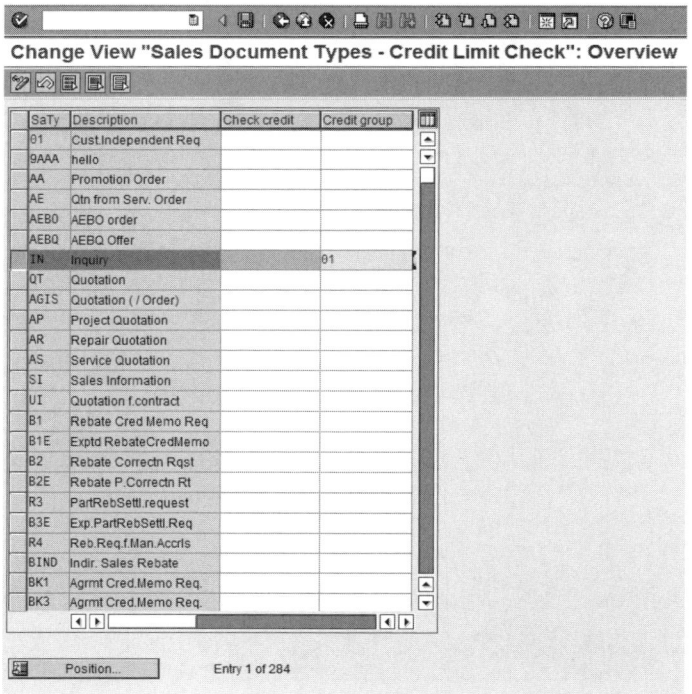

© SAP AG. All rights reserved.

FIGURE 8.15 Specifying and saving the credit group to Inquiry document

> **Note:** The process of assigning a credit group to the delivery document type is similar to the process of assigning a credit group to the sales document type.

Creating Automatic Credit Control

You can configure the mySAP ERP system to automatically manage the credit control by defining the details for automatic credit control, such as the type of credit check and the warning message displayed when a customer reaches the assigned credit limit. You can create a simple and effective automatic credit control by specifying the following entries in the **Change View "View for Maintenance of Automatic Credit Control": Overview** screen (Figure 8.16):

- **Credit Control Area**—Represents an organizational unit that determines a customer's credit limit.
- **Risk Category**—Segregates customers into various risk groups on the basis of their previous payment records.
- **Credit Group**—Represents a group of business documents, such as inquiry and quotation.
- **Credit Control Definition**—Represents a user-defined definition of automatic credit control. In the credit control definition entry, a user provides the description of the automatic credit control that needs to be created.
- **Type of Credit Check**—Represents the credit check that the mySAP ERP system executes on the document types. Table 8.1 lists the most commonly used credit checks.
- **System Response**—Specifies the message or error that the mySAP ERP system generates when a customer's credit limit is reached. Table 8.2 lists the standard system responses in the mySAP ERP system.
- **Document Status**—Specifies whether the document should be blocked according to the system response.
- **Include Open Order Value**—Specifies whether the open order value is included in the automatic credit control.
- **Include Open Delivery Document Value**—Specifies whether the open delivery document value is included in the automatic credit control.

Credit Check Type	Description
Static Credit Check	Ensures that the credit amount given is **not more** than the credit limit assigned to the customer. The credit amount is the sum of the following values: - **Open Sales Document Value**—Refers to an item for which an order is created but has not yet been delivered. - **Open Delivery Document Value**—Refers to a delivery item for which an invoice has not yet been created. - **Open Invoice Value**—Refers to the invoice value in the billing document that has not yet been sent to the accounting department. - **Open Items**—Refers to the items that are passed to the accounting department but have not yet been finalized by the customer.
Dynamic Credit Check	Ensures that the customer's credit limit does not exceed the credit amount plus the open order value of the specified items.
Document Value Check	Ensures that the goods value must not exceed the specified credit limit.

TABLE 8.1: Types of Credit Checks

System Response Type	Description
A	Refers to a warning message
B	Refers to an error message
C	Refers to a warning message displayed if the credit provided exceeds the credit limit
D	Refers to an error message displayed if the credit provided exceeds the credit limit

TABLE 8.2: Types of System Responses

Let's now perform the following steps to create the automatic credit control:

1. Select **SAP Customizing Implementation Guide > Sales and Distribution > Basic Functions > Credit Management/Risk Management > Credit Management > Define Automatic Credit Control** (Figure 8.13).
2. Click the **IMG Activity** icon (🔍) beside the **Define Automatic Credit Control** option (Figure 8.13). The **Change View "View for Maintenance of Automatic Credit Control": Overview** screen appears (Figure 8.16). This screen shows the existing automatic credit controls.
3. Click the **New Entries** button to create a new automatic credit control according to your business requirements, as shown in Figure 8.16.

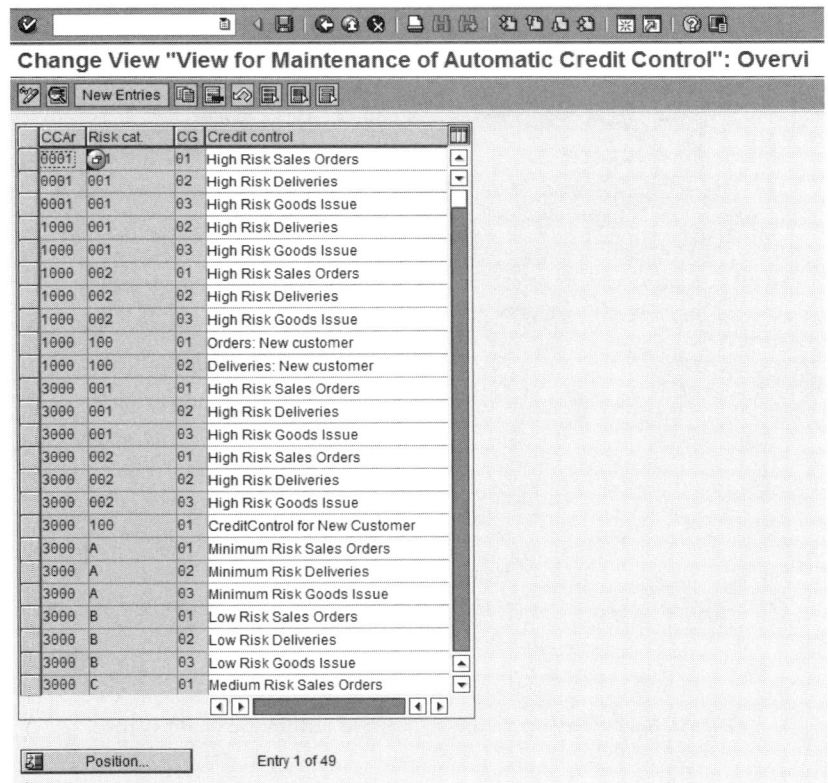

© SAP AG. All rights reserved.

FIGURE 8.16 Displaying existing automatic credit control

The **New Entries: Details of Added Entries** screen appears (Figure 8.17).

4. Specify the entries, according to your business requirements, in the **New Entries: Details of Added Entries** screen. Figure 8.17 displays the screen with the entries that we have specified in our example.
5. Click the **Save** icon (🖫) on the standard toolbar to save the newly created automatic credit control, as shown in Figure 8.17.

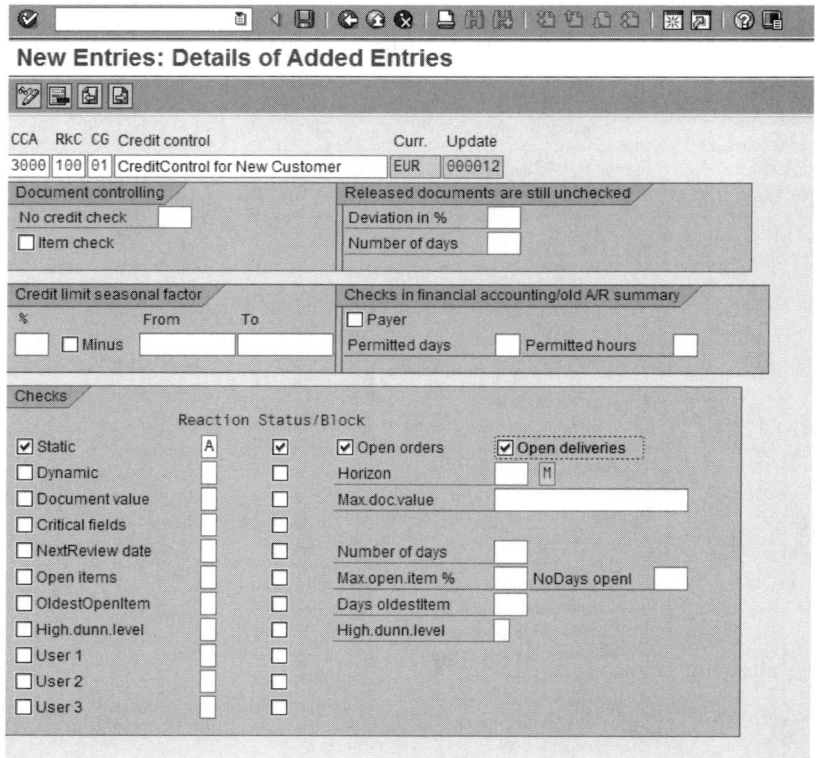

© SAP AG. All rights reserved.

FIGURE 8.17 Saving the newly created automatic credit control

The newly created automatic credit control can now be viewed in the **Change View "View for Maintenance of Automatic Credit Control": Overview** screen.

Figure 8.17 is the basis for a credit limit configuration in an organization. You can do the settings to define how the system should behave at different stages of a sales process for the customers assigned with different risk categories, as shown in Figure 8.17.

Creating Master Data for Customer Credit Management

In the customer credit management system of the mySAP ERP system, you assign the risk categories to the customers, according to your organization's standards. Perform the following steps to create master data for customer-specific credit management:

1. Select **SAP menu > Logistics > Sales and Distribution > Credit Management > Master data > FD32-Change**, as shown in Figure 8.18.

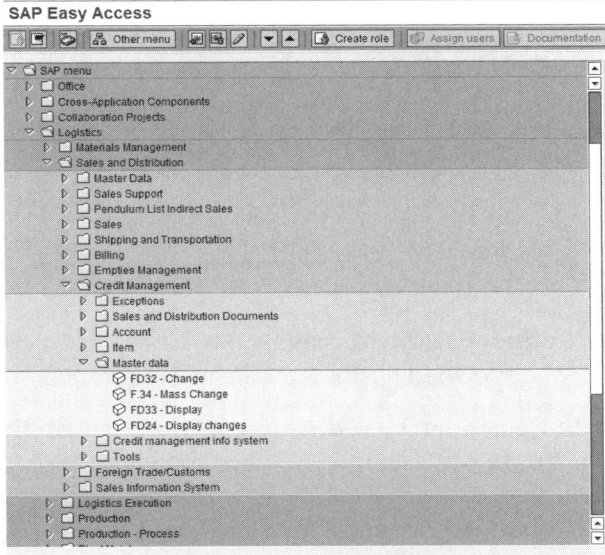

© SAP AG. All rights reserved.

FIGURE 8.18 Selecting the FD-32 Change option

The **Customer Credit Management Change: Initial Screen** appears (Figure 8.19).

2. Specify a customer code (Figure 8.19). In this example, we have specified 3391 as the customer code.
3. Specify the credit control area for the specified customer (Figure 8.19). In this example, we have specified 1000 as the credit control area.
4. Select the **Status** check box in the **Credit control area data** section (Figure 8.19).
5. Click the **Enter** icon ( ) on the standard toolbar, as shown in Figure 8.19.

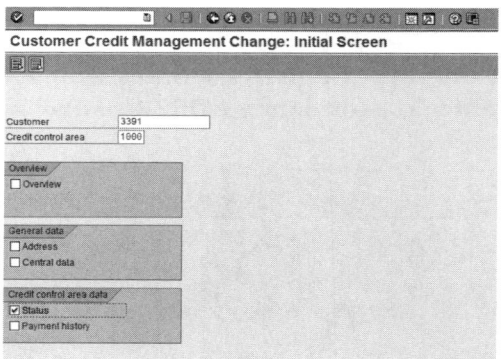

© SAP AG. All rights reserved.

FIGURE 8.19 Specifying a customer's specific details

The **Customer Credit Management Change: Status** screen showing the details of the specified customer appears (Figure 8.20).

6. Specify the customer's credit limit in the **Credit limit data** section (Figure 8.20). In this example, we have specified 30,000.00 Euro as the credit limit.
7. Specify the risk category in the **Internal data** section (Figure 8.20). In this example, we have specified 002 as the risk category.
8. Click the **Save** icon ( ) on the standard toolbar to save the specified values, as shown in Figure 8.20.

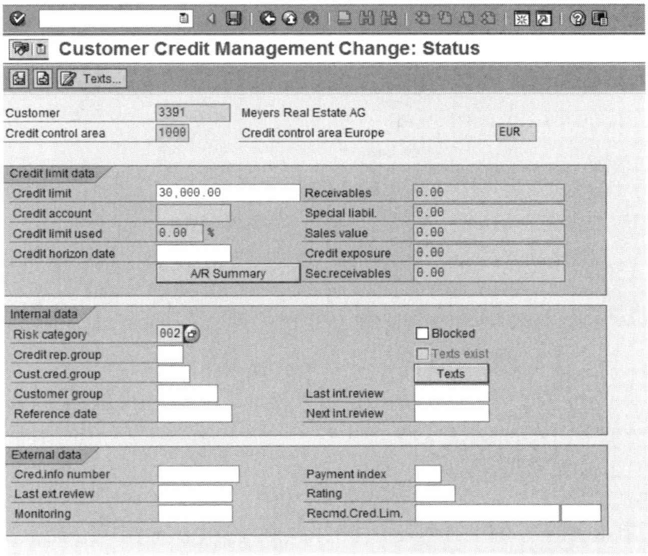

FIGURE 8.20 Specifying a customer's credit limit and risk category

As shown in Figure 8.20, we have assigned the credit limit and the risk category to a customer.

After discussing credit management, now let's describe risk management in SD.

IMPLEMENTING RISK MANAGEMENT IN SD

When an organization sells a good or a service to customers on credit, an associated risk of whether the customer will pay the credit amount arises. To minimize the risk of nonpayment, the guarantee against the payment is taken from the customer. In other words, to minimize the risk, an organization offers the goods and services to customers on credit based on guarantee, which is known as payment guarantee. This guarantee serves as an assurance to the organization for the due payment to be received from a customer. In the mySAP

ERP system, the process of assigning a guarantee against the payment is known as risk management.

In the mySAP ERP system, you need to perform the following tasks to implement risk management:

- Creating forms of payment guarantee
- Implementing the payment guarantee procedure

Creating Forms of Payment Guarantee

In the mySAP ERP system, the payment guarantee can be provided in various forms, such as document payment guarantee, payment cards, or export credit insurance. Therefore, you need to create the relevant form of payment guarantee to provide a payment guarantee for an item in a sales document.

The following entries must be specified while creating the forms of payment guarantee:

- **Payment Guarantee Key**—Refers to an alphanumeric key, which can be a maximum of two characters. The first character of this key must start with 9, Y, or Z; otherwise, the form of payment guarantee will not be created. The payment guarantee key is a necessary entry of the payment guarantee form. If you do not specify the payment guarantee key, you cannot save the payment guarantee form.
- **Payment Guarantee Category**—Refers to the basis on which the payment guarantee can be provided, such as payment card and export credit insurance.
- **Payment Guarantee Description**—Refers to the description of the payment guarantee form.

Let's now perform the following steps to create a form of payment guarantee:

1. Select **SAP Customizing Implementation Guide > Sales and Distribution > Basic Functions > Credit Management/Risk Management > Receivables Risk Management > Define Forms of Payment Guarantee** (Figure 8.21).
2. Click the **IMG Activity** icon (⊕) beside the **Define Forms of Payment Guarantee** option, as shown in Figure 8.21.

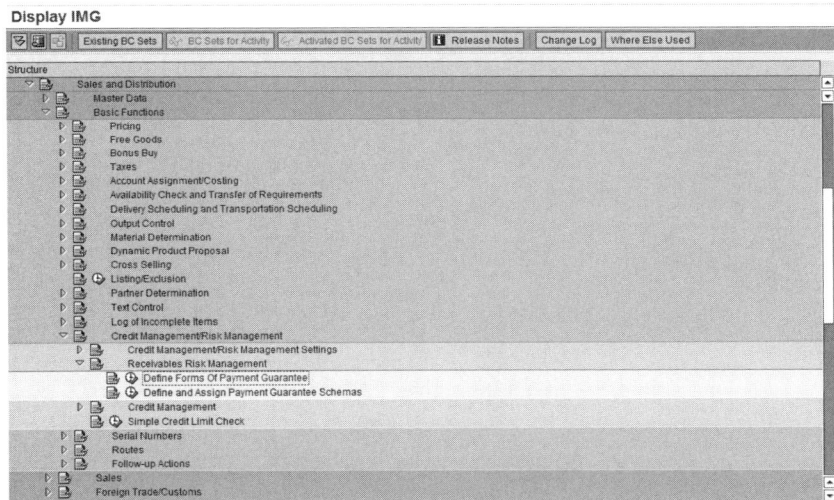

© SAP AG. All rights reserved.

FIGURE 8.21 Selecting the Define Forms of Payment Guarantee option

The **Change View "Maintain forms of payment guarantee": Overview** screen appears (Figure 8.22), showing the existing payment guarantee forms.

3. Click the **New Entries** button to create your own payment guarantee form, as shown in Figure 8.22.

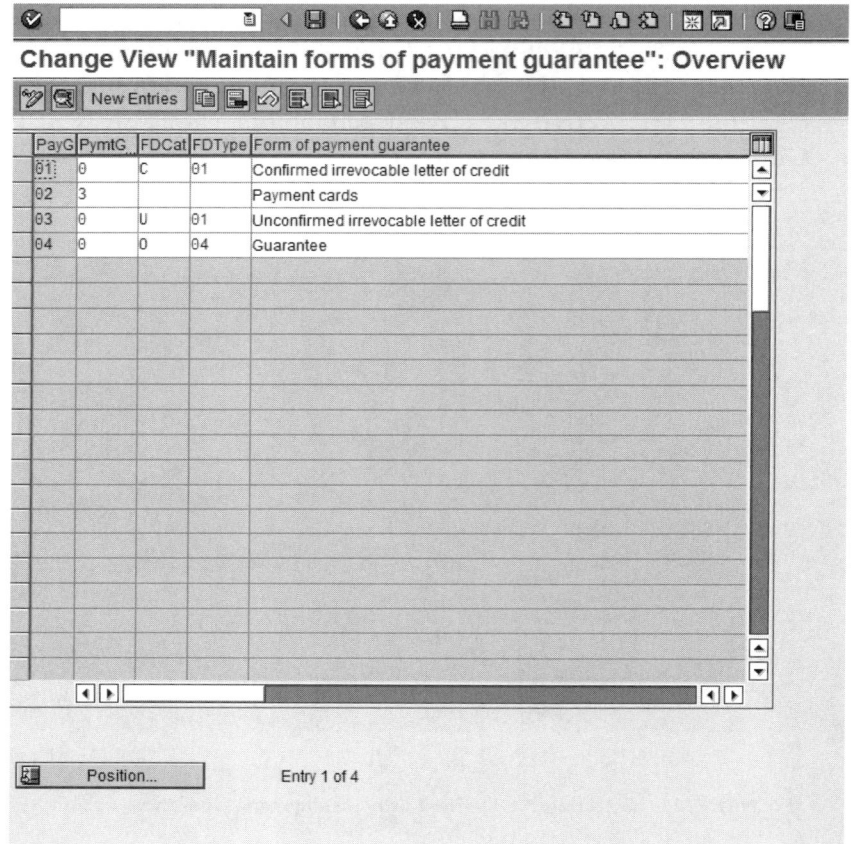

© SAP AG. All rights reserved.

FIGURE 8.22 Creating a new payment guarantee form

The **New Entries: Details of Added Entries** screen appears (Figure 8.23).

4. Specify the required entries (Figure 8.23). In this example, we have specified the following entries:

- Z5 as the payment guarantee form key in the **Paymt guarantee form** field
- 1 as the payment guarantee category key in the **Paymt guarantee cat.** field.
- `Export Credit Insurance` as the description of payment guarantee form in the **Paymt guarantee form** text box

5. Click the **Save** icon (🖫) on the standard toolbar to save the newly created form of the payment guarantee, as shown in Figure 8.23.

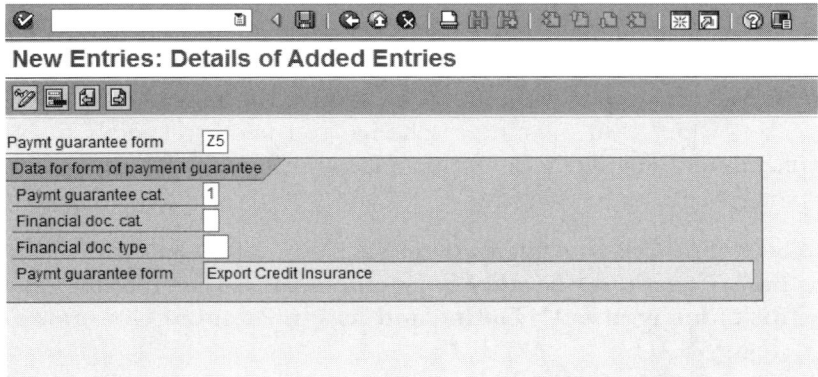

© SAP AG. All rights reserved.

FIGURE 8.23 Saving the specified entries

The newly created form of the payment guarantee can be viewed in the **Change View "Maintain forms of payment guarantee": Overview** screen.

Implementing the Payment Guarantee Procedure

The payment guarantee procedure helps you to define the type of payment guarantee forms and the sequence in which the mySAP ERP system uses them. In this section, we learn to:

- Create the payment guarantee schema
- Create the customer determination schema
- Create the document determination procedure

Creating the Payment Guarantee Schema

The payment guarantee schema is a payment guarantee procedure that specifies the form of payment guarantee and the sales document type. The basic objective of payment guarantee schema is to ensure the payment guarantee. While creating a payment guarantee schema, you need to specify a six-character alphanumeric key and its description. Let's perform the following steps to create a payment guarantee schema:

1. Select **SAP Customizing Implementation Guide > Sales and Distribution > Basic Functions > Credit Management/Risk Management > Receivables Risk Management > Define and Assign Payment Guarantee Schemas** (Figure 8.21).
2. Click the **IMG Activity** icon (⊕) beside the **Define and Assign Payment Guarantee Schemas** option (Figure 8.21). The **Choose Activity** dialog box appears (Figure 8.24).
3. Select the **Define Payment Guarantee Schema** activity in the **Choose Activity** dialog box (Figure 8.24).
4. Click the **Choose** button, as shown in Figure 8.24.

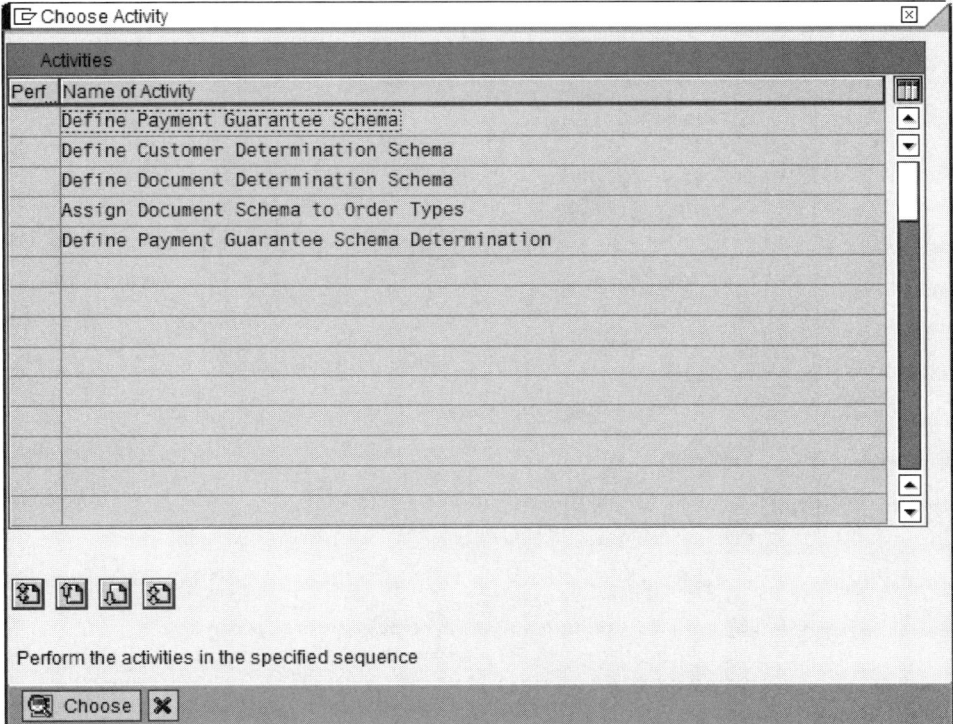

FIGURE 8.24   Selecting the Define Payment Guarantee Schema activity

The **Change View "Payment guarantee determination procedure": Overview** screen appears (Figure 8.25). This screen shows the existing payment guarantee procedures and their descriptions.

5. Click the **New Entries** button to create a new payment guarantee procedure, as shown in Figure 8.25.

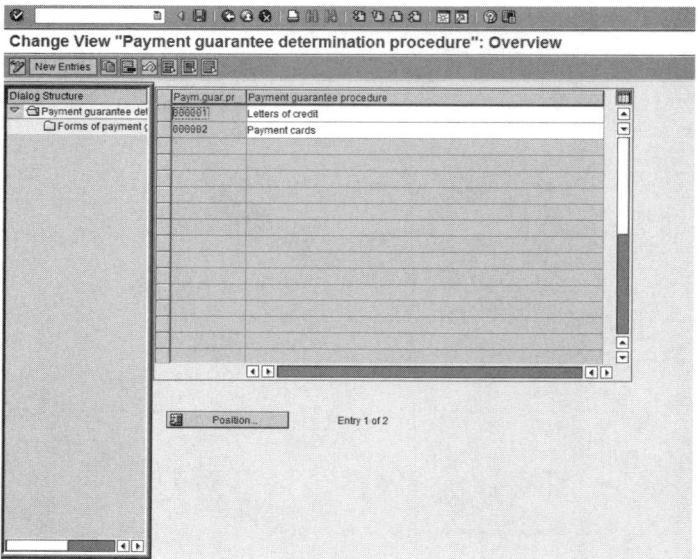

FIGURE 8.25 Creating a new payment guarantee procedure

The **New Entries: Overview of Added Entries** screen appears (Figure 8.26).

6. Specify the payment guarantee procedure key in the **Paym.guar.proc.** column and the payment guarantee procedure description in the **Payment guarantee procedure** column (Figure 8.26).
7. Click the **Save** icon (🖫) on the standard toolbar to save the payment guarantee procedure (Figure 8.26).

Now, when the payment guarantee procedure is created, you can assign a sequence number and the form of payment guarantee to it.

8. Select the newly created payment guarantee procedure and double-click the **Forms of payment guarantee** folder in the left pane, as shown in Figure 8.26.

IMPLEMENTING RISK MANAGEMENT IN SD   437

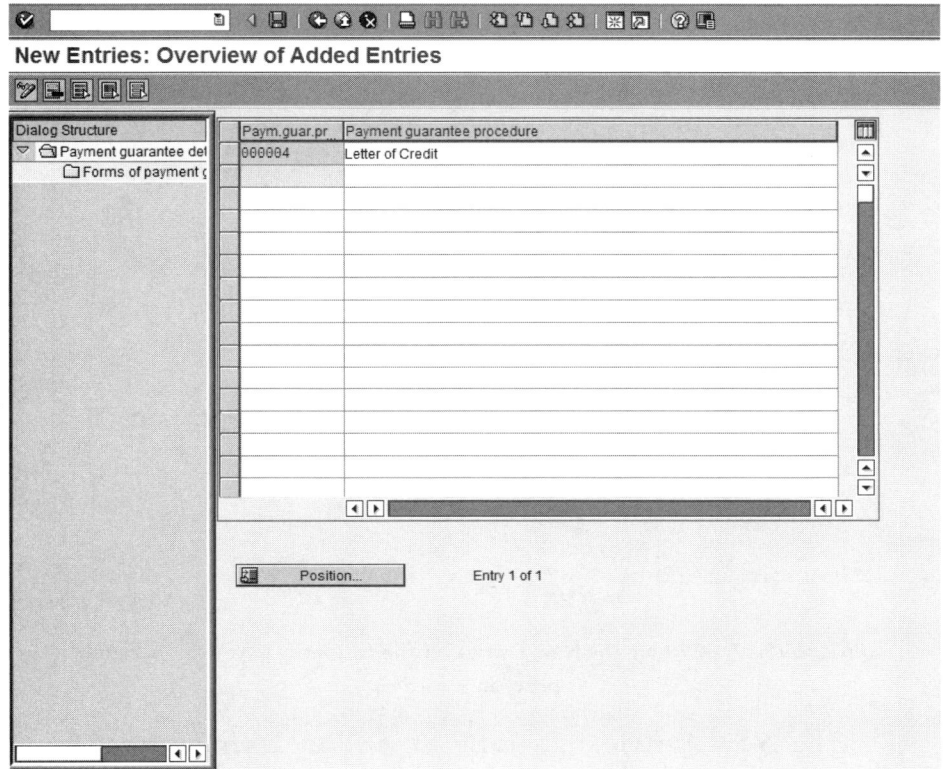

FIGURE 8.26   Saving the newly created payment guarantee procedure

The **Change View "Forms of payment guarantee": Overview** screen appears (Figure 8.27).

9. Click the **New Entries** button, as shown in Figure 8.27.

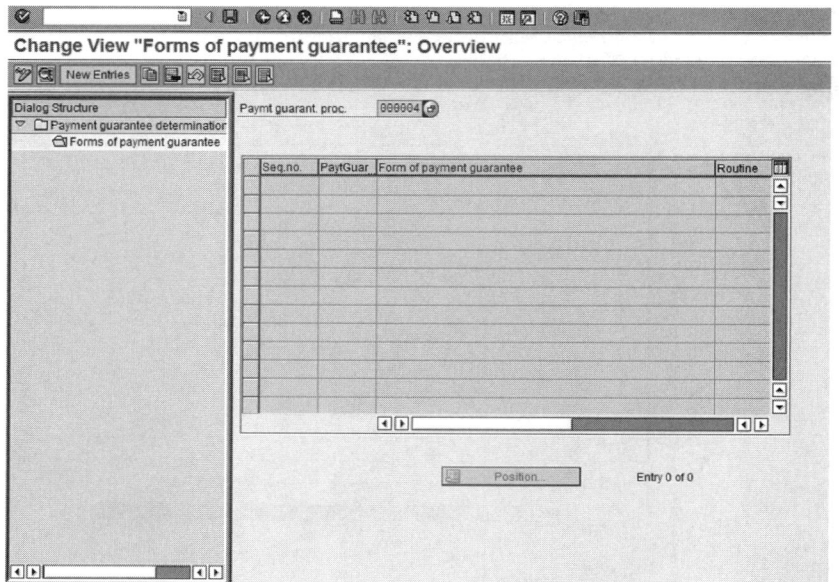

© SAP AG. All rights reserved.

FIGURE 8.27 Clicking the New Entries button to specify payment guarantee procedure entries

The **New Entries: Details of Added Entries** screen appears (Figure 8.28).

10. Specify the required entries. In this case, we have specified the following entries:

    - 40 as the sequence number
    - 01 as the payment guarantee form type

11. Click the **Save** icon ( ) on the standard toolbar to save the payment guarantee procedure with the specified entries, as shown in Figure 8.28.

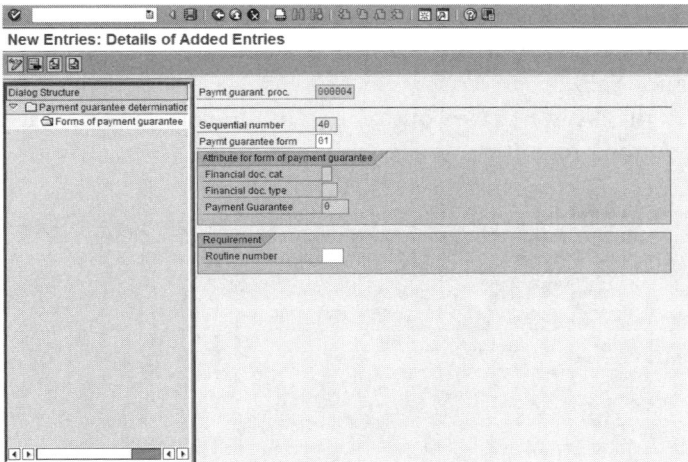

FIGURE 8.28 Saving the specified entries

The newly created payment guarantee procedure can be viewed in the **Change View "Payment guarantee determination procedure": Overview** screen.

Creating the Customer Determination Schema

The customer determination schema helps the mySAP ERP system to automatically use the payment guarantee procedure while creating a sales document. While creating the customer payment guarantee procedure, you must specify the customer payment guarantee procedure key (which is a four-character alphanumeric key) and its description. Let's now perform the following steps to create the customer guarantee procedure schema:

1. Select **SAP Customizing Implementation Guide > Sales and Distribution > Basic Functions > Credit Management/Risk Management > Receivables Risk Management > Define and Assign Payment Guarantee Schemas** (Figure 8.21).
2. Click the **IMG Activity** icon ( ) beside the **Define and Assign Payment Guarantee Schemas** option (Figure 8.21). The **Choose Activity** dialog box appears (Figure 8.24).
3. Select the **Define Customer Determination Schema** activity in the **Choose Activity** dialog box (Figure 8.24).

4. Click the **Choose** button (Figure 8.24). The **Change View "Maintain customer payment guarantee procedures": Overview** screen appears (Figure 8.29).
5. Click the **New Entries** button to continue creating the customer payment guarantee procedure, as shown in Figure 8.29.

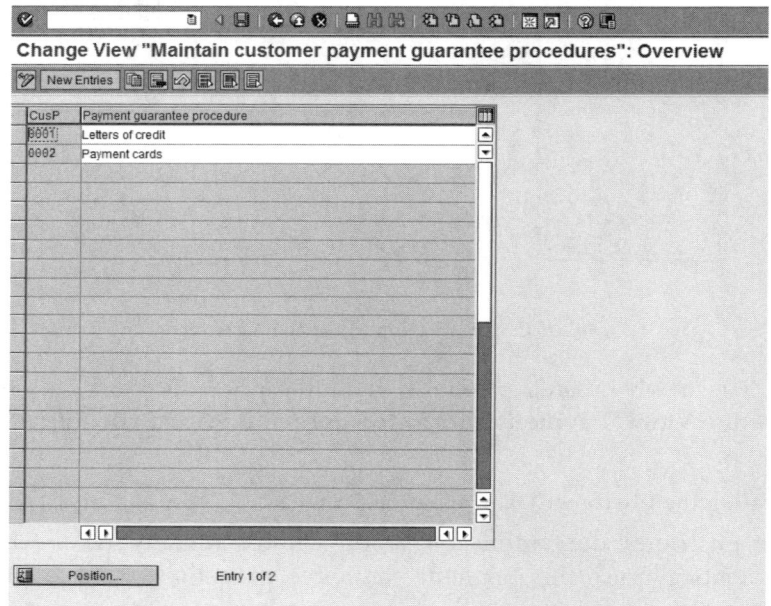

© SAP AG. All rights reserved.

FIGURE 8.29 Continuing creating the customer payment guarantee schema

The **New Entries: Overview of Added Entries** screen appears (Figure 8.30).

6. Specify the customer payment guarantee key in the **CusP** column and its description in the **Payment guarantee procedure** column (Figure 8.30). We have specified 0003 as the customer payment guarantee key and Confirmed Letter of Credit as the key description.

> **Note:** The customer payment guarantee key must be assigned in the billing view of the Customer Master Record.

7. Click the **Save** icon (💾) on the standard toolbar to save the newly created customer payment guarantee procedure, as shown in Figure 8.30.

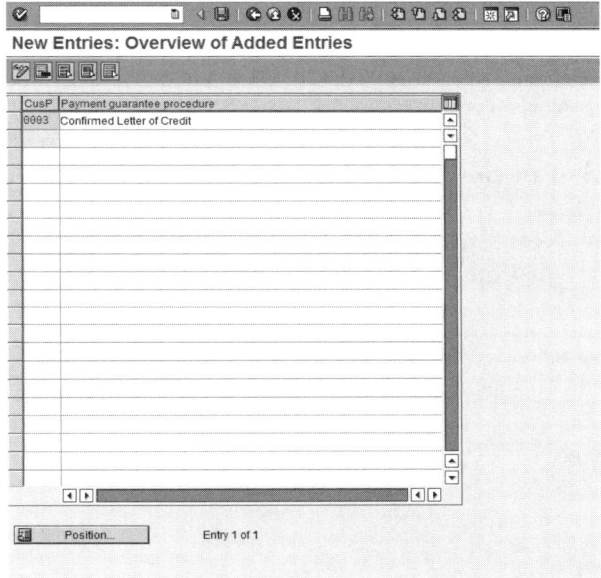

© SAP AG. All rights reserved.

FIGURE 8.30 Saving the newly created customer payment guarantee procedure

Now, you can view the newly created customer payment guarantee procedure in the **Change View "Maintain customer payment guarantee procedures": Overview** screen.

Creating the Document Determination Procedure

The document determination procedure helps the mySAP ERP system to automatically select a payment guarantee procedure while creating a sales document type. Perform the following steps to create the document payment guarantee procedure:

1. Select **SAP Customizing Implementation Guide > Sales and Distribution > Basic Functions > Credit Management/Risk Management > Receivables Risk Management > Define and Assign Payment Guarantee Schemas** (Figure 8.21).
2. Click the **IMG Activity** icon (⊕) beside the **Define and Assign Payment Guarantee Schemas** option (Figure 8.21). The **Choose Activity** dialog box appears (Figure 8.24).
3. Select the **Define Document Determination Schema** activity in the **Choose Activity** dialog box (Figure 8.24).
4. Click the **Choose** button (Figure 8.24). The **Change View "Maintain control of payment guarantee procedure": Overview** screen appears (Figure 8.31).
5. Click the **New Entries** button to continue creating the document payment guarantee procedure, as shown in Figure 8.31.

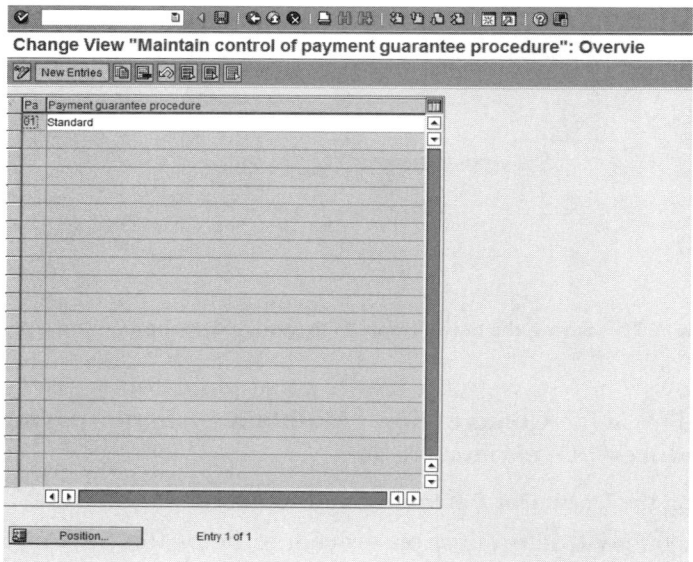

© SAP AG. All rights reserved.

FIGURE 8.31 Continuing creating the document payment guarantee procedure

The **New Entries: Overview of Added Entries** screen appears (Figure 8.32).

6. Specify the document payment guarantee procedure key in the **Pa** column and its description in the **Payment guarantee procedure** column (Figure 8.32). The document payment guarantee procedure key is a two-character alphanumeric key. In this example, we have specified 02 as the document payment guarantee procedure key and **Payment Cards** as its description (Figure 8.32).
7. Click the **Save** icon ( ) on the standard toolbar to save the newly created document payment guarantee procedure, as shown in Figure 8.32.

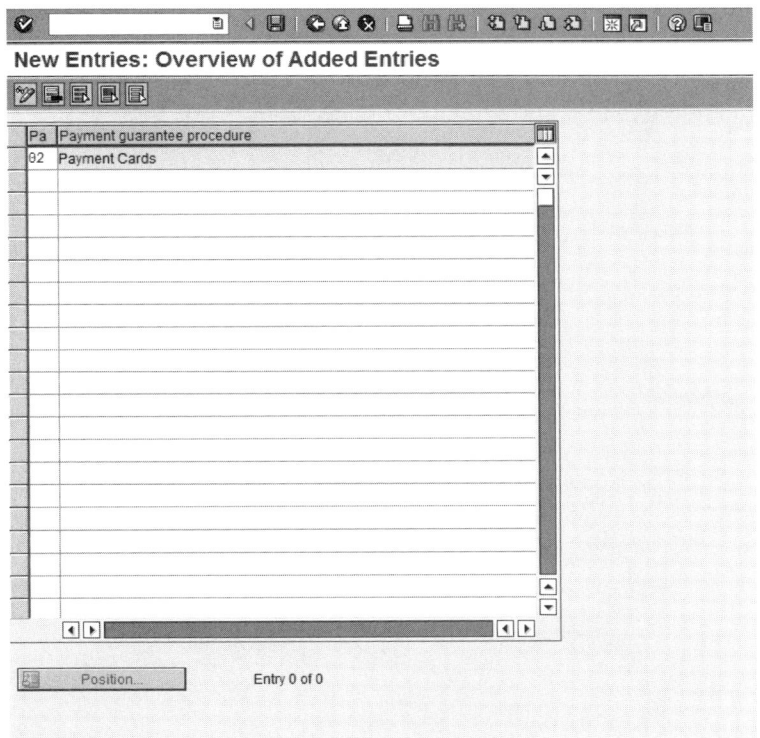

© SAP AG. All rights reserved.

FIGURE 8.32 Saving the newly created document payment guarantee procedure

This ends the discussion about the payment guarantee procedures. Let's summarize what we have learned in this chapter.

SUMMARY

In this chapter, you learned about the process of credit management in the SD module, and you also learned how to create or modify the credit control area. You learned how you can configuration the SAP system to behave as per the requirement of business process and learned the procedure to automate credit management. In addition, you learned how to create a customer risk category, credit groups, and automatic credit control. Toward the end of the chapter, the chapter discussed how to implement the payment guarantee procedure in the SD module.

In the next chapter, you explore the relationship of SAP SD with the Service Management (SM) and Quality Management (QM) modules.

Chapter 9
Relationship of SD to SM and QM Modules

If you need information on:	See page:
Implementing Service Management in SD	446
Implementing Quality Management in SD	462

When a company sells a product, the services related to that product are provided to the customer. A company can provide the services either free of cost, or it can bill the customer for the services offered. For example, when you purchase a new motorbike, you are provided few free services from the manufacturer. However, a motorbike requires regular servicing; therefore, when the time duration of free services expires, you need to pay the service amount to the service provider. Similar to motorbikes, many other products also require regular services. The process of offering services and managing service details is called service management. In the mySAP™ ERP system, the service management process is defined in the Service Management (SM) module; it records the activities associated with customer services. The services are provided to a customer against the sales order placed for a product, which is implemented in the Sales and Distribution (SD) module of SAP®. The service management process is a part of the SM module, and consequently, the SD and SM modules are interrelated. This chapter explores the relationship of the SM and SD modules.

Apart from the service management process, a company also needs to check the quality of the product (to be delivered to the customer) against various constraints or requirements. The process of managing the products' quality is defined in the Quality Management (QM) module. In addition, if the customer returns a product or a complaint against it, the QM module helps record the details of the complaint made against the sales order specified in the SD module. This chapter also discusses the relationship of the QM and SD modules; these two modules go hand in hand along with the Materials Management (MM) module to provide the best satisfaction for the customer.

Figure 9.1 shows the relationship of the QM and SD modules with the SD module.

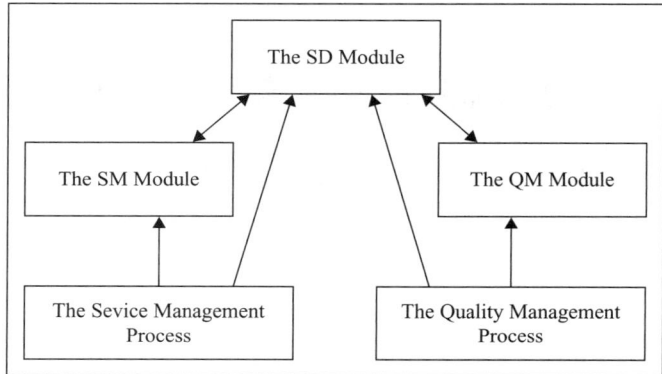

FIGURE 9.1 The relationship of the QM and SM modules with the SD module

Figure 9.1 shows that the service management process (part of the SM module) is implemented in the SD module, exhibiting the relationship between the SM and SD modules. On similar grounds, the quality management process is implemented in the SD module, exhibiting the relationship between the QM and SD modules.

In this chapter, you learn how to implement the service management and quality management processes in the SD module of SAP.

Now, let's explore each of them in detail.

IMPLEMENTING SERVICE MANAGEMENT IN SD

The types of services that an organization provides to its customers depends on the products that an organization sells. For example, a mobile manufacturing company provides product-related services to its customers through its service outlets, and a bank provides customer-care numbers to its customers to avail them the bank's services. We learned earlier that this process of providing and handling services to customers is called service management. Figure 9.2 provides a general flowchart to help you understand the concept of service management in a company.

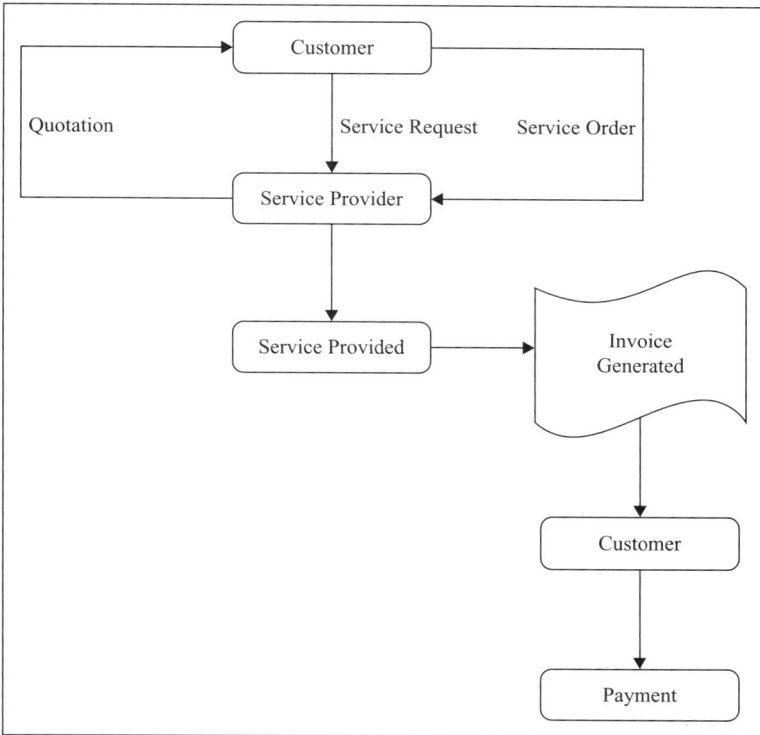

FIGURE 9.2 Service management flowchart

As shown in Figure 9.2, a customer sends a service request to the service provider. Based on the service requested by the customer, the service provider sends a quotation.

The quotation sent to a customer includes the terms and conditions that are connected to the service. A quotation is considered to be a legal document that can be referred to in case of any dispute between a customer and the service provider.

Note: The service provider might be a business entity within or outside the company that has initially sold the products to the customers.

If the customer accepts the quotation, the service order is placed with the service provider. The service provider then provides the services and generates an invoice. The invoice is then provided to the customer, and the customer pays the invoiced amount. In this way, the services are managed in an organization.

To implement service management in the SD module, you must learn how to do the following:

- Work with customer services in SD
- Work with service orders in SD
- Work with complaints and returns in SD

Let's explore these in detail.

Working with Customer Services in SD

In the SD module, customer service refers to a service management process that helps an organization to provide and manage services. An organization may provide various types of services to its customers. In SAP, the details related to the type and cost of customer services is provided in the customer and material master record defined in the SD module. The customer's master record includes the customer's personal details, which help provide the customer with a specific quotation. The material master record contains material details, such as material availability and cost. The documents, such as a service order and a sales order, are maintained while providing the customer services.

The following topics provide you with detailed knowledge about the concepts related to the customer service process and its configurations in the SD module:

- Exploring the material master
- Exploring document types
- Setting up notification types
- Working with catalogs

Exploring the Material Master

The material master helps store the information or records pertaining to a customer or material. The material master records are also defined in the mySAP ERP system for customer services purposes. The information about the services to be provided to a customer, such as the type of service and taxes charged for a service, is stored in the material master. These details of the service can be entered either in a sales order or in a contract made for the respective customer. The material master for a service item is the reflection of the kind of product that includes information about the basics of the product such as valuation class, plant-level maintenance data, accounting, and VPRS (moving average price or standard price).

When the services for a specific part of a product are required, the invoice for the service is generated depending upon the serial number of that part of the product. Therefore, you need to define a technical object that stores the serial numbers of various parts of a product.

Apart from the material master, you must also understand the document types used for services.

Exploring the Document Types in Customer Service

While managing the customer services, you need to work with various documents in order to process the customer service requests. These documents are as follows:

- **Service Notification**—Represents the customer inquiry about the service for a specific product.
- **Service Order**—Represents the order that a customer places after inquiry that will avail the service for a specific product.
- **Customer Repair Order**—Represents the returns and repairs processing. It is similar to a sales order and is generated when a customer returns any product for repairing. After the product is repaired, you generate a bill and deliver the product to the customer.
- **Sales Order**—Represents an order that a customer places in an organization to purchase products or services.

Setting up Notification Types

A notification type is a two-character alphanumeric key, which represents the notification category and its origin. A notification category represents the type of notification. The following notification categories are available in the mySAP ERP system:

- **Plant Maintenance**—Represents the mySAP ERP system's standard category key **01**. While managing customer services, you define this notification when the notification origin is a general maintenance notification, a malfunction report, or an activity report.
- **Quality Notification**—Represents the mySAP ERP system's standard category key **02**. You define this notification when the notification origin is a customer complaint, a complaint against a vendor, an internal problem notification, or a mySAP notification to the mySAP support line.
- **Service Notification**—Represents the mySAP ERP system's standard category key **03**. You define this notification when the notification origin is a problem notification, a service activity report, or a general service notification.
- **Claim**—Represents the mySAP ERP system's standard category key **04**. You define this category when the notification origin is a claim on a customer or a vendor or a claim by a customer or a vendor.
- **General Notification**—Represents the mySAP ERP system's standard category key **05**. You define this notification when the notification origin is general notification.

To configure the notification type, you must perform the following steps:

1. **Define Notification Type**—In the mySAP ERP system, you can create a new notification type by providing relevant information. To define a notification type, navigate the following menu path:

Menu Path

SAP Customizing Implementation Guide > Plant Maintenance and Customer Service > Maintenance and Service Processing > Maintenance

and Service Notifications > Notification Creation > Notification Types > Define Notification Types

2. **Maintain Screen Templates**—When you create notifications through a notification type, the screen templates appear. You can configure or maintain these screen templates by navigating the following menu path:

Menu Path

SAP Customizing Implementation Guide > Plant Maintenance and Customer Service > Maintenance and Service Processing > Maintenance and Service Notifications > Notification Creation > Notification Types > Set Screen Templates for Notification Types

3. **Maintain Long Text and Field Selection for Notification Types**—After configuring the screen templates for a notification type, you also need to maintain long text to specify the reasons to provide the services. You must navigate the following menu path to maintain long text for notification types:

Menu Path

SAP Customizing Implementation Guide > Plant Maintenance and Customer Service > Maintenance and Service Processing > Maintenance and Service Notifications > Notification Creation > Notification Types > Define Long Text Control for Notification Types

Apart from long text, you also need to configure the field selection by navigating the following menu path:

Menu Path

SAP Customizing Implementation Guide > Plant Maintenance and Customer Service > Maintenance and Service Processing > Maintenance and Service Notifications > Notification Creation > Notification Types>Set Field Selection for Notifications

4. **Define and Assign Order Types**—After configuring the long text and the field selection, you need to assign the defined notification type to an order type. Before assigning the order type, you must ensure that the order type is

already defined. However, if you want to define a new order type, navigate the following menu path:

Menu Path

SAP Customizing Implementation Guide > Plant Maintenance and Customer Service > Maintenance and Service Processing > Maintenance and Service Notifications > Notification Creation > Notification Types > Define Order Types and Special Notification Parameters

After defining the order type, you can assign it to a notification type by navigating the following menu path:

Menu Path

SAP Customizing Implementation Guide > Plant Maintenance and Customer Service > Maintenance and Service Processing > Maintenance and Service Notifications > Notification Creation > Notification Types > Assign Notification Types to Order Types

5. **Define Action Boxes**—After the notification type is assigned to an order type, it is essential to configure the actions so that the notification type is triggered automatically. For example, suppose a motorbike is sold to a customer stating that service is required every 6 months. In such a case, it is difficult to remember the service dates of all products sold to various customers. Therefore, you can define a notification type for a product against a sales order made for a customer. You also need to configure the action boxes for a notification type so that the mySAP ERP system automatically prompts and shows a message specifying the date on which the service for a product is due. To configure the action boxes, navigate the following menu path:

Menu Path

SAP Customizing Implementation Guide > Plant Maintenance and Customer Service > Maintenance and Service Processing > Maintenance and Service Notifications > Notification Processing > Additional Functions > Define Action Box

After discussing configuring a notification type, let's now discuss the catalog profiles and how they are created.

Working with Catalogs

A catalog profile is a combination of code groups that ensure that a correct technical object is used to resolve a customer's problem. For example, if a technical object X can be used only in motorbikes, then that object must not be referred to when resolving the problems related to other products. When you create a catalog profile, you specify the code group and its description. The code group is alphanumeric and can be a maximum of eight characters. Perform the following steps to create the catalog profile:

1. Select **SAP Customizing Implementation Guide > Maintenance and Service Processing > Maintenance and Service Notifications > Notification Creation > Notification Content > Define Catalog Profile** (Figure 9.3).
2. Click the **IMG Activity** icon (⊕) beside the **Define Catalog Profile** option, as shown in Figure 9.3.

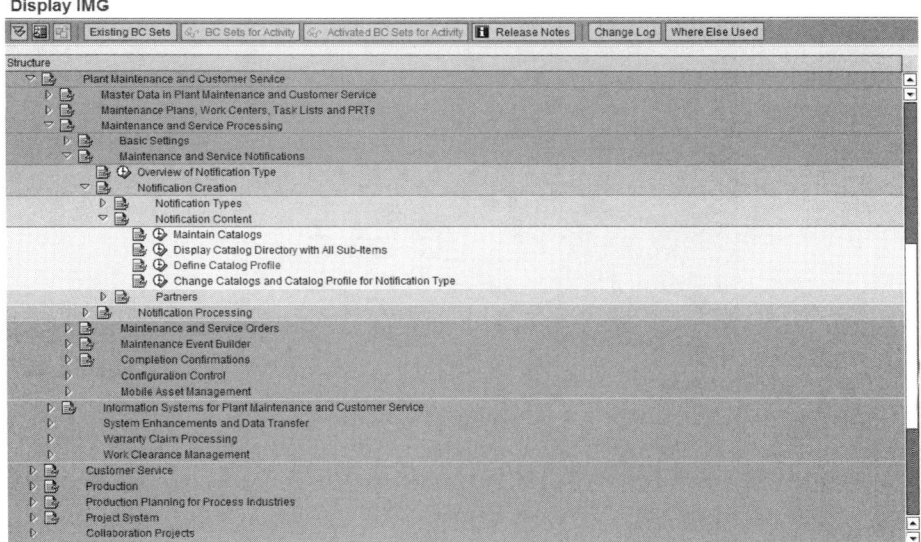

© SAP AG. All rights reserved.

FIGURE 9.3 Selecting the Define Catalog Profile option

The **Change View "Catalog profiles": Overview** screen appears (Figure 9.4). This screen shows the previously created catalog profiles.

454 CHAPTER 9 RELATIONSHIP OF SD TO SM AND QM MODULES

> **Note:** It should also be noted that the creation of a new catalog is as per the requirement of business.

3. Click the **New Entries** button to create a new catalog profile, as shown in Figure 9.4.

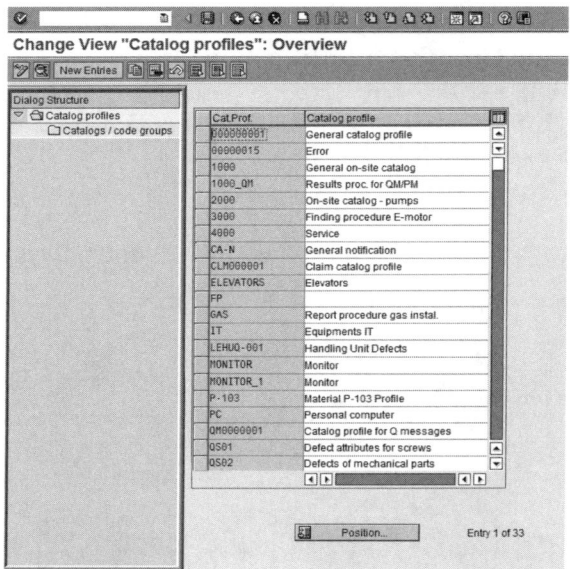

© SAP AG. All rights reserved.

FIGURE 9.4 Creating a new catalog profile

The **New Entries: Details of Added Entries** screen appears (Figure 9.5).

4. Specify the catalog profile code group and its description (Figure 9.5). We have specified 00000015 as the code group and Computer Error as its description (Figure 9.5).
5. Click the **Save** icon (🖫) on the standard toolbar to save the newly created catalog profile, as shown in Figure 9.5.

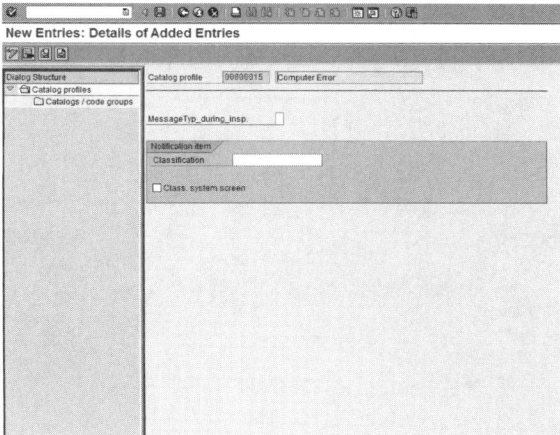

© SAP AG. All rights reserved.

FIGURE 9.5 Saving the newly created catalog profile

The newly created catalog program is saved and can be viewed in the **Change View "Catalog profiles": Overview** screen.

After learning how to implement the customer service process, let's now discuss how to define a service order in the mySAP ERP system.

Working with Service Orders in SD

A service order is defined as an order that a customer places to get a desired service from an organization. You can create a service order from a notification. Use the following menu path to create a service order from a notification:

Menu Path

SAP menu > Logistics > Customer Service > Service Processing > Notification > Create (Special) > IW54 – Problem Notification (Figure 9.6).

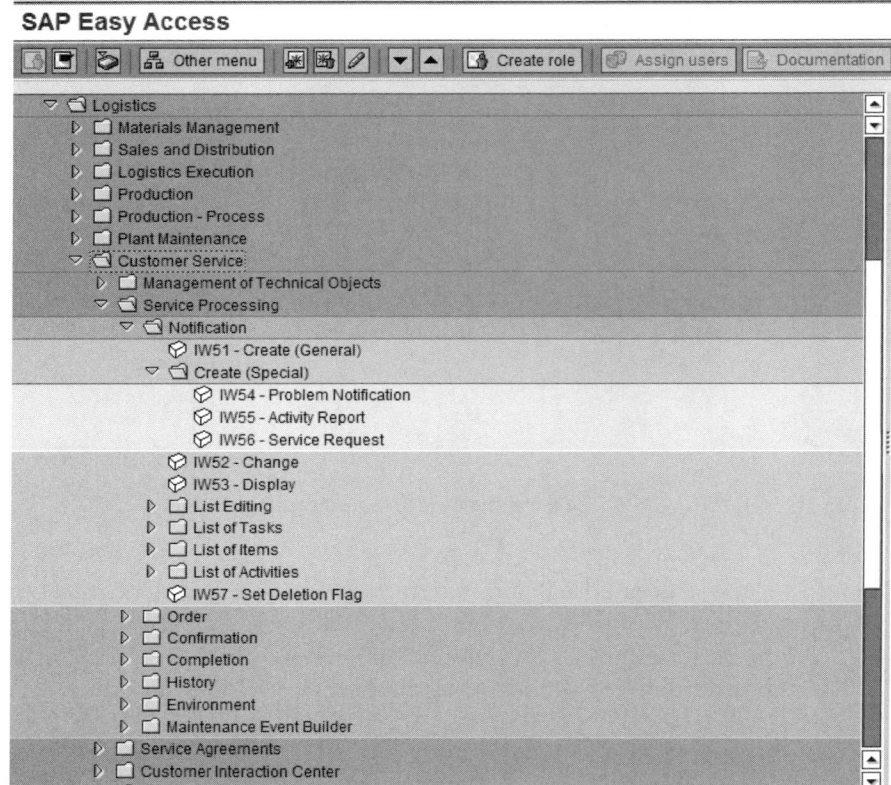

© SAP AG. All rights reserved.

FIGURE 9.6 Selecting option to create a service order from notification

When you double-click the **IW54 – Problem Notification** option, the **Create Service Notification: Service Notification** screen appears, as shown in Figure 9.7.

IMPLEMENTING SERVICE MANAGEMENT IN SD   457

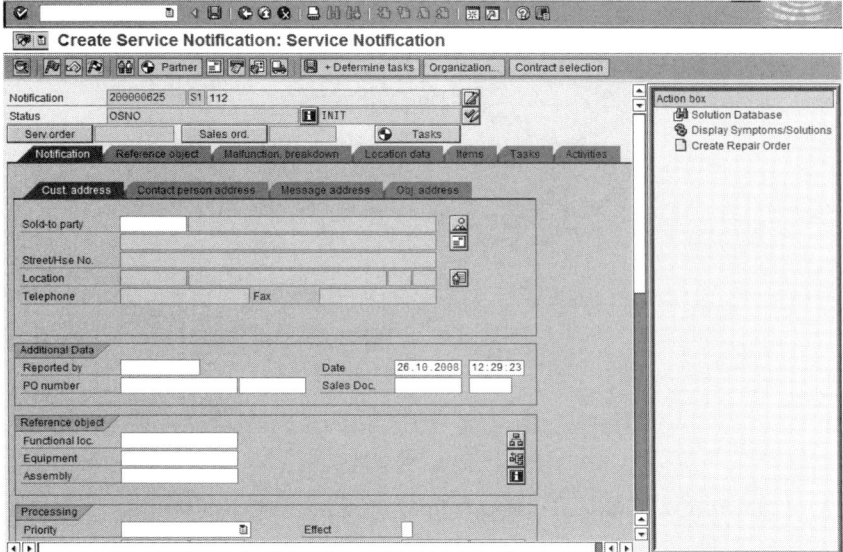

© SAP AG. All rights reserved.

FIGURE 9.7   Screen to specify notification and service order details

Specify the notification and service order details in the **Create Service Notification: Service Notification** screen according to your requirement. After specifying the details, save the service order. Now, after you have created the service order, you have to confirm its creation. You can use the following menu path to confirm the service order creation:

Menu Path

SAP menu > Logistics > Customer Service > Service Processing > Confirmation > Entry > IW42 − Overall Completion Confirmation (Figure 9.8).

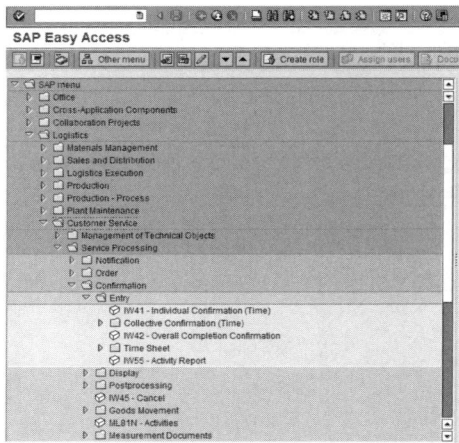

© SAP AG. All rights reserved.

FIGURE 9.8 Selecting option to confirm the service order creation

When you double-click the **IW42 – Overall Completion Confirmation** option, the **Overall Completion Confirmation** screen appears, as shown in Figure 9.9.

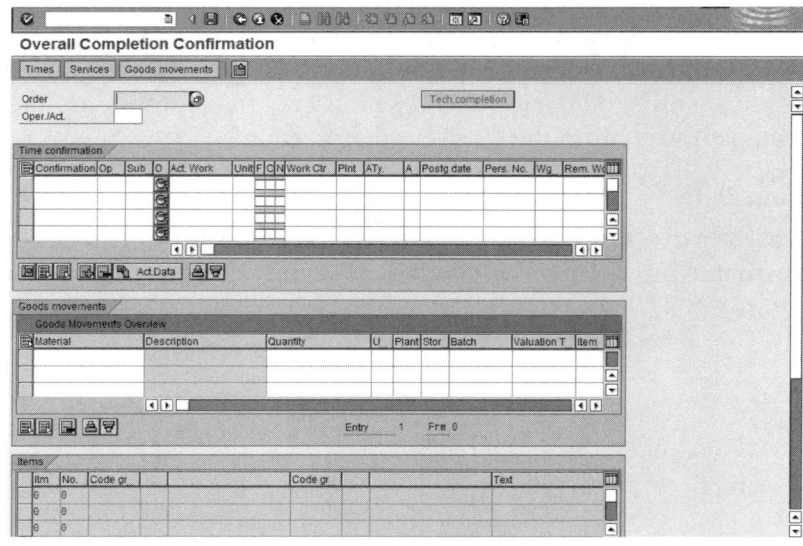

© SAP AG. All rights reserved.

FIGURE 9.9 Confirming the service order

Implementing Service Management in SD

Specify the service order in the **Overall Completion Confirmation** screen and save it.

After discussing service order processing, let's now discuss the process of complaints and returns in the mySAP ERP system.

Working with Complaints and Returns

An organization provides repair processing when a request is made by a customer to repair a defective item. In the mySAP ERP system, you need to create a service notification and then define a customer repair order with respect to the customer's request of repairing. To define a customer repair order, perform the following steps:

1. Select the following menu path:

Menu Path

SAP menu > Logistics > Customer Service > Service Processing > Order > Customer Repair > VA01 - Create (Figure 9.10).

2. Double-click the **VA01 - Create** option, as shown in Figure 9.10.

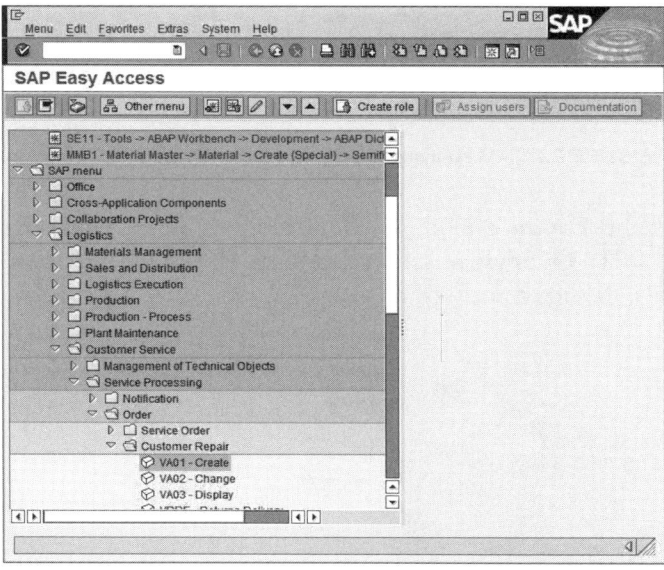

© SAP AG. All rights reserved.

FIGURE 9.10 Displaying the menu path for defining a customer repair order

The **Create Sales Order: Initial Screen** appears (Figure 9.11).

3. Enter the relevant details, as shown in Figure 9.11.

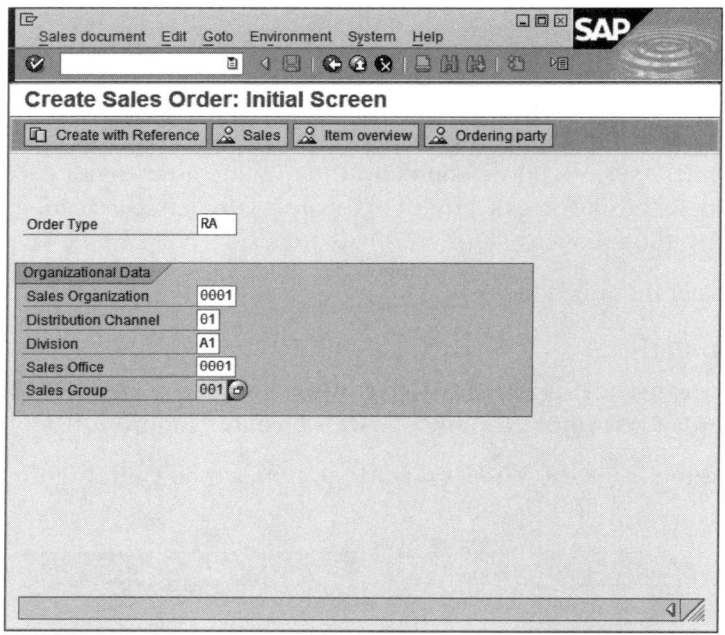

© SAP AG. All rights reserved.

FIGURE 9.11 Displaying the Create Sales Order: Initial Screen

4. Click the **Execute** icon (☑)(Figure 9.11). The **Create Repairs /Service 5000001: Overview** screen appears (Figure 9.12). Enter the required details, as shown in Figure 9.12.

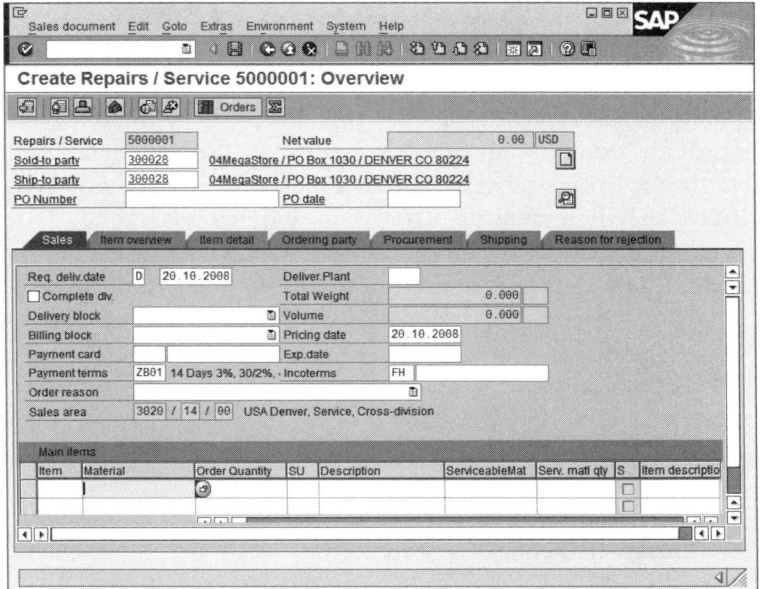

FIGURE 9.12 Displaying the details for creating repairs or services

5. Click the **Save** icon (🖫) on the standard toolbar to save the entered details.

As shown in Figure 9.12, you need to fill in the name of the Service Item Code in the material field for which you maintain the material master in the standard system. Other details like storage location would also be prompted by the system. Since it is a service item, it may not have a storage location. However, for a material master it is internal data that you must save during the creation of a material master, according to your requirement.

After discussing the service management implementation in SD processing, let's now learn how to implement quality management in SD.

IMPLEMENTING QUALITY MANAGEMENT IN SD

Before the goods are delivered to a customer, they are inspected for quality assurance. In other words, in the mySAP ERP system, while processing a sales order, a quality management process is also scheduled for the delivery of the goods. In this process, the technicians verify the goods and provide a certificate specifying that the inspection of the goods has been done. After the certificate is provided, the shipment processing is done in the SD module. To implement quality management in the SD module, you must learn how to do the following:

- Identify the phases of quality certification
- Manage quality during delivery

Now, let's explore each of these in detail.

Identifying the Phases of Quality Certification

After the quality inspection is performed, a quality certification is created, specifying that the product has been inspected for quality and can be shipped for delivery. These certificates might be created depending upon the agreements made with customers. The following are the two phases of managing the quality assurance and certification process:

- Planning Phase
- Processing Phase

Now, let's discuss each of them in detail.

The Planning Phase

The planning phase allows you to specify the layout, design, product, and customer-related information for the certificates. The layout of the certificate form to be printed is done with the help of variables created by a SAP user. In addition, you can also create a profile containing the details, such as characteristics and usage of the certificate form. You can view the certificate profile for material by performing the following steps:

1. Select **SAP menu > Logistics > Quality Management > Quality Certificates > Outgoing > Certificate Profile > QC03 - Display**, as shown in Figure 9.13.

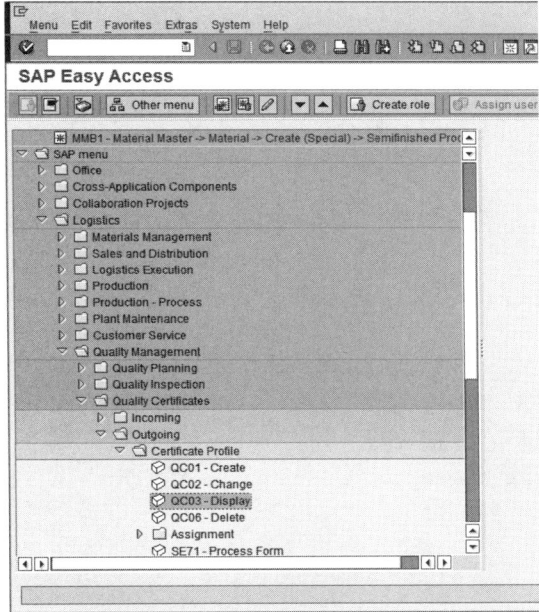

© SAP AG. All rights reserved.

FIGURE 9.13 Displaying the menu path for displaying a certificate profile

2. Double-click **QC03 - Display**; the **Display Certificate Profile: Initial Screen** appears (Figure 9.14).
3. Enter the certificate profile number whose details you want to display. In our example, we have entered `QC400-99` as the profile number (Figure 9.14).
4. Click the **Enter** icon ( ) as shown in Figure 9.14.

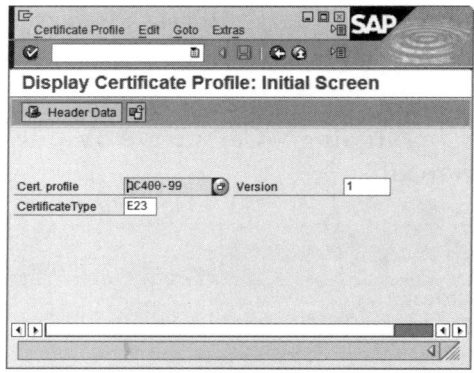

FIGURE 9.14 Displaying the entered details for a certificate profile

The header data of the QC400-99 certificate profile appears, as shown in Figure 9.15.

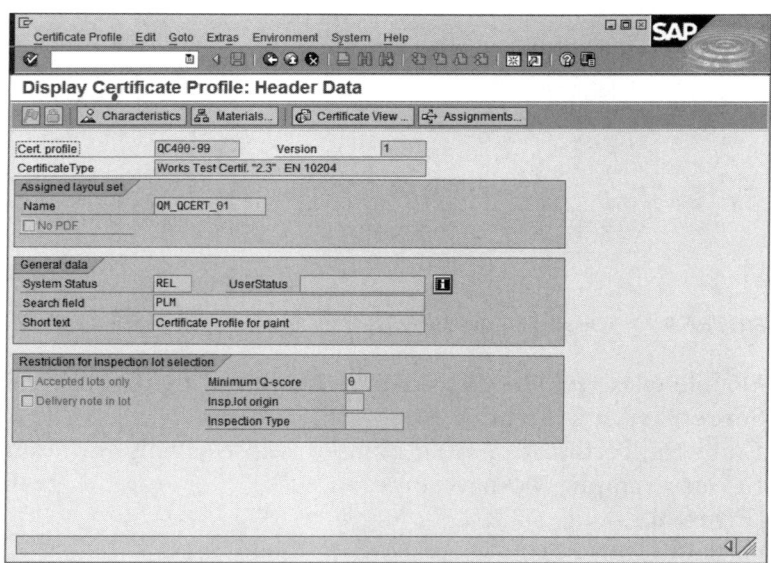

FIGURE 9.15 Displaying the header data of a certificate profile

You can also create a new certificate profile by double-clicking the **QC01 - Create** activity (Figure 9.13).

After learning about the planning phase, let's now explore the certificate processing phase.

The Processing Phase

The processing phase allows you to define the recipient of the certificate, specify the time required to create the certificate, and specify the language to be used in creating the certificate. You can view the recipient information by navigating the following menu path in the mySAP ERP system:

Menu Path

SAP menu > Logistics > Quality Management > Quality Certificates > Outgoing > Certificate Recipient > VV23 - Display, as shown in Figure 9.16.

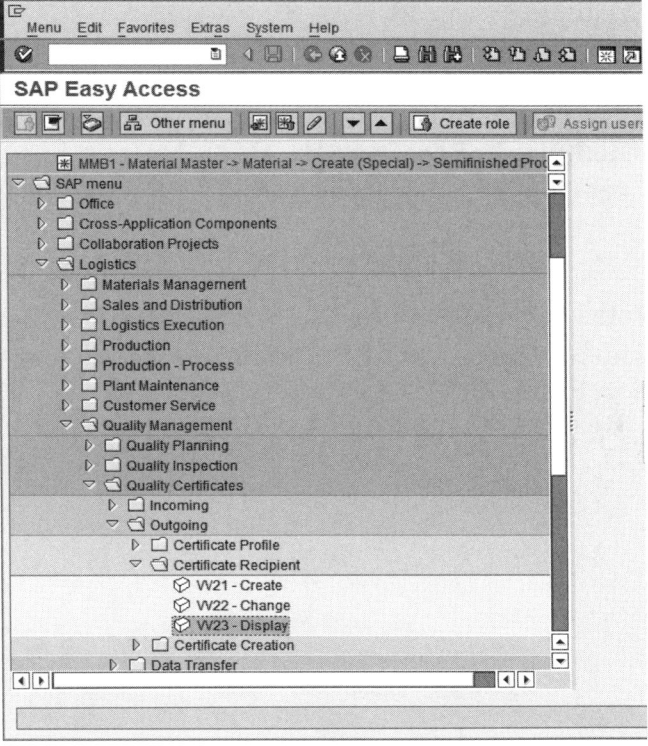

© SAP AG. All rights reserved.

FIGURE 9.16 Displaying the menu path to display the recipient details

Apart from viewing the details of existing certificate recipients, you can also define a new certificate recipient by selecting the **VV21 - Create** activity, as shown in Figure 9.16.

Let's now explore how quality is managed during delivery of products.

Managing Quality during Delivery

The QM module automatically performs the inspection of goods that need to be delivered to the customer before the products or services are delivered. For automatic inspection, the products for QM inspection should be activated in the material master of the MM module. The quality test may be configured in a way that a sample batch from the delivery lot is created and sent for quality testing. The delivery lot is cleared for delivery only after meeting the required quality standard, which is confirmed by the quality management report. Moreover, you can also view the quality details relevant to the SD module by navigating the following menu path:

Menu Path

SAP menu > Quality Management > Quality Planning > Logistics Master Data > Quality Info Records: SD

By navigating the preceding menu path, you can create, modify, or display the quality information relevant to the SD module. After inspection, the results are recorded, and you can view the results using the following menu path:

Menu Path

SAP menu > Logistics > Quality Management > Quality Inspection > Inspection Result > QE51N - Results Recording

The **Results Recording Worklist** screen appears, as shown in Figure 9.17.

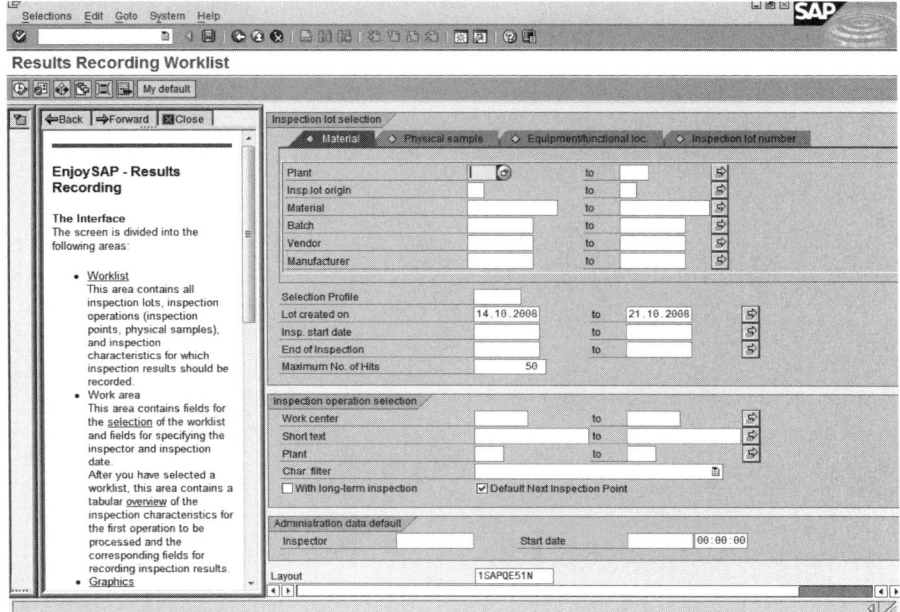

FIGURE 9.17 Displaying the Results Recording Worklist screen

You can enter the relevant details in the required fields, as shown in Figure 9.17 and click the **IMG Activity** icon ( ) to display the quality details.

Let's now summarize this chapter.

SUMMARY

In this chapter, you learned to implement service management in the SD module. Moreover, the chapter explored how to work with customer services, service orders, complaints, and returns in the SD module. Apart from service management, the chapter also explained the implementation of quality management in the SD module by exploring the phases of quality certification. Toward the end of the chapter, the quality management process during delivery was discussed.

The next chapter discusses how to generate views, reports, and lists in the SD module.

Chapter 10
Working with Reports and Analysis in SD

If you need information on:	See page:
Working with SD Reporting Tools in SAP	470
Working with the Sales Information System	489
Analyzing Data Using SAP Business Information Warehouse	499

Reporting and analysis are important post-sales activities in the SAP® Sales and Distribution (SD) module, and are carried out in an organization in order to analyze the outcome of a sales process. The reporting activity is primarily related to the generation of reports on the basis of the data related to a particular activity or process. The analysis activity entails observation of the reports to either draw a conclusion or to ascertain the market trends. Consequently, both the reporting and analysis activities contribute to formulating new strategies and plans for the organization. The reporting and analysis activities include tasks such as collecting information about an activity, preparing a report, and analyzing the report in order to draw conclusions. For example, the reporting of the credit sales data of a particular commodity reveals the total credit amount provided by an organization to its customers. In addition, the reporting and analysis activities of organizational data depict the situation of either over- or under-utilization of funds or resources. As a result, new policies can be initiated to avoid such situations.

The SAP standard system provides various standard reports that are very useful. However, according to the needs of the business, it may be necessary to develop some business-specific reports in addition to the standard reports. You can develop specific reports by using the data stored in specific tables of the SAP system. These reports are developed using the ABAP™ module.

If you have the Business Warehouse (BW) module, you are able to generate all sorts of records and data depending on your requirements.

The SAP SD module provides a rich set of reporting and analysis tools for the sales and distribution process. For example, the QuickView, Query, and List and Report tools are used for reporting. The commonly used tools for analysis are individual sales documents, listings, evaluations, and work lists. In this chapter, we explore these SD analysis and reporting tools in detail. Apart from the SD reporting tools, we discuss the Sales Information System (SIS), which is used to review the entire sales and distribution process. Lastly, the concept of the SAP business information warehouse is discussed.

Let's start the next section with a discussion about SD reporting tools.

WORKING WITH SD REPORTING TOOLS IN SAP

The SD reporting tools are used to generate reports based on specific needs and present data according to a customer's query, and to develop an ABAP report from system data. The following are the most commonly used tools to perform reporting activities for the sales and distribution process:

- QuickView
- SAP Query
- List and Report

Let's discuss each of them in detail.

Exploring the QuickView Tool

QuickView is an elementary tool used to generate reports simply by entering the data in the mySAP® ERP system instead of creating SAP queries. Therefore, the SAP consultants who do not have programming experience to create SAP queries can also generate reports using the QuickView tool.

Note: The QuickView tool is important for functional consultants.

QuickViewer is a reporting tool that is used to generate QuickViews assigned to particular data for which the report is to be created. The QuickViewer tool is similar to an ABAP Query, which is created using ABAP programming language. QuickViewer is more useful when you need to query more than one table, such as sets of master data to obtain the information you require. In this way, QuickViewer helps you to access multiple tables.

For creating a QuickView, we first need to define a database containing tables, views, or other data sources that are used to access data. Perform the following steps to create a QuickView using the QuickViewer tool:

1. Select **SAP menu > Tools > ABAP Workbench > Utilities > SQVI - QuickViewer** to launch QuickViewer, as shown in Figure 10.1.

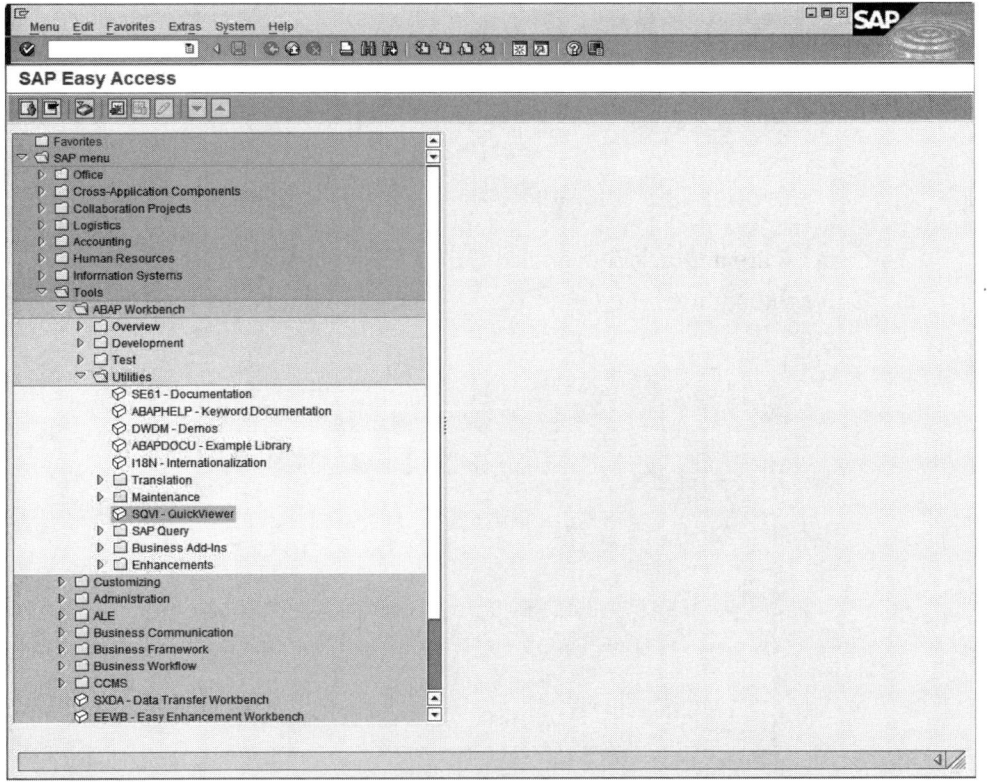

© SAP AG. All rights reserved.

FIGURE 10.1 Displaying the menu path for launching QuickViewer

The **QuickViewer: Initial Screen** appears as shown in Figure 10.2.

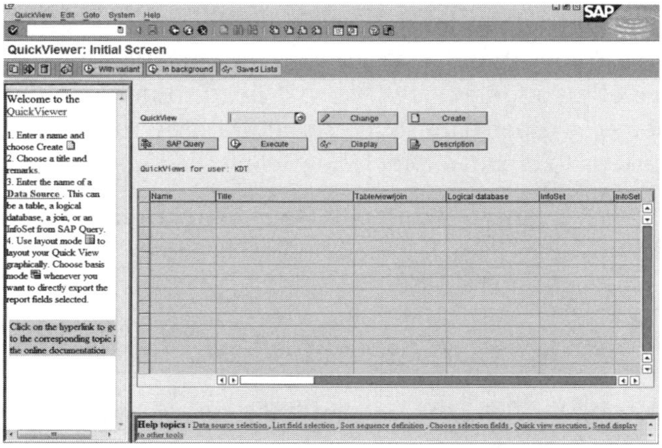

© SAP AG. All rights reserved.

FIGURE 10.2 Displaying the QuickViewer: Initial Screen

You can create a QuickView in the **QuickViewer: Initial Screen**.

2. Enter the name of the QuickView (**Z002**) and then click the **Create** button (Figure 10.3).

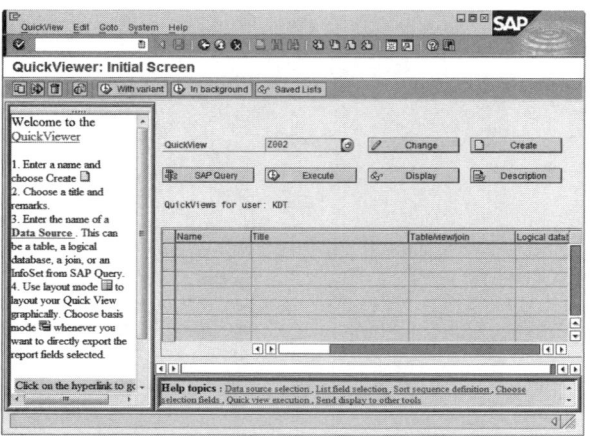

© SAP AG. All rights reserved.

FIGURE 10.3 Creating a QuickView (Z002)

Figure 10.3 shows the **QuickViewer: Initial Screen** that is used to create QuickView (**Z002**).

The **Create QuickView Z002:Choose Data Source** dialog box appears as shown in Figure 10.4.

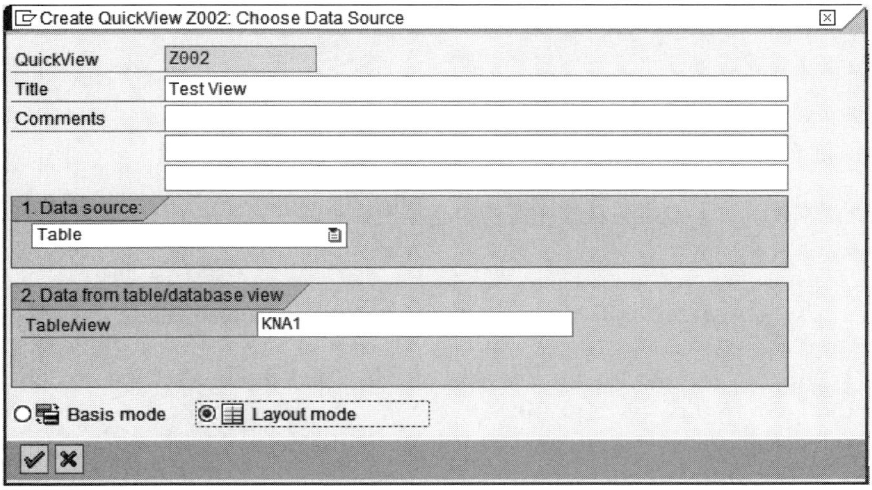

© SAP AG. All rights reserved.

FIGURE 10.4 Choosing layout mode of display

Figure 10.4 shows the **Create QuickView Z002:Choose Data Source** dialog box, which is used to create a QuickView (**Z002**). It displays the name of the QuickView report that had been entered in the **QuickViewer: Initial Screen**. Enter the required information in the text boxes beside the **Title, Test View, Data Source**, and **Table/View** labels. In the text box beside the **Title** label, we have entered `Test View`, and in the data source, we have selected the **Table** option as the data source. `KNA1` is entered in the text box beside the **Table/View** label to retrieve the data. Lastly, we have selected **Layout mode** as the mode to display data.

3. Press the **Enter** key (Figure 10.4). The **Choose Data Source** dialog box appears as shown in Figure 10.5.

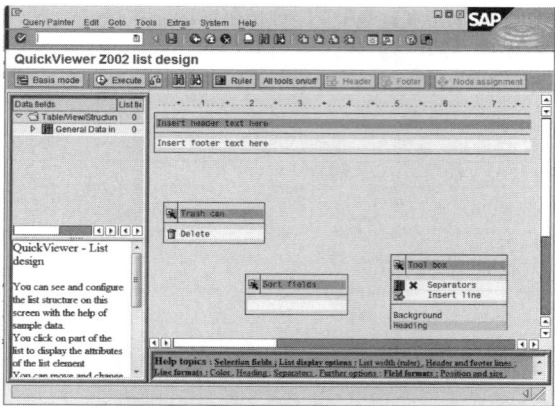

© SAP AG. All rights reserved.

FIGURE 10.5 Displaying the QuickView in the Layout mode

Figure 10.5 shows the **QuickViewer Z002 list design** screen, which displays the layout mode of the **Z002** QuickView. Apart from the **Layout mode**, you can also display a QuickView in the **Basis mode**.

As discussed previously, when you click the **Create** button on the **QuickViewer Initial Screen** (Figure 10.3), the **Create QuickView Z002:Choose Data Source** dialog box appears. This dialog box allows you to choose the mode in which to display a QuickView. Previously, we selected the **Layout mode** (Figure 10.4).

4. Choose the **Basis mode** from the **Create QuickView Z002: Choose Data Source** dialog box to display QuickView in **Basis mode**, as shown in Figure 10.6.

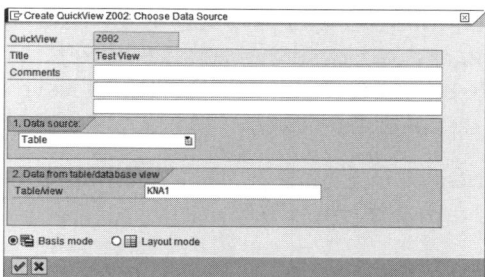

© SAP AG. All rights reserved.

FIGURE 10.6 Choosing the Basis mode of display

Figure 10.6 shows the **Create QuickView Z002: Choose Data Source** dialog box used to create a particular view (**Z002**). By default, the **Basis mode** is selected in Figure 10.6; therefore, the result of a QuickView is displayed in the **Basis mode**. The **QuickViewer: Initial Screen** appears after pressing the **Enter** key, as shown in Figure 10.7.

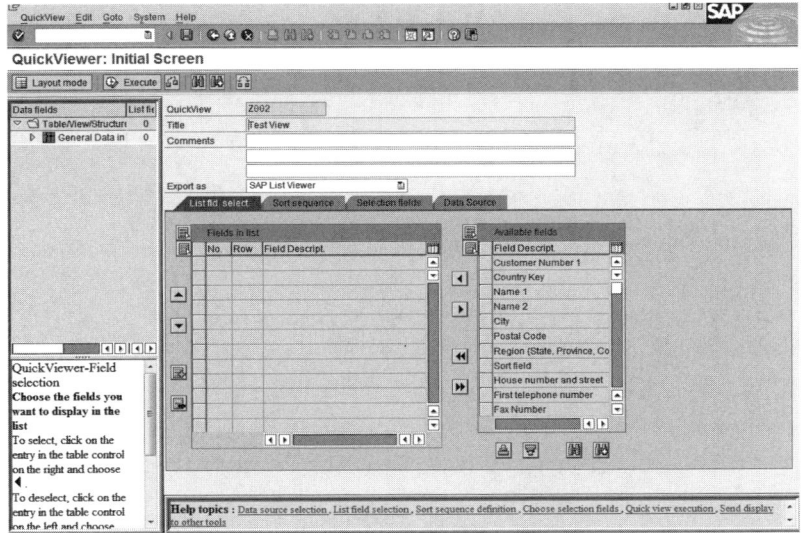

© SAP AG. All rights reserved.

FIGURE 10.7 Displaying the QuickView in the Basis mode

Figure 10.7 shows the following sections with reference to the **Z002** QuickView:

- **List fld. select**—Provides information related to various fields. To display the fields in a list format, you can add the fields displayed in the **Available fields** section (Figure 10.7) to the **Fields in list** section.
- **Sort sequence**—Provides information related to the sorted fields with reference to the **Z002** QuickView.
- **Selection fields**—Provides information related to the selection fields with reference to the **Z002** QuickView.
- **Data Source**—Provides data related to the data source, such as a table or view, to select data.

Now, let's select the **Data Source** section to view the data source related information of the **Z002** QuickView. The **QuickViewer: Initial Screen** appears, displaying the **Data Source** section as shown in Figure 10.8.

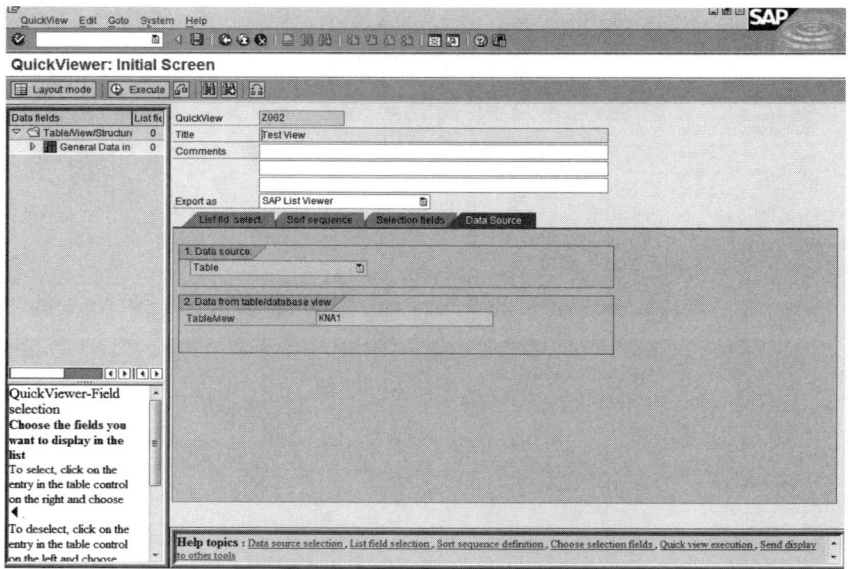

© SAP AG. All rights reserved.

FIGURE 10.8 Displaying the Data Source menu item

Figure 10.8 displays the **Data Source** section, which shows the data source (**Table**), and the table (**KNA1**), which are referenced to generate the QuickView.

You can also send the results of a QuickView to other external sources, such as Microsoft Excel or Word, for further analysis. The results of QuickView include the name of QuickView, title, and fields to be displayed in the list format. In addition, the QuickView results also include the data source used to create the QuickView, such as customer master records. Depending upon the requirement of the SAP user, the QuickView results can be exported in various formats. For example, if it is necessary to export the QuickView results in Microsoft Excel, the results are exported in that format. Figure 10.9 shows the exporting options; that is, external sources where the results of QuickView can be exported.

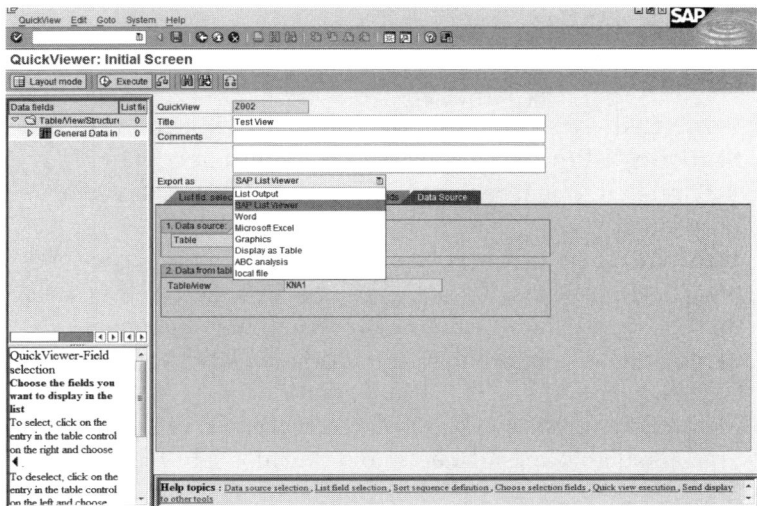

FIGURE 10.9 Displaying the external views to export quickview result

After discussing the QuickViews, now let's discuss the SAP Query.

Exploring SAP Query

SAP Query is a comprehensive tool used to generate reports from the input provided by QuickView. SAP Query can generate reports without ABAP programming. As a result, SAP Query hastens the process of report generation. We know that SAP provides a customized environment to create and execute an SAP Query. The main purpose of an SAP Query is to generate various types of reports, such as basic lists, statistics, and ranked lists.

Let's now explore the following aspects related to SAP Query:

- Lists available with SAP Query
- Components of an SAP Query
- SAP Query area
- Creating an SAP Query

Lists Available with SAP Query

An SAP Query generates resulting data in the form of some specific lists:

- **Basic List**—Provides a simple list, such as collection of orders.
- **Statistics**—Provides a special type of list that contains data related to mathematical functions such as average or percentage.
- **Ranked List**—Provides lists that have been prepared for analytical purposes. Examples of rank lists are the lists sorted on specific attributes, such as order number, customer identification, ascending sales, or other related types.

The preceding lists can be displayed in various formats such as tables, ALV grids, downloadable spreadsheets, and downloadable flat files.

Components of an SAP Query

The components of an SAP Query are used to accept and process the user's query and to generate the desired results. These components combine the process flow, which is used to create and execute an SAP Query. The SAP Query is organized into the following four noteworthy components:

- **Queries**—Defines, changes, and executes the queries, as well as generates the SAP lists.
- **InfoSet**—Contains the views of data used in the execution of SAP Query. An InfoSet is assigned to a particular user group. The role or user group is used to decide the relevance of InfoSet for a particular end user. If the role or user group is assigned to an InfoSet, an end user can work with that InfoSet. Apart from InfoSet, InfoSet Query is also used for creating reports.
- **User Group**—Helps administer and maintain user groups. Every user is assigned to a particular user group to create and execute the queries. Moreover, roles and user groups can be assigned to an InfoSet using the **Role/User Group Assignment** button (Figure 10.11).
- **Translational/Query**—Helps translate text created in an SAP Query. We can also compare the text created in an SAP Query by using the transactional query components.

The SAP menu path and transaction codes for each SAP Query component are listed in Table 10.1.

SAP Query Components	Menu Path	Transaction Code
Queries	SAP menu > Tools > ABAP Workbench > Utilities > SAP Query > Queries	SQ01
InfoSet	SAP menu > Tools > ABAP Workbench > Utilities > SAP Query > InfoSet	SQ02
User Group	SAP menu > Tools > ABAP Workbench > Utilities > SAP Query > User Groups	SQ03
Translational Query	SAP menu > Tools > ABAP Workbench > Utilities > Translation	SE63, SQ03

TABLE 10.1 Displaying menu path and transaction codes of SAP query components

SAP Query Area

The SAP query area is a place to hold a query. There are two types of query areas:

- **Global**—Denotes the global query areas that are developed and distributed throughout the SAP system. In other words, global query areas are not client specific; rather, they are connected to the change and transport organizer for global access and manipulation. Therefore, queries created in the global SAP query area can be accessed by all of the clients. Today, most of the query areas used in SAP are global.
- **Standard**—In a standard query area, all the query components, such as queries, InfoSet, and user groups, are created and managed for a specific individual client. In other words, the standard query area is client specific. The query objects are not attached to the workbench organizer. As a result, they are not created and managed according to the standard procedures for

creating and executing queries. The main advantage of using a standard query area is the flexibility of creating queries for specific clients.

After describing SAP query areas in detail, let's discuss how to create an SAP Query.

Creating an SAP Query

The following are the tasks to be performed to create a query:

- Creating an InfoSet [**SQ02**]
- Assigning a user group to the InfoSet [**SQ03**]
- Creating a query based on InfoSet [**SQ01**]
- Specifying the Display Format

Let's explore these in detail. In addition to these, we also compare QuickView and SAP Query.

Creating an InfoSet [SQ02]

To create a query, you need to declare a user group and to assign specific users to it. Each user group has an InfoSet or functional area that determines the database tables being accessed by an SAP Query. When a query is executed, the ABAP program runs in the background, and the InfoSet works as a template for the program. When a user creates a query by choosing an InfoSet, the query is known as an InfoSet query. For example, in the case of the HR module, an InfoSet is used for ad-hoc reporting; therefore, the corresponding query is called Ad-Hoc Query. The InfoSet is also used as a data source to create and execute subqueries within the SAP query areas.

To create an SAP Query, you need to create an InfoSet that determines the database tables and fields that can access a query. You need to navigate the following menu path to create an InfoSet:

Menu Path

SAP menu > Tools > ABAP Workbench > Utilities > SAP Query > SQ02 – InfoSets, as shown in Figure 10.10.

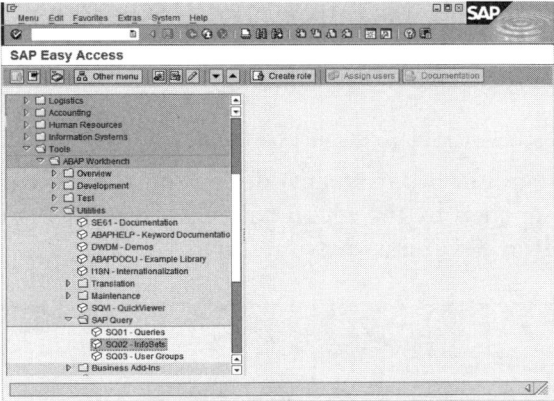

FIGURE 10.10 Displaying menu path for creating an Infoset

Now double-click the **SQ02 - InfoSets** menu item. The **InfoSet: Initial Screen** appears, where you can create an InfoSet, as shown in Figure 10.11.

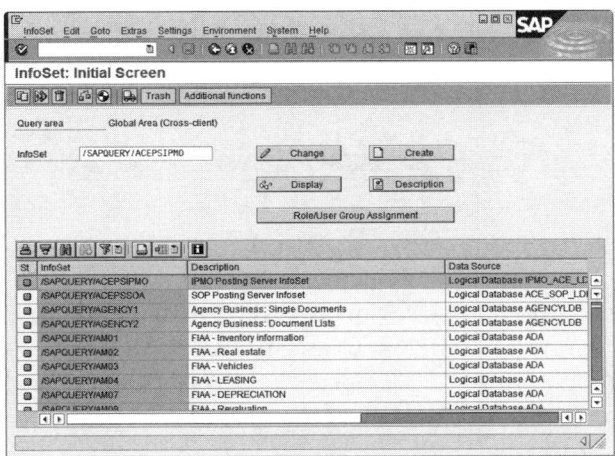

FIGURE 10.11 Displaying the Infoset: Initial Screen

Figure 10.11 shows the **InfoSet: Initial Screen**, which is used to create an InfoSet. After creating an InfoSet, the next step in the query creation process is to assign a user group to the InfoSet.

Assignment of a User Group to the InfoSet [SQ03]

For assigning a user group to an InfoSet, the **User Groups: Initial Screen** needs to be opened by the menu path displayed in Figure 10.10. The **User Groups: Initial Screen** is shown in Figure 10.12.

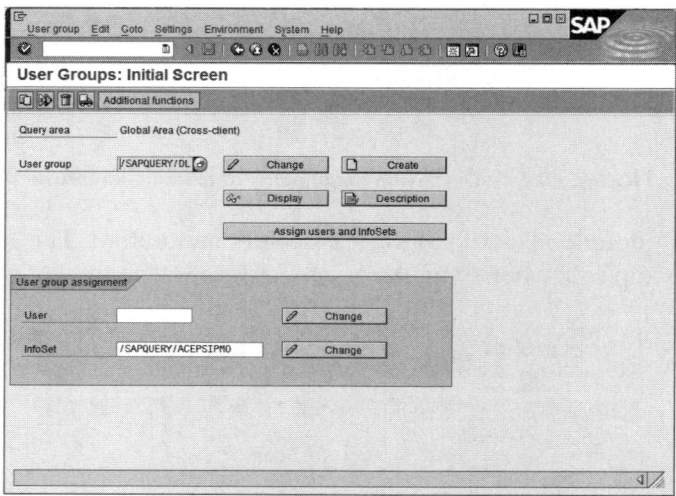

© SAP AG. All rights reserved.

FIGURE 10.12 Displaying the User Groups: Initial Screen

In Figure 10.12, the **User group** assignment section displays the previously created InfoSet, ACEPSIPMO. To assign a user group to this InfoSet, select the user group (/SAPQUERY/DL) and click the **Assign users and InfoSets** button. The **User Group/SAPQUERY/DL: Assign Users** screen appears as shown in Figure 10.13.

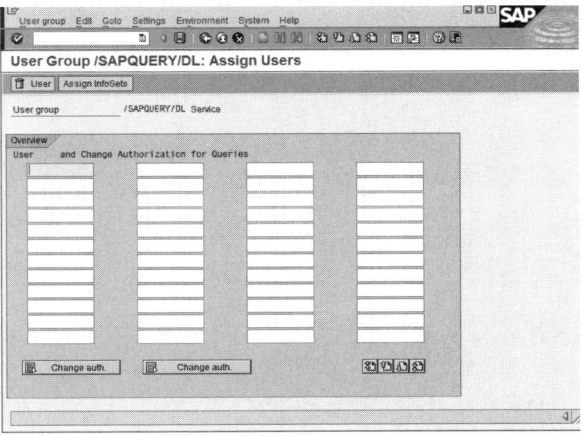

FIGURE 10.13 Displaying the User Group/SAPQUERY/DL: Assign Users screen

Now in the **User Group/SAPQUERY/DL: Assign Users** screen, click the **Assign InfoSets** button. The **User Group/SAPQUERY/DL: Assign InfoSets** screen appears as shown in Figure 10.14.

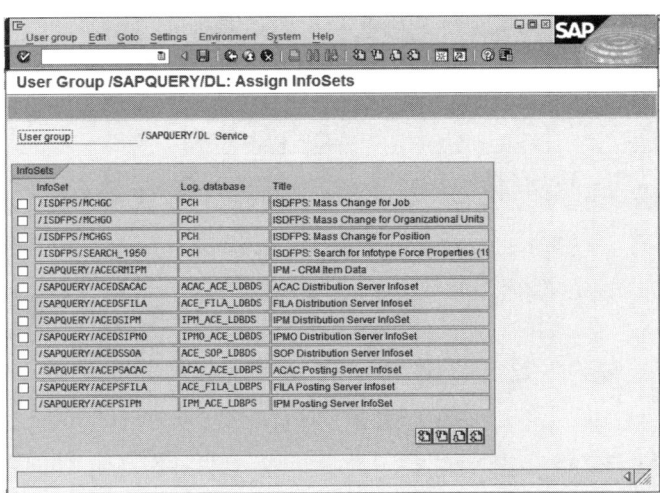

FIGURE 10.14 Displaying the User Group/SAPQUERY/DL: Assign InfoSets screen

484 CHAPTER 10 WORKING WITH REPORTS AND ANALYSIS IN SD

Figure 10.14 shows the **User Group/SAPQUERY/ES: Assign InfoSets** screen, which displays the list of InfoSets that needs to be selected. After assigning a user group to the InfoSet, the next step in the query creation process is to create a query based on the InfoSet.

Creation of a Query Based on InfoSet [SQ01]

To create the query based on the previously created InfoSet, navigate the following menu path:

Menu Path

SAP menu > Tools > ABAP Workbench > Utilities > SAP Query > SQ01 - Queries

Double-click the **SQ01 - Queries** activity; the **Query from User Group/SAPQUERY/DL: Initial Screen** appears as shown in Figure 10.15.

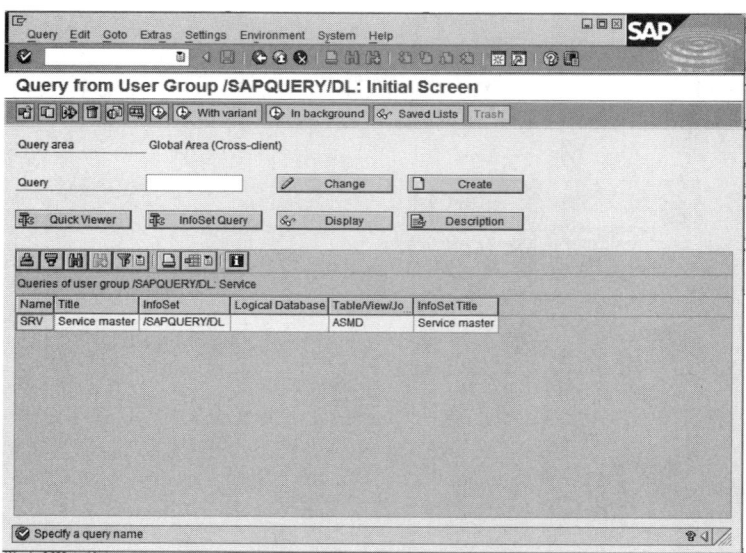

© SAP AG. All rights reserved.

FIGURE 10.15 Displaying the User Group/SAPQUERY/DL: Initial Screen

Figure 10.15 shows the initial screen for query creation, which shows the previously created InfoSet. For creating a query based on the previously created InfoSet, click the **InfoSet Query** button. The **Restricted Value Range (1)** dialog box is displayed containing the **InfoSet** list. Select the relevant **InfoSet** and proceed further according to your requirement, to execute the query.

Specifying the Display Format

After creating an SAP Query, the result of that query can be displayed in the following formats:

- **SAP List Viewer**—Displays sorted and filtered lists on the basis of a particular attribute.
- **Graphics**—Displays query results in a graphical format, such as a pie chart or a bar chart.
- **ABC Analysis**—Displays the results of ABC analysis. ABC analysis is a concept to categorize given data into three categories, A, B, and C, based on certain attributes. In ABC analysis, category A includes data having the highest level of priority or relevance (based on the specified attributes), category B includes data having the second highest level of priority or relevance, and so on. Let's consider a scenario where you want to generate the ABC analysis report for the available materials in the stock based on the value of the materials. Thereby, you define the A, B, and C categories as follows:

  - **A**—Specifies the most valuable items, constituting 20% of the entire stock.
  - **B**—Specifies the items with an average value, constituting 50% of the entire stock.
  - **C**—Specifies the least valuable items, comprising 30% of the entire stock, i.e., the remaining stock.

The corresponding ABC analysis of data categorized under A, B, and C types, as shown in Figure 10.16.

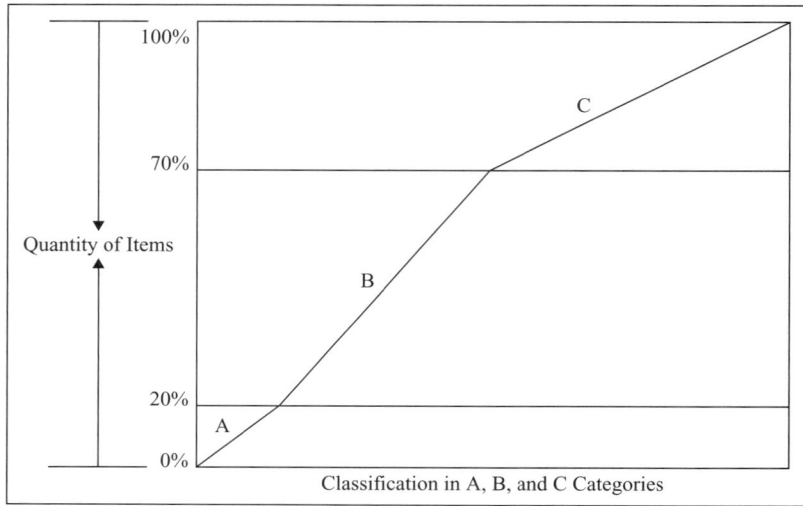

FIGURE 10.16 Displaying the ABC analysis

Figure 10.16 shows the ABC analysis of data.

Comparing QuickView and SAP Query

Table 10.2 lists the differences between QuickView and SAP Query:

QuickView	SAP Query
A basic tool for reporting and analysis	A comprehensive tool for reporting and analysis
No prior knowledge of programming is required	Knowledge of ABAP programming is required to generate reports in SAP Query
Assigning user groups is necessary	Assigning user groups is not required
InfoSets are not required to create QuickViews	InfoSets are required to create an SAP Query
Only basic lists may be defined	Highly customized and comprehensive lists can be defined

TABLE 10.2 Displaying differences between QuickView and SAP Query

After discussing the SAP Query tool, let's discuss reports and lists in the next section.

Exploring Reports and Lists

The results obtained by QuickViews or SAP Queries are used to generate either lists or reports. An SAP user runs an ABAP program to display the QuickView or SAP Query results in the report or list format. In this section, we discuss lists as well as SAP SD reports that are written in ABAP programs.

You need to enter the SA38 transaction code in the command field of the **SAP Easy Access** screen to run an ABAP program. The **ABAP: Program Execution** screen appears as shown in Figure 10.17.

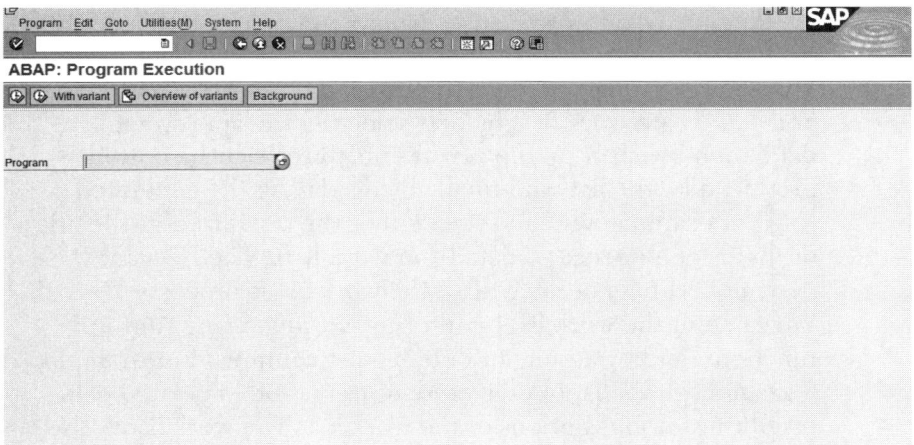

© SAP AG. All rights reserved.

FIGURE 10.17 Displaying the ABAP: Program Execution screen

Figure 10.17 shows the **ABAP: Program Execution** screen, which is used to run an ABAP program to generate the SAP SD report. The **With variant** button is used to select the variant, which restricts the data to be displayed on the report. After the variant is selected, we can run the ABAP program.

After discussing the reports, let's now discuss the lists in SAP SD. Lists display the data related to sales, delivery, material stocks, and billing for analysis purposes. Following are the categories of lists:

- **Online List**—Contains intermediate data that is required as input to process the current activity at a later stage. Online lists are also generated on the basis of an online query. Online query processing generates multiple instances of document views known as document flow. In other words, document flow is a part of the online lists, as document views are generated during online query processing. The document flow generates the data used to interpret and analyze the list details, such as history and past insertions and deletions made in the documents. In other words, it displays the entire status of a document.
- **Work List**—Generates lists to display the relevant data. You can create work lists by first selecting the appropriate data, then by applying the constraints to restrict the output produced by the list, and finally by displaying the generated list. For example, we can select either the organization-specific or the customer-related data from work lists. The relevant documents are generated after the work list is processed. We can edit the work list by filtering, sorting, using sum-up functions, and by adding or deleting list columns. For example, we can display a list of delivered items and other related data by editing various options of the work list. The work list is also categorized into two lists: delivery due list and billing list.

To access the SAP work lists, you need to navigate the following menu path:

Menu Path

SAP menu > Logistics > Sales and Distribution > Sales > Information System > Worklists, as shown in Figure 10.18.

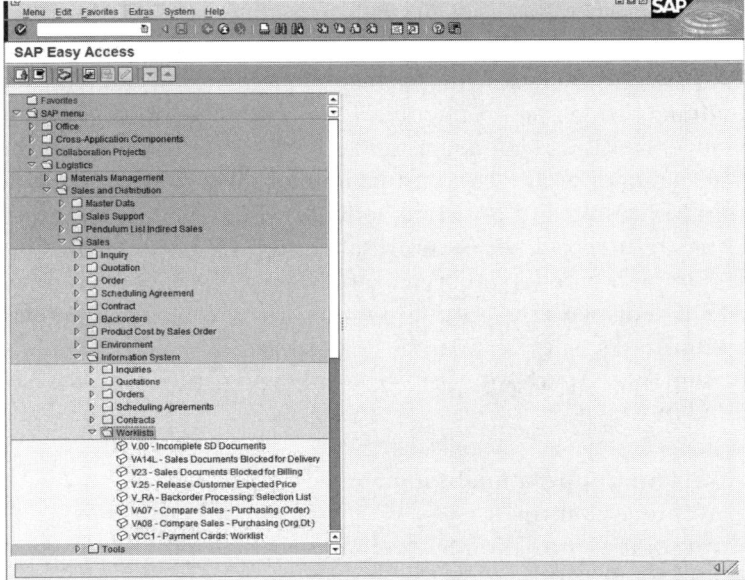

FIGURE 10.18 Displaying menu path to find work lists

Figure 10.18 displays the navigation path to display the work lists in the **SAP Easy Access** screen. The appropriate work list can be chosen from the screen by navigating to the corresponding menu path.

In the next section, let's discuss the sales information system.

WORKING WITH THE SALES INFORMATION SYSTEM

The Sales Information System (SIS) is used to analyze sales data of the overall sales process, such as orders (completed and pending), contracts, and quotations (incomplete, expired, or completed). By using SIS, online data related to sales activities can be accessed and used to generate real-time lists or reports. In other words, SIS offers customized information about the activities related to the sales process. Therefore, right from the beginning of the sales process until the collection of payment, the required master data and reports are retrieved from SIS.

SIS is a part of the Logistics Information System (LIS), which deals with the logistics process followed by an organization. In the SAP SD module, the logistics process includes the management of various activities starting from the manufacturing of a product until the product is sold. Therefore, SIS helps to manage the sales-related logistics activities, such as transportation, shipping, and packaging of products. Apart from managing the sales data, SIS also helps to link the presale and post-sale activities of a business. In other words, SIS works as an interface between presale and post-sale activities in the logistics process implemented in an organization.

SIS also displays the output in either list or report format, which are used for several tasks, such as analysis of post-sale data and to create invoice and tax documents. Apart from SIS, the following information systems are also included in LIS:

- Purchase Information System
- Inventory Control
- Transport Information System
- Shop Floor Information System
- Quality Management Information System
- Plant Management Information System

Figure 10.19 shows the architecture of SIS:

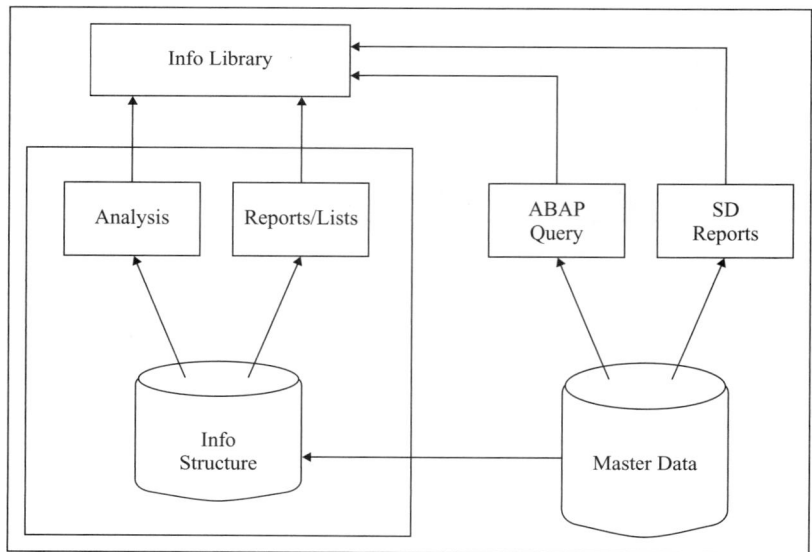

FIGURE 10.19 Displaying the Sales Information System (SIS)

Figure 10.19 shows the information structure (the main component of SIS) that contains historical data stored in statistical tables, such as customer, sales organization, sales office, material, and sales order. The data stored in the info structure is generated by the logistics processes of the business and is used for analysis and reporting purposes. The following types of information are stored in the info structures:

- **Selection Criteria**—Provides the criteria to store data in the info structure.
- **Time Period**—Represents the standard time scheduled for data collection.
- **Actual Data**—Contains information regarding a particular service, such as sales, delivery, and related items.

Analyses and reports are produced based on the data stored in the info structure. The data is ultimately stored in the info library, which acts as a centralized data source for the logistics process. The data generated by the logistics process and master data are used as data sources in SIS. Apart from this, master data is also used to produce standard SD lists, reports, and ABAP queries, which are stored in the info library.

In summation, SIS is used in the following ways:

- Summarize the sales data
- Analyze the sales data and produce analyses and reports
- Store sales-related transactional data, such as sales history
- Produce drill-down list (a list that is produced from the basic list by selecting a particular item and preparing the sublists)
- Provide analyses and reports that help management with decision making
- Provide the facility to export data into Excel™ or other PC files

We have learned earlier that SIS is used to analyze the sales data and generate reports. The following two types of analysis are performed with the help of SIS:

- Standard Analysis
- Flexible Analysis

In the following subsections, let's discuss implementation of these analyses in SIS.

Exploring Standard Analysis

Standard analysis is a way to analyze the data based on certain restrictions, such as displaying user-defined lists or reports based on specific data parameters and creating evaluation structure. Standard analysis is done on the sales data stored in tables of an info structure and is used to generate drill-down lists, which are discussed later. For standard analysis, first the data from the statistical tables of an info structure is selected on the basis of certain attributes, such as sales item, quantity, period of sales, and credit sales. Then, the selected data is drilled down to generate a drill-down list.

Let's consider a sales list of an organization located at Karol Bagh, as shown in Table 10.3.

Table 10.3 shows the sales data of the Karol Bagh location. Now, to find details regarding the amount of goods delivered at a Karol Bagh location, we need

Location	Quantity (units sold)	Amount
Karol Bagh	2,000	100,000

TABLE 10.3   Displaying the sales data

to drill down the sales data on the basis of quantity, as shown in Table 10.4.

Table 10.4 represents the quantity list that is further drilled down to find out the details of the delivered item, as shown in Table 10. 5.

Quantity (units delivered)	Location	Quantity (units sold)	Amount
15,000	Karol Bagh	5,000	250,000

TABLE 10.4   Displaying the drilled-down quantity list

SAP provides the following tools to represent the analyzed statistical data:

Item ID	Name	Quantity (units)
001	Electrical Components-A	1,000

TABLE 10.5   Displaying the drilled-down item list

- **ABC Analysis**—Analyzes results in terms of three distinct types, A, B, and C, based on certain predefined attributes, such as the quantity and value of material.
- **Time Series**—Analyze the data recorded at successive time intervals or in sequence.
- **Cumulative Curves**—Analyze data from the graphical curves and locate the changes in the statistical data with the help of the axis of the graphical curve.
- **Correlations**—Analyze the linear relationship between two items according to the X and Y coordinates.

After discussing the tools used to display the analysis report, let's learn how to perform the standard analysis for data in the SAP system.

You need to navigate the following menu path to perform the standard analysis:

Menu Path

SAP menu > Logistics > Sales and Distribution > Sales Information System > Standard Analyses

Figure 10.20 shows the preceding navigated menu path.

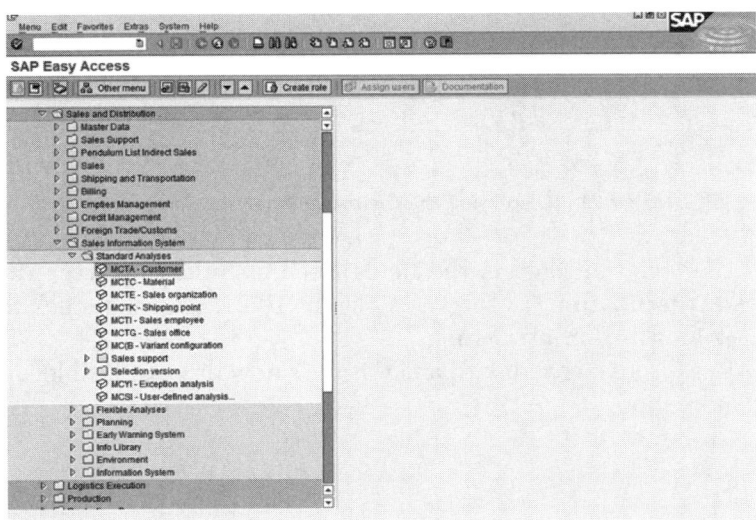

© SAP AG. All rights reserved.

FIGURE 10.20 **Displaying menu path for standard analysis**

Figure 10.20 shows the factors on the basis of which standard analyses can be performed in the mySAP ERP system. You need to select any one standard analysis according to your requirement. For example, to analyze customer-related data, double-click the **MCTA - Customer** option. The **Customer Analysis: Selection** screen appears as shown in Figure 10.21.

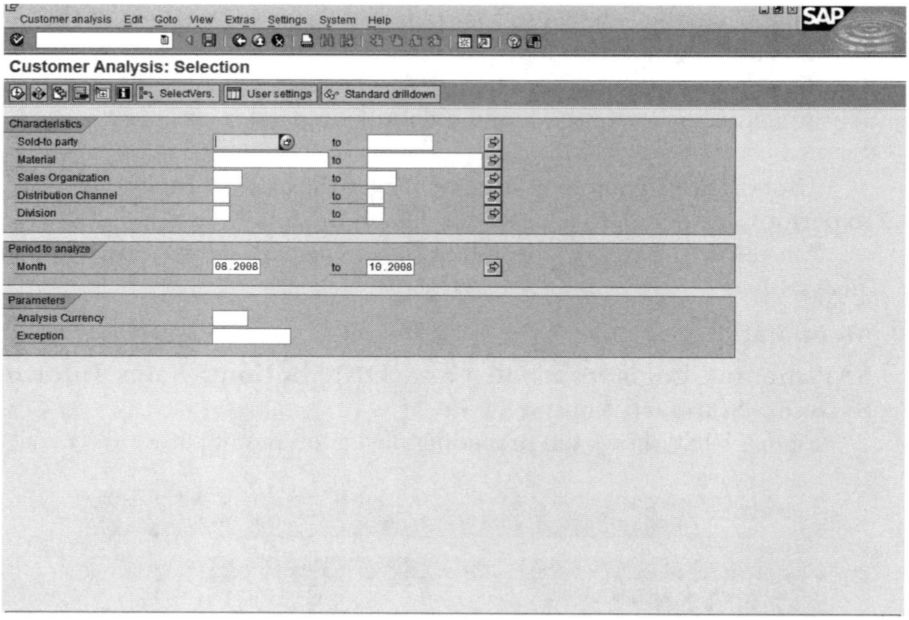

© SAP AG. All rights reserved.

FIGURE 10.21 Displaying the Customer Analysis: Selection screen

Enter relevant data in the fields, such as **Sold-to-party**, **Material**, and **Sales Organization**, as shown in Figure 10.21, and then click the **Execute** icon ( ) for further processing.

After discussing standard analysis, let's now discuss flexible analysis in the next subsection.

Exploring Flexible Analysis

Flexible analysis provides freedom to select the data used for analysis purposes. In this analysis, you can define the format and the content of a list. After finalizing the format and content of the list, you need to create an evaluation structure, which is required to perform flexible analysis of data. The evaluation structure consists of the characteristics (information suitable for analysis) and key figures (information gathered in relation to specific objects). Later, the evaluation structure is used to create the principles and guidelines for the evaluation process, which help the user to complete the flexible analysis process.

You need to navigate the following menu path to perform the flexible analysis:

Menu Path

SAP menu > Logistics > Sales and Distribution > Sales Information System > Flexible Analyses > Evaluation structure, as shown in Figure 10.22.

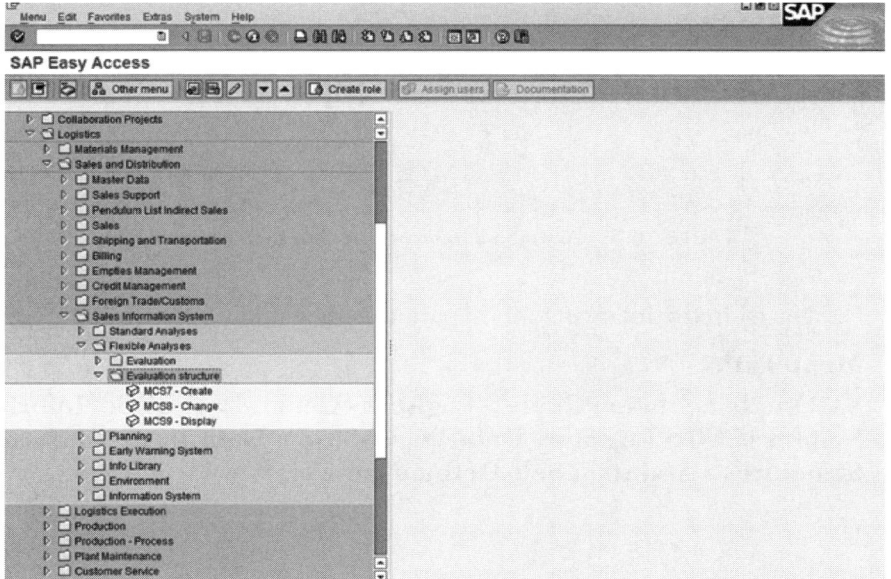

© SAP AG. All rights reserved.

FIGURE 10.22 Displaying menu path to create an evaluation structure

Figure 10.22 displays the menu path for creating an evaluation structure. After discussing the types of SIS analyses, let's discuss how to create an info structure.

Creating the Info Structure

As described in the previous section, the info structure is the main component of SIS; it contains statistical data for standard analysis and reporting. Note that the info structures from **S001** to **S501** are reserved as SAP standard info structures. Some of the common types of info structures and their purposes are listed in Table 10.6.

Info Structure	Purposes
S001	Customer
S002	Sales Office
S003	Sales Organization
S004	Material
S005	Shipping Point
S006	Sales Employee

TABLE 10.6 Common info structures and their purpose

Navigate the following menu path to create an info structure:

Menu Path

SAP Implementation Guide > Logistics - General > Logistics Information System (LIS) > Logistics Data Warehouse > Data Basis > Information Structures > Maintain Self-Defined Information Structures

Figure 10.23 shows the preceding menu path.

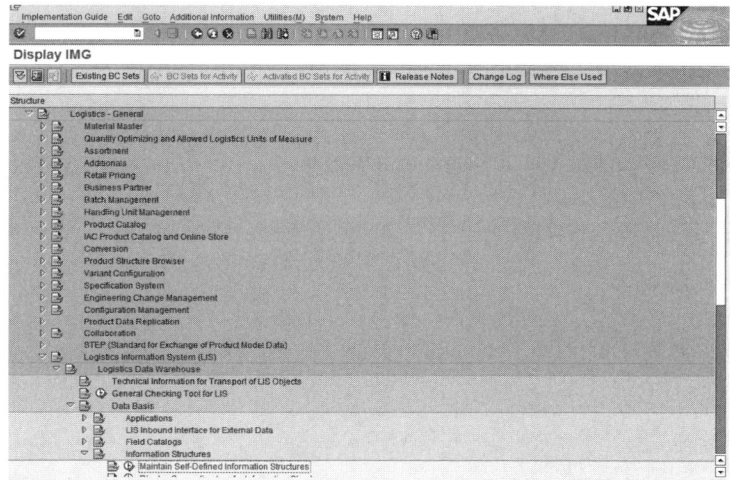

FIGURE 10.23 Displaying menu path to create an information structure

Now, click the **IMG Activity** icon (⊕) next to the **Maintain Self-Defined Information Structures** activity. The **Choose Activity** dialog box appears as shown in Figure 10.24.

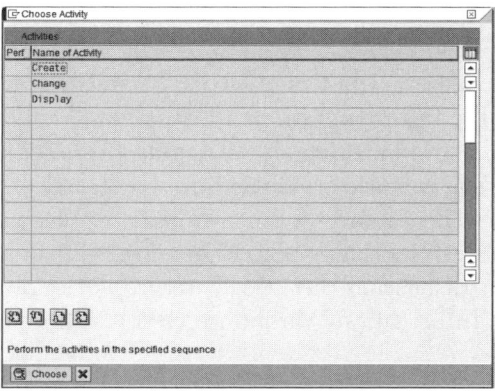

FIGURE 10.24 Displaying the Choose Activity dialog box

Figure 10.24 shows the **Choose Activity** dialog box, which contains the options to create, change, and display an info structure. To create an info structure, you need to double-click the **Create** option. The **Create Info Structure: Initial screen** appears as shown in Figure 10.25.

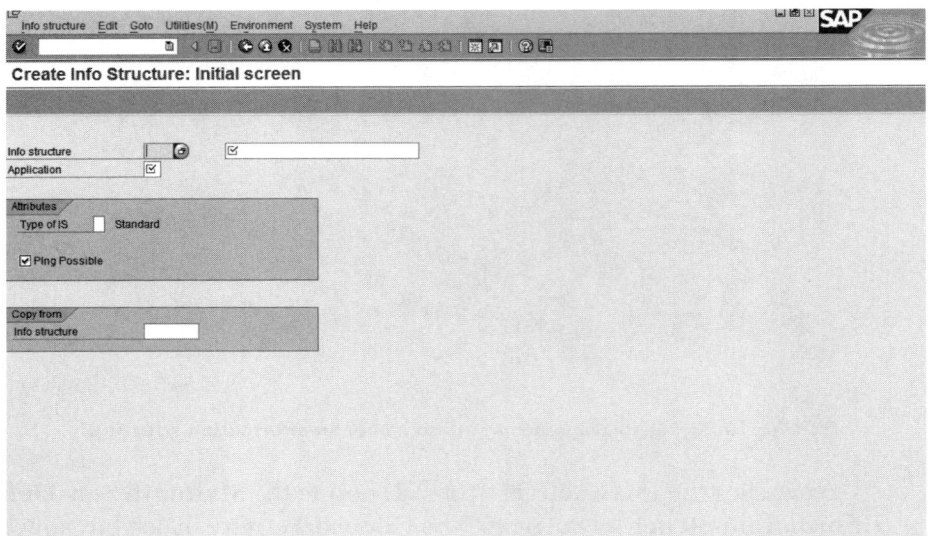

© SAP AG. All rights reserved.

FIGURE 10.25 Displaying the Create Info Structure: Initial screen

Figure 10.25 shows the **Create Info Structure: Initial Screen**, which is used to create the info structure. Enter the name and description in the **Info structure** field. After entering all the details, press the **Enter** key to create the info structure. You can also create an info structure by entering an existing info structure in the **Copy from** section. Similarly, you can use other options given in the **Choose Activity** dialog box (Figure 10.24) to change and display an info structure. After discussing the info structure, let's now describe data analysis using Business Information Warehouse (BW), in the next section.

ANALYZING DATA USING SAP BUSINESS INFORMATION WAREHOUSE

The SAP Business Information Warehouse (BW) is used to analyze large volumes of data from multiple sources within or outside the SAP® R/3® system. The following are the multiple sources from where SAP BW collects the data:

- **Internal/Operational Data Sources**—Include data generated from the SAP R/3 system, such as data from SD, FI, and other modules.
- **External Data Sources**—Include data collected from outside the SAP R/3 system, such as data repository and XML documents.

After understanding the features of BW, let's next explore the basic concepts, architecture, and business content of BW.

Understanding the Basic SAP BW Concepts

Similar to other information systems, SAP BW contains some basic sets of concepts and terminologies that are primarily used for notations and reference purposes. These concepts can be grouped into basic concepts, architecture and data flow, reporting, and others. The common concepts and terminologies include the following:

- InfoObject
- InfoCube
- InfoProvider

> **Note:** In addition to InfoObject, InfoCube, and InfoProviders; the data source, exact structures, transfer rules, InfoSource, MultiCube, InfoSet query, Report to Report query, User Exit, Transfer Structure, Persistent Staging Area (PSA), Update Rules, Operational Data Store (ODS), Master Data are some other SAP BW concepts, which are beyond the scope of this book.

InfoObject

An InfoObject contains attributes and characteristics of data used to generate reports in SAP BW. Moreover, the InfoObject is also used to group the data in SAP BW. The data contained in InfoObject can be any entity, such as customer, sales, or order. The InfoObject is further classified into characteristics and keys. The InfoObject classification is represented in Figure 10.26.

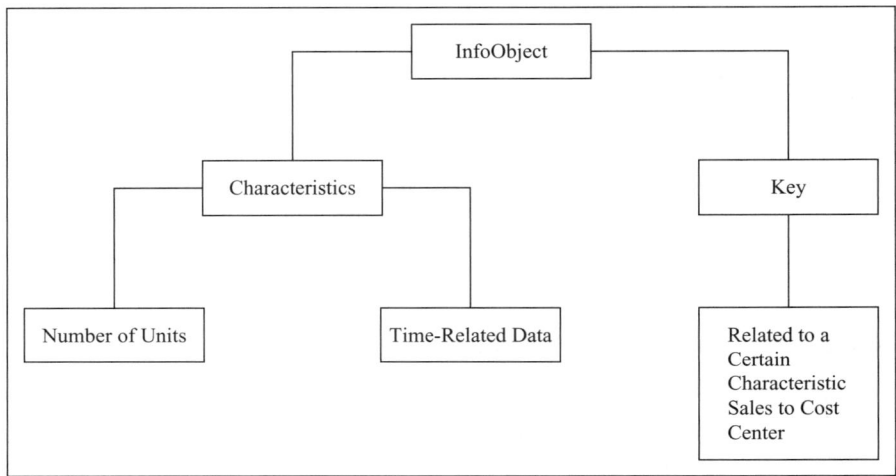

FIGURE 10.26 Displaying the InfoObject classification

Figure 10.26 shows the classification of InfoSet based on characteristics and keys. The characteristics of an InfoObject include the number of InfoObjects and the time period from which an InfoObject is included in the mySAP ERP system. The key refers to a particular attribute of the data stored in the InfoSet.

Let's now discuss the next SAP BW concept, the InfoCube.

InfoCube

An InfoCube is a self-contained dataset, such as data related to customer, sales, or organizational data. The InfoCube contains attributes of data that can be referenced by Business Explorer (BEx) query designer for reporting and analysis purposes.

> **Note:** BEx is a reporting tool in SAP BW that consists of the query designer to create and manipulate queries.

InfoCube can be categorized into the following types:

- **Transactional InfoCube**—Supports parallel write access (data written by several users at a single point in time), which is important to complete a transaction.
- **Basic InfoCube**—Stores data in the SAP BW staging area (intermediate data storage used to manage services such as data transformation and data extraction).
- **Remote InfoCube**—Manages the transaction of data outside the SAP BW system using BAPI®.
- **Virtual InfoCube**—Used to display data from non-BW sources.

After discussing InfoSet, let's now discuss InfoProviders.

InfoProviders

SAP BW InfoProviders refers to objects present in the SAP BW system. These objects are used to create and execute queries. InfoProviders contain data called data target, which includes data stores, ODS objects, and master data tables. InfoProviders can contain the following types of objects:

- **Data Target Objects**—Contain data related to InfoCubes, ODS objects, and InfoObjects.
- **Physical Storage Objects**—Contain logical views, such as InfoSet, RemoteCubes, SAP RemoteCubes, and MultiProviders.

After discussing the basic concepts of SAP BW, let's discuss its features.

Features of SAP BW

SAP BW acts as a centralized system for reports and analysis. In other words, the SAP BW interprets as well as analyzes the data and finally helps in generating reports. The SAP BW works as information warehouse for the entire SAP SD implementation. The following are the features of the SAP BW:

- Includes data extractors to access data from a data source, analysis and reporting tools, and business process models. The SAP BW infrastructure is similar to data warehouse.
- Helps to establish connection between SAP R/3 and non-SAP R/3 applications with the help of Business Application Programming Interfaces (BAPIs).
- Includes business content, an integrated Online Analytical Processing (OLAP) processor, automated data extraction and loading routines, metadata repository, administrative tools, multiple language support, BEx, and a Web-based user interface.
- Provides the facility to structure data in a consistent and standard format.
- Provides flexible reporting and analysis tools for strategic analyses.

After discussing the concepts of BW, let's now briefly explore the BW architecture.

Exploring the BW Architecture

The BW architecture is a three-tier structure composed of presentation front ends, BW server, and source systems. The presentation front end helps in the reporting of data. The BW server performs data warehouse management. The source systems represent data sources, such as SAP or non-SAP systems. The architecture of SAP BW is shown in Figure 10.27.

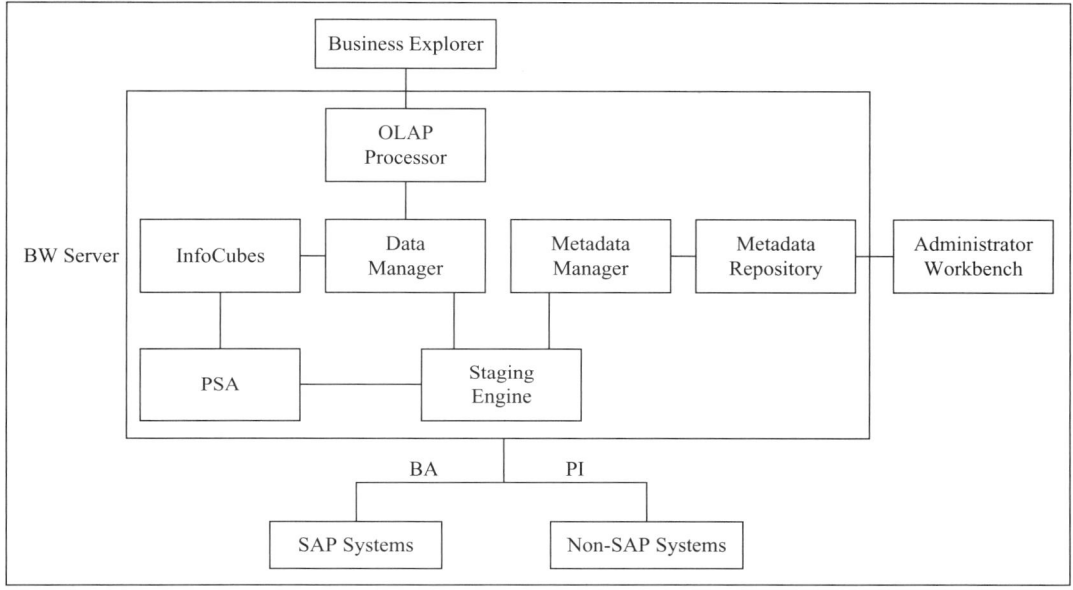

FIGURE 10.27   Displaying the SAP BW architecture

As shown in Figure 10.27, BEx is the topmost layer, which contains the reporting environment and tools, such as BEx Analyzer and Browser. The BW server is at the middle layer, and it performs the following tasks:

- Administers BW systems with the help of data extractors, staging engines, and administrator workbench (ABW). The SAP BW administrative services are used to administer a SAP BW system. The administrative workbench is used for administration, maintenance, and development of the SAP BW system.
- Stores and releases data with the help of InfoCube, data manager, metadata repository, PSA, and the operational data source. OLAP, an important component of the SAP BW server, is used for fast and consistent access to the various possible views of data. The basic functions of OLAP include retrieving data from data stores or repository and generating and executing query programs. In addition, OLAP is used for functions such as filtering data and performing runtime calculations and authoritative checks on data.

At the bottom level, the source systems serve as data sources for business data. A source system server communicates with the BW server by using BAPI. According to the SAP guidelines, the components of a source system server are the following:

- SAP R/3 components, such as 3.H
- mySAP components, such as mySAP SEM and mySAP CRM
- Non-SAP systems

Data processing in SAP BW can be virtually grouped into the following areas:

- **Data Warehousing**—Consists of higher-level and complex data mainly used for decision-making purposes. SAP BW organizes data in the format similar to a data warehouse for optimized data and reporting.
- **Business Intelligence Platform**—Includes transactional infrastructures and analysis technologies, such as OLAP processors, metadata repositories, and reporting agents.
- **Business Intelligence Suite and Business Explorer**—Includes business explorers, such as BEx Analyzer and BEx Web Applications, which are used to manage query reporting and analytical functions.
- **Development Technologies**—Develops analytical applications with the help of BI Java Connector. These analytical applications are used to access both multidimensional (OLAP) and tabular (relational) data.

After discussing the SAP BW architecture, let's now discuss business content.

Explaining Business Content

While generating reports, you can also provide business content; that is, additional information such as the details of the personnel generating the report. The objective of providing the additional information is to have a clear idea of the context in which the report has been prepared. In other words, the business content specifies the scope and nature of the reports that are generated.

The following attributes of business content are included as additional information in the reports:

- **Roles**—Specify the role of an employee in the company, such as the designation of an employee in an organization.
- **Queries**—Specify the queries that are used to generate reports by generating the required data.
- **InfoProviders**—Specify the objects present in the SAP BW system, such as InfoSet, InfoCubes, ODS objects, and master data tables. The InfoProviders serve as the basis of report generation.
- **Update Rules**—Specify the rules to update the business content to avoid business conflicts.
- **Data Extractors**—Specify the mechanism to extract data from SAP source system datasets and also transfer the extracted data as business content.

Let's now summarize this chapter.

SUMMARY

This chapter explored reporting and analysis in the SD module of SAP in detail. You learned about various development tools for SD reporting, such as QuickViews, SAP Queries, Lists, and Reports. Then, you explored sales information system in detail, including standard analysis and information structures. Finally, you explored SAP BW in depth including the concepts, architecture, and business content of SAP BW. You also learned how different applications play their roles in helping to analyze the entire business process. In other words, organizations basically use SAP in order to have all of these analytical tools on hand and to optimize their control of the processes. Therefore, you can say that this portion of SAP represents its essence.

Next, you learn about the relevant transaction codes of the SAP SD module in Appendix A.

Appendix A
Relevant Transaction Codes for the SD Module

You can navigate the menu path in order to perform various tasks, such as defining a sales document and performing text determination in the SAP Sales and Distribution (SD) module. Apart from using the menu paths, you can also use Transaction Codes (Tcodes) to perform the specific task and to easily access the relevant screens in the SAP GUI. A transaction code is a four-character code that specifies the task that needs to be performed to the mySAP™ ERP system.

The transaction codes are executed from the command field (Figure A.1, circled area) available on the **SAP Easy Access** screen. You need to enter the transaction code in the command field and press the **Enter** key to execute it. For example, to access the **Customizing: Execute Project** screen, you need to execute the SPRO transaction code, as shown in Figure A.1.

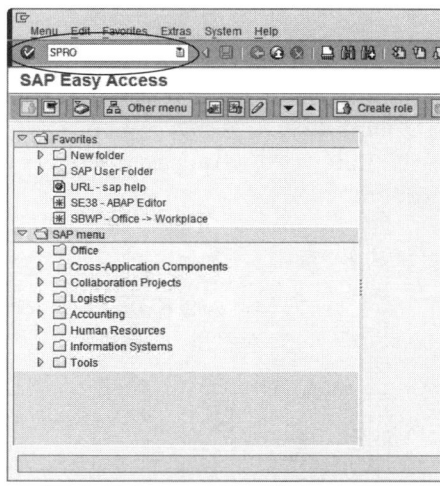

© SAP AG. All rights reserved.

FIGURE A.1 Displaying the SAP Easy Access screen

After entering the transaction code and pressing the **Enter** key, the **Customizing: Execute Project** screen appears as shown in Figure A.2.

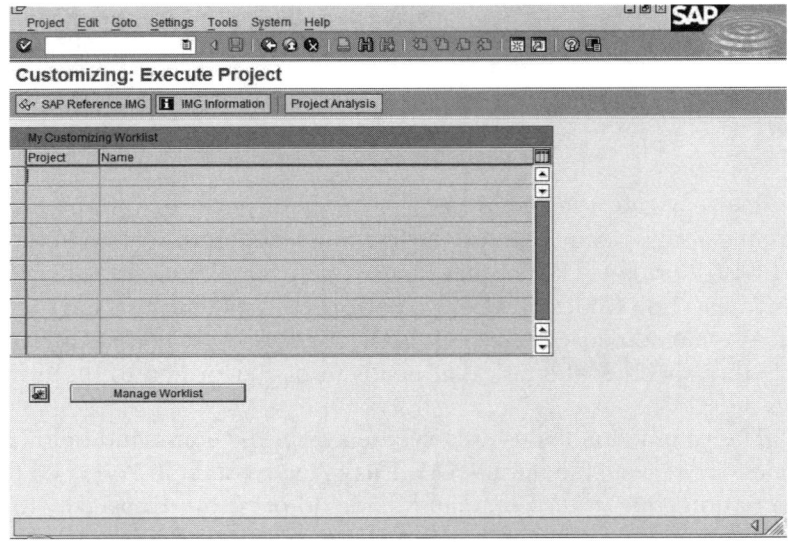

© SAP AG. All rights reserved.

FIGURE A.2 Displaying the Customizing: Execute Project screen

In this way, you can perform various activities using the transaction codes in the mySAP ERP system. This appendix describes the various transaction codes used in the SAP SD module.

Table A.1 lists the noteworthy transaction codes used in the SD module of the mySAP ERP system.

Transaction Code	Provides the functionality to
V	Quickstart RKCOWUSL
V+01	Create Sales Call
V+02	Create Telephone Call
V+03	Create Sales Letter

Continued

Appendix A Relevant Transaction Codes for the SD Module

Transaction Code	Provides the functionality to
V+11	Create Direct Mailing
V+21	Create Sales Prospect
V+22	Create Competitor
V+23	Create Sales Partner
V-01	Create Sales Order
V-02	Create Quotation
V-03	Create Ordering Party (Sales)
V-04	Create Invoice Recipient (Sales)
V-05	Create Payer (Sales)
V-06	Create Consignee (Sales)
V-07	Create One-Time Customer (Sales)
V-08	Create Payer (Centrally)
V-09	Create Ordering Party (Centrally)
V-11	Create Carrier
V-12	Create Customer Hierarchy Nodes
V-31	Create Freight 1
V-32	Create Freight 1 with Reference
V-33	Change Freight 1
V-34	Create Freight 2
V-35	Create Freight 2 with Reference to the Actual Freight Charges
V-36	Create Freight 2 with Reference
V-37	Change Freight 2
V-38	Display Freight 2
V-40	Display Taxes (Export)

Continued

Transaction Code	Provides the functionality to
V-41	Create Material Price
V-42	Create Material Price with Reference
V-43	Change Material Price
V-44	Display Material Price
V-45	Create Price List
V-46	Create Price List with Reference
V-47	Change Price List
V-48	Display Price List
V-49	Create Customer-Specific Price
V-50	Create Customer-Specific Price with Reference
V-51	Change Customer Price
V-52	Display Customer Price
V-61	Create Customer Discount or Surcharge
V-62	Create Customer Discount or Surcharge with Reference
V-63	Change Customer Discount or Surcharge
V-64	Display Customer Discount or Surcharge
V-65	Create Material Discount or Surcharge
V-66	Create Material Discount or Surcharge with Reference
V-67	Change Material Discount or Surcharge
V-68	Display Material Discount or Surcharge
V-69	Create Price Group Discount or Surcharge
V-70	Create Price Group Discount or Surcharge with Reference
V-71	Change Price Group Discount or Surcharge
V-72	Display Price Group Discount or Surcharge
V-73	Create Material Price Group Discount or Surcharge

Continued

Transaction Code	Provides the functionality to
V-74	Create Material Price Group Discount or Surcharge with Reference
V-75	Change Material Price Group Discount or Surcharge
V-76	Display Material Price Group Discount or Surcharge
V-77	Create Customer or Material Price Group Discount or Surcharge
V-78	Create Customer or Material Price Group Discount or Surcharge with Reference
V-79	Create Customer or Material Price Group Discount or Surcharge
V-80	Display Customer or Material Price Group Discount or Surcharge
V-81	Create Customer or Material Discount or Surcharge
V-82	Create Customer or Material Discount or Surcharge with Reference
V-83	Change Customer or Material Discount or Surcharge
V-84	Display Customer or Material Discount or Surcharge
V-85	Create Price Group or Material Price Group Discount or Surcharge
V-86	Create Price Group or Material Price Group Discount or Surcharge with Reference
V-87	Change Price Group or Material Price Group Discount or Surcharge
V-88	Display Price Group or Material Price Group Discount or Surcharge
V-89	Create Price Group or Material Discount or Surcharge
V-90	Create Price Group or Material Discount or Surcharge with Reference
V-91	Change Price Group or Material Discount or Surcharge
V-92	Display Price Group or Material Discount or Surcharge
V-93	Create Domestic Taxes
V-94	Create Domestic Taxes with Reference
V-95	Change Domestic Taxes
V-96	Display Domestic Taxes

Continued

Transaction Code	Provides the functionality to
V-97	Create Cross-Border Taxes
V-98	Create Cross-Border Taxes with Reference
V-99	Change Cross-Border Taxes
V.00	List Incomplete Documents
V.01	Sales Order Error Log
V.02	List Incomplete Sales Orders
V.03	List Incomplete Inquiries
V.04	List Incomplete Quotations
V.05	List Incomplete Scheduled Agreements
V.06	List Incomplete Contracts
V.07	Periodic Billing
V.14	Display the Sales Orders Blocked for Delivery
V.15	Display Backorders
V.20	Display Collective Delivery Process
V.21	Display the Log of Collective Runs
V.22	Display Collective Runs
V.23	Release Orders for Billing
V.24	Display Work List for Invoice Lists
V.25	Release Customer Expected Price
V.26	Display Selected Object Status
V/03	Create Condition Table (SD Price)
V/04	Change Condition Table (Sales Price)
V/05	Display Condition Table (Sales Price)
V/06	Start the Condition Categories: SD Pricing Application
V/07	Start the Maintain Access (Sales Price) Application

Continued

Transaction Code	Provides the functionality to
V/08	Start the Conditions: Procedure for A V Application
V/09	Start the Condition Types: Account Determination Application
V/10	Start the Account Determination: Access Sequence Application
V/11	Start the Conditions: Account Determination Procedure Application
V/12	Create the Condition Table for Account Determination
V/13	Change the Condition Table for Account Determination
V/14	Display the Condition Table for Account Determination
V/21	Start the View V_TVSA_NAC Application
V/22	Start the View V_TVTY_NAC Application
V/23	Start the View V_TVST_KOM Application
V/24	View V_TVTK_NAC
V/25	View V_TVFK_NAC
V/26	View V_TVKK_NAC
V/27	Create Conditions for Output Determination
V/30	Output Types (Sales Document)
V/31	View V_TNAPN Application V3
V/32	Create Sales Document Output Determination Procedure
V/33	View V_TNAPN Application V7
V/34	Maintain Condition-Type Application V2
V/35	Customize for Output Determination
V/36	Create Delivery Output Determination Procedure
V/37	Assign Customer
V/38	Maintain Condition-Type Application V4
V/39	View V_TNAPR Application V6

Continued

Transaction Code	Provides the functionality to
V/40	Maintain Condition-Type Application V3
V/41	View V_TVST_NAC
V/42	Output Determination Procedure (Billing Document)
V/43	View V_TVAK_NAC
V/44	Maintain Condition-Type Application DB
V/45	View V_TNAPN Application K1
V/46	Output Determination Procedure Customer
V/47	View V_TNAPN Application V1
V/48	Access Sequence (Sales Document)
V/49	View V_TNAPN Application V2
V/50	Access Sequence (Delivery)
V/51	View V_TNAPN Application V6
V/52	Access Sequence Application V3
V/53	View V_TNAPR Application V4
V/54	Access Sequence (Billing Document)
V/55	View V_TVBUR_NA
V/56	Output – Condition Table – Create Order
V/57	Output – Condition Table – Change Order
V/58	Output – Condition Table – Display Order
V/59	Output – Condition Table – Create Delivery
V/60	Output – Condition Table – Change Delivery
V/61	Output – Condition Table – Display Delivery
V/62	Output – Condition Table – Create Bill Document
V/63	Output – Condition Table – Change Bill Document
V/64	Output – Condition Table – Display Bill Document

Continued

Transaction Code	Provides the functionality to
V/65	Output Condition Table or Create Sales Support
V/66	Output Condition Table or Change Sales Support
V/67	Output Condition Table or Display Sales Support
V/68	Maintain Access Sequence (Sales Activity)
V/69	View V_TVAP_NAC
V/70	Maintain Condition-Type Application K1
V/71	View V_TVLK_NAC
V/72	Output Determination Procedure (CAS)
V/73	View V_TVLP_NAC
V/76	Maintain Product Hierarchy
V/77	Output – Condition Table – Create Transport
V/78	Output – Condition Table – Change Transport
V/79	Output – Condition Table – Display Transport
V/80	Access Sequence (Transport)
V/81	View V_TNAPR Application V7
V/82	Maintain Condition-Type Application V7
V/83	View V_TNAPR Application V3
V/84	Output Determination Transport
V/85	View V_TVKO_NAC
V/86	Create Conditions: V_T681F for B V1
V/87	Create Conditions: V_T681F for B V2
V/88	Create Conditions: V_T681F for B V3
V/89	Create Conditions: V_T681F for B V5
V/90	Create Conditions: V_T681F for B V6

Continued

Transaction Code	Provides the functionality to
V/91	Create Conditions: V_T681F for B V7
V/92	Create Conditions: V_T681F for B K1
V/93	Output – Condition Table – Create Packaging
V/94	Output – Condition Table – Change Packaging
V/95	Output – Condition Table – Display Packaging
V/96	Access Sequence (Packaging)
V/97	Output-Type Packaging
V/99	Output Determination Procedure Packaging
V/C1	Create Strategy Types: Batch Determination SD
V/C2	Access: Maintain Batch Determination SD
V/C3	Create Batch Determination Procedure for SD
V/C4	Search Types: Optimize Access
V/C5	SD Table T683C Search Procedure Determination
V/C6	Create Conditions: V_T681F for H V
V/C7	Create Condition Table: Create (Batches, SD)
V/C8	Create Condition Table: Change (Batch, SD)
V/C9	Create Condition Table: Display (Batches, SD)
V/CA	Automatic Batch Determination in Sales Order
V/CL	Automatic Batch Determination in Delivery
V/G1	Output Condition Table or Create Group
V/G2	Output Condition Table or Change Group
V/G3	Output Condition Table or Display Group
V/G4	Access Sequence (Groups)
V/G5	View V_TNAPR Application K1
V/G6	Maintain Condition-Type Application V5

Continued

Appendix A Relevant Transaction Codes for the SD Module

Transaction Code	Provides the functionality to
V/G7	View V_TNAPR Application V1
V/G8	Output Determination Procedure Groups
V/G9	View VN_TNAPR Application V2
V/I1	Activation of Condition Index
V/I2	Set Up Condition Indices
V/I3	Conditions: Pricing SD – Index
V/I5	Conditions: Pricing SD – Index in Background
V/I6	Display Conditions Using Index
V/LA	Create Pricing Report
V/LB	Change Pricing Report
V/LC	Display Pricing Report
V/LD	Execute Pricing Report
V/LE	Generate Pricing Reports
V/N1	Maintain Accesses (Free Goods – Sales)
V/N2	Provide the Functionality to Create Free Goods Table
V/N3	Provide the Functionality to Display Free Goods Table
V/N4	Create Free Goods Types – Sales
V/N5	Create Free Goods: Procedure for SD
V/N6	Create Free Goods Procedure Determination SD
V/T1	Maintain Profile
V/T2	Network Types
V/T3	Create Deadline: Assign Network Profile to Delivery Type
V/T4	Maintain Deadline Functions
V/T5	Maintain Deviation Reasons

Continued

Transaction Code	Provides the functionality to
V/T6	Maintain Assignment to Plant
V/T7	Assign Shipping Deadlines to Shipment
V/T8	Create Shipping Deadlines - Graphics Settings
V101	Create Initial Sales Menu
V12LDV_A	Create Pricing Report
V12LDV_B	Change Pricing Report
V12LDV_C	Display Pricing Report
V12LDV_D	Execute Pricing Report
V12LEV_A	Create Pricing Report (Rebate)
V12LEV_B	Change Pricing Report (Rebate)
V12LEV_C	Display Transactions (Rebate)
V12LEV_D	Execute Pricing Report (Rebate)
V23	Create Sales Documents Blocked for Billing
V633	Create Coupling: Conversion of Customer Key
VA00	Create Initial Sales Menu
VA01	Create Sales Order
VA02	Change Sales Order
VA03	Display Sales Order
VA05	Create List of Sales Orders
VA07	Compare Sales Purchasing (Order)
VA08	Compare Sales – Purchasing (Organization Department)
VA11	Create Inquiry
VA12	Change Inquiry
VA13	Display Inquiry
VA14L	Create Sales Documents Blocked for Delivery

Continued

Transaction Code	Provides the functionality to
VA15	Create Inquiries List
VA21	Create Quotation
VA22	Change Quotation
VA23	Display Quotation
VA25	Create Quotations List
VA25N	Create List of Quotations
VA26	Create Collective Processing for Quotations
VA31	Create Scheduling Agreement
VA32	Change Scheduling Agreement
VA33	Display Scheduling Agreement
VA35	Create List of Scheduling Agreements
VA41	Create Contract
VA42	Change Contract
VA42W	Create Workflow for Master Contract
VA43	Display Contract
VA44	Create Actual Overhead: Sales Order
VA45	Create List of Contracts
VA46	Create Collective Subsequent Processing of Contracts
VA51	Create Item Proposal
VA52	Change Item Proposal
VA53	Display Item Proposal
VA55	List Item Proposals
VA88	Create Actual Settlement: Sales Orders
VA94	Load Commodity Codes for Japan

Continued

Transaction Code	Provides the functionality to
VA95	Merge Commodity Code or Import Code No.
VACF	Commit. Carried Forward: Sales Orders
VAKC	Create Items in Sales Order Configuration
VAKP	Configuration: Maintain T180
VALU	Valuation Analysis
VAL_RELN	Release Note Approval
VAM4	Merge: Japan – Commodity Code
VAN1	Actual Revaluation: Sales Order
VAP1	Create Contact Person
VAP2	Change Contact Person
VAP3	Display Contact Person
VARC	SD: User Guide to Archiving
VARCH	Change Report Variant
VARD	Display Report Variant
VASK	Delete Groups
VB(1	Rebate Number Ranges
VB(2	Rebate Agreement-Type Maintenance
VB(3	Condition-Type Groups Overview
VB(4	Condition Types in Condition-Type Groups
VB(5	Assignment Condition – Condition-Type Group
VB(6	Rebate Group Maintenance
VB(7	Rebate Agreement Settlement
VB(8	List Rebate Agreements
VB(9	Maintain Sales Deal Types
VB(A	Promotion-Type Maintenance

Continued

Appendix A Relevant Transaction Codes for the SD Module

Transaction Code	Provides the functionality to
VB(B	Copying Control Maintenance
VB(C	Maintain Copying Control
VB(D	Rebate Agreement Settlement
VB01	Create Material Listing or Exclusion
VB02	Change Material Listing or Exclusion
VB03	Display Material Listing or Exclusion
VB04	Reference Material Listing or Exclusion
VB11	Create Material Substitution
VB12	Change Material Substitution
VB13	Display Material Substitution
VB14	Reference Material Substitution
VB21	Create Sales Deal
VB22	Change Sales Deal
VB23	Display Sales Promotion
VB25	List Sales Deals
VB31	Create Promotion
VB32	Change Promotion
VB33	Display Promotion
VB35	Promotions List
VB41	Create Cross-Selling
VB42	Change Cross-Selling
VB43	Display Cross-Selling
VB44	Copy Cross-Selling
VBBLOCK	Documents Blocked for Billing

Continued

Transaction Code	Provides the functionality to
VBELN_SET_GENERATE	Generate Sales Order Set
VBG1	Create Material Grouping
VBG2	Change Material Grouping
VBG3	Display Material Grouping
VBK0	Bonus Buy Selection
VBK1	Create Bonus Buy
VBK2	Change Bonus Buy
VBK3	Display Bonus Buy
VBK6	Delete Bonus Buy
VBKA	Bonus Buy: Access Sequences
VBKB	Bonus Buy: Create Condition Table
VBKC	Bonus Buy: Display Condition Table
VBKD	Bonus Buy: Condition Types
VBKE	Bonus Buy: Calculation Schema
VBKF	Bonus Buy: Schema Determination
VBKG	Bonus Buy: Field Catalog
VBN1	Free Goods – Create (SD)
VBN3	Free Goods – Display (SD)
VBO1	Create Rebate Agreement
VBO2	Change Rebate Agreement
VBO3	Display Rebate Agreement
VBOE	Currency Conversion Rebate Agreements
VBOF	Rebate: Update Billing Documents
VC/1	List of Customers

Continued

Appendix A   Relevant Transaction Codes for the SD Module

Transaction Code	Provides the functionality to
VC/2	Customer Master Data Sheet
VC/A	Sales Activity Description 01
VC/B	Sales Activity Description 02
VC/C	Sales Activity Description 03
VC/D	Sales Activity Description 04
VC/E	Sales Activity Description 05
VC/F	Sales Activity Description 06
VC/G	Sales Activity Description 07
VC/H	Sales Activity Description 08
VC/I	Sales Activity Description 09
VC/J	Sales Activity Description 10
VC00	Sales Support
VC01	Create Sales Activity
VC010102	Only Follow-Up Activities
VC010104	Internet Mailing
VC01N	Edit Sales Activity
VC01N_M	Edit Mailing
VC02	Change Sales Activity
VC03	Display Sales Activity
VC05	Sales Support Monitor
VC06	Parallel Processing for Address List
VC10	Report Tree – Select Addresses
VC15	Cross-Matching
VCC1	Payment Cards: Worklist

Continued

Transaction Code	Provides the functionality to
VCH1	Create Batch Search Strategy
VCH2	Change Batch Search Strategy
VCH3	Display Batch Search Strategy
VCHECKBONUS	Customizing Checks for Rebate
VCHECKT683	Customizing Check Pricing Procedure
VCHECKT685A	Customizing Check Condition Types
VCHECKTVCPF	Customizing Check Copying Control
VCHECKVOFA	Customizing Check Billing Types
VCHP	SD Table TVLP Deliveries: Items
VCOMP	Completed SD Documents
VCR1	Competitive Products
VCTP	Maintain Allocation Structure
VCU3	Display Incompletion Log
VCUAC	Display Anti-Dumping – Qty-Dependent
VCUAE	Display Anti-Dumping – Weight-Dependent
VCUDC	Display 3rd Country – Quantity-Dependent
VCUDE	Display 3rd Country – Weight-Dependent
VCUN	Reload
VCUP1	Display Preference – Quantity-Dependent
VCUP2	Display Preference – Weight-Dependent
VCUPC	Display Pharmaceuticals Production – Quantity-Dependent
VCUPF	Display Pharmaceuticals Production – Weight-Dependent
VCUST	Customer List
VCUZ1	Display Ceiling – Quantity-Dependent
VCUZ2	Display Ceiling – Weight-Dependent

Continued

Transaction Code	Provides the functionality to
VCUZC	Display Quota – Quantity-Dependent
VCUZE	Display Quota – Weight-Dependent
VCUZP	Display Ceilings – Percentage
VD01	Create Customer (Sales)
VD02	Change Customer (Sales)
VD03	Display Customer (Sales)
VD04	Customer Changes (SD)
VD05	Block Customer (Sales)
VD06	Mark Customer for Deletion (Sales)
VD07	Reference Doc Determination for Referring Customer
VD51	Create Customer-Material Info
VD52	Starts the Maintain Customer-Material Info Application
VD53	Display Customer-Material Info
VD59	List Customer-Material-Info
VDBLOCK	Documents Blocked for Delivery
VDDI EMU	Currency Conversion Customer Master
VDF1	Display Format Date Type/Period
VDH1	Customer Hierarchy Maintenance (SD)
VDH1N	Display/Maintain Customer Hierarchy
VDH2	Display Customer Hierarchy
VE01	INTRASTAT: Selection Dispatch to EU
VE02	INTRASTAT: Create Form – Germany
VE03	INTRASTAT: Create File – Germany
VE04	EXTRASTAT: Data Selection for Export

Continued

Transaction Code	Provides the functionality to
VE05	EXTRASTAT: Create File – Germany
VE06	INTRASTAT: Paper Form – Belgian
VE07	Create INTRASTAT Form for France
VE08	Create INTRASTAT File for Italy
VE09	Create INTRASTAT File for Belgium
VE10	Create INTRASTAT File for Holland
VE11	Create INTRASTAT File for Spain
VE12	Create INTRASTAT Form for Holland
VE13	KOBRA Data Selection: Export Germany
VE14	Create KOBRA File for Germany
VE15	Create Disk – INTRA/EXTRA/KOBRA/VAR
VE16	Create INTRASTAT Form for Austria
VE17	Create INTRASTAT Form for Sweden
VE18	SED Data Selection for USA Exporters
VE19	Create SED Form for USA
VE20	Create AERP File for USA
VE21	VAR: Selection of Bill. Docs Switzerland
VE22	Create VAR Form for Switzerland
VE23	VAR File – Switzerland
VE24	Commodity Code Number Information (Old)
VE25	SED: Selection: USA Carriers
VE26	Number of CAP Products List
VE27	HMF: Selection – USA
VE28	Name of Market Organization
VE29	Assigned Documents for Each License

Continued

Appendix A Relevant Transaction Codes for the SD Module

Transaction Code	Provides the functionality to
VE30	Existing Licenses
VE31	Blocked SD Documents
VE32	INTRASTAT: Paper Form – Ireland
VE33	INTRASTAT: Paper Form – UK
VE34	INTRASTAT: Paper Form – Belgian
VE35	Number of Market Organization
VE36	Group for CAP Products
VE37	INTRASTAT: File – France
VE38	INTRASTAT: Selection Simulation – EU
VE39	EXTRASTAT: Selection Simulation
VE40	KOBRA: Selection Simulation
VE41	VAR: Selection of Bill. Docs Switz
VE42	INTRASTAT: File – Denmark
VE43	SED: Selection Exp. USA Simulation
VE44	SED: Select Carrier USA Simulation
VE45	INTRASTAT: Paper Form – Greece
VE46	INTRASTAT: File – Finland
VE47	PRODCOM No.
VE48	Customs Quota Code
VE49	Code for Pharmaceutical Products
VE50	Legal Regulations
VE51	Legal Regulation/License Type
VE52	Country or Legal Regulations
VE53	Export Situation for a Country

Continued

Transaction Code	Provides the functionality to
VE54	Preference Determination: Collective
VE55	Preference Determination: Individual
VE56	Check Export Control for Consistency
VE57	Country Classification
VE58	Product Classification
VE59	Legal Regulations or Country Grouping
VE60	Expenditure Control Class According to Legal Regulations
VE61	Legal Regulations or Embargo Group
VE62	Material Group According to Legal Regulations
VE63	Customs Areas
VE64	Commodity Code or Customs Areas
VE65	Preference Regulations or Percentage Rates
VE66	Preference Procedure
VE67	Aggregate Vendor Declarations
VE68	Request Vendor Declarations
VE69	Incompletion Log
VE70	Place of Manufacture
VE71	Preference: Determine Customs Area
VE72	Export – Billing Documents
VE73	Goods Catalog: Create Document
VE74	Goods Catalog: Create Diskette
VE75	Preference Code
VE76	Anti-Dumping Code
VE77	Preference: Tariff Alternation
VE78	Plant Parameters for Vendor Declaration

Continued

Appendix A Relevant Transaction Codes for the SD Module

Transaction Code	Provides the functionality to
VE79	Quota Code Determination
VE80	Assign Chapter to Section
VE81	Check Report: General FT Data
VE82	Check Report: Export Control Data
VE83	Check Report: Preference Data
VE85	Change Statistical Value – Import
VE86	Display Statistical Value – Import
VE87	Change Statistical Value – Subcontracting
VE88	Change Statistical Value – Export
VE89	Display Statistical Value – Export
VE90	Change Preference Values
VE91	Display Preference Values
VE92	Create INTRASTAT Tape Luxembourg
VE93	EDI-CUSTEC Austria
VE94	Load Commodity Code for EU Countries
VE95	Create INTRASTAT Papers: Portugal
VE96	EXTRASTAT Data Select: Initial. Screen
VE97	Create EXTRASTAT Tape: Netherlands
VE98	Sales Invoice Values per Period
VE99	Create Document – Austria
VEA1	FT-Create Commodity Code Import
VEA2	FT: Create Commodity Code Export
VEA3	EXTRASTAT: File Version France
VEA4	EXTRASTAT: File Version France

Continued

Transaction Code	Provides the functionality to
VEB1	Period-End Closings: Control
VEB5	Calculate Assemblies Individually
VEB6	Calculate Assemblies Collectively
VEB9	Customer Exits: Print Control
VECN	Profitability and Sales Accounting
VECS	Legal Control: Special Character Code
VECZ	INTRASTAT: File – Czech Republic
VED1	Print Parameters for Export Docs
VED2	Form Data Control
VEFU	Foreign Trade: Add INTRASTAT Data
VEG1	Handling Unit Group 1
VEG2	Handling Unit Group 2
VEG3	Handling Unit Group 3
VEG4	Handling Unit Group 4
VEG5	Handling Unit Group 5
VEGK	FT: Combination Bus Transaction Type – Procedure
VEGR	Material Group: Packaging Materials
VEHU	INTRASTAT: File – Hungary
VEI0	Create INTRASTAT CUSDEC EDI IE
VEI1	Display IDoc Import
VEI3	Display Statistical Value – Subcontracting
VEI4	Merge: Remaining Commodity Codes
VEI5	Create Value Limit Subcontracting
VEI6	EDI: IDoc List – Import Basis
VEI7	Create INTRASTAT CUSDEC EDI GB

Continued

Appendix A Relevant Transaction Codes for the SD Module

Transaction Code	Provides the functionality to
VEI8	Create INTRASTAT CUSDEC EDI AT
VEI9	Create INTRASTAT CUSDEC EDI ES
VEIA	Create INTRASTAT CUSDEC EDI SE
VEIAI	INTRASTAT Archiving
VEIB	Create INTRASTAT CUSDEC EDI PT
VEIC	Create INTRASTAT CUSDEC EDI FI
VEID	Create INTRASTAT CUSDEC EDI LU
VEIE	SAPMSED8: Call EXPINV02
VEII	SAPMSED8: Call IMPINV01
VEIV	Foreign Trade: Add EXTRASTAT Data
VEIW	Create file INTRA or EXTRA or KOBRA
VEKU	Change KOBRA Documents
VEM4	Merge: EU – Commodity Code
VEPL	Create INTRASTAT CUSDEC EDI PL
VEPR	Customs Log
VESK	Create INTRASTAT CUSDEC EDI SK
VEU4	Load Commodity Code - Other Countries
VF00	Access Billing
VF01	Create Billing Document
VF02	Change Billing Document
VF03	Display Billing Document
VF04	Maintain Billing Due List
VF05	List Billing Documents
VF06	Batch Billing

Continued

Transaction Code	Provides the functionality to
VF07	Display Billing Document from Archive
VF08	Billing for External Delivery
VF11	Cancel Billing Document
VF21	Create Invoice List
VF22	Change Invoice List
VF23	Display Invoice List
VF24	Edit Work List for Invoice Lists
VF25	List of Invoice Lists
VF26	Cancellation Invoice List
VF27	Display Invoice List from Archive
VF31	Output from Billing Documents
VF42	Update Sales Documents
VF44	Revenue Recognition: Worklist
VF45	Revenue Recognition: Revenue Report
VF46	Revenue Recognition: Cancellation
VF47	Revenue Recognition: Consistency Check
VFBZ	Scale Basis for Pricing
VFLI	Log Tax Exemption
VFP1	Set Billing Date
VFRB	Retro-Billing
VFS3	Adjusting Info Structure S060
VFSN	Reorganization Info Structure S060
VFUN	Reload
VFX2	Display Blocked Billing Documents
VFX3	List Blocked Billing Documents

Continued

Appendix A Relevant Transaction Codes for the SD Module

Transaction Code	Provides the functionality to
VG01	Create Group
VG02	Change Group
VG03	Display Group
VGK1	Create Group for Delivery
VGK2	Change Group for Delivery
VGK3	Display Group for Delivery
VGL1	Create Group for Delivery
VGL2	Change Group for Delivery
VGL3	Display Group for Delivery
VF48	Revenue Recognition: Compare Report
VFAE	Archive EXTRASTAT Documents
VFAI	Archive INTRASTAT Documents
VFBS	Next Screen Control
VFBV	Reorganization of Discount-Rel. Data
VFBWG	Bulkiness and Minimum Weights
VGM1	Create Group for Freight List
VGM2	Change Group for Freight List
VGM3	Display Group for Freight List
VGW1	Create Picking Wave
VGW2	Change Picking Waves
VGW3	Display Picking Waves
VHAR	Maintain or Create Packaging Material Types
VHZU	Allowed Packaging Material Types
VI00	Shipment Costs

Continued

Transaction Code	Provides the functionality to
VI01	Create Shipment Costs
VI02	Change Shipment Costs
VI03	Display Shipment Costs
VI04	Create Shipment Cost Worklist
VI05	Change Shipment Cost Worklist
VI06	Collective Run in Background
VI08	Display FT Data in Purchasing Document
VI09	Change FT Data in Purchasing Document
VI10	Display FT Data in Billing Document
VI11	List Shipment Costs: Calculation
VI12	List Shipment Costs: Settlement
VI14	Change FT Data in Billing Document
VI15	Display Logs (Application Log)
VI16	Logs for Worklist Shipment
VI17	Display FT Data in Inbound Delivery
VI18	Display Anti-Dumping
VI19	Display Third-Country Customs Duties
VI20	Display Customs Quota
VI21	Display Pharmaceutical Products
VI22	Display Customs Exemption
VI23	Display Preferential Customs Duties
VI24	Code Number Information – Import
VI25	Display Gross Price – Customs
VI26	Display Surcharge/Discount – Customs
VI27	Display Freight – Customs

Continued

Transaction Code	Provides the functionality to
VI28	EDI: Customs ID Number – Vendor
VI29	Incompletion – Foreign Trade Data
VI30	Declaration to Authorities: Exclusion
VI31	Code Determination – Pharmaceutical Products
VI32	Code Determination – Anti-Dumping
VI33	Customs Exemption
VI34	Preferential Customs Duty Rate
VI35	Third-Country Customs Duty Rate
VI36	CAS Number
VI37	Import Simulation Control
VI38	Determination of Verification Docs
VI39	Authority for Verification Docs
VI40	Preference Type
VI41	Verification Document Type
VI42	Document Type (Export/Import)
VI43	Definition of Section
VI44	Assign Chapter to Section
VI45	Export → Import Conversion
VI46	Conversion: Mode of Transport
VI47	Conversion of Business Transaction Type
VI48	Conversion of Customs Offices
VI49	Foreign Trade Data Control in Document
VI50	Conversion: Import or Export Procedure
VI51	Define Payment Guarantee Procedure

Continued

Transaction Code	Provides the functionality to
VI52	Define Form of Payment Guarantee
VI53	Change FT Data in Inbound Delivery
VI54	Customs Approval Numbers
VI55	Approval Number per Plant
VI56	EDI: Customs ID Number – Customer
VI57	Legal Control – Order Header
VI58	Legal Control – Order Item
VI59	Legal Control – Delivery Header
VI60	Legal Control – Delivery Item
VI61	Conversion – Reference Country
VI63	Assign Delivery Item Categories
VI64	Display FT Data in Outbound Delivery
VI65	Maintains Market Organizations
VI66	Maintains Number of Market Organizations
VI67	Maintains CAP Products List Numbers
VI68	Control Commodity Code/Code Number
VI69	Maintains CAP Products Group
VI70	Default Values – Stock Transport Order
VI71	Change Preference Values
VI72	Display Insurance – Customs
VI73	Maintains Vendor Declaration
VI74	Display Vendor Declaration
VI75	Vendor Declarations – Dunning Notice
VI76	Mode of Transport – Office of Exit
VI77	Change FT Data in Outbound Delivery

Continued

Transaction Code	Provides the functionality to
VI78	Foreign Trade: Country Data
VI79	Display FT Data in Goods Receipt
VI80	Change FT Data in Goods Receipt
VI81	Check Report: CAP Products
VI82	Check General Customer Master Data
VI83	Check Customer Master/Legal Control
VI84	Document Payments: Check Customer Master
VI85	Incompleteness: Foreign Trade Vendor
VI86	Incompleteness: Cross-Plant
VI87	Foreign Trade: Header Data Proposal
VI88	Input Table for Preference Determination
VI89	Customs Law Description
VI90	Fill Foreign Components in BOMs
VI91	Display Foreign Components in BOMs
VI92	Preference: Alternative Comm. Code
VI93	Foreign Trade: Import Control
VI94	Load Import Code Numbers – EU Countries
VI95	Default Value of Foreign Trade Header Data
VI96	Customer Exits: Default Values
VI97	Define Control Codes
VI98	Receipt-Basis for Intercompany Billing
VI99	Returns and Credit Memos
VIAR	Archive Shipment Costs
VIB1	Sends IDoc Output

Continued

Transaction Code	Provides the functionality to
VIB2	Calls Print Program from VI10 or VI14
VIB3	Foreign Trade Output Status
VIB4	Print Transaction: Initial Processing
VIB5	Print Transaction: Repeat Processing
VIB6	Print Transaction: Error in Processing
VIB7	Send IDoc Output – Initial Processing
VIB8	Send IDoc Output – Repeat Processing
VIB9	Send IDoc Output – Error in Processing
VIBA	Send IDoc Output-AES-Initial Processing
VIBB	Send IDoc Output-AES-Repeat Processing
VIBC	Send IDoc Output-AES-Error in Processing
VIBD	Printing: Analysis from Data Audit
VIBN	Monitor Messages
VIC00	Consistency Check IMG Shipment Cost Calculation
VICC	Converts Format of the Currency Field
VICI	Call Shipment Info via CALL TRANS
VIE4	Incompleteness Periodic Declarations
VIFBW	Reorganization Shipment Costs in BW
VII4	Merge: Rest – Import Code Number
VII5	Import Control in the Material Document
VIIM	FT: Optional Cockpit: Purchase Order
VIJ1	Journal Import
VIJ2	Journal Export
VILG	FT: Country Group Definition
VILI	FT: Export Deliveries Journal

Continued

Transaction Code	Provides the functionality to
VIM4	Merge: EU – Import Code Number
VIM6	Customer Exits: Data Selection
VIMM	Declaration Receipts or Dispatches Mineral Oil Production
VIMU	Foreign Trade: Comparison of Codes
VINC	List of Incomplete SD Documents
VINK	Import Processing: Quota Number
VINP	Import Processing: Ceiling Numbers
VIPL	Display Customs Duty for Ceiling
VIR1	Import Reorganization – Incompleteness
VIR2	Export Reorganization – Incompleteness
VIRL	Reload Shipments
VIS3	Check program: Cross-Plant
VISW	Service: Information: Keywords
VIU4	Load Import Code No.-Other Countries
VIUC	FT Upload: Convert Custom Duty Types
VIUL	Foreign Trade: Data Upload
VIZB	Import Processing Means of Transport
VIZN	Import Processing Type of Goods ID Seal
VIZP	Import Processing: Package Type
VK+C	Condition Master Data Check
VK01	Conditions: Dialog Box for Condition Element
VK03	Create Condition Table
VK04	Change Condition Table
VK05	Display Condition Table

Continued

Appendix A Relevant Transaction Codes for the SD Module

Transaction Code	Provides the functionality to
VK11	Create Condition
VK12	Change Condition
VK13	Display Condition
VK14	Create Condition with Reference
VK19	Change Condition without Menu
VK20	Display Condition without Menu
VK30	Maintain Variant Conditions
VK31	Condition Maintenance: Create
VK32	Condition Maintenance: Change
VK33	Condition Maintenance: Display
VK34	Condition Maintenance: Create with Reference
VKA1	Archiving Conditions
VKA2	Deleting Conditions
VKA3	Reloading Conditions
VKA4	Archiving Agreements
VKA5	Deleting Agreements
VKA6	Reloading Agreements
VKAR	Read Archive File
VKAW	Generate Archive File
VKC1	Create General Strategy
VKC2	Change General Strategy
VKC3	Display General Strategy
VKDV	Number Range Maintenance: RV_SNKOM
VKM1	Blocked SD Documents
VKM2	Released SD Documents

Continued

Transaction Code	Provides the functionality to
VKM3	Sales Document
VKM5	Delivery
VKOA	Account Determination
VKOE	Assign GL Accounts
VKP0	Sales Price Calculation
VKP2	Display POS Conditions
VKP3	Pricing Document for Material
VKP4	Pricing Document for Organizational Structure
VKP5	Create Calculation
VKP6	Change Pricing Document
VKP7	Display Pricing Document
VKP8	Display Price Calculation
VKP9	Currency Conversion in Price Calculation
VKPA	Archiving File
VKPB	Sales Price Calculation in Background Run
VKPR	Read Archive File
VKU1	Report: Revaluation at Retail for Retail Price Change
VKU10	Correction of Valuation at Retail
VKU11	Delete Count Document Items
VKU2	Total Revaluation at Retail
VKU3	Partial Revaluation at Retail
VKU4	Retail Revaluation Docs for Material
VKU5	Display Retail Revaluation Document
VKU6	Revaluation at Retail: Selection of Retail Price Changes

Continued

Transaction Code	Provides the functionality to
VKU7	Report: Total Revaluation for Retail Price Change
VKU8	Test Transaction BAPI Count List
VKU9	Retail Revaluation Correction: List Display
VKUN	Reload File
VKVF	Conditions: Dialog Box for Condition Element
VKVG	Maintain Condition Elements
VKVI	General View Maintenance: Enter Values – Transaction VKVI
VKXX	Create Test for RKA
VKYY	Change Test for RKA
VKZZ	Test for RKS-Surcharge Conditions
VL00	Shipping of Goods
VL01	Create Delivery Document
VL01N	Create Outbound Delivery with Order Reference
VL01NO	Create Outbound Delivery w/o Order Reference
VL02	Change Outbound Delivery
VL03	Display Outbound Delivery
VL04	Process Delivery Due List
VL06	Delivery Monitor
VL06C	List Outbound Deliveries for Confirmation
VL06D	Outbound Deliveries for Distribution
VL06F	General Delivery List – Outbound Delivery
VL06G	List of Outbound Deliveries for Goods Issue
VL06I	Inbound Delivery Monitor
VL06IC	Confirmation of Putaway Inbound Delivery
VL06ID	Inbound Deliveries for Distribution

Continued

APPENDIX A RELEVANT TRANSACTION CODES FOR THE SD MODULE   543

Transaction Code	Provides the functionality to
VL06IF	Selection Inbound Deliveries
VL06IG	Inbound Deliveries for Goods Receipt
VL06IP	Inbound Deliveries for Putaway
VL06L	Outbound Deliveries to Be Loaded
VL06O	Outbound Delivery Monitor
VL06P	List of Outbound Deliveries for Picking
VL06T	List Outbound Deliveries (Transport Planning)
VL06U	List of Unchecked Outbound Deliveries
VL08	Confirmation of Picking Request
VL09	Cancel Goods Issue for Delivery Note
VL10	Edit User-Specific Delivery List
VL10A	Sales Orders Due for Delivery
VL10B	Purchase Orders Due for Delivery
VL10BATCH	VL10 Background Planning
VL10BATCH_A	Background Planning VL10 (0 Tbstrps)
VL10BATCH_B	Background Planning VL10 (3 Tbstrps)
VL10C	Order Items Due for Delivery
VL10CU	Delivery Scenarios
VL10CUA	User Roles (List Profiles)
VL10CUC	Create Profile – Delivery
VL10CUE	Exclude Function Code Profile
VL10CUF	F Code VL10 Profile
VL10CUV	Delivery Scenarios
VL10CU_ALL	User Roles (List Profiles)

Continued

Transaction Code	Provides the functionality to
VL10D	Purchase Order Items Due for Delivery
VL10E	Order Schedule Lines Due for Delivery
VL10F	Purchase Order Schedule Lines Due for Delivery
VL10G	Documents Due for Delivery
VL10H	Items Due for Delivery
VL10I	Schedule Lines Due for Delivery
VL10U	Cross-System Deliveries
VL12	Delivery Creation in Background
VL21	Post Goods Issue in Background
VL22	Display Delivery Change Documents
VL23	Goods Issue (Background Processing)
VL30	Shipping of Goods for Dispatching
VL31	Create Inbound Delivery
VL31W	Create Inbound Delivery Notification (WEB)
VL32	Change Inbound Delivery
VL32W	Change Inbound Delivery Notification (WEB)
VL33	Display Inbound Delivery
VL34	Worklist Inbound Deliveries
VL35	Create Wave Picks: Delivery/Time
VL35_S	Create Wave Picks: Shipment
VL35_ST	Create Wave Picks: Shipment/Time
VL36	Change Picking Waves
VL37	Wave Pick Monitor
VL38	Groups Created: Wave Picks
VL39	Billing Documents for Wave Picks

Continued

Transaction Code	Provides the functionality to
VL41	Create Rough GR
VL42	Change Rough GR
VL43	Display Rough GR
VL51	Create Route Schedule: Initial Screen
VL52	Change Route Schedule: Initial Screen
VL53	Display Route Schedule: Initial Screen
VL70	Output from Picking Lists
VL71	Output from Outbound Deliveries
VL72	Output from Groups of Deliveries
VL73	Selection Program for Issuing Output
VL74	Output from Handling Units
VL75	Shipping Notification Output
VL76	Output from Rough Goods Receipt
VLAL	Archive Deliveries
VLBT	Plan Delivery Creation as a Job
VLE1	Picking with Picking Waves
VLLA	RWE: Picking/Goods Issue Analysis
VLLC	RWE: Archive Data
VLLD	Rough Workload Forecast: Delete Log
VLLE	RWE: Goods Receipt/Putaway Analysis
VLLF	Picking Waves: Archive Data
VLLG	RWE: Analyze Complete Overview
VLLP	Rough Workload Forecast: Display Log
VLLQ	RWE: Returns to Vendor Analysis

Continued

Transaction Code	Provides the functionality to
VLLR	RWE: Customer/Store Return Analysis
VLLS	Standard Analyses Setting App 42
VLLV	W&S: Control RWE/Picking Waves
VLMOVE	HU Goods Movements
VLPOD	POD – Change Outbound Delivery
VLPODA	POD – Display Outbound Delivery
VLPODF	Worklist: POD Subsequent Processing
VLPODL	Worklist: POD Deliveries
VLPODQ	Automatic Proof of Delivery Confirmation
VLPODW1	Proof of Delivery (Communicator)
VLPODW2	Proof of Delivery via WEB
VLPP	Packing Request for Item Categories
VLRL	Reload Delivery
VLSP	Subsequent Outbound-Delivery Split
VLSPS	Outbound Delivery Split via HU Scan
VLUNIV	Change Delivery (General)
VM01	Create Hazardous Material
VM02	Change Hazardous Material
VM03	Display Hazardous Material
VM04	Filling Hazardous Substance Table MGEF
VMG1	Create Material Group 1
VMG2	Create Material Group 2
VMG3	Create Material Group 3
VMG4	Create Material Group 4
VMG5	Create Material Group 5

Continued

Transaction Code	Provides the functionality to
VN01	Number Assignment for SD Documents
VN03	Number Assignment for Document Conditions
VN04	Number Assignment for Master Conditions
VN05	Number Assignment for Address List
VN06	Create Number Interval-Sales Activities
VN07	Maintain Number Range for Shipments
VN08	Number Range for Shipment Costs
VN10	Number Range Maintenance: SD_SCALE
VNE1	Output: Create Condition Table-Shipment Notification
VNE2	Output-Condition Table-Change Shipment Notification
VNE4	Access Sequences (Shipment Notification)
VNE5	View V_TNAPN Appl. E1
VNE6	Output Determination Procedure-Shipment Notification
VNE7	View V_TVLK_NLA (Shipment Notification)
VNE8	View V_TVLK_NGW (Rough GI)
VNE9	Conditions: V_T681F for B E1
VNEA	Output: Create Condition Table – Rough GR
VNEB	Output-Condition Table-Change Shipment Notification
VNEC	Output Types (Rough Goods Receipt)
VNED	Access Sequences (Rough GR)
VNEE	View V_TNAPN Appl. M1
VNEF	Output Determination Procedure – Rough GR
VNEG	Conditions: V_T681F for B M1
VNEH	View V_TNAPR Appl. E1

Continued

Transaction Code	Provides the functionality to
VNEI	View V_TNAPR Appl. M1
VNKP	Number Range Maintenance: RV_VEKP
VNOP	C SD-VN Maintain TVAK
VNPU	Partner Conversion
VN_TP02	Salutation
VN_TP04	Marital Property Regime
VN_TP05	Employee Group
VN_TP06	Rating
VN_TP07	Credit Rating Institute
VN_TP10	Loan to Manager
VN_TP11	Employment Status
VN_TP12	German Banking Act Credit Info
VN_TP13	Target Group
VN_TP18	Undesirable Customer
VOA0	Order Information Configuration
VOA01	User Exit Lists Sales
VOA1	Inquiry Information Configuration
VOA2	Quotation Information Configuration
VOA3	Configuration of Scheduled Agreement Info
VOA4	Contract Information Configuration
VOA5	Product Proposal Info. Configuration
VOB3	Comparison: Bill. Docs and Stats
VOBO	Configuration for Backorder Processing
VOC0	Contract List Configuration
VOC1	Customizing for List of Addresses

Continued

Transaction Code	Provides the functionality to
VOD5	Configuration Customer Independent Requisition Info
VOE1	Maintain EDPST
VOE2	SD EDI Customer/Vendor
VOE3	SD EDI Partner Functions
VOE4	SD EDI Conversion
VOEX	Incompleteness: Billing Document
VOF0	Configuration of Billing Information
VOF01	User Exit Lists Sales
VOF1	Configuration: Collective Billing
VOF2	Configuration Invoice List Info
VOF3	Edit Work List for Invoice Lists
VOFA	Billing Doc: Document Type
VOFM	Configuration for Requisition Formulae
VOFN	Call Up Transaction VOFM
VOIM	Incompleteness: Purchase Order
VOK0	Conditions: Pricing in Customizing
VOK1	Account Determination: Customizing
VOK2	Output Determination
VOK3	Message Determination: Purchasing
VOK4	Output Determination: Inventory Management
VOK8	Condition Exclusion Assign Procedure V
VOKF	Configuration Release of CustPrice
VOKR	Configuration of Credit Release
VOL0	Delivery Information Configuration

Continued

Transaction Code	Provides the functionality to
VOL01	User Exit Lists Sales
VOL1	Configuration: Collective Delivery Procedure
VOL6	Configure Information On
VOL7	Settings for Packing
VOLI	Incompleteness: Delivery
VONC	Output Form for Each Group
VOP2	Configuration: Partner
VOPAN	Customizing Partners
VOR1	Joint Master Data: Distribution Channel
VOR2	Joint Master Data: Division
VORA	Archiving Control for Sales Doc
VORB	Group Reference Sales Document Types
VORI	Archiving Control Shipment Costs
VORK	Archiving Control for Sales Activity
VORL	Archiving Control for Delivery
VORN	Central Archiving Control
VORP	Repairs Procedure: Short Texts Transaction
VORR	Archiving Control for Billing Docs
VORS	Group Reference Procedures
VORT	Archiving Control for Shipments
VORV	Repair Procedure
VOTX	Configuration: Texts
VOV6	Maintain Schedule Line Categories
VOV7	Maintain Item Categories
VOV8	Document-Type Maintenance

Continued

Transaction Code	Provides the functionality to
VOVA	Default Values for Material
VOVB	Screen Sequence Group Maintenance
VOVC	Item Field Selection Group Maintenance
VOVD	Header Field Selection Group
VOVF	Variant Matching Procedure
VOVG	Define Characteristic Overview
VOVL	Cancellation Rules
VOVM	Cancellation Procedures
VOVN	Assignment Rules/Cancellation Procedure
VOVP	Rule Table for Date Determination
VOVQ	Cancellation Reasons
VOVR	Default Values for Contract
VOVS	Define Status in Overview Screen
VOW1	User Assignment GRUKO_WF
VOWE	Incompleteness: Goods Receipt
VP01	Maintain Print Parameters
VP01SHP	Print Parameter Maintenance Shipping
VP01TRA	Print Parameter Maintenance Transport
VP01_PAG	Maintain Print Parameters
VP01_SD	Maintain Print Parameters SD
VP01_TC	Print Parameter Maintenance Trading Center
VP94	Load Import Code No. for Japan
VPAR	Archiving Preference Logs
VPBD	Requirement for Packing in Delivery

Continued

Transaction Code	Provides the functionality to
VPE1	Create Sales Representative
VPE2	Change Sales Representative
VPE3	Display Sales Representative
VPM4	Merge: Japan – Import Code Number
VPN1	Number Range for Contact Person
VPNR	View of the Active PNR in 1A
VPRE	PRICAT Manual Creation
VPRICAT	Maintain and Create Price Catalog
VPW1	Portal Workset Administration
VPWL	Portal Target Administration
VRLI	FT: Reorganization T609S Delivery
VRRE	Returns Delivery for RMA Order
VRWE	FT: Reorganization T609S Goods Receipt
VS00	SD Main Menu for Customer
VS01	Create Scale
VS02	Change Scale
VS03	Display Scale
VS04	Create Scale with Reference
VS05	List Scales
VS06	List Scales for Shipment Costs
VSAN	Number Range Maintenance: RV_SAMMG
VSB1	Self-Billing Proc. Inbound Monitor
VSCAN	Configuration of Virus Scan Servers
VSCANTEST	Test for Virus Scan Interface
VSTK	Picking Confirmation

Continued

APPENDIX A   RELEVANT TRANSACTION CODES FOR THE SD MODULE

Transaction Code	Provides the functionality to
VT00	Transportation
VT01N	Create Shipment
VT03N	Display Shipment
VT04	Transportation Worklist
VT05	Worklist Shipping: Logs
VT06	Select Shipments: Materials Planning
VT07	Collective Run in Background
VT09	Number Ranges for Log VT04
VT10	Select Shipments: Start
VT11	Select Shipments: Materials Planning
VT12	Select Shipments: Transport Processing
VT13	F4-Help Shipment Number
VT14	Select Shipments: Utilization
VT15	Select Shipments: Free Capacity
VT16	Select Shipments: Check In
VT17	Extended Help (F4) Shipment Number
VT18	Start F4 Help Shipping
VT19	Shipment Tendering Status Monitor
VT20	Overall Shipment Process Monitor
VT22	Display Change-Document Shipment
VT30	Initial Internet Transport for Shipment
VT31	Shipment Tendering
VT31C	Customizing Screen for Shipment Tendering
VT32	Shipment Status List

Continued

Transaction Code	Provides the functionality to
VT33	Shipment Planning for Carriers
VT34	Event Reports for Carriers via HTML
VT34M	Event Reports for Carriers via WML
VT60	Transfer Location Master Data to TPS
VT61	Extending Transport Planning Deliveries
VT62	Send Deliveries to Forwarding Agent
VT63	Freight Planning Status from Deliveries
VT68	Deallocate Delivery from TPS
VT69	Plan Deliveries from Freight Planning
VT70	Output for Shipments
VTAA	Order to Order Copying Control
VTAF	Billing Doc. to Order Copying Control
VTAR	Archive Shipments
VTBT	Report for Definition of Batch Run
VTBW	Reorganization: Shipment Data in BW
VTCM	List of Continuous Moves
VTDOCU	Tech. Documentation Transportation
VTFA	Order to Bill Copying Control
VTFAKT	Bill Deliveries
VTFF	Bill to Bill Copying Control
VTFL	Delivery to Bill Copying Control
VTLA	Order to Delivery Copying Control
VTR1	XSI: Master Data: Service Codes
VTR2	XSI: Master Data: Routing Info
VTRC	XSI Cockpit

Continued

Transaction Code	Provides the functionality to
VTRC_VVTR0011	Delivery Tracking – Collective Request
VTRK	Tracking
VTRL	Reload Shipments
VTRS	XSI: Carrier: Master Data
VTRT	XSI: Carrier
VTWABU	Post Goods Issue
VUA2	Maintain Doc. Type Incompletion Procedure
VUA3	Display Doc. Type Incompletion Procedure
VUA4	Assignment Delivery Type Incompletion Procedure
VUA5	Display Assignment Delivery Type to Incompletion Procedure
VUC2	Maintain Incompletion Log
VUE2	Maintain Schedule Line Incompletion Procedure
VUE3	Display Schedule Line Incompletion Procedure
VUP2	Maintain Item Incompletion Procedure
VUP3	Display Item Incompletion Procedure
VUP4	Assignment Delivery Items to Incompletion Procedure
VUP5	Display Assignment Delivery Items Incompletion Procedure
VUPA	Display Partner Incompletion Procedure
VV11	Create Output: Sales
VV12	Change Output: Sales
VV13	Display Output: Sales
VV21	Create Output: Shipping
VV22	Change Output: Shipping
VV23	Display Output: Shipping

Continued

Transaction Code	Provides the functionality to
VV31	Create Output: Billing
VV32	Change Output: Billing
VV33	Display Output: Billing
VV51	Create Output: Sales Activity
VV52	Change Output: Sales Activity
VV53	Display Output: Sales Activity
VV61	Create Output: Handling Unit
VV62	Change Output: Handling Unit
VV63	Display Output: Handling Unit
VV71	Create Output: Transportation
VV72	Change Output: Transportation
VV73	Display Output: Transportation
VVCB	Maintain Activity Authorization
VVG1	Create Output: Group
VVG2	Change Output: Group
VVG3	Display Output: Group
VW01	SD Scenario 'Incoming Orders'
VW02	SD Scenario 'Freedom to Shop'
VW10	SD Scenario 'Order Status'
VX00	Export Control
VX01	Create License (Old)
VX02	Change License (Old)
VX03	Display License (Old)
VX05	Customers for License
VX06	Export Control Classes for License

Continued

Transaction Code	Provides the functionality to
VX07	Simulation: License Check
VX08	Simulation: Boycott List Check
VX09	Simulation: Embargo Check
VX0C	Foreign Trade: Customizing Menu
VX10	Countries of Destination for License
VX11	Create Financial Document
VX12	Change Financial Document
VX13	Display Financial Document
VX16	BAFA Diskette: Selection
VX17	Create BAFA Diskette
VX22	Change License Data (Old)
VX23	Display License Data (Old)
VX30	Legal Control: Export Control Class
VX49	Doc. Payment Guarantee: Doc.Types
VX50	Doc. Payment Guarantee: Fin.Doc.Types
VX51	Doc. Payment Guarantee: Bank Function
VX52	Doc. Payment Guarantee: Field Ctrl ID
VX53	Doc. Payment Guarantee: Fin.Doc.Type ID
VX54	Doc. Payment Guarantee: Field Ctrl-Bank Function
VX55	Doc. Payment Guarantee: Export/Import Docs
VX56	Doc. Payment Guarantee: Bank IDs
VX57	Doc. Payment Guarantee: Export Docs Default
VX58	Doc. Payment Guarantee: Export Docs Assignment
VX70	Sanctioned Party List: Legal Regulation

Continued

Transaction Code	Provides the functionality to
VX71	Sanctioned Party List: Departure
VX72	Sanctioned Party List: Scope of Check
VX73	Sanctioned Party List: Aliases
VX74	Sanctioned Party List: ExclusiveTexts
VX75	Sanctioned Party List: List Types
VX76	Sanctioned Party List: References
VX77	Sanctioned Party List: Delimiter
VX78	Sanctioned Party L.: Normalization
VX79	Sanctioned Party List: Phon. Check
VX80	CAP: CAP Products List Number
VX81	CAP: CAP Products Group
VX83	CAP: Components Leading Good
VX84	CAP: CAP Material Components
VX85	CAP: CAP Bill of Material
VX86	Maintain Market Organizations
VX87	Maintain Number of Market Organizations
VX94	Declarations to Authorities: Check
VX98	Display FT Data in Purch.Doc.-INTERNET
VX99	FT/Customs: General Overview
VXA1	Docs Assigned to Financial Documents
VXA2	Existing Financial Documents
VXA3	Financial Documents: Blocked Docs
VXA4	Financial Documents: Simulation
VXA5	Document Payments: Print Monitoring
VXA7	Documentary Payments: Simulation

Continued

APPENDIX A RELEVANT TRANSACTION CODES FOR THE SD MODULE

Transaction Code	Provides the functionality to
VXBC	SLS: List of Blocked Customers
VXCZ	INTRASTAT: Form – Czech Republic
VXDA	SLS: Audit Trail – Customer Master
VXDG	Export Control
VXDP	Declarations to the Authorities
VXDV	List of Expiring SLS Records
VXGK	Export Control
VXHU	INTRASTAT: Form – Czech Republic
VXIE	Maintain Foreign Trade Data
VXJ0	Foreign Trade: MITI Decl. – Japan
VXJ1	MITI Declarations
VXJ2	Declaration of Import Billing Docs Japan
VXJ3	Foreign Trade: Import Declaration Japan
VXKA	SLS: Audit Trail: Vendor Master
VXKD	Declarations to the Authorities
VXKP	Configuration: Maintain Tables T180*
VXL1	Legal Control: SLS – Scenario 1
VXL2	Legal Control: SLS – Scenario 2
VXL3	Legal Control: SLS – Scenario 3
VXL4	Legal Control: SLS – Scenario 4
VXL5	Legal Control: SLS – Scenario 5
VXL6	Legal Control: SLS: Sim.: Customer
VXL7	Legal Control: SLS: Search Terms
VXL8	Legal Control: SLS: Change History

Continued

Transaction Code	Provides the functionality to
VXL9	Legal Control: SLS: Sim.: Vendor
VXLA	Legal Control: SLS – Audit Trail
VXLB	Legal Control: SLS: Sim.: Address
VXLC	SLS: Vendor Check – Scenario 3
VXLD	Legal Control: SLS – List Display
VXLE	SLS: Scenario 5 – Vendor Master
VXLP	Legal Control: SLS: Keyword: Address
VXLU	Legal Control: SLS – Data Service
VXLX	Legal Control: SLS: Sim. Customer
VXLY	Legal Control: SLS: Sim. Delivery
VXLZ	Sanctioned Party List Screen
VXME	Declarations to the Authorities
VXMO	Common Agricultural Policy
VXPL	INTRASTAT: Form – Poland
VXPR	Export Control
VXS1	Legal Control: SLS: Create Entry
VXS2	Ges. Kontrolle: SLS: Change Entry
VXS3	Legal Control: SLS: Display Entry
VXSE	Declarations to the Authorities
VXSIM	Simulate Import
VXSK	INTRASTAT: Form – Slovakia
VXSL	Foreign Trade: Area Menu SLS
VXSW	Mass Change Material Commodity Code
V_BPID003_E	Identification Number Categories
V_BPUM_CTL	BP: Activate Parallel Maintenance

Continued

Appendix A Relevant Transaction Codes for the SD Module

Transaction Code	Provides the functionality to
V_FMAC	Table Maintenance for FMAC
V_FMITPOC1	View Maintenance V_FMITPOC1
V_FMITPOC2	View Maintenance V_FMITPOC2
V_FMITPOC3	View Maintenance V_FMITPOC3
V_FMITPOC4	View Maintenance V_FMITPOC4
V_FMPY	Table Maintenance for FMPY
V_I7	Condit: Pricing SD – Index in Background
V_I8	Conditions: Pricing SD – Index
V_MACO	Completion of Sales Documents
V_NL	Edit Net Price List
V_R1	List of Backorders
V_R2	Display List of Backorders
V_RA	Backorder Processing: Selection List
V_SA	Collective Processing Analysis (Delivery)
V_TBC001	Business Partner: Grouping to Account Group
V_TBPID	Characteristics of ID Numbers
V_TP019	Values Table Group Category Fields
V_TP23	Maintain Different Type Criterion
V_TP23S	Control Different Type Criterion
V_TP24	Partner Grouping Characteristics
V_TPR1	BP: Assignment Categories
V_TPR2	BP: Assignment Category - Application
V_TPR4	BP: Assign Modules to Time Periods
V_TPR5	BP: Role Categories – Application

Continued

Appendix A Relevant Transaction Codes for the SD Module

Transaction Code	Provides the functionality to
V_TPR6	BP: Role Categories – Application
V_TPR9	BPR: Role for Grouping/Address Type
V_TPZ18	Category of Additional Data Fields
V_UC_7	Incomplete SD Documents
V_V1	Updating Unconfirmed Sales Documents
V_V2	Updating Sales Documents by Material

TABLE A.1 List of the noteworthy transaction codes

You can simplify and hasten the processing of various tasks in the mySAP ERP system by accessing the transaction codes listed in Table A.1.

Appendix B
Advanced Sales and Distribution Functions

Apart from the various processes that we learned about earlier, such as billing, pricing, and invoice generation, there are a few advanced functions in the Sales and Distribution (SD) module. This appendix discusses the miscellaneous SD functions, such as partner determination, output determination, and text determination. It is quite possible that while entering details for various documents, such as sales documents, one can enter invalid values. To handle such types of situations, you can maintain sales incompletion logs, which is also described in this appendix. Moreover, while working with the mySAP™ ERP system, you must have noticed that automatic partner determination occurs in the sales documents. These functionalities are an important part of the SD module, and they help you to control the processes in sales and distribution. In this appendix, we configure the automatic partner determination process. Apart from partner determination, the mySAP ERP system also copies the data within a text line from one text object to another. This appendix describes these functions under the following sections:

- Implementing Sales Incompletion Logs
- Setting Up Partner Determination in SD
- Text Determination in SD
- Output Determination in SD

Let's discuss each of them in detail one by one.

IMPLEMENTING SALES INCOMPLETION LOGS

When you enter data in a sales document, the mySAP ERP system automatically proposes relevant data from the customer and material master. However, you can also add data manually in the sales document, as the data provided in the sales document helps perform multiple functions, such as delivery process, billing, and shipping.

Depending upon the sales document type, sometimes the mySAP system allows you to save an incomplete sales document; however, at times, it does not allow saving a sales document. For example, if you save an incomplete quotation, the mySAP ERP system allows you to save it; however, you cannot save an incomplete sales order as the missing data may affect the processing of other sales documents related to the sales order. To avoid such a situation, incompletion logs are maintained to remind you that important data required for further processing is missing from the respective document.

To implement the sales incompletion log in the mySAP ERP system, you need to perform some activities, such as defining and assigning an incompletion procedure. To perform these activities, you need to navigate the following menu path:

Menu Path

SAP Customizing Implementation Guide > Sales and Distribution > Basic Functions > Log of Incomplete Items, as shown in Figure B.1.

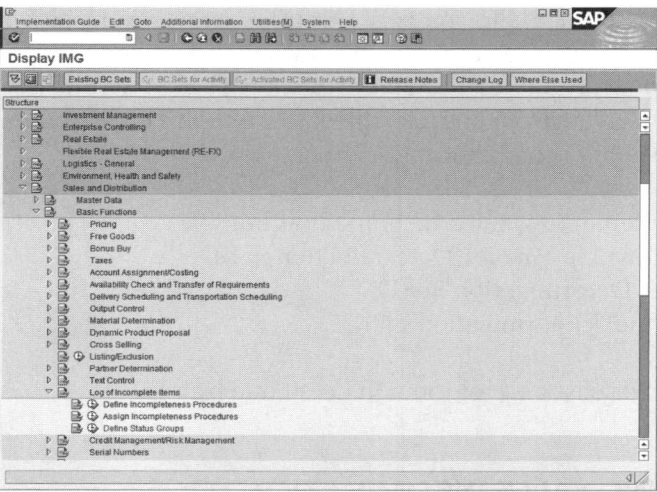

© SAP AG. All rights reserved.

FIGURE B.1 Displaying the menu path to Log of Incomplete Items

Figure B.1 shows the following activities to specify when a sales document is considered as incomplete and how the mySAP ERP system responds when you create an incomplete document:

- Define Status Groups
- Define Incompleteness Procedures
- Assign Incompleteness Procedures

Now, let's discuss each of them in detail.

Defining Status Groups

The **Define Status Groups** activity allows you to define a status group to specify the status of incomplete sales and distribution documents. Status groups provide the selection for activating an incompletion log at various stages of a sales process. To define the status group, navigate the following menu path:

Menu Path

SAP Customizing Implementation Guide > Sales and Distribution > Basic Functions > Log of Incomplete Items > Define Status Groups

After navigating the preceding menu path, click the **IMG Activity** icon (⊕) besides the **Define Status Groups** activity (Figure B.1). The **Change View "Incompletion Control: Status Groups": Overview** screen appears, as shown in Figure B.2.

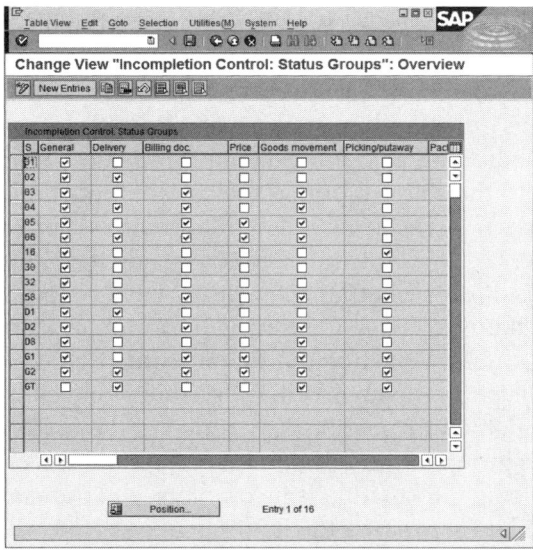

© SAP AG. All rights reserved.

FIGURE B.2 Displaying the existing status groups

Figure B.2 shows the existing status groups for which various fields, such as delivery and billing documents, are defined. The following are the details of the status fields shown in Figure B.2:

- **General**—Indicates whether the mySAP ERP system should record a status message for general information provided in a sales document. Selecting the **General status** field for a status group will cause the mySAP ERP system to check whether general information is provided in the fields assigned to the status group in the relevant incompletion procedure. If some of the general information is incomplete, the status message prompts the user to provide it.
- **Delivery**—Indicates whether the mySAP ERP system should record a status message for delivery information specified in a sales document. Selecting the **Delivery status** field for a status group will cause the mySAP ERP system to check whether delivery-related information is provided in the fields assigned to the status group in the relevant incompletion procedure. If some of the delivery information is incomplete, the status message prompts the user to provide it.
- **Billing doc.**—Indicates whether the mySAP ERP system should record a status message for billing information specified in a sales document. Selecting the **Billing doc. status** field for a status group will cause the mySAP ERP system to check whether billing-related information is provided in the fields assigned to the status group in the relevant incompletion procedure. If some of the billing information is incomplete, the status message prompts the user to provide it.
- **Price**—Indicates whether the mySAP ERP system should record a status message for pricing information specified in a sales document. Selecting the **Price status** field for a status group will cause the mySAP ERP system to check whether pricing-related information is provided in the fields assigned to the status group in the relevant incompletion procedure. If some of the pricing information is incomplete, the status message prompts the user to provide it.

- **Goods movement**—Indicates whether the mySAP ERP system should record a status message for the status of goods movement specified in a sales document. Selecting the **Goods movement status** field for a status group will cause the mySAP ERP system to check whether information related to goods movement is provided in the fields that are assigned to the status group in the relevant incompletion procedure. If some of the goods movement data is incomplete, the status message prompts the user to provide it.
- **Picking/putaway**—Indicates whether the mySAP ERP system should record a status message for the picking information specified in a sales document. Selecting the **Picking/putaway status** field for a status group will cause the mySAP ERP system to check whether the picking/putaway-related information of an item is provided in the fields that are assigned to the status group in the relevant incompletion procedure. If some of the picking/putaway data is incomplete, then the status message prompts the user to provide it.
- **Packing**—Indicates whether the mySAP ERP system should record a status message for the packing information specified in a sales document. Selecting the **Packing status** field for a status group will cause the mySAP ERP system to check whether the packing-related information is provided in the fields that are assigned to the status group in the relevant incompletion procedure. If some of the packing data is incomplete, then the status message prompts the user to provide it.

To define a new status group, click the **New Entries** button (Figure B.2). Then specify the name for the status group along with its details and select the status fields, such as **General** and **Delivery**. After providing the relevant information, click the **Save** icon (📄) to save the entered details. Now, let's move ahead to discuss the next activity, **Define Incompleteness Procedures**.

Define Incompleteness Procedures

The **Define Incompleteness Procedures** activity allows you to define the incompleteness procedures to be applied to multiple incompleteness objects. The incompleteness procedure allows you to group the fields that need to be checked for completeness. Incomplete data in either of the grouped fields implies that the document is incomplete. Moreover, on the basis of the status group, you can also block activities for a particular document. Apart from these, you also need to specify whether the warning message should be prompted when no data are provided in a field for each field. After defining the incompletion procedure, we further assign this to sales process.

To define an incompleteness procedure, navigate the following menu path:

Menu Path

SAP Customizing Implementation Guide > Sales and Distribution > Basic Functions > Log of Incomplete Items > Define Incompleteness Procedures

After navigating the preceding menu path, click the **IMG Activity** icon (☼) beside the **Define Incompleteness Procedures** activity (Figure B.1). The **Display View "Groups": Overview** screen appears as shown in Figure B.3.

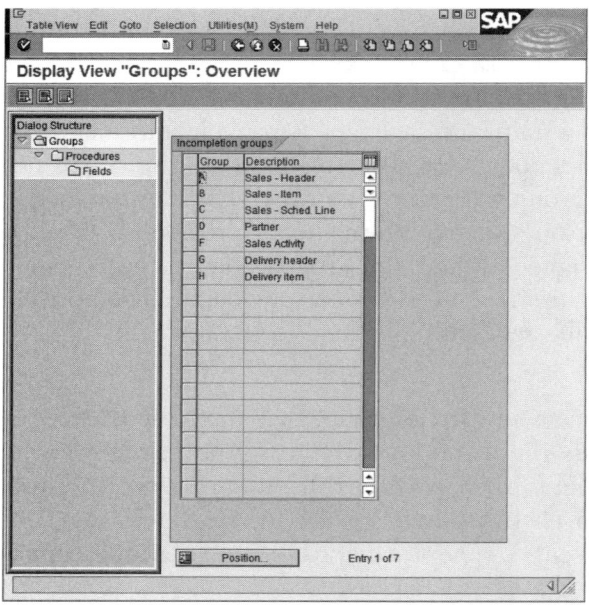

© SAP AG. All rights reserved.

FIGURE B.3 Displaying the existing incompletion groups

Figure B.3 shows the existing incompletion groups defined in the mySAP ERP system. You can also define a new error group by creating a copy of an existing group. For example, in our case we select **Group B – Sales Item** to define a new error group. After selecting the **Group B – Sales Item** group, double-click the **Procedures** folder (Figure B.3). The **Display View "Procedures": Overview** screen appears as shown in Figure B.4.

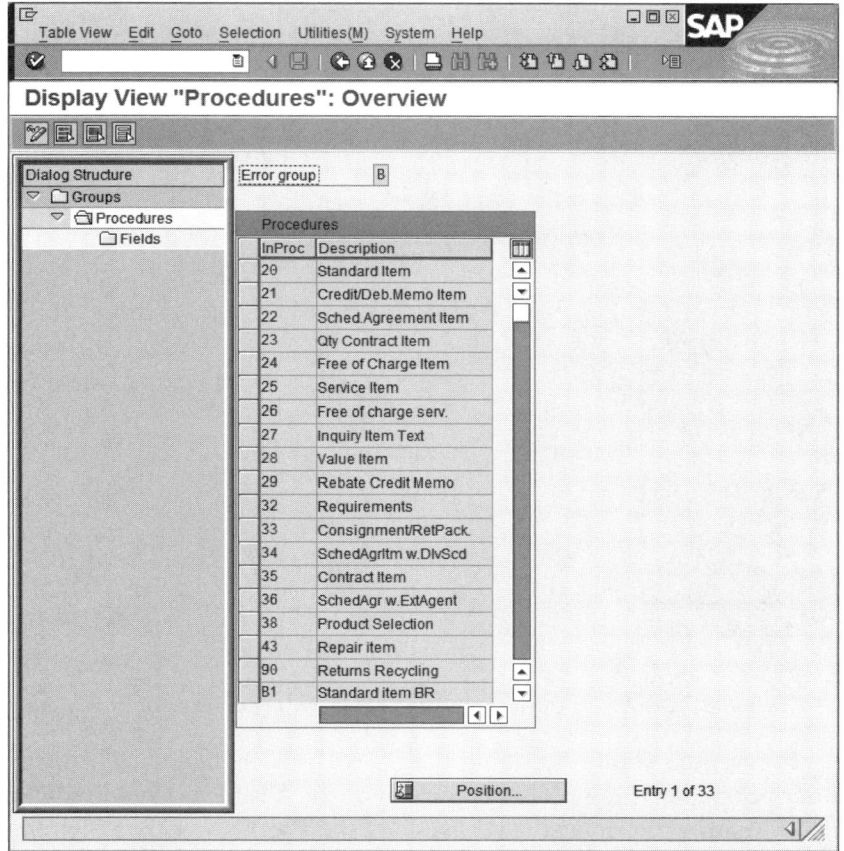

© SAP AG. All rights reserved.

FIGURE B.4 Displaying the procedures defined for a specific error group

Figure B.4 displays the procedures defined for the sales document items. To add or delete an entry in a procedure, you can create a copy of the existing procedure assigned to a particular error group. For example, in our case, we select the **21-Credit/Deb.Memo Item** procedure. Now, double-click the **Fields** folder (Figure B.4), and click the **Display>Change** icon ( ). The **Display View "Fields": Overview** screen appears, as shown in Figure B.5.

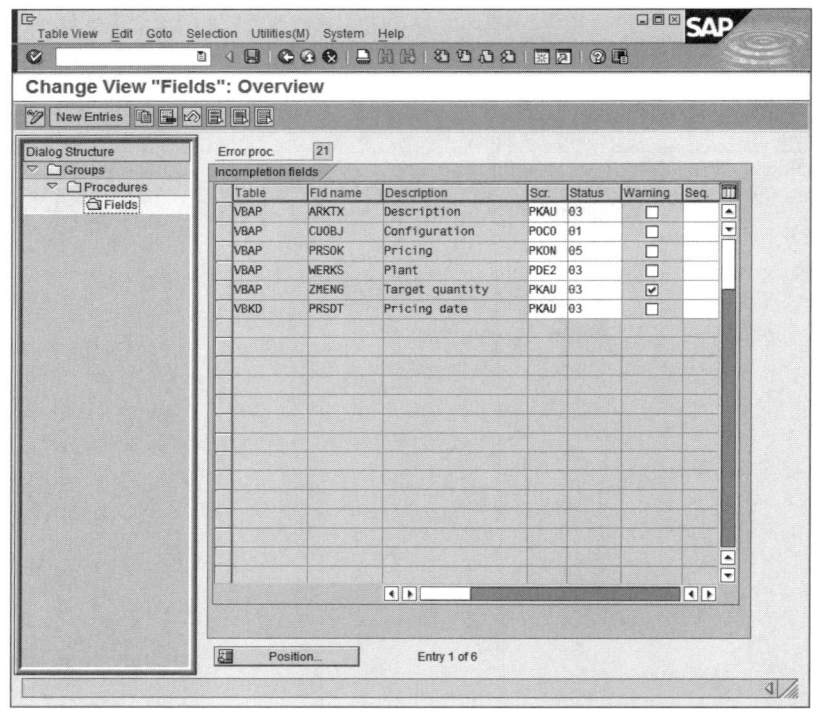

© SAP AG. All rights reserved.

FIGURE B.5 Displaying the incompletion fields for a specific error procedure

Figure B.5 shows the table names with the assigned field name and its description. For example, in Figure B.5, the **VBAP** table and **PRSOK** field names related to pricing data is assigned the **PKON** screen, which the mySAP ERP system uses to prompt the SAP® users for entering incomplete data. To define a new incompletion field, click the **New Entries** button (Figure B.5) and enter the relevant details, such as **Table, Fld name, Description**, and assigned **Scr**. After entering the relevant details, click the **Save** icon ( ) on the standard toolbar to save the entered data.

Let's now explore the **Assign Incompleteness Procedures** activity.

Assign Incompleteness Procedures

Now, to implement the defined procedure, you must assign it to multiple incompleteness objects, such as sales document types, item categories, and schedule line categories. Assigning incompleteness procedures to incompleteness objects ensures that incomplete data are provided to the multiple incompleteness objects. The **Assign Incompleteness Procedures** activity allows you to assign procedures to multiple incompleteness objects. To assign incompleteness procedures, navigate the following menu path:

Menu Path

SAP Customizing Implementation Guide > Sales and Distribution > Basic Functions > Log of Incomplete Items > Assign Incompleteness Procedures

After navigating the preceding menu path, click the **IMG Activity** icon (⊕) beside the **Assign Incompleteness Procedures** activity (Figure B.1). The **Choose Activity** dialog box appears as shown in Figure B.6.

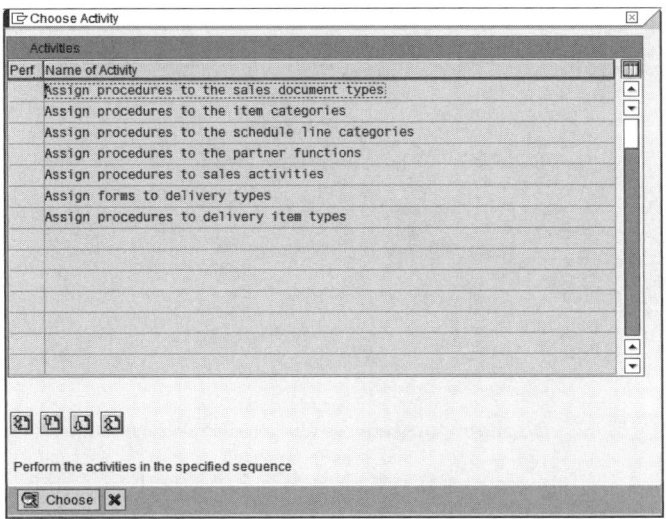

© SAP AG. All rights reserved.

FIGURE B.6 Displaying the Choose Activity dialog box for assigning procedures

Figure B.6 shows the various activities to assign an incompletion procedure. In our case, we chose the **Assign procedures to the sales document types** activity by double-clicking the activity. The **Change View "Error Logs for Sales Document Header": Overview** screen appears as shown in Figure B.7.

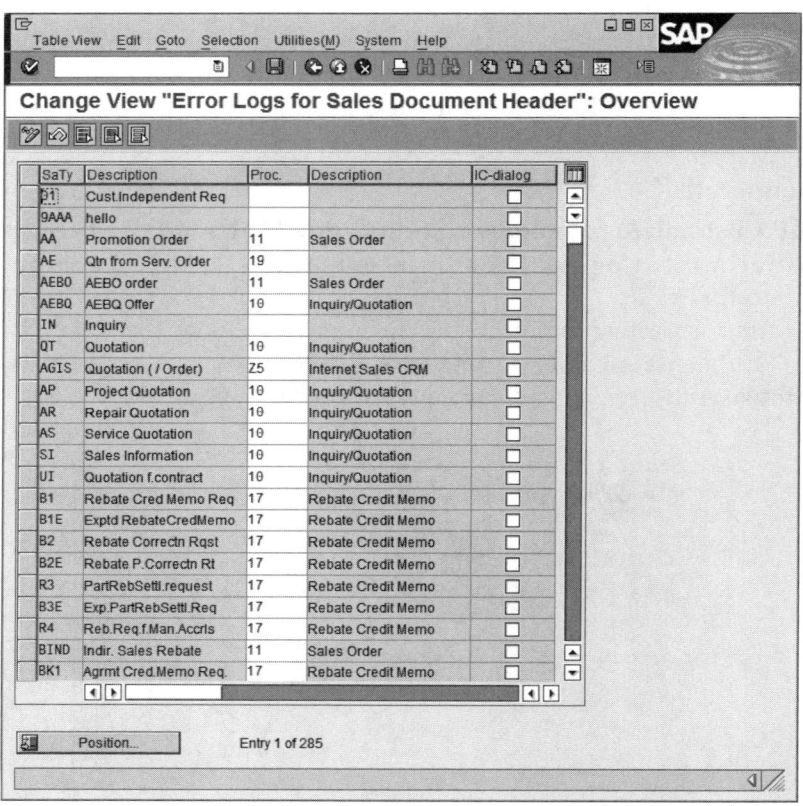

© SAP AG. All rights reserved.

FIGURE B.7 Displaying procedures assigned to sales document types

Figure B.7 shows the **IC-dialog** check box, which indicates whether the mySAP ERP system would allow you to save an incomplete document. You can specify the procedure in the **Proc.** column for a specific sales document type and then click the **Save** icon (🖫) on the standard toolbar to save the changes made.

After discussing how to implement sales incompletion logs, let's now discuss the concept of partner determination.

> **Note:** This section has discussed how to assign the incompletion procedures to a sales document. Similarly, you can assign procedures to either of the following:
>
> - Item categories
> - Schedule line categories
> - Partner functions
> - Sales activities
> - Delivery types
> - Delivery item types

SETTING UP PARTNER DETERMINATION IN THE SD MODULE

The mySAP ERP system provides various standard partner functions, such as sold-to party, bill-to party, and payer-to party. Moreover, the sales employee associated with that particular customer may also be considered for definition as partner in the partner function of customer master. The process of automatically determining these partner functions, while creating various documents, is known as partner determination. Although the mySAP ERP system provides automatic partner determination for some documents, we can also set up partner determination for various other documents, such as customer master and sales document header.

The process of automatic partner determination occurs based on various rules that we define while defining partner determination. Navigate the following menu path to set up partner determination:

Menu Path

SAP Customizing Implementation Guide > Sales and Distribution > Basic Functions > Partner Determination > Set up Partner Determination, as shown in Figure B.8.

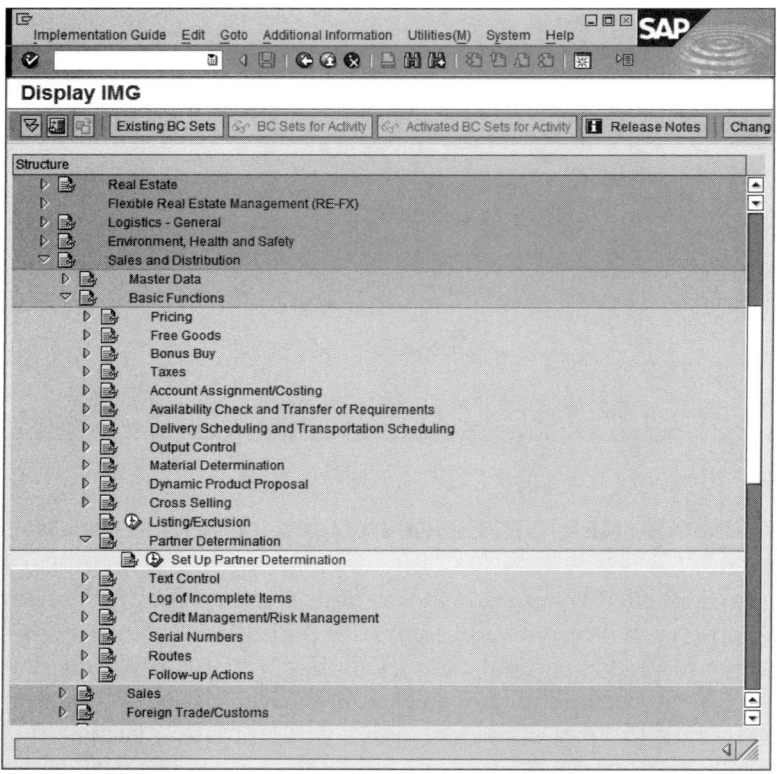

© SAP AG. All rights reserved.

FIGURE B.8 Displaying the menu path to set up partner determination

After navigating the preceding menu path, click the **IMG Activity** icon (⊕) beside the **Set Up Partner Determination** for customer master activity. The **Choose Activity** dialog box appears as shown in Figure B.9.

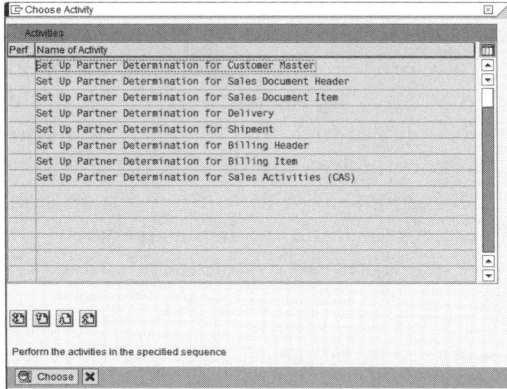

© SAP AG. All rights reserved.

FIGURE B.9 Displaying the Choose Activity dialog box to set up partner determination

Figure B.9 shows the various activities used to set up partner determination. The **Set Up Partner Determination for Customer Master** activity allows you to configure partner determination for the customer master. When you double-click this activity, the **Change View Partner Determination Procedures": Overview** screen appears as shown in Figure B.10.

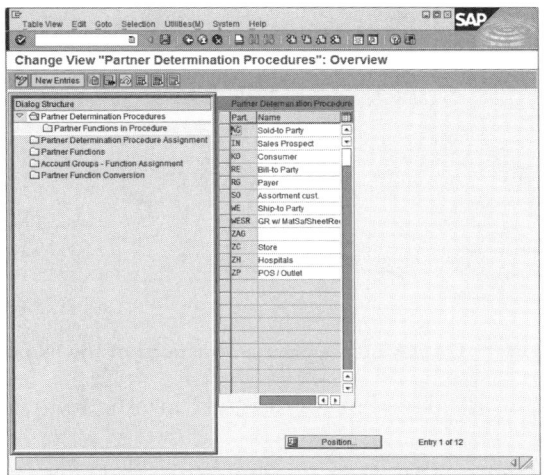

© SAP AG. All rights reserved.

FIGURE B.10 Displaying the existing partner determination procedures

Figure B.10 shows the list of already defined partner determination procedures. You can also define a new partner determination procedure by either creating a new procedure or by copying and modifying an existing one. To create a new procedure, you need to click the **New Entries** button and enter the relevant details in order to define the partner determination procedure.

To display the partner functions defined for a procedure, we first select the **IN** partner determination procedure and then double-click the **Partner Functions in Procedures** folder to display its partner functions. The **Change View "Partner Functions in Procedure": Overview** screen appears as shown in Figure B.11.

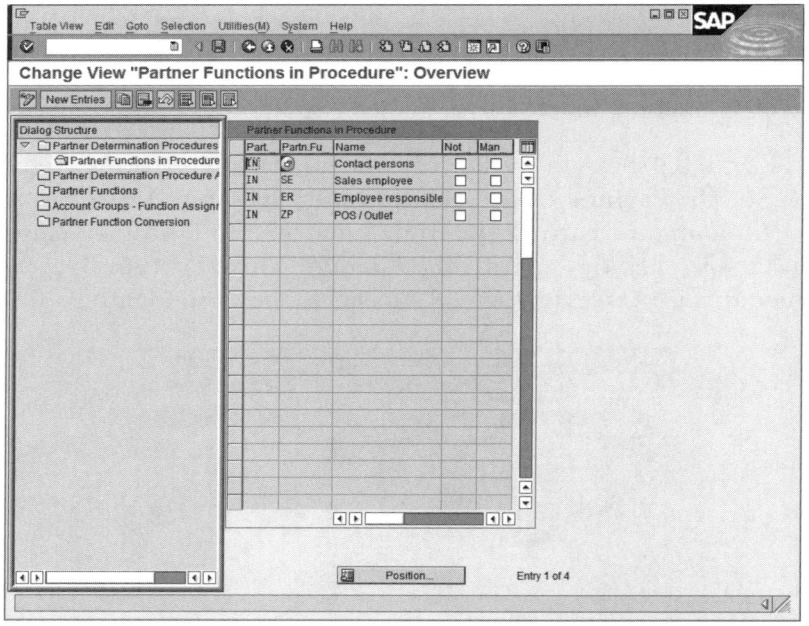

© SAP AG. All rights reserved.

FIGURE B.11 Displaying the partner functions of the IN procedure

The columns displayed in Figure B.11 are the following:

- **Partner Determination Procedure**—Specifies the partner determination procedure for which the partner functions are defined. In our example, we have selected the **IN** partner determination procedure.

- **Partner Function**—Specifies the partner function assigned to the **IN** partner determination procedure.
- **Name**—Specifies the name of the partner functions.
- **Not Mandatory**—Indicates that a partner cannot be changed after it is defined.
- **Mandatory**—Indicates whether the partner function is mandatory in a specific partner object.

You can define a partner determination procedure and partner functions by clicking the **New Entries** button shown in Figure B.11. Then, enter the relevant details and click the **Save** icon (■) on the standard toolbar to save the entered data. Apart from defining the procedures, you can also view the list of existing partner determination procedures assigned to various groups. To display the assignment of partner determination procedures, double-click the **Partner Determination Procedure Assignment** folder (Figure B.11). The **Change View "Partner Determination Procedure Assignment": Overview** screen appears as shown in Figure B.12.

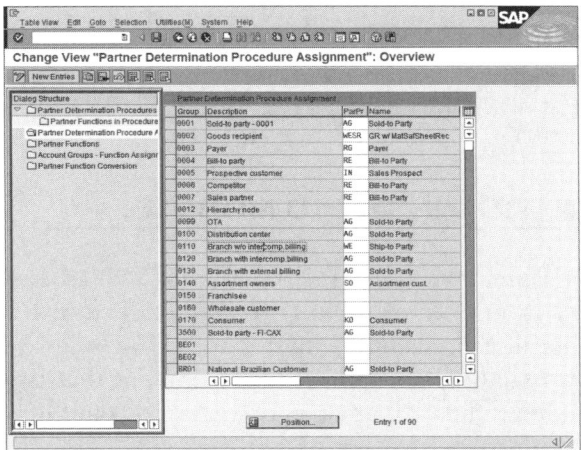

© SAP AG. All rights reserved.

FIGURE B.12 **Displaying the partner determination procedure assignment**

Figure B.12 shows the assignment of various partner determination procedures to the associated groups. For example, the AG partner determination procedure is assigned to the **0001** group. When the customer master record associated with the **0001** group is displayed, the AG partner determination procedure assigned to it is invoked. Then, the list of partners associated with the AG partner determination procedure is displayed automatically.

> **Note:** This section has explained how to set up a partner determination for the customer master. Similarly, you can set up a partner determination for any of the following:
>
> - Sales Document Header
> - Sales Document Item
> - Delivery
> - Shipment
> - Billing Header
> - Billing Item
> - Sales Activities (CAS)

After discussing the setup of partner determination procedures, let's explore the concept of text determination.

TEXT DETERMINATION IN THE SD MODULE

The text determination process allows the mySAP ERP system to copy data automatically from one text object to another. The text object refers to the sales text data in the customer master record or sales document header. It defines what exactly is needed on the document that is sent to a customer. Figure B.13 shows the various types of text objects in the SD module used for text determination.

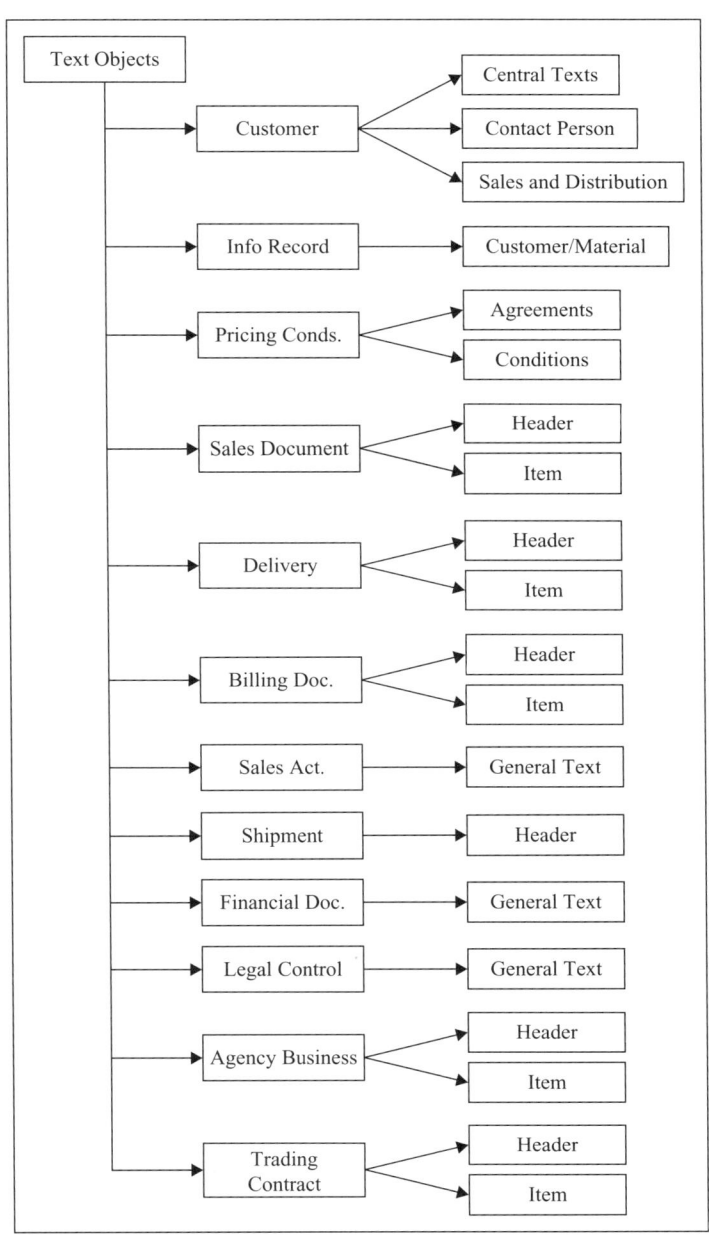

FIGURE B.13 Displaying various text objects in the SD module

Figure B.13 shows various types of text objects in the SD module that are used to configure text determination. Navigate the following menu path to configure the text determination:

Menu Path

SAP Customizing Implementation Guide > Sales and Distribution > Basic Functions > Text Control, as shown in Figure B.14.

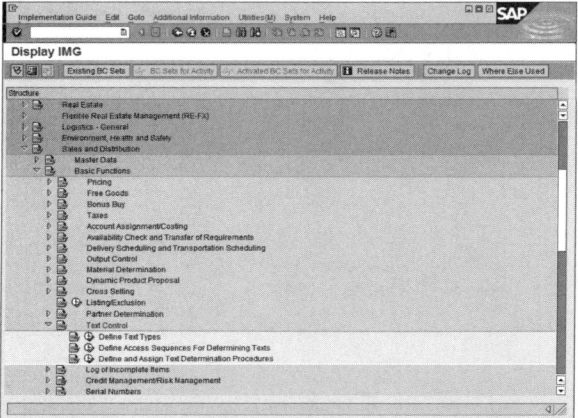

© SAP AG. All rights reserved.

FIGURE B.14 Displaying the menu path for text determination

Figure B.14 shows the activities associated with text control. Let's explore the following activities in detail to control the text in the SAP system:

- Define Text Types
- Define Access Sequences For Determining Texts

Define Text Types

For text determination, you need to define the procedures by specifying the text types. You can define text types for every text object by providing relevant information, such as key, description, and text name of the text type. This text type passes on the information to appear on the document. To define text types, navigate the following menu path (Figure B.14):

Menu Path

SAP Customizing Implementation Guide > Sales and Distribution > Basic Functions > Text Control > Define Text Types

After navigating the preceding menu path, click the **IMG Activity** icon (🔘) beside the **Define Text Types** activity. The **Customizing Text Determination** screen appears as shown in Figure B.15.

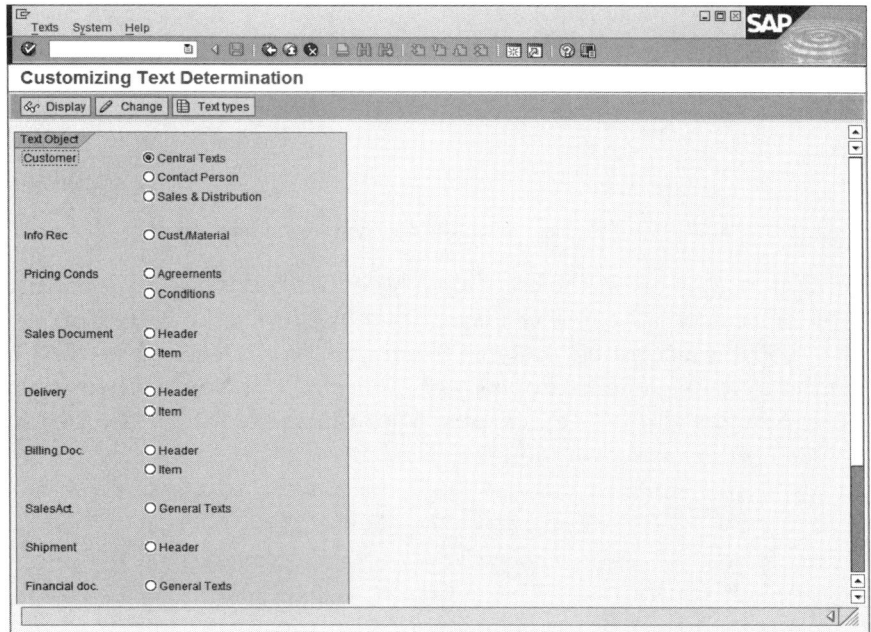

© SAP AG. All rights reserved.

FIGURE B.15 Displaying the Customizing Text Determination screen

Select the appropriate text object and then click the **Text types** button to modify the text object. In our example, we selected the **Sales & Distribution** option within the **Customer** text object. The **Change View "Text Types: Maintain Text ID for TxtObj KNVV": Overview** screen appears as shown in Figure B.16.

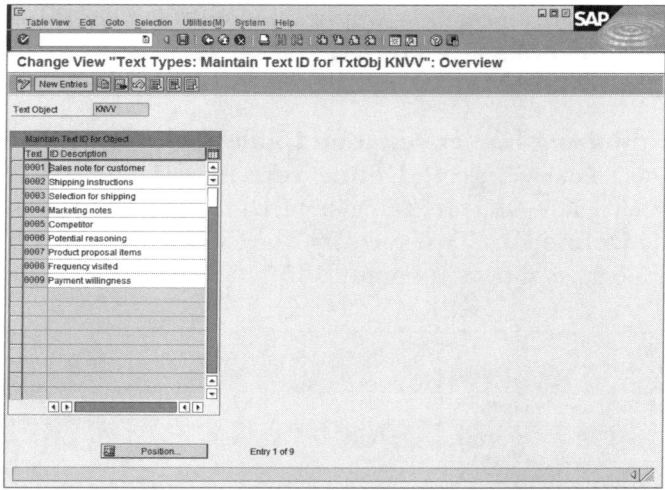

FIGURE B.16 Displaying the text types for a text object

Figure B.16 shows the list of already defined text types. To define a new text type, you can create a new text type either by clicking the **New Entries** button or by copying an existing text type. In our example, we clicked the **New Entries** button to define a new text type. After clicking the **New Entries** button, the **New Entries (View "Text Types: Maintain Text ID for TxtObj KNVV")** screen appears as shown in Figure B.17.

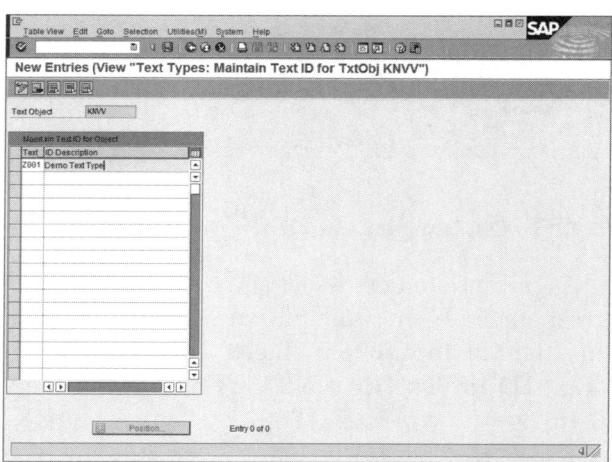

FIGURE B.17 Displaying the details entered to define a text type

Text Determination in the SD Module 583

After entering the text type name and its description, click the **Save** icon (🖫) on the standard toolbar to save the entered data.

Let's now learn how to define access sequence for text determination.

Define Access Sequences For Determining Texts

After defining the text types, you need to define the access sequences for text procedures that help in performing text determination as the whole process is driven through the condition technique. The **Define Access Sequences for Determining Texts** activity allows you to define the access sequence for text determination. Navigate the following menu path to perform the **Define Access Sequences for Determining Texts** activity (Figure B.14):

Menu Path

SAP Customizing Implementation Guide > Sales and Distribution > Basic Functions > Text Control > Define Access Sequence For Determining Texts

After navigating the preceding menu path, click the **IMG Activity** icon (⊕) beside the **Define Access Sequence For Determining Texts** activity. The **Customizing Text Determination** screen appears (Figure B.15). Select the **Sales & Distribution** option within the **Customer** text object and click the **Change** button. The **Change View "TxtDetProc Customer SD": Overview** screen appears as shown in Figure B.18.

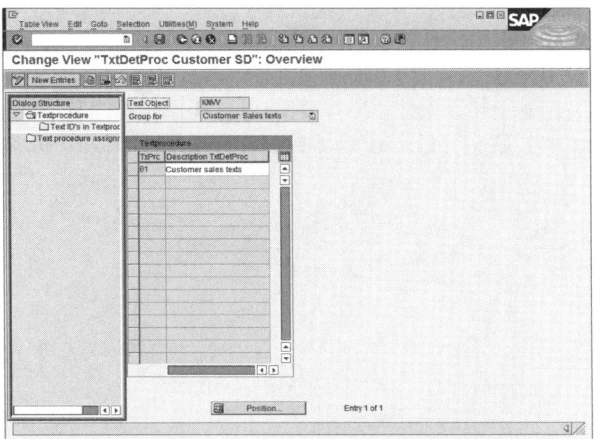

© SAP AG. All rights reserved.

FIGURE B.18 Displaying the text procedures associated with a text object

Select the text procedure **01** and double-click the **Text ID's in Textprocedure** folder. The **Change View "Customer SD Text IDs in Txt Det. Proc 01": Overview** screen appears as shown in Figure B.19.

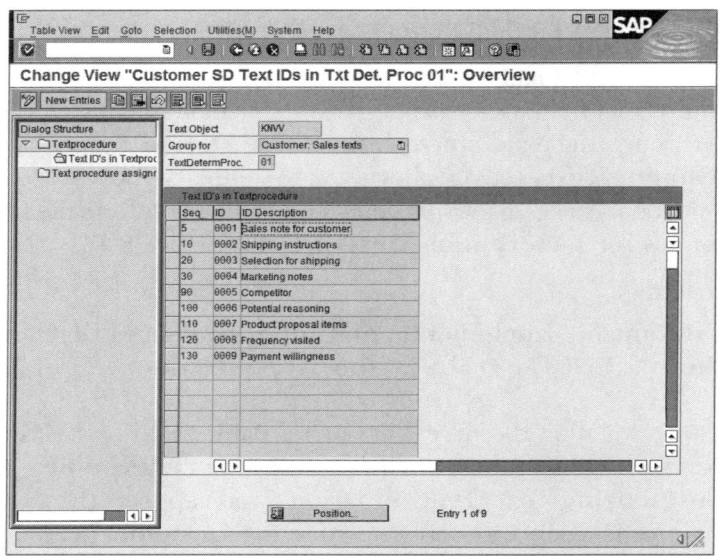

© SAP AG. All rights reserved.

FIGURE B.19 Displaying the access sequence for various text IDs

Figure B.19 shows the access sequence specified for various text IDs. For example, the **0001** text ID is assigned to the **5** access sequence. To define an access sequence, click the **New Entries** button. The **New Entries (View "Customer SD Text IDs in Txt Det. Proc 01")** screen appears as shown in Figure B.20.

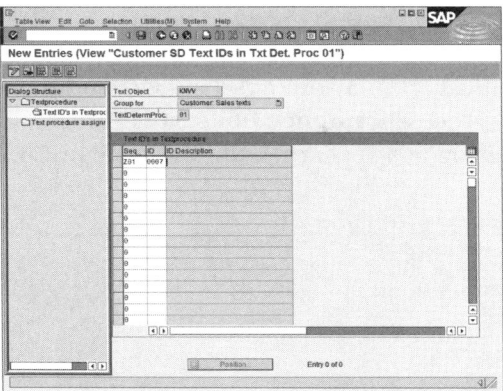

FIGURE B.20 Displaying the details entered for a text ID

Figure B.20 shows the details for a new text ID. Now, select the **Header** option within the **Sales Document** text object and click the **Change** button to display the access sequence for text determination (Figure B.15). The **Change View "TextDetProc Sales Doc. Header": Overview** screen appears as shown in Figure B.21.

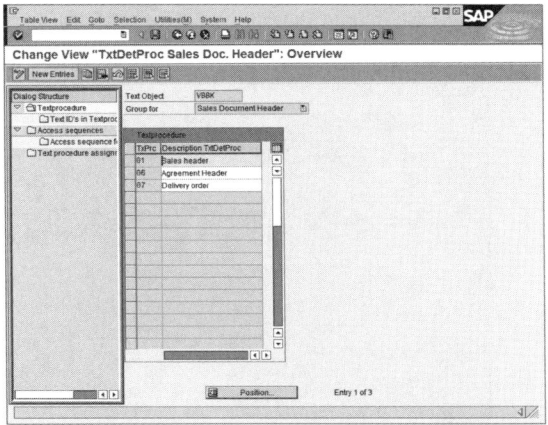

FIGURE B.21 Displaying text procedures for a sales document header

To display the access sequence defined for a text procedure, you need to select a text procedure and then click the **Access sequence for Text ID's** folder (Figure B.21). In our example, we selected the **01** text procedure and then clicked the **Access sequence for Text ID's** folder. The **Determine Work Area: Entry** dialog box appears, as shown in Figure B.22.

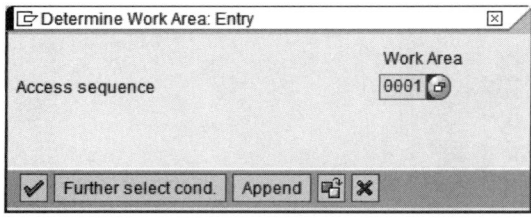

© SAP AG. All rights reserved.

FIGURE B.22 Displaying the Determine Work Area: Entry dialog box

Figure B.22 shows that we have entered the **0001** work area. Now click the **Continue** icon ( ); the **Change View "Sales Doc. Header Access Sequence 0001": Overview** screen appears as shown in Figure B.23.

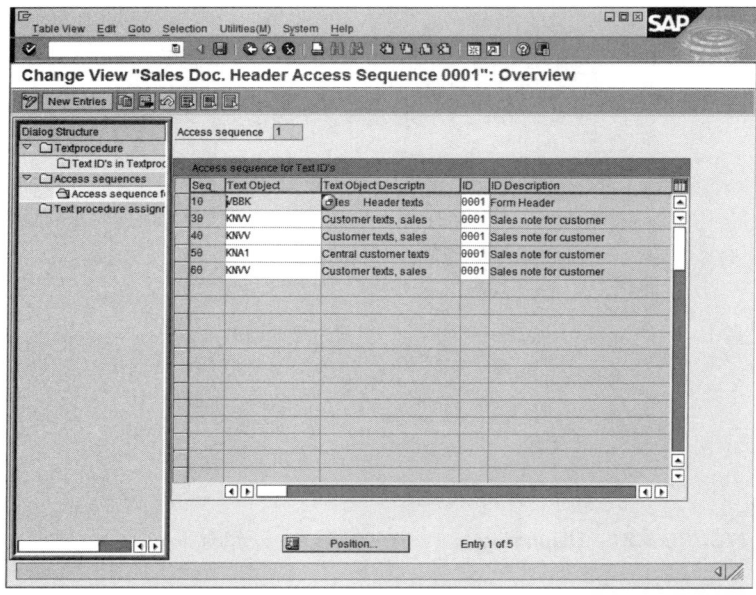

© SAP AG. All rights reserved.

FIGURE B.23 Displaying the access sequences for a sales document header

You can define a new access sequence for a sales document header by clicking the **New Entries** button and entering the relevant details. After entering the details, click the **Save** icon (🖫) on the standard toolbar.

Let's now move ahead to discuss output determination.

OUTPUT DETERMINATION IN THE SD MODULE

The concept of output determination helps the mySAP ERP system to select and process the output from every sales transaction on the basis of a specified condition. The two techniques, output determination from the customer master record and output determination using condition, are used to control output determination for each output proposal. To implement output determination, navigate the following menu path:

Menu Path

SAP Customizing Implementation Guide > Sales and Distribution > Basic Functions > Output Control > Output Determination, as shown in Figure B.24.

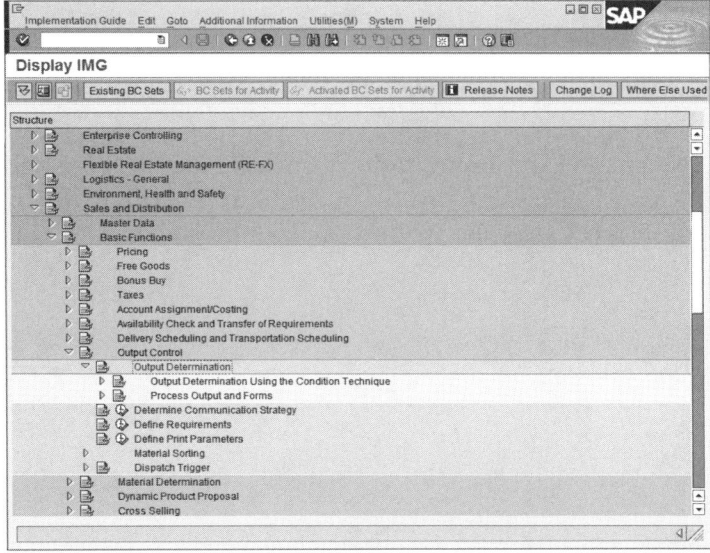

© SAP AG. All rights reserved.

FIGURE B.24 Displaying the menu path for output determination

Figure B.24 shows the following two tasks to be performed for output determination:

- Output Determination Using the Condition Technique
- Process Output and Forms

Let's now discuss each of them in detail.

Output Determination Using the Condition Technique

The concept of determining output based on a criteria or condition is known as output determination using the condition technique. Output is the document or communication that is given to a customer such as quotations and billing document. The condition technique allows you to process output separately for every recipient. In the mySAP ERP system, you can implement the output determination process for the following:

- Sales Activities
- Sales Documents
- Billing Documents

To implement the output determination process for these activities and documents, you need to navigate the following menu path:

Menu Path

SAP Customizing Implementation Guide > Sales and Distribution > Basic Functions > Output Control > Output Determination > Output Determination Using the Condition Technique, as shown in Figure B.25.

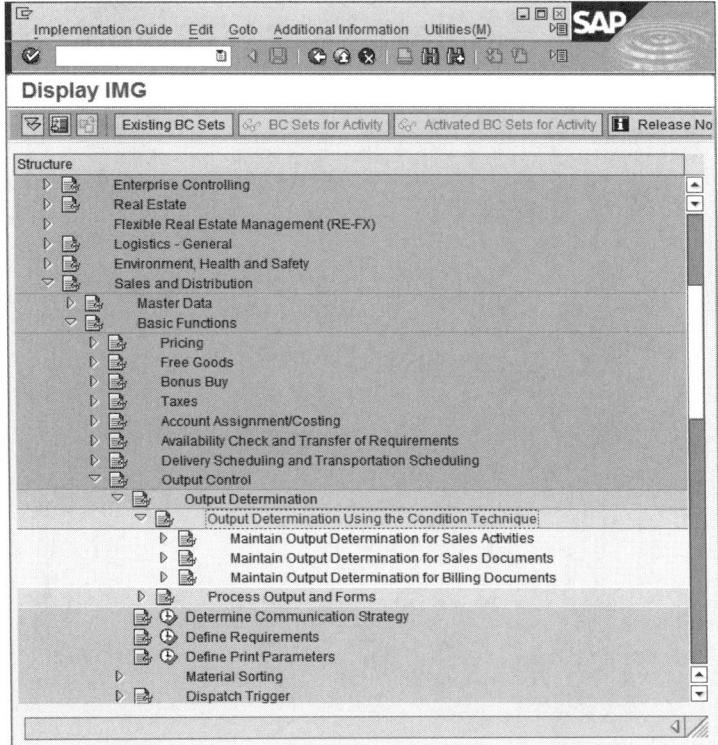

FIGURE B.25 Displaying the menu path for Output Determination Using the Condition Technique

Let's discuss how to implement the output determination process for sales documents in detail. For this, navigate the following menu path:

Menu Path

SAP Customizing Implementation Guide > Sales and Distribution > Basic Functions > Output Control > Output Determination using the Condition Technique > Maintain Output Determination for Sales Documents, as shown in Figure B.26.

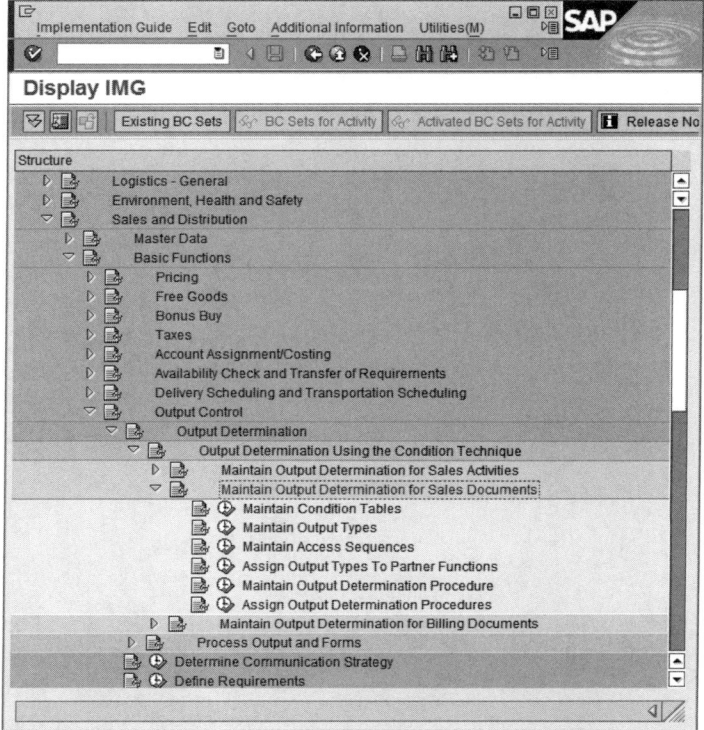

© SAP AG. All rights reserved.

FIGURE B.26 Displaying the menu path for Maintain Output Determination for Sales Documents

Figure B.26 shows the list of activities that you need to perform to maintain output determination for sales documents. Let's discuss each of these activities in detail.

Maintain Condition Tables

The **Maintain Condition Tables** activity allows you to define the condition tables for sales documents and helps define the condition fields to create output condition records. To maintain condition tables, navigate the following menu path (Figure B.26):

Menu Path

SAP Customizing Implementation Guide > Sales and Distribution > Basic Functions > Output Control > Output Determination > Output Determination using the Condition Technique > Maintain Output Determination for Sales Documents > Maintain Condition Tables

After navigating the preceding menu path, click the **IMG Activity** icon (⊕) beside the **Maintain Condition Tables** activity. The **Choose Activity** dialog box appears as shown in Figure B.27.

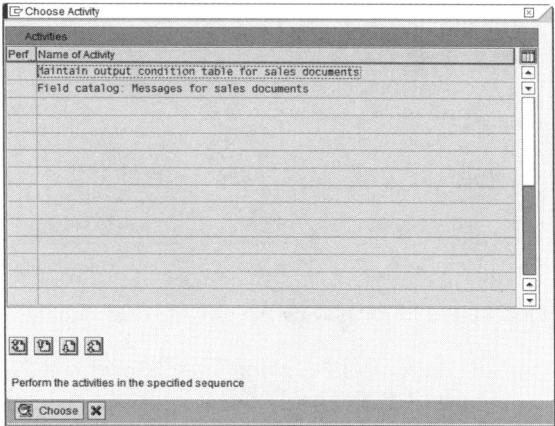

© SAP AG. All rights reserved.

FIGURE B.27 Displaying the Choose Activity dialog box

The **Maintain output condition table for sales documents** activity shown in Figure B.27 allows you to maintain condition tables for sales documents. The **Field catalog: Messages for sales documents** activity allows you to place fields into the field catalog. Select the appropriate activity according to the task you want to perform. In our example, we selected the **Field catalog: Messages for sales documents** activity and then clicked the **Choose** button. The **Change View "Field Catalog (Output Sales)": Overview** screen appears as shown in Figure B.28.

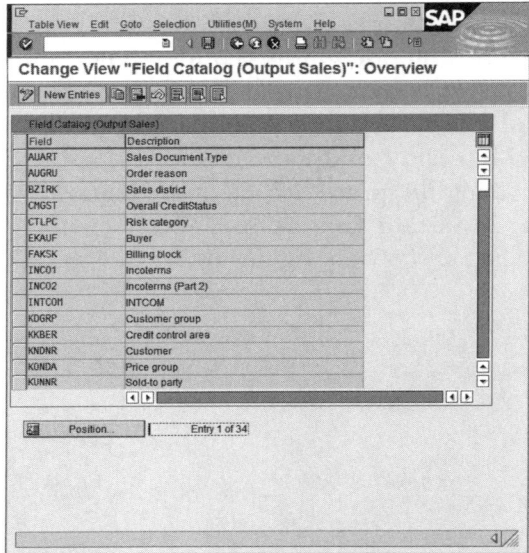

© SAP AG. All rights reserved.

FIGURE B.28 Displaying the existing field catalogs

You can define a new field catalog by clicking the **New Entries** button, entering the relevant details, and saving the entered data. Moreover, you can also modify the existing field catalog by selecting it and clicking the **Change > Display** icon ( ). After clicking the **Change > Display** icon ( ), modify the details and then click the **Save** icon ( ) on the standard toolbar to save the entered data.

After defining a field catalog, let's move ahead to discuss the next activity, **Maintain Output Types**.

Maintain Output Types

The **Maintain Output Types** activity allows you to maintain output types, such as quotations and order confirmations, for various output type records. It is similar to that of maintaining condition types in the pricing procedure. To maintain output types, navigate the following menu path (Figure B.26):

Menu Path

SAP Customizing Implementation Guide > Sales and Distribution > Basic Functions > Output Control > Output Determination > Output Determination using the Condition Technique > Maintain Output Determination for Sales Documents > Maintain Output Types

After navigating the preceding menu path, click the **IMG Activity** icon (🔵) beside the **Maintain Output Types** activity. The **Display View "Output Types": Overview** screen appears as shown in Figure B.29.

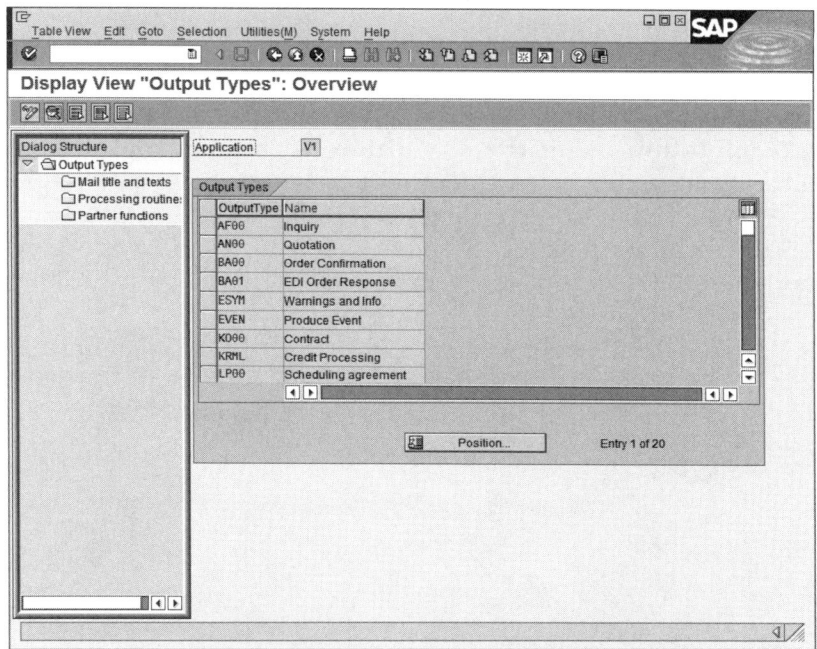

© SAP AG. All rights reserved.

FIGURE B.29 Displaying the existing output types

Figure B.29 shows the list of already defined output types. You can also view their details, such as partner functions, by double-clicking the appropriate folder under the **Output Types** folder. Moreover, you can also modify the output types by selecting it and clicking the **Change-->Display** icon (📝). After clicking the **Change>Display** icon (📝), modify the details and then click the **Save** icon (💾) on the standard toolbar to save the entered data.

Let's now discuss how to maintain access sequence for output determination.

Maintain Access Sequences

The **Maintain Access Sequences** activity allows you to define access sequences to search conditional records for a specified condition type. To maintain access sequences, navigate the following menu path:

Menu Path

SAP Customizing Implementation Guide > Sales and Distribution > Basic Functions > Output Control > Output Determination > Output Determination using the Condition Technique > Maintain Output Determination for Sales Documents > Maintain Access Sequences

After navigating the preceding menu path, click the **IMG Activity** icon (🔧) beside the **Maintain Access Sequences** activity. The **Change View "Access Sequences": Overview** screen appears, as shown in Figure B.30.

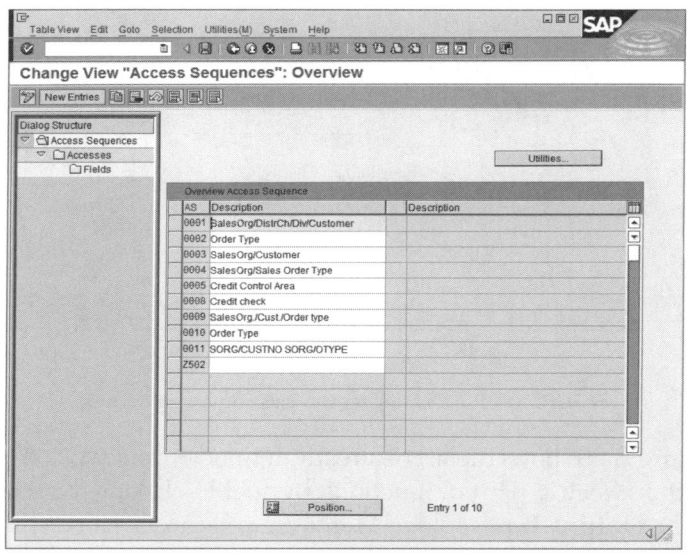

© SAP AG. All rights reserved.

FIGURE B.30 Displaying the existing access sequences defined for output determination

You can define the new access sequence for output determination by clicking the **New Entries** button, entering relevant details, and then saving the entered data. Moreover, you can also maintain the already defined access sequences for output determination by selecting an access sequence and then clicking the appropriate folder to display and modify the relevant details of that access sequence.

After discussing how to define and maintain access sequences for output determination, let's now discuss how to assign the defined output types to partner functions.

Assign Output Types to Partner Functions

The **Assign Output Types To Partner Functions** activity allows you to assign the output types defined in the **Define Output Types** activity to the various partner functions. To assign an output type to a partner function, navigate the following menu path (Figure B.26):

Menu Path

SAP Customizing Implementation Guide>Sales and Distribution > Basic Functions > Output Control > Output Determination > Output Determination using the Condition Technique > Maintain Output Determination for Sales Documents > Assign Output Types To Partner Functions

After navigating the preceding menu path, click the **IMG Activity** icon () beside the **Assign Output Types To Partner Functions** activity. The **Change View "Output Control: Output By Partner Function": Overview** screen appears as shown in Figure B.31.

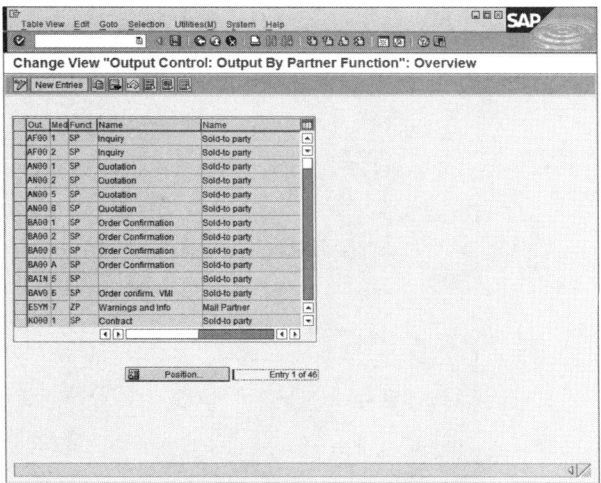

© SAP AG. All rights reserved.

FIGURE B.31 Displaying existing output types assigned to partner functions

Figure B.31 displays the list of output types that have been assigned to various partner functions; for example, the **AF00** output type is assigned to the

SP partner function. To assign a new output type to a function, click the **New Entries** button and enter the required details, such as the name of the output type and partner function. Then click the **Save** icon (🖫) on the standard toolbar to save the relevant details.

Let's now discuss the process of maintaining output determination procedures.

Maintain Output Determination Procedure

The **Maintain Output Determination Procedure** activity allows you to define output determination procedures for various sales documents. Then this procedure is assigned to a document type. To a define an output determination procedure, navigate the following menu path (Figure B.26):

Menu Path

SAP Customizing Implementation Guide > Sales and Distribution > Basic Functions > Output Control > Output Determination > Output Determination using the Condition Technique > Maintain Output Determination for Sales Documents > Maintain Output Determination Procedure

After navigating the preceding menu path, click the **IMG Activity** icon (⊕) beside the **Maintain Output Determination Procedure** activity. The **Change View "Procedures": Overview** screen appears, as shown in Figure B.32.

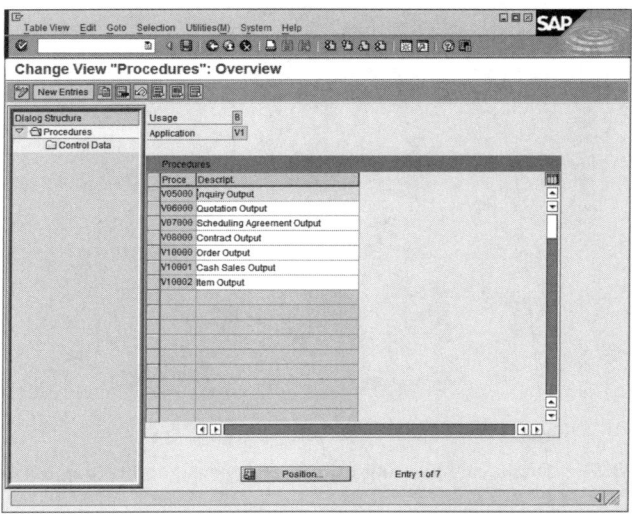

© SAP AG. All rights reserved.

FIGURE B.32 Displaying the procedures defined for output determination

Figure B.32 shows the list of already defined procedures used for output determination. To define a new output determination procedure, click the **New Entries** button (Figure B.32). The **New Entries: Overview of Added Entries** screen appears as shown in Figure B.33.

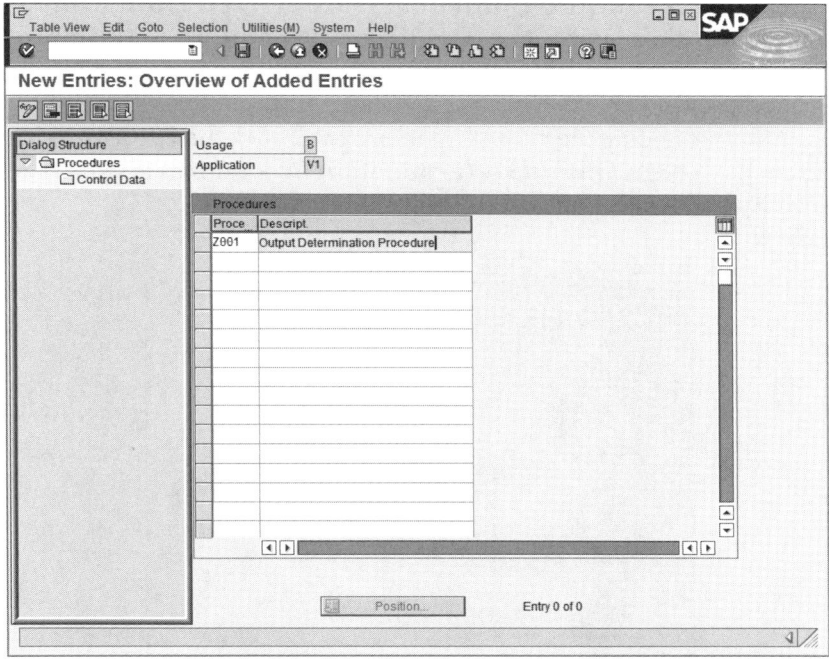

© SAP AG. All rights reserved.

FIGURE B.33 Displaying details entered for a new output determination procedure

After entering the details for an output determination procedure, click the **Save** icon (🖫) on the standard toolbar to save the entered details. Now, you can assign the defined procedure to a sales document header or sales document item, which are discussed in the next section.

Assign Output Determination Procedures

The **Assign Output Determination Procedures** activity assigns an output determination procedure to either a sales document header or a sales document item. You also need to specify an output type to be displayed when the associated document is either displayed or modified. To assign an output determination procedure, navigate the following menu path (Figure B.26):

Menu Path

SAP Customizing Implementation Guide > Sales and Distribution > Basic Functions > Output Control > Output Determination > Output Determination using the Condition Technique > Maintain Output Determination for Sales Documents > Assign Output Determination Procedures

After navigating the preceding menu path, click the **IMG Activity** icon ( ) beside the **Assign Output Determination Procedures** activity. The **Choose Activity** dialog box appears, as shown in Figure B.34.

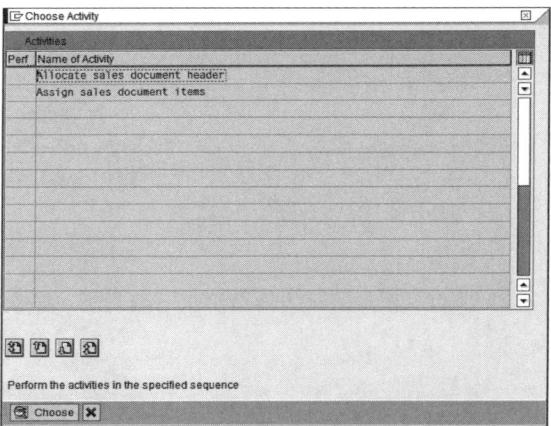

© SAP AG. All rights reserved.

FIGURE B.34 Displaying the activities to assign output determination procedures

Figure B.34 shows the following two activities:

- **Allocate sales document header**—Assigns a sales document header to an output determination procedure.
- **Assign sales document items**—Assigns a sales document item to an output determination procedure.

Depending upon the task you want to perform, you can select either of these activities and click the **Choose** button. In our case, we selected the **Allocate**

sales document header activity and click the **Choose** button. The **Change View "Sales Document Types - Output Assignment": Overview** screen appears as shown in Figure B.35.

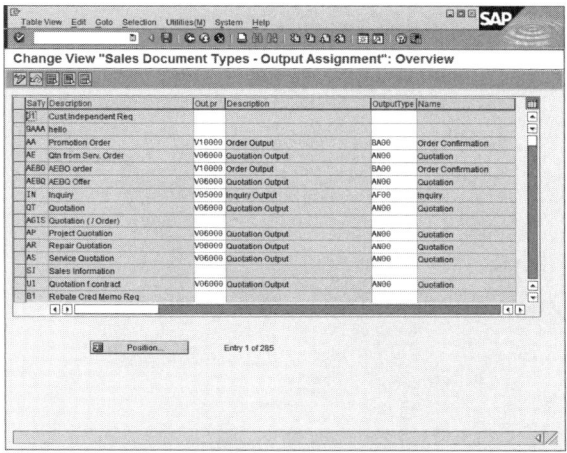

© SAP AG. All rights reserved.

FIGURE B.35 Displaying the existing procedures assigned to a sales document header

Figure B.35 shows the existing defined procedures assigned to various sales documents. You can specify the output determination procedure in the **Out.pr** column for a sales document header and then click the **Save** icon ( ) on the standard toolbar to save the modified details.

Let's now explore how to define the layout of output documents in the next section.

Process Output and Forms

In this section, we discuss how to define the layout of an output document; for example, the text that should be displayed and text position in an output document. The layout of an output document is defined in a form. To process output and define forms, navigate the following menu path:

Menu Path

SAP Customizing Implementation Guide > Sales and Distribution > Basic Functions > Output Control > Output Determination > Process Output and Forms, as shown in Figure B.36.

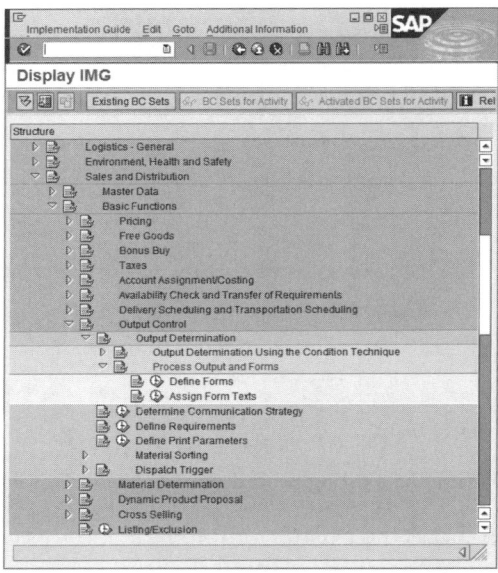

© SAP AG. All rights reserved.

FIGURE B.36 Displaying the menu path to process output and define forms

Figure B.36 shows the activities you need to perform to process output and define the layout for an output document. In this section, we discuss how to define layouts in a form.

The **Define Forms** activity allows you to define forms that specify the layout of an output document. To create a new form, you need to navigate the following menu path (Figure B.36):

Menu Path

SAP Customizing Implementation Guide > Sales and Distribution > Basic Functions > Output Control > Output Determination > Process Output and Forms > Define Forms

After navigating the preceding menu path, click the **IMG Activity** icon (☻) beside the **Define Forms** activity. The **Form Painter: Request** screen appears as shown in Figure B.37.

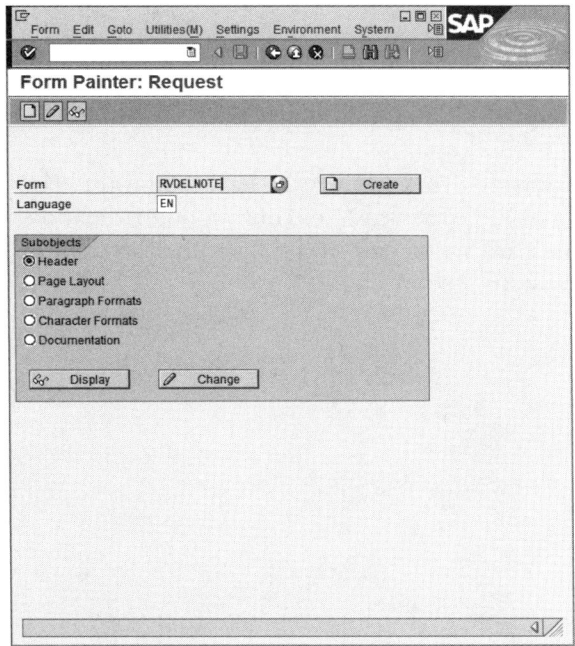

© SAP AG. All rights reserved.

FIGURE B.37   Displaying the Form Painter: Request screen

In Figure B.37, the details of a new form from an SAP standard form are displayed. You can modify the relevant details of the new form according to your requirements. Figure B.37 shows the following subobjects:

- **Header**—Specifies the general information, such as user name and description with regard to form layout.
- **Pages**—Specifies the number of pages for the form layout.
- **Windows**—Provides windows, which is displayed as a separate section on a page in a form.

- **Page Windows**—Arranges the windows specified in the Windows subobject.
- **Paragraph Formats**—Provides paragraph styles for the form layout. For example, whether the paragraph should be right aligned or justified.
- **Character Formats**—Provides the style for a string of characters. For example, a word might need to be either bold or italic.

To summarize, this appendix has explained the concepts of sales incompletion logs, partner, text, and output determination. As discussed earlier, these processes are a vital part of the sales and distribution process and help to customize the SAP system.

Glossary

Access sequence
The creation and arrangement of condition records in a logical sequence.

Automatic credit management
A process that helps the mySAP™ ERP system to automatically determine the action to be taken for a customer who has reached the credit limit.

Availability To Promise (ATP)
It serves as the basis for availability check in which the mySAP ERP system automatically evaluates the available quantity to promise or commit to a sales document.

Backorder processing
The processing of a sales order that has either not been fully confirmed or has not been confirmed at a specific date.

Billing
The process of creating a legal document that contains the details of quantity, price, discounts, and taxes for the materials sold or services rendered to a customer.

Billing plan
A plan that contains a list of dates according to which the mySAP ERP system generates billing request items. After generating billing request items, the mySAP ERP system also creates a billing document based on each billing request item. Note that if a billing plan is defined at the header level of a sales document, the billing plan is valid for all the items that are assigned to it.

Cancellation invoice
An invoice that is created after billing document is found to have errors and needs to be cancelled or recreated.

Catalog profile
A combination of code groups ensuring that a correct technical object is used to resolve a customer's problem.

Collective requirements
A group of requirements created over a certain period of time, such as daily, weekly, or monthly, that are transferred to the MRP department.

Collective shipment
A shipment having one or more departure and destination points.

Condition master data
Data determined based on the business logic or configuration settings.

Configuration data
Configuration data in the mySAP ERP system are linked to the application processing logic and are stored in configuration tables.

Consignment fill-up
When the stock ordered by a customer is delivered to the customer on the basis of the order placed.

Consignment stock process
A special process that is used to place the stock or material reserved for a customer at the customer's or organization's end.

Controlling (CO) module
The CO module is designed for planning, reporting, and monitoring business operations in an organization.

Copying control
A process in which some important transaction parameters are copied from an original document to a target document. It controls the flow of data from one document to another. For example, the copying control process is used to create a new billing document from an existing billing or sales document.

Credit management system
Allows the management of the customer's credit limit and credit period as specified in the customer master record.

Credit memo
A sales document that is created on the basis of customer's complaints, such as defective goods or overcharging of the goods or services by the vendor.

Customer master data
A collection of records related to a customer, sales area, and other transaction-related units.

Customer Services (CS) module
The CS module provides support for customer services; for example, customer support services for computers and equipment.

Debit memo
A sales document that is created because the customer is not charged enough by the vendor.

Decentralized warehouse management
The process of implementing the warehouse management system on another system instead of the mySAP ERP system.

Delivery block
A situation in which the ordered goods are blocked for delivery.

Delivery process
The process of delivering the product from a shipping point to the customer's destination. A product is said to be delivered when it finally reaches the customer's destination. The shipment process usually ends at a shipping point such as a harbor, post office, or local distribution office.

Delivery split
The process of splitting one consignment of delivery into multiple shipments.

Distribution channel
In SAP, a distribution channel specifies a medium to supply the products or services of an organization to the customers.

Division
An organizational unit in the SD module that is used to logically group products into separate categories.

Down payment
The partial payment of goods paid by a customer at the time of purchasing of goods. For example, a customer may purchase plant engineering and construction or capital goods on installment. The customer is required to pay a one-time initial amount at the time of purchasing the goods.

ERP system
In the term ERP, E stands for Enterprise, which includes an organization, firm, or company; R stands for Resource, which involves the four M's (i.e., man, machine, material, and money); and P stands for Planning, which means efficient use of the available resources.

Financial/Accounting (FI) module
The Financial/Accounting (FI) module is designed to handle the financial and accounting-related tasks of an organization. This module helps create and maintain financial records such as general ledger, accounts payable, and accounts receivable.

Human Capital Management (HCM) module
The HCM module is designed to plan and control personnel activities. This module is also known as the Human Resources (HR) module, which is responsible for performing the HR-related activities.

Individual shipment
A shipment that has a single departure and destination point is referred.

Individual transfer of requirements
A single transfer of demand that occurs in the MRP department for each schedule line.

InfoCube
A self-contained dataset, such as data related to customer, sales, or organizational data.

InfoObject
It contains attributes and characteristics of data used to generate reports in SAP® BW.

InfoProviders
Objects present in the SAP BW system. These objects are used to create and execute queries.

Installment payment
When a customer makes a payment in installments, it is known as an installment payment. Only one billing document is created for all of the installments. Then a printed invoice is created on the basis of the billing document, which includes a list of all the individual payment dates, the total amount to be paid by the customer, and the terms and conditions of the installment.

Investment (IM) module
The IM module is designed to manage various investment securities, such as shares and bonds, to meet the investment goals for the benefits of the investors of a company.

Logistics Execution (LE) module
The LE module is designed to implement the shipping and delivery activities of the SD module. This module works closely with the MM and SD modules.

Master contracts
In SAP, the quantity, service, or value contracts can be grouped under one main contract, known as the master contract.

Master data
Master data in the mySAP ERP system represents a business entity that consists of company code, cost centers, customer master accounts, and vendor master accounts.

Material Management (MM) module
The MM module is designed to procure and manage the material resources of a company. This module also handles the inventory functions, such as purchasing, inventory management, and re-order processing, which are performed as daily business operations.

Material master data
All the records related to the products/materials and services offered by the organization.

Milestone billing
A billing arrangement in which a customer is billed in installments spread over a specific period of time on the achievement of a predefined milestone for a work.

Notification type
A two-character alphanumeric key that represents the notification category and its origin.

Payment terms
The terms of payment that specify the conditions agreed to by a company and a customer for the payment of invoices.

Periodic billing
Billing of a good or service might be distributed over a period of time, where the customer has to pay a specific predefined amount at predefined periods or intervals.

Picking location
A place from where the goods ordered by a customer are picked up to be transported to another location.

Pricing procedure
A technique to determine the price of goods and services in the mySAP ERP system.

Pricing reports
ABAP/4 programs used in the SD module of SAP® to analyze condition records based on different criteria.

Pro forma invoice
An invoice that needs to be created when exporting goods. It contains the details regarding the quantity and cost of the goods. It is created on a paper and provided to the custom/governing authorities of the receiving country, so that they can verify the forthcoming shipment. A pro forma invoice is created on the basis of a sales order or a delivery.

Production Planning (PP) module
The PP module is designed to plan the production phase of a product, such as the type of the product and the quantity to be produced on the basis of demand.

Project System (PS) module
The PS module is designed to handle both small- and large-scale projects. For instance, it can handle large-scale projects such as building a factory, and small-scale projects such as organizing a schedule for recruitment.

Quality Management (QM) module
The QM module is designed to check and enhance the quality of products developed by a company.

QuickView
An elementary tool for generating reports simply by entering the data in the mySAP ERP system, instead of creating the SAP queries.

Rebate agreement
A rebate is a special discount given by a company to its customers retroactively; the agreement of a rebate between the company and the customer is called a rebate agreement. The special discount is based on the sales volume (or target) of the customer over a specific period of time, which is configured in the rebate agreement.

Rebates
Rebates are the amounts deducted from the price of goods and services on the basis of certain criteria.

Replenishment lead time
The time required to produce the required stock.

Returnable packaging process
A special type of packaging process in which the packing material used for packaging is returned by the customer after the delivery of goods.

Rounding difference
A technique used to round off a fraction number to the nearest integer.

Sales and Distribution (SD) module
The SD module is one of the logistics modules that helps manage the sales and distribution activities in an organization.

Sales document type
Specifies the functionality of a sales document.

Sales group
An organizational unit that represents the group of people involved in the sales activities.

Sales Information System
A part of Logistics Information System (LIS) that deals with the logistics process followed by an organization.

Sales office
Organizations selling their goods and services need to have their sales units or teams in different geographical areas. These geographically separated teams work in separate premises.

Sales order
A sales document or agreement that is created when a customer places an order in an organization to receive goods or services.

Sales organization unit
In SAP, a sales organization unit represents an organization unit used to distribute and sell the goods and services offered by the organization.

SAP
Systems Applications and Products (SAP) in data processing is a business software

that can be customized according to the requirements of a user.

SAP Business Information Warehouse (BW)
Used to analyze large volumes of data from multiple sources within or outside the SAP® R/3 system.

SAP Customizing Implementation Guide
The SAP Customizing Implementation Guide is the backbone of the mySAP ERP system and helps to determine how the system functions. The SAP Customizing Implementation Guide is an implementation guide or a customizing screen introduced with the SAP R/3 system.

SAP Graphical User Interface (GUI)
The SAP GUI is a standard SAP user interface that displays menus to perform various business activities.

SAP Query
A comprehensive tool to generate reports from the input provided by QuickView. SAP Query can generate reports without ABAP™ programming.

SAP® R/1 system
The development process of SAP began in 1972, with five IBM employees: Dietmar Hopp, Hans-Werner Hector, Hasso Plattner, Klaus Tschira, and Claus Wellenreuther in Mannheim, Germany. A year later, the first financial and accounting software was developed; it formed the basis for continuous development of other software components, which later came to be known as the SAP R/1 system.

Scheduling agreements
Detailed agreements between an organization and a customer.

Shipment
Refers to the process of transporting goods from one place to another.

Shipping point
Either a departure or a destination point for the goods.

Standard invoice
A sales document that contains the sales records of a customer. In other words, it is a bill given to a customer against the delivery of goods or services. It is created by referring either a sales order or a delivery. You create an invoice on the basis of a delivery if you want to ensure that goods are sent before the invoice is created.

Taxes
Taxes are the amount paid by the customer as well as the seller of the goods and services.

Transaction data
Any business activity in an organization generates data, which is known as transaction data and is handled by the mySAP ERP system either at the document level or at the summary level.

Warehouse management
The process of managing, storing, and facilitating the movement of goods in and out of the warehouse of an organization.

Warehouse Management (WM) module
The WM module divides the storage location defined in the Inventory Management submodule into storage types, storage sections, and then into storage bins.

INDEX

A

Access sequence, 75, 117, 118, 133–135
Accounts Payable, 21, 22, 351
Accounts Receivables, 21, 22, 34, 112, 351, 394
Activity-Based Costing, 23
Application layer, 6, 10, 11–13, 14
Asset Accounting, 22
Automatic credit management, 407, 413–416
Availability to promise, 164
Availability to Promise (ATP), 164, 173–177, 191

B

Backorder Processing, 172
Bank Accounting, 22
Billing, 2, 27, 34, 35, 36, 70, 79, 81, 87, 111, 112, 141, 147, 231, 232, 339–366, 374–404, 424, 488
Billing plan, 339, 366–374, 395

C

Cancellation invoice, 342, 350, 352
Cash sale document, 111
Catalog profile, 452–455
Checking group, 168, 172–180
Checking rule, 166, 168, 173, 175, 179–181, 185–186
Collective requirements, 212
Collective shipment, 263, 266–268
Condition exclusion, 136–139
Condition master data, 69, 75
Configuration data, 32, 33
Consignment fill-up, 254–255
Consignment stock process, 253–257
Consolidation, 22
Contracts, 164, 222–243, 249
Controlling (CO) Module, 21–23
Copying control, 85, 98, 356–361
Cost Center Accounting, 23
Cost Element Accounting, 23
Country code, 149–153
Credit management system, 405–429
Credit memo, 80, 110, 111–112, 342, 347, 350, 357, 362, 372, 374–376
Credit memo document, 111–112
Customer master data, 32, 39, 69–73, 117, 146
Customer Services (CS) Module, 21, 31, 37

D

Database layer, 6, 8, 10–11, 13, 14
Debit memo, 80, 110, 112, 340, 342, 349–350, 357, 362, 363, 374–375
Debit memo document, 112
Decentralized warehouse management, 319, 327–329
Delivery blocks, 213, 217–219, 302–307, 310
Delivery process, 35, 36–37, 175, 259, 264, 274–318, 319, 322, 323–328, 335–337
Delivery split, 275, 316–318
Discount, 27, 93, 95, 115, 116, 118, 125, 126, 129, 136, 139, 140, 141–142, 143, 158, 222, 339, 362, 363, 374, 384, 390, 397, 402
Distribution channel, 39, 41, 44–45, 55, 58, 59, 60–61, 63, 66–68, 70, 73, 74, 77, 87, 227
Division, 39, 41, 45–47, 51, 58, 62, 63, 70, 87, 88, 392
Down payment, 395

E

ERP system, 3–4

F

Financial/Accounting (FI) Module, 21, 35, 73, 147, 340, 395, 413
Funds Management, 22

G

General Ledger, 21, 22, 348
Group conditions, 135, 136

H

Header level, 80–81, 88, 91, 306, 314, 349, 366
Hierarchy Pricing, 140, 141
Human Capital Management (HCM) Module, 26, 28

I

Individual shipment, 263–266, 273
Individual transfer of requirements, 212
InfoCube, 499, 500–501, 503, 505
InfoObject, 499, 500, 501
InfoProviders, 499, 501, 505
Installment Payment, 340, 395, 396, 402, 403
Internal Orders, 23
Investment (IM) Module, 23–24, 31
Item category, 80, 93–103, 106, 108–109, 110, 112, 171, 174, 184–185, 254, 279–280, 282, 283, 329–331
Item level, 81, 346, 356

L

Logical view, 8, 9–10, 501
Logistics Execution (LE) Module, 21, 29

M

Manual pricing, 140
Master Contracts, 223, 234–243
Master data, 14, 24, 26, 27, 28, 32–33, 37, 39–78, 80, 81, 117, 146, 155, 413, 427, 489, 491, 499, 501, 505

Material Management (MM) Module, 3, 4, 20, 21, 27–28, 29, 31, 32, 37, 39, 40, 47, 163, 163–258, 211, 261, 446
Material master data, 26, 32–33, 37, 39, 69, 73–75, 81
Milestone billing, 232, 368, 372–374
Minimum Price Value Pricing, 140, 141
MySAP ERP, 5, 7, 18, 20–22, 24, 26–37, 80, 93, 99, 100, 103, 104, 107, 109, 110–111, 112, 115–119, 121, 125, 126, 129, 133, 140–142, 146–147, 149–161, 164, 168, 170, 173–175, 178, 185, 186, 193, 195, 205–206, 212–223, 232, 238, 243–249, 253–254, 264–267, 270–280, 301, 306, 320–322, 327, 329, 337, 340–342, 347–349, 362, 366–368, 371, 372, 374–377, 384, 392, 394–397, 405–407, 410, 413, 420, 422, 423, 430, 439, 441, 449–452, 459, 462, 494, 500

N
Notification type, 448, 450–452

P
Payment terms, 382, 397–404
Payroll Management (PY), 26
Periodic Billing, 368–372
Personnel Administration (PA), 26
Personnel Development (PD), 26
Picking location, 295–301
Plant, 25, 27, 40, 41, 54–59, 66–68, 147, 153–155, 164, 166, 178, 185, 186, 205, 224, 257, 261, 284, 290, 294–295, 297, 298, 490
Presentation layer, 6, 10, 11, 12–13, 14
Pricing procedure, 115, 116–125, 133, 135, 139, 141, 142, 143, 346, 348, 384
Pricing reports, 117, 143
Pro forma invoice, 340, 342, 350–351, 357, 388
Product allocation, 173, 187–205
Product Cost Controlling, 23
Production Planning (PP) Module, 26, 28, 31, 40, 212
Profit Center Accounting, 23
Profitability Analysis, 23
Project System (PS) Module, 24

Q
Quality Management (QM) Module, 29–30, 37, 47, 445–446, 462–467
Quantity contract, 223–225
QuickView, 470–477, 480–486, 487
Quotation document, 110–111

R
Rebate Agreement, 141, 158, 339, 340, 374–394
Rebates, 145–160, 340, 375, 376, 384, 390
Regional codes, 149–153
Replenishment lead time, 165, 174
Requirement class, 168–171, 181–182, 199–200, 211–214
Requirement types, 168, 170–171, 175, 211–215
Rescheduling, 164

Returnable packaging process, 260, 333–337
Rounding difference, 140, 142
Rush order document, 111

S

Sales and Distribution (SD) Module, 1–4, 20, 21, 26–37, 39, 79–112, 259–260, 339–341, 406, 429–444, 445–467, 469–505
Sales document type, 80–112, 122–123, 210, 212, 235–239, 254, 278, 307–310, 420–422, 434
Sales group, 48–52, 59, 65–66
Sales Information System, 489–497
Sales office, 48–51, 59, 64–67, 70, 491
Sales order, 26–27, 33, 35–37, 49, 76–79, 80–84, 103, 112, 141, 156, 163–164, 168–172, 175–176, 186–187, 206, 208–212, 225, 253–254, 259–260, 262, 279, 305–310, 323–328, 341–342, 349–350, 357, 375, 395, 417, 448–449, 460, 462, 491
Sales order process, 80, 164, 175, 420
Sales organization unit, 40, 42
SAP, 1–37
SAP Business Information Warehouse (BW), 470, 499–505
SAP Customizing Implementation Guide, 18–20, 47–68
SAP GUI, 10–18, 504
SAP Query, 470, 477–487
SAP R/1 system, 5
SAP R/2 system, 5–6, 7
SAP R/3, 2, 6–15, 18, 499

Schedule line, 33, 80, 81, 103–109, 168, 173–174, 183–184, 188, 201–202, 211–217, 243–249, 278–279, 306, 310–314
Scheduling agreements, 243–252
Service and maintenance contract, 223, 231–234
Shipment, 259–274, 275, 337, 350, 462
Shipping point, 55–59, 67–68, 258–260, 262, 274–275, 284–301, 326, 335, 337
Software-oriented view, 8, 10–11
Special Purpose Ledger, 22
Splitting rules, 243, 246–250
Standard invoice, 349–350
Standard order, 80, 110, 112, 419
Surcharges, 116, 125, 129, 140–142

T

Tax determination, 146–155
Taxes, 115–116, 125, 145–160, 339, 384, 385, 449
Transaction data, 13, 14, 32–33
Transfer of requirement, 168, 211–221
Travel Management, 22

V

Value contract, 223, 225–231, 234

W

Warehouse management, 29, 30–31, 36, 37, 73, 259–260, 319–329
Warehouse Management (WM) Module, 30–31, 37